HANDBOOK OF EARLY CHILDHOOD TEACHER EDUCATION

This handbook synthesizes both contemporary research and best practices in early childhood teacher education, a unique segment of teacher education defined by its focus on child development, the role of the family, and support for all learners. The first volume of its kind, the *Handbook of Early Childhood Teacher Education* provides comprehensive coverage on key topics in the field, including the history of early childhood teacher education programs, models for preparing early childhood educators, pedagogical approaches to supporting diverse learners, and contemporary influences on this quickly expanding area of study.

Appropriate for early childhood teacher educators as well as both pre- and in-service teachers working with children from birth through 8, this handbook articulates the unique features of early childhood teacher education, highlighting the strengths and limitations of current practice as based in empirical research. It concludes by charting future directions for research with an aim to improve the preparation of early childhood educators.

Leslie J. Couse is Associate Professor of Education at the University of New Hampshire, USA, and Adjunct Assistant Professor of Pediatrics at the Geisel School of Medicine at Dartmouth College, USA.

Susan L. Recchia is Professor of Education, Co-coordinator of the Program in Integrated Early Childhood Education, and Faculty Director of the Rita Gold Early Childhood Center at Teachers College, Columbia University, USA.

HANDBOOK OF EARLY CHILDHOOD TEACHER EDUCATION

Edited by Leslie J. Couse and Susan L. Recchia

NEW YORK AND LONDON

First published 2016
by Routledge
711 Third Avenue, New York, NY 10017

and by Routledge
2 Park Square, Milton Park, Abingdon, Oxon OX14 4RN

Routledge is an imprint of the Taylor & Francis Group, an informa business

Library of Congress Cataloging-in-Publication Data
Handbook of early childhood teacher education / edited by Leslie J. Couse and Susan L. Recchia.
pages cm
Includes bibliographical references and index.
1. Early childhood educators—Training of—Handbooks, manuals, etc.
2. Early childhood education—Handbooks, manuals, etc. I. Couse, Leslie J., editor of compilation. II. Recchia, Susan, editor of compilation.
LB1732.3.H36 2016
372.21—dc23
2015007995

ISBN: 978-0-415-73675-6 (hbk)
ISBN: 978-0-415-73676-3 (pbk)
ISBN: 978-1-315-81824-5 (ebk)

Typeset in Bembo
by Apex CoVantage, LLC

Printed and bound in Great Britain by
TJ International Ltd, Padstow, Cornwall

To our students and the teachers we've had the honor to work with and learn from, and to the children in ECE settings who continue to inspire us to watch, listen, and remember what matters most

CONTENTS

ILLUSTRATIONS

Figures

Tables

FOREWORD

Not too long ago, I was sitting on the couch beside one of my grandchildren, then two and a half, who was slowly waking from his nap and gently sucking his thumb. He took his thumb out of his mouth, turned to me, and quietly said, "Granny, did you suck your thumb when you were little?" "I did," I replied. He went back to his reverie for a while. Then, he stopped again and said, "Don't you think the right one's the best?"

I begin with this story because it clearly and directly puts the focus on the relationship that we want those who care for and educate our youngest children to have with them. My grandson could only have had that conversation with someone whom he trusted and felt completely comfortable with; someone who was interested in him and would give him the time for such musing; someone who was present for him. Developing such relationships requires of adults working with children what Dewey (1933) describes as *being alive to the moment*; what Maxine Greene (1973) describes as *wide-awakeness*; what Rogers & Raider-Roth (2006) describe as *presence* and define as "*a state of alert awareness, receptivity, and connectedness to the mental, emotional, and physical workings of both the individual and the group in the context of their learning environments, and the ability to respond with a considered and compassionate best next step*" (p. 265).

Presence is essential to all good teaching and especially to the teaching of young children. It requires that, in these hurried, pressured times, the adults/teachers in children's lives learn how to be IN the moment so that they can hear, make sense, and respond appropriately. For teachers, presence requires both self-knowledge and self-understanding as well as knowledge and understanding of those with whom we interact. Presence is hard to teach and it is hard to learn.

If any of us remembers a wonderful teacher, it almost goes without saying that the memory is shaped by presence—by the "connectedness" that we felt with that person. Most of our memories of great teachers are developed sometime during and after third grade. This is because third grade used to be the moment when school began to assume a remarkable sameness that we learned to count on: teacher at the front of the room calling on us periodically; conversation going on between students and teacher like a tennis match with the teacher on one side lobbing balls to interested students on the other. Those teachers who changed the routine in some way and connected with us as individuals are the ones who stood out.

Few remember their preschool years and almost no one remembers infancy and toddlerhood. Yet, brain science tells us that the major work of understanding the world and ourselves in it is done in these earliest years—that time between birth and age 8. Brain science suggests that those who, like my grandson, are fortunate to have someone who will listen to them, who know what to expect, who can shape environments that enable them to think and discern and move—those are the ones who move into later childhood and adulthood with capacity for living deeply and well.

The question then becomes not how to remember the earliest years but how to make the earliest years as sensually, physically, emotionally, and intellectually rich for young children as we can so that they can come to their later educational life as the expert learners that nature has equipped them to be. That means that those who care for them in the nursery and in child care, at home, in preschool, in kindergarten, and in first and second grades have to know what they are doing! It means that the education of adults for work in early childhood is really important because those adults have to see children as incredibly exciting, powerful knowers whose every move is something of a milestone. It means that the ways in which we prepare and support those who work with our youngest children must be thoughtful, and well-informed by science, research, and practical knowledge. And, because none of us really remember our earliest years, the education of early childhood professionals must be well structured so as to enable them to learn how to learn from and with children—in the company of children. This is what this *Handbook of Early Childhood Teacher Education* is all about.

It takes up issues critical to every aspect of early childhood teacher education, from the practical and theoretical to the political and ontological, and it does all of this within a landscape that is bifurcated by third grade understandings of school and new understandings of learning that suggest that the mind blossoms with complexity. Given this situation, the major problem of educating teachers for early childhood becomes one of changing perceptions AND understandings of learning: first, among early childhood teachers themselves, and, second, among the general public.

To enable early childhood teachers to let go of the front-of-the-room/teacher-knows-all model, they must find themselves in settings where they can see children deeply engaged in their play. One thinks of Reggio Emilia in Italy or the Play Settings of Anji in China. These are "schools" in which teachers can learn the clinical skills of observation and experimentation, noting how children shape the environment and determining how to develop opportunities for them to engage further and more imaginatively. These are venues in which teachers/professionals, like those in Japan and Finland who have made Lesson Study and teacher research famous, learn to discuss their findings so as to become better clinicians and to create settings in which powerfully engaging opportunities to learn are the norm for all students.

As difficult as the task of shifting teacher perceptions and understandings is, revising those of the general public regarding the potential of early childhood education is even greater. It is hard for most people, even many parents, to look at early childhood environments as places of powerful learning. What, after all, do infants do but eat and sleep? And isn't play all that toddlers and older preschoolers do? *Real school (their third grade model)* is what most parents and policy-makers focus in on; their focus does not involve the authentic play and experimentation from which children learn. Rather, they want skill development NOW.

Equipping teachers to recognize, identify, and explain children's learning is one aspect of this shift. Another is the will and confidence from leaders in the field to stand firm behind what brain research is so clearly showing: linearity does not beget wonder, imagination, deep knowing; it is time and puzzling with complexity and engagement in making sense alone and with others that leads to creativity, confidence, and competence.

This *Handbook of Early Childhood Teacher Education* offers those of us in this field a rich opportunity to examine the unique features of early childhood teacher education, to consider the strengths and limitations of current practice based upon empirical research, and to chart future directions for research to improve the preparation of early childhood educators. While it cannot and will not tell us exactly what to do, it does offer us pathways for thinking about how to develop in our own practice the presence that will enable our students to tell us, as my grandson did, how they are making sense of the moment. For all the children that our students will teach, my hope is that we all will find those pathways here.

Frances O'Connell Rust
University of Pennsylvania—Graduate School of Education

References

Dewey, J. (1933). *How we think.* Buffalo, NY: Prometheus Books.

Greene, M. (1973). *Teacher as stranger.* Belmont, CA: Wadsworth.

Rogers, C. R., & Raider-Roth, M. B. (2006). Presence in teaching. *Teachers and Teaching: Theory and Practice, 12*(3), 265–287.

INTRODUCTION

The importance of early education is widely recognized across the world, as evidenced by the United Nations Convention on the Rights of the Child (CRC). The CRC, the most widely ratified international treaty on human rights, establishes global standards to ensure the protection, survival, and development of all children (UNICEF, 2014). Research continues to increase our understanding of the critical role early education plays in the long-term success of an individual (Peisner-Feinberg et al., 2001; Shonkoff & Phillips, 2000). The influential nature of teaching quality on academic achievement (Hamre & Pianta, 2005; Peisner-Feinberg et al., 2001) has focused attention on the preparation of teachers. Globally, fewer than 75% of early care and primary teachers are prepared to national standards in 34 of 98 countries reporting (UNESCO, 2014).

In the United States, the importance of early learning to both healthy development and future economic capacity (Barnett & Masse, 2007; National Scientific Council on the Developing Child and National Forum on Early Childhood Policy and Programs, 2010; Heckman & Kautz, 2012) is reflected in increased public funding and access to early learning (Duncan, 2014; RTT-ELC, 2013). Coupled with an accountability movement for quality education, the need to understand how to best prepare teachers for young children is paramount.

The purpose of this handbook is to compile a synthesis of landmark and contemporary research on early childhood teacher education that will complement and extend the existing research on teacher preparation, as well as articulate an agenda for future research, as there is no text currently that does this. Early childhood teacher education is a unique segment of teacher education that is defined by its focus on child development, the role of family, and support for all learners. The preparation of teachers for early childhood education draws on a unique blend of research and theory that informs best practice for child learning and drives the learning experiences of future teachers in a way that is different from other areas of teacher education. As the first of its kind, this handbook will: articulate the unique features of early childhood teacher education; clarify the strengths and limitations of current practice based upon empirical research; and chart future directions for research to improve the preparation of early childhood educators.

Many handbooks and texts focus on early childhood education from a developmental or curricular point of view, articulating what young children need to know and how to teach young children. Yet, there is little focus on how to prepare high-quality teachers of young children. What are the elements of high-quality early childhood teacher education? What does the research tell us? What models have been successful? And once teachers complete initial certification, what are their continuing professional development needs and how can they best be met? This handbook examines the research and best practices in early childhood teacher education for both preservice and inservice teachers. It articulates the content and pedagogy of early childhood teacher education within a research framework and responds to questions regarding how adult learning principles influence the form, function, and duration of teacher education.

Early childhood is a stage of life with unique considerations for learning. The range of typical development for a child from birth to 8 years of age is broad, with rapid physical, cognitive, linguistic, and social emotional growth. Children move through two to three periods of development, depending upon the theoretical frame of reference, during the early childhood years, resulting in direct implications for teaching and learning. Consequently, early childhood is typically grouped in three periods of practice: infants and toddlers, preschool-kindergarten, and primary school years (first through third grade). These developmental periods affect pedagogy and shape decisions teachers make regarding curriculum. Therefore, in defining what teachers need to know, these three groups are evident in the organization of the text. Traditionally, early education has been marked by a developmental approach, one that considers what is individually appropriate, age appropriate, and culturally appropriate within an intentional curricular framework. This frame of reference recognizes that a range of development, experiences, and practices is reflected within any early education setting. The work of ECE is challenged by efforts to support increasingly diverse learners and provide challenging learning opportunities that are responsive to the children in early education settings. How teachers are best prepared to support diversities in the classroom, including ability, linguistic knowledges, cultural practices, and family lifestyles, as well as how teachers collaborate with other professionals to accomplish this, is at the heart of early childhood teacher education.

The role of families in early education is viewed as central to establishing a partnership in educating young children. Developing such a partnership hinges upon trusting reciprocal relationships between parents and educators, where both parents and educators inform practice. In the preparation of early childhood educators, how are parent relationships brought to the forefront? What methods are the most fruitful in developing teacher competence in partnering with parents? How are challenges of cultural practice, parent and teacher expectations, and responsive teaching ethically negotiated?

Finally, societal influences shape teacher education. Shifting social and political paradigms offer opportunities to critically examine and improve practice. How can early childhood teacher education be responsive to changing demographics, public policy, globalization, and advances in technology in the preparation of teachers? The handbook culminates with enduring research questions to advance the field of early childhood teacher education. This handbook leads the way to compile the contemporary context of teacher education research that supports research-based practices and future directions for early childhood teacher education.

Leslie J. Couse and Susan L. Recchia

References

Barnett, W.S., & Masse, L. N. (2007). Early childhood program design and economic returns: Comparative benefit-cost analysis of the Abecedarian program and policy implications, Economics of Education Review, *26*, 113–125. Retrieved from http://nieer.org/sites/nieer/files/BenefitCostAbecedarian.pdf

Duncan, A. (2014). Preschool development grants. Retrieved from: http://www.ed.gov/news/press-releases/18-states-awarded-new-preschool-development-grants-increase-access-high-quality-

Heckman, J. J., & Kautz, T. D. (2012). Hard evidence on soft skills. National Bureau of Economic Research, Working Paper 18121. Retrieved from http://www.nber.org/papers/w18121

Hamre, B. K., & Pianta, R. C. (2005). Can instructional and emotional support in the first-grade classroom make a difference for children at risk of school failure? *Child Development*, *76*(5), 949–967.

National Scientific Council on the Developing Child and National Forum on Early Childhood Policy and Programs. (2010). *Foundations of Lifelong Health Are Built in Early Childhood.* The Center on the Developing Child at Harvard University. Retrieved from http://www.developingchild.harvard.edu

Peisner-Feinberg, E. S., Burchinal, M. R., Clifford, R. M., Culkin, M. L., Howes, C., Kagan, S. L., & Yazejian, N. (2001). The relation of preschool child-care quality to children's cognitive and social developmental trajectories through second grade. *Child Development*, *72*(5), 1534–1553.

Race to the Top Early Learning Challenge (RTT-ELC). (2013). Retrieved from: http://www2.ed.gov/programs/racetothetop-earlylearningchallenge/2013-early-learning-challenge-flyer.pdf

Shonkoff, J. P., & Phillips, D. A. (Eds.). (2000). *From neurons to neighborhoods: The science of early childhood development.* Washington, DC: National Academy of Press.

United Nations Children's Fund (UNICEF). (2014, November). *25 years of the convention on the rights of the child: Is the world a better place for children?* New York: Author. Retrieved from http://www.unicef.org/publications/files/CRC_at_25_Anniversary_Publication_compilation_5Nov2014.pdf

United Nations Educational, Scientific, and Cultural Organization. (2014). EFA Global Monitoring Report 2013/4: *Teaching and Learning,* UNESCO, Paris, p. 85–86.

ACKNOWLEDGEMENTS

There are so many people to thank who have helped to make this handbook a reality. First we would like to express our appreciation for our colleagues at the National Association for Early Childhood Teacher Education (NAECTE), where the idea for this book was born. Their support and encouragement to take this project forward and their belief in our ability to make it happen were the impetus that got us started. We are grateful to our Routledge editor, Alex Masulis, and editorial assistant, Daniel Schwartz, who were always available to respond to our questions and offer advice. Our chapter authors shared their wisdom and expertise while working with us to realize the vision for this handbook. Their willingness to engage fully with the process inspired our work as editors, and energized us when we needed refueling. We were fortunate to have assistance from two exemplary graduate assistants at the University of New Hampshire, Paige Belisle and Erika Baril. Their attention to the details of references and format in our final draft was invaluable. We are thankful to our friends and colleagues who offered a listening ear, shared good advice, and reinforced our efforts in so many kind and caring ways. And finally, we offer heartfelt thanks to our families, who lived through the process with us. We are especially grateful to our husbands and children for their support and encouragement, their respect for our work, their concern for our well-being, and their ability to make us laugh.

PART I

Context, History, and Public Policy of Early Childhood Teacher Education

1

21st CENTURY EARLY CHILDHOOD TEACHER EDUCATION

New Frames for a Shifting Landscape

Rebecca S. New

The *Handbook of Early Childhood Teacher Education* is a unique and timely contribution to ongoing debates about the early care and education of children and what it will take to recruit and retain qualified, competent early childhood (EC) professionals. After decades of resistance, there is widespread acknowledgement at national and global levels of children's early learning potentials and the risks we take—for children and society—in ignoring this special period in human development. Unfortunately, this latter awareness has surged due to mounting evidence of the consequences of adult ignorance or indifference to this highly responsive period in human development, including a widening gap in school achievement.

The convergence of understandings about the significance of the early years has led to calls for increased funding for child care and early childhood education (ECE) at local, state, and national levels. ECE's economic capital is based on the premise of well-educated children being key to the nation's future fiscal health and global standing. This argument informs new research initiatives, more technological devices targeted to increasingly younger children, policy treatises, and magazine articles on the importance of high-quality early care and education.

What's exciting about this is the level of advocacy—local, state, national—for the importance of our work with young children, families, and teachers. What is so daunting is the extraordinary gap between rhetoric and reality. The continued juxtaposition of long-held cultural biases with new understandings about the importance of children's early childhoods is painfully apparent in EC's current landscape. The stakes for more effectively responding to social prejudices with compelling principles, as well as data, have never been higher. The children at the center of U.S. social and political discourses are more ethnically and linguistically diverse than at any time in our history and represent the largest percentage of Americans living in poverty. This handbook represents a much-needed opportunity to add our voices to ongoing efforts to comprehend and respond to 21st century challenges in a nation that proclaims American exceptionalism in spite of global perspectives to the contrary (OECD, 2006).

The editors envisioned this handbook as an occasion for us to think deeply, critically, and constructively about *where we've come from*, *why we do what we do*, and *what we might do differently*. In the course of writing this chapter, I was repeatedly provoked and occasionally thrown off-course by events of natural and man-made disasters in a world that continues to whirl beneath our feet. I returned often to a guiding principle—*that all children deserve and are capable of much more than many are granted*—and wondered why we must still make that social justice argument on children's behalf. This tension pushed me to take yet another look at the EC teacher education landscape to better understand the origins of our image as a profession. In the pages that follow, I consider the sources of that image in light of their relevance to our future work with EC teachers on behalf of more equitable early educations and socially just childhoods in America.

The metaphor of landscape is a helpful way to consider U.S. early care and education (within which teacher education is firmly planted), although the depiction of such a vast territory raises questions of method. To *survey* a landscape generally entails standardized tools with which to measure and describe the terrain in ways recognizable to those within and outside the boundaries. Such precise plotting and appraisal of U.S. ECE is unlikely, given overlapping boundaries, confusing labels, and public and private settings for children from infancy through age eight. What we do know, however, is not encouraging, as described at length in other chapters. Large-scale surveys on the costs, quality, availability, and professional salaries of those working in child care and early education services in the U.S. confirm the perennial unevenness of the terrain in which EC teacher education is planted and hint at further erosion if we don't diagnose causes and find new ways to nourish the soil.

I borrow from the tradition of landscape painting to illustrate alternative perspectives on the unfulfilled rhetoric of ECE in American society. The representational genre of *figurative* landscapes depicts both people *and* context in relationships, with selective attention to critical details. A wide-angled format permits the inclusion of temporal aspects, thus conveying the dynamic relationship between how things were and how they are.

With those potentials in mind, the landscape portrayed illustrates a *cultural model of U.S. ECE* including philosophical, socio-political, and social science contributions to what drives us as a profession. The figurative elements of this landscape are limited to brief sketches of enduring practices and professional discourses guided by ideological foundations. The contemporary portion of this composition includes cracks and shifts in the terrain, evidence of the weight of socio-cultural and political change. The chapter concludes with an unfinished image of a radicalized EC teacher education as a creative hybrid of some of our field's long-held values and traditions, re-invigorated with imagined possibilities better suited to children growing up in a new world.

Cultural Models of Child Development

To understand U.S. ECE requires recognition of cultural roots beneath the surface of the more visible landscape. Cultural influences on adult ideologies and child-rearing patterns have been demonstrated in decades of anthropological research (LeVine & New, 2008). The cumulative impact of this work has informed new theories of the cultural nature of human development (Rogoff, 2003) and the central role of parental belief systems (Goodnow, Miller, & Kessel, 1995), drawing attention to the role of the environment, as "developmental niches" (Super & Harkness, 1986) that support culturally desirable behaviors and competencies (Harkness & Super, 1996). Current scholarship continues to challenge universal theories of development—processes *and* outcomes—in learning and cognition language development, attachment, and socio-emotional development, highlighting the subjective nature of concepts of competence, deviance, and developmental disorder (Lancy, Bock, & Gaskins, 2010).

Psychological anthropologists interpret culturally diverse parental goals and child care practices as mutually supporting components of cultural models of child care (LeVine et al., 1994). The concept of cultural models is understood as a core set of values and beliefs that guide decision making, made "visible" through social traditions, discourses, and norms of behavior and development. Scholars highlight the importance of cultural values and beliefs, describing them as a "moral direction" (LeVine et al., 1994) or, more recently, as a "moral imperative"—a "permeating light under which adults guide and children develop" (Li, 2012, p. x). Of special relevance to this chapter is the strength of a given cultural model as evidenced by the unquestioned acceptance of the moral direction and its resistance to change across boundaries and generations.

The concept of cultural models is useful in interpreting differences in other nations' approaches to non-familial care and early education. EC researchers working in the tradition of psychological anthropology have demonstrated relationships between cultural values, national policies, and EC services in such diverse nations as: Italy, Japan, and China (Edwards & Gandini, 2001; New, Mallory, & Mantovani, 2000; Tobin, Wu, & Davidson, 1989). These studies include ethnographies of infants and toddlers napping and playing outside in cold and inclement weather; teachers who allow children to sharpen knives and climb trees and boulders without adult supervision; and preschoolers seriously engaged in solving complex math problems, negotiating social and physical conflicts, and debating the ethics of child labor. These diverse cultural practices defy age-based expectations of attention spans, stage-theory interpretations of cognitive or moral development, standardized measures of "quality" EC environments, and universal conceptions of "developmentally appropriate" practices (New, 1999).

Cross-cultural research on child care and early education suggests children are highly motivated to learn what they need to know and do in order to be competent participants in family and community settings. Evidence of the wide range of potential child development "outcomes" highlight the limits of socio-cultural goals for children ("moral goods") associated with any cultural model, such that child care practices like encouraging compliance to adult authority, are unlikely to co-occur with the purposeful promotion of autonomy or creative thinking. Further, this "packaging" of a society's hopes for and expectations of children—reflected in routinized parenting, child care arrangements, and institutional supports for early learning—is embedded within the larger socio-cultural-political context. A cultural model of ECE in a pluralistic U.S. society is inextricably linked to legal and political perspectives on children's rights, the place of families within society, and the meanings and means of achieving equity and social justice. The following depiction of a U.S. cultural model notes this complex array of socio-cultural and political relationships and directs attention to changes and continuity across the EC landscape, including images of children, families, and EC professionals, and the ideological rationale for an early education.

U.S. ECE: A Cultural Model for the Century of Childhood

EC teacher education is deeply embedded in the history of ECE, and some of the earliest advocates of children became leaders in designing teacher education programs. Other historians (e.g., Barbara Beatty [1995] and Blythe Hinitz [see Chapter 2]) have provided detailed and fascinating descriptions of the evolution of EC and teacher education within the context of a rapidly growing, turbulent, and far-from-child-centered society. For the purposes of this chapter, the following discussion highlights three features sustained over our shared histories: (1) an image of young children as needy recipients of compensatory services or eager learners; (2) the dominant role of developmental science in establishing norms of competence and deviance in child development, parenting, child care, and education; and (3) the continued resistance to public support for children and families in our increasingly diverse and wealthy society.

ECE to the Rescue

Beginning in the early part of the 19th century, U.S. ECE was primarily a form of **social activism** characterized by religious and philanthropic efforts on behalf of children and families living in poverty. Ideas from Western Europe—notably those of Locke, Pestalozzi, Froebel, and Montessori—spurred the conviction that children were *not* just small adults and could be taught to take care of themselves and be socialized to be more like middle-class children, albeit with the aim of becoming more capable workers and productive citizens if provided the right materials and environments when young.

These ideas were compelling to those committed to the 20th century's "modernist project" of building a new American society through social progress (Lubeck, 2000). Some early leaders were inspired by John Locke's writings on the child's malleability to environmental influences. More progressive EC educators sought out more "modern" sources of inspiration, setting up an eventual competition between those convinced of the merits of Froebel's educational toys-in-the-form-of "gifts" and those who rejected his rigid pedagogy in favour of Montessori's self-correcting materials.

Throughout the early 1900's, many of the most widely known ECEs and advocates focused on poor and minority families, in part due to a lack of social services. Gradually attention shifted from charity kindergartens to the benefits of these out-of-home programs for middle-class children. As the availability of tools for **standardized measurements** of "normal" intelligence began to take hold of the American imagination, EC educators began to explore Dewey's ideas about **child-initiated and play-based** activities and **project-based curriculum** (Dewey, 1926). Classroom teachers became increasingly dedicated **observers** of children's behavior, sometimes inviting mothers to join in record keeping. These early beginnings contributed to dual images of young children as either eager to learn and ready to benefit from out-of-home early education *or* in urgent need of compensatory experiences to make up for what lacked in the home.

As interest grew in more standardized developmental assessments, university child study institutes were established and trained observers began to replace mothers and teachers in collecting and comparing data on children's early behavior and development. Emerging theories from the social sciences inspired researchers to design and implement their own studies on child development, often distancing their efforts from (and potential relevance to) real children in actual classrooms. EC professionals were eager consumers of this growing body of research. It is notable that the first national organization dedicated to EC professionals (National Association of Nursery Educators—precursor to NAEYC) was formed in the same year (1922) as the National Research Council's endorsement of Child Development as a separate discipline. It is hardly surprising that EC educators increasingly turned to studies conducted by scholars as a basis for working with children and families both in and out of the classroom or child care setting. This shift away from classroom-based child studies (precursor to teacher research) to an **objective science** established a knowledge base for the EC profession (Bloch, 1987) and bolstered an image of child development as an applied science (Rutter, 2002). This marriage of early childhood and developmental science was also deemed necessary to protect children from "rash, unwise, and potentially damaging policy decisions" (Sherrod, 1998, p. 3).

As knowledge grew about the pace and processes of early learning and development, these understandings also generated new questions about the contributions of early experiences to subsequent development. Parents and EC caregivers concerned about spoiled children welcomed Skinner's demonstrations of the power of positive reinforcement and behavior management strategies. Erikson's interpretation of healthy psycho-sexual development influenced interpretations of "normal" child development and raised anxieties about the consequences of unresolved stage-based "crises." Other 20th century theories offered new ways of measuring children's development and generated hypotheses about group differences as a function of early experiences. Gesell's theory of maturational readiness was translated into checklists of developmental milestones that could easily be completed by pediatricians and middle-class parents. Bowlby's theory of attachment and separation, grounded in the experiences of thousands of children separated from their families in Western Europe, was reassuring to 1950's "stay-at-home" mothers (in spite of successful experiences with federally funded child care for mothers who worked during the WWII "war effort"). Collectively, these theories and the research they inspired profoundly influenced lay and professional perceptions of good parenting, healthy development, and the place of early care and education in American society. This scholarship also contributed to professional discourses of risk as a function of school readiness and secure relationships.

Three features of this history are relevant to the current status of EC teacher education: the evolution of scientific interest in children's cognition into a pre-occupation with school readiness and achievement; legislative and social changes associated with perceptions of ability and "difference"; and the struggle within the EC field to establish a professional identity. The "cognitive revolution" launched by Piagetian scholars is regarded by some as the beginning of the end of the field's long-standing resistance to academic expectations. Changes in the form of a "trickle-down curriculum" began to show up following the 1983 report on *A Nation at Risk* (National Commission on Excellence in Education), which pointed to mediocre school achievement and linked the need for higher expectations to the nation's future well-being and international standing. Research findings were translated into lay publications for parents and the general public, and newspaper headlines supported growing interest in children's early vulnerabilities and learning potentials.

While middle-class parents sought out and enrolled their children in private nursery schools and kindergartens, state and local funds supported a variety of compensatory and parent-education programs. Civil rights activists took advantage of this growing interest in children's learning to successfully advocate for the passage of Head Start, federally funded comprehensive EC services for low-income children, fueling new debates about discourses of cultural deprivation. Another dramatic change in the EC landscape occurred in 1975 with passage of IDEA (*Individuals with Disabilities Education Act*). This authorized early intervention services and public school access for young children with special needs, transforming expectations of American classrooms and teacher education programs while adding discourses of intervention, integration, mainstreaming, and inclusion to the professional repertoire.

As EC professionals acquired new roles and skills in promoting learning in multicultural and inclusive classrooms, concerns about children's achievement contributed to a growing press for academic education in kindergarten. Under NAEYC leadership, EC professionals went directly, albeit selectively, to the child development literature as the basis for delineating "appropriate" or "inappropriate" forms of early care and education practices, resulting in NAEYC's *Guidelines for Developmentally Appropriate Practice* (Bredekamp, 1987); the acronym DAP became code and the publication the go-to source to ward off pressures for more academics in the EC classroom. Critics of DAP guidelines focused on its singular reliance on an ethnocentric outdated body of scientific knowledge, a marked lack of attention to developmental differences, and a less than professional interpretation of teachers as in need of such a script (Mallory & New, 1994). Revisions incorporated Vygotskian theory and examples from Reggio Emilia to illustrate the social and cultural dimensions of child *and adult* learning (Bredekamp & Copple, 1997, Copple & Bredekamp, 2009). In the final decade of the 20th century, child development research, brain imaging and increasingly sophisticated statistical modeling validated assumptions of risks inherent in the earliest years of life, helped launch *Early Head Start* and were central to the growing press for "universal" pre-kindergarten for four-year-olds.

What Does the U.S. Cultural Model of ECE "Look Like"?

How does this cultural model of ECE get translated within child care and early learning settings? Many contemporary EC programs share qualities with those from the last two decades of the 20th century, suggesting a consistent translation of professional beliefs into core professional practices associated with our ECE cultural model. That these characteristics are salient to international visitors gives me confidence that they are fair representations of key principles that inform our work, though I'm aware of the risks of caricature given the extreme variability in the form, function, size, costs, and quality of what falls within the boundaries of this landscape. Throughout the U.S., some of the most salient features of ECE environments include:

1. Principle of **child-*not group*-centeredness**, reflected in small groups and low teacher-child ratios, an emphasis on self-esteem, child-accessible arrangement of space/separate private spaces, frequent opportunities for individualized activities.
2. Focus on the **autonomous individual with choices**, reflected in discourses of "child-initiated" and "free-play," with environments and daily routines that require children to choose and develop self-help skills.
3. Belief in **play** as a primary source and context for children's early learning and development, evidenced by the availability of constructive materials, large or small blocks, special places for socio-dramatic play, sand or water tables, and, subject to safety concerns, time for outdoor play.
4. Instructional decisions informed by **developmental goals *and compensatory* orientation**, reflected in discourses of child and family needs (rarely assets), linguistic and developmental differences, and differentiated curriculum; expectations for particular forms of "parent involvement" and teacher-led "parent-education programs."
5. Staffing includes lead and assistant teachers, and a variety of others; roles, teacher qualifications, and **professional expertise** are associated with specific age groups (infant/toddler, preschool, school-age), intervention specialists (OT, PT), or content areas, i.e., art, music, physical activities.
6. Concerns about **physical safety and emotional "well-being"** are apparent in classroom discipline/management strategies; restrictions on outdoor or "risky" play; and adult-child discourses that emphasize self-esteem; and teacher scripts to *be careful!*
7. **Inclusive** classrooms are now within the normal array of EC settings, although private settings may not accept children with special needs; classrooms frequently include additional adults, some who work within or outside the classroom based on goals outlined in the child's IEP (Individualized Education Plan).
8. U.S. EC educators are proud of their programs, especially when accredited and highlighting diverse curriculum approaches. Parents who can afford options may choose from a variety of "name brand" **options** from abroad (e.g., Montessori, Waldorf, Reggio Emilia) or other well-respected U.S. curriculum models (e.g., High Scope, Creative Curriculum, Project Approach; Roopnarine & Johnson, 2013).

A philosophy based on science. If asked about these ways of relating to and educating children, many if not most U.S. EC teacher educators will reference a shared philosophy that values early childhood as a special time when children evidence "potential" that requires adult support and nurturance. They may point to the results of longitudinal studies that demonstrate "lifetime effects" of children's early experiences in programs characterized by the features outlined above (Schweinhart et al., 2005). Teachers and student teachers might emphasize concern for the "total child" and the roles of families and professionally trained educators in children's early development. In describing our field's rationale for child-initiated and play-based activities, teacher educators may expect students to give credit to Dewey for the EC mantra of "learning by doing" and convey an understanding of Piagetian theories implied by the simple mantra that children "construct their own knowledge" through "hands-on activities."

Echoing larger cultural values, U.S. EC educators typically explain the importance of attending to children's individual differences. Those with more recent degrees and/or advanced courses in child development proffer contemporary theories of learning, including Vygotskian principles about the contributions of peers as "more capable others" and the power of play as a context for observing children's zones of proximal development. If called upon to defend arrangements of space and learning materials, EC educators may reference Montessori's belief in the importance of a prepared environment and standardized measures of quality learning environments. Reggio Emilia's interpretation of "space as a third teacher" may be cited as a more recent inspiration. If visitors ask for further explanations of our taken-for-granted goals and practices, EC teachers and teacher educators will surely acknowledge NAEYC's research-based guidelines for developmentally appropriate practice, now available in grade-specific publications (Copple, Bredekamp, Koralek, & Charner, 2013). What our current and future EC educators **cannot say** is that children in the U.S. have a right to this or any other kind of an ECE.

This account of ECE has served as an American ideal for much of the past century and continues to be held up as a model for the profession. These characteristics of child-centered early care and education in the U.S. are consistent with NAEYC accreditation standards, legal mandates, parental preferences, and research findings on the importance of the environment and teacher-child relationship. The terms *nurturant, warm, child-centered, play-based,* and *informed by research* can be found in EC mission statements across the U.S. The continuity of so many of these characteristics is surprising, given the number and scope of changes over these decades; yet, the resilience of this model is consistent with the premises of a cultural model, which sustains an image of coherence by minimizing distractions and detractors, though there are plenty increasingly visible in this 21st century landscape.

A New Century for Children and Families in a Globalized Society

The globalization of American society is apparent in ways both large and small. Social demographics reveal a growing number and diversity of immigrants, including groups of adults and unaccompanied child refugees. Dual language programs for children and adults are increasingly common, indicating the international dimensions of our increasingly pluralistic society. Economic indicators reveal a growing disparity between the haves and have-nots, leading some to despair of a new class-based "opportunity gap" for children growing up in poverty (Putman, 2015). More children with special needs are now enrolled in early intervention and inclusive EC settings, the number a reflection of earlier detection in some cases and lack of prenatal care in others. American children under the age of 6 years are increasingly likely to live with a single and/or employed mother and debates about minimum wage reveal an empathy gap. Other changes in American society of significance to the well-being of children and families include the growing presence of violence, not just on television but in homes, schools, and communities, and omnipresent technology as means of communication, entertainment, and information. These features are more than mere data. In combination with poverty, they function as contexts of children's development (Gershoff, Mistry, & Crosby, 2014).

Given cost and availability, fewer than half of America's young children spend time with EC professionals. The current plateau in state-funded pre-kindergarten programs (Barnett, Carolan, Squires, & Brown, 2013) will hopefully change in response to the White House's *early learning initiatives*; yet solutions to the chronic lack of affordable high-quality child care for children of any age, especially infants and toddlers (Lally, 2013), are not easily imagined in the current political and fiscal context and recurrent concerns about whether child care is actually "good for babies" (Belsky et al., 2007). When children are enrolled in a child care center, persistent inequities in salaries and workplace conditions (Whitebook, Phillips, & Howes, 2014) contribute to chronically high turnover rates and may dampen the enthusiasm of teachers, thus hampering the sort of teacher-child relationship repeatedly identified as a primary source of quality care. Teachers in public preschools and Head Start have moderately improved salaries and working conditions, but are also increasingly likely to experience stress given new pressures of performance standards (Head Start Bureau, 2000) and more teacher-directed, sedentary, pre-academic activities. These are just some of many topics being debated (Zigler, Gilliam,

& Barnett, 2011) as private foundations and charitable trusts add leverage to the idea that preschool is an investment in the next generation (Kirp, 2007).

Some of the changes in U.S. EC programs reflect a new confidence in children's early learning abilities. Most, however, reflect the blizzard of accountability policies that have buried schools across the country with requirements of evidence of compliance and testing outcomes. Researchers have noted kindergarten teachers' frustrations with attempts to comply with new (district/state-level) mandates to include more time for academic instruction (Gallant, 2009). Those with EC credentials voice concerns about the growing contradictions between their professional philosophies (and professional development) and what they are now expected to do. As kindergarten takes on the mantle of what used to be first grade, primary grades are increasingly dedicated to high-stakes test preparation, to the dismay of children, parents, and teachers alike. Collaborative efforts such as the *FirstSchool* initiative encourage teachers across the pre-K–primary grades to make better use of colleagues and school-wide data to improve children's experiences within the classroom and promote more "seamless transitions" across grade levels and between homes and schools (Ritchie & Gutmann, 2013). Yet some caution against moving too quickly to tie ECE to elementary schools given the groups' historic differences in philosophical orientations to teaching and learning, power differentials, and the unrelenting press for an increasingly narrow curriculum (Halpern, 2013).

As research continues on the children of immigrants expands (Suárez-Orozco, Suárez-Orozco, & Todorova, 2008), new questions are emerging about declines in immigrant achievement across generations (García Coll & Marks, 2012). Some scholars now focus on teachers' perceptions of their roles and relationships with children's parents, assumptions about family socio-economic backgrounds, and professional resistance to supporting children's heritage languages (Qin, 2006). An entirely different body of brain research provides new insights on the interface between cognition and emotion (Blair, 2002) and raises new concerns about potential neurological and behavioral consequences of growing up in contexts of "adversity." These studies underscore the challenges facing children growing up in the U.S., and those of scholars seeking to understand the complex dimensions of children's lives. Before considering how our field could respond to these chronic and new challenges, it's necessary to consider what we might have contributed to this state of affairs.

ECE Contributions to Contemporary Dilemmas

Our history of activist intervention has focused on both real and presumed needs of children and continues to be influenced by a holistic view of child development extending to children's family lives. The science of child development has retained its place of prominence as evidenced by our continued reliance on developmental theories and research paradigms—that incorporate standardized measurements and complex statistical models to explain what's most important to children's development and identify professional "best practices" (Shonkoff & Phillips, 2000; Hyson & Tomlinson, 2014).

That we haven't made enough of a difference as a society and profession in child poverty (Harrington, 1962; Huston, 1994; 2014) or school achievement of children from low incomes/ethnic minorities (Duncan et al., 2007) is cause for critical self-reflection, a habit of mind that doesn't come easily given our history of "evangelical" efforts to effect change in *others* (Goffin, 2013). Recent publications in teacher education (Genishi & Goodwin, 2008; Grieshaber & Cannella, 2001) raising provocative questions about social justice aims in ECE. A consistent thread throughout contemporary reflections is an emphasis on the diversities within our field, classrooms, and society.

The following discussion picks up this thread to consider some of the unintended consequences of our field's orientation to *difference,* including (1) our professional discourses, (2) a reliance on ethnocentric and reductionist developmental science, and (3) the policy implications of these scientific and professional interpretations for children and families.

Professional discourses that keep us at bay. The way we talk about children and families and some of the terms used more broadly in the field may be problematic if they inhibit productive conversations with others. For example, discussions about a 'play-based curriculum' are easily misunderstood by people outside ECE. More intentional descriptions can help us be more effective advocates for ECE—e.g., reference to "early care and education" instead of "daycare" highlights children's learning and may counter negative connotations associated with non-familial child care (Rhodes & Huston, 2012). Other features of ECE discourse are less obviously problematic. Discourses of "*developmental appropriateness*" may work against children's best interests because they elicit insufficient curiosity about the children themselves and their capabilities for learning and doing. Age-based interpretations of DAP discourage teachers from providing more challenging activities that could lead to surprising insights into *what children can actually do.* Adherence to a textbook version of what's "developmentally appropriate" also precludes the possibility that *we're wrong,* as research with families from diverse cultural groups has noted. *Discourses of difference in children* miss the mark by limiting our expectations of children and the learning opportunities provided to them. Even when teachers use their knowledge of children's cultural and individual differences to determine "appropriate," deficit labels keep us from "seeing" the children (Fennimore & Goodwin, 2011). As we speak about children, our language influences our own and others' intellectual and emotional orientations. We've learned to reference the child before mentioning the disability (*the autistic child* is now *the child with autism),* yet this semantic shift doesn't change the impression that what's most important about the child is a diagnosis distinguishing her from her classmates.

Discourses of difference in families can also impede our efforts, yet are typical in research studies, titles of professional publications, and descriptions of school populations. For example, large-scale statistical studies frequently highlight ethnic and social class differences in relation to children's early education (e.g., Barbarin et al., 2008); other studies make oblique references to "family processes" associated with "economically disadvantaged children's school transitions (Crosnoe & Cooper, 2010). Such labels contribute to a narrow view of diversity ignoring the variability within sub-cultural and linguistic groups subsumed within singular concepts, such as immigrant status. The pervasive discourse of what families "lack" also makes it difficult for educators to imagine "how non-mainstream parents could contribute to their children's education" (Doucet, 2011, p. 2235).

Deficits in developmental science. Scattered throughout the history of child development are criticisms of its inadequacies at capturing and explaining the characteristics and consequences of children's development. Twentieth century critiques included early concerns about insufficient attention to context in child development research (Anderson, 1956), social science's racial biases (Baratz & Baratz, 1970), and its very "strangeness" (Bronfenbrenner, 1986), leading some to question its relevance to our work in ECE (Lubeck, 2000). In spite of hopes that developmental scientists had finally "discovered the world" (LeVine, 1980), very little cross-cultural research on child development, parenting, socialization, teaching strategies has made its way into mainstream developmental literatures (Hagen & Conley, 1994; Abu-Zena & New, 2012). Instead, child development researchers continue to rely on standardized measurements of children's development and quality indicators of early care and education (Belsky et al., 2007). Such decontextualized empirical/analytic approaches to early educational research illustrate the distance between researchers and children and the professionals engaged in the dynamic and situated processes of teaching and learning (Iorio & Adler, 2013).

Social consequences of deficit policies. The U.S. welfare approach reflects class assumptions about which children need which type of early educational experiences (Cahan, 1997). In turn, educational institutions providing those experiences define and then delimit services for particular groups of children and reinforce an "expert culture" of specialized and differentiated areas of expertise. This combination of EC specialists and compensatory policies sustains a fragmentation of services *and* conflicting views of best interests for children and families. Many of the services squeezed under the umbrella of ECE correspond with this definition, as evidenced by income eligibility criteria for Head Start and most state-funded pre-K programs (Barnett et al., 2013). The welfare stigma of targeted services have helped keep the demand low for universal services due to welfare stigmas (Saraceno, 1984) in contrast to other welfare states where government support is associated with societal aims of social justice and equity (Bennett, 2006; Einarsdottir & Wagner, 2006). What is most clear is that different forms of early care and education contribute to and *create* differences that are apparent as soon as children enter formal schooling (Duncan et al., 2007; Lareau, 2003).

What to Do About Inequitable, Unaffordable, and Unavailable EC Services?

Recent reflections on ECE offer an array of recommendations for how to improve EC (teacher) education, a diversity of perspectives seemingly incompatible with the call for "one strong voice" to speak on behalf of common purpose in response to crises both internal and external (Goffin, 2013, p. 15). Yet, a diversity of perspectives need not be incompatible with the aim of a common purpose for our field. The following sketch of a new cultural model of ECE capitalizes on the concept of diversity as a unifying principle and strategic response to challenges facing ECTE.

The Social Construction of a New Cultural Model of EC

An American childhood was once described as a "cultural invention" (Kessen, 1979), an insight consistent with theoretical premises of cultural models as representations of a society's traditional ways of interpreting and supporting childhood. However, the notion of a cultural model as *invention* suggests a purposeful, creative, and situated response to EC. The status of young children in America supports the imperative to not only imagine a different sort of childhood, but to recalibrate our professional roles and responsibilities in light of this new image of the child.

Inspirations for such an endeavor come from places like Reggio Emilia, whose municipal EC services are guided by an image of a "new culture of childhood" constructed by and for the community. That Reggio Emilia's cultural model has been sustained over a half century of socio-demographic and political changes (New & Kantor, 2013) serves as evidence of what is possible given a collective will, imagination, and determination. Australian educators are also seeking to disrupt a commercialized view of the child, proposing that EC services can serve as democratic contexts for constructing an alternative image of the child as citizen (Peers & Fleer, 2014). With these examples in mind, what follows is an imagined 21st century version of our traditional cultural model of EC (teacher) education that is a purposeful hybridization of strengths and lessons learned from our history.

Selective Traditions

Courtney Cazden introduced me to the concept of *selective traditions*, a term used by Marxist philosopher Raymond Williams to describe the process by which we "select from the legacy of the past to explain, support, and justify actions in the present" (Cazden, 1996, p. 165). Such an orientation to our field's complex history is consistent with my aim to both provoke and inspire by means of an "intentionally selective version of a shaping past . . ." that conveys ". . . a sense of *predisposed continuity*" (italics in the original; Williams, 1977, pp. 115, 116). There are many aspects of our history that could affirm and support the hard work ahead, including the following iterations of some selective traditions:

A new image of children. Our field remains dedicated to the concept of *child-centeredness* and its "translation" into arrangements of the environment and curriculum foci. What's problematic about this image is *what we see* when we look at the child. Our traditional cultural model has maintained an image of children as needy and dependent upon our expertise, a deficit conception supported by Piagetian stage-theory that highlights a "configuration of deficits," distinguishing children from adults blinding us to children's unrecognized and undervalued capacities. A new image that could bring children "closer to us" (so we could *see them better*) would be one in which they too, have capacities for empathy, kindness, creativity, and philosophical reflections. By proposing an image of the child that is not so different from adults, we could invite families and community members to imagine how children are "positioned" in the larger society. By considering children as protagonists capable of interpreting their world, adults might value the importance of an early education that engages children's minds (Katz & Chard, 1989) and "makes sense" to them (Genishi & Goodwin 2008).

Reclaim our roles as teacher researchers. The field's tradition of child study anticipates contemporary interpretations of teacher research and the principle of inquiry as an ethical stance (Cochran-Smith & Lytle, 2009). Documentation is one way EC educators can update traditions of Child Study, as is inviting parents and other family members to assist in observing and recording children's behaviors at home. This sort of home-school partnership can help make families' funds of knowledge (Gonzalez, Moll, & Amanti, 2005) more accessible to teachers. As teachers invite parents to identify areas of interest or concern, they gain a better understanding of the classroom culture. Relationships that result from such collaborations support children as they move between home and school. Teacher research partnerships can also include school- or community-based colleagues, contributing to smoother transitions.

Teacher collaborations with teacher educators could focus their inquiry on a common developmental or classroom curiosity; in turn, they could seek out policy makers willing to exchange insights and concerns across their respective "cultural divides" (Granger, Tseng, & Wilcox, 2013, p. 208). Such collaborations and conversations might counter the sometimes "idiosyncratic" nature of policy making and teacher decision making (Huston, 2014, p. 227). Researchers who gain deeper understandings of teachers' roles are more likely to appreciate their "clinical" knowledge and subjective insights. In turn, teachers who better understand research will be more likely to utilize it in classrooms (Granger et al., 2013). Such research-practice partnerships can subvert the conventional "research to practice" model by creating learning communities conducive to *adult* learning and improved educational experiences for children.

Seeing is believing. Child development institutes and university-based laboratory schools are part of our field's history, promoting a keen interest in children's learning. As those institutions disappeared, knowledge about child development was increasingly disseminated via professional and lay publications (increasingly available online). Setting aside the critique of this narrow approach to understanding development, children would be better served if there were alternative (re)sources to counter or complement decontextualized forms of knowledge representation. Teacher research as described above is one such example, although decisions about dissemination will be critical to its usefulness outside of immediate classroom settings. With the aim of informing a larger public, narratives such as those by Vivian Paley and Cynthia Ballenger represent reflections that can compel others to envision more nuanced and authentic images of children *and their teachers*. Documentation, in the form of photographs and video recordings of children, is an especially powerful way to let others "see for themselves" what children and teachers are learning-by-doing. Reggio Emilia has done the most to illustrate documentation's potentials as an advocacy tool, a source of theory-building, hypothesis-generating, and way to engage families and policy makers. U.S. ECEs have incorporated documentation into school-wide projects and as a key component of professional learning communities (e.g., Moran, Desrochers, & Cavicchi, 2007). We have yet to fully utilize the social media potentials that could also help in *Making Learning Visible* (Project Zero, 2003), nor have early educators taken the next step to use these representations to inform policy makers about children's early learning in the context of caring for and stimulating early learning environments.

These recommendations—in the form of new iterations of selective traditions from our field—call for a new image of children that highlights their *competencies* and new roles for teachers as *collaborative* researchers and *intentional* advocates on behalf of children and the field of ECE. This cultural-model-in-transition has direct implications for the parent field of EC teacher education.

Conclusion

So what are the implications of this briefly sketched revision of our field's selective traditions in a landscape that continues to change in a society that refuses to budge? In spite of a century of effort and good intentions, we have yet to insure that all children have safe homes and access to nutritious food, healthcare, and schools where they and their families are welcome. Although ECE cannot resolve issues of our society (Hyson & Tomlinson, 2014), we can and must do more on behalf of more equitable education and socially just childhoods. We must also do things differently. The following recommendations are based on images of children as competent, not needy; and teachers as collaborative and intentional learners who don't always know what's best, but are motivated by the promise of "diversity within unity" (Banks et al., 2001).

Some critical *first steps* are to:

- Redefine our responsibilities to include the promotion of social justice and educational equity.
- Reconstruct our self-image as professionals resist artificial boundaries and have the courage to step outside our areas of expertise.
- Let go of textbook depictions child development research as our primary knowledge base.
- Reject the language of deficits (children, families) and exceptionalism ("best practice").
- Acknowledge the need for multiple perspectives and develop skills for asking good questions.
- Look in the mirror—examine and claim responsibility for our own cultural biases.
- Envision self and other awareness as fundamental to our professional expertise (New, 2013).

What public actions could we take to inform our *learning*, heighten our *visibility*, and increase *our viability* as a profession?:

- Learn new languages by: (a) enrolling in Spanish or Chinese; (b) listening to ourselves; practicing how to talk about children so that others can see them; and (c) staying informed so we can enter into conversations with colleagues, community members, and policy makers.
- Get back in the EC classroom—not just to supervise students, but to experience the teaching and learning taking place (or not) and the life of the teacher(s). *Courtney Cazden went back to first grade each sabbatical.*
- Be a good citizen and get out in the community (school board, city council, PTA) to learn what others see as important, observe power distributions, and the nature of local discourses; use occasions to advocate and build social capital.
- Use out-of-building conversations and observations to identify potential relationships with other teacher educators; researchers in social sciences, health, and allied professions; and local teachers and school administrators.
- Take first steps at reclaiming child study by identifying research foci based on knowledge of local issues in early care or education, community concerns, or state challenges.

And how do we bring these goals, understandings, skills, and uncertainties to our students?

We can begin by stepping away from our traditional "learn and *then* do" and purposefully positioning future EC teachers within multiple terrains of the early childhood landscape. The following suggestions are only some of the many ways in which we might re-conceptualize EC teacher education programs:

- Widen the scope of our ***commitment to children*** by requiring future teachers to take account of their larger surroundings—beyond children's families, including neighborhoods and the community—to better understand their childhoods. Such "bridge constructions" will help new teachers make connections with families and community members—essential components of a "learning-to-teach" professional development program (Bales & Mueller, 2008). These bridges can serve as scaffolds to build reciprocal relationships (Berk & Winsler, 1995). EC teacher educators can model effective strategies of bridge building, including the respectful eliciting ideas, sharing resources, and establishing a common ground, by inviting teacher education colleagues in other specialty areas to join class discussions. When teacher educators demonstrate how to leverage diversity (Day, 2006) for children's benefit, they gain access to funds of knowledge, and new understandings, of once divisive issues (Cochran-Smith & Dudley-Marling, 2012). Such participative learning environments have a dual "educational-cultural edge" given the potential for both personal and institutional growth (Gorodetsky & Barak, 2008).
- ***Curriculum and pedagogy*** for preservice teacher education students, no less than those in EC settings, should be informed by what we know about processes of social cognition (Solomon, 1993), what we understand about cultural practices that characterize their former and future environments (Dickinson & Tabors, 2001), and what we can learn together about topics where no one is expert (Berk & Winsler, 1995). Such a pedagogy of collaborative inquiry can be instantiated through assignments that ask students to observe and listen to children, develop a tentative research agenda, and work in small groups to generate "common core" learning goals for particular age groups. Future teachers could read qualitative studies such as Gillander's (2007) documentation of a Spanish-speaking child's relationship with her English-speaking pre-K teacher; Valdes' (1996) ethnography about the development of respectful relationships between teachers and culturally diverse families, or Hong's (2011) study of how immigrant families get engaged in children's school communities. Student teachers need parallel opportunities to observe and interact with children in both in and out-of-school contexts to remind them that children are more than students—they are members of families and communities.
- Prepare teachers to be ***critical consumers of alternative theories and research paradigms.*** Preservice teacher education students need to know more than how to supplement and critique child development theories and work successfully with children's families. In addition to using inquiry to focus on specific aspects of development, students can be assigned articles to critique, including those critical of contemporary educational practices (i.e., Biesta, 2007 *or* Graue, Kroeger, & Prager, 2001). Field work could include partnering with community-based child care professionals, to study early learning and relationships in infant-toddler settings and examine the validity and relevance of commonly used quality indicators in child care research.

These are just some of the ways in which future teachers could be supported to develop the skills and dispositions of inquiry, collaboration and critical thinking—each indispensable to adults hoping to facilitate the learning and development of children who are not only ready to learn (Bowman, Donovan & Burns, 2001) but are increasingly more worldly than we are (Bloch, Kennedy, Lightfoot, & Weyenberg, 2006).

In this chapter, I have sketched the early childhood landscape as it has grown and spread over the past century in support of a cultural model of early care and education in the U.S. Our cultural model is apparent in our discourses, our values and beliefs—a set of morally infused principles that guides both our assessment and reparation of perceived faults in the EC terrain, many of which are better described by others in this volume. My goals were more, however, than to ground the reader in the current landscape of ECTE, but to imagine another cultural model that is more in line with the growing diversity within the field, in classrooms and communities, and across our large and complex nation. What seems most clear to me is that we cannot strive for that singular voice that Goffin and others are now advocating unless that voice incorporates other voices as well—not always in harmony, perhaps, but none-the-less part of the narrative. I used to take comfort in John Dewey's interpretation of "education as conversation" (1926), but this only works if we speak the same language and are able to listen to each other. We haven't yet figured out how to do that within our own profession, much less with others—elementary teachers and teacher educators, immigrant parents, community members, policy makers. This new image of a radicalized profession requires some significant changes in our ways of being—changes that none-the-less draw upon our rich history of advocacy for children, their families, and our profession as well as our philosophical underpinnings. In honor of yet another philosopher of education, I hope we can find inspiration in Maxine Greene's imperative to "keep the conversation going" (2001) as we take a radical turn in our sense of professional identity and commit to learning from and with others on behalf of children's current and future early childhoods.

References

Abu-Zena, M., & New, R. (2012). Children are ready to learn, but are we? The role of adult relations in school readiness. *Zero to Three, 33*(1), 28–36.

Anderson, J. E. (1956). Child development: An historical perspective. *Child Development, 27*(2), 181–196.

Bales, B. L., & Mueller, J. J. (2008). Preparing teachers for a new era: Building bridges in the learning-to-teach professional sequence. *The New Educator, 4*(2), 152–168.

Banks, J. A., Cookson, P., Gay, G., Hawley, W. D., Irvine, J. J., Nieto, S., Schofield, J. W., & Stephan, W. G. (2001). Diversity within unity: Essential principles for teaching and learning in a multicultural society. *Phi Delta Kappan, 83*(3), 196–212.

Baratz, S. S., & Baratz, J. C. (1970). Early childhood intervention: The social science base of institutional racism. *Harvard Educational Review, 40*(1), 29–50.

Barbarin, O. A., Early, D., Clifford, R., Bryant, D., Frome, P., Burchinal, M., & Pianta, R. (2008). Parental conceptions of school readiness: Relation to ethnicity, socioeconomic status, and children's skills. *Early Education & Development, 19*(5), 671–701.

Barnett, W. S., Carolan, M. E., Squires, J. H., & Brown, K. C. (2013). *The state of preschool 2013: State preschool yearbook.* Rutgers University, NJ: National Institute for Early Education Research.

Beatty, B. (1995). *Preschool education in America: The culture of young children from the colonial era to the present.* New Haven, CT: Yale University Press.

Belsky, J., Vandell, D. L., Burchinal, M., Clarke-Stewart, K. A., McCartney, K., & Owen, M. T. (2007). Are there long-term effects of child care? *Child Development, 78*(2), 681–701.

Bennett, J. (2006). Selected developments in the early childhood field since Starting Strong II. *Revue internationale d'éducation de Sèvres, 13*(53), 129–140. Special issue on Qualite', equite' et diversite' dans le prescolaire. ["Quality, equity and diversity in preschoool education"], S. Rayna (guest editor).

Berk, L., & Winsler, A. (1995). *Scaffolding children's learning: Vygotsky and early childhood education.* Washington, DC: National Association for the Education of Young Children.

Biesta, G. (2007). Why "what works" won't work: Evidence-based practice and the democratic deficit in educational research. *Educational Theory, 57*(1), 1–22.

Blair, C. (2002). School readiness: Integrating cognition and emotion in a neurobiological conceptualization of children's functioning at school entry. *American Psychologist, 57*(2), 111–127.

Bloch, M. N. (1987). Becoming scientific and professional: An historical perspective on the aims and effects of early education. In T. S. Popkewitz (Ed.), *The formation of school subjects* (pp. 25–62). Basingstoke, UK: Falmer.

Bloch, M. N., Kennedy, D., Lightfoot, T., & Weyenberg, D. (Eds.). (2006). *The child in the world/the world in the child: Education and the configuration of a universal, modern, and globalized childhood.* New York: Palgrave Macmillan.

Bowman, B. T., Donovan, M. S., & Burns, M. S. (Eds.). (2001). *Eager to learn: Educating our preschoolers.* Washington, DC: National Academy Press.

Bredekamp, S. (1987). *Developmentally appropriate practice in early childhood programs serving children from birth through age eight.* Washington, DC: National Association for the Education of Young Children.

Bredekamp, S., & Copple, C. (Eds.). (1997). *Developmentally appropriate practice for early childhood programs serving children from birth through age eight* (Rev. ed.). Washington, DC: National Association for the Education of Young Children.

Bronfenbrenner, U. (1986). Ecology of the family as context for human development: Research perspectives. *Developmental Psychology, 22*(6), 723–742.

Cahan, E. (1997). On the uses of history for developmental psychologists or on the social necessity of history. *SRCD Newsletter, 40*(3), 2, 6, 8. Ann Arbor, MI: Society for Research in Child Development.

Cazden, C. B. (1996). Selective traditions: Readings of Vygotsky in writing pedagogy. In D. Hicks (Ed.), *Discourse, learning, and schooling* (pp. 165–185). New York: Cambridge University Press.

Cochran-Smith, M., & Dudley-Marling, C. (2012). Diversity in teacher education and special education: Issues that divide. *Journal of Teacher Education, 63*(4), 237–244.

Cochran-Smith, M., & Lytle, S. (2009). *Inquiry as a stance: Practitioner research in the next generation.* New York: Teachers College Press.

Copple, C., & Bredekamp, S. (2009). *Developmentally appropriate practice (in early childhood programs, serving children from birth through age 8).* Washington, DC: National Association for the Education of Young Children.

Copple, C., Bredekamp, S., Koralek, D., & Charner, K. (2013). *Developmentally appropriate practice: Focus on infants and toddlers.* Washington, DC: National Association for the Education of Young Children.

Crosnoe, R., & Cooper, C. E. (2010). Economically disadvantaged children's transitions into elementary school: Linking family processes, school contexts, and educational policy. *American Educational Research Journal, 47*(2), 258–291.

Darling-Hammond, L. (2010). *The flat world and education: How America's commitment to equity will determine our future.* New York: Teachers College Press.

Day, C. B. (2006). Leveraging diversity to benefit children's social-emotional development and school readiness. In B. Bowman & E. K. Moore (Eds.), *School readiness and social-emotional development: Perspectives on cultural diversity* (pp. 23–32). Washington, DC: National Black Child Development Institute.

Dewey, J. (1926). *Art and education.* Merion, PA: Barnes Foundation Press.

Dickinson, D. K., & Tabors, P. O. (Eds.). (2001). *Beginning literacy with language: Young children learning at home and school.* Baltimore, MD: Brookes Publishing.

Doucet, F. (2011). (Re)constructing home and school: Immigrant parents, agency, and the (un)desirability of bridging multiple worlds. *Teachers College Record, 113*(120), 2705–2738.

Duncan, G. J., Dowsett, C. J., Claessens, A., Magnuson, K., Huston, A. C., Klebanov, P., & Japel, C. (2007). School readiness and later achievement. *Developmental Psychology, 43*(6), 1428–1446.

Edwards, C., & Gandini, L. (2001). *Bambini: The Italian approach to infant/toddler care.* New York: Teachers College Press.

Einarsdottir, J., & Wagner, J. T. (2006). *Nordic childhoods in early education.* Greenwich, CT: Information Age Publishing.

Fennimore, B. S., & Goodwin, A. L. (Eds.). (2011). *Promoting social justice for young children.* New York: Springer.

Fung, H., & Smith, B. (2010). Learning morality. In D. Lancy, J. Bock, & S. Gaskins (Eds.), *The anthropology of learning in childhood* (pp. 261–285). New York: Alta-Mira Press/Rowman & Littlefield.

Gallant, P. (2009). Kindergarten teachers speak out: "Too much, too soon, too fast!" *Reading Horizons, 49*(3), 201–220.

García Coll, C., & Marks, A. (Eds.). (2012). *The immigrant paradox in children and adolescents: Is becoming American a developmental risk?* Washington, DC: American Psychological Association.

Genishi, C., & Goodwin, A. L. (Eds.). (2008). *Diversities in early childhood education: Rethinking and doing.* Oxon, UK: Routledge.

Gershoff, E. T., Mistry, R. S., & Crosby, D. A. (Eds.). (2014). *Societal contexts of child development: Pathways of influence and implications for practice and policy.* New York: Oxford University Press.

Gillanders, C. (2007). An English-speaking prekindergarten teacher for young Latino children: Implications of the teacher–child relationship on second language learning. *Early Child Education Journal, 35*(1), 47–54.

Goffin, S. G. (2013). *Early childhood education for a new era: Leading for our profession.* New York: Teachers College Press.

Gonzalez, N., Moll, L. C., & Amanti, C. (2005). *Funds of knowledge: Theorizing practices in households and classrooms.* Mahwah, NJ: Lawrence Erlbaum Associates.

Goodnow, J. J., Miller, P. J., & Kessel, E. (Eds.). (1995). *Cultural practices as contexts for development. New directions for child development (67).* San Francisco, CA: Jossey-Bass.

Gorodetsky, M., & Barak, J. (2008). The educational-cultural edge: A participative learning environment for co-emergence of personal and institutional growth. *Teaching and Teacher Education, 24*(7), 1907–1918.

Granger, R., Tseng, V., & Wilcox, B. (2013). Connecting research and practice. In E. Gershoff, R. Mistry, & D. Crosby (Eds.), *Societal contexts of child development: Pathways of influence and implications for practice and policy.* New York: Oxford University Press.

Graue, M. E., Kroeger, J., & Prager, D. (2001). A Bakhtinian analysis of particular home-school relations. *American Educational Research Journal, 38*(3), 467–498.

Greene, M. (2001). Interpretation and re-vision: Toward another story. In J. T. Sears & J. Dan Marshall (Eds.), *Teaching and thinking about curriculum: Critical inquiries* (pp. 75–78). Troy, NY: Educator's International Press.

Grieshaber, S., & Cannella, G. (2001). *Embracing identities in early childhood education: Diversity and possibility.* New York: Teachers College Press.

Hagen, J. W., & Conley, A. C. (1994, Spring). Ethnicity and race of children studied in *Child Development,* 1980–1993. *SRCD Newsletter,* 6–7. Los Angeles, CA: Society for Research in Child Development.

Halpern, R. (2013). Tying early childhood education more closely to schooling: Promise, perils and practical problems. *Teachers College Record, 115*(1), 1–28.

Harkness, S., & Super, C. (Eds.). (1996). *Parents' cultural belief systems: Their origins, expressions, and consequences.* New York: Guilford Press.

Harrington, M. (1962). *The other America—Poverty in the United States.* New York: Macmillan.

Head Start Bureau. (2000). *The Head Start child outcomes framework.* Washington, DC: Author.

Hong, S. (2011). *A cord of three strands: A new approach to parent engagement in schools.* Cambridge, MA: Harvard Education Press.

Huston, A. C. (1994). Children in poverty: Designing research to affect policy. *Social Policy Report, 8*(2), 1–12.

Huston, A. C. (2014). Epilogue: The ecology of human development in the 21st century. In E. T. Gershoff, R. S. Mistry, & D. A. Crosby (Eds.), *Societal contexts of child development: Pathways of influence and implications for practice and policy* (pp. 220–229). New York: Oxford University Press.

Hyson, M., & Tomlinson, H. B. (2014). *The early years matter: Education, care, and the well-being of children, birth to 8.* New York: Teachers College Press.

Iorio, J. M., & Adler, S. M. (2013). Take a number, stand in line, better yet, be a number get tracked: The assault of longitudinal data systems on teaching and learning. *Teachers College Record.* Retrieved from http://www.tcrecord.org

Katz, L., & Chard, S. (1989). *Engaging children's minds: The project approach.* Norwood, NJ: Ablex.

Kessen, W. (1979). The American child and other cultural inventions. *American Psychologist, 34*(10), 815–820.

Kirp, D. (2007). *The sandbox investment: The preschool movement and kids-first politics.* Boston, MA: Harvard University Press.

Lally, R. (2013). *For our babies: Ending the invisible neglect of America's infants.* New York: Teachers College Press.

Lancy, D., Bock, J., & Gaskins, S. (Eds.). (2010). *The anthropology of learning in childhood.* New York: Alta-Mira Press/Rowman & Littlefield.

Lareau, A. (2003). *Unequal childhoods: Class, race, and family life.* Berkeley, CA: University of California Press.

LeVine, R. A. (1980). Anthropology and child development. In C. Super & S. Harkness (Eds.), *Anthropological perspectives on child development. New directions for child development, 1980*(8), (pp. 71–86). San Francisco, CA: Jossey-Bass.

LeVine, R. A., Dixon, S., LeVine, S., Richman, A., Leiderman, P. H., Keefer, C. H., & Brazelton, T. B. (1994). *Child-care and culture: Lessons from Africa.* Cambridge, UK: Cambridge University Press.

LeVine, R., & New, R. (Eds.). (2008). *Anthropology and child development: Selected readings.* Malden, MA: Blackwell Publishers.

Li, J. (2012). *Cultural foundations of learning: East and West.* Cambridge, UK: Cambridge University Press.

Lubeck, S. (2000). On reassessing the relevance of the child development knowledge base to education: A response. *Human Development, 43*(4–5), 273–278.

Mallory, B., & New, R. (Eds.). (1994). *Diversity and developmentally appropriate practices: Challenges for early childhood education.* New York: Teachers College Press.

Maxwell, K. L., Lim, C-I., & Early, D. M. (2006). *Early childhood teacher preparation programs in the United States: National report.* Chapel Hill, NC: University of North Carolina, FPG Child Development Institute.

Moran, M. J., Desrochers, L., & Cavicchi, N. (2007). Progettazione and documentation as sociocultural activities: Changing communities of practice. *The Journal of Theory Into Practice, 46*(1), 81–90.

National Commission on Excellence in Education. (1983). A nation at risk: The imperative for educational reform: A report to the nation and the Secretary of Education, United States Department of Education. U.S. Government Printing Office (Stock No. 065-000-00177-2). Retrieved from http://datacenter.spps.org/uploads/sotw_a_nation_at_risk_1983.pdf

New, R. (2013). Looking back and moving forward. *Journal of Early Childhood Teacher Education, 34*(1), 113–118.

New, R. (1999). "What should children learn? Making choices and taking chances." *Early Childhood Research and Practice, 1*(2), 1–25. Retrieved from www.eric.org/ecrp

New, R., & Kantor, R. (2013). Reggio Emilia in the 21st century: Enduring commitments amid new challenges. In J. Roopnarine & J. Johnson (Eds.), *Approaches to early childhood education* (6th ed.) (pp. 331–354). Boston, MA: Pearson.

New, R., Mallory, B., and Mantovani, S. (2000). Cultural images of children, parents, and teachers: Italian home-school relations. *Early Education and Development, 11*(5), 597–616.

OECD. (2006). *Starting strong: Early childhood education and care* (vols. I & II). Paris, FR: Author.

Peers, C., & Fleer, M. (2014). The theory of 'belonging': Defining concepts used within Belonging, Being and Becoming—The Australian early years learning framework. *Educational Philosophy and Theory, 46*(8), 914–928.

Project Zero. (2003). Making teaching visible: Documenting individual and group learning as professional development. Cambridge, MA: Project Zero, Harvard University.

Putnam, R. (2015). *Our kids: The American dream in crisis.* New York: Simon & Schuster.

Qin, D. B. (2006). "Our child doesn't talk to us anymore": Alienation in immigrant Chinese families. *Anthropology & Education Quarterly, 37*(2), 162–179.

Rhodes, H., & Huston, A. C. (2012). Building the workforce our youngest children deserve. *SRCD Social Policy Report, 26*(1), 1–26.

Ritchie, S., & Gutmann, L. (Eds.). (2013). *FirstSchool: Transforming preK-3rd grade for African American, Latino, and low-income children.* New York: Teachers College Press.

Rogoff, B. (2003). *The cultural nature of human development.* Oxford, UK: Oxford University Press.

Roopnarine, J., and Johnson, J. (Eds.). (2013). *Approaches to early childhood education* (6th ed.). Boston, MA: Pearson.

Rutter, M. (2002). Nature, nurture, and development: From evangelism through science toward policy and practice. *Child Development, 73*(1), 1–21.

Saraceno, C. (1984). The social construction of childhood: Child care and education policies in Italy and the United States. *Social Problems, 31*(3), 351–363.

Schweinhart, L., Montie, J., Xiang, Z., Barnett, W. S., Belfield, C. R., & Nores, M. (2005). *Lifetime effects: The High/Scope Perry Preschool study through age 40.* (Monographs No. 14, High/Scope Educational Research Foundation). Ypsilanti, MI: High/Scope Press.

Sherrod, L. (1998). Report from the committee on child development, public policy, and public information. *Society for Research on Child Development Newsletter, 41*(1), 3–7.

Shonkoff, J. P., & Phillips, D. A. (Eds.). (2000). *From neurons to neighborhoods: The science of early childhood development.* Washington, DC: National Academy Press.

Solomon, G. (Ed.). (1993). *Distributed cognitions: Psychological and educational considerations.* Cambridge, UK: Cambridge University Press.

Suárez-Orozco, C., Suárez-Orozco, M., & Todorova, I. (2008). *Learning a new land: Immigrant students in American society.* Cambridge, MA: Harvard University Press.

Super, C., & Harkness, S. (1986). The developmental niche: A conceptualization at the interface of child and culture. *International Journal of Behavioral Development, 9,* 545-569.

Tobin, J., Wu, Y. H., & Davidson, D. (1989). *Preschools in three cultures: Japan, China and the U.S.* New Haven, CT: Yale University Press.

Valdes, G. (1996). *Con respeto: Bridging the distances between culturally diverse families and school: An ethnographic portrait.* New York: Teachers College Press.

Whitebook, M., Phillips, D., & Howes, C. (2014). *Worthy work, STILL unlivable wages: The early childhood workforce 25 years after the National Child Care Staffing Study.* Berkeley, CA: Center for the Study of Child Care Employment, University of California, Berkeley.

Williams, R. (1977). *Marxism and literature.* New York: Oxford University Press.

Zigler, E., Gilliam, W., & Barnett, W. S. (2011). *The Pre-K debates: Current controversies and issues.* Baltimore, MD: Brookes Publishing Company.

2

HISTORY OF EARLY CHILDHOOD TEACHER EDUCATION

Blythe Farb Hinitz and Betty Liebovich, with Charlotte Jean Anderson

Early childhood teacher education (ECTE) in the United States (U.S.) is first a story of people and later of philosophies, theories, organizations, and institutions. We will examine the history of U.S. ECTE in preparing professionals for kindergarten, nursery, child care, and primary education groups and classrooms, highlighting the rich variety of ECTE from the 1800s to today. The diversity of ECTE probably matches that of its "clients"—preservice and inservice teachers (female/male; African-American, Hispanic-American, American Indian, Asian-American, and European-American; professing a variety of religious and cultural beliefs and practices)—and the children and families with whom they work. We will synthesize previously published research focused predominantly on European-American teacher preparation and add relevant recent information. The earliest literature about U.S. ECTE focused on a population that was first male and White, then female and White. In reality, there was an active parallel group of African-American early childhood teacher educators whose important contributions will be discussed. We also include highlights of the available research about other under-represented ECTE populations.

The definition of early childhood teacher education is inclusive of the definition of early childhood education (ECE). In the U.S., ECE encompasses children from birth to age eight, whereas in other countries the age parameters vary. U.S. teacher education programs historically prepared educators to work in kindergartens and primary level programs, then later expanded to nursery school and child care settings.

The roots of U.S. ECTE lie in Europe, with the German Froebelian kindergartens, Montessori's Children's House in Italy, and the work of the McMillan sisters and Grace Owen in England. For a comprehensive review of the German beginnings of kindergarten teacher education in the United States, starting with Mathilda Kriege and Maria Kraus-Boelte, see Hewes (1990) and Lascarides & Hinitz (2011). Some of the originators of early education programs in the U.S., including Margaret Naumburg, founder of Walden School (and later teacher educator in art therapy), studied with Maria Montessori; others, like Elizabeth Harrison, visited Rome and reported observations. Hampton Institute's kindergarten teacher training program affirmed a Montessorian influence toward learning practical life skills. When academics such as William Heard Kilpatrick disparaged the Montessori Method, there was a fifty-year hiatus in the acceptance of Montessori training and schools in the U.S. (Lascarides & Hinitz, 2011).

Roots of U.S. Kindergarten Teacher Preparation

The earliest kindergartens in the U.S., both German-speaking and English-speaking, had teacher training departments, often apprenticing young women and basing the theoretical portion of the preparatory course on observations made in the classroom. Hewes reminds us that the development of teacher training classes for young women in the early 1800s was dependent upon market demand (i.e. school financial considerations, women's salaries were lower than men's) and the use of more humane disciplinary measures that did not necessitate "strong men to carry out the whippings that had been common in colonial schools" (Hewes, 1990, p. 3). The majority of the classes, such as those begun by William and Eudora Hailmann, were in private academies and training schools (Lascarides & Hinitz, 2011). Susan Blow began free training classes for assistants in her St. Louis kindergartens.

The introduction of kindergarten teacher training into normal schools and colleges was difficult. The genesis of National Louis University is illustrative of the process. Elizabeth Harrison became a student of Alice Putnam's Kindergarten Training School in 1879. Nine months later, she received both a diploma and a certificate to train kindergarten teachers. Harrison continued her study at Susan Blow's Kindergarten School in St. Louis and with John Kraus and Maria Kraus-Boelte in New York. Upon returning to Chicago in 1883, Harrison began the Chicago Kindergarten Club, and in 1886 she opened Miss Harrison's Training Class, later renamed the Chicago Kindergarten Training School, and, in 1891, the Chicago Kindergarten College. The College required completion of a high school education for admission. Following several name changes, it incorporated and affiliated with the National Kindergarten Association in 1912. As the National Kindergarten and Elementary College, it was accredited to award bachelor's degrees. In 1920 Harrison retired and turned the presidency of the College over to Edna Dean Baker. Her sister Clara Bell Baker supervised the new Demonstration School for kindergarten and elementary students. In 1930, the College adopted a four-year undergraduate curriculum and changed its name to National College of Education. The most recent name change, to National Louis University, came in 1990 with the separation of the Colleges of Arts & Sciences and Management & Business from the National College of Education (Goddard, 2007a, 2007b, n.d.). Chicago was a hub of progressive early childhood education and teacher education from 1885 to 1930. Colonel Francis Parker became the head of the Cook County Normal School in 1883, turning it into a well-respected teacher preparation institution that included an ECE program (Hinitz, 2013b).

Roots of U.S. Nursery School Teacher Preparation

Among the purposes for starting nursery schools in the U.S. was teacher training. Other purposes included research and parent education (Hymes & Eliot, 1978). The fields represented by the founders included: social work, home economics, nursing, psychology, education, and medicine/psychiatry (Hymes & Eliot, 1978). Consequently, the preparatory curriculum for both nursery school teachers and directors encompassed necessary content, skills, and dispositions from the six representative fields. The English roots of nursery school teacher preparation are the precursor of preschool teacher education in the U.S. The majority of the original U.S. nursery school teachers, directors, and teacher educators were trained in England by Margaret McMillan or Grace Owen.

Margaret McMillan (1860–1931)

In England, up until The Education Act of 1918, Grant Regulations No. 6, little notice was taken of the need for early years (EY) settings for children under the age of five. Any prior education act merely acknowledged that young children were attending primary schools but did little to acknowledge a need to create widespread provision for children under five. McMillan battled continuously for the general public to accept nursery schools as desirable and the training of their teachers as necessary (Bradburn, 1989). The 1918 Education Act was ground-breaking, stating a need for the creation of more nursery schools and defining the aims of nursery schools to include "definite training—bodily, mental and social—involving the cultivation of good habits in the widest sense, under the guidance and oversight of a skilled and intelligent teacher" (EA, 1918, p. 88). Further, this Act maintained that children would be supported by "women who possess qualifications and experience for the training and teaching of young children" (EA, 1918, p. 123). Money was allocated to Local Education Authorities instructed to "encourage persons in their [nursery schools] employment to obtain, if they do not already possess, qualifications for work in elementary and other schools and departments for young children" (EA, 1918, p. 124). Nursery schools were intended to be a separate institution from infant schools (institutions for children ages five to seven years), but could be settings attached to other organizations, such as a day nursery or infant department of a public school.

The Education Act of 1921 (EA, 1921) made provision for grants to organize nursery schools for children over two and under five, to be administered and overseen by Local Education Authorities. With this in mind, Margaret McMillan and Grace Owen were instrumental in contributing to the national approach to educating teachers of young children. McMillan inaugurated initial teacher training in the open-air nursery in Deptford in 1919, and Owen became the principal of the Mather Training College in Manchester, England in 1924.

In 1923, the Nursery School Association (NSA) was established, with McMillan as president and Owen as honorary secretary. Both led the group in determining guidelines for EY teacher education in England. They respected each other's ideals for teacher education, but differed in their principles of that training. "McMillan's insistence on economies of scale and a schooling that acknowledged the pattern of working-class life, brought her into conflict with the NSA" (Steedman, 2004–2014, p. 3). McMillan was adamant that working-class women who were interested in pursuing a career in EY education be considered for EY teacher education. The NSA insisted that only women who had experience with young children or a background education, which working-class women would not necessarily possess, be considered for EY teacher education.

McMillan was passionate about the importance of "well trained" teachers and felt that children were "cheated" when subjected to inadequately trained teachers. In her opinion, two years with two teaching practices was insufficient; she believed that the job of educating young children could not be achieved without more rigorous and extensive training. According to McMillan, "they [teacher trainees] should have three years sound practice in teaching before they are allowed to be responsible for the education of children" (McMillan, 1927, p. 198). (In the minutes of the NSA meeting regarding creation of a standardized teaching program, McMillan was quoted as being unsupportive of the two-year course of study.)

The Rachel McMillan Training College began with Margaret McMillan and her sister Rachel opening what is now called the Rachel McMillan Nursery in 1914 in Deptford, Southeast London, an area characterized by the squalor of its tenements and rampant poverty. From its inception, the nursery was a training center for EY teachers. McMillan felt that there would be no future for the growing number of nursery schools in England without carefully trained teachers and workers. McMillan had difficulty recruiting teachers to work in the nursery due to a lack of understanding of the need for teaching young children. She realized that nursery schools could only grow if there were sufficient well-trained teachers to staff them. In her words:

> Many people supposed that training of any kind was unnecessary—that any kind of nice, motherly girl would do for a nursery teacher. Nurseries were to be, in other words, a dumping ground for the well-intentioned but dull women of today.
>
> *(McMillan, 1919, p. 15)*

The program of study in "The College" reflected McMillan's ethos of caring for the whole child, involving parents and the community in education, and the need for specially trained teachers. She believed young children needed education and care, which she saw as inseparable, and specially-trained teachers as teacher-nurses. She espoused "a nursery teacher is dealing with a brain and a soul even if she's dealing with a nose and a lip" (McMillan, 1919, p. 15).

In response to her repeatedly encountering trained teachers who could not cope with the poverty of the community and who fell into despair when confronted with large classes of deprived children, her student teachers in "The College" began working with children immediately. It was not until the second and third year of study that students began working with theory, equipped with "a thousand memories to give it new interest" (McMillan, 1919, p. 19).

The final step of attaining her dream of offering young children a sound education was for McMillan to build a training college specifically designed for educating EY teachers. Using her network of social connections, she obtained financial and political support mainly through Nancy Astor and Lloyds of London. New buildings in Creek Road, Deptford connected to the existing nursery were opened on May 8, 1930 by Queen Mary a year before Margaret's death. Students took a three-year full-time course of study leading to a Froebel Certificate.

Grace Owen (1873–1965)

In organizing the teacher training program at Mather Training College (overseen by the Manchester Education Committee), Grace Owen drew on her understanding and respect for Friedrich Froebel's ideal of greater freedom of activity for young children in a learning environment and the use of "occupations" to educate young children and their teachers "through play and contact with nature" (Owen, 1923, p. 12). Owen was dedicated to the Nursery School Movement and stated "staffing will need the utmost care, since inefficiency would bring about the failure of the movement" (Owen, 1923, p. 16). She found that in the 1923 climate of primary education, a "teacher of young children may or may not be specially trained" counter to the Education Act (1918) specifically stating women teaching young children should possess qualification and experience (Owen, 1923, p. 17). Owen felt strongly that there was a need to offer teacher training for women in the "adequate provision of skilled care and hygienic conditions" and that Local Authorities would be instrumental in providing this training (Owen, 1923, p. 17). Following from the Froebel model of supporting young children's development, Owen sought to train teachers to embrace and support the idea of young children not having formal instruction.

When recruiting trainee teachers of young children, Owen sought those with a "complete sincerity of character," which would allow the child to develop trust in the future teacher (Owen, 1923, p. 133). She firmly believed that special training for the teacher of young children was necessary and that training should be commensurate with that of teachers "recognized as trained and certified by the Board of Education" (Owen, 1923, p. 134). Although the training of an EY teacher needed to be specialized, Owen felt strongly that the status of an EY teacher should be the same as that of an infant school teacher (Owen, 1923, p. 134).

Owen's views on the duration of teacher training differed from McMillan's. Owen embraced the ideal that two years (the typical Government Training College program) were sufficient to prepare the EY teacher. Further, she felt that, with appropriate prior experience, a one-year program focusing on EY teaching was adequate "top up" training. The candidates that Owen found most worthy of studying to teach young children were women with varied gifts—including a desire to support children with special needs, an interest in psychology and child development, and the aspiration to support fellow women in developing a career rather than toiling away in mindless work (Owen, 1923).

In January 1925, The NSA of Great Britain proposed a suggested course of training for nursery school teachers that was approved by the Board of Education and adopted by many teacher training colleges—one exception being "The College," as Margaret McMillan did not support a two-year course of study. The NSA proposed that entrance qualifications, as required by the Board of Education for teacher trainees, include either a two-year course of study leading to a Teacher's Certificate or a one-year course of study for college-trained certificated teachers.

The foundations of EY teacher training in England are largely credited to the work and determination of Margaret McMillan and Grace Owen. Although they did not agree on the details of the curriculum offered in training colleges, they did agree that a specialist teacher of young children was necessary and that young children deserved the expertise of a professional educated to understand and nurture their minds, bodies, and spirits. Both influenced training and practice worldwide, making it their mission to spread their understanding and technique as far as possible. Each spent her life in the pursuit of offering young children a high-quality learning environment provided by dedicated teachers attuned to their specific developmental needs and interests.

From the beginning of the twentieth century, both McMillan and Owen had connections to early education teacher training and practice in the United States. The Rachel McMillan Nursery and "The College" had many visitors from across the world. Grace Owen attended Teachers' College of Columbia University (TC) between 1900 and 1905, graduating with a Bachelor of Science degree. As a student, she attended a lecture course given by Patty Smith Hill and took the ideas of her blocks and block play back to England. While in New York, Owen published an article about her impressions of the kindergarten movement in *Child Life* and took the ideas she learned about Froebel and kindergarten back to Manchester, England where she incorporated these ideals into her teacher training program (Owen, 1900).

There was no professional training for nursery school educators in the United States during the early 1920s. Prospective teacher-educators and administrators had two choices: to go to England to study or to hire a teacher trained there. One American who studied with McMillan in Deptford and observed the nursery organized and run by Owen in Manchester, England was Abigail Adams Eliot. In 1921, funded by the Women's Education Association of Boston, Eliot sailed to England for the sole purpose of learning about teaching young children and studying with Margaret McMillan.

Eliot found the educational experience at "The College" very stimulating and commented that "by actual work, guided by the skillful teacher's example and suggestion, we learned what young children could do, what help they needed, what attitude toward them brought the best results, what makes up a young child's day. We were involved in their learning and their physical welfare and development" (Eliot, 1960). Eliot realized that her experiences in England were invaluable to her developing understanding of learning and teaching in the early years. Upon returning home to Boston at the end of 1922, Eliot began following through on her plans for creating the Ruggles Street Nursery School and Training Center in the Roxbury section of Boston (Eliot, 1972).

Eliot was also responsible for bringing a teacher from England to assist the group of mothers who established the Cambridge Nursery School in Massachusetts. The cooperative ran a ten-week experimental summer program during which the middle-class mothers assisted the McMillan teacher. The first purpose-built nursery school building was erected and officially opened in the fall of 1923 (Hewes, 1998, p. 40–41).

Edna Noble White worked and studied with McMillan at Deptford in 1920–1921. She returned to Detroit as the founding director of the Merrill-Palmer Motherhood and Home Training School, funded by the bequest of Lizzie Merrill Palmer. White realized that McMillan's theory and practice in support of children's physical health blended well with her previous training in home economics and nutrition at the University of Illinois and her work as a home economics professor at the Ohio State University (1908 to 1919). White utilized these understandings as the basis for establishing a nursery school that, in 1922, became the second center for child development research in the U.S. (the first was the Iowa Child Welfare Research Station, opened in 1917, and supported by Rockefeller funds from 1922 through the 1930s). White demonstrated that child development and parent education were worthy of college-level study by initiating a research program and interdisciplinary course of study, including education, home economics, nutrition, pediatrics, psychology, and social work at the only research station not attached to a university (Lascarides & Hinitz, 2011).

Alice V. Keliher of New York University visited the McMillan nursery while she was a doctoral student at TC in 1929. She took moving pictures widely shown throughout the U.S. and was hired by Arnold Gesell for a three-year naturalistic study of babies at Yale University (Shipley, 1992). Ida Jones Curry used part of her 1935 Rockefeller Foundation Fellowship to spend a summer studying at the Rachel McMillan Training College and working in the nursery, and Oneida Cockrell visited the McMillan nursery. They brought lessons learned home to the Hampton Institute Nursery School and Early Childhood Development and Preschool Education courses, the Rosenwald-Garden Apartment Nursery School and Kindergarten, and several Chicago institutions of higher education.

Diverse Early Childhood Teacher Education

Gender and race continue to play a role in the makeup of the early childhood teacher education field. The contributions of its culturally and linguistically diverse population are a rarely discussed segment of U.S. ECTE. As recorded in many sources, the ECTE system trained students with diverse heritages to become teachers in private and public schools. However, the student population of the "mainstream" tertiary teacher-training institutions was almost entirely European-American. The African-American and bilingual—particularly Spanish-speaking—teacher educators within the under-researched multicultural/multilingual population must be acknowledged to provide a comprehensive understanding of U.S. ECTE.

The profession of early childhood teacher education began in the U.S. in the early 1800s with European-American and African-American ECTE people, programs, and publications. Horace Mann discerned a need for teacher training institutions and began the first normal schools in 1838. He was the president of Antioch College from 1853 to 1859, an institution of higher education (IHE) that educated both Black and White students. Henry Barnard, the first U.S. Commissioner of Education, advocated kindergarten education and related teacher training through his *American Journal of Education*. Superintendent of Schools William Torrey Harris insisted that Susan Blow receive specific professional training prior to opening the first free public school kindergarten in St. Louis in 1873. Haydee Campbell, the first Black graduate of Blow's kindergarten training program, received the highest score on the test for kindergarten supervisor, and in 1882 became the supervising principal of the "kindergartens for colored children" in the St. Louis Public Schools (Lascarides & Hinitz, 2011, p. 513; Children's Defense Fund, n.d.). Campbell was the organizer of the kindergarten department of the National Association of Colored Women (NACW), formed by the merger of The Colored Women's League of Washington and the National Federation of Afro-American Women in 1896.

William Hailmann and his wife, Eudora, established and conducted German-speaking and English-speaking kindergarten training schools in Milwaukee, Wisconsin; Detroit, Michigan; LaPorte, Indiana; and Winona, Minnesota from 1878 to 1894. After Eudora's death in 1904, William taught ...ormal schools in Chicago and Cleveland, and in his later years at the Broadoaks Kindergarten ...l School in Pasadena, California.

Parallel Systems

...teenth and the first half of the twentieth century, the U.S. had two parallel systems of ...Es founded by European-Americans and others founded by African-Americans. Most ...ources agree that Merrill Palmer in Detroit, the Ruggles Street Training Center in Boston, ... of Educational Experiments (now Bank Street College of Education), and Teachers Col... New York City were among the first European-American early childhood teacher ...utions in the U.S. These were followed by Yale University; the University of Califor... ...les; the University of Cincinnati; Johns Hopkins University; and Institutes of Child ...rted by Rockefeller funds) at several universities around the country, including Iowa,

Minnesota, and the University of California at Berkeley. Chapter XII of the *Twenty-Eighth National Society for the Study of Education Yearbook*, "Professional training for research and instruction in preschool education," describes the growth in professional training when study of the development of the preschool child was becoming a "new movement in education" (Whipple, 1929, p. 405). Scholarships to prepare applicants for "research in child development; resident instruction in child development and welfare in school, college, and University; child welfare services in clinics, institutions, social service, health organizations, schools, nursery school teaching, etc.; and parent education, in field organization, study—group leadership, extension programs, and resident instruction in college or university" are discussed (Whipple, 1929, pp. 406–407). The majority of the scholarship recipients (71%) held bachelor's degrees, 25% had master's degrees, and 3% had doctorates. These scholars were registered in university courses in research, psychology of childhood, general psychology, statistics, mental hygiene, education (curricular research, nursery school supervision, training of the teachers of young children, problems in preschool education, educational methods of young children, advanced educational psychology, mental and educational tests, educational measurements, problems of the training school, educational economics, rural education and psychology, character education, philosophy of education, and modern and experimental schools in Europe), parental education, sociology, nutrition and biochemistry, physiology and physical growth, art appreciation, contemporary American literature, and special problems in home economics, among others (Whipple, 1929).

The Traditional History of Early Childhood Teacher Education in the U.S.

European-American training institutions begun after the Civil War included the kindergarten training classes established by the Krieges (1868), the New York Seminary for Kindergartners (Maria Kraus-Boelte and John Kraus, 1872), the Chicago Kindergarten Club (Elizabeth Harrison, 1874), the first kindergarten training school in California (Emma Marwedal, 1876), the Louisville Free Kindergarten Association (Anna Bryan, 1887–1893; Patty Smith Hill, 1893–1905), the Chicago Froebel Kindergarten Association training school (Alice Putnam, 1874, later moved to Cook County Normal School, then to Hull House, 1898), Wheelock College (1889), Clark University (G. Stanley Hall, 1889), and Armour Institute (Chicago, 1893). Julia Tutwiler, the first woman president of an Alabama college (1890), instituted a number of innovative practices at the Alabama Normal College for Girls (ANC). Among them was the European system of combining the liberal arts (the academic program taught at the related Livingston Female Academy) with pedagogical methods (taught at the ANC) into a progressive teacher preparation program. The late 1890s found Nina Vandewalker directing the Milwaukee Normal School Kindergarten Department (1897–1920) and Susan Blow teaching at TC (1896–1909). In 1905, Blow was joined by Patty Smith Hill, with whom she debated about ECE for four years. Hill rose rapidly through the academic ranks, becoming a full professor in 1922. She retire[illegible] from the TC faculty, but not from professional work, in 1935.

Alice Temple (1871–1946), who considered the "education of teachers as the major source [illegible] education at all age levels" (Snyder, 1972, p. 195), was a staunch proponent of unified kinderg[illegible] grade curriculum and teaching. She was influenced by Anna Bryan as a student, and later [illegible] at the Chicago Free Kindergarten Association, and by John Dewey as a student and a [illegible] School teacher at the University of Chicago. According to *Unified Kindergarten and First-Gr*[illegible] which Temple co-authored with Samuel Chester Parker, teacher training for a unified curric[illegible] include the subject matter to be taught, certain skills, the use of many devices, and the abil[illegible] stand and apply general principles of teaching (Parker & Temple, 1925).

Ella Flagg Young (1845–1918), a teacher trainer and principal in Chicago for thir[illegible] Dewey's department at the University of Chicago in 1899. In a paper presented to the [illegible] cation Association (NEA) in 1887, Young stated that teachers "ought to know what th[illegible] to accomplish in the classroom, why, and how they were doing it," a foreshadowing of h[illegible]

When the Dewey family left for New York City in 1904, Young spent a year in Europe, returning to head the Chicago Normal School from 1905 to 1909. As the Normal School leader, Young insisted that its "programs respond directly to the needs of the city's school children." She innovatively sent teacher candidates into typical city schools each morning, followed by the study of academic subjects and psychology in the afternoon, a pattern similar to the one followed by kindergarten and nursery school educators. She "demanded free and independent judgment on the part of both faculty and students" (Goddard, 2007a, p. 4; Goddard, 2003, p. 9).

Two educators who made important personal research contributions to the early childhood field as professors, authors, and mentors are Lois Hayden Meek Stolz (1891–1984) and Millie Almy (1915–2001), both of whom received doctorates from TC. Stolz was a project director at the Laura Spelman Rockefeller Fund, the Education Secretary of the American Association of University Women (AAUW), and a faculty member at three universities. During her tenure at the University of California at Berkeley Institute of Child Welfare, Stolz became the Executive Director of the World War II Kaiser shipyard Child Service Centers. Millie Almy taught at TC (1944–1948 and 1952–1971), the University of Cincinnati College of Home Economics (1948–1951), and the University of California at Berkeley (1971–1980), where she founded the Interdisciplinary Day Care and Child Development Project (Almy & Snyder, 1947). Almy's research focused on young children's mental and affective development and on how young children understand science, math, and literature. Almy served as regional director of federally funded preschools in Buffalo, New York during the Works Progress Administration (WPA).

Unexplored Populations in Early Childhood Teacher Education in the U.S.

Each of the populations discussed in the sections below had (and some still have) a specific set of difficulties with which to contend and overcome or circumvent in order to become an integral part of ECTE. Most African-Americans arrived as slaves or were born into slavery in the U.S. Schooling was forbidden under slavery. Immediately prior to and during the Civil War, this situation led to contentious debates. The founding of a parallel set of specifically Black normal schools and seminaries, which became the Historically Black Colleges and Universities (HBCUs) of the present era, resulted from these events. There were many funding difficulties and the institutions required the support of religious groups, industrial leaders, women's clubs, and foundations. During the past several years, there have been a growing number of doctoral dissertations about Black (particularly female) ECTE leaders. The increasing recognition given to these individuals supports the theses promulgated in this chapter.

Hispanic-Americans faced, and continue to face, numerous language and cultural barriers. Until the most recent U.S. census, they constituted a mainly immigrant population, with limited primary, secondary, and tertiary education and career skills development. Asian-Americans have likewise historically constituted an immigrant population with initially limited English language skills. Unlike Hispanic-Americans, they fought for U.S. educational opportunities. However, until the upsurge in Asian-American ECE doctoral students in recent decades, they mainly taught their own populations. The dissimilarities of these two ECTE populations from the "mainstream" have led to the small percentage of Latino-/Latina- and Asian-American early childhood teacher educators working today. It is likely that the demographic trends in ECTE doctoral programs will soon impact this situation.

Historically, early childhood teacher education was designed to prepare women for motherhood; therefore, women taught practical courses and founded kindergarten and nursery training institutions. The men who became teacher educators or professors of ECE, such as Hailmann, Dewey, Kilpatrick, Hymes, and Spodek, had a strong theoretical and historical background, a specific philosophy, and ties to practical aspects of the field. However, with the exception of Booker T. Washington, they did not found schools and colleges; rather, they were founded by psychologists, such as Gessell (Yale Clinic of Child Development, 1911) and Hall (Clark University, 1887). Asa Hilliard, III (1933–2007), Fuller E. Callaway Professor of Urban Education at Georgia State University (1980–2007), was unique. He was a renowned expert on Africa and its culture, and the author of hundreds of articles and books (APA, 2014; Hillard, 1974).

African-American Early Childhood Teacher Education

African-American ECTE developed in parallel, blossoming after the end of the Civil War with the founding of several normal and industrial institutes and seminaries that became major HBCUs. Institutions founded during that time period included: Atlanta University (AU, 1865), Fisk University (1866), Howard University (1867), Hampton Institute (HI, now University, 1868), Spelman College (SC, 1881), Tuskegee Institute (now University, 1881), and the Haines Normal and Industrial Institute (1886), which featured the first kindergarten in Augusta, Georgia, established by Lucy Craft Laney (1854–1933) as a separate Kindergarten Department within the Institute. Each of these institutions included preparation of early education teachers under the auspices of either the Department of Home Economics or the Child Development segment of the Psychology Department.

The description of Hampton Institute is indicative of the scope and purpose of many early HBCUs. Hampton Normal and Agricultural Institute (for freedmen) was founded in April 1868 on land purchased by the American Missionary Association (AMA) in June 1867, in order to meet a

> need for teachers in the country public schools of the South. . . . With the improvement of the colored race, more thoroughly equipped teachers are necessary, not only for the public schools, but for the workshops, and for the industrial and agricultural schools that have started up all through the South and among the Indians of the West. To meet this need Hampton provides an Academic Department with a corps of able teachers, mostly graduates of normal schools and colleges, who give thorough instruction in the English branches. Beside this manual training is given to the boys, and sewing, cooking and bench work to the girls. . . . Those who wish to fit themselves to become teachers in the public schools, after graduation from the Academic Department, enter the Normal Department, where they receive instruction in methods of teaching, and have practice in the Whittier School, in which there are over three hundred children, with a kindergarten and classes in cooking, gymnastics, and the English branches.
>
> *(Richings, 1904, pp. 445, 453, 456)*

However, some institutions were universities from the beginning. Howard University was founded in the District of Columbia in 1867. From its inception, it awarded diplomas in kindergarten education and in 1902 provided advanced work leading to a kindergarten director's diploma (Richings, 1904; Cunningham & Osborn, 1979).

The HBCUs discussed above were sponsored and financially supported by religious groups or by the philanthropic funds of wealthy industrialists and business people. The Rockefeller-funded General Education Board, Rockefeller Foundation, and Spelman Fund provided start-up and continuing financial support for numerous research and curriculum projects, IHEs, and schools over many decades. The Julius Rosenwald Fund, using Sears and Roebuck profits, supported the training of numerous Black teachers and administrators and the building of many Black schools and homes in the South, as well as child care centers and schools in its home city of Chicago. Other funders included the Peabody Fund, Slater Fund, Phelps-Stokes Fund, and the Anne Jeanes Foundation. Many of the kindergartens for African-American children and later the nursery and child care programs that served as training sites were supported by Black women's clubs and organizations.

A predominantly "industrial education" philosophy and curriculum with related "normal" courses to train teachers was supported. However, there were overt and covert "pockets of resistance." Under Black control, their schools "quickly became teacher-training institutions whose academic emphasis was more literary than industrial and agricultural." The opposing philosophies of Black education and teacher education are symbolized by Booker T. Washington (1856–1915), educated at HI and founder of Tuskegee Institute, and W.E.B. DuBois (1868–1963), a graduate of Fisk with a Harvard University Ph.D. Born a slave, Washington believed that the hope of his people lay in hard work and submission to authority. "He argued that by producing good workers, industrial education would reduce white hostility toward black schooling and slowly lead to greater economic security." DuBois publicly challenged "Washington's policies of submission, gradualism and compromise," stating that "industrial training should be secondary to a literary and professional education for black leaders" (Allison, 1995, 146–148, 150–152).

During the decades from 1865 to 1965, a group of teacher education programs existed at HBCUs that were run for and by Black lay and clerical leaders. The women who populated this impressive body of African-American ECT educators spearheaded the introduction of current theories and practice of the time period and more recently "developmentally appropriate practice" in ECE, in primary schools, kindergartens, and later nursery schools for Black children (Bredekamp, 2014).

Some outstanding Black ECT educators began teaching out of fiscal necessity in their mid-teens, with or without higher education; these include Ida Wells Barnett, Charlotte Hawkins Brown, and Oneida Cockrell. Some, like Margaret Murray Washington and Oneida Cockrell, worked full time while attending college on a part-time basis. Others, such as Ida Wells Barnett at Fisk and Evangeline Ward at Cornell, attended professional courses during the summer. Some, like Josephine Silone Yates, were the first Black applicants certified to teach in a specific state. Most received their bachelor's (B) and master's (M) degrees from HBCUs. Mary Church Terrell and Haydee Campbell (B—Oberlin), Josephine Silone Yates (B—Rhode Island State Normal School, M—National University of Illinois), Charlotte Hawkins Brown (B—Wellesley), and Ida Jones Curry (M—TC) were exceptions. Curry, a 1932 Rockefeller Foundation Fellowship recipient, served as a Graduate Assistant to Roma Gans. Curry received a second Rockefeller Foundation Fellowship to study and observe nursery schools and kindergartens in England, France, Belgium, and Holland in 1935 and completed her Master of Arts in Child Development in 1936 (Personal communication, Registrar TC, May, 2014). All of the women discussed above returned to HBCUs to teach. In those days, a master's degree in Child Development from TC was the equivalent of a doctorate today (Aldridge & Christensen, 2013; Christensen & Rababah, 2013; Funeral Services for Ida Louise J. Curry Saturday June 26, 1993, copy 2014; Wadelington, 1984, Revised 1997).

Those Black students who attended one of the very few integrated colleges had experiences similar to that of Mary Eliza Church Terrell at Oberlin College. She obtained a Bachelor of Arts degree in the "gentlemen's course," a four-year program consisting of classical studies, including Greek and Latin. Terrell avoided the "ladies' curriculum," a two-year Literary Course leading only to a certificate. Oberlin was strongly abolitionist and had served as a station on the Underground Railroad, providing safe houses for slaves escaping to the North (Lascarides & Hinitz, 2011, p. 512–513).

The late 1800s also saw the beginnings of cooperation, if not collaboration, between fledgling organizations for Black and White early childhood educators, spearheaded by leaders like Patty Smith Hill. The Louisville Free Kindergarten Association (LFKA), which Hill headed, invited the Louisville Colored Kindergarten Association to become a branch. This practice was unheard of at that time (Hinitz, 2013b, p. 14).

During the twentieth century, two widely heralded African-American women founded institutions of higher education in the South. Charlotte Hawkins Brown (1883–1961) founded the Alice Freeman Palmer Memorial Institute (PMI), named for the first woman president of Wellesley College, her Massachusetts mentor, in 1902. Benefactors, including the Julius Rosenwald Foundation (1916) and the AMA (1926–1934), funded the construction of buildings on the North Carolina campus and PMI operations. Following the closing of PMI in 1972, ownership of the grounds passed through several hands until the State of North Carolina purchased forty acres in 1987 for development of the state's first historic site commemorating the contributions of African-American education and women's history.

Mary McCleod Bethune (1875–1955) presided over HBCU Bethune-Cookman College, formed by the merger of the Daytona Normal and Institute for girls (founded by Bethune in 1904) and Cookman Institute for men, from 1923 to 1942. The Methodist Episcopal Church (MEC)-affiliated school included elementary and secondary courses, industrial training, and religious instruction. Bethune was a major figure in Black educational and organizational work. Her work with the NACW, the National Association for the Advancement of Colored People (NAACP), and the Association for the Study of Negro Life and History, the black history organization founded by Carter G. Woodson, brought her to the attention of U.S. Presidents Calvin Coolidge, Herbert Hoover, and Franklin Delano Roosevelt. She was the director of the Division of Negro Affairs in Roosevelt's New Deal administration, the only African-American who distributed funds for scholarships. Bethune often shared speaking platforms with Eleanor Roosevelt and was appointed by President Truman as a delegate to and advisor on interracial relations at the San Francisco Conference which led to the organization of the United Nations (Lewis, n.d.).

HBCU faculty sustained their promising undergraduate students by encouraging them to obtain higher academic degrees, assisting them in obtaining scholarships and jobs to cover the expenses they incurred, and providing them with a support network. For example, Flemmie Kittrell received a bachelor's degree from HI in 1928, one year prior to the opening of the Home Economics nursery school under the direction of Mrs. Phyllis Jones Tilly (Cunningham & Osborn, 1979). She taught at SC for Pearlie Reed (founder of the SC laboratory nursery school in 1930) who also mentored Dorothy Neal (Simpson & McConnell-Farmer, 2013).

Dorothy Nell Eberhardt Neal Birchette (c. 1918/1920–2013), a 1940 graduate of SC, received her Master of Arts degree from the Department of Education of AU in 1942. Her thesis, "A Study of Two Anthropometric Measures of the Children of the Spelman College Nursery School Atlanta, Georgia" (Eberhardt, 1942), closely paralleled work being done on White children at the Iowa Child Welfare Research Station and other research institutes during the same time period. In her literature review, Eberhardt cites responses from the very few people who had available data on Black children to share: Myrtle Thompson of Bennett College and Nina M. Kellog of the Mary Crane Nursery School at Hull House in Chicago.

Hampton Institute, Spelman College (founded as the Atlanta Baptist Female Seminary), and Atlanta University were the institutions of choice for study and jobs of the best and brightest Black education students. Hampton bachelor's alumni included Booker T. Washington, Flemmie Pansey Kittrell (1904–1980), and Evangeline Howlett Ward (1920–1985). Ida Louise Jones Curry (1912–1993), a graduate of Spelman guided by Pearlie Reese, became Director of the Hampton Nursery School and Instructor in Early Childhood Development and Preschool Education in 1937. She mentored Evangeline Bysshe (Somerville) Jones (Ward) (Marquis Who's Who, 1974–1975), whom she inspired with the realization "that there was such a thing as actual education of children below the age of six" (Simpson & McConnell-Farmer, 2013, p. 146). Curry, like Stolz and Almy, was a leader in the National Association for Nursery Education (NANE, now the National Association for the Education of Young Children—NAEYC) and a model for her students.

Drs. Kittrell and Ward returned to Hampton as Chair of the Department of Home Economics, Kittrell from 1940 to 1944 and Ward from 1946 to 1953. From that point, their paths diverged; Kittrell, the first Black recipient of a doctorate from Cornell University in Home Economics, became a professor at HBCU Howard University (1944–1971). Ward went to AU on scholarship and worked in the SC nursery school while completing her master's degree. She left Hampton a second time to pursue her doctoral studies at TC, completing her degree and Graduate Research Assistantship with Kenneth Wann in 1955. She remembered mirroring all of Wann's activities, from answering phone calls to library research to teaching courses (Personal communication with Hinitz in 1975). She held several administrative and faculty positions across the U.S. prior to joining the Temple University faculty in 1963. She continued her own professional development with summer study at Oxford University (1966) and the University of St. Andrews in Scotland (1968; Marquis Who's Who, 1974–1975).

Ward took pride in her influential roles in NAEYC, and the formulation of a Code of Ethics for the profession of early childhood education in 1976. The current (2015) NAEYC Code of Ethics is a testament to her belief that teacher educators and all early childhood professionals should adhere to specific ethical principles in working with students, families, and each other. After her retirement in June 1985, she looked forward to continuing her leadership on the World Organization for Early Childhood Education (OMEP) Working (Executive) Committee, where she served as an International Vice President. Her life was cut short by a brain aneurysm following her keynote speech at the Australian ECE national conference in October 1985. More than a dozen past and current ECT educators are her legacy, as she was a legacy for Ida Jones Curry (Hinitz, 2013b; Lascarides & Hinitz, 2011; Peltzman, 1998; Simpson & McConnell-Farmer, 2013).

One wonders whether Evangeline Ward realized that she and her mentor Ida Jones Curry are the link between the two parallel systems of early childhood teacher education. Both women earned degrees from prominent HBCUs, each received a higher level degree from a renowned European-American institution of higher education, and each passed the mantle of knowledge and practice to numerous teachers and teacher educators through their tenure on higher education faculties. However, Ward is the stronger link between the two systems, due to her teaching at Temple University, while Curry returned to an HBCU institution after completing her master's degree.

Hispanic-/Latina-/Latino- and Asian-American Early Childhood Teacher Education

The diversity of the ECTE community has rarely been noted in the literature. Three research-based volumes on early childhood teacher preparation appeared between 1988 and 1994. Although they discussed the role of the Early Childhood Educator (Almy, 1988), history and pedagogy of ECTE (Spodek & Saracho, 1990), and the competencies of the practitioner (Goffin & Day, 1994), with the exception of one chapter on men (Seifert, 1988) and one chapter providing a cross-cultural perspective (Saracho & Spodek, 1990), no mention is made of the increasing multiplicity of cultures and ethnicities represented by early education clientele and professional (preschool, kindergarten, and primary) staff. There is a particular dearth of information about Latin-American and Asian-American early childhood teacher educators.

Although there is a modest literature that addresses the rich historical contributions made by members of the Hispanic/Latina/Latino community, there are influential educationists from this heritage making history through their contributions to the field of early childhood and teacher education today. Some, like Josué Cruz, Dean of the College of Education and Human Development at Bowling Green State University, and Linda Espinosa, University of Missouri, Columbia, and Principal Investigator at the Center for Early Care and Education Research–Dual Language Learners (CECER-DLL) at the Frank Porter Graham Child Development Institute of the University of North Carolina, Chapel Hill, created change through their active involvement in higher education.

Olivia Saracho (University of Maryland) focuses on teacher preparation to meet the specific needs of young children from diverse populations. Her chapter discussing educational implications of teaching and approaches to Mexican-American students and their culture (Saracho & Hancock, 1983) was the only piece of this genre published prior to 2006.

Many prominent Hispanic ECT educators have headed and/or served on professional boards, drawing attention to an underserved and overlooked population of children and families' needs. Their organizational work focused on the Hispanic community and educational groups and those in early childhood and higher education. Dr. Espinosa was the lead consultant for the Best Practices for Young Dual Language Learners Project in the Child Development Division of the California State Department of Education. Ana Berdecía, whose work embraces directing the Center for Public Policy and the Positive Development of Urban Children of the John S. Watson Institute of Thomas Edison State College (NJ), chairing the Advisory Board of Professional Impact New Jersey, and community college teaching, utilizes a multi-modal approach to assist urban EC educators in obtaining the college degree that confers professional status.

Eugene E. Garcia, Distinguished Professor of Research at The National Hispanic University (NHU) and former Vice President for Education Partnerships at Arizona State University, chaired the National Task Force on Early Childhood Education for Hispanics (NTFECEH; NTFECEH, 2007). From the release of its report to the present, the Task Force, through its research-based recommendations to governments, educational researchers, and institutions of higher education, has become a major influence in improving the design, funding, and evaluation of the preparation of bilingual and culturally knowledgeable teachers (García, Jensen, & Cuellar, 2006).

In a similar manner to Latin-Americans, the contributions of Asian-American early childhood teacher educators rarely find their way into histories of the field. A few examples from the work of Chinese-, Japanese-, Korean-, Indian-American, and other Pacific Rim university educators provide a glimpse of the significance of their work. Constance Kamii (University of Alabama, Birmingham) reinvented arithmetic for young children in the U.S. utilizing Piagetian principles, including the theory of logico-mathematical development. Dr. Kamii disseminates research-based knowledge through her publications and work with preservice and inservice teachers (Beatty, 2013). In addition to their teaching and research responsibilities, two colleagues have taken leadership roles in professional organizations. Karen Liu (Indiana State University) is a Past President of the Association for Childhood Education International, and X. Christine Wang, Interim Director of the Early Childhood Research Center at the State University of New York at Buffalo, holds executive roles in components of the American Educational Research Association.

Men in Early Childhood Teacher Education

Men who have achieved leadership roles in recent ECTE history reached that status through stellar higher education teaching, research, and (sometimes) clinical practice. They have contended with the perception of ECE as "women's work," and societal proscriptions against males interacting closely with young children and female teacher preparation candidates. Many have backgrounds and undergraduate degrees in other fields, such as music, human development, sociology, or anthropology. These men have historically been a diverse group in terms of philosophy, theoretical foundations, and cultural heritage, ranging from participation in the Kindertransport in Europe during World War II to urban or small town U.S. upbringing and attendance at local schools. All of them possess(ed) characteristics and accomplishments that permitted them to explore opportunities within this female-dominated teacher-education field, including earned doctorates, teacher education faculty positions in higher education, authoring publications, grant-funded research, and government positions, creating a new male niche.

Twentieth Century Male ECTE Leaders

James L. (Jimmy) Hymes, Jr. (1913–1998) participated in every major ECE breakthrough of the twentieth century. After completing master's and doctoral degrees in a program emphasizing human development and the integration of disciplines at TC, he was recruited by his advisor, Stolz, to direct the Kaiser Child Service Centers in Oregon during World War II (Hymes, 1979; Teachers College, Columbia University Announcement of Teachers College School of Education, School of Practical Arts, 1934–1935; Department of Special Collections and University Archives, Stanford University Libraries, 1957–1958; Hymes & Stolz, 1978). As an author and teacher educator at the State University of New York at New Paltz, George Peabody College for Teachers (now a part of Vanderbilt University), and the University of Maryland, Hymes was influential through his championship of specialized certification for preschool teachers (Anderson, 2003; Hymes, 1976).

Donald Keith Osborn (1927–1994) was a division chair at Merrill-Palmer Institute in Detroit (1952–1968) and a faculty member at the University of Georgia (1968–1994). A historian of education, Osborn is remembered by former students for his attention to individuals, extensive preparation for lectures, and his unusual ability to simplify complex child development data and communicate it in an accessible manner (NAEYC, 1994). Osborn and Hymes are remembered for their significant roles in shaping the parameters and staffing of Projects Head Start and Follow Through (Hymes & Osborn, 1979).

Twenty-First Century Male ECTE Leaders

Edgar Klugman, Professor Emeritus and former Director of Continuing Education at Wheelock College, is the author and editor of influential publications on early childhood, play, and policy. A revered colleague and collaborator, he is known for his research on play and work in support of men in early education (Nelson, 2009).

Bernard Spodek is Professor Emeritus at the University of Illinois at Urbana-Champaign. He has written extensively about all aspects of ECTE, including its history, candidates, curriculum, and standards. Well-known in international venues, he is the founding President of the Pacific Early Childhood Educational Research Association (PECERA; UIUC, n.d.; Spodek, 1972).

Jerry Aldridge drew on his early experiences teaching in special education and general early childhood/elementary classes in rural counties of Alabama throughout his career in higher education. He retired as Professor Emeritus from the University of Alabama at Birmingham to teach at Bogor Agricultural University in Indonesia, where he continued to share his knowledge of curriculum, instruction, and multicultural education.

Edward M. Greene was a staff member at the High/Scope Educational Research Foundation during the early phases of the model's development, later serving as an online faculty member, and currently working in the fields of bilingual and transmedia education (E.M. GREENE). He has focused on helping preservice and inservice teachers know themselves, extend their knowledge of children's social and cultural milieu, and utilize this knowledge base in the classroom (Greene, 2014).

Thomas Moore (Benedict College, Columbia, South Carolina) is a musician extraordinaire. He teaches content and pedagogical skills to preservice and inservice teachers through music and other modalities (Moore, n.d.).

These men, along with Drs. Josué Cruz and Eugene E. Garcia, discussed earlier, have utilized their standing with government agencies and the public, conference presentations, and leadership and service on the boards of multiple professional, business, and charitable organizations to make a difference by transforming the field of ECTE. The hard work and determination of the ECT educators mentioned in this section on unexplored populations have contributed to what will become a historic account of creating change for the entire ECTE community.

Conclusion

Early childhood teacher education in the U.S. has evolved and diversified over the decades of its existence. It began in the 1800s with the advent of Normal Schools (Horace Mann), private kindergarten teacher training (Maria Kraus-Boelte and John Kraus, Matilda Kriege), public school kindergarten teacher preparation (William Torrey Harris, Susan Blow), and kindergarten training schools (Elizabeth Harrison, Eudora and William Hailmann). It developed on the East Coast through work at Teachers College of Columbia University (William Heard Kilpatrick, John Dewey, Susan Blow, and Patty Smith Hill), the Cooperative School for Student Teachers (now Bank Street College of Education; Caroline Pratt, Harriet Merrill Johnson and Lucy Sprague Mitchell) and the Ruggles Street Nursery School and Training Center (Abigail Adams Eliot). In the Midwest, Anna Bryan (Chicago Free Kindergarten Association), Alice B. Temple (University of Chicago), and Edna Noble White (the Merrill-Palmer Motherhood and Home Training School) expanded the boundaries of the ECTE field. On the West Coast, the work was advanced by Kate Douglas Wiggin (Silver Street Kindergarten). Henry Barnard (the first United States Commissioner of Education) was a kindergarten advocate who supported teacher education.

A majority of the initial training programs were begun for European-American students. Therefore, a parallel group of "normal and industrial" institutions for Black ECT educators was established in the South through efforts of religious groups and individuals. They included Haines Normal and Industrial Institute (Lucy Craft Laney), Bethune-Cookman College (Mary McLeod Bethune), and Hampton Institute and Tuskegee Institute (Booker T. Washington, Margaret Murray Washington). Secondary and tertiary education for Black students interested in teaching children was provided. Some Black teacher preparation candidates attended existing institutions, such as the St. Louis Kindergarten Training School (Haydee Campbell) and Columbia College Chicago (Oneida Cockrell). Several IHEs with a predominantly Black student body were founded in the aftermath of the Civil War. The students of Atlanta (Janice Hale, Evangeline Ward), Fisk (Ida Wells Barnett), and Howard Universities and Spelman College (Ida Jones Curry, Dorothy Eberhardt Neal Birchette) became educational leaders and advocates. HBCUs continue to educate ECTE professionals today because there is still a need for the perspectives these institutions provide.

In recent decades, members of diverse U.S. populations have entered a variety of ECTE programs, and a few became leaders in the field. It is important to acknowledge the fact that ECT educators bring with them their cultural, racial, ethnic, and religious backgrounds. Now, as in the past two hundred years, these characteristics add depth and breadth to ECTE. However, it is both the similarities and the differences among ECT educators that make the field accessible to all candidates who meet the standards for admission to EC teacher preparation programs today. The authors agree with Hutchinson that

> a competent early childhood teacher educator is one who, as a student of children, knows how to support children in their natural quest for knowledge and provides opportunities for prospective teachers to attain that skill with children living in real-life circumstances. Furthermore, the competent teacher educator provides these experiences in optimal surroundings in order to reinforce the efficacy of good practices.
>
> *(Goffin & Day, 1994, p. 154)*

In a 1976 speech, Evangeline Ward discussed "a style of ethics to which those of us who teach children and who teach teachers can adhere or support." She continued, "As conscious professionals, we owe it to ourselves as well as to those who teach or hope to teach and to the children whose education is likely to be affected by us . . . to be 'scrupulously ethical.'' Ward then shared her struggle to flesh out the following principles as guidelines for the profession of early childhood teacher education:

1. We can guarantee respect for the unique capacities and styles of each learner: adult and child.
2. We can defend vigorously the right of each potential teacher to <u>know what is presently known</u> in this broad-based changing field of early childhood care and education.

3. We must assure that the individually different styles of learning are meshed with individually different styles of teaching and that people grow in their abilities well in this way—both adults hoping to be teachers and children.
4. We can acknowledge and work at our own capacities to continuously learn. We can pursue new ideas and study new practices by informal and formal means in order to be able to put into practice what emerges.
5. We can admit our own biases as the first evidence of true professionalism.
6. We can admit to being well experienced in our own ethnic—cultural value systems—and at the same time admit the limitations this imposes on total immersion in any other. This imposes on each of us, however, a special responsibility to seek the knowledge, understanding and acceptance of the chosen ways of others in the multicultural currents of America. As early educators, no other ethical choice is permissible; we owe it to the children as well as to future teachers.

(Ward, 1976, pp. 7–8)

The authors of this chapter suggest that in taking to heart the principles enumerated above, we honor the selected colleagues whose lives and work are highlighted in this chapter, and the many unsung heroines and heroes of early childhood teacher education whose work we have yet to discover.

There is much work waiting to be done by members of the field—graduate students and tenured academics alike. The growing literature on Black ECTE needs parallel growth in dissertations and publications about Hispanic-American, Asian-American, and other ECTE populations. Additionally, biographies of specific individuals who have made outstanding contributions to the field should continue to be researched and shared. Volumes similar to Aldridge & Christiansen (2013) and Hinitz (2013a) that disseminate completed research should be published on a regular basis. The threads of the research reported in this chapter should be picked up and woven into increasingly clearer pictures of what actually happened in the past and how it affects ECTE today.

Acknowledgement

A note of thanks from the authors is tendered to Ms. Andreese Scott of the Hampton University Museum Archives and Drs. Jerry Aldrich, Lois McFadyen Christensen, Harlene Galen, and W. Jean Simpson for their support of this work.

Note

For more information about many of the people and programs mentioned in this chapter see Lascarides and Hinitz (2011).

References

Aldridge, J., & Christensen, L. M. (Eds.). (2013). *Stealing from the mother: The marginalization of women in education and psychology from 1900–2010*. Lanham, MD: Rowman & Littlefield Education.

Allison, C. B. (1995). *Past and present: Essays for teachers in the history of education*. New York: Peter Lang.

Almy, M. (1988). The early childhood educator revisited. In B. Spodek, O. N. Saracho, & D. L. Peters (Eds.), *Professionalism and the early childhood practitioner* (pp. 48–55). New York: Teachers College Press.

Almy, M. C., & Snyder, A. (1947). The staff and its preparation. In H. B. Nelson (Ed.), *46th National Society for the Study of Education Yearbook, Part II Early childhood education* (pp. 231–232). Chicago, IL: University of Chicago Press.

American Psychological Association (APA). (2014). *Featured psychologist: Asa Hilliard, III, PhD.* Retrieved from http://www.apa.org/pi/oema/resources/ethnicity-health/psychologists/asa-hilliard.aspx

Anderson, C. J. (2003). *Contributions of James Lee Hymes, Jr. to the field of early childhood education* (Unpublished doctoral dissertation). University of Texas, Austin, TX.

Beatty, B. (2013). Playing with numbers: Constance Kamii and reinventing arithmetic in early childhood education. In B. F. Hinitz (Ed.), *The hidden history of early childhood education* (pp. 238–262). New York: Routledge.

Bradburn, E. (1989). *Margaret McMillan: Portrait of a pioneer.* London, UK: Routledge.

Bredekamp, S. (2014). *Effective practices in early childhood education: Building a foundation* (2nd ed.). Boston, MA: Pearson.

Children's Defense Fund. (n.d.). *Haydee E. Campbell.* Retrieved from http://www.childrensdefense.org/child-research-data-publications/data/haydee-e-campbell.pdf

Christensen, L. M., & Rababah, E. Q. (2013). Josephine Silone Yates. In J. Aldridge & L. M. Christensen (Eds.), *Stealing from the mother: The marginalization of women in education and psychology from 1900–2010* (pp. 29–33). Lanham, MD: Roman & Littlefield.

Cunningham, C., & Osborn, D. K. (1979). A historical examination of Blacks in early childhood education. *Young Children, 34*(3), 20–29.

Department of Special Collections and University Archives, Stanford University Libraries. (1957–1958). *Guide to the Lois Meek Stolz psychology case interviews (SC0277).* Retrieved from http://www.oac.cdlib.org/findaid/ark:/13030/kt9w1023b1/

Eberhardt, D. N. (1942). *A study of two anthropometric measures of the children of the Spelman College Nursery School, Atlanta, Georgia.* Retrieved June 2014, from Dissertations & Theses from 1942: Digital Commons, Atlanta University Center, Robert W. Woodruff Library: http://digitalcommons.auctr.edu/dissertations/index.html#year1942

Education Act of 1918. (EA 1918). (n.d.). Retrieved January 2015 from Legislation UK Government: http://www.legislation.gov.uk/ukpga/1918/39/pdfs/ukpga_19180039_en.pdf

Education Act of 1921. (EA 1921). (n.d.). Retrieved January 2015 from Education in England: http://www.educationengland.org.uk/documents/acts/1921-education-act.html

Eliot, A. A. (1960). *Reflection letter on the 100th Anniversary of Margaret McMillan's birth.* London, UK: Dreadnought Library Archives, University of Greenwich.

Eliot, A. A. (1972). Nursery schools fifty years ago. *Young Children, XXVII*(4), 208–213.

EM GREENE Associates International. (n.d.). *Edward M. Greene director of early learning—EM GREENE Associates International.* Retrieved from http://edgreene.net/

Funeral Services for Ida Louise J. Curry Saturday June 26, 1993. (2014). Hampton, VA: pamphlet—reproduction courtesy of Hampton University Museum.

García, E. E., Jensen, B., & Cuellar, D. (2006). Early academic achievement of Hispanics in the United States: Implications for teacher preparation. *The New Educator, 2*(2), 123–147.

Goddard, C. (2003). *Democracy in the school: Ella Flagg Young's ideas about preparing teachers in turn-of-the-century Chicago.* Unpublished manuscript.

Goddard, C. (2007a). *An intertwined heritage: Progressive teacher education in Chicago.* Unpublished manuscript.

Goddard, C. (2007b, October 18). Releasing the child's emotional drive: Clara Belle Baker, the Progressive tradition in Chicago, and the origin of the Demonstration School. *A talk for the Parent Education Committee of Baker Demonstration School.* Lecture conducted from Chicago.

Goddard, C. (n.d.). *Elizabeth Harrison and the kindergarten movement in Chicago.* Unpublished manuscript.

Goffin, S. G., & Day, D. E. (Eds.). (1994). *New perspectives in early childhood teacher education: Bringing practitioners into the debate.* New York: Teachers College Press.

Greene, E. M. (2014, November). Electronic mail message to Charlotte Anderson.

Hewes, D. W. (1990). Historical foundations of early childhood teacher training: The evolution of kindergarten teacher preparation. In B. Spodek & O. N. Saracho (Eds.), *Early childhood teacher preparation: Yearbook in early childhood education* (Vol. I) (pp. 1–22). New York: Teachers College Press.

Hewes, D. W. (1998). *It's the camaraderie: A history of parent cooperative preschools.* Davis, CA: Center for Cooperatives.

Hilliard III, A. G. (1974). Moving from abstract to functional teacher education: Pruning and planting. In B. Spodek (Ed.), *Teacher education of the teacher, by the teacher, for the child* (pp. 7–23). Washington, DC: National Association for the Education of Young Children.

Hinitz, B. F. (Ed.). (2013a). *The hidden history of early childhood education.* New York: Routledge.

Hinitz, B. F. (2013b). History of early childhood education in multicultural perspective. In J. L. Roopnarine & J. E. Johnson (Eds.), *Approaches to early childhood education* (6th ed.) (pp. 3–33). Upper Saddle River, NJ: Pearson.

Hymes, J. L. (1976). James L. Hymes, Jr. Papers, Pacific Oaks College, box 7. *An Attempt at Autobiography: Curriculum Vitae.* Unpublished manuscript.

Hymes, J. L. (1979). *Early childhood education living history interviews. Book 3: Reaching large numbers of children.* Carmel, CA: Hacienda Press.

Hymes, J. L., & Eliot, A. A. (1978). America's first nursery schools. In J. L. Hymes (Ed.), *Early childhood education living history interviews. Book 1: Beginnings* (pp. 6–25). Carmel, CA: Hacienda Press.

Hymes, J. L., & Osborn, D. K. (1979). The early days of Project Head Start. In J. L. Hymes (Ed.), *Early childhood living history interviews. Book 3: Reaching large numbers of children* (pp. 28–33, 40–55). Carmel, CA: Hacienda Press.

Hymes, J. L., & Stolz, L. M. (1978). The Kaiser child service centers. In J. L. Hymes (Ed.), *Early childhood education living history interviews. Book 2: Care of the children of working mothers* (pp. 26–56). Carmel, CA: Hacienda Press.

Lascarides, V. C., & Hinitz, B. F. (2011). *History of early childhood education* (paper ed.). New York: Routledge Taylor & Francis.

Lewis, J. J. (n.d.). *Mary McKeod Bethune facts.* Retrieved from http://womenshistory.about.com/od/bethune/a/mary_bethune.htm

Marquis Who's Who. (1974–1975). Evangeline Ward. In *Who's Who of American Women* (p. 1006). New Providence, NJ: Author.

McMillan, M. (1919). *The nursery school.* London, UK: J.M. Dent and Sons.

McMillan, M. (1927). *The life of Rachel McMillan.* London, UK: J.M. Dent and Sons.

Moore, T. (n.d.). *About Dr. Moore.* Retrieved from http://drthomasmoore.com/index.php/about

National Association for the Education of Young Children (NAEYC). (1994). In memoriam: D. Keith Osborn. *Young Children, 49*(4), 64.

National Task Force on Early Childhood Education for Hispanics. (2007). *Para nuestros niños: Expanding and improving early education for Hispanics: Main report.* Retrieved from http://www.ecehispanic.org

Nelson, B. G. (2009). *Dr. Edgar Klugman talks about his 59 years in the early childhood profession.* Retrieved from http://www.menteach.org/news/dr_edgar_klugman_talks_about_his_59_years_in_the_early_childhood_profession

Owen, G. (1900). An English student's impressions of American kindergartens. *Child Life, II*(6), 97–102.

Owen, G. (Ed.). (1923). *Nursery school education.* London: EP Dutton.

Parker, S. C., & Temple, A. (1925). *Unified kindergarten and first-grade teaching.* Boston, MA: Ginn and Company.

Peltzman, B. R. (1998). *Pioneers of early childhood education: A bio-bibliographical guide.* Westport, CT: Greenwood Press.

Richings, G. F. (1904). *Evidences of progress among colored people* (11 ed.). Philadelphia, PA: Geo. S. Ferguson.

Saracho, O. N., & Hancock, F. M. (1983). Mexican-American culture. In O. N. Saracho & B. Spodek (Eds.), *Understanding the multicultural experience in early childhood education* (pp. 3–15). Washington, DC: National Association for the Education of Young Children.

Saracho, O. N., & Spodek, B. (1990). Early childhood teacher preparation in cross-cultural perspective. In B. Spodek & O. N. Saracho (Eds.). *Early childhood teacher preparation* (pp. 102–117). New York: Teachers College Press.

Seifert, K. (1988). Men in early childhood education. In B. Spodek, O. N. Saracho, & D. L. Peters (Eds.), *Professionalism and the early childhood practitioner* (pp. 105–116). New York: Teachers College Press.

Shipley, F. (1992). Alice V. Keliher. In V. E. Schmidt & A. L. Meyer (Eds.), *Profiles in childhood education 1931–1960* (pp. 91–98). Wheaton, MD: Association for Childhood Education International.

Simpson, W. J., & McConnell-Farmer, J. L. (2013). Selected African-American pioneers of early childhood education. In B. F. Hinitz (Ed.), *The hidden history of early childhood education* (pp. 143–158). New York: Routledge.

Snyder, A. (1972). *Dauntless women in childhood education, 1856–1931.* Washington, DC: Association for Childhood Education International.

Spodek, B. (1972). Staff requirements in early childhood education. In I. J. Gordon (Ed.), *Early childhood education: The seventy-first yearbook of the National Society for the Study of Education* (pp. 359–361). Chicago, IL: University of Chicago Press.

Spodek, B., & Saracho, O. N. (Eds.). (1990). *Early childhood teacher preparation: Yearbook in early childhood education* (Vol. I). New York: Teachers College Press.

Steedman, C. (2004–2014). *Oxford dictionary of national biography.* Oxford, UK: Oxford University Press.

Teachers College Columbia University. (1934). *Announcement of Teachers College School of Education School of Practical Arts 1934–35.* New York: Author.

University of Illinois at Urbana-Champaign (UIUC). (n.d.). *Bernard Spodek.* Retrieved from http://faculty.education.illinois.edu/b-spodek/

Wadelington, C. W. (1984, Revised 1997). *Important dates in the life of Dr. Charlotte Eugenia Hawkins Brown and the Alice Freeman Palmer Memorial Institute.* Retrieved from http://www.nchistoricsites.org/chb/time-line.htm

Ward, E. H. (1976 July 2). Through the lives of others: A perpetual memorial. *Conference Honoring Kenneth Wann.* Coral Gables, Florida.

Whipple, G. M. (Ed.). (1929). *Twenty-eighth yearbook of the National Society for the Study of Education: Preschool and parental education.* Bloomington, IL: Public School Publishing Company.

3

PUBLIC POLICY AND WORKFORCE IN EARLY CHILDHOOD EDUCATION

W. Steven Barnett and Shannon Riley-Ayers

Introduction and Policy History

The fault lines that define early childhood education policy and divide the early childhood education field have been evident in the United States for hundreds of years (Beatty, 1997). Should it be a public or private responsibility? Should it be part of the public schools? Is the primary goal child care or education? Should programs focus on children in poverty or serve all children? Can states be trusted to administer federally funded programs? Ambivalence and differences of opinion about the answers to these questions have shaped early childhood policy from colonial times and continue to do so today (Beatty, 1997; Cahan, 1989; Karch, 2013). As policy has evolved, it has intensified the divisions within the field, perhaps making them more difficult to resolve. As a result, there is no single early childhood care and education (ECCE) workforce. Instead, there are three (or four) distinct workforces.

Federal and state policies have combined to create three broadly separate early childhood sectors: Head Start, child care, and public education. The last can be subdivided into regular and special education. Head Start is a federal program that makes grants directly to local organizations; while most of these are private nonprofits, some are public schools. Child care is largely provided by private organizations (for profit as well as nonprofit) and individuals in homes and centers as well as by family, friends, and neighbors. Public education includes kindergarten through grade three, and includes both regular education and special education for children with disabilities. Nearly all public education, beginning at kindergarten, is provided in public schools. Special education is an entitlement under federal and state law for children that begins at age three. Preschool education for children without disabilities is a more recent, and complicated, development.

Although the title of this chapter refers to the workforce, the focus of this chapter is on teachers. We define a teacher as the adult in charge of an individual classroom. We recognize that there are other members of the early childhood workforce. Teacher assistants are common in many preschool classrooms, and we devote a section to them. Administrators, other support staff, and the many informal providers of education to young children are beyond the scope of this chapter. We discuss only the numbers of these other members of the workforce to provide a context to understand the data on teachers.

The separate early childhood sectors have changed over time with respect to the numbers and characteristics of teachers and other staff, and they continue to evolve. Including kindergarten through grade 3 (K-3) teachers of children, the largest sector today is public education. This is followed by child care, with Head Start now the smallest sector. Even if only teachers for children under age 5 were to be considered, it is likely that the number of teachers is larger in public education than in Head Start. This would not have been true a decade ago. As public education has grown, it also has blurred the fault lines that define these sectors.

Although we continue to treat these four sectors as distinct, programs are being blended, and the distinctions between public and private education and child care are becoming blurred. This creates problems for defining and identifying the early childhood workforces. Some teachers belong to more than one group. The extent to which these workforces will merge in the future or just continue to be blurred around the edges is a central topic of our chapter. A number of recent federal and state policy developments can be seen as efforts to bridge the fault lines that have led to fractured policy. However, we begin by considering policy in each of these sectors separately and discussing the implications of each for teachers.

Child Care and the Private Sector

Young children participate in a wide range of privately provided care and education from the first year of life into the school years (including before- and after-school care). Many of these arrangements are informal and provided by family and friends, often without financial compensation. Public policy influences these services and their workforces through funding and regulation. Historically, most of these services have been viewed as child care that was the responsibility of the family. Help for families in obtaining such services was regarded as charity. The U.S. government's role was extremely limited, with the exception of during WWII when the provision of child care was seen as necessary to bring women into the labor force to support the war effort. Consistent with this tradition, Congress enacted a small tax deduction for low-income families in 1954.

Since then, child care policy has been shaped as much by failures as by successes. Attempts to develop comprehensive approaches to federal regulation and funding of early care and education for all children have failed, beginning with the Comprehensive Child Development Act of 1971 (Karch, 2013). Broad support for the Act and subsequent attempts foundered on an inability to agree on the role of public schools, state control, and early education as a child's right. Instead, child care policy moved forward primarily through an expansion of tax credits and as a welfare program. Under these policies, the public schools have no role, education is not a priority, and parents are given maximum discretion by limiting state authority. The primary federal role is to provide funding to lower income families, and child care quality is not regulated at the federal level. State regulations have focused largely on health, safety, and the role of child care as a welfare program rather than a form of education.

Judged by funding amounts, the most substantial federal and state child care policies are subsidies, tax credits, and the Child Care Food Program (Barnett & Haskins, 2010). In theory, these policies should raise the quality of care by increasing the funds available. In addition, associated regulations might raise quality. However, the vast majority of subsidies have been distributed through vouchers that can be used for any form of care, including kith and kin home-based care that is subject to little or no regulation (Adams & Rohacek, 2002). The net effects of subsidy and regulation are debated, particularly the extent to which they have increased or reduced the availability of center-based programs in low-income communities and whether or not they have improved or harmed the development of children (Hawkinson, Griffen, Dong, & Maynard, 2013; Herbst & Tekin, 2010; Hotz & Xiao, 2011; Ryan, Johnson, Rigby, & Brooks-Gunn, 2011). There is some evidence that subsidies have increased the use of licensed care and center care (Ryan et al., 2011).

It is hardly surprising that the child care sector has the lowest level of quality and highest rate of teacher turnover compared to Head Start and public education (Bassok, Fitzpatrick, Greenberg, & Loeb, 2013). Low wages and poor benefits contribute to ill health, depression, poverty, turnover, and little investment in ongoing professional development (Ryan & Whitebook, 2012). The characteristics of the workforce make it difficult for teachers to provide a highly supportive, developmentally enriching experience for young children, especially those who experience the same stresses of growing up in poverty (Institute of Medicine [IOM]& National Research Council [NRC], 2012).

Head Start

Head Start was launched in 1965 as part of Lyndon Johnson's War on Poverty (Zigler & Valentine, 1979). The program had broad goals and has been viewed as a tool for community development and political mobilization as well as a child development program. Eligibility for Head Start was primarily defined by the federal poverty line, with exceptions for up to 10 percent of the total served (for example, children with disabilities or in foster care do not have to be in poverty). With its broad goals, the program emphasized: parent education and training, direct employment of parents, comprehensive health and social services, and supporting the development of the whole child. Most programs operate only for a part day and more than a quarter only serve children four days a week. Those that meet families' needs for child care do so by providing these services with other funding streams.

Head Start's political fortunes have waxed and waned over its 50-year history. It began as a massive summer program during its first year, but later shrank as the summer option was eliminated in favor of the school-year model. After experiencing substantial enrollment growth in the 1990's, the program leveled off to enroll a little over 900,000 three- and four-year-old children a year. After more than 50 years, it is notable that Head Start still reaches less than half the eligible population. Nearly 2 million children are in poverty in this age range, and many children in Head Start live in households above the federal poverty line (poverty status changes for many after program entry). Recently, Head Start has been expanded to serve children under age 3 rather than to expand enrollment in the two years prior to kindergarten.

Head Start began with virtually no requirements for teacher qualifications and the provision of very brief training. As with other sectors, Head Start was heavily influenced by the popular notion that formal education was not required to teach young children. In addition, the rush to implement the program on a massive scale from the beginning and the imperatives of imparting maximum control to local communities and maximizing parental employment were obstacles to formal educational requirements. Justified as a political necessity to maintain support for the program, it ultimately backfired as one evaluation after another later found Head Start to be weakly effective in providing a good education (Barnett, 2011a; U.S. Department of Health and Human Services, 2010). Expert advice at the time from Jerome Bruner, Frances Degen Horowitz, and others stating that the program as designed was unlikely to succeed in providing a good education to young children was ignored (Rose, 2010; Zigler & Valentine, 1979).

Gradually, Head Start teacher qualifications have increased. However, until very recently, regulations required only a Child Development Associate's credential for lead teachers in classrooms. Such a policy was consistent with the program's broad mandate but modest budget, and its continued emphasis on hiring adults in low-income communities who were in need of jobs, especially parents. As recently as 1997, almost half of the teachers had no education beyond high school, and about half of center directors and teachers had been Head Start parents (Barnes, Guevara, Garcia, Levin, & Connell, 1999). By 2004, 70 percent of Head Start teachers had at least an associate's degree, with more than half of these having a bachelor's degree (Center for Law and Social Policy [CLASP], 2014).

In the 2007 Reauthorization of Head Start, Congress required all teachers to have at least an associate's degree by the 2011–2012 year and 50 percent to have a bachelor's degree by fall of 2013. The degrees must relate to early childhood education or include additional coursework in early childhood education. By 2012, 93 percent of Head Start teachers had at least an associate's degree and 62 percent had at least a bachelor's degree. Unfortunately, Congress did not dedicate increased funding to raise compensation to levels comparable to those that higher degrees would earn in the public schools or other fields. Salaries and benefits remain far below those of teachers in public schools with similar degrees.

The low salaries of Head Start teachers raise several concerns. The average Head Start teacher salary in 2012 was $29,650 (Office of Head Start, 2014). This is basically what was required to keep up with inflation from the average Head Start teacher salary in 2004 of $24,221 (CLASP, 2014) *without any increase to account for the improvement in degree levels.* Low salaries also give rise to higher turnover and may contribute to the fact that more than one-third of Head Start teachers report symptoms of mild to severe depression (Aikens et al., 2011).

Early Head Start was created in 1994 to provide comprehensive child and family development services to low-income children under age 3 and pregnant women. Early Head Start enrollment was quite modest, with about 60,000 prior to 2010. In 2012–2013, the program enrolled about 110,000 (because of turnover, cumulative enrollment was about 165,000 including 150,000 children). About half of the children served attend center-based programs. To put this number in context, about 3 million children under age 3 are in poverty, and Early Head Start reaches less than 4 percent of that number. Nearly 60 percent of Early Head Start classroom teachers have at least an associate's degree, and nearly 30 percent have a bachelor's (Office of Head Start, 2014). Early Head Start teacher salaries averaged $25,495 in 2012; they were lower than those of Head Start teachers because of lower average qualifications (Office of Head Start, 2014).

Public Education

Public education includes several subsectors of the early childhood workforce. These include teachers grades K-3, preschool special education, and state-funded pre-K programs (which are not always in public schools). In addition, public schools provide some preschool programs outside of state-funded pre-K at their own discretion, though data on these programs are not systematically collected. The largest group of these teachers is in kindergarten through grade three classrooms.

About 1 million early childhood teachers serve in kindergarten through grade 3 (Bureau of Labor Statistics [BLS], 2014). These teachers are essentially integrated into the K-12 workforce and have more in common with their colleagues than with teachers of younger children. However, until relatively recently, kindergarten teachers would not have been included in this group. The Kindergarten Movement in the United States began in the 1800s, but it was a very long time before kindergarten became a widely accepted part of public education. In the early 1960s, about 70 percent of children attended kindergarten, and public kindergarten enrolled around 50 percent of children at age 5 (Tanner & Tanner, 1973; United States Census Bureau, 1966). By 1975, about 75 percent of children attended public kindergarten. It was barely 25 years ago that kindergarten reached near universal enrollment.

The incorporation of kindergarten into the public school brought kindergarten teachers into the K-12 teaching force. Today they have qualifications and compensation comparable to those of other teachers in the primary grades. These are quite different from those in other sectors. The entry level educational qualification expected of all teachers is a bachelor's or higher degree. Public school teachers also must obtain a state license, or certification. How policy continues to develop regarding the preparation of K-12 teachers is beyond the scope of this chapter. Our primary point is that full inclusion of kindergarten into the public school system was a route to professionalization of kindergarten teachers including their preparation.

State-funded pre-K is much more diverse than other parts of public education. Although most are administered by state education agencies, some are under other agencies, and many are jointly administered with human services (Barnett, Carolan, Squires, & Horowitz, 2013). Provision is often through a mixed delivery system that includes the private sector and Head Start, as well as the public schools. Most teachers in state-funded pre-K are not fully integrated into the public education system. Even when working in public school buildings, preschool teachers do not always have the same qualifications, status, and compensation as other public school teachers, though they are paid much better on average than teachers in state-funded pre-K programs in the private sector and the other sectors generally (Barnett et al., 2013; Bassok, Fitzpatrick, Loeb, & Paglayan, 2013). The pay advantage for preschool teachers in public schools compared to state-funded preschool outside the public schools or private programs generally was about 60 percent (Barnett et al., 2013; NIEER, 2014; NSECE Project Team, 2013; Whitebook, Phillips, & Howes, 2014). The continued outsider status of preschool with respect to public education is evident within the state-funded pre-K sector. In some states pre-K is essentially part of public schooling, even if provided by private providers contracting with public schools (Barnett et al., 2013). Here preschool teachers have preparation, working conditions, and pay comparable to that of K-12 teachers. In some states, a mixed delivery system results in a split workforce, with teachers in contracted private providers having lower levels of qualifications (often an associate's degree) and lower levels of compensation (Barnett et al., 2013). In yet other states, qualifications requirements are low for all teachers, but where preschool is administered by public schools at the local level, preschool teachers may have the same qualifications and compensation as other teachers.

In 1986, the provision of intervention services to children with a delay or disability under the age of 5 and their families became a national policy. Currently, all states and eligible territories participate in early intervention for children from birth to age 2 (early intervention) and preschool special education. Preschool special education teachers have largely followed kindergarten teachers into the public education system. Federal legislation incentivized, supported, and eventually required the provision of a free appropriate public education to all children ages 3 to 5 with disabilities (Shonkoff & Meisels, 2000). The preschool special education workforce is relatively small, with about 24,000 teachers (BLS, 2014). Their qualifications and compensation are comparable to that of other teachers in the public schools. The Division of Early Childhood (DEC) of the Council for Exceptional Children has developed standards for the preparation of teachers in partnership with the National Association for the Education of Young Children, and worked with the accreditation organizations for teacher preparation programs (Klein & Gilkerson, 2000; Lifter et al., 2011). These efforts appear to have had greater success in influencing higher education programs than shaping state requirements.

Annual funding to each state for early intervention is based upon census figures of the number of children, birth through age 2, in the general population. Federal fiscal support via formula grants to states exceeded $419 million annually in 2013 (Early Childhood Technical Assistance Center [ECTAC], 2014a), with roughly 350,000 infants and toddlers, or just under 3 percent of the population aged birth through 2, served. Improved access has been a great success of early intervention, but the percentage of those served can vary by state by as much as 5 percent. This can suggest that there are substantial numbers of infants and toddlers who are identified for services in some states and are not being identified in others (Hebbeler, Spiker, & Kahn, 2012). While other early childhood programs have used Quality Rating and Improvement Systems (QRIS) to measure, report, and improve quality, nothing comparable exists for early intervention (Spiker, Hebbeler, & Barton, 2011). Collecting outcome data on children participating in early intervention is relatively new, with a start in 2007, and many states continue to work on the quality of these data collected. However, what has been collected demonstrates children achieving more growth than would have been expected without intervention (ECTAC, 2014b). Work is still needed on the transition between the two programs of early intervention and preschool special education.

Summary Description of the Current Workforces

Burton et al. (2002) estimated 2.3 million people are paid to provide early care and education, with roughly 24 percent working in center-based programs, 28 percent working in family child care programs, and the majority of individuals working as family, friend, and neighbor caregivers. More recently, and similarly, the National Survey of Early Care and Education Project Team (2013) published information from surveys in 2012 with an estimate of 1 million paid staff in home-based programs and 1 million in center-based programs. Somewhat less than 450,000 of these are identified as lead teachers. Other estimates have been somewhat higher (IOM & NRC, 2012). Center-based programs show 6 percent in school-sponsored centers, 14 percent in Head Start, 21 percent in public pre-K programs, and 59 percent in "other centers, all remaining programs offering ECE" (p. 9). Although these reports provide a general look at the landscape, there are several challenges in identifying and accurately describing the early childhood care and education workforces (Rhodes & Huston, 2012).

The ECCE workforces vary in location (homes, houses of worship, centers, public schools), funding source (tuition, subsidies, state or federal dollars), and licensing status (licensed or unlicensed). Responsibilities and expectations for the workforces also vary from providing basic safety and care (feeding, dressing, etc.) to implementing high-level educational goals (implementing a research-based curriculum, individualizing instruction based on assessment, etc.). Data systems are generally maintained separately by sector (child care, Head Start, state pre-K programs) causing difficulties in aggregating the information for a complete picture of the workforce landscape. Additionally, imperfect labor categories in federal data systems often group preschool teachers with kindergarten teachers, and within the child care sector, teachers may not be distinguished from assistants. This makes even a basic description of education, wages, qualifications, knowledge, and beliefs difficult to produce.

Nevertheless, we provide a brief comparative description by sector of *center-based* teachers of children under age 5 as an aid to understanding the impacts of past policies and future policy improvements. As noted earlier, this is about 500,000 teachers, which is roughly half the number employed in K-3. The characteristics and preparation of teachers of older children are extensively addressed elsewhere (Cochran-Smith, Feiman-Nemser, McIntyre, & Demers, 2008; Cochran-Smith & Zeichner, 2010; Darling-Hammond & Sclan, 1996).

The Importance of the Teacher

Early childhood teachers are working with children at the most critical and impressionable stages of children's development (Kagan, Kauerz, & Tarrant, 2008). Genetic studies indicate that although genetics can account for some development, a larger percentage of variability in skills is open to interventions. ECCE has the opportunity to provide the experiences necessary to support learning at this critical point of rapid brain development. The science of teaching and learning affords us a strong understanding of the types of experiences young children need. However, the complexity of the delivery of these experiences is sophisticated and teachers in these roles need extensive training and support to do so effectively (Dickinson, 2011).

Kagan et al. (2008) describe the specific demands placed upon teachers of young children. They note that teachers are responsible for all domains of young children's development; they need to attend to children's different learning styles, meet the needs of individual learners, and understand theoretical and practical pedagogy as they interact with the children. Teachers must wear the hats of teacher, researcher, and advocate as they enhance the learning outcomes of children. To be effective, early education teachers must have a strong knowledge base of content and child development. They must understand the role of culture and the value of family engagement. They need to assess children, deliver curriculum, and be intentional in their teaching and interacting with children. There are also high professional and moral expectations.

Challenges to a High-Quality Workforce

Given the demands of early education for highly intellectual, well-educated personnel, we see a serious mismatch between the demands and responsibilities of this workforce and the professional preparation, support, and compensation afforded those who work with children under age 5 (Whitebook & Ryan, 2011; Kagan et al., 2008). In the next part of this chapter, we discuss three interrelated challenges for recruiting, developing, supporting, and maintaining a high-quality workforce. These three challenges relate to compensation, education, and training. All three challenges are rooted in a fundamental economic problem. Current levels of funding (public and private) severely limit three things: (1) teacher compensation, (2) the pay-off to teachers and the organizations in which they work from investing in education and training, and (3) the desirability of staying in the preschool classroom as teachers acquire greater skills and experience.

For two reasons, this fundamental economic problem is more severe in the preschool years than at older ages and becomes even more severe among teachers of younger children. First, as the age of child falls, the staff-child ratio that is considered appropriate increases, which raises the cost per child (National Association of Child Care Resource and Referral Agencies [NACCCRA], 2011). Second, as the age of the child falls, the extent to which the public believes anyone (or, at least, any woman) can perform the work with no specialized education or training rises. Preschool special education is an exception, as it has come to be viewed as requiring highly specialized skills and knowledge. Kindergarten for children at age 5 was viewed this way prior to its incorporation into public education (Child Care Aware of America, 2013).

Compensation

To the extent that the teaching of young children is viewed as requiring no preparation to acquire specialized skills and knowledge, teachers in the formal sector essentially compete with workers in the informal sector. This severely limits pay. Yet, even if public attitudes change there remains the problem that a higher ratio of teachers to children is more expensive. For infants, the appropriate ratios may be 1 to 3 or 4 children. For preschoolers, this is commonly 10 children or less, though staffed by a teacher and an assistant rather than two co-teachers. Compare this to K-3, where teachers commonly have many more children and do not have an assistant.

There is relatively little research regarding the relationship of higher wages with lower turnover, better classroom practices, and outcomes for children, and the existing results are mixed (Early et al., 2007; Whitebook & Sakai, 2003). Evidence regarding teacher compensation is similarly mixed for K-12 education, but it is difficult to eliminate confounding factors in such studies (Darling-Hammond, Amrein-Beardsley, Haertel, & Rothstein, 2012; Hanushek & Rivkin, 2012). The basic principles of supply and demand dictate that better compensation would permit the hiring and retention of better teachers (Barnett, 2003). It is difficult for the ECCE workforces to have sustained commitment to the field if not compensated in a manner reflective of the importance of their work and the demands placed upon them.

Wages for early childhood workers overall are relatively low. In 2009 American Community Survey data showed that 61 percent of full-time workers in ECCE occupations earned less than $22,000 per year, approximately the federal poverty level for a family of four (USGAO, 2012). Teaching assistants averaged $13,000 and preschool teachers averaged $18,000. However, there is considerable variation across workforces, as previously discussed (NSECE Project Team, 2013). Teachers in K-3 are the best paid and teachers in public pre-K are next, followed at quite a distance by teachers in Head Start and then teachers in private sector preschool programs. Differences in fringe benefits contribute to even greater disparities between those in public and private programs.

There is additional diversity within the public pre-K sector. Preschool special education teachers are on par with primary school teachers. Teachers in state-funded programs receive quite different salaries from state to state and even within states (Barnett, Epstein, Friedman, Sansanelli, & Hustedt, 2009). While seven states require the same pay and qualifications regardless of whether state pre-K is provided in public schools or private programs, others have different standards for the qualifications and pay of teachers in the two settings. In state pre-K programs able to report salary ranges for pre-K teachers in public settings, 83 percent were paid less than $50,000; in nonpublic settings, 88 percent were below that figure. The median salary range for teachers in public school settings was $40,000 to $44,999, while in private settings the range was $30,000 to $34,999. Knowledge about compensation in state-funded pre-K is limited, as most states could not even report data on pay range.

Assistant teachers are paid even more poorly than teachers (NSECE Project Team, 2013). Although the majority of states could not report data on salaries of assistant teachers, the available data indicate that assistants generally are paid at quite low levels even in state-funded pre-K. In the 2008–2009 state pre-K program survey, no program reported an average starting salary for an assistant teacher above the $25,000 to $30,000 range (Barnett et al., 2009). Across public and nonpublic settings, the most commonly reported pay range for assistants was $15,000-$24,999.

Educational Preparation

The National Survey of Early Care and Education Project Team (2013) reports data that showed more than half of center-based classroom teachers had some level of college degree with one quarter having four-year degrees and 9 percent having a graduate or professional degree. The home-based staff reported less educational attainment than the center-based staff, about 30 percent with college degrees. Interestingly, these data show that the educational attainment differs for teachers of older versus younger children. Educational attainment was higher for those serving children ages 3 through 5 than for those serving younger children.

The National Institute of Early Education Research (NIEER, 2014) conducted a national survey of over 2,500 lead teachers of 3- and 4-year-old children in 2011. The vast majority of teachers reported at least an associate's degree. In public preschools, 41 percent of teachers held bachelor's degrees and 47 percent held master's degrees or higher. Forty-nine percent of Head Start teachers reported a bachelor's degree, with 20 percent reporting master's degrees or higher. Thirty-eight percent of teachers in private centers held bachelor's degrees, but only 14 percent had master's degrees or higher. However, there are great differences in auspice when looking at those teachers with high school degrees, some college, or less. Here, private centers had 24 percent of teachers in this degree category while there were 4 percent in public preschools and 5 percent in Head Start.

Over time, qualifications requirements have increased for the early childhood workforces, including preschool teachers. The National Association for the Education of Young Children is among the organizations that have advocated for this change (Willer, Lutton, & Ginsberg, 2011). Government also has increased its requirements for teachers of older preschoolers. Data from 2012–2013 show 57 percent of state pre-K programs require a bachelor's degree to teach in state-funded preschool, up from 45 percent in 2001–2002 (Barnett et al., 2013). Additionally, Head Start has consistently increased the education requirements for its workforce over time. These requirements explain the high percentage of degreed teachers. However, researchers caution that a bachelor's degree alone without other considerations may not be sufficient (Barnett, 2011b; Bowman, 2011).

More generally, there is a lack of agreement among researchers about the value of requiring that preschool teachers have preservice educational requirements comparable to those of primary school teachers. Those who have advocated for higher educational qualifications have limited this to teachers of children ages 2 and above (Burns, Donovan, & Bowman, 2000). Others oppose even this requirement (Fuller, 2011). Some researchers have concluded that inservice training is much more effective and might even serve as the primary route for preschool teacher preparation (Pianta, 2011). This might be accomplished through a certification for acquired training or competencies (Kagan et al., 2008).

Among those who advocate for a bachelor's degree, there appears to be an emerging consensus on several points. There is a general agreement that the empirical links between teacher degree attainment and observed quality or child academic gains have been weak across the literature as a whole

(Burchinal, Hyson, & Zaslow, 2011; Tout, Zaslow, & Berry, 2005). However, researchers also have pointed to many reasons that the bachelor's degree—properly implemented and compensated—may be one important component of ECCE teacher preparation nevertheless (Bowman, 2011; Barnett, 2011b; Burchinal et al., 2011; Kagan & Gomez, 2011). These same authors concur that a bachelor's alone is not sufficient to prepare highly effective teachers and that the content of bachelor's degree preparation for teachers currently is far from ideal and much too variable (Bowman, 2011; Kagan & Gomez, 2011). It also is recognized that preschools involve teaching teams that include other workers as well as teachers and that the quality of teaching depends on all team members, so that the preparation and training of administrators and assistants also requires attention (Willer et al., 2011).

The acquisition of higher education requirements for early childhood teachers including degrees and certifications are complicated by low wages in the field. Often, early childhood teachers can be deterred from advancing in their field with further education due to the cost of these schooling and training requirements or opportunities in relation to their wages. This returns us to the fundamental economic problem. One proposed solution is to increase ratios, allowing for increased compensation without increasing the budget. This is essentially the approach taken in the French École Maternelle (Peer & Burbank, 2004).

Another proposed remedy is the use of scholarship programs to award funds to ECCE workers to cover the costs of such higher education or training. Wage incentives and subsidies have yielded modest improvements in education and training (Bridges, Fuller, Huang, & Hamre, 2011). One such program, the T.E.A.C.H.™ Early Childhood Project, is implemented in several states. The scholarship helps increase compensation and the retention of skilled teachers. Typically, once T.E.A.C.H. participants have reached their educational goals, they receive a salary increase, often with the requirement to stay in their current position for one year or more. This program supports educational attainment for the ECCE workforce and also addresses increases in wages based on professional development. However, the funds provided by T.E.A.C.H. are quite modest and far too little to provide pay parity with primary education.

Small incentives will have only small effects on staff education and training (Bridges et al., 2011). If preschool teachers acquire the same level of qualifications as primary teachers, but their pay remains lower, there will be strong pull for them to leave to teach in primary schools. If they invest only in easily acquired, but lower quality higher education, then their actual qualifications will remain lower than those of primary school teachers. In this case, it will be much more difficult for them to obtain jobs in primary schools. However, their effectiveness as preschool teachers should not be expected to be much improved.

Training

Content and pedagogical knowledge is critical for the ECCE workforce as we place great demands on their expertise for guiding the learning and development of our youngest children. Teachers need a broad understanding of how children learn and their role in supporting and increasing children's learning. First, teachers need a firm understanding of child development, both the typical trajectories and early learning expectations and standards. Further, teachers need to recognize the differences in young children by assessing their strengths and identifying their struggles and then responding appropriately. Teachers need to do this in all domain areas, including physical well-being and motor development, social and emotional development, approaches to learning, language and literacy, and cognitive skills (including early mathematics and early science knowledge; Snow & Van Hemel, 2008).

This is no small feat. Surely, to be able to do this for all children, each child with his or her unique set of circumstances and rate of development, requires extensive training and support. The definitive amount of support or training has yet to be identified. As a start, 81 percent of state preschool programs report 15 hours or more of inservice training (Barnett, Jung, Youn, & Frede, 2013), up nearly 20 percent from 2002.

Ongoing intensive training demonstrates an improvement of both classroom quality and child outcomes (e.g., Wasik & Hindman, 2011; Fukkink & Lont, 2007). Research also supports the role of coaching in improving teachers' practices and enhancing student learning (Pianta, 2011). Although there is not a standard definition of coaching across the field, most agree that coaching entails developing a supportive collaborative professional relationship between an expert and a practitioner (Joyce & Showers, 2002). This relationship is used to provide feedback based on performance, individual goal setting, and supportive implementation (through procedures such as model lessons, topic study, and collaboration) to guide improvement. The coaching cycle is not unlike that of formative assessment that teachers implement for their students.

As with any other development of knowledge and skills, such training also increases the value of the worker and can lead to increased demands for compensation as well. If there is no cost to the employee and the knowledge and skills are not transferable to other work, then it is possible for compensation to remain relatively low without increasing the extent to which the workforces leave for primary education and other employment. However, the existing levels of turnover become more expensive as the costs of inservice training rise. To the extent that compensation has to rise to retain workers who develop much stronger competencies through experience and training, the fundamental economic problem must be confronted again.

Promising Policy Developments

Public policy has had, and continues to have, tremendous implications for the early childhood workforces. Policies that favor a low-cost, nonprofessional workforce favor low wages, poor qualifications and training, and high turnover. Such a workforce has little control over its own preparation and development. Two alternative policy approaches that might dramatically change the workforces are currently under development and discussed here. One is the creation of Quality Rating and Improvement Systems (QRIS). The other is to incorporate preschool into public education, as was done with kindergarten. Earlier it was noted that many advocate for policies that could raise the quality of teaching through highly directed on-the-job training (Pianta, 2011; Kagan & Gomez, 2011). This is a key component of both policies described below.

Quality Rating and Improvement Systems (QRIS)

About half of the states have implemented QRIS policies in recent years and the rest have QRIS under development. The QRIS approach seeks to improve quality by introducing rating systems that provide more information to the purchasers of early care and education services regarding the quality of those services. There are multiple ways in which QRIS can influence the workforce.

The most obvious influence is by including qualifications and training of teachers in the rating system (Office of Child Care, 2014). All of the QRIS that had been implemented by 2011 included teacher preservice educational qualifications with higher ratings linked to more education. Two thirds included a bachelor's degree as part of the standard for achieving the highest level or rating in the system for centers. Only 30 percent of states that included home-based providers in the QRIS required a bachelor's degree for the highest rating of home-based programs. Most require just a Child Development Associate (CDA) credential or similar state qualification of home-based providers for the highest rating level. By contrast, this was the qualification most often required at the lowest center-based programs. Most QRIS also have requirements for continuing professional development, typically beginning with child care licensing requirements and then increasing the number of hours with each level of the rating system.

QRIS has the potential to reduce fragmentation of the workforce to the extent that different types of programs—private child care, Head Start, and state pre-K—are brought into a single system with shared career paths. However, QRIS are voluntary for private programs that do not receive public money and often include only programs that are licensed by state child care agencies. States may exempt not only some private providers, but also Head Start and public school programs (Office of Child Care, 2014). Staff in programs that do not participate in a QRIS are unlikely to be much affected by it.

The effects of QRIS fundamentally depend on the extent to which the QRIS redirects resources based on teacher quality, qualifications, and professional development. Some QRIS require providers to reach the top levels of the QRIS in order to be eligible to provide relatively well-funded state pre-K services (Office of Child Care, 2014). In such cases, payment and teacher compensation levels may be substantially higher, providing considerable incentive for programs to help teachers to improve their qualifications, ongoing professional development, and teaching quality. However, more generally parents may not respond significantly to ratings (assigning much more importance to such other factors as location) and public funding increases associated with moving up levels may be very modest. Another complicating factor is that some QRIS levels may not be well-aligned with actual quality (Sabol, Hong, Pianta, & Burchinal, 2013).

Public Education: New Jersey's Abbott Preschool Model

In 1998 New Jersey's Supreme Court ordered education reforms that included universal, well-planned, high-quality preschool education for all 3- and 4-year-olds in 31 districts throughout the state. This ruling was a part of the landmark *Abbott v. Burke* (1985) and affected districts that collectively serve approximately one quarter of the state's children. This decision began one of the most significant changes in early childhood policy anywhere in the United States.

Policymakers in New Jersey addressed many of the challenges outlined above when developing an adequately funded, high-quality public education system for children beginning at age 3. Essentially they did this by bringing the existing workforces and programs into the public education system and transforming them rather than replacing them with a new system. The result is a new model of public education in some key respects. In this section, we will outline the relevant NJ Abbott preschool program policies and effects on the workforce.

Mixed-delivery model. School districts and the state were assigned the responsibility of ensuring that all classrooms met the standards of a high-quality preschool education regardless of program auspice. These were clearly specified. However, school districts were encouraged to contract with private providers and Head Start to provide services. Roughly two thirds of children are served by these other providers. To help maintain a highly qualified staff, the preschool teacher's salary was equivalent to those teachers in the public school regardless of auspice. It was established that each classroom would have a maximum class size of 15 students. Teachers also are required to have the same early childhood certification (i.e., license) regardless of auspice.

Degrees and certification. As one step toward quality, the state created a new preschool through grade 3 (P-3) teacher certificate. This enabled all early childhood educators to receive relatively uniform specialized training at the bachelor's degree level. The state instituted incentive programs and deadlines for teachers to acquire this certification and bachelor's degrees. Perhaps the greatest motivator was that teachers in private programs and Head Start received very large salary increases when they completed the degree and certification.

Coaching and professional development. In addition to a highly qualified teaching staff, master teachers, also known as coaches, played an integral role in implementing and maintaining high levels of program quality. It is recommended that one master teacher be available for support for every 20 teachers. The master teachers are responsible for providing direct classroom coaching using a reflective coaching model. Here the coaches observe, provide feedback in a collaborative manner, and model exemplary practices. In addition to this direct in-classroom support, master teachers are involved in planning professional development opportunities to match the needs of the teachers.

Leadership. Aware of the importance of the administrator in early education, New Jersey also offered a training series for P-3 educational leaders. The goal of the program was to provide the administrators with strategies and techniques to effectively implement high-quality programs (Rice & Lesaux, 2012). The program reached nearly 500 administrators, many of whom had little to no previous experience with or knowledge of effective early childhood program implementation. This may be viewed as transforming the leadership in public education to support appropriate practice in the new early childhood programs that have been incorporated into public education.

Home language support. The growing population of Spanish-speaking children in New Jersey mandated an approach where the home language of children is valued and developed in the preschool classroom. A variety of approaches have been used to support home language in these programs. With limited resources of qualified Spanish-speaking teachers, two-way bilingual immersion (TWI) was one approach adopted to address the needs of dual-language learners. TWI is full-immersion into the language for a set period of time rotating from the English "world" to the Spanish "world" between two teaching teams. One team speaks only English and the other speaks only Spanish. A randomized control trial demonstrated positive results for TWI, noting positive outcomes for both Spanish-speaking children and native English-speaking children (Barnett et al., 2007).

Overall impacts of the Abbott public education approach on the workforce. The incorporation of the early childhood workforces serving 3- and 4-year-olds into the public education system has been transformational. The essential reason for this success is that the Abbott policy addressed the fundamental economic problem. The policy began by setting out the goals to be accomplished and specifying a preschool education that could accomplish those goals. Program funding was determined by these requirements rather than the reverse. The program was fundamentally defined by its educational goals and fully incorporated into public education. Because it began with the teachers who were already serving the children, the resulting preschool teaching force was more diverse than the K-12 teaching force. However, teachers are now much more effective, better educated, better supported, and better compensated than previously.

We note that some early childhood workforces remain outside the public education system, despite the Abbott transformation. Although some programs have tried to provide seamless service quality whenever the child is present, those who provide wrap-around care outside the school day need not have the same qualifications and compensation. The "education solution" in this example addressed much but not all of the teaching force for children ages 3 to 5 and did not address teachers of infants and toddlers at all. Whether it is desirable and politically and financially feasible to bring more or even all hours of care into public education are questions for the future. If this is viewed as a continuation of the process that brought kindergarten teachers into the public education system, it may be a necessary step before those questions can be effectively addressed. Even such wealthy Nordic countries as Norway, that are willing to spend much more per pupil on young children than the United States, have not yet accomplished this goal (Organisation for Economic Co-operation and Development [OECD], 2006, 2011).

Conclusion

Clearly, the ECCE workforce is a critical component in the system for the care and education of young children. But this workforce is complicated. First, there is a fragmentation into several workforces including Head Start, child care, and public education (regular and special education). Second, there is the overlap of these sectors that blurs the lines across programs. Third, these teachers vary greatly on key characteristics such as preparation, qualifications, responsibilities, and compensation.

Policies are doing their part to shape the workforce and perhaps work toward cohesiveness. The increased qualifications now required for teachers of Head Start is one example of how over time there have been increases in the requirements for some teachers in ECCE. Another example is the expansion of public pre-K in some states. However, policies in this arena still vary greatly from state to state. Lastly, the advent of the QRIS will also impact the educational qualifications of teachers in the ECCE field and holds some potential to merge the workforces of the separate sectors in many aspects.

References

Abbott v. Burke, 100 N.J. 269, 495 A.2d 376, (N.J., 1985).

Adams, G., & Rohacek, M. (2002). More than a work support? Issues around integrating child development goals into the child care subsidy system. *Early Childhood Research Quarterly, 17*, 418–440.

Aikens, N., Hulsey, L.K., Moiduddin, E., Kopack, A., Takyi-Laryea, A., Tarullo, L., and West, J. (2011). Data Tables for FACES 2009 Head Start Children, Families, and Programs: Present and Past Data from FACES Report. OPRE Report 2011–33b. Washington, DC: Office of Planning, Research and Evaluation, Administration for Children and Families, U.S. Department of Health and Human Services.

Barnes, H. V., Guevara, M. D., Garcia, G., Levin, M., & Connell, D. B. (1999). How do Head Start staff characteristics relate to parent involvement and satisfaction? Paper presented at the Biennial Meeting of the Society for Research in Child Development, Albuquerque, NM.

Barnett, W.S. (2003). Low wages=low quality: Solving the real preschool teacher crisis. *Preschool Policy Matters, 3.* New Brunswick, NJ: NIEER.

Barnett, W.S. (2011a). Effectiveness of early educational intervention. *Science, 333*(6045), 975–978.

Barnett, W.S. (2011b). Minimum requirements for preschool teacher educational qualifications. In E. Zigler, W.S. Gilliam, & W.S. Barnett (Eds.), *The preK debates: Current controversies & issues* (pp. 48–54). Baltimore, MD: Brookes Publishing.

Barnett, W.S., Carolan, M.E., Squires, J.H., & Horowitz, M. (2013). *The state of preschool 2013: State preschool yearbook.* New Brunswick, NJ: National Institute for Early Education Research.

Barnett, W.S., Epstein, D. J., Friedman, A.H., Sansanelli, R., & Hustedt, J.T. (2009). *The state of preschool 2012: State preschool yearbook.* New Brunswick, NJ: National Institute for Early Education Research.

Barnett, W.S., & Haskins, R. (2010). *Investing in young children: New directions in federal preschool and early childhood policy.* Washington, DC: The Brookings Institute.

Barnett, W.S., Jung, K., Youn, M., & Frede, E. C. (2013). *Abbott preschool program longitudinal effects study: Fifth grade follow-up.* New Brunswick, NJ: National Institute for Early Education Research.

Barnett, W.S., Yarosz, D. J., Thomas, J.H., Jung, K., & Blanco, D. (2007). Two-way monolingual English immersion in preschool education: An experimental comparison. *Early Childhood Research Quarterly, 22*, 277–293.

Bassok, D., Fitzpatrick, M., Greenberg, E., & Loeb, S. (2013). *The extent of within- and between-sector quality differences in early childhood education and care.* Charlottesville, VA: Center on Education Policy and Workforce Competitiveness, UVA.

Bassok, D., Fitzpatrick, M., Loeb, S., & Paglayan, A. (2013). *The early childhood care and education workforce from 1990 through 2010: Changing dynamics and persistent concerns.* Charlottesville, VA: Center on Education Policy and Workforce Competitiveness, UVA.

Beatty, B. (1997). *Preschool education in America: The culture of young children from the colonial era to the present.* New Haven, CT: Yale University Press.

Bowman, B. (2011). Bachelor's degrees are necessary but not sufficient: Preparing teachers to teach young children. In E. Zigler, W.S. Gilliam, & W.S. Barnett (Eds.), *The pre-K debates: Current controversies & issues* (pp. 54–57). Baltimore, MD: Brookes Publishing.

Bridges, M., Fuller, B., Huang, D.S., & Hamre, B.K. (2011). Strengthening the early childhood workforce: How wage incentives may boost training and job stability. *Early Education & Development, 22*(6), 1009–1029.

Burchinal, P., Hyson, M., & Zaslow, M. (2011). Competencies and credentials for early childhood educators: What do we know and what do we need to know. In E. Zigler, W. Gilliam, & W.S. Barnett (Eds.), *The pre-k debates: Current controversies and issues* (pp. 73–77). Baltimore: Brookes Publishing.

Bureau of Labor Statistics, U.S. Department of Labor (BLS). (2014). *Occupational outlook handbook, 2014–15 edition: Preschool teachers*, Retrieved from http://www.bls.gov/ooh/education-training-and-library/preschool-teachers.htm

Burns, M. S., Donovan, M. S., & Bowman, B. T. (Eds.). (2000). *Eager to learn: Educating our preschoolers.* Washington, DC: National Academies Press.

Burton, A., Whitebook, M., Young, M., Bellm, D., Wayne, C., Brandon, R., and Maher, E. (2002). *Estimating the size and components of the U.S. child care workforce and caregiving population: Key findings from the child care workforce and caregiving population.* Washington, DC: Center for the Child Care Workforce and Seattle, WA: Human Services Policy Center, University of Washington.

Cahan, E. D. (1989). *Past caring: A history of US preschool care and education for the poor, 1820–1965.* New York: National Center for Children in Poverty.

Center for Law and Social Policy (CLASP). (2014). *The United States Head Start by the numbers: 2012 PIR profile.* Retrieved from http://www.clasp.org/resources-and-publications/publication-1/HSData2012US.pdf

Child Care Aware of America. (2013). *We can do better: 2013 update: Child Care Aware® of America's ranking of state child care center regulations and oversight.* Arlington, VA: Author.

Cochran-Smith, M., Feiman-Nemser, S., McIntyre, D. J., & Demers, K. E. (Eds.). (2008). *Handbook of research on teacher education: Enduring questions in changing contexts.* London, UK: Routledge.

Cochran-Smith, M., & Zeichner, K. M. (Eds.). (2010). *Studying teacher education: The report of the AERA panel on research and teacher education.* London, UK: Routledge.

Darling-Hammond, L., Amrein-Beardsley, A., Haertel, E., & Rothstein, J. (2012). Evaluating teacher evaluation. *Phi Delta Kappan, 93*(6), 8–15.

Darling-Hammond, L., & Sclan, E. M. (1996). Who teaches and why: Dilemmas of building a profession for twenty-first century schools. *Handbook of Research on Teacher Education, 2*, 67–101.

Dickinson, D. K. (2011). Teachers' language practices and academic outcomes of preschool children. *Science, 333*(6045), 964–967.

Early Childhood Technical Assistance Center (ECTAC). (2014a). *Annual Appropriations and Number of Children Served Under Part C of IDEA.* Retrieved from http://ectacenter.org/partc/partcdata.asp

Early Childhood Technical Assistance Center (ECTAC). (2014b). *Child Outcomes Highlights for FFY2012.* Retrieved from http://ectacenter.org/eco/assets/pdfs/childoutcomeshighlights.pdf

Early, D. M., Maxwell, K. L., Burchinal, M., Alva, S., Bender, R., Bryant, D. . . . Zill, N. (2007). Teacher education, classroom quality, and young children's academic skills: Results from seven studies of preschool programs. *Child Development, 79*(2), 558–580.

Fukkink, R. G., & Lont, A. (2007). Does training matter? A meta-analysis and review of caregiver training studies. *Early Childhood Research Quarterly, 22*(3), 294–311.

Fuller, B. (2011). College credentials and caring: how teacher training could lift young children. In E. Zigler, W. Gilliam, & W. S. Barnett (Eds.), *The pre-k debates: Current controversies and issues* (pp. 57–64). Baltimore, MD: Brookes Publishing.

Hanushek, E. A., & Rivkin, S. G. (2012). The distribution of teacher quality and implications for policy. *Annual Review of Economics, 4*(1), 131–157.

Hawkinson, L., Griffen, A., Dong, N., & Maynard, R. (2013). The relationship between child care subsidies and children's cognitive development. *Early Childhood Research Quarterly, 28*, 388–404.

Hebbeler, K., Spiker, D., & Kahn, L. (2012). Individuals with Disabilities Education Act's early childhood programs: Powerful vision and pesky details. *Topics in Early Childhood Special Education, 31*(4), 199–207.

Herbst, C., & Tekin, E. (2010). Child care subsidies and child development. *Economics of Education Review, 29*, 618–638.

Hotz, V. J., & Xiao, M. (2011). The impact of regulations on the supply and quality of care in child care markets. *The American Economic Review, 101*(5), 1775–1805.

Institute of Medicine (IOM) and National Research Council (NRC) (2012). *The early childhood care and education workforce: Challenge and opportunities. A workshop report.* Washington, DC: National Academies Press.

Joyce, B., and Showers, B. (2002). *Student achievement through staff development* (3rd ed.). Alexandria, VA: Association for Supervision and Curriculum Development.

Kagan, S. L., & Gomez, R. E. (2011). B.A. plus: Reconciling reality and reach. In E. Zigler, W. Gilliam, & W. S. Barnett (Eds.), *The pre-k debates: Current controversies and issues* (pp. 68–73). Baltimore, MD: Brookes Publishing.

Kagan, S. L., Kauerz, K., & Tarrant, K. (2008). *The early care and education teaching workforce at the fulcrum: An agenda for reform.* New York: Teachers College Press.

Karch, A. (2013). *Early start: Preschool politics in the United States.* Ann Arbor, MI: University of Michigan Press.

Klein, N., & Gilkerson, L. (2000). Personnel preparation for early childhood intervention programs. In J. Shonkoff & S. Meisels (Eds.), *Handbook of early childhood intervention* (pp. 454–478). Cambridge, UK: Cambridge University Press.

Lifter, K., Chandler, L. K., Cochran, D.C., Dinnebeil, L. A., Gallagher, P. A., Christensen, K. A., & Stayton, V. D. (2011). DEC personnel preparation standards revision 2005–2008. *Journal of Early Intervention, 33*(2), 151–167.

National Association of Child Care Resource and Referral Agencies (NACCCRA). (2011). *We can do better: NACCRRA's ranking of state child care center standards and oversight.* Washington, DC: NACCRRA.

National Institute for Early Education Research (NIEER). (2014). *National teacher survey.* New Brunswick, NJ: NIEER.

National Survey of Early Care and Education (NSECE) Project Team. (2013). Number and characteristics of early care and education (ECE) teachers and caregivers: Initial findings from the National Survey of Early Care and Education (NSECE). OPRE Report #2013–38, Washington, DC: Office of Planning, Research and Evaluation, Administration for Children and Families, U.S. Department of Health and Human Services.

Office of Child Care. (2014). *A foundation for quality improvement systems state licensing, preschool, and QRIS program quality standards.* Washington, DC: DHHS.

Office of Head Start. (2014). 2012–2013 *Head Start program information report (PIR), PIR summary report national level, May 27, 2014.* Washington, DC: Administration on Children and Families.

Organisation for Economic Co-operation and Development (OECD). (2006). *Starting strong II: Early childhood education and care.* Paris, FR: OECD Publishing.

Organisation for Economic Co-operation and Development (OECD). (2011). *Starting strong III: A quality toolbox for early childhood education and care.* Paris: OECD Publishing.

Peer, S., and Burbank, J. (2004). *Focus on early learning: Lessons from the French Écoles Maternelles.* Seattle, Washington: Economic Opportunity Institute. Retrieved from http://www.eoionline.org/wp/wp-content/uploads/early-learning/EcolesMaternelles-Jan04.pdf

Pianta, R. (2011). A degree is not enough: Teachers need stronger and more individualized professional development supports to be effective in the classroom. In E. Zigler, W. Gilliam, & W. S. Barnett (Eds.), The *pre-K debates: Current controversies & issues.* (pp. 64–68). Baltimore, MD: Brookes Publishing.

Rhodes, H., & Huston, A. (2012). Building the workforce our youngest children deserve. *Social Policy Report: The Society for Research in Child Development, 26*(1), 3–6.

Rice, C. C., & Lesaux, N. K. (2012). *Early learning instructional leaders and strong preK-3rd student assessment systems: The New Jersey story.* Newark, NJ: Advocates for Children of New Jersey.

Rose, E. (2010). *The promise of preschool.* Oxford, UK: Oxford University Press.

Ryan, R., Johnson, A., Rigby, E., & Brooks-Gunn, J. (2011). The impact of child care subsidy use on child care quality. *Early Childhood Research Quarterly, 26*, 320–331.

Ryan, S., & Whitebook, M. (2012). More than teachers: The early care and education workforce. In B. Pianta (Ed.), *Handbook of early education* (pp. 92–110). New York: Guilford Press.

Sabol, T. J., Hong, S. S., Pianta, R. C., & Burchinal, M. R. (2013). Can rating pre-K programs predict children's learning? *Science, 341*(6148), 845–846.

Shonkoff, J. P., & Meisels, S. J. (Eds.). (2000). *Handbook of early childhood intervention.* Cambridge, UK: Cambridge University Press.

Snow, C. E., & Van Hemel, S. B. (Eds.). (2008). *Early childhood assessment: Why, what, and how.* Washington, DC: National Academies Press.

Spiker, D., Hebbeler, K. M., & Barton, L. R. (2011). Measuring quality of ECE programs for children with disabilities. In M. Zaslow, I. Martinez-Beck, K. Tout, & T. Halle (Eds.), *Quality measurement in early childhood settings* (pp. 229–256). Baltimore, MD: Brookes.

Tanner, L. N., & Tanner, D. (1973). Unanticipated effects of federal policy: The kindergarten. *Educational Leadership, 31*(1), 49–52.

Tout, K., Zaslow, M., & Berry, D. (2005). Quality and qualifications: Links between professional development and quality in early care and education settings. In M. Zaslow & I. Martinez-Beck (Eds.), *Critical issues in early childhood professional development* (pp. 77–110). Baltimore, MD: Brookes Publishing.

United States Census Bureau (1966). Current population survey tables. Retrieved from http://www.census.gov/hhes/school/data/cps/1966/tables.html

U.S. Department of Health and Human Services, Administration for Children and Families (2010). *Head start impact study.* Final report. Washington, DC: Author.

U.S. Government Accountability Office (USGAO). (2012). *Child Care Workforce Quality.* GAO-12–248. Washington, DC: Author.

Wasik, B., & Hindman, A. (2011). Improving vocabulary and pre-literacy skills of at-risk preschoolers through teacher professional development. *Journal of Educational Psychology, 103*(2), 455–469.

Whitebook, M., Phillips, D., & Howes, C. (2014). *Worthy work, STILL unlivable wages: The early childhood workforce 25 years after the National Child Care Staffing Study.* Berkeley: Center for the Study of Child Care Employment, University of California

Whitebook, M., & Ryan, S. (2011). *Degrees in context: Asking the right questions about preparing skilled and effective teachers of young children.* New Brunswick, NJ: NIEER.

Whitebook, M., & Sakai, L. (2003). Turnover begets turnover: An examination of job and occupational instability among child care center staff. *Early Childhood Research Quarterly, 18*(3), 273–293.

Willer, B. A., Lutton, A., & Ginsberg, M. R. (2011). College credentials and caring: How teacher training could lift young children. In E. Zigler, W. Gilliam, & W. S. Barnett (Eds.), *The pre-k debates: Current controversies and issues* (pp. 57–64). Baltimore, MD: Brookes Publishing.

Zigler, E., & Valentine, J. (1979). *Project Head Start: A legacy of the war on poverty.* New York: Free Press.

4

BEYOND THE STATUS QUO

Rethinking Professional Development for Early Childhood Teachers

Pamela J. Winton, Patricia A. Snyder, and Stacie G. Goffin

Forming professional development (PD) systems that prepare and support a knowledgeable and skilled early childhood education (ECE) workforce is receiving unprecedented attention (Barnett, 2011; Rhodes & Huston, 2012; Yoshikawa et al., 2013). These PD systems are expected to ensure early childhood teachers have the knowledge, skills, and dispositions to design high-quality learning environments, implement evidence-based interactional and instructional practices, and use child progress and outcomes information to inform and refine their practices. Based on expectations that PD will result in improved interactional and instructional practices that, in turn, promote children's development and learning, PD has become a "hot topic" (Diamond, Justice, Siegler, & Snyder, 2013).

Yet, despite the mounting number of documents and policy initiatives promoting the importance of PD, as well as promising approaches for its effective design and delivery, too many early childhood teachers experience PD that is episodic, disconnected from practice, and based on a "train-and-hope" mentality (Snyder, Hemmeter, & McLaughlin, 2011; Winton, McCollum, & Catlett, 2008). Policy makers and others involved in initiatives such as the Race to the Top Early Learning Challenge are requesting research evidence to inform public investments in PD and PD systems. Significant efforts have been directed to recognizing and coordinating ECE as a field of practice with associated implications for the design and delivery of coherent and aligned PD and PD systems. Those responsible for initial teacher preparation and ongoing PD are seeking guidance for their efforts. Yet, given the lack of consensus across ECE's sectors on key concepts, organizing frameworks, and PD terms and definitions, providing united and informed responses to these requests remains challenging.

At the center of the challenges is a lack of coherent and aligned PD systems.[1] Closing systemic gaps requires a demanding process of addressing some of the field's most fundamental issues of purpose and identity (Goffin & Washington, 2007). For instance, ECE, as a field of practice, is comprised of multiple sectors, each with its own agencies and organizations, history, culture, terminology, funding streams, standards, definitions of PD, and interpretations of PD practices (Goffin, 2013; Rhodes & Huston, 2012; Snyder, Denney, Pasia, Rakap, & Crowe, 2011; Winton et al., 2008). Leaders in ECE cannot even consistently respond to questions of who is considered an early childhood teacher; the knowledge, skills, and dispositions needed by early childhood teachers in different roles; and the outcomes to be achieved from PD. Consequently, what is considered ECE PD varies greatly, from a finite set of training hours typically outlined in child care facility licensing requirements in states, to certification or licensure requirements for pre-K teachers and specialists working in public schools or in early intervention, to continuing education requirements within each ECE sector.

In response to ECE's fragmentation in general and specifically related to PD, Goffin (2013; Goffin & Washington, 2007) declared the time has come to "call the question" and accept responsibility for defining ECE as a professional field of practice, one that is responsible for developing a competent, accountable workforce. Goffin (2013) suggested ECE should consider becoming a field comprised of specialties, unified in part by a workforce prepared with core or common competencies. The inclusion of specialties would recognize the shared knowledge, skills, and dispositions among the ECE workforce, while also acknowledging unique scopes of practice and associated competencies tied to different roles and responsibilities. Responding to Goffin's (2013) proposal, Winton (2013) agreed with her logic but stressed the challenges inherent to defining and implementing the "devilish details" associated with defining, delivering, and evaluating PD within a unified field of practice.

The purpose of this chapter is to respond to these and other PD practice and system challenges. We begin the chapter by offering a unifying definition for PD from the National Professional Development Center on Inclusion (NPDCI, 2008). We then describe essential features of PD (the *who*, *what*, and *how*) that must be considered and integrated in designing effective PD. Included are promising research findings to inform rethinking approaches to PD. Next, we offer a framework and propose action steps that might be taken to advance toward coherent and aligned PD systems capable of supporting ECE as a unified field of practice. We conclude with recommendations that we believe can move us beyond the status quo of professional development for early childhood teachers.

A Unifying Definition for Early Childhood Education Professional Development

An agreed-upon definition for ECE PD that can consistently be used in a unified field of practice with various specialties for the purposes of planning, implementing, evaluating, and systems building is non-existent (Maxwell, Feild, & Clifford, 2005). Answers are needed to questions such as: Does the term PD encompass both preservice preparation and inservice training? Does PD include diverse forms of delivery, such as mentoring, coaching, reflective supervision, and other job-embedded approaches, or is it limited to formal instruction?

Forming coherent and aligned PD systems is destined to be continually problematic in the absence of an agreed-upon definition. The definition of PD in this chapter comes from the National Professional Development Center on Inclusion (NPDCI), a federally funded project focused on developing cross-sector PD systems to support inclusion and inclusive practices for young children with disabilities. NPDCI defines professional development as "facilitated teaching and learning experiences that are transactional and designed to support the acquisition of professional knowledge, skills, and dispositions as well as the application of this knowledge in practice" (NPDCI, 2008, p. 3). This definition encompasses many forms and formats of PD, including teacher preparation (i.e., preservice) and ongoing preparation and growth (i.e., inservice). The definition promotes coherent and aligned PD systems by bridging traditional divides among institutions of higher education with responsibility for preparing teachers and agencies/organizations that determine training or licensure requirements and provide ongoing training and implementation supports (Buysse, Winton, & Rous, 2009). With its emphasis on application of knowledge in practice, this definition reflects growing recognition that effective interactional and instructional practices are central to professional competence and achieving desired child outcomes (National Council for Accreditation of Teacher Education [NCATE], 2010; Snyder, Denney et al., 2011).

Core Components of Professional Development

The NPDCI definition emphasizes the alignment of three core and interrelated PD components: (1) *the who*—the individual learners (early childhood teachers as defined in this chapter) and those who support their learning (faculty and PD providers); (2) *the what*—the content focus of PD; and

(3) *the how*—the facilitated teaching and learning experiences used to achieve desired PD outcomes. Details about each of these core components and why they are critical considerations for rethinking PD practices and moving toward coherent and aligned PD systems are described below.

The Who: *Defining the Early Childhood Education Workforce*

Early childhood teachers. For the purposes of this chapter, *early childhood teachers* are individuals working directly with children as well as those who work with early childhood teachers to advance their competence in supporting children's learning and development. This definition, which is inclusive of teachers addressing the learning and development of children from birth to the start of kindergarten[2] in center- and home-based programs, includes child care, Early Head Start/Head Start, preschool/Pre-K, early intervention (birth-to-three programs for infants and toddlers with or at risk for disabilities under Part C of the Individuals with Disabilities Education Act (IDEA), and early childhood special education for preschool children with disabilities (Section 619 of IDEA).

Information on the biggest segment of the ECE workforce—the 2 million teachers working in Head Start, public pre-K, and child care—is available in a report from the Office of Planning, Research, and Evaluation (OPRE; U.S. Department of Health and Human Services, 2013). Several OPRE findings are notable in their implications for PD practices and systems. These 2 million teachers are divided evenly between those working in center- and home-based settings, with a slim majority (53%) of center-based and one third (30%) of home-based teachers having a college degree of some kind. Workforce characteristics, such as education level and compensation, varied considerably depending on the center-based program's auspices and funding stream and the age of children being served. Children ages birth to 3, for example, were less likely to have degreed teachers (36% degreed) than were children ages 3 through 5 (62% degreed). Teachers were likely to receive lower wages in comparison to others with similar levels of education.

Early childhood special education teachers and other specialists serving infants and toddlers through IDEA Part C early intervention programs[3] and children ages 3 through 5 through Section 619 of IDEA may be working as an inclusive or specialized public school classroom teacher or with families and children in home- or community-based settings, sometimes in collaboration with other teachers and with parents to support inclusion of children with disabilities in natural environments. These individuals are highly likely to have a BA degree or higher.[4]

Faculty and professional development providers. Another, and too often overlooked, component of *the who* included in our definition of the ECE workforce are the early childhood faculty, coaches, consultants, mentors, trainers, supervisors, and technical assistance (TA) specialists who provide PD, in some cases in conjunction with directly serving children. Although some information exists on the demographics of early childhood two- and four-year faculty (Hyson, Horm, & Winton, 2012; Maxwell, Lim, & Early, 2006), no national picture exists of PD providers working outside institutions of higher education. Education, experience, knowledge, dispositions, pedagogical skills, funding sources, and wages likely vary considerably. Titles (e.g., coaches, itinerant teachers, technical assistance practitioners, mentors) are numerous and lack agreed-upon definitions and consistently assigned responsibilities or role-associated knowledge, skills, and dispositions. It is generally expected that these individuals should know and be able to implement evidence-based practices that support children's learning and development and also be capable of implementing evidence-based PD approaches on those topics with adult learners (Snyder, Denney, et al., 2011). Typically, these individuals are being entrusted with accomplishing this two-pronged task without specialized licensure, credentials, or formal oversight and without a PD system to support their ongoing growth and development in these two essential areas of content and pedagogical expertise.

This portrait of *the who* illustrates the wide variability of the ECE workforce in terms of education levels, work settings, roles, and responsibilities. This variability highlights the necessity of considering the unique and common needs and characteristics of individuals in designing coherent and aligned PD systems.

The What: *Knowledge, Skills, Dispositions, and Practice Application*

A variety of documents that might fall into the category of PD content or practice standards co-exist, each identifying knowledge, skills, dispositions, and competence in implementing evidence-based practices needed for interacting with or teaching young children. This array of options associated with *the what* of PD further reinforces the fragmented state of ECE PD and underscores the need to unify sources of possible PD content.

Content standards. Among these documents are the voluntary personnel preparation standards (i.e., content standards) promulgated by national organizations, such as the National Association for the Education of Young Children (NAEYC, 2011) and the Council for Exceptional Children/Division for Early Childhood (CEC/DEC, 2008), with the intent of defining standards or competencies for their members. These documents have particular salience for teacher education programs because they serve as benchmarks for teacher preparation accreditation systems such as the Council for the Accreditation of Educator Preparation (CAEP, formerly NCATE) (Chandler et al., 2012). In addition to recommended national standards, most states have competency documents or licensure requirements for early childhood teachers in targeted sectors, indicating state-specific expectations for these teachers. Focused examination of these competencies revealed they are not consistently aligned with national standards (Center to Inform Personnel Preparation Policy and Practice in Early Intervention and Preschool Education, 2008), nor have states taken a uniform approach to how standards or licensing requirements are organized (Winton & West, 2011). Many are organized by knowledge, skills, or dispositions needed to teach content-focused domains (e.g., math, literacy, visual-performing arts) or level of education in contrast to observable interactional and instructional practices linked to early learning standards for children (Florida Expanding Opportunities for Early Childhood Inclusion, 2012). In some states, multiple sets of competencies co-exist without being aligned, contributing further to systemic fragmentation in ECE PD.

Practice standards. Expectations for *the what* of PD extend beyond developing and supporting early childhood teachers' knowledge, skills, and dispositions. PD must also support teachers to implement interactional and instructional practices in their work settings. In keeping with this expectation, national professional organizations have issued policy statements for their membership identifying practices that benefit young children's development and learning. For instance, NAEYC has a position statement, *Developmentally Appropriate Practice in Early Childhood Programs Serving Children from Birth through Age 8* (NAEYC, 2009); CEC/DEC has a set of *Recommended Practices in Early Intervention/ Early Childhood Special Education* (DEC, 2014), specific practices based on the best available empirical research as well as the wisdom and experience of the field, that builds upon and extends NAEYC's position statement on developmentally appropriate practices.

Aligning standards and competencies. These disparate, potentially duplicative national and state sources of content standards and practice competencies will need to be aligned to unify ECE as a professional field of practice by establishing a shared as well as specialized knowledge base along with practice competencies (*the what* of PD). Toward this end, a workgroup of CEC/DEC members aligned the CEC/DEC and NAEYC personnel standards (Chandler et al., 2012). Not surprisingly, the authors found areas of convergence as well as areas of difference representing each organization's differing emphasis on general and specialized knowledge and skills for working with young children with and without disabilities and their families. The workgroup's efforts resulted in a detailed alignment matrix of the two sets of standards available at the DEC website (www.dec-sped.org/). In the move toward defining ECE as a field of practice comprised of specialties, this matrix could serve as a guide for states interested in developing an integrated set of general and specialized practice standards within coherent and aligned PD systems.

The How: *Professional Development Strategies*

Promising professional development strategies. A growing body of research identifies PD strategies demonstrated to be effective in supporting early childhood teachers in terms of their knowledge, skills related to implementing practices with fidelity, and confidence in using data to make informed practice-based decisions. This rigorous, empirical evidence is an important supplement to general principles of adult learning (e.g., Knowles, Holton, & Swanson, 1998) that have guided PD for decades. For the present chapter, we identified select empirical evidence, drawing from a larger set of 154 studies reviewed by Snyder et al. (2012). We identified 32 studies[5] published between 2006 and 2012 in peer-reviewed journals that used experimental designs in which participants were randomly assigned to PD intervention conditions. These 32 studies examined PD interventions that included coaching, consultation, or mentoring delivered on-site or remotely, involved early childhood teachers who worked with children from birth through 5 years of age, and reported empirical evidence about PD outcomes for either early childhood teachers or for the children with whom they work.

With respect to *the who* of PD, across the 32 reviewed studies, participants' practice settings included Head Start (n = 22 studies), public or private pre-K programs (n = 14 studies), child care center-based programs (n = 7 studies), child care home-based programs (n = 2 studies), and preschool classrooms including children with disabilities (n =1 study). None of the 32 studies was conducted in early intervention Part C practice settings.

The content (*the what*) most often focused on a specific curricula or content domain (e.g., literacy, social emotional) with some studies focused on multiple domains. Literacy was the content focus in 22 of the 32 studies, social-emotional in five studies, general instructional practices in three studies, teacher-child interactions or relationships in three studies, classroom environmental quality or classroom management in two studies, and general instructional strategies in two studies. One study focused on joint attention and another on instructional practices for young children with autism.

With respect to *the how* of PD, the experimental interventions in the 32 reviewed studies included two key features: (1) provision of detailed, concrete, and specific information about environmental, interactional, or instructional practices related to the content focus with explicit descriptions and demonstrations of these practices (often through workshops or learning objects on websites) and (2) provision of sustained and individualized support and feedback on implementing these practices in job-embedded settings (often described as coaching, mentoring, or consultation). When implemented in combination, these two features showed promise across studies for improving dimensions of classroom quality and teaching practices and, in some studies, for improving select child outcomes.

Study authors referred to the sustained and often individualized support and feedback provided to early childhood teachers as *coaching* (14 studies), *consultation* (nine studies), *mentor coaching* (five studies), or *mentoring* (four studies). Despite differences in terminology, most of the sustained and individualized support appeared to incorporate similar strategies based on the authors' descriptions. For example, teachers were provided models or video exemplars of practices, were observed implementing practices, and were provided feedback about their practice implementation. While the aforementioned terms are often used interchangeably in the literature, several authors have asserted a need to distinguish and clarify these terms (Howard et al., 2013; NAEYC/National Association of Child Care Research and Referral Agencies [NACCRRA], 2011; Sheridan, Edwards, Marvin, & Knoche, 2009; Snyder et al., 2012). This includes not only distinguishing and clarifying definitions but also the purposes, forms, functions, and implementation support strategies (e.g., observation, feedback) associated with each term.

Overall, findings from the 32 studies suggest that ECE PD that (1) defines dimensions of classroom or environmental quality, (2) explicitly links interactional and instructional practices to these dimensions, and (3) is most likely to be associated with effective interactional and instructional practices has at least three important features. First, the environmental, interactional, or instructional practices that are the focus of the PD are explicitly defined and multiple exemplars are provided of what these practices look like when implemented in authentic ECE settings. Second, the PD provides teachers with job-embedded opportunities to learn and implement the practices with explicit feedback about their implementation. Third, the PD includes information that links improvements or changes in environmental quality or teachers' interactional and instructional practices to child progress monitoring and child learning outcomes.

Realities of professional development implementation. Notwithstanding the growing body of knowledge about effective PD strategies, the availability of evidence on how PD is implemented is limited. What we do know suggests that large amounts of money are being spent on inservice ECE PD[6] with little assurance that desired outcomes in teacher knowledge, skills, and dispositions or child and family outcomes are being achieved. In addition, national survey data from state agencies with IDEA 619 and Part C responsibilities suggest the majority of states do not have systemic, sustainable approaches to PD and technical assistance, with workshops being the dominant approach to PD delivery (Bruder et al., 2009). These findings, even within one small sector of ECE, coupled with what we know about effective PD, underscore the gap between what we are learning about promising approaches to PD and the inadequacies of current ECE PD systems with respect to the how of PD.

What remains to be learned about effective professional development. In spite of a growing body of research on promising PD strategies, the effects of PD interventions on the distal outcome of child learning and development have not been robust, particularly when child outcomes are examined relatively close in time to when teachers begin implementing environmental, interactional, or instructional practices with fidelity. Therefore, additional questions remain to be addressed through research about the magnitude of distal (child) effects in PD intervention studies, particularly what type of child effects might be expected and when these effects might be expected in relation to teachers' implementation of practices.

A review by Hill, Beisiegel, and Jacob (2013) described important implications gleaned from what has been learned and what remains to be learned from "experimenting" with PD in pre-K through 12 settings. While acknowledging many factors could account for the variable or modest student outcomes reported in their review (e.g., poorly specified PD content, extent to which PD intervention features were implemented with fidelity, misaligned teacher or child outcome measures, small sample sizes, insufficient statistical power), Hill et al. proposed a revised roadmap for improving PD experimental research. Among their recommendations was a need to conduct more rigorous experimental comparisons of PD design features at the initial stages of development, including gathering information about feasibility, acceptability, and utility of the intervention from the perspectives of end-users such as teachers and PD providers.

Although promising evidence is accruing about features of effective PD, still more needs to be known about which facilitated teaching and learning strategies or approaches are most effective and efficient for helping teachers improve classroom quality and their interactional and instructional practices (Diamond et al., 2013; Hill et al., 2013). Specifically, which facilitated teaching and learning experiences at what levels of intensity are necessary for practitioners to acquire, become fluent with, generalize, and maintain practices most likely to result in positive child learning and developmental outcomes? For example, is it better for *the what* (content) of early childhood PD to be structured to support implementation of one or a small set of interactional or instructional practices or for the PD to support implementation of a literacy or social-emotional framework that includes a larger number of practices? In addition, information is needed about costs of PD interventions demonstrated to be effective along with cost-benefit or cost-effectiveness analyses.

Given research evidence to date suggests a central role for sustained implementation support (often referred to as coaching) as an active ingredient of effective PD, more research is needed to identify formats and features of effective coaching (National Center on Quality Teaching and Learning, 2014; Snyder, Hemmeter, Fox, & Conroy, 2014). For example, is coaching more or less effective when provided by a colleague or instructional leader from one's own program or by a coach from outside the program? What is the role of communities of practice in relation to individualized coaching? How might these two types of facilitated teaching and learning experiences be combined, and for which teachers might the combination be most relevant and effective? How frequently should the coach consult with a teacher, and how much coaching is needed for teachers to acquire, become fluent with, generalize, and sustain implementation of practices? Is there a threshold for coaching with respect to amount and duration beyond which improvements in practices are minimal and therefore not justified? On what basis are decisions made about which teachers should receive more intensive implementation supports such as coaching? How should these decisions be linked to other competency components, including training and staff selection, as described in implementation science frameworks (Fixsen, Naoom, Blase, Friedman, & Wallace, 2005)?

Questions also remain with respect to delivery and pedagogical approaches. Is it better for teachers to analyze others' teaching practices or their own teaching practices, or both? How many and what types of teaching practice exemplars are sufficient based on the teachers' pace and phase of learning (e.g., acquisition, fluency, generalization, maintenance)? Which features of early childhood PD are important for teachers without formal preservice preparation versus those with formal preparation?

Finally, as technology becomes more prominent in early childhood PD, more information is needed about how facilitated teaching and learning experiences should be designed and delivered using technological advancements. Snyder, Hemmeter, and McLaughlin (2011) have cautioned that as technology becomes increasingly used, we should not assume web-based modules, blogs, discussion boards, and the posting of resources online include the structural and substantive features of PD necessary for achieving meaningful proximal (teacher) and distal (child) outcomes. We need to determine which technology-based PD experiences hold the most promise for supporting teachers' learning and application of evidence-based interactional and instructional practices. Despite many remaining research questions, what has been learned to date from experimenting with PD suggests it is time to rethink *the how* of PD.

Aligning the Core Components (*Who, What, and How*) of Professional Development

Becoming a unified professional field of practice responsible for developing a competent ECE workforce requires intense effort directed toward designing facilitated teaching and learning experiences that intentionally address the core *who, what, and how* components of PD. We must recognize that one size—one set of competencies or one approach to PD—will not fit all. There are individual differences within and across the field's specialties in terms of unique needs, strengths, and desired outcomes for PD. Depending on the PD outcomes being sought, various levels of impact are possible, including (a) raising awareness, (b) acquiring or enhancing knowledge, (c) acquiring or enhancing skills, or (d) shaping or modifying dispositions. These outcomes might be achieved, as suggested by Sheridan et al. (2009), by focusing on a variety of topics: changes in teachers' interactions with children or families, the design of learning environments, or the use of specific curricular or teaching strategies for particular groups of children or an individual child. In coherent and aligned PD systems, the delivery and type of facilitated teaching and learning experiences will vary depending on the content and level of impact desired for different levels of needs within and between sub-specialty groups.

Figure 4.1 shows an approach for addressing the fit between the how of PD and desired teacher outcomes (*the who and what*). It shows that PD strategies (e.g., reading, case study, self-reflection, coaching) should be selected for use based on their proven association with achieving a desired PD outcome. For example, if a desired PD outcome is for teachers to be aware of a new regulation related to the natural environments provision of IDEA, then a reading or self-guided instructional module followed by a learning check on a website might be appropriate for achieving the desired awareness outcome. If

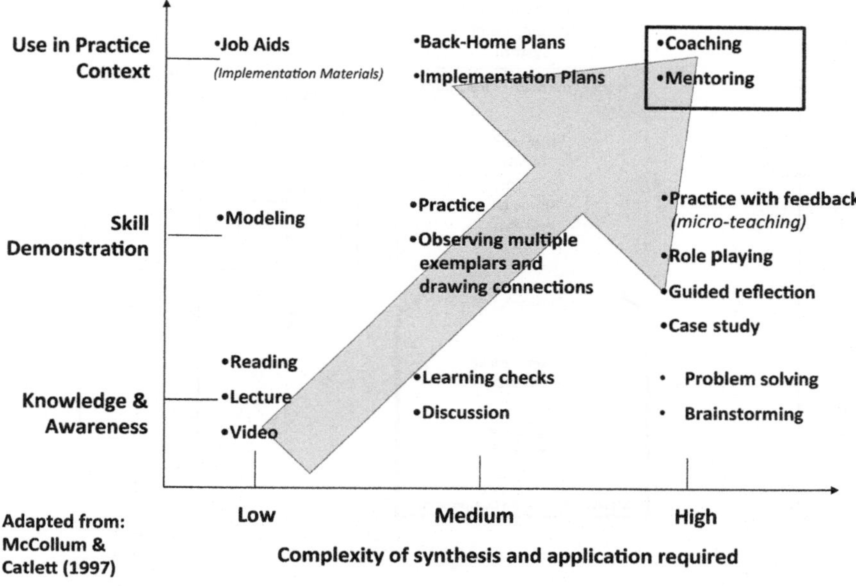

Figure 4.1 Aligning Instructional Strategies to Desired Professional Development Outcomes

the desired PD outcome is focused on skill implementation in practice contexts, then more complex experiential strategies identified in the ECE PD literature will likely be needed. Experiential strategies include coaching (Hanft, Rush, & Shelden, 2004; National Center on Quality Teaching and Learning, 2014), consultation (Buysse & Wesley, 2005), and communities of practice (Wesley & Buysse, 2006). As described earlier, much is being learned about these latter PD strategies, particularly in relation to supporting the highest level of impact—application of interactional and instructional practices in job-embedded contexts. It should be noted, however, that these intensive PD strategies are typically expensive. Using these intensive strategies intentionally as part of PD sequences that are integrated with less expensive approaches, like webinars and workshops that are reliably associated with awareness/knowledge-related outcomes, is an important aspect of rethinking PD practices.

Putting the Pieces Together: Taking Steps toward Coherent and Aligned Professional Development Systems

As stated in the introduction, momentum is strong for transforming ECE's fragmented PD into coherent and aligned systems. The intent of this chapter is to provide a framework, selected resources, and recommendations for how the ECE field might seize this moment in time. We have proposed a unifying definition of PD that includes discussion of current realities associated with the three key components of PD (*the who, what, and how*) and have shared what is being learned from research about promising approaches to effective PD, particularly for supporting the crucially important element of practice implementation. However, knowledge does not lead to action without a roadmap for putting the pieces together. We acknowledge that creating change in deeply entrenched, highly siloed PD systems can be daunting. In the remaining section of the chapter, using Figure 4.2 as a framework, we elucidate a few of the "devilish details" or interrelated steps that might be taken to move forward in designing and implementing coherent and aligned PD systems at various levels (i.e., ECE teacher, program, and system) within the context of broader early childhood systems-building initiatives.

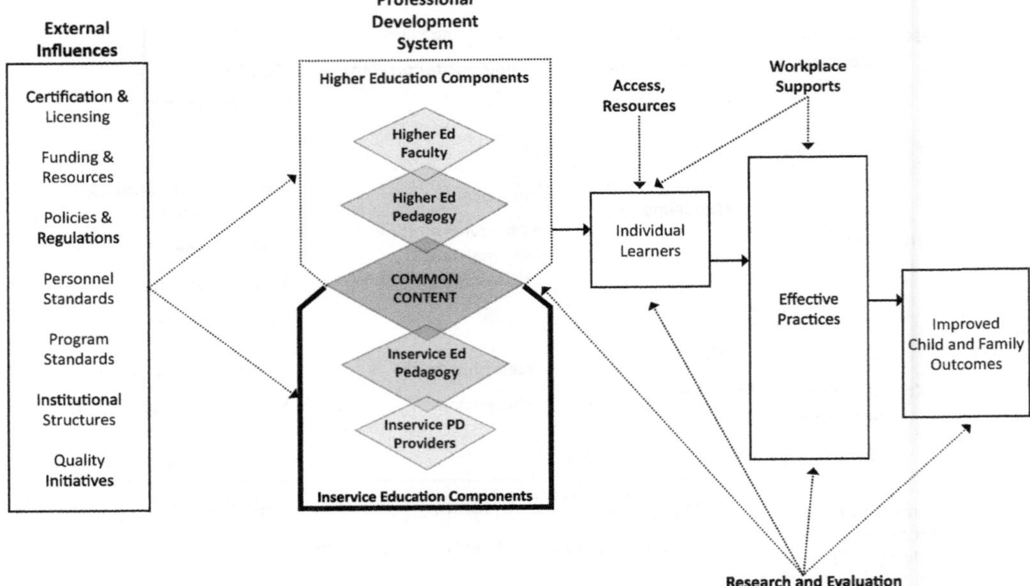

Figure 4.2 Professional Development within the Context of a Theory of Change. Adapted from Hyson, M., Horm, D. M., & Winton, P. J. (2012). Higher education for early childhood educators and outcomes for young children: Pathways toward greater effectiveness. In R. Pianta, L. Justice, S. Barnett, & S. Sheridan (Eds.), *Handbook of early education* (p. 554). New York, NY: Guilford Press.

Map Backward from Desired Outcomes

In a seminal article on examining PD outcomes, Guskey (1986) suggested a logical but rarely considered starting place for designing PD systems that begins with mapping backward from desired outcomes. Consistent with Guskey's suggestion, we describe Figure 4.2 in an unorthodox way, moving not from left to right but beginning with the right-hand rectangle: the child and family outcomes, and then associating each rectangle with a proposed next step.

One source for identifying child outcomes to guide PD planning, implementation, and evaluation decisions are the early learning standards focused on what young children should know and be able to do that states have developed as part of early childhood systems-building activities (Kagan, 2012). Another set of outcomes that could guide PD are those reported annually by state IDEA programs in State Performance Plan/Annual Performance Reports (U.S. Department of Education, 2012). For the 2015 submission, OSEP added new indicators for both Part C and Part B, which require each state to identify a child-level outcome that they will focus on improving. States must develop a comprehensive, multi-year State Systemic Improvement Plan (SSIP) that demonstrates how they will build their capacity to support local educational agencies and early intervention service programs and providers in improving the identified result for children with disabilities (Vinh, Lucas, Taylor, Kelley, & Kasprzak, 2014). The indicator requires that states make linkages to other state and federal quality initiatives such as states' early learning standards, which is a clear incentive for historically separate ECE sectors to work together to develop a set of integrated outcomes that could then shape PD. A third accountability structure that guides ECE PD is the Head Start Child Development and Early Learning Framework (Office of Head Start, 2010). We propose that the accountability systems across these various sectors be aligned to create a coherent set of child and family outcomes for use in PD systems.

Focus Professional Development on Practices with Strongest Evidence Base

Once desired child and family outcomes and data sources across sectors are aligned, mapping backward to the specific environmental, interactional, and instructional practices (the second rectangle from the right in Figure 4.2) most reliably associated with the desired child and family outcomes is a logical next step. Specification of these practices helps identify the content focus for PD and informs the selection of strategies for learning about and applying those practices (*the how* of PD). Careful selection of practices creates an important link in the causal chain between PD (facilitated teaching and learning experiences) and proximal (teacher) and distal (child and family) outcomes. We propose that an integrated set of common/shared cross-sector ECE practice standards, focused on those practices with the strongest evidence base, be identified and updated in an ongoing fashion as a centerpiece within coherent and aligned PD systems.

Plan Professional Development to Address Individual Learners

The third rectangle from the right in Figure 4.2 depicts the learners (i.e., *the who*). It is important to consider how to identify diverse needs while fully embracing the expertise of ECE specialties so PD practices and approaches are more effectively and efficiently designed within coherent and aligned PD systems. For instance, depending upon their sub-specialty, some early childhood teachers might need support in learning about process features of ECE environments that support quality interactions; early childhood teachers may also need support for learning about intentional teaching practices for children with special learning needs. We propose that PD be planned and implemented in ways that effectively and efficiently address and capitalize on the diverse needs and characteristics of the ECE workforce in terms of education, expertise, role, responsibilities, and work setting.

Bring Higher Education and Agencies Closer Together

As depicted in the central rectangle in Figure 4.2, preservice and inservice are intentionally presented as connected system components because to do otherwise would undermine cohesive systemic change. The integration of higher education into broader ECE PD systems in active and meaningful ways cannot be assumed (Hyson et al., 2012). Too often we hear early childhood program administrators complain that college graduates are ill-prepared for the realities of ECE settings. Likewise, higher education faculty complain that it is hard to find community-based ECE practica sites that reflect the ethnic, cultural, socio-economic, and ability diversity of children and families being served in ECE settings and provide exemplars of practices with the strongest evidence base. Intentional and systematic initiatives are necessary to build quality and strong connections between higher education and state agency PD (Winton & Catlett, 2009). We propose federal funding be earmarked to strengthen these connections—connections that would be further strengthened by having a set of validated and agreed-upon content and practice standards (*the what*) to guide faculty and PD providers in developing aligned PD, as depicted in the middle of the central rectangle in Figure 4.2.

Align Professional Development Systems with External Factors

As shown in the left-hand rectangle in Figure 4.2, organizational structures influencing present and future ECE PD systems include licensing and certification, funding streams, policies, personnel and program standards, institutional structures, and accountability initiatives such as Quality Rating and Improvement Systems (QRIS). Because of ECE's fragmentation, however, these external factors do not uniformly affect the field as each sector (e.g., Head Start, child care, pre-K, etc.) is typically driven by its own version of these factors. Linking high-quality, tailored PD options, intentionally designed to address unique learner needs as those evolve and change, to incentives and requirements (the "carrots and sticks"), such as licensure, certification, training credits, and career and salary advancement, is an important component of coherent and aligned ECE PD systems. Too often, early childhood teachers report taking the same workshop year after year to meet state training requirements because no motivation exists for pursuing PD options that will extend their learning.

In the absence of field-wide leadership driving unification of ECE as a professional field of practice, we propose creating a centralized leadership cadre at the federal level focused on strengthening organizational, structural, and policy connections to create coherent and aligned ECE PD systems (1) vertically across sector demarcations at national, state, and local levels serving different age groups of children and (2) horizontally across the multiple ECE-related disciplines in higher education and the various agencies and entities comprised of different specialties providing PD to early childhood teachers. The extent to which early childhood teachers can implement learned practices with fidelity—which is essential to achieving desired child and family outcomes associated with the practice—is dependent on organizational supports for implementing what has been learned (e.g., access, resources, and workplace supports as indicated in Figure 4.2).

Research that informs how to rethink the design, delivery, and evaluation of facilitated teaching and learning experiences, as depicted by the arrows in Figure 4.2, is necessary for addressing many questions and issues raised in this chapter. In addition, focused evaluations of PD systems are needed to ensure data are available to inform decisions related to continuous improvement and determine the extent to which PD is resulting in desired teacher and child or family outcomes. We propose that cross-sector federal funding be earmarked for research and evaluation of ECE PD.

Figure 4.2 presents a framework illustrating the way in which the three core components of PD (*the who, what, and how*) are embedded within ECE systems building, and the proposals in this section of the chapter offer a roadmap for moving from fragmented to coherent and aligned ECE PD systems. From an implementation science perspective (Tout, Metz, & Bartley, 2013), a perspective too often overlooked in systems development work, the planning and delivery of ECE PD must be aligned with organizational structures and leadership to achieve the intended teacher, child, and family outcomes.[7]

Conclusion

Based on (1) a unifying definition for ECE PD, (2) specification of essential PD components (*the who, what, and how*), (3) a growing body of research from experimenting with ECE PD, and (4) a holistic framework for coherent and aligned PD systems, we are better positioned to address policymakers' questions on investments in PD that will likely result in desired outcomes for early childhood teachers and for children and families. ECE PD should (1) promote intentional application of interactional and instructional practices associated with children's improved learning and development; (2) target specific, observable practices; (3) be set in a practice context with aligned support inclusive of feedback about practice implementation; and (4) have high potential for effective execution of teaching and learning experiences of sufficient duration and intensity to achieve intended results for children and families. Yet, unless part of a small demonstration or research project, few early childhood teachers are exposed to PD experiences meeting these criteria, a reality driven in large measure by a fragmented field of practice that thwarts development of coherent and aligned ECE PD systems and also insufficient use of the knowledge base associated with effective practice implementation.

Those committed to a competent and confident workforce and optimal learning and developmental outcomes for young children are at an important juncture, one that offers both opportunities and challenges. More than ever before, a bright light is shining on ECE and its potential to provide high-quality early learning experiences that set a course toward children's future school and life successes. Central to realizing the promise of high-quality early learning is high-quality professional development for those who directly and indirectly support the development and learning of all and each young child and family. This leads us to pose the following recommendations for moving beyond the status quo and rethinking ECE PD practices and PD systems.

Recommendations

- Accept responsibility across all ECE sectors for developing a professionally competent workforce bound by a shared core of knowledge, skills, and dispositions, and comprised of sub-specialties with unique scopes of practice associated with different roles, responsibilities, and/or specializations.
- Address the absence of organized field-wide leadership with a strategic long-term focus on developing ECE as a professionally coherent field of practice so an institutional foundation exists for orchestrating development of coherent and aligned professional development systems as recommended in this chapter.
- Adopt and implement a comprehensive blueprint for building coherent and aligned PD systems whose starting point is desired child and family outcomes, whose center-piece is agreed upon ECE standards of practice that recognize and align common and specialized competencies for guiding PD, and whose PD delivery methods reflect the research on effective PD strategies and approaches as well as the diverse composition of the ECE workforce.
- Conduct rigorous research to further refine knowledge about the "essential ingredients" that comprise effective PD and identify comparatively effective and efficient strategies for achieving desired PD outcomes.
- Insist that every early childhood teacher has rights and responsibilities to participate and engage actively in PD that prepares him or her to support with competence and confidence the development and learning of each and every child and family with whom they interact.

In an article published in 1966 in the *American Psychologist*, Nicholas Hobbs made the following observation about children's early experiences: "We start with the assumption that each day, that every hour in every day, is of great importance to a child, and that when an hour is neglected, allowed to pass without reason and intent, teaching and learning go on nonetheless and the child may be the loser" (p. 1109). Given what is known from the science of early childhood development and learning, we no longer can afford to waste precious early learning opportunities by having young children spend so many of their waking hours with teachers who do not receive the PD and infrastructure supports that allow them to be competent and confident practitioners focused on optimizing the development and learning of all young children. As a field of practice, ECE has the opportunity to embrace a blueprint for change that rethinks PD. Not moving forward would be an injustice to our field and the children and families we serve.

Acknowledgements

The authors wish to thank Beth Caron, Christy Kavulic, and Catherine Scott-Little for comments on an earlier draft of the chapter.

Notes

1. For the purposes of this chapter, coherent and aligned PD systems within a state or community have a shared mission and vision, assume responsibility for developing a competent and accountable workforce, and implement a logical, well-organized, consistent, and easy-to-understand approach for accomplishing coherence and alignment.
2. Our choice of chronological scope rests on the two premises offered by Goffin & Rous (2015): (1) Retaining the field's core values and diverse sectors is strengthened by a birth to age 5 focus and (2) a coherent ECE system is essential to forging connections between ECE and kindergarten-3rd grade.

3. We recognize that many specialists who work within early intervention are therapists (e.g., occupational therapists, physical therapists, speech-language therapists, nurses) and are unlikely to think of themselves as early childhood teachers. Additionally, there are Part C early intervention instructional specialists who we include as part of our definition of the ECE workforce. We believe the Part C component of the ECE workforce brings expertise that, if appropriately harnessed, strengthens ECE PD systems. At the same time we acknowledge the difficulty of ensuring these personnel have the knowledge, skills, and dispositions to work with infants and toddlers and their families related to their licensure or credential requirements, which may permit them to practice across the life span without specialized training focused on infants and toddlers with disabilities and their families (Bruder, Mogro-Wilson, Stayton, & Dietrich, 2009). Clearly, early intervention specialists can benefit from PD that extends their expertise about early childhood development and inclusive early childhood environments.
4. Data collected from states by the U.S. Department of Education (U.S. Department of Education, 2012), indicate that 95.9% of the 41,203 special education teachers serving children ages 3 through 5 are "highly qualified," defined as: (1) having a bachelor's degree, (2) having state certification or licensure, and (3) demonstrating subject-matter knowledge for the subjects they teach. The personnel representing multiple disciplines, including special instructors, serving the 332,982 infants and toddlers and their families receiving Part C services must also be "appropriately and adequately prepared and trained," meaning they have "qualifications consistent with state-approved or recognized certification, licensing, registration, or other comparable requirements that apply to the area in which the personnel provide early intervention services."
5. A list of the 32 studies is available from the second author.
6. Based on the example of California First 5 state and local commissions' expenditures of more than $157 million over a five-year period (an average of more than $2,700 per teacher), Hamre, Downer, Jamil, and Pianta (2012) estimated millions of dollars are spent by states each year on ECE PD.
7. Tools and structures designed to assist cross-sector stakeholders in engaging in PD systems building using the framework offered by the National Professional Development Center on Inclusion definition and the three key components of PD (NPDCI, 2011) as well as other PD planning tools (Professional Development Workforce Center, 2014) are online.

References

Barnett, W. S. (2011). Effectiveness of early educational intervention. *Science, 333*, 975–978.

Bruder, M. B., Mogro-Wilson, C. M., Stayton, V. D., & Dietrich, S. L. (2009). The national status of in-service professional development systems for early intervention and early childhood special education practitioners. *Infants and Young Children, 22*(1), 13–20. doi:10.1097/01.IYC.0000343333.49775.f8

Buysse, V., & Wesley, P. W. (2005). *Consultation in early childhood settings*. Baltimore, MD: Brookes.

Buysse, V., Winton, P. J., & Rous, B. (2009). Reaching consensus on a definition of professional development for the early childhood field. *Topics in Early Childhood Special Education, 28*, 235–243.

Center to Inform Personnel Preparation Policy and Practice in Early Intervention and Preschool Education. (2008). *Analysis of state certification requirements for early childhood special education data report*. Farmington: University of Connecticut Health Center, Author.

Chandler, L. K., Cochran, D. C., Christensen, K. A., Dinnebeil, L. A., Gallagher, P. A., Lifter, K., . . . Spino, M. (2012). The alignment of CEC/DEC and NAEYC personnel preparation standards. *Topics in Early Childhood Special Education, 32*(1), 52–63. doi:10.1177/0271121412437047

Council for Exceptional Children (CEC), Division for Early Childhood (DEC). (2008). *Early childhood special education/early intervention (birth to age 8) specialist standards with CEC advanced common core*. Retrieved from http://www.cec.sped.org/Standards/Special-Educator-Professional-Preparation/CEC-Initial-and-Advanced-Specialty-Sets

Diamond, K. E., Justice, L. M., Siegler, R. S., & Snyder, P. A. (2013). *Synthesis of IES research on early intervention and early childhood education* (NCSER 2013–3001). Washington, DC: U.S. Department of Education, Institute of Education Sciences, National Center for Special Education Research. Retrieved from http://ies.ed.gov/ncser/pubs/20133001/pdf/20133001.pdf

Division for Early Childhood (DEC). (2014). *DEC recommended practices in early intervention/early childhood special education*. Retrieved from http://www.dec-sped.org/recommendedpractices

Fixsen, D. L., Naoom, S. F., Blase, K. A., Friedman, R. M., & Wallace, F. (2005). *Implementation research: A synthesis of the literature* (FMHI Publication #231). Tampa: University of South Florida, Louis de la Parte Florida Mental Health Institute, The National Implementation Research Network. Retrieved from http://www.fpg.unc.edu/~nirn/resources/detail.cfm?resourceID=31

Florida Expanding Opportunities for Early Childhood Inclusion. (2012, April). *Florida targeted competencies for specialists supporting inclusion*. Retrieved from http://www.centraldirectory.org/uploads/ACF2B00.pdf

Goffin, S.G. (2013). *Early childhood education for a new era: Leading for our profession.* New York: Teachers College Press.

Goffin, S.G., & Rous, B. (2015). Revisiting early childhood education's governance choices. In S.L. Kagan & R. Gomez (Eds.), *Governance of early childhood education: Polemics and possibilities.* New York: Teachers College Press.

Goffin, S.G., & Washington, V. (2007). *Ready or not: Leadership choices in early care and education.* New York: Teachers College Press.

Guskey, T.R. (1986). Staff development and the process of teacher change. *Educational Researcher, 15*(5), 5–12.

Hamre, B.K., Downer, J.T., Jamil, F.M., & Pianta, R.C. (2012). Enhancing teachers' intentional use of effective interactions with children. In R.C. Pianta, W.S. Barnett, L.M. Justice, & S.M. Sheridan (Eds.), *Handbook of early childhood education* (pp. 507–532). New York: Guilford Press.

Hanft, B.E., Rush, D.D., & Shelden, M.L. (2004). *Coaching families and colleagues in early childhood.* Baltimore, MD: Brookes.

Hill, H.C., Beisiegel, M., & Jacob, R. (2013). Professional development research: Consensus, crossroads, and challenges. *Educational Researcher, 42*, 476–487. doi:10.3102/0013189X13512674

Hobbs, N. (1966). Helping disturbed children: Psychological and ecological strategies. *American Psychologist, 21*, 1105–1115.

Howard, E.C., Rankin, V.E., Fishman, M., Hawkinson, L.E., McGroder, S.M., Helsel, F.K., . . . Wille, J. (2013). *The descriptive study of the Head Start early learning mentor coach initiative* (OPRE Report #2014–05a). Washington, DC: U.S. Department of Health and Human Services, Administration for Children and Families, Office of Planning, Research, and Evaluation.

Hyson, M., Horm, D.M., & Winton, P.J. (2012). Higher education for early childhood educators and outcomes for young children: Pathways toward greater effectiveness. In R. Pianta, L. Justice, S. Barnett, & S. Sheridan (Eds.), *Handbook of early education* (pp. 553–583). New York: Guilford Press.

Individuals with Disabilities Education Act (IDEA). (2004). Pub. L. No. 108-446, U.S.C. 20, 1400 et seq.

Kagan, S.L. (2012). Early learning and development standards: An elixir for early childhood systems reform. In S.L. Kagan & K. Kauerz (Eds.), *Early childhood systems: Transforming early learning* (pp. 55–70). New York: Teachers College Press.

Knowles, M., Holton, E., & Swanson, R. (1998). *The adult learner: The definitive classic in adult education and human resource development* (5th ed.). Houston, TX: Gulf.

Maxwell, K.L., Feild, C.C., & Clifford, R.M. (2005). Defining and measuring professional development in early childhood research. In M. Zaslow & I. Martinez-Beck (Eds.), *Critical issues in early childhood professional development* (pp. 21–48). Baltimore, MD: Brookes.

Maxwell, K.L., Lim, C.-I., & Early, D.M. (2006). *Early childhood teacher preparation programs in the United States: National report.* Chapel Hill, NC: The University of North Carolina, FPG Child Development Institute.

McCollum, J. & Catlett, C. (1997). Designing effective personnel preparation for early intervention: Theoretical frameworks. In Winton, McCollum & Catlett (Eds.). Reforming personnel preparation in early intervention: Issues, models, and practical strategies. Baltimore, MD: Brookes Publisher.

National Association for the Education of Young Children (NAEYC). (2009). *Developmentally appropriate practice in early childhood programs serving children from birth through age 8* (Position statement). Retrieved from http://www.naeyc.org/files/naeyc/file/positions/position%20statement%20Web.pdf

National Association for the Education of Young Children (NAEYC). (2011, June). *2010 NAEYC standards for initial & advanced early childhood professional preparation programs for use by associate, baccalaureate and graduate degree programs.* Retrieved from: http://www.naeyc.org/ecada/files/ecada/file/Standards/NAEYC%20Initial%20and%20Advanced%20Standards%203_2012.pdf

National Association for the Education of Young Children (NAEYC) & National Association of Child Care Research and Referral Agencies (NACCRRA). (2011). *Early childhood education professional development: Training and technical assistance glossary.* Washington, DC, and Arlington, VA: Authors. Retrieved from http://www.naeyc.org/GlossaryTraining_TA.pdf

National Center on Quality Teaching and Learning. (2014). *Making decisions about practice-based coaching.* Seattle, WA: Author.

National Council for Accreditation of Teacher Education (NCATE). (2010). *Transforming teacher education through clinical practice: A national strategy to prepare effective teachers.* Washington, DC: Author.

National Professional Development Center on Inclusion (NPDCI). (2008). *What do we mean by professional development in the early childhood field?* Chapel Hill, NC: The University of North Carolina, FPG Child Development Institute, Author.

National Professional Development Center on Inclusion (NPDCI). (2011). *The big picture: Building cross-sector professional development systems in early childhood* (3rd ed.). Retrieved from http://npdci.fpg.unc.edu/sites/npdci.fpg.unc.edu/files/resources/NPDCI-Big-Picture-Planning-Guide-3rd-edition-7–2011_0.pdf

Office of Head Start. (2010). *The Head Start child development and early learning framework: Promoting positive outcomes in programs serving children 3–5 years old.* Washington, DC: U.S. Department of Health and Human Services, Administration for Children and Families, Author. Retrieved from https://eclkc.ohs.acf.hhs.gov/

Professional Development Workforce Center. (2014). *Strengthening the early childhood and school-age workforce: A tool to improve workplace conditions, compensation, and access to professional development.* Retrieved from https://childcareta.acf.hhs.gov/sites/default/files/strengtheningworkforce_tool.pdf

Rhodes, H., & Huston, A. (2012). Building the workforce our youngest children deserve. *Social Policy Report, 26*(1), 3–26.

Sheridan, S. M., Edwards, C. P., Marvin, C. A., & Knoche, L. L. (2009). Professional development in early childhood programs: Process issues and research needs. *Early Education and Development, 20,* 377–401.

Snyder, P., Denney, M., Pasia, C., Rakap, S., & Crowe, C. (2011). Professional development in early childhood intervention: Emerging issues and promising approaches. In C. Groark (Series Ed.) & L. Kaczmarek (Vol. Ed.), *Early childhood intervention: Shaping the future for children with special needs and their families: Vol. 3. Emerging trends in research and practice* (pp. 169–204). Santa Barbara, CA: Praeger/ABC-CLIO.

Snyder, P., Hemmeter, M. L., & Fox, L. (in submission). Supporting implementation of evidence-based practices through coaching.

Snyder, P., Hemmeter, M. L., & McLaughlin, T. (2011). Professional development in early childhood intervention: Where we stand on the 25th anniversary of P.L. 99–457. *Journal of Early Intervention* (Special issue in honor of the 25th anniversary of IDEA's early childhood programs), *33,* 357–370.

Snyder, P., Hemmeter, M. L., Meeker, K. A., Kinder, K., Pasia, C., & McLaughlin, T. (2012). Characterizing key features of the early childhood professional development literature. *Infants and Young Children, 25,* 188–212. doi:10.1097/IYC.0b013e31825a1ebf

Tout, K., Metz, A., & Bartley, L. (2013). Considering statewide professional development systems. In T. Halle, A. Metz, & I. Martinez-Beck (Eds.), *Applying implementation science in early childhood programs and systems* (pp. 21–42). Baltimore, MD: Brookes.

U.S. Department of Education, Office of Special Education and Rehabilitative Services, Office of Special Education Programs. (2012). *31st Annual Report to Congress on the Implementation of the Individuals with Disabilities Education Act, 2009.* Retrieved from https://explore.data.gov/Education/2012-IDEA-Part-C-Child-Count-and-Settings/dg4k-psxe

U.S. Department of Health and Human Services, Administration for Children and Families, Office of Planning, Research, and Evaluation (OPRE). (2013). *Number and characteristics of early care and education teachers and caregivers: Initial findings from the national survey of early care and education* (OPRE report 2013–38). Retrieved from http://www.acf.hhs.gov/sites/default/files/opre/nsece_wf_brief_102913_0.pdf

Vinh, M., Lucas, A., Taylor, C., Kelley, G., & Kasprzak, C. (2014, August). *SSIP phase I roadmap.* Retrieved from Early Childhood Technical Assistance Center (ECTA) website: http://ectacenter.org/~pdfs/calls/2014/ssip/SSIP_Phase_I_Roadmap_081914.pdf

Wesley, P. W., & Buysse, V. (2006). Building the evidence base through communities of practice. In V. Buysse & P. W. Wesley (Eds.), *Evidence-based practice in the early childhood field* (pp. 161–193). Washington, DC: Zero to Three Press.

Winton, P. J. (2013). Leapfrogging complexities of the status quo [Invited commentary]. In S. G. Goffin, *Early childhood education for a new era: Leading for our profession* (pp. 66–70). New York: Teachers College Press.

Winton, P. J., & Catlett, C. (2009). Statewide efforts to enhance early childhood personnel preparation programs to support inclusion: Overview and lessons learned. *Infants and Young Children, 22*(1), 63–70.

Winton, P. J., McCollum, J. A., & Catlett, C. (Eds.). (2008). *Practical approaches to early childhood professional development: Evidence, strategies and resources.* Washington, DC: Zero to Three Press.

Winton, P. J., & West, T. (2011). Early childhood competencies: Sitting on the shelf or guiding professional development? In C. Howes & R. C. Pianta (Eds.), *Foundations for teaching excellence: Connecting early childhood quality rating, professional development, and competency systems in states* (pp. 69–92). Baltimore, MD: Brookes.

Yoshikawa, H., Weiland, C., Brooks-Gunn, J., Burchinal, M. R., Espinosa, L. M., Gormley, W. T., Ludwig, J., Magnuson, K. A., Phillips, D., & Zaslow, M. (2013, October). *Investing in our future: The evidence base on preschool education.* Society for Research in Child Development. Retrieved from: http://www.srcd.org/policy-media/policy-updates/meetings-briefings/investing-our-futureevidence-base-preschool

5

ACCREDITATION AND PATTERNS OF LICENSURE

Achieving the Potential

Marilou Hyson and Marica Cox Mitchell

A Systems Perspective on Accreditation and Licensure

Like other teacher education sectors, the early childhood field includes systems of higher education program accreditation and systems of individual teacher licensure. Also like other teacher education sectors, in early childhood these two systems share a common purpose: to define, assess, enhance, and ensure teacher quality. The accreditation system focuses on quality at the level of college or university teacher preparation, while licensure (or certification) focuses on the quality of individual teachers. As Figure 5.1 illustrates, the characteristics of these two systems are influenced by many factors: political and policy imperatives, research findings, professional organizations' recommendations, and more. Keeping those influences in mind, accreditation and licensure have potentially significant effects on what happens within early childhood teacher preparation programs and, ultimately, what happens when graduates enter the work force—both in their professional practices and in their impact on children's development and learning.

These kinds of effects should cause us to pay a great deal of attention to accreditation and patterns of licensure. Far from being simply bureaucratic processes, the standards, criteria, procedures, and assessments employed within these systems can—at their best—make a positive difference in what future early childhood educators learn, how they are judged ready to practice, and how they function when they take up their professional roles. Yet, the flip side is that if accreditation and licensure are poorly aligned with what future early childhood professionals should know and be able to do, or if the systems are ineffectively implemented, their effects will be at best negligible and at worst pernicious.

Of course, even the best accreditation and teacher licensure systems cannot, by themselves, transform the quality of services for young children and their families. Teacher effectiveness relies on more than just the quality of preparation or type of licensure. Narrow reforms—whether directed at preschool programs or at teacher preparation—are doomed to failure without being embedded within broader improvements and without attention to a broader network of influences and constraints.

Aims and Scope of this Chapter

With those contexts and cautions in mind, this chapter will describe the current status of higher education program **accreditation** and individual teacher **licensure** by examining these systems' potential to promote high-quality early childhood teacher education and, as a result, high-quality

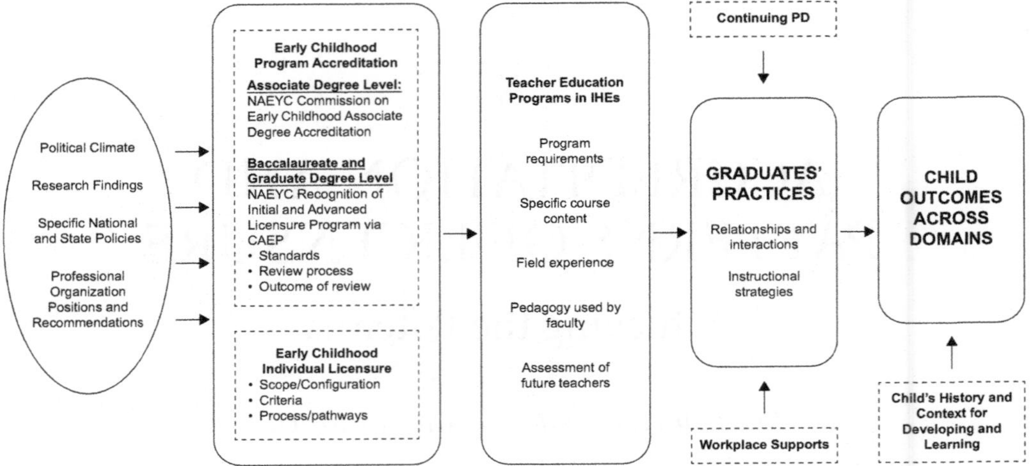

Figure 5.1 Why Care About Early Childhood Teacher Licensure and Higher Education Accreditation? A Model for Potential Influence on Practices and Outcomes.

Note: While alternative certification programs play a critical role in teacher preparation, this model focuses solely on IHEs.

professional practices and child outcomes. To this end, we will draw upon currently available research as well as anecdotal evidence from some promising innovations.

Higher education program accreditation. With respect to accreditation, the chapter will focus on the standards and approval processes for teacher education units as administered by the newly formed Council for the Accreditation of Educator Preparation (CAEP), comprised of two previously separate entities, the National Council for Accreditation of Teacher Education (NCATE) and the Teacher Education Accreditation Council (TEAC). CAEP identifies the National Association for the Education of Young Children (NAEYC) as the Specialized Professional Association (SPA) responsible for setting standards for early childhood preparation programs and granting national recognition. These programs primarily prepare graduates to work in public school settings.

Individual teacher licensure. As far as individual licensure, the chapter's main emphasis will be state-awarded teacher certification/licensure within the birth-to-age-8 early childhood scope. We will use available data to describe current configurations or licensure patterns across states as well as trends over time. States' use of "blended" licensure (i.e., general early childhood and early childhood special education through a single certificate) will be briefly noted but not discussed in depth. While states offer alternative pathways to licensure, the traditional higher education route to early childhood licensure will be this chapter's focus.

Clarifying Some Terms

The early childhood field has been bedeviled by issues and discrepancies in nomenclature and terminology. In part, these discrepancies have arisen from the distinctive history of the early childhood field; its holistic, comprehensive scope; the diversity of settings and auspices for programs serving young children; and the implications for how early childhood professionals are and should be prepared to practice. Some examples of terminology issues that are relevant to this chapter follow.

"Early childhood." The chapter follows and supports the "birth through age 8" scope of the early childhood field, reflected in position statements by NAEYC (2009), the National Association of Early Childhood Teacher Educators (NAECTE, 2009), the United Nations (UNESCO & UNICEF,

2012), and others. However, we also note that states' licensure configurations and teacher preparation programs themselves often address only certain segments of that continuum.

"Teachers." We use the term "teachers" as shorthand for those who work with young children and their families in multiple roles and settings. In our field, the terms "early childhood educator" and "early childhood professional" are often used interchangeably or even in preference to "teacher." Similarly, early childhood "teacher preparation" encompasses a wider range of roles and work settings than is common in the preparation of elementary and secondary teachers.

"Accreditation" and "national recognition." Early childhood professionals often think of "accreditation" as referring to the recognition of programs directly serving young children. In this chapter the term refers to the recognition of higher education programs. To further complicate this usage, those familiar with CAEP know that within that system the term "accreditation" has been reserved for the baccalaureate or graduate level teacher education "unit" or educator preparation program as a whole, rather than specialized programs within the unit. Such programs (early childhood being only one example) may receive so-called "national recognition" if the umbrella unit—or overall educator preparation program—is CAEP-accredited and if the specialized program is judged by the relevant professional association or "SPA" to meet its standards. However, for early childhood associate degree programs, which are not part of the CAEP system, accreditation is granted by NAEYC through its Early Childhood Associate Degree Accreditation (ECADA) system. In the interest of simplicity, this chapter will use "accreditation" to refer to (a) NAEYC's recognition of baccalaureate and graduate degree programs via CAEP and (b) NAEYC's accreditation of associate degree programs via its ECADA system.

"Certification" and "licensure." In this chapter we use these terms interchangeably to describe government-granted permission to practice as an early childhood educator. However, the early childhood field has also used the term "certification" to describe the Child Development Associate (CDA) or other forms of recognition outside of the state licensure system. "Certification" is also the term used by the National Board of Professional Teaching Standards (NBPTS) for their advanced teaching credential, for which a state teaching license is the usual prerequisite.

A Chapter Preview

Following this introduction, we will describe key features of the current map of higher education program accreditation and individual licensure, presenting some history and current descriptive data while noting gaps in the available data. Next, we will discuss research on the impact of accreditation and licensure today, looking at what is known and, more notably, what is not known, about their effects on various dimensions of quality. The chapter concludes with recommendations about the research, public policies, and higher education practices that will be needed to realize the full potential of accreditation and licensure as levers for quality improvement.

The Accreditation and Licensure Map

This section will begin with a brief history of early childhood program accreditation and a description of existing and emerging accreditation systems. Following that, we will turn to the related and even more complicated map of early childhood teacher licensure.

Accreditation

Some History and Context

Judith Eaton describes accreditation in the United States as a more than century-old process of external quality review created and used by higher education to scrutinize colleges, universities, and programs for quality assurance and quality improvement (Eaton, 2009). The foundation for accreditation of early childhood preparation programs began in 1978, when NAEYC responded to the lack of national criteria for early childhood professional preparation by using a consensus-building process to develop guidelines (later known as standards) that could serve as a tool for quality improvement (Seefeldt, 1988). Following Governing Board approval of the guidelines in 1981, NAEYC entered into a partnership with NCATE, becoming one of the first professional associations to have its specialty guidelines NCATE-approved and thus linking NAEYC's review process to the overall NCATE accreditation system. Today, there are close to 270 institutions in 38 states with NCATE- (now CAEP-) accredited teacher education units *and* NAEYC-recognized programs.

As Head Start, some state pre-kindergarten programs, and other early learning settings began to require specialized degrees in early childhood education, the importance of associate degree programs became more evident. Associate degrees serve as a pathway to baccalaureate degrees and/or to direct entry into the workforce. NAEYC, in collaboration with the Associate Degree Early Childhood Teacher Educators–ACCESS to Shared Knowledge and Practice (ACCESS), began to explore the accreditation of associate degree programs in the 1990s. The NAEYC Early Childhood Associate Degree Accreditation (ECADA) system was launched in 2006 after a feasibility study and pilot. There are currently 162 institutions in 31 states with accredited associate degree programs. Using Race to the Top Early Learning Challenge grants and other sources of funding, states like North Carolina, Tennessee, South Carolina, Michigan, and Rhode Island have launched statewide initiatives to encourage and support associate degree programs seeking accreditation. An additional 115 institutions have programs in self-study. As Figure 5.2 illustrates, these two accreditation systems are similar but have distinct characteristics.

Accreditation Standards and Processes

Earning accreditation in both systems is largely based on evidence of candidate performance in relation to the *2010 NAEYC Standards for Initial and Advanced Early Childhood Professional Preparation Programs* (see Table 5.1).

These standards are derived from NAEYC's (2009) Position Statement, *Preparing Early Childhood Professionals: NAEYC Standards for Early Childhood Preparation Programs*, the third revision to NAEYC's 1982 *Early Childhood Teacher Education Guidelines for Four- and Five-Year Programs* and its 1985 *Guidelines for Early Childhood Education Programs in Associate Degree Granting Institutions.* Meeting these standards requires evidence that programs (1) offer learning opportunities aligned with the key elements of the standards, (2) design key assessments that measure candidates' performance on key elements of the standards, (3) collect and aggregate data on candidate performance related to the standards, and (4) use that data in intentional, responsive ways to improve the quality of teaching and learning in the program (NAEYC, 2010).

The Prevalence of Nationally Accredited Early Childhood Programs

Data on the prevalence of national accreditation are not encouraging. At the time of Maxwell, Lim, and Early's national survey (2006), there were 1,349 early childhood teacher preparation programs in the United States including associate and baccalaureate programs (the number is probably greater, as this study focused only on those that prepared individuals to work with children ages birth through age 4). Of these programs, we estimate that no more than 33% hold some form of NAEYC accreditation: 162 with ECADA accreditation and approximately 270 with NAEYC recognition via CAEP/NCATE.

These low percentages may be attributed, at least in part, to the voluntary nature of accreditation. Unlike law schools and medical schools, institutions that prepare education professionals are

	NAEYC Early Childhood Associate Degree Accreditation (ECADA)	NAEYC Early Childhood Program Recognition through NCATE (now transitioned to CAEP)
Year of Launch	2006	Early 1980s
Type of Early Childhood Degree Program	Associate degree	Baccalaureate or graduate degrees that primarily prepare graduates to work in public school settings; often called licensure programs. These may include alternate certification programs if applicable.
Pathway to NAEYC Accreditation	Direct Programs apply directly to NAEYC for accreditation	Indirect via CAEP Teacher education units apply to CAEP for accreditation; if expected or encouraged in the state, CAEP submits the ECE programs that sit within the teacher education units to NAEYC for review.
Accreditation Decision Makers	ECADA Commission; the Commission also establishes all policies	NAEYC Reviewers and/or Auditors
Competencies that Drive Accreditation Decision (The process requires programs to provide evidence of their candidates' competencies—What do they know? What can they do?)	NAEYC *Initial* Standards for Professional Preparation along with other programmatic requirements	NAEYC *Initial or Advanced* Standards for Professional Preparation *Initial – initial role in the field* *Advanced – advanced role in the field*
Review and Decision Process for the Early Childhood Program	1. Eligibility determination by NAEYC 2. Submission of Self-Study Report to NAEYC 3. Site visit conducted by NAEYC reviewers 4. Presentation of evidence to Commission 5. *Accreditation* decision by Commission	1. Presentation of evidence to NAEYC via CAEP 2. Electronic review of evidence by NAEYC reviewers 3. *Recognition* decision by NAEYC reviewers and/or auditors
Number of Institutions with Accredited Programs as of May 2015	170	Approximately 256; includes "blended" programs meeting both NAEYC and DEC/CEC standards
Primary Purpose for Pursuing Accreditation	1. Voluntary commitment to quality 2. State support and/or policy	1. State teacher licensure and approval policy 2. Voluntary commitment to quality

Figure 5.2 Overview of NAEYC Higher Education Accreditation Systems for Early Childhood Programs

Table 5.1 Overview of the 2010 NAEYC Standards for Initial and Advanced Early Childhood Professional Preparation Programs

Candidates should be able to:
Standard 1. Promote child development and learning
Standard 2. Build family and community relationships
Standard 3. Observe, document, and assess to support young children and families
Standard 4. Use developmentally effective approaches
Standard 5. Use content knowledge to build meaningful curriculum
Standard 6. Become a professional
Standard 7. Participate in early childhood field experiences (for programs seeking NAEYC recognition as part of CAEP accreditation)

Note: Diversity, inclusive practices, technology, and the focus on the birth through age 8 age span are integrated threads across all standards.

usually not required to become accredited. Likewise, specialized or programmatic accreditation, such as national accreditation of early childhood preparation programs, is often not required or is a function of state government rather than of national professional associations. State policies about accreditation vary greatly; as a result, some states (e.g., New Mexico, South Dakota, Washington, and Maine) do not have any institutions with nationally accredited early childhood degree programs.

Another factor influencing the low number of nationally accredited early childhood programs is the narrow scope of the current accreditation system, which—at the baccalaureate and graduate level—accredits almost exclusively those programs leading to state licensure. However, many early childhood degree programs were not designed to prepare professionals for state licensure or to teach in public school settings. Such degree programs (often designated by names such as Bachelor of Science in Child Development or Bachelor of Science in Early Childhood Studies) are currently ineligible to participate in accreditation. To try to address this issue, NAEYC is beginning to explore a new model that would support such programs by expanding its ECADA accreditation beyond the associate level to include non-licensure baccalaureate programs.

Early Childhood Teacher Licensure

In addition to accreditation, early childhood teacher licensure is another system intended to ensure teacher quality and effectiveness. Licensure is often a requirement for teachers planning to work in elementary schools or other publicly-funded educational settings. To earn licensure, candidates typically provide evidence that they graduated from an approved teacher preparation program, earn a passing score on state-identified assessments, and meet state requirements related to moral character or professional fitness.

State Variations in Early Childhood Licensure Configurations

Widely varying early childhood licensure configurations exist across states and even within states. A report from The New America Foundation (Bornfreund, 2011) illustrates this complexity by highlighting the range of state licensure options available for teachers working with young children birth through age 8 in public elementary school settings or other settings that require licensure.

As seen in Figure 5.3, licensure categories may include Birth to Kindergarten, Birth to Grade 3, Pre-K to Grade 3, Pre-K to Grade 6, Kindergarten to Grade 6, and other patterns. Additionally,

State	Licenses Available	State	Licenses Available
AL	B-K; K-5; P-3	MT	K-8
AK	P-3; K-6; K-8	NE	B-3; K-6; K-8
AZ	B-3; K-8	NV	B-K; B-2; K-8
AR	P-4; 4-8	NH	P-3; K-6; K-8
CA	P-12 (in self-contained classroom)	NJ	P-3; K-5
CO	P-3; K-6	NM	B-3; K-8
CT	B-K; N-3; K-6	NY	B-2; 1-6
DC	P-3; 1-6; 4-8	NC	B-K; K-6
DE	B-2; K-6	ND	B-3; K-6; 1-6; K-8; 1-8
FL	B-Age 4; Age 3-3rd; K-6	OH	P-3; 4-9
GA	B-Age 5; P-5; 4-8	OK	B-Age 3; P-3; 1-8
HI	P-3; K-6	OR	K-8 (in self-contained classrooms)
ID	B-3*; K-8	PA	P-4; 4-8
IL	B-3; K-9**	RI	P-2; 1-6
IN	B-K; K-3; 4-6	SC	P-3; 2-6
IA	B-3; P-K; K-6	SD	B-Age 4; B-3; K-8
KS	B-K*; B-3*; K-6	TN	B-K*; P-3; K-6; 4-8
KY	B-K*; K-5	TX	P-4; P-6; 4-8
LA	P-3; 1-5; 4-8	UT	1-8***
ME	B-Age 5; K-3; K-8	VT	B-3; B-Age 6*; K-3; K-6
MD	P-3; 1-6; 4-8	VA	P-3; P-6
MA	P-2; 1-6	WA	P-3; K-8
MI	B-3; K-5	WI	B-Age 8; B-Age 11; Age 6-Age 12
MN	B-3; K-6	WV	B-P; P-K; K-4
MS	N-1; P-K; K-3; 4-8; K-6	WY	B-Age 5*; Ages 3-5; Age 3-3rd; K-6; 7-8 (in self-contained classroom)
MO	B-3; 1-6		

Figure 5.3 State Licensure: A National Perspective Comparing Licenses for Teaching in an Elementary School (Bornfreund, 2011)

The number represents a grade level, unless otherwise specified:
B = birth; P = pre-k; K = kindergarten; N = nursery
* = Blended Program ECE/Special Ed ** = Additional Requirements to Teach Middle Grades
*** = To teach kindergarten, teachers who have a 1-8 license can obtain a K-3 endorsement.

Note: In self-contained classrooms, students have the same teacher for all core subject areas.

Source: New America Foundation reporting based on state teacher licensure web page

most states have licensure provisions for those intending to work with young children who have disabilities. These provisions are at least as varied as licensure provisions for "general" early childhood educators, including some provisions for blended or unified early childhood education (ECE) and early childhood special education (ECSE) licenses, either as requirements or options in states with multiple certification pathways (Stayton et al., 2009). A recent NAEYC survey of states' certification profiles (NAEYC, 2014) shows that certificates continue to be varied, often quite broad and overlapping, and use varied terminology that makes comparisons and data collection challenging.

How Licensure Affects Teacher Preparation

Within each state, the specific licensure structure influences the way education schools prepare prospective teachers for the early childhood profession (Bornfreund, 2011). Gaps in preparation are often attributable to the programs' need to align with the state's scope of licensure, which, as seen in Figure 5.3, often emphasizes preschool, kindergarten, and the early elementary grades. For example, NAEYC (2009) has noted that many teacher education programs give inadequate attention to children's critical early years, especially the birth-to-age-3 period.

The influence of licensure on teacher preparation programs can also be seen in state-specific studies like *The State of Early Childhood Higher Education in New Jersey: The New Jersey Early Childhood Higher Education Inventory* (Kipnis, Whitebook, Austin, & Sakai, 2013). This study found that most degree programs in New Jersey were far less likely to focus coursework on infants and toddlers than on preschool and the early elementary grades. Most likely, this preschool emphasis stems from the influence of New Jersey's licensure configurations (P-3 and K-6) on the coursework and overall design of teacher preparation programs at the baccalaureate and graduate degree levels. In contrast, New Jersey associate degree programs, which are not directly influenced by state licensure requirements, were more likely to report focusing their course content on infants and toddlers. Other Higher Education Inventory reports for New Hampshire (Kipnis, Austin, Sakai, Whitebook, & Ryan, 2013) and Rhode Island (Austin, Kipnis, Sakai, Whitebook, & Ryan, 2013) also showed close relations between state licensure configurations and baccalaureate course emphases.

Early Childhood Licensure Recommendations from Professional Associations

More than 20 years ago, NAEYC and the Association of Teacher Educators issued a joint position statement intended to address these kinds of challenges in early childhood licensure (ATE & NAEYC, 1991). The position statement recommended that state departments of education and certifying agencies create free-standing early childhood birth-through-age-8 certification (licensure) distinctive from existing certifications for elementary and secondary education.

More recently, the National Association of Early Childhood Teacher Educators (2009) issued a position statement with similar recommendations, endorsed by the American Associate Degree Early Childhood Educators (ACCESS), the Association for Childhood Education International (ACEI), the National Association for the Education of Young Children (NAEYC), the Southern Early Childhood Association (SECA), the National Association of Early Childhood Specialists in State Departments of Education (NAECS/SCE), and the National Coalition for Campus Children's Centers (NCCCC). This position statement was also supported by the American Association of Colleges for Teacher Education (AACTE). An accompanying toolkit (NAECTE, 2008) summarizes the research base and proposes advocacy strategies.

Although Figure 5.3 shows that some state licenses follow the 0–8 configuration recommended by this series of position statements, this method remains a rarity. Pressures against a distinctive birth-to-age-8 license include school administrators' desire for flexibility in assigning teachers to higher elementary grades.

In Summary: The Accreditation and Licensure Map

The preceding description shows that both higher education program accreditation and teacher licensure are "all over the map." Great variability exists in whether early childhood teacher preparation programs are eligible for accreditation review, and even those that might be eligible may or may not apply, depending on their state and institutional requirements. Patterns of teacher licensure are equally variable, both across states and graduates' intended work settings. Adding further difficulty to reading this map is the lack of comprehensive, up-to-date, easily interpretable data on the prevalence and patterns of accreditation and licensure.

The Impact of Accreditation and Licensure Today

With this map in mind, the following section will summarize what is known about the effects of early childhood accreditation and licensure on various dimensions of quality. Looking back at the graphic representation in Figure 5.1, ideally this section of the chapter would include robust data on early childhood accreditation and licensure's effects on (a) policies and practices within higher education, (b) graduates' professional competence, and (c) children's development and learning. That ideal will not be realized here. As will become evident, we know a good deal more about the number and prevalence of various accreditation and licensure patterns—incomplete and outdated as these data often are—than we do about what difference they make. The early childhood field is not alone in lacking good research on this question, however. Reviews of research within the broader field of teacher education (e.g., Boyd, Goldhaber, Lankford, & Wykoff, 2007; Wilson & Youngs, 2005) also find either that evidence of the impact of accreditation and licensure is simply absent, or that it lacks sufficient rigor to be a useful guide to policy and practice.

Impacts of Higher Education Program Accreditation

Before summarizing the limited evidence about the impact of early childhood program accreditation, we will take a brief look at accreditation impacts within the general field of teacher education—although there, too, the research is meager.

Impacts of National Accreditation I: Research from Teacher Education in General

As noted earlier, in teacher education there is no requirement that preparation programs be accredited by a national body. But does national accreditation affect the quality of schools of education or their graduates? Darling-Hammond (2010) notes that this question remains controversial. NCATE describes multiple benefits (e.g., "NCATE's performance-based system of accreditation fosters the development of competent classroom teachers, specialists, and administrators," NCATE, n.d.), but it relies on assertions of accreditation's value combined with testimonials from graduates of accredited institutions and other stakeholders (Williams, 2000) rather than on empirical evidence. In contrast, interviews by Goodlad (1990) and colleagues showed that many higher education administrators saw accreditation as a high-cost, low-benefit process imposed from outside the institution. The researchers were left with the impression that NCATE accreditation was "so costly and so demanding of time that it pushes aside other kinds of long-term planning and renewal in teacher education" (p. 167). On a more positive note, another study (Gitomer, Latham, & Zionek, 1999) summarized in Wilson and

Youngs' (2005) literature review found that students' passing rates on the Praxis I and II exams were higher for those attending NCATE-accredited programs. However, it is not possible to know whether these differences were directly related to quality features linked to accreditation, to other factors such as selection bias (better students might choose to enroll in NCATE-accredited teacher education programs), or to accreditation alignment with standardized tests of teacher knowledge.

Impacts of National Accreditation II: Research on Early Childhood Teacher Education Programs

The dearth of research on accreditation impacts in teacher education in general is also typical of early childhood teacher education. Although it would be valuable to know whether early childhood program accreditation affects variables such as program content and pedagogy; faculty or student knowledge, attitudes, and skills; institutional practices; competencies of graduates; and a host of other outcomes, what we have is a fairly blank slate. Following are examples of the few studies that have looked at impacts, first for baccalaureate and graduate programs and then for accreditation of early childhood associate degree programs.

Baccalaureate and graduate programs. One study of faculty from a national sample of early childhood programs (Hyson, Tomlinson, & Morris, 2009) included a number of questions about NCATE/NAEYC accreditation in a larger survey of programs' quality improvement priorities and challenges. About 50% of the survey's respondents held positions in programs accredited by NCATE/NAEYC. Comparisons of responses provided by representatives of accredited and non-accredited programs revealed no significant differences in their self-reported quality improvement priorities, program climate, or other variables. However, the authors emphasize that one cannot conclude that accreditation makes no difference, as many early childhood programs were housed in non-NCATE institutions and thus would have been ineligible for NAEYC/NCATE program review.

Whether their programs were accredited or not, survey respondents were asked their impressions of the accreditation process as a quality-improvement activity. Most responses were positive. Those from accredited programs reported that the process had given them a "clearer sense of our program's mission, strengths, and needs" (60%). Other frequently cited benefits included "improved assessment of our students' competence" (51%), "improved learning opportunities for our students" (43%), "better ability to use data for program improvement" (39%), and "enhanced reputation of our program" (40%). These attitudes are more favorable toward accreditation than those of the higher education administrators in Goodlad's (1990) report, perhaps because the Hyson et al. sample focused only on faculty and administrators working in early childhood programs.

ECADA accreditation and associate degree programs. Turning to accreditation of associate degree programs through ECADA, research on impacts is even more limited because the system is so new. A recent survey by NAEYC of the primary-contact faculty from ECADA-accredited programs examined their perceptions of accreditation impacts (Huss-Hage & Mitchell, 2013). Overwhelmingly, faculty reported that, as a result of the accreditation process, they had increased their knowledge of how to align student learning outcomes to course assignments and assessments. Faculty also reported that students now had more opportunities to demonstrate their understanding of the NAEYC standards (93% agreed) and had increased their engagement in active, collaborative learning opportunities (75% agreed). It is important, however, to note that the data are self-reported, no data were collected on graduates' competencies, and the survey was not able to compare these responses with those of faculty whose programs had not been successful in achieving accreditation.

Direct comparison with the previously cited data on accreditation of baccalaureate and graduate programs (Hyson et al., 2009) is difficult because of the differences in the two systems, as was shown in Figure 5.2. Unlike the program review process used in the NCATE (CAEP)/NAEYC system, ECADA accreditation includes inputs (such as faculty qualifications and regional accreditation as eligibility requirements) and also requires a campus visit by a team from the NAEYC ECADA pool of peer reviewers. Although both systems use essentially the same professional preparation standards, these factors may influence differences in faculty perceptions and contribute to other impacts that may be studied in the future.

Impacts of Teacher Licensure/Certification

Moving now from program accreditation to individual licensure, we begin by summarizing what is known from research on the impacts of licensure within the broader teacher education field before turning to specific studies of early childhood licensure.

Research from the Broader Teacher Education Field

Does being a certified teacher confer certain benefits? The research is far from persuasive. A paper by Boyd, Goldhaber, Lankford, and Wykoff (2007) reviewed the literature on relationships between teacher licensure patterns, performance on "teacher tests," and children's learning outcomes. Their review led the researchers to conclude that although some positive associations can be found, the evidence—like that for accreditation—is insufficient to serve as a guide for policy. Others (e.g., Darling-Hammond, 2010) interpret the evidence more optimistically. As with the results of research on accreditation, it is difficult to know if the certification glass is half empty or half full.

Within this ambiguous picture, there is some evidence that teachers who are certified—in comparison to those who are teaching without state certification—are less likely to leave the profession within five years (Darling-Hammond, 2010). It is possible that teachers who are certified benefited from better college or university preparation, and thus are in a better position to deal with the classroom challenges faced by all new teachers. However, the correlational designs used in this research cannot confirm cause-effect relationships.

A few studies have tried to examine impacts on students' academic achievement when the teacher holds a specialized teaching license. For example, one study (Boyd, Grossman, Lankford, Loeb, & Wyckoff, 2009) compared certified and non-certified teachers in New York City public secondary schools. The researchers found that students achieved more when teachers were certified in the field in which they taught. Caution is needed when applying such findings to the early childhood field, as this and other research on licensure impacts has been limited to middle and secondary schools and to one field, mathematics.

Looking beyond licensure per se, Boyd et al. (2009) also found that within the group of teachers holding specialized licenses, those from certain teacher preparation programs had a more positive impact on their students' achievement than graduates of other programs, with a key factor seeming to be a strong emphasis on practice within the more-effective programs. As summarized in a research brief on the issue (Indiana University-Purdue University Indiana, 2009), the relatively limited evidence on licensure impacts suggests that it is difficult to disentangle licensure impacts from other factors. Student achievement is most enhanced when teachers are fully certified, have completed a traditional teacher education program (as compared with licensure via alternative routes), are strong academically, and have more than two years' experience. Such findings further underscore the need for higher education quality improvement and the use of accreditation as a lever to promote improvement.

Research on the Specific Impacts of Early Childhood Licensure

As in the broader teacher education field, there is little rigorous research on the impact of early childhood teacher licensure, whether one looks at impacts on teachers' beliefs, classroom practices, or child outcomes. In their literature review, Maxwell, Feild, and Clifford (2006) found no studies of state-level early childhood teacher certification that met their criteria for inclusion in the review. In their recommendations, Maxwell and colleagues suggest that future research should include specific questions about state teacher licensure, worded in ways that would allow cross-state comparisons.

Early childhood licensure as predictor of teachers' beliefs. A few studies have compared the pedagogical beliefs or attitudes of those certified in early childhood or currently enrolled in ECE certification programs with the beliefs of those prepared in elementary education. For example, Vartuli (1999) found that teachers who had been certified in early childhood had attitudes that were more consistent with developmentally appropriate practices (DAP) than those with certification in elementary education. Looking at preservice settings, Smith (1997) found similar patterns, comparing those certified only in elementary education with those who also had an early childhood endorsement on their elementary certificate. File and Gullo (2002) collected data on students within one university, comparing those who had enrolled either in an elementary (ELED) or early childhood (ECED) certification option. Although the beliefs of these two groups were similar early in their programs, by the time they entered student teaching their beliefs had diverged somewhat, with ECED students being less likely to agree with teacher-directed practices than elementary education students.

Although none of these studies directly examined classroom practices, it is likely that, as File and Gullo (2002) say "prospective teachers from ECED and ELED are 'primed' through their beliefs to shape their classrooms in somewhat different ways" (p. 126), a point consistent with research on the connections between teachers' beliefs and their behaviors (e.g., Raths & McAninch, 2003), although the contexts within which teachers end up working may inhibit or skew these connections (e.g., Stipek & Byler, 1997).

Early childhood licensure and classroom practices. Moving from beliefs to practices, the research is even more sparse and inconclusive. In general, researchers have not found strong connections between early childhood licensure per se and teachers' use of specific classroom practices. In a study of state pre-kindergarten programs, Pianta and his colleagues (2005) found some evidence that if teachers had a bachelor's degree specifically in ECE/child development (regardless of whether they held a license in ECE), their classrooms had a more positive emotional climate and better provision for learning compared to the classrooms of teachers with a different college degree.

Early childhood licensure and child outcomes. Unfortunately, we have the least evidence on what is arguably the most important question: Does the type of teacher licensure (or even licensure itself, versus not holding a license) have any impact on children's developmental and learning outcomes? As summarized in many publications, there is little evidence of impact (e.g., Burchinal, Hyson, & Zaslow, 2008; Tout, Zaslow, & Berry, 2006; United States Department of Education, 2010). Looking closely at the effects of teachers' preparation and qualifications, Early and colleagues (Early et al., 2006, 2007) reanalyzed data from seven large studies of early care and education for 4-year-olds, combining Head Start, pre-kindergarten, and other child care settings, using consistent definitions of teachers' education and children's academic outcomes across studies. No significant impacts on outcomes were found for either teachers' level of education or teachers' college major (e.g., a major in early childhood education). The specific question of whether ECE licensure/certification had an impact could not be addressed with the available data, but given the overall lack of impact, it is unlikely.

A few hints of positive impacts may be found, however. In a recent literature review on early childhood credentials and certification, Bredekamp and Goffin (2012) noted positive, though indirect, evidence from two states (New Jersey and Oklahoma) that had mandated early childhood teacher licensure as one of the requirements for their redesigned early childhood systems. In both cases, implementing these requirements required the states to create new teaching licenses or radically redesign existing ones. States also needed to work with their higher education systems to revamp teacher preparation consistent with these expectations. In the wake of implementing these requirements (which involved working with the states to create or redesign early childhood licensure, and working with higher education to increase access and redo programs), positive outcomes have been seen in the development and learning of children enrolled in programs taught by those meeting the new licensure requirements. However, that evidence cannot demonstrate in itself a cause-effect relationship between specialized early childhood certification and improved child outcomes.

Some thought-provoking evidence may be found in a recent study (Son, Kwon, Jeon, & Hong, 2013) in which the investigators explored the impact of teacher qualifications and training using a secondary analysis of a large data set from the Head Start FACES study. Consistent with other research, the investigators did not find effects of teachers' levels of formal education. However, those who had majored in early childhood/child development (both at the associate and bachelor's level) generally had higher-quality classroom environments—and, in turn, those positive environments predicted more positive child outcomes as seen in school readiness scores. However, the investigators did not find that early childhood licensure/certification made a difference; instead, it was the college major that mattered. Discussing why a major in ECE/child development was such a good predictor whereas ECE certification was not, the authors point out the great variability in how "early childhood certification" is defined and implemented from one state to another—a point emphasized repeatedly in this chapter.

Summarizing the Impacts of Accreditation and Licensure: Minimal, or Minimally Researched?

In summary, we see only minimal evidence of impacts related to early childhood program accreditation and licensure/certification. Turning first to accreditation, aside from some self-reported data, there is little evidence that accredited early childhood programs affect either those programs' quality, graduates' practices, or outcomes for the children that graduates teach, whether we look at the associate or the baccalaureate/graduate level. Does that mean that there are no differences in quality related to accreditation? The data cannot answer that question, in part because of the complexity of eligibility requirements for accreditation review, as well as the lack of objective, valid measures of quality. At the individual level, again there is very sparse evidence that it is better for teachers to hold an ECE license than to lack such a license or to hold a license in another field. But the state-level variability in licensure scope and expectations creates challenges for research on this question; further challenges are posed by the confounding of licensure status with graduates' college majors, which may have some effect independent of whether the major leads to licensure. Clearly, much more study of these issues is needed, together with reforms in policies and higher education practices based on current and future research.

Toward Transformative Systems: Recommendations

In a discussion of the processes by which professions such as medicine and law ensure that their knowledge base is transferred and updated, Linda Darling-Hammond (Darling-Hammond, Holtzman, Gatlin, & Heilig, 2005) described three standards-driven elements connected firmly like a three legged stool: program **accreditation** by a professional body, **licensure** (typically by a professional body, not a state agency), and advanced **certification** or credentialing, together promoting quality assurance. In contrast to these "mature professions," Darling-Hammond observes that "the three legged stool has been notably wobbly in teaching" (p. 471). Evident in teacher education in general, this wobbliness has been equally problematic in early childhood teacher education.

Based on our review of research and professional position statements on early childhood accreditation and licensure, a number of steps can be recommended to strengthen accreditation and licensure both as individual systems and as connected supports for our profession. We divide these into recommendations for **policies, research**, and **higher education practices**.

Policies

Accreditation

- Require all higher education programs that prepare early childhood educators to be accredited. This is consistent with the norm in professions such as medicine, nursing, and law.
- Use authentic, practice-focused assessments of graduates' competence as the key factor in accreditation decisions. Ensure that assessments are comprehensive, valid, and based on evidence about the competencies' potential impacts on young children's development and learning.

Licensure

- Move toward a uniform system of early childhood teacher certification, encompassing the birth-to-age-8 range but with possible areas of emphasis within that scope (Bredekamp & Goffin, 2012). Almost 30 years ago, Carol Seefeldt (1988) asserted that "[be]cause many states either do not certify early childhood educators or narrowly define early childhood . . . many programs that are controlled by certification requirements do not meet the early childhood profession's standards for teacher preparation" (p. 248). Fifteen years ago, in a chapter on "The State of the Art in Early Childhood Professional Preparation," Joan Isenberg (2000) said that "without . . . a universally accepted early childhood license, the field will continue to prepare teachers inadequately to work with these age groups" (p. 20). The call continues in a key recommendation of the New America Foundation's recently released policy brief *Beyond Subprime Learning* (Bornfreund, McCann, Williams, & Guernsey, 2014). Change is long overdue.
- Move toward a unified system of licensing or credentialing early childhood professionals across settings and auspices, using criteria that reflect essential competencies related to different roles and responsibilities.

Both Accreditation and Licensure

- Use professional expertise to regularly review accreditation and licensure standards, ensuring that they reflect the best research on what early childhood professionals should know and be able to do, and what higher education institutions need to do to produce those outcomes.

Research

Accreditation

- Conduct well-designed studies of the impact of accreditation, including accreditation of associate degree and "non-licensure" programs. Include impacts on the program and institution as a whole: for example, descriptive research or case studies of impacts on (a) program faculty (e.g., effects on knowledge, attitudes, pedagogy, and working conditions), (b) the program's curriculum (courses, course content, etc.), (c) the larger institution (e.g., allocation of resources), and (d) other institutions and stakeholders—including in the case of associate degree programs, impact on articulation and transfer to baccalaureate programs.
- In studying accreditation of early childhood teacher education programs, consider questions such as those posed by Wilson and Youngs (2005) when they discussed accreditation across the general field of teacher education: "Does participation in a national accreditation program have a differential effect? What is the effect of aligning a teacher education program with various standards [such as state- or nationally developed standards]? Do some forms of accreditation have more impact on student learning?" (p. 619).

Accreditation and Licensure

- Conduct well-designed studies of the impacts of various licensure/certification options, including alternative certification in ECE, as well as elementary licensure vs. early childhood-specific licensure.
- In research both on accreditation and licensure, include study of impacts on the institution as well as impacts on graduates' beliefs and practices.
- Use research results as a basis for future modifications of accreditation and licensure standards and of their implementation.

Practices in Higher Education

Accreditation and Licensure

- Intentionally use the self-study phase of preparing for accreditation review to reflect on programs' alignment with national standards and on the quality of and uses of student assessment data.
- Provide released time and other opportunities for full-time and adjunct faculty, students, graduates, and other stakeholders to collaborate and use the process for professional renewal and goal-setting.
- Ensure that, while complying with existing state licensure criteria, programs also align with evidence-based national standards and recommendations about the scope and key components of quality teacher preparation.
- Establish credible criteria for assessing the impact of accreditation and licensure, especially the impact upon graduates' practices. Use results to improve accreditation/licensure standards and their implementation within higher education programs.

Final Thoughts

Throughout this chapter, we have tried to provide an objective assessment of the current condition and impact of early childhood accreditation and licensure systems. Although in many ways the picture is discouraging, it also reveals multiple opportunities to build the systems' capacity to contribute to quality improvement through enhanced policies, research, and higher education practices. Such actions are particularly urgent at this critical time of unprecedented federal and local investment in early childhood services. These investments and other proposed expansion initiatives will have a far better chance to produce their intended outcomes if evidence-based, unified systems of early childhood accreditation and licensure are ready to support teacher quality and effectiveness.

References

Association of Teacher Educators (ATE) & National Association for the Education of Young Children (NAEYC). (1991). *Early childhood teacher certification: A position statement of the Association of Teacher Educators and National Association for the Education of Young Children.* Retrieved from www.naeyc.org

Austin, L.J.E., Kipnis, F., Sakai, L., Whitebook, M., & Ryan, S. (2013). *The state of early childhood higher education in Rhode Island: The Rhode Island Early Childhood Higher Education Inventory.* Berkeley, CA: Center for the Study of Child Care Employment, University of California at Berkeley.

Bornfreund, L. (2011). *Getting in sync: Revamping licensing and preparation for teachers in Pre-K, kindergarten, and the early grades.* Washington, DC: New America Foundation.

Bornfreund, L., McCann, C., Williams, C., & Guernsey, L. (2014). *Beyond subprime learning: Accelerating progress in early education.* Washington, DC: New America Foundation.

Boyd, D., Goldhaber, D., Lankford, H., & Wyckoff, J. (2007). The effect of certification and preparation on teacher quality. *The Future of Children,* 17(1), 45–68.

Boyd, D., Grossman, P., Lankford, H., Loeb, S., & Wyckoff, J. (2009). Teacher preparation and student achievement. *Educational Evaluation and Policy Analysis, 31*(4), 416–440.

Bredekamp, S., & Goffin, S. G. (2012). Making the case: Why credentialing and certification matter. In R. Pianta, S. Barnett, L. Justice, & S. Sheridan (Eds.), *Handbook of early childhood education* (pp. 584–604). New York: Guilford Press.

Burchinal, M., Hyson, M., & Zaslow, M. (2008). Competencies and credentials for early childhood educators: What do we know and what do we need to know? *NHSA Dialog, 11*(1), 1–7.

Darling-Hammond, L. (2010). Teacher education and the American future. *Journal of Teacher Education, 61*(1–2), 35–47.

Darling-Hammond, L., Holtzman, D. J., Gatlin, S. J., & Heilig, J. V. (2005). Does teacher preparation matter? Evidence about teacher certification, Teach for America, and teacher effectiveness. *Education Policy Analysis Archives, 13*(42), 1–47.

Early, D. M., Bryant, D., Pianta, R., Clifford, R., Burchinal, M., Ritchie, S., Howes, C., & Barbarin, O. (2006). Are teachers' education, major, and credentials related to classroom quality and children's academic gains in pre-kindergarten? *Early Childhood Research Quarterly, 21*(2), 174–195.

Early, D. M., Maxwell, K. L., Burchinal, M., Alva, S., Bender, R. H., Bryant, D., Cai, K., Clifford, R. M., Ebanks, C., Griffin, J. A., Henry, G. T., Howes, C., Iriondo-Perez, J., Jeon, H-J., Mashburn, A. L., Peisner-Feinberg, E., Pianta, R. C., Vandergrift, N., & Zill, N. (2007). Teachers' education, classroom quality, and young children's academic skills: Results from seven studies of preschool programs. *Child Development, 78*(2), 558–580.

Eaton, J. S. (2009). Accreditation in the United States. *New Directions for Higher Education, 145,* 79–86.

File, N., & Gullo, D. F. (2002). A comparison of early childhood and elementary education students' beliefs about primary classroom teaching practices. *Early Childhood Research Quarterly, 17*(1), 126–137.

Gitomer, D. H., Latham, A. S., & Zionek, R. (1999). The academic quality of prospective teachers: The impact of admissions and licensure testing. *ETS Teaching & Learning Report Series, ETS RR03–25.* Princeton, NJ: Educational Testing Service.

Goodlad, J. (1990). *Teachers for our nation's schools.* San Francisco, CA: Jossey-Bass.

Huss-Hage, E. A., & Mitchell, M. C. (2013). Celebrating excellence in associate degree programs that prepare early childhood professionals. *Young Children, 68*(5), 54–56.

Hyson, M., Tomlinson, H. B., & Morris, C. (2009). Quality improvement in early childhood teacher education: Faculty perspectives and recommendations for the future. *Early Childhood Research & Practice, 11*(1), n1.

Indiana University–Purdue University Indiana, Center for Urban and Multicultural Education. (2009). *Teacher licensure (certification)* (Research brief). Retrieved from http://education.iupui.edu/CUME/pdf/Teacher%20Licensure%20Brief.pdf

Isenberg, J. P. (2000). The state of the art in early childhood professional preparation. In National Institute on Early Childhood Development and Education, U.S. Department of Education (Eds.), *New teachers for a new century: The future of early childhood professional preparation* (pp. 17–52). Washington, DC: National Institute on Early Childhood Development and Education.

Kipnis, F., Austin, L. J.E., Sakai, L., Whitebook, M., & Ryan, S. (2013). The state of early childhood higher education in New Hampshire: The New Hampshire Early Childhood Higher Education Inventory. Berkeley, CA: Center for the Study of Child Care Employment, University of California at Berkeley.

Kipnis, F., Whitebook, M., Austin, L., & Sakai, L. (2013). *The state of early childhood higher education in New Jersey: The New Jersey Early Childhood Higher Education Inventory.* Berkeley, CA: Center for the Study of Child Care Employment, University of California at Berkeley.

Maxwell, K. L., Feild, C. C., & Clifford, R. M. (2006). Defining and measuring professional development in early childhood research. In M. Zaslow & I. Martinez-Beck (Eds.), *Critical issues in early childhood professional development* (pp. 21–48). Baltimore, MD: Paul H. Brookes.

Maxwell, K. L., Lim C.-I., & Early, D. M. (2006). *Early childhood teacher preparation programs in the United States* (National Report). Chapel Hill, NC: University of North Carolina, FPG Child Development Institute.

National Association for the Education of Young Children (NAEYC). (2009). *NAEYC standards for early childhood professional preparation: Position statement.* Washington, DC: Author.

National Association for the Education of Young Children (NAEYC). (2010). *2010 NAEYC standards for initial & advanced early childhood professional preparation programs.* Washington, DC: Author. Retrieved from http://www.naeyc.org/files/ecada/file/2010%20NAEYC%20Initial%20&%20Advanced%20Standards.pdf

National Association for the Education of Young Children (NAEYC). (2014). *Early childhood teacher certification: The current state policies landscape and opportunities.* Washington, DC: Author. Retrieved from http://www.naeyc.org/files/naeyc/Early%20Childhood%20Teacher%20Certification%20%283%29_1.pdf

National Association of Early Childhood Teacher Educators. (2008). *Early childhood teacher certification toolkit.* Washington, DC: Author. Retrieved from http://www.naecte.org/docs/Toolkit%20for%20use%20with%20NAECTE%20Position%20Statement%20on%20Teacher%20Certification.pdf

National Association of Early Childhood Teacher Educators (NAECTE). (2009). National Association of Early Childhood Teacher Educators (NAECTE) position statement on early childhood certification for teachers of children 8 years old and younger in public school settings. *Journal of Early Childhood Teacher Education, 30*(2), 188–191.

National Council for Accreditation of Teacher Education (NCATE). (n.d.). *Why should schools of education be NCATE accredited?* Retrieved from http://www.ncate.org/LinkClick.aspx?fileticket=69DJO%2BxykzQ%3D&tabid=392

Pianta, R., Howes, C., Burchinal, M., Bryant, D., Clifford, R., Early, D., & Barbarin, O. (2005). Features of prekindergarten programs, classrooms, and teachers: Do they predict observed classroom quality and teacher-child interactions? *Applied Developmental Science, 9*(3), 144–159.

Raths, J., & McAninch, A. (Eds.). (2003). *Teacher beliefs and classroom performance: The impact of teacher education.* Greenwich, CT: Information Age Publishing.

Seefeldt, C. (1988). Teacher certification and program accreditation in early childhood education. *Elementary School Journal, 89*(2), 241–251.

Smith, K. (1997). Student teachers' beliefs about developmentally appropriate practice: Pattern, stability, and the influence of locus of control. *Early Childhood Research Quarterly, 12*(2), 221–243.

Son, S.-H., Kwon, K.-A., Jeon, H.-J., & Hong, S.-Y. (2013). Head Start classrooms and children's school readiness benefit from teachers' qualifications and ongoing training. *Child & Youth Care Forum, 42*(6), 525–553. doi:10.1007/s10566–013–9213–2

Stayton, V., Dietrich, S. L., Smith, B. J., Bruder, M. B., Mogro-Wilson, C., & Swigart, A. (2009). State certification requirements for early childhood special educators. *Infants and Young Children, 22*(1), 4–12. doi:10.1097/01.IYC.0000343332.42151.cd

Stipek, D., & Byler, P. (1997). Early childhood education teachers: Do they practice what they preach? *Early Childhood Research Quarterly, 12*(3), 305–325.

Tout, K., Zaslow, M., & Berry, D. (2006). Quality and qualifications: Links between professional development and quality in early care and education settings. In M. Zaslow & I. Martinez-Beck (Eds.), *Critical issues in early childhood professional development.* (pp. 77–110). Baltimore, MD: Paul H. Brookes.

UNESCO & UNICEF (2012). Asia Pacific end-of-decade notes on Education for All. *EFA Goal 1: Early Childhood Care and Education.* Bangkok, Thailand: Author. Retrieved from http://www.unicef.org/rosa/217145e.pdf

United States Department of Education Policy and Program Studies Service. (2010). *Toward the identification of features of effective professional development for early childhood educators: Literature review.* Washington, DC: Author.

Vartuli, S. (1999). How early childhood teacher beliefs vary across grade levels. *Early Childhood Research Quarterly, 14*(4), 489–514.

Williams, B. C. (Ed.). (2000). *Telling our story: Reforming teacher education through accreditation.* Washington, DC: NCATE.

Wilson, S. M., & Youngs, P. (2005). Research on accountability processes in teacher education. In M. Cochran-Smith & K. M. Zeichner (Eds.), *Studying teacher education: The report of the AERA Panel on Research and Teacher Education* (pp. 591–643). Washington, DC: American Educational Research Association.

PART II

The Knowledge Base of Early Childhood Teacher Education

6

PREPARING TEACHERS FOR INFANT CARE AND EDUCATION

Susan L. Recchia

New knowledge about the powerful and long-lasting impact of responsive care giving on early brain development has created a compelling need for early childhood practice and policy to develop deeper understandings of how infants learn and how to best support their learning (National Scientific Council on the Developing Child, 2007; Schore, 2005). The significance of the first years of life as foundational to all later learning brings a moral imperative to the field of early childhood education to find better ways to prepare teachers and leaders to work effectively with infants and families (Lally, 2013). Promoting high-quality infant care and education has become a national policy focus in the U.S. (Obama-Biden "Zero-to-Five Plan" [White House, n.d.]), where more than half of the 12 million infants and toddlers regularly spend their time in a child care program (Hyson & Tomlinson, 2014; Horm, Hyson, & Winton, 2013). Evidence from other countries also reflects a heightened focus on early care and education (Dalli, White, Rockel, & Duhn, 2011; Mathers, Eisenstadt, Sylva, Soukakou, & Ereky-Stevens, 2014) which has led to changes in policy and practice.

This chapter begins with a brief synthesis of what we know from interdisciplinary research about the unique characteristics of infants as learners and a review of the most agreed-upon essential components of high-quality infant care and education. Promising practices, enduring questions, and continuing challenges for the field are explored with particular regard to the role of early childhood teacher education in preparing exemplary practitioners for work with infants and families.

Most professional preparation programs, service agencies, and educational settings address the years from birth through age 3 as distinct from later periods of childhood. For the purpose of this chapter, the birth-to-3 age span is referred to as infancy and viewed as a period of continuous and rapid development, which is complex, integrated, and multi-faceted, and which requires specialized knowledge to be fully understood (Dalli et al., 2011). Preparing teachers to provide responsive early care and education for this age group similarly reflects both the complexity and the uniqueness of teaching and learning for the youngest children.

Unique Characteristics of Infants and Toddlers as Learners and Implications for Early Care and Education

There is a consensus in the literature that infants learn in ways that are different from older preschoolers and thus a specialized understanding of teaching and learning is required for children from birth to 3 years old. This is due, in part, to infants' distinct non-verbal communication styles, their increased need for individualized physical care and emotional nurturing, their primarily physical and sensory ways of exploring and learning about the world, and their quickly changing cognitive, linguistic, social-emotional, and physical competencies due to rapid growth and brain development unique to this period of life (Fogel, 2009). There is a well-developed body of literature addressing infant development that undergirds our understandings of infant learning, which I will touch on only briefly here to highlight particular ways that this knowledge base informs early childhood teacher education for infant teachers. Three conceptual constructs are focused on: relationships as an essential context for infant development; the integral nature of play as a facilitator of infant learning; and infants' individual contributions to their own learning and development.

Human Relationships as a Context for Infant Learning

Although once considered passive recipients of the environment, we now see infants as active social beings who are predisposed to learning from others and from the experiences they encounter in their everyday lives (Shonkoff & Phillips, 2000). Lally (2013) has conceptualized the infant as a "*Vulnerable Competent Learner*" who expects social interactions; is driven to make meaning of the environment and learn to communicate; and is biologically ready to form attachments to and learn from caregivers. However, in order to maximize their developmental potential, infants "need adults not only to help them survive, as we have always known, but to provide them with experiences that build their brains" (Lally, 2013, p. 21).

Just as infants develop prenatally within a physical womb, Lally (2013) demonstrates how infants need a "social womb" during the first years of life, which serves as a nurturing extra-uterine environment to support dramatic changes in brain development during the infancy period (p. 14). Ideally, this social womb surrounds babies with an environmental space that both protects them from harm and helps them learn about their social and cultural worlds. Conversely, when early environments are unable to nurture infants "through supportive relationships that facilitate adaptive coping" (Shonkoff, 2010, p. 359), they may be exposed to "toxic stress." This occurs when infants have little control over negative situations and experiences that impact their lives and little access to adults who can help them integrate their emotional responses and become calm in the face of these challenges (National Scientific Council on the Developing Child, 2005). Low quality care, at home or outside the home, can produce toxic stress, which may contribute to potentially serious, and possibly enduring, threats to infants' overall development and well-being (Cryer, Hurwitz, & Wolery, 2000). Sadly, far too many babies are being cared for in settings which are providing mediocre care, at best (Howes, Phillips, & Whitebook, 1992; Lally, 2013).

We understand unequivocally that infants grow and learn within the context of human relationships (Lally, 2013; Shonkoff & Phillips, 2000). They rely on their caregivers to observe and understand their non-verbal communication systems, to create safe opportunities for them to move and explore their physical environment, and to respond to them socially and emotionally through interactions that promote reciprocal and synchronous connections. Through the establishment of emotional "intersubjectivity" (Trevarthen, 1979) with attuned caregivers, babies are provided a context for building trusting relationships with others that serve as the foundation for exploration and learning (Whitington & Ward, 1999).

Relationship-based care. Sensitive and responsive relationships in child care have been consistently correlated with advanced levels of cognitive, language, and social skills in young children (NICHD Early Child Care Research Network, 2001). Scholars have argued that responsive care should be a priority in early care and education for infants (Howes & Hamilton, 1993; Howes & Ritchie, 2002; Lally, 2009; Raikes, 1996; Shonkoff & Phillips, 2000), and early childhood organizations in the U.S., such as the National Association for the Education of Young Children (NAEYC) and Zero to Three, strongly support relationship-based care, particularly for the youngest children in child care (Elicker, Ruprecht, & Anderson, 2014). Recommendations that help promote responsive and relationship-based caregiving in infant group care include small group size (six to eight infants); low caregiver-to-child ratios (no greater than 1:3); primary caregiver assignments; low caregiver turnover and continuity of care; cultural and familial continuity; and meeting the needs of the individual within the group context (Dalli et al., 2011; Howes, Phillips, & Whitebook, 1992; Lally, Mangione, & Singer, 2002; Zero to Three, 2007).

Providing relationship-based care includes the notion of caregiver continuity, which implies that infants remain with the same teacher for an extended period during their first years in child care. The National Association for the Education of Young Children (NAEYC, 1991) has long endorsed that "every attempt is made to have continuity of adults who work with children, particularly infants and toddlers" (NAEYC, 1991, p. 40). Yet, it is practiced only rarely in U.S. infant child care settings, in part due to the characteristically high turnover among infant child care staff and the challenge of providing care at costs that parents can afford (Cryer et al., 2000; Lally, 2013).

One highly recommended practice for providing continuity of care is the enactment of a primary care system in infant group care (Lally et al., 2002; Margetts, 2005; McMullen & Apple, 2012). Viewed as an ideal framework for providing individualized and responsive relationship-based care, a primary care system assures that each infant is assigned to a key caregiver, who is primarily responsible for the infant's caregiving needs and responsive to the infant's cues. Each caregiver has only a few key infants to focus on, with other caregivers' providing support and back-up as part of the caregiving team (Lally, 2009). Within a primary care system, the caregiver takes on the role of adapting to the child, rather than expecting the child to conform to a particular set of center expectations (Theilheimer, 2006). A primary care system ideally allows caregivers the necessary time and space to learn about their key infants' individual needs and preferences for daily care, such as how they like to fall asleep, prefer to be fed, and react to sensory stimuli, including touch, smells, and sounds (Dalli et al., 2011). Primary caregiving in infant child care promotes a deeper understanding of individual infants; increases opportunities for effective and individualized caregiving; enhances team teaching and overall staff empowerment; and provides a richer context for relationships with families (Dalli & Kibble, 2010; Lee, Shin, & Recchia, under review; Margetts, 2005).

Play as a Facilitator of Early Learning

Among the factors that support infant development, play is believed to be one of the most powerful (Fromberg, 2002). The infant curriculum comes to life within the daily moments that comprise a young child's world and gains power through teachers' playful responses and scaffolding (Jung & Recchia, 2013). Play is viewed as the "natural habitat" of young children, making it the most appropriate medium for infant learning (Bergen, 1998). Play "serves as a communications channel between adults and children, provides the creative material through which they organize and understand their experiences . . . and determines the context for their social-emotional development" (Bergen, Reid, & Torelli, 2001, p. 6). In play, infants experiment with the world and practice their social, cognitive, and physical abilities (Honig, 2006; Manning-Morton & Thorp, 2003). They explore objects and their properties, imitate others' actions, try out their intended thoughts in reality, and learn how to modify and adapt their skills (Lillard, 2007; Lindahl & Samuelsson, 2002). Infants' capacity for understanding others and the world grows from what they initially experience through playful explorations and interactions (Manning-Morton & Thorp, 2003).

Infants learn to socialize and inherit their culture through playing with peers and adults. In a recent collaborative study focused on infant child care in different countries, researchers found that both infant teachers and parents across cultures considered play the most important learning context for young children (Pramling-Samuelsson & Fleer, 2010). However, adult roles in play were viewed differently within different cultures. Caregivers' beliefs and values impact their ways of interpreting the infants' world and filter cultural understandings to infants in both subtle and powerful ways (Rogoff, 2003).

Play-based, integrated, and responsive pedagogy. Teaching and learning with infants takes place through the playful engagements that are part of everyday caregiving routines and rituals with both caregivers and peers. Because so much of infants' learning and communication happens through their active physical and sensory engagement with the environment, infant pedagogy needs to include ongoing awareness of children's bodies, with particular attention and responsiveness to their movements and gestures (Manning-Morton, 2006). Recent studies that have explored teachers' roles in play with infants in child care have also indicated a high level of reciprocity in quality teaching, where infants take the lead while teachers respond to their expressed interests (Jung, 2013; Jung & Recchia, 2013; Lee, 2006; Stover, White, Rockel, & Toso, 2010). Teachers adapt their responses based on children's individual ways of engaging in play, sometimes offering more support and other times standing back to let the children act as agents in their own learning. Because infant learning unfolds in a naturally holistic way, infant teaching requires a deeply integrated approach, which starts with creating synchronous teacher-child connections (Recchia & Shin, 2012). This type of pedagogy goes beyond simply developing curricular content and "developmentally appropriate" activities that are commonly enacted in preschool programs. More than a specific set of teaching techniques, it draws on teachers' intimate knowledge of the actual infants in their care.

Teaching in this way requires a great deal of consciousness and intellectual effort for teachers. In Jung & Recchia's (2013) study, teachers shared that individualized scaffolding of infants' play can be quite difficult at times. Teachers need to recognize infants' often subtle cues, expressed through non-verbal communication. Careful observation of changes in behavior, which can happen quickly, is indispensable to gaining a better understanding of an individual infant's interests, desires, and challenges. Failure to identify these capacities can lead teachers to act on their own assumptions in their interactions with infants, eventually disrupting their play. Recchia and her colleagues underscore that observation and reflective practice are critical skills, especially for infant teachers, because they enable teachers to gain greater insight into individual infants' characteristics and to respond to infants in more relevant and authentic ways (Recchia & Loizou, 2002; Recchia & Shin, 2010).

It is important to note that the notion of "scaffolding" can be misconstrued as direct teaching in a way that disenfranchises infants. When teachers focus on what they think the infant should know without considering the infant's own interests, competencies, and actions in play, they may inadvertently dominate the play with an imposed teaching agenda and undermine infants' self-motivations and agency (Canning, 2007). Jung and Recchia (2013) suggest that teachers' empowerment of infants' play not only serves as an essential means for scaffolding, but also strengthens the nature of the play itself, endorsing play as a meaningful source of infants' learning (Bruner, 1983).

Supporting Infants' Distinct Contributions to Their Own Learning

Child development texts and assessment guides articulate normative developmental milestones, contributing to the notion that infant development follows a universal lock-step pattern. Those who work closely with infants, however, realize how distinctly different even two babies of the same age and culture can be (Fogel, 2009). Differences in temperament, reactivity, responsiveness, and expressiveness are apparent from the start of life, and these individual differences affect infants' physical, cognitive, social, and emotional experiences in the world (Brazelton, 1969; Stern, 1985). As responsive caregivers observe babies and come to recognize the subtle nuances in their non-verbal communication and behavior, they are able to offer differential responses that speak to infants' individual needs and interests (Jung, 2013). These ways of being together in unique relationships provide opportunities for building intersubjectivity with infants and help create the "social womb" discussed by Lally (2013) that nurtures infants' sense of themselves as valued, understood, and cared for.

Early learning is integrated and holistic, fueled by infants' active explorations of the environment and interactions with others (Bergen et al., 2001). Within their learning relationships, infants interject their own perspectives, communicating their preferences, interests, and concerns (Hammond, 2009). When caregivers allow space for infants to initiate in this way, they attend to what Shonkoff (2010) articulates as the important role infants play in their own development. Being "in sync" with a particular infant is a reciprocal process between infant and caregiver which requires the caregiver not only to see and make sense of the world through the infant's eyes, but also to communicate this understanding back to the infant (Recchia & Shin, 2012). Teacher-caregiver synchrony requires a level of comfort, engagement, and communicative persistence that can take time to establish. Synchrony is also a dynamic process which changes with development (Howes & Ritchie, 2002). Infants' interests, skills, and competencies continue to change quickly in the first years of life. As infants develop and change, caregivers also need to adapt and transform their responses within this dynamic context to continue to provide responsive nurturing and support (Jung & Recchia, 2013).

Structural, Programmatic, and Philosophical Support for Quality Care and Early Education

Developing relationships with infants takes time and requires opportunities for focused attention and individualized interactions. Quality care and education for infants unfolds within a constellation of dynamic, caring relationships, connecting teachers and children; teachers and teachers; administrative staff and teachers; and teachers, staff, children, and families. A center's structural organization and policies, its philosophical approach to teaching and caring, its ability to provide ongoing mentoring and support to staff, and the leadership style it embraces come together in synthesizing the overall experience of quality care (Dalli et al., 2011).

Even teachers who are prepared to embrace responsive and relationship-based pedagogy will be hard-pressed to enact it if the environmental conditions in which they work cannot support these constructs in practice (White, 2009). The imposition of a set curriculum with rigid routines and systems of caring for babies that are focused primarily on health and safety regulations are standard practice in many infant centers (Lally, 2013). These types of environments cannot support the level of intimacy and individualized interaction necessary for developing authentic relationships with infants that promote intersubjectivity, mutual understanding, and responsive care. There are also concerns about the levels of stress for both infants and teachers that can be generated when supports are not in place (Shonkoff, 2010). In order to create "a membrane of supportive connections" (p. 89), Dalli et al. (2011) recommend employment conditions that encourage staff to feel valued and decrease teacher turnover; recognition of the specialized nature of infant teachers' work; and teaching practices that reduce environmental stress for infants.

Characteristics of Exemplary Infant Teachers

Infant teachers require highly specialized knowledge, skills, education, and a particular kind of professionalism, for which they should be carefully and deliberately prepared (Beck, 2013; Lally et al., 2002; Lee, 2006; Recchia, Beck, Esposito, & Tarrant, 2009; Shonkoff & Phillips, 2000). Exemplary infant teachers are able to establish meaningful caregiving relationships with infants; have expertise and specialized knowledge regarding the birth to age 3 developmental continuum; can enact responsive caregiving practices with diverse children and families; and have the capacity to reflect on and transform their practice in response to feedback (Dalli et al., 2011; Degotardi & Davis, 2008; Manning-Morton, 2006).

Historically there has been a division in the field between early care and education that often places those who teach the youngest children (infants and toddlers) in a lower status group (Manning-Morton, 2006). This is reflected in staffing policies and practices in the U.S. as well as in other countries, where the educational preparation required of infant "caregivers" is less rigorous than that required of "teachers" of older children. Manning-Morton (2006) argues that the skills required of infant caregivers are under-valued in the field. There is a growing interest in and support for the professionalization of infant teachers in the U.S. and abroad, with new early years' policies emerging in countries such as Australia, England, and New Zealand (Abbott & Langston, 2004; Branscomb & Ethridge, 2010; Manning-Morton, 2006; Norris, 2010; Rockel, 2009).

Teacher Competencies Applied to Practice

Although many of the competencies that are expected of infant teachers can also be applied in teaching across the early childhood birth through age 8 continuum, the uniqueness of the earliest years makes particular strengths especially critical for working with this age group. These strengths are embedded in the broad competencies articulated in Dalli et al.'s (2011) review of the literature on quality care.

Emotional engagement with infants, families, and colleagues. Intimate relationships are a necessary foundation for developing infants' basic ability to trust others and their sense of self-worth. Thus, it is important for infant caregivers to create emotionally safe environments as well as to be emotionally available for infants (Elfer & Dearnley, 2007). The ability to be emotionally available and responsive also applies to work with families and other staff members. Because infants' sense of themselves and the world is so embedded in their experiences within their families, making connections with their primary caregivers is an essential component in understanding infants' expectations of being cared for and their responses to care (Gonzales-Mena & Eyer, 2012). Caring for infants in groups is almost always characterized as a team effort, with multiple adults sharing responsibilities for a group of children. Teaching teams that are able to make strong and supportive connections with each other are positioned to create a learning environment that reduces stress for infants and families (Shonkoff, 2010), as well as for themselves as professionals.

Critical reflection. Teacher reflection is a skill that has been articulated in the teacher education literature as an essential element of quality teaching (Pedro, 2006; Schön, 1983). In a recent study of new early childhood teachers, Recchia and Beck (2014) found that teachers who were able to reflect on and question their beliefs, particularly around disorienting experiences, were able to better process the details of what was happening in their work with children and families to make meaningful changes in their practice. Given the demands of teaching and caring for infants and the complexities of working with diverse learners and their families (Recchia & Shin, 2012), reflection is a competency that can be applied broadly in infant teaching. Reflecting on emotional encounters with children and families is equally important to reflecting on philosophical beliefs that inform particular teaching practices, and both forms of reflection are associated with responsive pedagogy (Dalli et al., 2011).

Child development knowledge. There is great consensus among researchers and teacher educators that a strong grounding in child development knowledge is critical to work with very young children (Copple & Bredekamp, 2009; Mathers et al., 2014). This knowledge base crosses disciplines and continues to grow and change with new research and insights from the field. Child development knowledge supports teachers' understanding of children's ways of being in the world and guides decisions for responsive teaching and caring.

Although there is a strong resistance among critical theorists to viewing child development as the primary lens through which we understand children's experience (Ryan & Grieshaber, 2005), recent neurobiological research on infants' developing brains has reignited a developmental/neuropsychological focus on early learning with findings that are too powerful to ignore. This new knowledge provides empirical evidence for infants' experiences that were previously only partially understood. The complexity of development and learning in the early years reflects a need for multi-disciplinary knowledge to inform our understandings of what is known and what we can continue to learn. Meltzoff (2009) has advocated for "translational studies" which bring together knowledge from different disciplines in a cross-fertilization process to further inform understandings of complex interactions between experience and biology. Infant teachers who take a stance of inquiry benefit from many sources of knowledge and information, which can be integrated and synthesized to inform their practice.

A strong grounding in child development knowledge takes on increased significance for teachers who work with infants for several reasons. First, the broad range of developmental competencies that span the birth through age 3 age group requires that teachers be prepared to address children at multiple developmental levels. Infants' skills also change rapidly, and teachers need to be able to adjust their responses to children to match their increasing competencies (Jung, 2013). Additionally, infant teachers are in a front-line position to recognize children's developmental difficulties. A strong understanding of the nuances of development can help them to better assess children's learning and potential, and communicate their understandings with families. Teachers who have a firm understanding of early development are better positioned to help families seek out special education services if needed and navigate the complexities of the referral process. Applying child development knowledge within mixed age groups of infants creates the possibility for early childhood professionals to expand their learning and better understand developmental differences (Recchia & Lee, 2004).

Awareness of diversity. As the population of infants in child care continues to grow and to become increasingly diverse, infant teachers need to enact culturally responsive teaching. Questions regarding how teachers negotiate discrepancies between their own expectations for behavior, and infants' and families' actual ways of being, have yet to be fully explored (Recchia & Shin, 2012). This concern is particularly important for work with families of very young children, given infants' limited ability to speak for themselves.

When different experiences and world views create a "disconnect" between the ways practitioners and families view children's competence, culturally relevant expectations for behavior may be misinterpreted, interfering with the process of meaningful communication with families. Early childhood teachers, notoriously strong advocates for children, may find it hard to make connections with families who do not share their belief systems. In their struggle to continue to support what they believe children need for optimal development and learning, teachers may position themselves as adversaries with families, inadvertently undermining opportunities for collaboration (Barrera, 2003).

Cultural differences in child-rearing practices and adult-child communication styles can create confusion for practitioners' as they attempt to make meaning of what they see. Recchia and Williams (2006) explored these differences through a series of vignettes focused on families of infants and toddlers, with or at risk for disabilities, who were in a variety of early education programs. They discuss the need for teachers and families to work within what Barrera (2003) refers to as a "third space," or a place where different points of view are not only recognized, but allowed to co-exist. Within this space, boundaries become more permeable and fluid, making way for multi-layered understandings of how things might be, and allowing for the possibility that not all phenomena can be clearly explained. Understanding their own cultural identities, and the ways in which their world views influence their actions, is essential to understanding children's and families' cultural identities (Ramsey & Williams, 2003).

Research/evaluation focus. Given the changing nature of early care and education and the rapidly increasing breadth of new information on infant development and learning, the need for infant teachers to keep abreast of research in the field is particularly compelling. Recommended practices suggest that teachers' decisions about their ways of being with, responding to, and planning curriculum for young children be based on the best-available empirical evidence as well as the wisdom and experience of the field (DEC, 2014). Teacher education scholars also call for teachers' active involvement in ongoing evaluation of children's learning and of their own practice through documentation and critical reflection (Lee, 2006). Additionally, as the complexity of infant teaching is best understood by those who engage in it directly, teacher research can greatly enhance our knowledge of classroom practice (Nimmo & Park, 2009).

The research base in infant teaching is both limited and complicated. It is difficult at best to separate the interconnected variables within a complex early education setting to see clear effects, and the diversity of settings makes it even harder to generalize outcomes from one setting to another (Dalli et al., 2011). Teachers' professional knowledge is built in part through their experiences in daily practice, which must be considered alongside research knowledge. By incorporating research knowledge into their work, carefully observing and reflecting on their teaching environments, and collaborating with colleagues in shared inquiry, infant teachers invest in continued learning and professional development which integrates research and practice (Nimmo & Park, 2009).

Developing Deeper Understandings of Professionalism

In looking across these expectations for exemplary infant teachers, it is clear that the nature of their work is complex, multi-faceted, and challenging (Jung, 2013), requiring professional preparation and professionalized practice. However, increasing the professional presence of infant teachers in the field has been a slow-moving process (Beck, 2013). The nature of teaching and caring for infants is physically and emotionally intense in ways that are different from work with older children (Colley, 2006; Manning-Morton, 2006), and this intensity can be recognized as an important element of professionalism in infant caregiving. Scholars who have included discussions of these notions of professionalism in their work have articulated the importance of infant teachers' awareness of their own personal relationship histories and attitudes toward intimacy, as a frame for understanding their responses to the children and families in their care (Degotardi & Davis, 2008; Recchia & Loizou, 2002; Recchia & Shin, 2010).

Interestingly, Recchia and Shin (2010) found that this important part of working and being with infants was viewed as less than professional to the preservice early childhood students in their study. Some students expressed concern that the special feelings they were developing for the babies in their care and the playful nature of their interactions felt "unprofessional." This dichotomy between work with infants and older children, and the ways it intersects with developing views of professionalism, reflects a lack of understanding regarding both infants' ways of learning, their need for intimate relationships, and the importance of responsive and playful caregiving as a critical element of early education (Dalli et al., 2011).

Preparing Infant Teachers for the Field

A call to re-envision early childhood teacher education to better prepare pre-service students to meet the needs of infants and their families has resonated both in the U.S. and abroad (Dalli & Kibble, 2010; Degotardi & Davis, 2008; Elfer & Dearnley, 2007; Margetts, 2005). Teacher educators have suggested alternative models of preparation, and there is a growing body of research which is exploring promising practices. Infancy scholars agree that teaching with this age group requires specialized preparation and continuing professional development (Dalli et al., 2011).

Positioning Infancy as Foundational to Early Childhood Education

Despite a documented need for better prepared teachers to provide high-quality child care and early intervention for infants (Lally, 2013), early childhood degree programs in the U.S. tend to give inadequate attention to these critical early years in preparing early childhood teachers for work in the field (Horm et al., 2013; NAEYC, 2009). Requirements for infant caregivers and systems for preparing teachers to provide early care and education for infants vary from state to state, as well as across programs (Hyson & Tomlinson, 2014; Norris, 2010). What preservice teachers learn from these teacher preparation programs often fails to meet the early care and education needs of infants because the curriculum and teaching strategies they were taught to use are more effective with older children (Horm et al., 2013; Lally et al., 2002; McMullen & Apple, 2012). Many early childhood programs fail to provide in-depth, multi-disciplinary knowledge, skills, and supervised practice focused on infants (Beck, 2013; Horm et al., 2013; Ray, Bowman, & Robbins, 2006). Thus, students have few opportunities to experience the ways that early development comes to life in practice.

Considering the gap between theories about teaching learned in coursework and actual teaching experiences in early education settings, what preservice students know about infancy often remains theoretical, academic, and superficial. Although most early childhood students have had some exposure to infants through babysitting or contact with family members, very few have had hands-on experience with babies or have worked with infants in groups; as a result they are less adept at applying their limited theoretical knowledge of this age group to actual classroom practice (Recchia & Shin, 2010). This lack of experience, coupled with ambiguous feelings about what it means to be an infant teacher (Beck, 2013; Rockel, 2009), can make students uncomfortable working with babies, and it often takes some time before they are able to fully immerse themselves in teaching and caregiving routines.

Given the importance of the early years as foundational to all later learning, deeper understandings of children from birth to age 3 would provide all early childhood teachers with seminal knowledge to inform their professional practice (Horm et al., 2013). Recent studies have found that fieldwork with infants helped preservice teachers to expand their knowledge and experience in ways that could be applied across the early childhood continuum (Beck, 2013; Recchia & Shin, 2010).

Engaging in Field Experiences with Infants and Families Informed by Theory and Research

Supportive faculty mentoring during field experiences can provide a framework for theory practice connections and help preservice teachers learn in the moments of actual practice about competencies such as communication with infants, the significance of joint attention, and engaging with families. Learning these highly specialized skills for providing responsive early care and education takes time and practice, and this process is not necessarily intuitive (Manning-Morton, 2006; Nimmo & Park, 2009). Because it takes time to develop relationships with infants and families, and it is within the context of relationships that deeper learning happens, field experiences must extend for an adequate amount of time (Recchia & Loizou, 2002; Recchia, Lee, & Shin, in press). Lee (2006) suggests that relationship building in infant care takes between six and eleven weeks and can be enhanced by a relationship-based framework (Lee, Shin, & Recchia, under review).

Relationship-based care. Meaningful interactive experiences in high-quality care settings can challenge students' previously held assumptions about the capacities of infants and their ideas about professional work with infants (Recchia, Lee, & Shin, in press). Relationship-based care provides a caregiving context that both nurtures infants' learning and is emotionally enriching for caregivers (Edwards & Raikes, 2002; Elicker & Fortner-Wood, 1995). Lee and colleagues (under review) explored the use of a primary caregiving system as a framework for learning to teach infants within an infant-toddler theory practice course. Preservice early childhood students were assigned "key" infants who they followed throughout the semester. Students reported that acting as "key" caregivers helped them learn to focus deeply on each individual infant; gain a richer understanding of each child through careful observations; read and respond to infants' cues appropriately; communicate with infants more fluidly and reciprocally; engage in longer and deeper play and exploration with infants; and develop authentic and meaningful relationships with infants and their families. These findings reinforce the notion that preparing preservice teachers for relationship-based practice with infants happens best when students are immersed in these practices through supported hands-on field experiences (Margetts, 2005).

The essential value of meaningful practice with infants. Because observation and interpretation of young children's characteristics, behaviors, and dispositions guide teaching practices, curricular decision-making processes, and interactions (Degotardi & Davis, 2008), it is essential that early childhood students have opportunities to engage in well-planned and supervised field-based practica with infants which take place over an extended time with a particular group of children. The quality of the placement environment must also be considered as students may be highly influenced by the nature of the early care and education practices that are modeled for them in the field. In Recchia and Shin's (2010) study, which explored preservice teachers' reflections on a semester-long practicum with infants, the infant classroom provided a unique context for challenging some previously held notions concerning early childhood teaching and learning, as the students encountered inner conflicts and tensions during the practicum. For instance, the students were asked to sit, actively engage through observation, and learn about children and their own ways of interacting with peers and the environment rather than always to "be in action" or "be useful" in the classroom. Through these challenges, and with the guidance and support of experienced classroom mentor teachers who demonstrated high-quality infant caregiving practices, students experienced a shift from seeing the teacher as an authority and control figure, to seeing the teacher as a learner being led by the children. These concepts can be equally powerful when applied across the early childhood spectrum, but seemed to be illuminated for the students in a more distinct way through the unique demands of working with infants, particularly in an environment that supported infant-led learning.

Attending to Emotional Experiences for Both Infants and Teachers

Engaging in infant early care and education can have a powerful emotional impact on caregivers (Elfer & Dearnly, 2007; Manning-Morton, 2006). Degotardi and Davis (2008) suggest greater emphasis be placed on understanding the unique psychological characteristics of infants, such as their temperaments and personalities, while also exploring teacher candidates' psychological understandings of and dispositions toward intimacy and relationships. Responsive caregiving relies on teachers' emotional presence, which allows them to be in the moment with infants and develop intersubjective understandings. These relational components are embedded in the infant curriculum such that they become more essential aspects of quality teaching than any particular teaching strategies or specific curricular content. The most meaningful infant learning takes place through this process of mutual engagement (Dalli et al., 2011).

Teacher educators can better prepare candidates for the emotional nature of infant teaching by bringing this focus into early childhood preparation. Working with infants requires that teachers invest both a high level of emotional engagement and a great deal of physical labor into teaching and caring. Teacher candidates can learn to critically analyze notions of professional practice in line with these realities by questioning their own taken-for-granted assumptions about what professionalism entails (Manning-Morton, 2006).

Learning to work as a team. Teaching older students is characterized by a model that places one adult "in charge" of a sizable group of children. Working with infants in groups, on the other hand, is by necessity a collaborative enterprise. Infant teachers who are able to establish positive working relationships with families and colleagues add substantively to their provision of high-quality care by enhancing their knowledge of infants' needs and orchestrating more continuous caregiving throughout the day. This essential component in infant-toddler teaching does not always come naturally to early childhood students who are often drawn to the field because of their interest in working with children. New teachers are frequently surprised by the challenges they encounter in the field in their necessary collaborations with adults (Recchia & Beck, 2014). Preparing teachers to explore their attitudes and feelings toward collaboration before they enter the field can be naturally integrated into preservice programs through group projects, peer review exercises, and field-based experiences

(Recchia et al., 2009). Because of the particular significance of this competency for infant teachers, it is especially important to articulate it as both a philosophical stance and a practice-based one in infant teaching. Infant practica offer an ideal environment for providing opportunities for students to develop the skills and dispositions they will need as collaborative infant teachers (Lee et al., under review).

Enduring Questions and the Need for Meaningful Research to Inform the Field

Research has shown that quality professional preparation can lead to changes in infant teachers' beliefs that can be translated to high-quality teaching practices (Dalli et al., 2011; Recchia et al., in press). Yet, infant teachers are often expected to hold only the minimum qualifications for teaching and frequently receive the lowest levels of professional development and support (Jung, 2013). Considering what we know about the growing need for infant care, and the significance of providing quality early care and education to the youngest children (Lally, 2013), it is critically important that qualifications for infant teachers be held to a higher set of expectations from the field (Norris, 2010). Infant teachers also need to be supported with opportunities for continuous and high-quality professional development.

It is clear that the nature of infant teachers' work is highly complex, and to do it well requires a sophisticated set of teaching practices that will evolve with new knowledge (Lee, 2006; Jung, 2013). What is less clear is how infants adapt to teacher expectations and interaction styles and whether and how teachers make decisions in the moments of their day-to-day practice to foster the ideals of a caring and supportive social environment in their work with infants and families (Recchia & Shin, 2012). Questions also remain about the parameters and characteristics of high-quality settings; what works best for different groups of infants, families, and teachers; and what kinds of adaptations teachers need to make in their caregiving practices to accommodate individual and cultural differences.

Horm and her colleagues (2013) lament the inadequate research base in infant teacher education and call for more mixed-methods studies to broaden our understandings of the complexities of infant teaching practice. They articulate concerns about the lack of emphasis on the youngest children in early childhood teacher education programs, which is also reflected in the small number of faculty members who are prepared to adequately address this important part of early childhood practice. They question whether doctoral preparation programs for early childhood teacher educators are doing enough to prepare their graduates to address the teaching and research needs of infant teacher education. Addressing these concerns can help to move the field of early childhood teacher education forward.

Scholars both in the U.S. and other countries have raised questions about what determines "quality" in infant teachers (Dalli et al., 2011). The complexities of the field and the multiple and diverse preparation pathways for work with infants make it difficult to define quality across contexts. Preparation means different things in different places, even within a given country, and standards for practice may be determined differently depending on local or national policy. Although structural elements that support programs can contribute greatly to quality, there is growing agreement that determinants of quality go far beyond elements of programs that can be easily regulated. Ecological understandings of quality emphasize the interactive and connected nature of structural and process variables in creating a physical and interpersonal context for early care and education. Because it is also now more readily understood that quality rests in large part in the relationships created in early care and education between teachers and infants, "[t]he factors that once occupied researchers' attention therefore are now seen as subsidiary to this pedagogical and relational emphasis" (Dalli et al., 2011, p. 25).

Many of the existing studies on child care quality have relied on quantitative rating scales to measure teachers' characteristics such as responsiveness and sensitivity, assessed in relatively brief periods of time (Jung, 2013). Although these measures can provide valuable information about some characteristics of programs and teachers, they are apt to miss more nuanced teacher behaviors or disregard behaviors that fall outside of predetermined categories. Qualitative studies which look closely and over an extended time period at teachers' interactions with infants (Degotardi & Davis, 2008; Jung, 2013) have shown that teachers' practice constantly changes in connection with the dynamic elements inherent in infant group care settings. Studies such as these, which reflect teachers' own thoughts and ideas, can also inform teacher preparation for infant teachers by providing rich descriptions and deeper analyses of teachers' actions and insight into their rationales for the choices they make in daily practice.

Conclusion

This chapter synthesizes powerful insights from research and practice on the uniqueness of infancy and its implications for preparing early childhood teachers to understand and work with this age group. The importance of early relationships as foundational to later social, emotional, and cognitive competencies has been well articulated in the literature, but slow to be enacted in infant care and education practice. There is an urgent need for new forms of hybrid research that can help us look more deeply at the processes through which teachers and children in an early care and education setting move together through teaching and learning moments in their everyday world, to describe them for the field, and to stimulate further thinking about the potential impact of our discoveries for early childhood teacher education. This work goes beyond recommended practices or health and safety policies which are widely disseminated in the literature, to provide a vision of how the elements of quality care can be enacted by teachers and supported by administrators. New knowledge gained from research of this nature can also serve as a powerful tool for talking back to increasingly restrictive policies in early childhood education that seem to have lost sight of consistent evidence from both scientific research and clinical practice regarding the nature of quality teaching and learning for infants, families, and teachers.

Acknowledgment

Deep appreciation is extended to Lisa Beck, Eleni Loizou, and Minsun Shin for their generous feedback on a previous version of this chapter. Their insights always help to illuminate my best thinking about infants and their teachers.

References

Abbott, L., & Langston, A. (2004). *Birth to three matters: Supporting the framework of effective practice.* Maidenhead, UK: Open University Press.

Barrera, I. (2003). From rocks to diamonds: Mining the riches of diversity for our children. *Zero to Three, 23*(5), 8–15.

Beck, L. M. (2013). Fieldwork with infants: What preservice teachers can learn from taking care of babies. *Journal of Early Childhood Teacher Education, 34*(1), 7–22.

Bergen, D. (Ed.). (1998). *Readings from play as a medium for learning and development.* Olney, MD: Association for Childhood Education International.

Bergen, D., Reid, R., & Torelli, L. (2001). *Educating and caring for very young children: The infant/toddler curriculum.* New York: Teachers College Press.

Branscomb, K. R., & Ethridge, E. A. (2010). Promoting professionalism in infant care: Lessons from a yearlong teacher preparation project. *Journal of Early Childhood Teacher Education, 31*(3), 207–221.

Brazelton, T. B. (1969). *Infants and mothers: Differences in development.* New York: Delacorte.

Bruner, J. S. (1983). Play, thought and language. *Peabody Journal of Education, 60*(3), 60–69.

Canning, N. (2007). Children's empowerment in play. *European Early Childhood Education Research Journal, 15*(2), 227–236.

Colley, H. (2006). Learning to labor with feeling: Class, gender and emotion in childcare education and training. *Contemporary Issues in Early Childhood, 7*(1) 15–29.

Copple, C., & Bredekamp, S. (Eds.). (2009). *Developmentally appropriate practice in early childhood programs* (3rd ed.). Washington, DC: National Association for the Education of Young Children.

Cryer, D., Hurwitz, S., & Wolery, M. (2000). Continuity of caregiver for infants and toddlers in center-based child care: Report on a survey of center practices. *Early Childhood Research Quarterly, 15*, 497–514.

Dalli, C., & Kibble, N. (2010). Peaceful caregiving as curriculum: Insights on primary caregiving from action research. In A. Meade (Ed.), *Dispersing waves: Innovation in early childhood education* (pp. 27–34). Wellington, NZ: NZCER.

Dalli, C., White, E. J., Rockel, J., & Duhn, I. (2011). *Quality early childhood education for under-two-year-olds: What should it look like? A literature review.* New Zealand: Ministry of Education.

DEC: The Division for Early Childhood of the Council for Exceptional Children. (2014). *DEC Recommended Practices in Early Intervention/Early Childhood Special Education.* Retrieved from DEC website: www.dec-sped.org

Degotardi, S., & Davis, B. (2008). Understanding infants: Characteristics of early childhood practitioners' interpretations of infants and their behaviors. *Early Years: Journal of International Research & Development, 28*, 221–234.

Edwards, C. P., & Raikes, H. (2002). Extending the dance: Relationship-based approaches to infant/toddler care and education. *Young Children, 57*(4), 10–17.

Elfer, P., & Dearnley, K. (2007). Nurseries and emotional well-being: Evaluating an emotionally containing model of professional development. *Early Years, 27*(3), 257–279.

Elicker, J., & Fortner-Wood, C. (1995). Adult-child relationships in early childhood programs. *Young Children, 51*(1), 69–78.

Elicker, J., Ruprecht, K. M., & Anderson, T. (2014). Observing infants' and toddlers' relationships and interactions in group care. In L. J. Harrison & J. Sumsion (Eds.), *International perspectives on early childhood education and development 11, Lived spaces of infant-toddler education and care: Exploring diverse perspectives on theory, research, and practice* (pp. 131–145). London, UK: Springer.

Fogel, A. (2009). *Infancy: Infant, family and society.* Cornwall-on-Hudson, NY: Sloan.

Fromberg, D. P. (2002). *Play and meaning in early childhood education.* Boston, MA: Pearson.

Gonzales-Mena, J., & Eyer, D. W. (2012). *Infants, toddlers, and caregivers: A curriculum of respectful, responsive, relationship-based care and education.* New York: McGraw-Hill.

Hammond, R. A. (2009). *Respecting babies: A new look at Magda Gerber's RIE approach.* Washington, DC: Zero to Three.

Honig, A. S. (2006). What infants, toddlers, and preschoolers learn from play: 12 ideas. *Montessori Life, 1*, 16–21.

Horm, D. M., Hyson, M., & Winton, P. J. (2013). Research on early childhood teacher education: Evidence from three domains and recommendations for moving forward. *Journal of Early Childhood Teacher Education (34)*1, 95–112.

Howes, C., & Hamilton, C. E. (1993). The changing experience of child care: Changes in teachers and in teacher-child relationships and children's social competence with peers. *Early Childhood Research Quarterly, 8*, 15–32.

Howes, C., Phillips, D., & Whitebook, M. (1992). Thresholds of quality: Implications for the social development of children in center-based child care. *Child Development, 63*, 449–460.

Howes, C., & Ritchie, S. (2002). *A matter of trust.* New York: Teachers College Press.

Hyson, M., & Tomlinson, H. B. (2014). *The early years matter: Education, care, and the well-being of children, birth-8.* New York: Teachers College Press.

Jung, J. (2013). Teachers' roles in infants' play and its changing nature in a dynamic group care context. *Early Childhood Research Quarterly, 28*, 187–198.

Jung, J., & Recchia, S. (2013). Scaffolding infants' play through empowering and individualizing teaching practices. *Early Education & Development, 24*(6), 829–850.

Lally, J. R. (2009). The science and psychology of infant–toddler care: How an understanding of early learning has transformed child care. *Zero to Three, 29*(2), 47–53.

Lally, J. R. (2013). *For our babies: Ending the invisible neglect of America's infants.* New York: Teachers College Press.

Lally, J. R., Mangione, P., & Singer, S. (2002, November). *The importance of intimacy in infant toddler care: Looking at how the combination of small groups, primary caregiver assignment, and continuity benefit the developing child.* Presented at the Annual Conference of the National Association for the Education of Young Children, New York.

Lee, S.-Y. (2006). A journey to a close, secure, and synchronous relationship: Infant-caregiver relationship development in a childcare context. *Journal of Early Childhood Research, 4*(2), 133–151.

Lee, S.-Y, Shin, M., & Recchia, S. L. (under review). Primary caregiving as a framework for preparing early childhood pre-service students to understand and work with infants.

Lillard, A. (2007). Pretend play in toddlers. In C. A. Brownell & C. B. Kopp (Eds.), *Socioemotional development in the toddler years: Transitions and transformations* (pp.159–176). New York: Guildford Press.

Lindahl, M., & Samuelsson, I. P. (2002). Imitation and variation: Reflections on toddlers' strategies for learning. *Scandinavian Journal of Educational Research, 46*(1), 25–45.

Manning-Morton, J. (2006). The personal is professional: Professionalism and the birth to three practitioner. *Contemporary Issues in Early Childhood, 7*(1), 42–52.

Manning-Morton, J., & Thorp, M. (2003). Key times for play: The first three years. Philadelphia, PA: Open University Press.

Margetts, K. (2005). Responsive caregiving: Reducing the stress in infant toddler care. *International Journal of Early Childhood, 37*(2), 77–84.

Mathers, S., Eisenstadt, N., Sylva, K., Soukakou, E., & Ereky-Stevens, K. (2014). *Sound foundations: A review of the research evidence on quality of early childhood education and care for children under three. Implications for policy and practice.* London, UK: The Sutton Trust.

McMullen, M. B., & Apple, P. (2012). Babies [and their families] on board! Directors juggle the key elements of infant/toddler care and education. *Young Children, 67,* 42–48.

Meltzoff, A. (2009). Roots of social cognition: The like-me framework. In D. Cicchetti & M. R. Gunnar (Eds.), *Minnesota Symposia on child psychology: Meeting the challenge of translational research in child psychology* (pp. 29–55). Hoboken, NJ: John Wiley.

National Association for the Education of Young Children (NAEYC) (1991). *Accreditation criteria and procedures of the National Academy of Early Childhood Programs. Rev. ed.* Washington, DC: Author.

National Association for the Education of Young Children (NAEYC). (2009). *NAEYC standards for early childhood professional preparation: Position statement.* Washington, DC: Author.

National Scientific Council on the Developing Child. (2005). *Excessive stress disrupts the architecture of the developing brain. Working Paper No. 3.* Updated June 2009. Harvard University. Retrieved from: www.developingchild.harvard.edu

National Scientific Council on the Developing Child. (2007). *The timing and quality of early experiences combine to shape brain architecture: Working paper No. 5.* Retrieved from www.developingchild.harvard.edu

NICHD Early Child Care Research Network. (2001). Child care and children's peer interaction at 24 and 36 months: The NICHD study of early child care. *Child Development, 72*(5), 1478–1500.

Nimmo, J., & Park, S. (2009). Engaging early childhood teachers in the thinking and practice of inquiry: Collaborative research mentorship as a tool for shifting teacher identity. *Journal of Early Childhood Teacher Education, 30*(2), 93–104.

Norris, D. J. (2010). Raising the educational requirements for teachers in infant toddler classrooms: Implications for institutions of higher education. *Journal of Early Childhood Teacher Education, 31*(2), 146–158.

Pedro, J. (2006). Taking reflection into the real world of teaching. *Kappa Delta Pi, 42*(3), 129–132.

Pramling-Samuelsson, I., & Fleer, M. (2010). Commonalities and distinctions across countries. In I. Pramling-Samuelsson & M. Fleer (Eds.), *Play and learning in early childhood settings* (pp.19–50). New York: Springer.

Raikes, H. (1996). A secure base for babies: Applying attachment concepts to the infant care setting. *Young Children, 51*(5), 59–67.

Ramsey, P., & Williams, L. R. (2003). *Multicultural education: A source book.* (2nd ed.) New York: Routledge/Falmer.

Ray, A., Bowman, B., & Robbins, J. (2006). *Preparing early childhood teachers to successfully educate all children: The contribution of four-year undergraduate teacher preparation programs.* New York: Foundation for Child Development.

Recchia, S. L., & Beck, L. (2014). Reflective practice as "enrichment": How new early childhood teachers enact pre-service values in their classrooms. *Journal of Early Childhood Teacher Education* (3), 203–225.

Recchia, S. L., Beck, L., Esposito, A., & Tarrant, K. (2009). Diverse field experiences as a catalyst for preparing high quality early childhood teachers. *Journal of Early Childhood Teacher Education, 30,* 105–122.

Recchia, S. L., & Lee, Y.-J. (2004). At the crossroads: Overcoming concerns to envision possibilities for toddlers in inclusive childcare. *Journal of Research in Childhood Education, 19*(2), 175–188.

Recchia, S. L., Lee, S.-Y., & Shin, M. (in press). Preparing early childhood professionals for relationship-based work with infants. *Journal of Early Childhood Teacher Education.*

Recchia, S. L. & Loizou, E. (2002). Becoming an infant caregiver: Three profiles of personal and professional growth. *Journal of Research in Childhood Education, 16*(2), 133–147.

Recchia, S. L., & Shin, M. (2010). 'Baby teachers': How pre-service early childhood students transform their conceptions of teaching and learning through an infant practicum. *Early Years, 30*(2), 135–145.

Recchia, S. L., & Shin, M. (2012). In and out of synch: Infant childcare teachers' adaptations to infants' developmental changes. *Early Child Development and Care, 182*(12), 1545–1562.

Recchia, S. L., & Williams, L. R. (2006). Culture, class, and diversity: Implications for practice. In G. Foley & J. Hochman (Eds.), *Infant mental health in early intervention: Achieving unity in principles and practice* (pp. 267–294). Baltimore, MD: Paul H. Brookes.

Rockel, J. (2009). A pedagogy of care: Moving beyond the margins of managing work and minding babies. *Australian Journal of Early Childhood, 34*(3), 1–8.

Rogoff, B. (2003). *The cultural nature of human development.* Oxford: Oxford University Press.
Ryan, S., & Grieshaber, S. (2005). Shifting from developmental to postmodern practices in early childhood teacher education. *Journal of Teacher Education, 56*(1), 34–45.
Schön, D. A. (1983). *The reflective practitioner: How professionals think in action.* New York: Basic Books, Inc.
Schore, A. (2005). Attachment, affect regulation, and the developing right bran: Linking developmental neuroscience to pediatrics. *Pediatrics in Review, 26,* 204–217.
Shonkoff, J. P. (2010). Building a new biodevelopmental framework to guide the future of early childhood policy. *Child Development, 81*(1), 357–367.
Shonkoff, J. P., & Phillips, D. A. (Eds.). (2000). *From neurons to neighborhoods: The science of early childhood development.* Washington, DC: National Academy Press.
Stern, D. N. (1985). *The interpersonal world of the infant: A view from psychoanalysis and developmental psychology.* New York: Basic Books.
Stover, S., White, J., Rockel, J., & Toso, M. (2010). Hunting the snark: The elusive nature of play. *The First Years: Nga Tau Tuatahi,* 12(1). Retrieved from: http://hdl.handle.net/2292/21732
Theilheimer, R. (2006). Molding to the children: Primary caregiving and continuity of care. *Zero to Three, 26*(3), 50–54.
Trevarthen, C. (1979). Communication and cooperation in early infancy. A description of primary intersubjectivity. In M. Bullowa (Ed.), Before speech: The beginning of human communication (pp. 321–347). London, UK: Cambridge University Press.
White, E. (2009). *Assessment in New Zealand early childhood education: A Bakhtinian analysis of toddler metaphoricity.* Melbourne, AU: Monash University.
White House, President Barack Obama. (n.d.). *The Agenda, Education.* Accessed August 9, 2014, from the Agenda @ The Whitehouse website at http://www.whitehouse.gov/agenda/education/
Whitington, V., & Ward, C. (1999). Intersubjectivity in caregiver-child communication. In L. E. Berk (Ed.), *Landscapes of development: An anthology of readings* (pp. 109–122). Belmont, CA: Wadsworth Publishing.
Zero to Three. (2007, January). *Improving quality child care for infants and toddlers* (Fact Sheet). Retrieved from http://www.zerotothree.org/

7

THE SIMPLICITY OF COMPLEXITY

Early Childhood Teacher Education for Pre-Kindergarten/Kindergarten (PRE-K/K)

Doris Pronin Fromberg

The Knowledge Base of Early Childhood Teacher Education (ECTE) in relation to Early Childhood Education (ECE) is value-laden within any particular socio-cultural, economic, historical, and political context. The editorial perspective of this paper is nurtured within the currently available socio-cultural, historical, political, and research context. Therefore, the complex non-linear (three-dimensional) nature of learning, as contrasted with a minimalist (two-dimensional) perspective, is central to the editorial perspective of this paper.

It is necessary to focus on complex non-linear perspectives in the context of a contemporary movement in the United States toward universalizing national standards within a Common Core. The Common Core tends to create a cascade of minimalist testing based on technical, easily scored data that flow toward minimalist teaching-to-the-tests that, in turn, create scripted simplistic lessons (see Ravitch, 2010; Singer, 2014). The idea of a formalized common standard skirts the issue of *equivalence of scholarship* that can reside in a variety of forms while judging achievement in absolute metrics rather than relative to the arc of individual children's or teachers' progress.

There is a self-similar, fractal relationship in the development of knowledge bases between the fields of ECTE and ECE that includes the nesting of at least three major perspectives: diversity, power, and ideology. These three major perspectives undergird the socio-political, economic, and substantive decisions that impact early education and teacher education; they influence the potential for an ethical education. A discussion of each perspective follows. Then, there is discussion of the distinctive nature of pre-K/K within these contexts. The continuing section outlines some key components for the preparation of early childhood professionals to work with pre-K/K children.

Professional refers to an ethical teacher who has completed a state-approved credential to teach young children from a registered early childhood teacher education program in an institution of higher education. The early childhood professional has a high tolerance for ambiguity. A technical/functionary can sometimes develop a repertoire of isolated activities and verbalize a list of important principles. It is the scope and depth as well as the capacity for juggling and employing pattern flexibility, however, that differentiates the functionary from the professional (Fromberg, 1999). The National Board of Professional Teaching Standards, which supports Common Core standards, includes an early childhood education component for experienced teachers to demonstrate expertise, including some interdisciplinary teaching and critical thinking skills (NBPTS, 2014). Higher education ECTE faculty also need to advocate with liberal arts and sciences colleagues to shift from mainly lecture deliveries toward engaging students in learning through active use of the distinctive inquiry tools within their respective fields.

Diversity, Power, and Ideology

Diversity (Children and Teachers)

Children. Youngsters between 40–72 months of age typically participate in United States pre-K/K. They begin school with different experiences and a distinctive range of capacities. Researchers have found that socio-economic situations affect significant differences in basic skills (United States Department of Education, 2012) and vocabulary development among five-year-olds (Hart & Risley, 1995; Heath, 1983; National Early Learning Literacy Panel, 2008). Professional early childhood teachers expect young children to have a varied profile of developmental achievements, ranging from the toddler's typical capacity through that of children older than five years of age. Although early differences may cause long-term achievement gaps, at the same time, rote vocabulary development within scripted test-preparation school programs that focus on phonics rather than content-rich activities under-utilizes the fast-growing brains of youngsters (Gopnik, 2009).

Teachers. Adults who prepare to teach pre-K/K children also bring a range of different academic and personal experiences and skills to their teaching. Undergraduate and graduate teacher candidates have a variety of liberal arts and sciences content concentrations. Graduate candidates usually come from a variety of career experiences. Preservice teacher candidates also have had different community experiences. At the same time, the pre-K/K teacher is a generalist who is ethically responsible for helping young children move toward the full range of what John Dewey (1933) called humanity's fund of knowledge.

Power (Children and Teachers)

Early childhood teachers' power to impact children's learning is often underestimated. The power of teachers to use ethical practice considers the diversity of children's prior experiences. Teachers depend on a strong guiding ideology based upon current empirical and clinical findings as well as ethical considerations. The *internal* power of teachers to adjust their practices is central to the capacity of teachers to implement a personal educational ideology. In the face of contemporary grading of individual teachers and schools, some school administrators—who are unfamiliar with the conditions by which young children learn and develop—feel anxious about high-stakes test scores and impose whole-group, lockstep expectations to impact curricular results. For example, the requirement for some teachers includes proof of a specific number of paper-and-pencil assignments with grades and quiz grades during particular marking periods. These administrative policies constrain teacher agency to differentiate instruction and employ active conditions for early learning.

External political, economic, and socio-cultural contexts change across time. Policies and administrator understanding of how young children learn can and often do influence teacher practices. Teachers who provide a reasonable organization and guidance of an early childhood classroom define the degree of respect for youngsters' capacity to self-regulate. Professional early childhood teachers are able to organize a decentralized classroom in which they work with individual children and small groups. Youngsters are able to select from among engaging educational experiences and interact with one another as teachers circulate, appreciate, assess, plan, and adapt instruction. In turn, young children's well-being and educational success depend upon their strong executive function abilities, which include self-regulation/impulse control; working memory/planning capacity; and attention-shifting capacity/adaptation, in order to sustain resilience in the path of various educational and personal challenges (Matthews, Ponitz, & Morrison, 2009; Mischel, Shoda, & Rodriguez, 1989; Nevills & Wolfe, 2009; Sigman, 2008). The built-in opportunities for children's social interaction and feedback through play and other collaborative engagements, as well as their independent pacing, foster executive function.

Teachers' degree of autonomy also defines their access to resources and methods. An ideal professional educator has the kind of style that includes and controls the range of alternatives (Whitehead, 1929). Their individual style includes the power to use alternative conditions for teaching flexibly with different children at different times.

Ideology

Power is nested within the context of society. Thus, there are absolutes and relatives with respect to ideology and values. Both pre-K/K children and teachers might encounter a *continuum* of educational opportunities that range from singular, concrete educational experiences through pluralistic, holistic, illuminative experiences. Table 7.1 is an intentionally dichotomous metaphor to illustrate two ends of the continuum of teaching ideologies, as follows:

Children. For some young children, the impact of a school's ideology is important because school might be the most stable place in their lives. Some children are generally anxious to please adults and willing to comply and conform, even to noxious demands. Then, there are children in passive settings, who might sometimes withdraw or become labeled as acting-out problems. Thus, the implemented ideology of the school provides a lens through which youngsters form their expectations about education and their own sense of competence going forward.

Teachers. Preservice teachers might be influenced by the university culture in which they are prepared to teach or succumb in varied degrees to the sometimes contrasting models in the field-based cultures in which they learn to practice. Their psychosocial development and prior experiences influence their capacity to enter the continuum across a culture of caring and egalitarianism or a culture of competition and elitism.

Distinctive Nature of Pre-K/K Education

ECE and ECTE are not newly hatched/erupted fields of practice. There is lots of folklore within existing practice that collides regularly with research findings and policy developments. This is not to suggest that research and policy always marry. Within these contexts, there are many interpretations.

It is noteworthy that there are a significant number of studies that have identified effective approaches to early learning (Barnett, Jung, Youn, & Frede, 2013; Bodrova & Leong, 2007; Campbell, Ramey, Pungello, Sparling, & Miller-Johnson, 2002; Jerrold, 2010; Reynolds, Temple, Robertson, & Mann, 2001; Schweinhart et al., 2005; Seplocha & Strasser, 2009; Stipek, Feiler, Daniels, & Milburn, 1995). The shared characteristics of these studies include teachers who are certified in early childhood education; provide action-based learning environments; have a broadly conceived, in-depth understanding of conceptual development; allow consideration for diversity; and demonstrate sensitivity

Table 7.1 Dichotomous Metaphor of the Continuum of Teaching Ideologies

Singular: How	*Plural: Whats and Whys*
Flatfooted, concrete listing of—and adherence to—ingredients in a recipe	Gracefully flowing, contextualized approach
Discrete courses, topics, separation of content and methods	Flexible integration of contextualized content and alternative methods
Recitative or repetitive, scripted approach	Potential for connection-making and building executive function
Uniform delivery to all, toward conformity and discrete, uniform, and singular summative assessment	Adaptive interactions and methods based upon ongoing multiple forms of assessment

to family and community involvement. However, ethical issues may surface when families prioritize values such as conformity, dependence, and unquestioned uniform compliance, while teachers educate for self-reliance, independent thought, and connection-making (Maldonado & DeBello, 2012). When teachers and communities differ, conceptual learning may suffer. For example, communities may differ from the school culture in (1) priorities (Nir-Janiv, 1982) and images of citizenship (e.g., voting versus consensus; Kingsolver, 1998); (2) the influence of personal relationships (Delpit, 2012); and (3) communication systems rich in storytelling and analogy rather than single, correct answers (Heath, 1983). Then, curriculum development and assessment could become incongruent with children's experiences unless teachers are aware, respectful, and competent in diversifying and sequencing learning experiences. In these instances, teachers who embody a sense of caring and egalitarian possibilities are most effective in educating children. Thus, it has been recommended that admission to ECTE includes careful ethical assessment, not only with academic records, but personal interviews (Haberman, 1995; Ladson-Billings, 1994; Sternberg, 2010). It is also important to consider candidates' previous experiences with young children.

Conditions for Learning

Professional early childhood teachers can impact the learning of individual children who have had diverse experiences when they use seven integrated conditions for learning. These conditions focus on building relationships and connections. (Indeed, these conditions have similar relevance for extending professional development within adult contexts.) These conditions include (1) comparisons/contrasts/induction; (2) surprises/cognitive dissonance; (3) physical engagements; (4) social interactions and competence; (5) play and imagination; (6) revisiting; and (7) a sense of competence (Fromberg, 2012).

Comparisons and contrasts (inductive learning) assist perception whereas isolated facts or sounds might be camouflaged within a rote environment (see also Fauconnier & Turner, 2002). A variety of field placements affords teacher candidates comparisons that can stimulate reflective analysis (see Recchia, Beck, Esposito, & Tarrant, 2009).

Surprise (cognitive dissonance) growing out of activities that include expectation-experience-comparison helps to embed perceivable new learning and, among other content learning, strengthens reading comprehension. Indeed, neuroscience confirms that expectation, a form of future simulation based upon prior models, is the essence of intelligence (Kaku, 2014). Moreover, children's sense of surprise is a relevant form in which teachers can assess their grasp of new meaning. (For teacher candidates and teachers, self-reflection along with focused peer and mentor feedback provides a parallel experience; see Schon, 1983).

Physical engagement with comparisons of concrete, three-dimensional objects is fundamental to early learning. Children develop the visual and spatial skills that are necessary for understanding concepts in science, technology, design engineering, and mathematics (STEM). Building with blocks, manipulations of three-dimensional objects, and games with objects contribute to building these learnings. Children also extend their three-dimensional representations to two-dimensional representations, a pathway along the continuum of symbolic development. Physical experiences also help English language learners/dual language learners to expand their language skills (see Gordon, 2007).

Social interaction affords children (and teacher candidates) the opportunity to build social competence as they practice communication and receive feedback from others. Thus, this feedback process can help children both expand and try out their perceptions and support English language learners (Espinosa, 2010; Johnson, Johnson, Holubec, & Roy, 1984). Children also come to appreciate that others may have perceptions and ideas different from their own, thereby strengthening their theory of mind (Astington & Pelletier, 2005; Blair & Razza, 2007; Harris & Kavanaugh, 1993; Leslie, 1995; Perner, 1991). Theory of mind is important to written as well as oral communication because effective communication requires appreciating that other people have thoughts, feelings, and beliefs. The transition that defines the *relationship* between a personally centered view and a decentered view reflects a growth of meaning and *social competence* (Piaget, 1965). Teacher candidates learn to decenter from focusing on their own performance toward caring about children's possible experiences. Cohort feedback and support can be helpful (see Berliner, 1994).

Play and imagination, particularly socio-dramatic pretend play when children interact with one another, is richly researched. Four main areas of extensive research indicate the value of socio-dramatic pretend play to improve (1) language development; (2) social competence; (3) IQ and conceptual knowledge; and (4) connection-making and problem solving. Socio-dramatic play is a form of collaborative, oral playwriting and lies on the continuum of drawing-writing-writing into reading-reading.

Children whose families engaged in pretense demonstrated more high-fantasy behavior and were able to persevere and be patient with others (Singer & Singer, 1979, 2015). They scored higher in imaginative storytelling, and made more analogic statements than low-fantasy children (Fromberg, 1999). Flexible thinkers with ethical attitudes could be well-suited to teaching in early childhood settings.

Revisiting makes it possible to build the fresh connections with which children's brains function (Bowman, Donovan, & Burns, 2001; Gopnik, 2009; Sylwester, 2000). With experiences across time, children can create additional connections and *compare* earlier with later perceptions (Piaget & Inhelder, 1973). Likewise, revisiting ECE knowledge bases provides opportunities for teachers to deepen their connections between outlooks and refined practices (see Tom, 1997).

A *sense of competence* builds as children meet challenges. Neuroscientists highlight the connection between intellect and emotion (Damasio, 2003; Kaku, 2014; National Scientific Council on the Developing Child, 2004, 2005, 2008). Children develop meaning within stronger or weaker emotions. They develop a sense of themselves as 'winners' or 'losers' very early in the process of schooling. Their motivation to retain curiosity, feel capable of learning, and the possibility of learning contrasts with the problems of feeling less competent, which may result in withdrawing or bullying. Preservice teachers build a sense of competence as they move through an arc of increasing field based responsibilities with support (Darling-Hammond & Bransford, 2007).

Some Areas of Study

Young children do not divide the world into formal school subject matter or skills. They expand their conceptual learning through direct experiences and connecting experiences, along with ways to represent their meanings in the arts, literacy, and mathematics. The center of early learning and the content of education is the pursuit of meanings. Active, direct experiences that represent the meaningful concepts typical within the sciences and social sciences become the center of pre-K/K education. As pre-K/K children engage in these active experiences, they acquire meaningful concepts and have reasons to represent their experiences symbolically through the arts, literacy, and mathematics that are discussed in turn (Vygotsky, 1997). The discussion that follows offers a perspective about some ECE conceptually-rich knowledge bases.

Integrated Literacy Experiences, the Arts, and Conceptual Learning

Language literacy begins with spoken language and young children represent their perceptions through the arts, including drawing. Research points to the beginnings of writing with (1) scribbles; (2) then groupings of symbols; (3) replaced by consonants to represent syllables; (4) then the contrast and conflict between groupings and consonants; and (5) followed by alphabetic writing that recognizes sound values shorter than syllables (Ferreiro & Teberosky, 1982). Writing is recursive with, and a significant entry into, beginning reading. Writing skills develop in multiple ways. For example, pre-K/K children see models of their spoken language recorded and professional teachers celebrate their drawing and early writing forms.

Pre-K/K children hear teachers read plenty of relevant trade books and poetry; join in song; and play games with sounds. Teachers provide lots of text with high predictability and repetition with a gradient of print for children to begin to read. When children role play stories, their story comprehension improves (Pellegrini & Galda, 1982).

During socio-dramatic and block play, teachers have provided labels and writing materials that fit children's play themes. Professional early childhood teachers *functionally integrate* language literacy as well as mathematical literacy experiences within meaningful conceptual content throughout the day.

Integrated Mathematical and Conceptual Science Learning

The foundations of *mathematics and science begin with motor activity*, rules in the physical world, and physical relationships. Mathematical and science literacy begin with movement through space and *three-dimensional experiences* with building and manipulating objects, as well as children themselves moving through different spaces. Children explore balance and symmetry and equivalency in number and measurement. The grammar of mathematics includes the elements of space and shape (geometry) as well as size (including numbers) and the *comparing and contrasting* ways in which youngsters manipulate objects and learn how quantities function.

Researchers have found that collaborative games are particularly valuable in building the imagery to support mathematical learning (Clements & Sarama, 2009) as well as science learning (Kamii, 2015; Kamii & DeVries, 1998; Zan & Geiken, 2010). Professional teachers integrate mathematical literacy throughout the day, including during routines and conceptual experiences as well as focused games. Thus there are skills, including attitudes and conceptual knowledge, which characterize children's achievements. The discussion now turns to early childhood teacher education where skills might be less generally self-evident.

Key Components of Early Childhood Teacher Education

The research base of early childhood teacher education mirrors general teacher education research. Professional journals, handbooks, and association papers focus on surveys of practices and beliefs, surveys of policies, quantitative study of short-term change and longer-term test scores, and qualitative reports of clinical findings (Zeichner, 2010; Cochran-Smith, Feiman-Nemser, McIntyre, & Demers, 2008; Sikula et al., 1996; Tisher & Wideen, 1990). Perhaps a self-evident palpable sense of high-quality teacher education outcomes, in contrast with narrowly conceived standardized test scores, is sometimes elusive because of the complex interactive, kaleidoscopic nature and the predictable unpredictability of educating young children.

Three major tasks of professional early childhood teacher education include bridging content knowledge (Dewey, 1933); building a stock of related activities; and understanding *why* to match content and activities. These are discussed in turn.

Bridging Content Knowledge

There is a unique need to bridge the distance between adult conceptions of knowing and young children's ways of learning about concepts. Therefore, content knowledge connects with pedagogy that includes knowledge of how children learn and develop. Professionals know how to plan content that includes (1) engaging activities that embrace the seven integrated conditions with which young children learn, as well as (2) the active methods of inquiry and tools that adults use to build content knowledge (Connelly & Clandinin, 1985; Eisner, 1985; Phenix, 1984).

Building a Stock of Meaningful Activities

Professionals need the power to select from alternative activities, materials, and procedures, in order to adjust instruction for different children. Among these alternatives is particular attention to the research about the influence of pretend play as a condition for early learning, as well as professional ways for teachers to provide for its inclusion along with playfulness in educational programs (Fromberg, 2002, 2012). Play is relevant for all pre-K/K children, including those who bring diverse cultural experiences to school or have individual and special learning needs (Wolfberg, 2009). However, some children might benefit from various curricular adaptations or peer models in order to develop pretend play with others as well as with objects (see Mindes & Jung, 2015; Stagnitti, 2010).

Understanding Why to Match Content and Activities

The most important, empowering component for professional early childhood teacher education is the development of 'why' rationales. It follows that professional teachers need to understand the research-based and clinical rationales necessary in order to select from among alternatives. Professional teachers who understand why they make decisions have the power to become immune from shifting policy caprices or internet fads while focusing on what is realistic, meaningful, and possible for pre-K/K children.

The choreography between understanding rationales and implementing curriculum with richly meaningful events is an ongoing development that begins with the thoughtful selection of teacher candidates and continues throughout professional studies and engagements with children. Novices might focus initially upon their own performance. However, as they review data collected during their interactions with children, receive sensitive feedback and coaching from mentors, and increasingly develop self-reflection through cognitive dissonance, they develop a focus on children's possible perceptions and experiences and skills to modify their own performance (Berliner, 1994). Then, they build toward planning and executing a sequence of activities as their skills expand.

Moreover, professionals who understand why they plan and engage in meaningful activities can explain (a form of advocacy) their rationales to other adults, including families, school administrators, and community members. It is particularly important in this era of accountability for early childhood teachers to be able to communicate the importance of action-based, integrated, meaningful learning environments because many adults, including school managers and policy makers, expect pre-K/K classrooms to enact sedentary, uniform curricular practices. Teachers also learn to negotiate with the socio-moral perspectives of families (see Maldonado & DeBello, 2012; Souto-Manning, 2013). In short, professional teachers have a systemic view of curriculum content that is meaningful and culturally sensitive as they plan and interact with children.

Early Childhood Teacher Education Program Development

Candidates who enter early childhood teacher education come from a mixed profile of different liberal arts majors and personal experiences. Undergraduate candidates are mainly female (99%) and European-American (78%) (Saluja, Early, & Clifford, 2002). They are frequently individuals who begin as child care teacher aides or assistants and then pursue a career ladder (Bredekamp, 2013). Graduate prospective teachers have been career changers from fields such as publishing, communications, business, and law. Therefore, the conduct of course work and field work needs to provide for differentiations in order to help candidates achieve a competent, professional level as novices, or for ongoing professional development. It is helpful, for example, if field placements include university supervised pre-kindergarten and kindergarten settings whose ideologies are congruent with the teacher education program.

There is a continuum of linear and non-linear models of early childhood teacher education. However, the potential for social reconstruction depends upon the distinctive knowledge base and field models within a particular preservice higher education program. Inner city public institutions typically serve more diverse populations than private suburban centers. However, rural poverty provides parallel challenges and opportunities for teachers to perceive and provide differentiated educational experiences. An outline of polar models ensues, followed by a discussion of the unique nature of early childhood group organization and the architecture of assessment that undergirds early childhood teacher education.

Linear Model (Two-Dimensional)

The courses in institutions of higher education (or alternative-route-to-certification separate course listings) might be based on a two-dimensional linear approach that is additive and provides separate courses about a variety of topics. For example, a course in child development separate from curricular implementation could yield slippage when actual teaching takes place. Similarly, a separate course in multicultural education that focuses on the unique perspectives of distinct families and children, while building an appreciation for the humanity of all children and families, needs connection with alternatives for curriculum implementation. In the linear approach, the teacher candidate would need to plan integrated learning experiences during a later field experience that might or might not demonstrate an ideology that is compatible with, or welcome, in a field setting.

Non-linear Model (Three-Dimensional)

A non-linear model would include an integrated course of curricular study co-requisite with supervised early childhood field based experiences. It is important that candidates have *supervised* field experiences with pre-kindergarten and kindergarten children in a variety of programs; multiple field placements offer preservice teachers an opportunity to establish a personalized approach to teaching through reflective evaluation and modification of their own teaching. Clinical supervision helps by involving (1) preliminary feedback about adaptable plans and (2) on-site data collection of candidates' interactions with children. Data collection occurs with video, audio, and/or transcribed records. (3) Records serve candidates as a database for feedback and reflective self-analysis along with individualized coaching (see Cochran-Smith et al., 2008; Darling-Hammond, 2012; Darling-Hammond & Bransford, 2007; Joyce, Weil, & Calhoun, 2008). (4) With a community of peers, shared data-collection and self-reflection also have served to help modify professional development (see Cunningham, 2011). Candidates' self-reflection across time with multiple models provides an opportunity for cognitive dissonance/surprises where the discrepancy analysis between one's expected performance and children's level of receptivity, engagement, and learning might create surprises to support new professional learnings. This process is similar to the ways that young human beings learn.

Participation in a variety of programs with children who have different socio-economic experiences offers candidates an opportunity for comparisons and the inductive development of a personal, professional, central knowledge base and guiding ideology. For example, candidates whose prior schooling formats have been mainly whole-class, teacher-directed, paper-and-pencil, and information-oriented would need direct teaching experiences that include cognitive dissonance. They would need theoretical understandings, alternative models, and ongoing respectful coaching and self-reflection in order to integrate alternative models that support the active conditions for early learning (see Joyce et al., 2008). Thus, empowered professionals could have the opportunity to develop their practices and insights within a complex, systemic perspective. Candidates in a non-linear program have the potential to develop independent thinking, deliberative action, and innovative interactions. Neuroscience study reports that direct experiencing entails more neural connections in the brain than do words or two-dimensional images

(Kaku, 2014). *Thus, no less than children, adults benefit from such direct professionally focused experiences and feedback.* When teachers' or candidates' data collection provides a discrepancy between what they intended and what they found, *the cognitive dissonance/surprise helps them to modify practices.*

The distinctive focus of ECTE is curriculum development, which includes engaging ways to help pre-K/K children expand their knowledge and refine their skills. Therefore, effective ECTE programs include particular attention to the distinctive organization of pre-K/K classrooms and the thoughtful questioning strategies that support the seven integrated conditions for learning.

Orchestrating Decentralized Pre-K/K Classroom Organization

Helping candidates and teachers to organize a decentralized classroom where children work simultaneously in small groups is a particular challenge for ECTE (Fromberg, 2012; Souto-Manning, 2013). The decentralized organization creates opportunities for teachers to adjust to the children's different paces and modes of learning. Models and coaching also can help candidates learn how to limit the number of daily transitions—which consume instructional time—by scheduling longer blocks of decentralized time. Candidates observe and practice how to negotiate smooth (staggered) transitions to maximize instructional time on task and respect the scholarship of pre-K/K children who flourish when not rushed (Elkind, 2001, 2007; Gross, 2014).

Pre-K/K children are capable of considerable self-direction and autonomy. Professional early childhood teachers learn how to schedule time, pace events, and provide resources and space in order to maintain currency with the diverse readiness to learn of different children. Effective organization provides a significant time (45–90 minutes daily, depending on the duration of the day) for small groups and individual children to focus on engaging, active educative events while the teacher circulates and coordinates instruction with small groups and individuals. (1) The teacher begins with everyone sharing their plans for the variety of activities available during that activity/work/play period that the teacher has planned and pre-selected; these plans include collaboration with children's expressed interests. (2) The teacher circulates and engages in the following actions: brief teaching; appreciating progress; assessing; re-planning; providing/adapting resources; and redirecting individuals or a small group. (3) Teachers also allot time for pre-K/K children to review and discuss their activities after the activity period.

Refining Questioning Strategies

The pre-K/K teacher's role also includes the capacity to interact and support children by astute and sensitive questioning, and positively worded feedback that empowers children to build their self-regulation. Candidates and teachers use audio-tape to record their discussion questions and interactions with the goal of empowering children to expand their spoken contributions. Their goal is to pose authentic questions that ask for children's perceptions, ideas, descriptions, and opinions. It is relevant to listen to their interactions and look at transcriptions of teacher-talk in order to reduce recitative single fact-stating and yes-no responses for which the teacher already knows the answers.

The teacher adjusts resources, and plans effective and engaging instruction, by listening to pre-K/K youngsters and interpreting the needs of expressively challenged children and those with different learning needs. As a diagnostician, the pre-K/K teacher engages in ongoing assessment in order to plan instruction.

The Architecture of Assessment

Effective teachers constantly assess what children know and can do in order to plan next steps. As generalists, early childhood teachers need to be broadly educated in the liberal arts and sciences, particularly in ways that stress the active tools used to attain content knowledge. Indeed, early childhood teachers face the need to translate adult understanding into perceivable and engaging activities for pre-K/K children. Therefore, they understand the particular assessment cycle as follows:

Contents. What are the contents and components within particular areas of study/domains, e.g., sciences, social sciences, the arts, literacy, and mathematics? What are the dynamic-themes/images cutting across particular domains that help children make connections? For example, multicultural considerations involve a range of social sciences, literacies, sciences, mathematics, and the arts. Design engineering involves physical sciences, the arts, and mathematics. Connection-making is itself a creative process that includes playfulness. (The next section discusses selected conceptual areas of study and interdisciplinary images.)

Pathways/sequences. What are the pathways/sequences that build on challenges to the provision of a manageable risk and chance for success? Within areas of study, pre-K/K teachers learn to control each new teaching variable by embedding a new variable within the repertoire of particular past experiences that have engaged the children's perception.

Assessment formats. Professional pre-K/K teachers attempt to connect plans with children's readiness for challenge. Multiple forms of assessment include listening, observing, and reviewing products, such as oral expression, physical coordination, drawings, writings, and constructions (see also Mindes & Jung, 2015; Zelazo, 2006). Assessment takes place with an eye for building a sense of competence and possibility so that pre-K/K children increasingly can become resilient and self-regulated. *In a similar way, candidates and teachers who build a sense of competence could have motives for ongoing professional development.*

Teacher scaffolds/interventions. The professional teacher who has knowledge of the content, imagery, and sequence of complexity is able to use the active, integrated seven conditions for learning in early childhood that make it possible for children to perceive fresh connections. Pre-K/K candidates and teachers continuously build a repertoire of active, direct experiences, some of which are modeled by teacher educators, cooperating teachers, staff developers, and other teacher candidates, based upon their field work.

Engaging Agenda of Meaningful Content Experiences

Professional pre-K/K teachers learn how to translate advanced learning standards into experiences that match the ways in which children can (a) conceptualize, (b) attend, and (c) learn. They consider the areas of study as well as the images/dynamic-themes that cut across areas of study; thus, the expanding networks of integrated brain connections serve as a supportive developing strength. In Table 7.2, relevant disciplines, selected examples of meaningful activities, and their learning value are presented, beginning with the social studies. Specific attention to social studies is warranted because of the need for conceptual richness to replace the practice of many teachers who narrowly define social studies curriculum as a string of holiday crafts and formal standardized testing that focuses mainly on memorization and literacy skills. In addition, the social studies receive little attention within the Common Core domains.

A critique of Common Core testing derides the notion of text complexity as technical sentence length and finding the pre-determined tester's answer in the text (Singer, 2014). However, active participation in the arts and literacy further helps children to engage in a continuum of representational forms. Thus, the *meaningful content* embedded in activities offers reasons for pre-K/K children to use symbols for representation. Moreover, when teachers select adjacent activities across content domains that represent similar underlying imagery/dynamic-themes, children are able to experience readiness for other experiences related to similar underlying imagery which reflects the integrated nature of early learning.

Table 7.2 Examples of Meaningful Content across Disciplines

Disciplines	*Activity-Based Domains*	*Sample Activities & Underlying Imagery*
THE SOCIAL STUDIES, the study of the social, embed social learning and the principles of the social sciences throughout the curriculum, which includes wholesome human interactions, as follows:	**History** includes the cyclical changes among animals, humans, and non-animate forms. The central tool of historians is the interpretation of events. . .	—through such means as oral histories, interviews, comparing biographies and books written from different viewpoints about the same subject. The *dynamic-theme/image* of cyclical change cuts across the social studies, sciences, and the arts.
	Economics deals directly with issues of scarcity, and the classification of community goods and services.	Pre-K/K teacher candidates build the study of economics into their role playing with props, thoughtful planning of events, and field trips. The *dynamic-theme/image* of contrasts-conflicts/dialectical processes cuts across the social sciences, sciences, and the arts.
	Geography is a study of the interaction between humans and environments.	Teachers provide for three-dimensional constructions that build spatial imagery through the arts, music, and movement activities, and a variety of three-dimensional mapping experiences before two-dimensional representations. Effective pre-K/K teachers typically provide experiences that involve families and/or guests in multicultural events. Teachers help pre-K/K children connect these and other experiences to the world globe. The *dynamic-theme/image* of synergy/interdependence of humans, terrain, and environment cuts across the social sciences, sciences, and the arts.
	Political Science/Civics concerns issues of power and governance.	Teachers help young children deal with daily issues of choice; resolving disputes and ethical issues by learning about mutually useful alternatives; and bringing the daily vocabulary of names and anti-bias roles within the community into the classroom through concrete, child-accessible formats. These formats might include interviews, field trips, role play based upon experience, and writing/dictating letters to school and community workers. The *dynamic-theme/images* of dialectical and cyclical change cut across the social sciences, sciences, and the arts. It is noteworthy that the images which cut across content areas integrate concepts in the inductive ways through which learning expands (see Fromberg, 2012).
SCIENCE, TECHNOLOGY, DESIGN ENGINEERING, AND MATHEMATICS integrate studies of the physical world.	**Physics and interdisciplinary physical sciences** deal with how objects can move through space and time.	Pre-K/K teachers plan opportunities for children to actively engage with physical interactions such as three-dimensional constructions; ramping; and comparing physical properties. These kinds of experiences can represent contrasting/conflicting *dynamic-theme/imagery*.
	Chemical events deal with the study of interactions and changes of substances and their properties.	*Experiences with chemical* phenomena (comparing solutions and changes such as popcorn) reflect a shared *dynamic-theme/image* of synergy.
	Biological sciences study living beings and life processes.	Experiences with *biological* sciences (observing plant and animal behavior, changes, and growth) reflect underlying *dynamic-theme/images* of change and cyclical change. At the same time, culturally sensitive teachers recognize that religious orientations to scientific issues might engender conflict for children. There are sensitive and respectful ways that teachers can plan direct personal and cognitive dissonance experiences.

MATHEMATICS	Numerical symbols and their operations represent and measure structural and spatial conditions.	Although *mathematical skills* become integrated throughout daily learning experiences, teachers use a *distinctive repertoire of planned, sequential experiences* in order to continue systematically and sequentially building the children's mathematical skills. They begin with three-dimensional experiences, then combine three- and two-dimensional experiences and representations, and then two-dimensional representations. Pre-K/K teachers learn that such content-rich experiences with active engagement in three-dimensional activities provide motives for children to measure, estimate, and calculate comparisons thereby reinforcing their mathematical learning and written representations.
THE ARTS AND LITERACY	Tools to represent perceptions, experiences, and meanings include language literacy and the visual, plastic, and movement arts.	Pre-K/K candidates learn how to sequence the pathways that develop the elemental sound-bases and visual-spatial bases of these tools. Within the context of conceptually engaging and meaningful social science and science experiences, candidates support children's development of literacy skills with increasing complexity. Thus, complexity of meanings and skills braid together. In turn, meanings include both conceptual and personal emotional complexity (Fromberg, 2002).

Some Present and Future Trends

Current practices in ECE and ECTE vary with respect to a three-dimensional view of flexible, collaborative education. The future needs creative thinkers and critical thinkers who can adapt to rapid change and conceive of more than a single answer to a question, even if the question seeks a uniform response (Kaku, 1997). Therefore, play, particularly socio-dramatic play and three-dimensional play, needs strong support. Also, teachers who use the conditions by which young children learn offer opportunities for collaborative child engagement and development of self-regulation.

The increased use of digital technology in classrooms and teacher education can take a variety of forms. Some teachers of young children have been able to retain important three-dimensional learning and social interaction for most of the time while using tablets and smart boards creatively with youngsters to focus attention and add playfulness for literacy, mathematics, problem solving, and the arts. This technology, likely to be eclipsed by molecular technologies, can build autonomy for children with physical and other disabilities.

Where high-quality diverse models of teaching are located at a distance, some institutions of higher education have expanded the models of instruction by providing on-site field data collection and sensitive feedback formats by supervisors through interactive computer use. However, it is essential that each candidate has opportunities to receive (1) direct on-site interactions with children and (2) reflective analysis of their contacts in (3) an arc of increasing responsibilities with a sequence of planning and follow through. Therefore, *an entirely online program of course work does not fit current research about the brain and how professionals learn their craft.*

Early childhood teacher professionalism in the United States is in an amateur state of development. Professional organizations need to set standards and control entry into their own profession. In turn, teacher preparation needs to include a healthy dose of practice in advocacy, not a small task in a largely polite, female population of candidates.

Teacher autonomy in curriculum development is an essential part of professionalism. Professional teachers as far away as highly performing Finland are highly educated, empowered to tailor curriculum to custom-fit their students and are not subject to micro-management, nor are children repeatedly measured to cover standardized tests (see Allington, 2002). High-performing school systems have moved on from administrative control and accountability; they support their teachers in developing innovations in pedagogy; in improving their performance and that of their colleagues; and creating a network of innovation (Schleicher, 2013, p. 3). Novice Japanese teachers participate in ongoing collaborative mentorship and have opportunities to interact with mentors throughout the day (Ahn, 2014). Reggio Emilia teaching is characterized by ongoing collaboration between teams of classroom teachers and art specialists (Edwards, Gandini, & Forman, 1998). These examples focus attention on the need for inservice early childhood teachers to have additional opportunities to collaborate through sharing experiences, collegial coaching, and ongoing self-study and learning. The predictable unpredictability of early childhood teaching deserves such customized attention.

Conclusion

Early childhood teacher education and pre-K/K childhood education develop within self-similar open systems of connection-making that nurture an expanding capacity for learning and independent actions. Both children and their teachers ideally engage in a distinctive repertoire of active, engaging learning experiences; social interactions; and activities that span a variety of modalities, such as visual, tactile, and auditory. Assessment for both pre-K/K children and their teachers takes place in multiple ways within the architecture of assessment discussed above.

Pre-K/K candidates and teachers, as well as teacher educators, need to know how to employ the seven conditions for early learning and have the power to employ alternative approaches. Both ECE and ECTE are human endeavors that often are predictably unpredictable.

Professionals can understand that different children and different adults at different times might have experiences with equivalent imagery. However, the same individuals exposed to the same events at the same time might have very different experiences. In turn, school administrators need preparation in early childhood curriculum in order to support high-quality teaching and learning in a decentralized setting. School administrators who have particular preparation in early childhood curriculum would be able to supervise, mentor, support an arc of ongoing teachers' professional development, and interpret high-quality pre-K/K practice to families and communities. In these systemic ways, both pre-K/K children and their teachers could have opportunities to feel supported, competent, and motivated to continue learning,

References

Ahn, R. (2014). How Japan supports novice teachers. *Education Leadership, 71*(8), 49–53.

Allington, R. L. (2002). *Big brother and the national reading curriculum: How ideology trumped evidence.* Portsmouth, NH: Heinemann.

Astington, J. W., & Pelletier, J. (2005). Theory of mind, language, and learning in the early years: Developmental origins of school readiness. In B. D. Homer & C. S. Tamis-LeMonda (Eds.), *The development of social cognition and communication* (pp. 205–230). Mahwah, NJ: Lawrence Erlbaum.

Barnett, W. S., Jung, K., Youn, M-J., & Frede, E. C. (2013). *Abbott preschool program longitudinal effects study: Fifth grade follow-up.* New Brunswick, NJ: New Jersey Institute of Early Education Rutgers University.

Berliner, D. C. (1994). Developmental stages in the lives of early childhood educators. In S. G. Goffin & D. E. Day (Eds.), *New perspectives in early childhood teacher education,* (pp. 120–123). New York: Teachers College Press.

Blair, C., & Razza, R. P. (2007). Relating effortful control, executive function, and false belief to emerging math and literacy ability in kindergarten. *Child Development, 78*(2), 647–663.

Bodrova, E., & Leong, D. J. (2007). *The Vygotskian approach to early childhood education* (2nd ed). Upper Saddle River, NJ: Pearson/Merrill/Prentice-Hall.

Bowman, B. T., Donovan, M. S., & Burns, M. S. (Eds.). (2001). *Eager to learn: Educating our preschoolers.* Washington, DC: National Academy Press.

Bredekamp, S. (2013). *Effective practices in early childhood education: Building a foundation* (2nd ed.). Upper Saddle River, NJ: Pearson/Merrill/Prentice Hall.

Campbell, F. A., Ramey, C. T., Pungello, E. P., Sparling, J., & Miller-Johnson, S. (2002). Early childhood education: Young adult outcomes form the Abecedarian Project. *Applied Developmental Science, 6,* 42–57.

Clements, D. H., & Sarama, J. (2009). *Early childhood mathematics educational research: Learning trajectories for young children.* New York: Routledge.

Cochran-Smith, M., Feiman-Nemser, S., McIntyre, D. J., & Demers, K. E. (2008). *Handbook of research in teacher education: Enduring questions in a changing context.* New York: Taylor and Francis/ATE.

Connelly, M., & Clandinin, J. (1985). Practical knowledge and the modes of knowing: Relevance for teaching and learning. In E. Eisner (Ed.), *Learning and teaching the ways of knowing: Part II* (Eighty-fourth yearbook of the National Society for the Study of Education), (pp.174–198). Chicago, IL: University of Chicago Press.

Cunningham, D. (2011). *Improving teaching with collaborative action research.* Alexandria, VA: Association for Supervision and Curriculum Development.

Damasio, A. (2003). *Looking for Spinoza: Joy, sorrow, and the feeling brain.* New York: Harcourt.

Darling-Hammond, L. (2012). The right start: Creating a strong foundation for the teaching career. *Kappan, 94*(3), 8–13.

Darling-Hammond, L., & Bransford, J. D. (Eds.). (2007). *Preparing teachers for a changing world: What teachers should learn and be able to do.* San Francisco, CA: Jossey-Bass.

Delpit, L. (2012). *'Multiplication is for White people': Raising expectations for other people's children.* New York: The New Press.

Dewey, J. (1933). *How we think.* Boston, MA: D.C. Heath.

Edwards, C. P., Gandini, L., & Forman, G. (1998). *The hundred languages of children* (2nd ed.). Westport, CT: Ablex/Greenwood.

Eisner, E. (1985). *Learning and teaching the ways of knowing: Part II* (Eighty-fourth yearbook of the National Society for the Study of Education). Chicago, IL: University of Chicago Press.

Elkind, D. (2001). *The hurried child: Growing up too fast too soon.* Philadelphia, PA: DaCapo Press/Perseus.

Elkind, D. (2007). *The power of play: Learning what comes naturally.* Philadelphia, PA: DaCapo/Perseus.

Espinosa, L. M. (2010). *English language learners/Dual language learners: Getting it RIGHT for young children from diverse backgrounds: Applying research to improve practice.* Boston, MA: Pearson.

Fauconnier, G., & Turner, M. (2002). *The way we think: Conceptual blending and the mind's hidden complexities.* New York: Basic Books.

Ferreiro, E., & Teberosky, A. (1982). *Literacy before schooling* (K. G. Castro, Trans.). Exeter, NH: Heinemann.

Fromberg, D. P. (1999). A review of research on play. In C. Seefeldt (Ed.), *The early childhood curriculum: Current findings in theory and practice* (pp. 27–53). New York: Teachers College Press.

Fromberg, D. P. (2002). *Play and meaning in early childhood education.* Boston, MA: Allyn & Bacon.

Fromberg, D. P. (2012). *The all-day kindergarten and pre-k curriculum: A dynamic-themes approach.* New York: Routledge.

Gopnik, A. (2009). *The philosophical baby.* New York: Farrar, Straus, & Giroux.

Gordon, T. (2007). *Teaching young children a second language.* Westport, CT: Praeger.

Gross, G. (2014). The effects of hurrying children through childhood. Retrieved from www.huffingtonpost.com/dr_gail_gross_the_effects_of_hurrying_children_through-childhood_b_382419/html

Haberman, M. (1995). *Star teachers of children of poverty.* Indianapolis, IN: Kappa Delta Pi.

Harris, P. L., & Kavanaugh, R. D. (1993). Young children's understanding of pretense. *Monographs of the Society for Research in Child Development No. 231, 58*(1).

Hart, B., & Risley, T. R. (1995). *Meaningful differences in the everyday experience of young American children.* Baltimore, MD: Paul H. Brookes.

Heath, S. B. (1983). *Ways with words: Language, life, and work in communities and classrooms.* New York: Cambridge University Press.

Jerrold, R. (2010). *A comparison of early childhood linear-academic and nonlinear-intellectual teacher methodologies.* Doctoral dissertation. Cypress, CA: Touro University.

Johnson, D. W., Johnson, P. T., Holubec, E. J., & Roy, P. (1984). *Circles of learning.* Washington, DC: Association for Supervision and Curriculum Development.

Joyce, B. R., Weil, M., & Calhoun, E. (2008). *Models of teaching* (8th ed.). Boston, MA: Allyn & Bacon.

Kaku, M. (1997). *Visions; Science revolution for the twenty-first century.* New York: Basic Books.

Kaku, M. (2014). *The future of the mind.* New York: Doubleday.

Kamii, C. (2015). Play and mathematics at age one to ten. In D. Fromberg & D. Bergen (Eds.), *Play from birth to twelve* (3rd ed.), (pp. 197–205). New York: Taylor and Francis Routledge.
Kamii, C. & DeVries, R. (1998). *Physical knowledge in preschool education.* New York: Teachers College Press.
Kingsolver, B. (1998). *The poisonwood bible.* New York: Harper Flamingo.
Ladson-Billings, G. (1994). *The dreamkeepers: Successful teaching for African-American students.* San Francisco: Jossey-Bass.
Leslie, A. M. (1995). Pretending and believing: Issues in the theory of ToMM. In J. Mehler & S. Franck (Eds.), *COGNITION on cognition* (pp. 193–202). Cambridge, MA: MIT Press.
Maldonado, N. S., & DeBello, L. L. (2012). *Hispanic/Latino American children and their families: A guide for educators and service providers.* Olney, MD: Association for Childhood Education International.
Matthews, J. S., Ponitz, C. C., & Morrison, J. S. (2009). Early gender differences in self-regulation and academic achievement. *Journal of Educational Psychology, 101*(3), 689–704.
Mindes, G., & Jung, L. A. (2015). *Assessing young children* (5th ed.). Upper Saddle River, NJ: Pearson.
Mischel, W., Shoda, Y., & Rodriguez, M. L. (1989). Delay of gratification in children. *Science, 244*(4907), 933–938.
National Board of Professional Teaching Standards (NBPTS). (2014). Retrieved from www.nbpts.org/newsroom/archive/2014
National Early Literacy Panel (2008). *National Early Literacy Panel research and dissemination to support early literacy development in young children.* Retrieved from http://www.nifl.gov/nifl/NELP/NELPreport.html
National Scientific Council on the Developing Child (2004). *Children's emotional development is built into the architecture of their brains. Working Paper No.2.* Cambridge, MA: Harvard University. Retrieved from http://www.developingchild.net
National Scientific Council on the Developing Child. (2005). *Excessive stress disrupts the architecture of the developing brain. Working paper No 3.* Cambridge, MA: Harvard University. Retrieved from http://www.developingchild.harvard.edu
National Scientific Council on the Developing Child. (2008). *The timing and quality of early experiences combine to shape brain architecture. Working Paper No. 5.* Cambridge, MA: Harvard University. Retrieved from http://www.developingchild.net
Nevills, P., & Wolfe, P. (2009). *Building the reading brain Pre-K-3.* Thousand Oaks, CA: Corwin/Sage.
Nir-Janiv, N. (1982). *Early childhood education: An international perspective.* New York: Plenum.
Pellegrini, A. D., & Galda, L. (1982). The effects of thematic-fantasy play training on the development of children's story comprehension. *American Educational Research Journal, 19,* 443–452.
Perner, J. (1991). *Understanding and the representational world.* Cambridge, MA: MIT Press.
Phenix, P. H. (1984). *Realms of meaning: A philosophy of the curriculum for general education.* New York: McGraw-Hill.
Piaget, J. (1965). *The moral judgment of the child* (M. Gabail, Trans.). New York: Free Press.
Piaget, J., & Inhelder, B. (1973). *Memory and intelligence.* New York: Basic Books.
Ravitch, D. (2010). *The death and life of the great American school system: How testing and choice are undermining education.* New York: Basic Books.
Recchia, S. L., Beck, L., Esposito, A., & Tarrant, K. (2009). Diverse field experiences as a catalyst for preparing high quality early childhood teachers. *Journal of Early Childhood Teacher Education, 30*(2), 105–122.
Reynolds, A. J., Temple, J. A., Robertson, D. L., & Mann, E. A. (2001). Long-term effects of an early childhood intervention on educational achievement and juvenile arrest: A 15-year follow-up of low-income children in public schools. *Journal of the American Medical Association, 285*(18), 2339–2346.
Saluja, G., Early, D. M., & Clifford, R. M. (2002). Demographic characteristics of early childhood teachers and structural elements of early childhood and education in the United States. *Early Childhood Research and Practice*, 4(1). Retrieved from www.ecrp.illinois.edu/abtecrp.html
Schleicher, A. (2013). What we learn from the PISA 2012 results. *OECD Education Today*. Retrieved from www.oecdeducationtoday/blogspot.com/2013/12/what-we-learn-from-pisa-2012-results.html
Schon, D. A. (1983). *The reflective practitioner: How professional think in action.* New York: Basic Books.
Schweinhart, L. J., Montie, J., Xiang, Z., Barnett, W. S., Belfield, C. R., Nore, M. (2005). *Lifetime effects: The High/Scope Perry preschool study through age 40.* Monograph of the High/Scope Educational Research Foundation Number Fourteen. Ypsilanti, MI: High/Scope Press.
Seplocha, H., & Strasser, J. (2009). *A snapshot of quality in kindergarten classrooms in low-income districts: Implications for policy and practice.* Trenton, NJ: New Jersey Department of Education.
Sigman, A. (2008). *Practically minded: The benefits and mechanisms associated with a craft-based curriculum.* Ruskin Mills Educational Trust. Retrieved from http://www.rmet.org.uk
Sikula, J. P., Buttery, T. J., Guyton, E., & the Association of Teacher Educators. (1996). *Handbook of research on teacher education* (2nd ed.). New York: Macmillan.
Singer, D. G., & Singer, J. S. (2015). Fantasy and imagination. In D. P. Fromberg & D. Bergen, (Eds), *Play from birth to twelve* (3rd ed.), (pp.806–824). New York: Routledge/Taylor and Francis.

Singer, J.S., & Singer, D. (1979). The value of imagination. In B. Sutton-Smith (Ed.), *Play and learning* (pp. 195–218). New York: Gardner.

Singer, A. (2014). How to pass Pearson tests or peeling the Pearson pineapple. Retrieved from http://www.huffigtonpost.com/how_to_pass_a_Pearson_testb5428565.html

Souto-Manning, M. (2013). *Multicultural teaching in early childhood classrooms: Approaches, strategies and tools.* New York: Teachers College Press.

Stagnitti, K. (2010). Helping kindergarten and preschool teachers foster play in the classroom. In A. A. Drewes & C. E. Schaefer (Eds.), *School-based play therapy* (pp. 145–161). Hoboken, NJ: John Wiley & Sons.

Sternberg, R. J. (2010). *College admissions for the 21st century.* Cambridge, MA: Harvard University Press.

Stipek, D., Feiler, R., Daniels, D., & Milburn, S. (1995). Effects of different instructional approaches on young children's achievement and motivation. *Child Development, 66*, 209–233.

Sylwester, R. (2000). *A biological brain in a cultural classroom.* Thousand Oaks, CA: Corwin.

Tom, A. R. (1997). *Redesigning teacher education.* Albany, NY: State University of New York Press.

Tisher, P., & Wideen, M. F. (Eds.). (1990). *Research in teacher education: International perspectives.* London: The Falmer Press.

U.S. Department of Education Institute of Education. (2012). *Program for international student assessment: Selected findings.* Retrieved from *http://nces.ed/gov/surveys/pisa/pisa2012*

Vygotsky, L. S. (1997). *The history of the development of higher mental functions vol. 2* (M. J. Hall, Trans.). New York: Plenum Press.

Whitehead, A. N. (1929). *The aims of education.* New York: Mentor.

Wolfberg, P. (2009). *Play and imagination in children with autism* (2nd ed.). New York: Teachers College Press.

Zan, B., & Geiken, R. (2010). Ramps and pathways: Developmentally appropriate, intellectually rigorous, and fun science. *Young Children, 65*(1), 12–17.

Zeichner, K. (2010). Rethinking the connections between campus courses and field experiences in college- and university-based teacher education. *Journal of Teacher Education 61*(69), 89–99.

Zelazo, P. D. (2006). The Dimensional Change Card Sort (DCCS): A method of assessing executive function in children. *Nature Protocols, 1*(1), 297–301. Retrieved from http://www.nature.com/natureprotocols

8

WHAT'S RESEARCH GOT TO DO WITH IT?

Moving Theory into Practice in Grades 1–3

Sam Oertwig, Adam Holland, Gisele M. Crawford, Sharon Ritchie, and Nitasha M. Clark

Introduction

Much has been written about high-quality teaching of content areas and the use of instructional practices that support diverse learners in the primary grades. Therefore, this chapter will not attempt to discuss every aspect of what teachers of young children and their school leaders need to know. Instead, the focus will be on two essential dispositions for teaching and three important, yet often unaddressed, 21st century educational principles that should undergird every primary teacher's approach to classroom practice in 1st through 3rd grade.

These essential dispositions permit teachers to function at the highest levels within a professional learning community and as instructional leaders in primary classrooms:

- Collectively and individually, teachers possess a mindset of continuous improvement.
- Teachers recognize that their own biases, both explicit and implicit, have a significant impact on how students behave and develop and can impede their progress, and are skilled at exploring those biases.

Basing curriculum, instruction, and classroom management decisions on research findings for these three foundational principles would genuinely transform early childhood teaching practice:

- High student motivation and engagement are more effectively promoted through a mastery approach rather than the performance-based approach that we typically see.
- Student progress is optimized when teachers understand and apply findings from current brain research, in particular what has been learned about the various aspects of executive function, to all instructional decisions.
- Well-designed collaborative opportunities build and strengthen skills needed to do well in school as well as the world of work.

By mastering these dispositions and principles, teachers and administrators maximize their own potential to inspire, nurture, and challenge children in primary grades, unleashing diverse students' potential to be successful in both school and life. Teacher educators can go beyond didactic instruction of these concepts. They can model these dispositions and enact these principles in their own instruction in the preservice classroom.

healthy development that will lead to lifelong productivity and quality social interactions. Helping new teachers understand this developmental progression and how to influence it will address one of the most stubborn issues in U.S. education: how to ameliorate the unacceptable educational disparities between racial and economic groups (Blair & Diamond, 2008; Clifford, Crawford, Garcia, & Cobb, 2014). Primary teachers who create a nurturing classroom community support the development of all aspects of the children, which can be particularly crucial for those who begin elementary school already lagging behind some of their more advantaged peers.

The importance of executive function in the classroom. While the brain itself begins to develop nearly at the moment of conception, neurological studies reveal that executive processes begin developing in infancy and continue until around 30 years of age. The developmental rate of the prefrontal cortex varies, and the corresponding cognitive skills themselves develop at different rates and over periods of time (Diamond, 2002). For example, the skills of inhibition and working memory are usually the first to show significant growth during the preschool years. Growth in the areas of organization, planning, and attention span generally increase around age 5, but these functions do not fully mature until our mid- to late 20's. Thus, a child's brain is in a constant, yet uneven, state of development that varies from one individual to the next, and development of different functions can vary as much as three years between peers (Barkley, Murphy, & Fischer, 2008). While many believe that IQ is the strongest predictor of success in school, the level of executive functioning skills, particularly working memory and inhibition, is actually the highest predictor of success in reading, spelling, and math (Alloway & Alloway, 2010; St Clair-Thompson & Gathercole, 2006). Young children from low socio-economic backgrounds are reported to come into school with lower levels of executive function more often than do their middle-class counterparts, and they fall further behind each year (Noble, McCandliss, & Farah, 2007). Therefore, teachers who support children's development of executive functioning are directly addressing the achievement gap.

When executive brain processes are not functioning at optimal levels, children experience academic and/or behavior difficulties. Often, the problems that children experience in school (lack of focus, disorganization, disruptive behavior) are attributed to low IQ, a possible learning disability, or lack of effort. However, these difficulties are perhaps more indicative of underdeveloped executive function skills (Barkely, 2012). Learning to pay attention, control impulses, and retain information in one's memory do not necessarily happen automatically as children mature, but there is some evidence that these skills can be improved through training and practice (Diamond, 2012; Gawrilow, Gollwitzer, & Oettingen, 2011). Although working memory difficulties affect all aspects of learning, they have been specifically identified as a contributing factor for 52% of all students who experience ongoing problems in math (Gathercole, Pickering, Ambridge, & Wearing, 2004). Imagine a child who experiences difficulty following instructions, is in trouble for not paying attention during whole group story time, cannot connect the story to his own life, lacks the ability to copy problems on the board, and scatters his papers and materials all over the place. This child needs scaffolded teaching support to help him practice each of these discreet skills. He needs a teacher who knows how to strategically weave learning opportunities that challenge executive functioning into the daily routine and curriculum (Diamond & Lee, 2011).

The role of relationships. The emotional well-being of children is quite fragile, and experiencing success in school can play an important role in cognitive development. High levels of stress and low self-concept can negatively impact the natural timeline for the development of executive function skills and the learning process (Blair, Zelazo, & Greenberg, 2005). According to Arnsten (2009), the prefrontal cortex is more sensitive to stress than any other area of the brain. Even mild uncontrollable stress causes the amygdala to trigger the release of dopamine and noradrenaline, which lowers the functioning of working memory and attention regulation. Therefore, teachers help support optimal levels of executive function when they keep children's emotional attitudes buoyant. Early on, children develop self-concepts about themselves as learners and their abilities to be successful in school. Children's academic trajectories are established early and are very difficult to turn around (Alexander, Entwisle, & Dauber, 1993). Part of this is owed to the fact that the brain responds to perceived social threats in the same way as threats to physical survival (Lieberman & Eisenberger, 2004). When a child feels incompetent or disliked, there is an accompanying emotional response. A child in a heightened emotional state is not able to take in and/or process new information, so less learning occurs during these incidents. In addition, each time the child experiences a sense of failure or incompetence, his own self-image of being a successful learner is negatively impacted.

The higher the level of anxiety, the more vigilant the individual becomes about looking for threats and the greater the tendency to overgeneralize, wherein small stressors are perceived as large stressors (Phelps, 2006). Unfortunately, once these mechanisms have been triggered, significant time is required for the body to again reach a state of balance. Time for recovery is an absolute necessity before the learning process can again begin. Through a dropout prevention grant from the North Carolina Department of Public Instruction, researchers at the University of North Carolina at Chapel Hill helped elementary school teachers learn more about the experiences of Black and Latino boys in their classrooms (Crawford, Cobb, Clifford, & Ritchie, 2014). One of the most compelling realizations for the participating teachers arose from watching boys who suffered a perceived injustice remain detached from learning for long periods of time. Teachers were able to effectively shorten that lost time by acknowledging boys' hurt feelings and encouraging them to re-engage.

Intentional teaching across developmental domains. When teachers understand some of the complexities of the brain and the way its response to emotional situations can impede learning, they are better able to intentionally develop classroom environments that feel safe and supportive. They recognize that much can be done to prevent negative emotional situations from ever occurring and they can effectively employ a number of strategies to help children cope quickly when their emotions are triggered. Teachers who have been well prepared to create respectful, nurturing environments in which *all* children thrive approach student behavior from a teaching and learning standpoint, rather than seeing it as a compliance problem. All primary education coursework can explicitly recognize that there is no separation between the teaching of academic content and the teaching of skills that help children focus and attend, recognize the needs and ideas of others, and comply with community rules and expectations. Preservice teachers can be systematically guided to value and plan instructional opportunities that help children increase their emotional and social well-being while mastering cognitive skills.

Well-prepared teachers come to understand that time spent engaging students in reciprocal caring relationships is foundational to the accomplishment of academic goals. The section above on motivation and student engagement outlines some of the counter-productive strategies, such as rewards and punishments, which many new teachers will find are entrenched in the schools where they teach. Teacher educators can coach aspiring teachers to demonstrate practices that build community more effectively. The *Responsive Classroom* approach describes how teacher educators can convey some of these ideas. Throughout the year, social content is emphasized as much as academic content, and the first six weeks in particular are recognized as a critical time for students to practice the skills and behaviors that will help them learn while taking care of each other and the classroom environment (Denton & Kriete, 2000). Two studies, the Responsive Classroom Efficacy Study (2008–2011) and the Social and Academic Study (2001–2004), documented that teachers who used this approach had higher student motivation, experienced higher student gains in reading and math, created classrooms that were more emotionally supportive and organized, and were more skillful in delivering standards-based instruction (Abry, Rimm-Kaufman, Larsen, & Brewer, 2013; Rimm-Kaufman & Chiu, 2007).

Because schooling is an inherently social activity, success depends in part on children's ability to successfully interact with those around them. Doing so requires children to master a wide array of social and emotional skills. It is important for teachers to understand, though, that social competence is a contextualized construct, affected by both the classroom environment as a whole as well as by children's individual abilities and behaviors (Holland, 2013). For example, in a classroom in which children are frequently asked to voice opinions and have some degree of physical freedom, specific children will be viewed as possessing a high level of social competence. These same children with a teacher who requires them to sit silently for long periods of time may be perceived as less socially competent. Therefore, in gauging children's needs and abilities, excellent teachers also recognize the environment's critical role in shaping children's expression of their social abilities.

On behalf of children's overall development, it is critical for teachers to think about their role in improving children's social competence through explicit interventions as well as a well-planned classroom environment. The *Getting Ready* intervention, which focuses on working with parents of preschool children living in poverty, has been shown to affect children's ability to develop positive relationships with their teachers and increase their initiative while decreasing anxiety and withdrawal behaviors after they transitioned to school (Sheridan, Knoche, Edwards, Bovaird, & Kupzyk, 2010). In elementary classrooms, Wilson, Pianta, and Stuhlman (2007) analyzed not only whether classroom climate affected children's social competence but also which attributes of the environment had significant effects. They found that classrooms in which children were exposed to greater positivity, sensitivity, allowance for autonomy, and evaluative feedback showed greater gains in competence. These results may suggest that no single approach is sufficient to significantly affect children's social competence. We contend that supporting social competence is complex and that teachers must negotiate forming positive relationships with their students, providing a nurturing classroom environment, and dedicating time to explicitly teaching and supporting social and emotional skills. Knowledge and understanding of how the classroom environment affects this domain of child development is still evolving, underscoring the need for educators to remain current on advances in the field throughout their careers.

Collaborative Learning

The need to rethink social and developmental supports in primary classrooms is certainly evident in the expectations of the Common Core State Standards (CCSS). Controversial as they are, we appreciate the CCSS viewpoint that children are deep thinkers and that it is the role of the teacher to capably guide and support them. The Standard for Math across K-3rd grade stipulates that children should be able to construct viable arguments and critique the reasoning of others, and the English Language Arts Standard similarly requires that students have ample opportunities to take part in a variety of rich, structured conversations—as part of a whole class, in small groups, and with a partner. Being productive members of these conversations requires that students contribute accurate, relevant information, respond to and develop what others have said, make comparisons and contrasts, and analyze and synthesize a multitude of ideas in various domains. Concurrently, states and districts, pushed by the expectations of universities and businesses, are working to develop students with 21st century skills, including the ability to engage in collaboration, problem solving, and reasoning (Partnership for 21st Century Skills, 2011).

The good news is that a large body of research has shown that collaborative approaches to learning can be effective in producing achievement gains, promoting critical thinking, and enhancing problem solving in face-to-face learning contexts (Steffe, Cobb, & von Glasersfeld, 1988; Webb, 1989). However, research also shows how seldom interactive group work actually takes place. Over the past eight years, data from the FirstSchool Snapshot have provided information about how pre-K-3rd grade children spend their days in school (Ritchie & Gutmann, 2014). Remarkably consistent results across states and districts indicate that generally only about 9% of the day is devoted to small group and collaborative work. Since children's voices are, as a rule, not prioritized, it is likely that students have not been taught how to engage in collaboration or given ample chance to practice.

The same data also establish the lack of time for children to play or engage in choice. The notion of play for children beyond age 4 is sadly a subject of much controversy. The result is that play is largely absent in K-3 classrooms despite solid evidence that it is the primary avenue for children to collaborate, negotiate, plan, and work together. Research makes it clear that children learn best through active questioning and information-gathering combined with hands-on experiences and direct social interactions. This process of active learning and knowledge acquisition occurs during play with materials, ideas, and other people (Chouinard, 2007, as cited in Drew, Christie, Johnson, Meckley, & Nell, 2008). Play also provides opportunities for children to develop socially and emotionally in contexts that provide natural opportunities for them to recognize and manage emotions, develop care and concern for others, make responsible decisions, negotiate and compromise, and navigate challenging situations. These skills are linked to improved self-concept, decreased conduct problems, and decreased stress and social withdrawal (Weissberg & Cascarino, 2013).

Play and choice, however, are not the only avenues for engaging in collaborative work. According to King (2007), in order to be effective collaborators, students need regular practice thinking out loud, explaining, elaborating, and arguing. In her Scripted Collaboration approach, she elaborates on how collaborative learning can and should be structured by teachers to help students focus on, remain engaged in, and regulate their actions in collaboration with others. *Thinking Aloud* makes thinking explicit and available to the student doing the thinking, as well as exposing that same thinking to the rest of the group. *Explaining* pushes students to use their own words rather than simply repeating what they have heard. *Elaborating* gives students the opportunity to add details and examples and relate new information to what they already know, and *Argumentation* provides students the opportunity to negotiate meaning by listening to others and asserting their point of view. These strategies can be used effectively in higher education classrooms as well, offering teacher educators another opportunity to model the practices aspiring teachers can use.

Johnson and Johnson (2007) further illuminate the importance of students working together. They found that children who engaged in cooperative structures spent more time on task than did students working individually, and students working cooperatively tended to be more engaged, to attach greater importance to success, and to be less distracted and disruptive. In addition, they found that cooperation, compared to competitive and individualistic efforts, tends to result in greater achievement, more positive relationships, and greater psychological health. They suggest that if schools genuinely want to prepare students to meet local and state standards, the use of cooperative learning should dominate instructional practice (Johnson & Johnson, n.d.).

Coursework on collaborative learning provides the opportunity for rich discussion of the ways that competition and individualism are emphasized in traditional educational models. Whereas individualism fosters and promotes independence, individual thinking, individual achievement, self-expression, and personal choice, a more collectivist approach fosters and values interdependence, group success through adherence to norms, respect for authority, and group consensus (Trumbull, Rothstein-Fisch, & Greenfield, 2000). Collaborative learning gives students the opportunity to learn to work with all types of people and to add their perspectives based on a variety of differences, including experiential and cultural. This exchange helps students value their own contributions and better understand other points of view and cultural values (Oertwig & Holland, 2014).

Inherent in collaboration is relationship building. Moving beyond stability, trust, and well-being, Johnson and Johnson (2012) also found the accompanying benefits of lowering the absenteeism and dropout rates, greater commitment to group goals, feelings of personal responsibility to the group, and willingness to take on challenges. This interaction between student's emotional well-being and the opportunity to achieve within a group structure surely evokes a strong need to increase the knowledge and skill base of educators to be purposeful in designing and delivering collaborative learning opportunities.

Conclusion

In this chapter we have used research grounded in developmental science and educational psychology to make the case for a 21st century approach to teacher education focused on the fundamental knowledge base for all teachers of young children. Two things are indisputable—too many young children are not doing well in school, and teacher education programs are under pressure to provide better support for new professionals and demonstrate results (Bornfreund, 2011). Educating ***all*** children effectively requires teachers and instructional leaders to create a culture of collaborative inquiry, where they continually seek to improve their practice, identify how implicit biases are operating in their classrooms, and base instructional and management decisions on research and an understanding of children's development and cultural context. In fact, we have strong evidence that many children, especially those of color and/or who live in poverty, will not acquire the skills and knowledge they need to gain in 1st through 3rd grade until and unless teachers can create the conditions for learning explored in this chapter. To ensure teacher candidates are well prepared to teach in culturally, racially, and ethnically diverse classrooms, teacher preparation programs should be structured in such a way that teacher educators consistently:

- Model their own continuous improvement process as educators, sharing struggles and celebrating intellectual risk-taking;
- Build in opportunities for diverse field experiences throughout the degree program, with opportunities to openly explore challenges encountered and make explicit connections to coursework;
- Offer students in the higher education classroom the same instructional strategies that help primary students learn: build classroom community; scaffold students' learning; and offer opportunities to collaborate;
- Examine instructional practices across the course of study for 1st through 3rd grade for ways to promote children's engagement and improve executive function, create opportunities to collaborate, and infuse culturally relevant materials and content; and
- Coach aspiring teachers to articulate their educational philosophy and the research base undergirding it, preparing them to advocate for appropriate practices and demonstrate the effectiveness of those practices.

The ability to persuade is essential for teachers to function at the highest level of their profession and for collaborative structures within schools and districts to function optimally as well. In an era of increasing scrutiny of children's academic progress at younger and younger ages, and unrelenting pressure on schools and districts to produce "results" (Crawford et al., 2014), primary teachers in particular are called upon to advocate for the practices that support all aspects of young children's learning and development. When teachers are well-versed in current educational research and able to think critically about it, not only will they make good instructional choices for their students but they will also be able to talk to colleagues, leaders, parents, and policy makers about why they believe in those choices and why different choices might be detrimental to children. If we expect the next generation of teachers to convince their school leaders and more experienced colleagues that a completely different approach is needed, we owe teacher candidates not only a mastery of new knowledge and a toolkit of promising practices, but the confidence to instigate a re-examination of even the most entrenched practices in schools.

References

Abry, T., Rimm-Kaufman, S. E., Larsen, R. A., & Brewer, A. J. (2013). The influence of fidelity of implementation on teacher-student interaction quality in the context of a randomized controlled trial of the Responsive Classroom approach. *Journal of School Psychology, 51*(4), 437–453.

Akiba, M. (2011). Identifying program characteristics for preparing pre-service teachers for diversity. *Teachers College Record, 113*(3), 658–697.

Alexander, K. L., Entwisle, D. R., & Dauber, S. L. (1993). First-grade classroom behavior: Its short-and long-term consequences for school performance. *Child Development, 64*(3), 801–814.

Alloway, T. P., & Alloway, R. G. (2010). Investigating the predictive roles of working memory and IQ in academic attainment. *Journal of Experimental Child Psychology, 106*(1), 20–29.

Ames, C., & Archer, J. (1988). Achievement goals in the classroom: Students' learning strategies and motivation processes. *Journal of Educational Psychology, 80*, 260–267.

Arnsten, A. (2009). Stress signalling pathways that impair prefrontal cortex structure and function. *Nature Reviews Neuroscience, 10*(6), 410–422.

Auwarter, A. E., & Aruguete, M. S. (2008). Effects of student gender and socioeconomic status on teacher perceptions. *The Journal of Educational Research, 101*(4), 242–246.

Barkely, R. A. (2012). *Executive functions: What they are, how they work, why they evolved.* New York: Gilford Press.

Barkley, R. A., Murphy, K. R., & Fischer, M. (2008). *ADHD in adults: What the science says.* New York: Guilford Press.

Bianco, M., & Harris, B. (2014). Strength-based RTI: developing gifted potential in Spanish-speaking English language learners. *Gifted Child Today, 37*(3), 169–176.

Blair, C. (2002). School readiness: Integrating cognition and emotion in a neurobiological conceptualization of children's functioning at school entry. *American Psychologist, 57*, 111–127.

Blair, C., & Diamond, A. (2008). Biological processes in prevention and intervention: The promotion of self-regulation as a means of preventing school failure. *Development and Psychopathology, 20*(3), 899–911.

Blair, C., Zelazo, P. D., & Greenberg, M. T. (2005). The measurement of executive function in early childhood. *Developmental Neuropsychology, 28*, 561–571.

Bornfreund, L. (2011, March). *Getting in sync: Revamping licensing and preparation for teachers in PreK, Kindergarten, and the early grades.* Washington, DC: New America Foundation. Retrieved from www.Newamerica.net

Chouinard, M. M. (2007). *Children's questions: A mechanism for cognitive development.* Boston, MA: Blackwell.

Clifford, R. M., Crawford, G. M., Garcia, S. C., & Cobb, C. T. (2014). Introduction. In S. Ritchie & L. Gutmann (Eds.), *FirstSchool: Transforming PreK-3rd grade for African American, Latino, and low-income children* (pp. 9–28). New York: Teachers College Press.

Coleman, M. R., Shah-Coltrane, S., & Harrison, A. (2010a). *Teacher's observation of potential in students: Individual student form.* Arlington, VA: Council for Exceptional Children.

Coleman, M. R., Shah-Coltrane, S., & Harrison, A. (2010b). *Teacher's observation of potential in students: Whole class form.* Arlington, VA: Council for Exceptional Children.

Crawford, G. M., Cobb, C. T., Clifford, R. M., & Ritchie, S. (2014). The groundswell for transforming prekindergarten through third grade. In S. Ritchie and L. Gutmann (Eds.), *FirstSchool: Transforming PreK-3rd grade for African American, Latino, and low-income children* (pp. 9–28). New York: Teachers College Press.

Deci, E. L., & Ryan, R. M. (2000). The "what" and "why" of goal pursuits: Human needs and the self-determination of behavior. *Psychological Inquiry, 11*, 227–268.

Denton, P., & Kriete, R. (2000). *The first six weeks of school.* Greenfield, MA: Northeast Foundation for Children.

Diamond, A. (2002). Normal development of prefrontal cortex from birth to young adulthood: Cognitive functions, anatomy, and biochemistry. In D. T. Stuss, R. T. Knight, & T. Robert (Eds.), *Principles of frontal lobe function* (pp. 466–503). New York: Oxford University Press.

Diamond, A. (2012). Activities and programs that improve children's executive functions. *Current Directions in Psychological Science, 21*(5), 335–341.

Diamond, A., & Lee, K. (2011). Interventions shown to aid executive function development in children 4 to 12 years old. *Science, 333*(6045), 959–964.

Dougherty, S., Goodman, J., Hill, D., Litke, E., & Page, L. (2014). Middle school math acceleration and equitable access to 8th grade algebra: Evidence from the Wake County public school system (Working paper RWP14–029). Retrieved from the Harvard Kennedy School of Government website: https://research.hks.harvard.edu/publications/workingpapers/citation.aspx?PubId=9434&type=WPN

Drew, W. F., Christie, J., Johnson, J. E., Meckley, A. M., & Nell, M. L. (2008). Constructive play: A value-added strategy for meeting early learning standards. *Young Children, 63*(4), 38–44.

Eccles, J. S., & Wigfield, A. (2002). Motivational beliefs, values, and goals. *Annual Review of Psychology, 53*, 109–132.

Elliot, A. J., McGregor, H. A., & Thrash, T. M. (2002). The need for competence. In E. L. Deci & R. M. Ryan (Eds.), *Handbook of self-determination research* (pp. 361–387). Rochester, NY: University of Rochester Press.

Gathercole, S. E., Pickering, S. J., Ambridge, B., & Wearing, H. (2004). The structure of working memory from 4 to 15 years of age. *Developmental Psychology, 40*(2), 177–190.

Gawrilow, C., Gollwitzer, P., & Oettingen, G. (2011). If-Then plans benefit executive functions in children with ADHD. *Journal of Social and Clinical Psychology, 30*(6), 616–646.

Gregory, A., Skiba, R. J., & Noguera, P. A. (2010). The achievement gap and the discipline gap two sides of the same coin? *Educational Researcher, 39*(1), 59–68.

Hamre, B. K., & Pianta, R. C. (2001). Early teacher–child relationships and the trajectory of children's school outcomes through eighth grade. *Child Development, 72*, 625–638.

Harradine, C. C., Coleman, M.R.B., & Winn, D. M. (2014). Recognizing academic potential in students of color: Findings of U-STARS~PLUS. *Gifted Child Quarterly, 58*(1), 24–34.

Holland, A. L. (2013). *Children's social competence across the transition to kindergarten: A latent growth curve analysis.* Doctoral dissertation. University of North Carolina at Chapel Hill. Retrieved from ProQuest. (3562913).

Holland, A. L., Crawford, G. M., Ritchie, S., & Early, D. M. (2014). A culture of collaborative inquiry. In S. Ritchie and L. Gutmann (Eds.), *FirstSchool: Transforming PreK-3rd grade for African American, Latino, and low-income children* (pp. 57–80). New York: Teachers College Press.

Jang, H. (2008). Supporting students' engagement, motivation, and learning during an uninteresting activity. *Journal of Educational Psychology, 100*, 798–811.

Johnson, D. W., & Johnson, F. P. (2012). *Joining together: Group theory and group skills* (11th ed.). Boston, MA: Allyn & Bacon.

Johnson, D. W., & Johnson, R. T. (2007). Social interdependence theory and cooperative learning: The teacher's role. In R. Gillies, A. Ashman, & J. Terwel (Eds.), *The teacher's role in implementing cooperative learning in the classroom* (pp. 9–37). New York: Springer.

Johnson, D. W., & Johnson, R. T. (n.d.). Introduction of cooperative learning. Retrieved from http://www.co-operation.org/home/introduction-to-cooperative-learning/

K-3 North Carolina Assessment Think Tank. (2013). *Assessment for Learning and Development in K-3* [online report]. Retrieved from http://www.dpi.state.nc.us/docs/earlylearning/k3-assessment.pdf

Kidd, J. K., Sánchez, S. Y., & Thorp, E. K. (2008). Defining moments: Developing culturally responsive dispositions and teacher practices in early childhood preservice teachers. *Teaching & Teacher Education, 24*(2), 316–329.

King, A. (2007). Scripting collaborative learning processes: A cognitive perspective. In F. Fischer, I. Kollar, H. Mand, & J. M. Haake, (Eds.), *Scripting computer-supported collaborative learning* (pp. 13–37). New York: Springer.

Lai, C. K., Hoffman, K. M., & Nosek, B. A. (2013). Reducing implicit prejudice. *Social and Personality Psychology Compass,* 7(5), 315–330.

Lieberman, M. D., & Eisenberger, N. I. (2004). Conflict and habit: A social cognitive neuroscience approach to the self. In A. Tesser, J. V. Wood, & D. A. Stapel (Eds.) *Building, defending, and regulating the self: A psychological perspective* (pp. 77–102). New York: Psychology Press.

McKown, C., & Weinstein, R. S. (2008). Teacher expectations, classroom context, and the achievement gap. *Journal of School Psychology, 46*(3), 235–261.

Meece, J. L., Anderman, E. M., & Anderman, L. H. (2006). Classroom goal structure, student motivation, and academic achievement. *Annual Review of Psychology, 57*, 487–503.

Milner, H. R. (2005). Stability and change in US prospective teachers' beliefs and decisions about diversity and learning to teach. *Teaching and Teacher Education, 21,* 767–786.

National Education Association. (2011, November*). Race against time: Education Black boys. Focus on Blacks* [research summary]. Retrieved from: http://www.nea.org/assets/docs/educatingblackboys11rev.pdf

Nickerson, R. S. (1989). Confirmation bias: A ubiquitous phenomenon in many guises. *Review of General Psychology, 2*(2), 175–220.

Niemiec, C. P., & Ryan, R. M. (2009). Autonomy, competence, and relatedness in the Classroom: Applying self-determination theory to educational practice. *Theory and Research in Education,* 7(2), 133–144.

Noble, K. G., McCandliss, B. D., & Farah, M. J. (2007). Socioeconomic gradients predict individual differences in neurocognitive abilities. *Developmental Science, 10*(4), 464–480.

Oertwig, S., & Holland, A. (2014). Improving instruction. In S. Ritchie & L. Gutmann (Eds.). *FirstSchool: Transforming PreK-3rd grade for African American, Latino, and low-income children* (pp.102–124). New York: Teachers College Press.

Partnership for 21st Century Skills. (2011). *Framework for 21st Century Learning.* Washington DC: author. http://www.p21.org/storage/documents/1.__p21_framework_2-pager.pdf

Phelps, E. A. (2006). Emotion and cognition: Insights from studies of the human amygdala. *Annual Review of Psychology, 57*, 27–53.

Pianta, R. C., Belsky, J., Vandergrift, N., Houts, R., & Morrison, F. J. (2008). Classroom effects on children's achievement trajectories in elementary school. *American Educational Research Journal, 45*(2), 365–397.

Pianta, R. C., & Stuhlman, M. W. (2004). Teacher-child relationships and children's success in the first years of school. *School Psychology Review, 33*(3), 444–458.

Pintrich, P. (2000). Multiple goals, multiple pathways: The role of goal orientation in learning and achievement. *Journal of Educational Psychology, 92*, 544–555.

Pintrich, P. R., & Schunk, D. H. (2002). *Motivation in education: Theory, research, and applications* (2nd ed.). Columbus, OH: Merrill-Prentice Hall.

Reeve, J. (2009). Why teachers adopt a controlling motivating style toward students and how they can become more autonomy supportive. *Educational Psychologist, 44*(3), 159–175.

Rimm-Kaufman, S. E., & Chiu, Y.J.I. (2007). Promoting social and academic competence in the classroom: An intervention study examining the contribution of the Responsive Classroom approach. *Psychology in the Schools, 44*(4), 397–413.

Ritchie, S. (2014). Directions for the future. In S. Ritchie and L. Gutmann (Eds.), *FirstSchool: Transforming PreK-3rd grade for African American, Latino, and low-income children* (pp. 170–186). New York: Teachers College Press.

Ritchie, S., & Gutmann, L. (Eds.). (2014). *FirstSchool: Transforming PreK-3rd grade for African American, Latino, and low-income children.* New York: Teachers College Press.

Rodriguez, M. A. (2012). "But they just can't do it": Reconciling teacher expectations of Latino students. *Journal of Cases in Educational Leadership, 15*(1), 25–31.

Rosenthal, R., & Jacobson, L. (1992). *Pygmalion in the classroom: Teacher expectation and pupils' intellectual development.* New York: Irvington Publishers.

Rudman, L. A. (2004). Social justice in our minds, homes, and society: The nature, causes, and consequences of implicit bias. *Social Justice Research, 17*(2), 129–142.

Ryan, R. M., & Deci, E. L. (2002). An overview of self-determination theory: An organismic-dialectical perspective. In R. M. Ryan & E. L. Deci (Eds.), *Handbook of self-determination research* (pp. 3–36). Rochester, NY: University of Rochester Press.

Rydell, R. J., & McConnell, A. R. (2006). Understanding implicit and explicit attitude change: A system of reasoning analysis. *Journal of Personality and Social Psychology, 91*(6), 995–1008.

Senko, C., & Harackiewicz, J. M. (2005). Regulation of achievement goals: The role of competence feedback. *Journal of Educational Psychology, 97*(3), 320–336.

Sheridan, S. M., Knoche, L. L., Edwards, C. P., Bovaird, J. A., Kupzyk, K. A. (2010). Parent engagement and school readiness: Effects of getting ready intervention on preschool children's social-emotional competencies. *Early Education and Development, 21*, 125–156.

Souto-Manning, M. (2012). Teacher action research in teacher education. *Childhood Education, 88*(1), 54+. Retrieved from http://go.galegroup.com/ps/i.do?id=GALE%7CA312618333&v=2.1&u=unc_main&it=r&p=AONE&sw=w&asid=0b2d751c727c98f2b97933ecd9e917f6

Staats, C. (2014). *State of the science: Implicit bias review 2014.* Columbus, OH: Kirwan Institute, Ohio State University. Retrieved from http://kirwaninstitute.osu.edu/wp-content/uploads/2014/03/2014-implicit-bias.pdf

St Clair-Thompson, H. L., & Gathercole, S. E. (2006). Executive functions and achievements in school: Shifting, updating, inhibition, and working memory. *The Quarterly Journal of Experimental Psychology, 59*(4), 745–759.

Steffe, L. P., Cobb, P., & von Glasersfeld, E. (1988). Construction of arithmetical meanings and strategies. New York: Springer-Verlag Publishing.

Stoughton, E. H. (2007). "How will I get them to behave?": Pre-service teachers reflect on classroom management. *Teaching and Teacher Education, 23*, 1024–1037.

Sugai, G., Horner, R. H., Dunlap, G., Hieneman, M., Lewis, T. J., Nelson, C. M., & Wilcox, B. (2000). Applying positive behavioral support and functional behavior assessment in schools. *Journal of Positive Behavioral Interventions, 2*, 131–143.

Tenebaum, H. R., & Ruck, M. D. (2007). Are teachers' expectations different for racial minority than for European American students? A meta-analysis. *Journal of Educational Psychology, 99*(2), 253–257.

Trumbull, E., Rothstein-Fisch, C., & Greenfield, P. M. (2000). *Bridging cultures in our schools: New approaches that work.* San Francisco, CA: WestEd.

Tversky, A., & Kahneman, D. (1974). Judgment under uncertainty: Heuristics and biases. *Science, 185*, 1124–1131.

Vansteenkiste, M., Lens, W., & Deci, E. L. (2006). Intrinsic versus extrinsic goal contents in self-determination theory: Another look at the quality of academic motivation. *Educational Psychologist, 41*(1), 19–31.

Webb, N. M. (1989). Peer interaction and learning in small groups. *International Journal of Educational Research, 13*(1), 21–39.

Weissberg, R. P., & Cascarino, J. (2013). Academic learning + social-emotional learning = national priority. *Phi Delta Kappan, 95*(2), 8–13.

Wilson, H. K., Pianta, R. C., & Stuhlman, M. (2007). Typical classroom experiences in first grade: The role of classroom climate and functional risk in the development of social competencies. *The Elementary School Journal, 108*, 81–96.

Zygmunt-Fillwalk, E. M. (2006). The difference a course can make: Preservice teachers' perceptions of efficacy in working with families. *Journal of Early Childhood Teacher Education, 27*(4), 327–342.

9

WHAT TEACHERS NEED TO KNOW ABOUT FAMILY-CENTERED PRACTICE

Douglas R. Powell and Sara A. Schmitt

Educators have long understood that effective teaching includes proactive efforts to connect home and school learning environments. Much of this understanding has been organized within a parent involvement rubric that has deep roots in the field of early childhood education. In recent decades, the idea of parent involvement has shifted to include emphasis on families as complex systems, mutuality in exchanges between teachers and parents, and the multidimensionality of family contributions to children's learning. There is an increasingly sophisticated set of knowledge and skills for teachers to master in becoming productive partners with families.

A growing corpus of empirical and theoretical literature offers useful points of departure for the preparation of teachers on approaches to working with families of young children. In this chapter, we summarize key information on the contributions of families and parents to children's development in the early years and on the concept and dimensions of family-centered practices in programs of early education and care. We also review strategies for preparing teachers to implement family-centered practice in early childhood settings.

Family and Parental Contributions to Child Development

Parenting in Context

Parents and children are inextricably linked and share a bond that is arguably the most si[...] intimate relationship among human beings. Parents play a powerful role in facilitating [...] development, and a large body of research has been dedicated to exploring the eff[...] behaviors on developmental outcomes. A common theme in extant literature is th[...] enting does not happen in isolation. The parent-child relationship is complex a[...] proximal and distal contexts within which families reside (Bronfenbrenner, 19[...]

One of the most important contextual factors influencing the parent-chi[...] Culture provides a lens through which families view the world; it shapes th[...] ted from generation to generation, and it provides guidelines for approp[...] practices. Two models, *individualism* and *collectivism*, are commonly used[...] ing cultural norms and expectations that have direct implications fo[...] whose cultural identity aligns with the individualistic model te[...] omy, value personal choice, support competition, and allow for [...] et al., 2006). In contrast, parents whose cultural identity is cha[...]

encourage interdependence between parent and child for longer periods of time, stress obedience to all adults (especially parents and older family members), and foster relatedness among individuals (Greenfield et al., 2006). In some cases, these parenting practices and developmental goals align with the dominant cultural climate, and in other situations, they do not. Incongruence between home and societal cultures can have implications for child development and for parent-school relationships. For example, the American educational system reflects a more individualistic model. In the early childhood years, educators are encouraged to utilize a more child-directed approach, facilitate dialogue among adults and children, promote independent exploration, support active learning, and expect parental involvement (Copple & Bredekamp, 2009). This is often in stark contrast to the values and experiences promoted and provided in the homes of parents who adhere to collectivist traditions. These barriers can lead to challenges for children in classroom contexts and may make it difficult for educators to involve parents in classroom activities. Moreover, there may be cultural differences in the *ways* that parents involve themselves in their children's academic lives. For example, whereas European Americans tend to be more involved in activities that occur at school, Chinese Americans are more involved in explicit academic teaching at home (Huntsinger & Jose, 2009).

It is important to note the growing recognition that dichotomous frameworks for understanding cultural influences on child-rearing practices and developmental goals may be too simplistic. Rather than pitting individualism and collectivism against one another, it may be more appropriate to recognize that these value systems often coexist within families (Tamis-LeMonda et al., 2008). Many parents, regardless of cultural background, view both autonomy and relatedness as fundamental for healthy child development. For example, some parents believe that social connectedness is a pathway to independence and success rather than a deterrent, and others see autonomy and relatedness as joint contributors to children's success (Tamis-LeMonda et al., 2008). Thus, although there is utility in nderstanding broad cultural frameworks as they relate to parenting practices, it is also essential to lize that many families endorse values that cross cultural lines.

ocial class or socioeconomic status (SES) is a second powerful contextual factor related to cul- that influences child-rearing practices. SES is based on family income, level of parent education, arent occupation. For years there has been general consensus in the research literature that rable variation exists between low SES families and high SES families in terms of parenting s and the transmission of values (Coontz, 2006). For example, in their seminal study, Hart (1995) reported that on average, parents from lower socioeconomic strata speak less to an parents from higher socioeconomic strata. This discrepancy in language input is vocabulary (i.e., less input is correlated with lower vocabularies; Hart & Risley, co ld, 2013). In another influential observational study, Lareau (2003) found that fo king-class, and poor American families shared some features (e.g., all par- cla ppy and healthy), several variations in parenting styles emerged. For pare active in their children's development, creating opportunities for betw rests, providing resources, and engaging in school activities. In incom and Fe used their efforts primarily on providing basic necessities from 67 al and extracurricular resources. In addition, working- In ad n's schooling. practices. nding how social class and culture influence critique is that there is striking variability kground. For example, among low- early language experiences. Weisleder d infants from low-SES families ranged

within-culture variation regarding parenting scripts they learned as children. For example, as a result of assimilation processes, immigrant parents may deviate from the cultural values that characterize their native communities (Glick, Hanish, Yabiku, & Bradley, 2012). Moreover, modern globalization has resulted in shifts from traditional collectivist belief systems to a more Western ideology in some families, particularly those from middle- to upper-middle social classes (Verma & Sharma, 2006). For these reasons, parenting practices within cultures are becoming increasingly heterogeneous. Thus, it is important to take a broader perspective when understanding child development and the parent-child relationship, and many theoretical perspectives support this notion (e.g., ecological systems theory; Bronfenbrenner, 1979; family systems theory; Broderick, 1993; sociocultural theory; Vygotsky, 1962).

Parenting Styles/Dimensions

Parenting styles have received considerable attention in the literature and are characterized by child-rearing behaviors that reflect a global or overall approach to parenting. In her seminal work, Diana Baumrind (1966, 1971) identified four patterns of behaviors or basic categories of parenting styles that influence child outcomes: authoritarian, permissive, uninvolved, and authoritative. These patterns are comprised of two dimensions: parental control/autonomy support and warmth/responsivity. Authoritarian parenting involves high parental control, low autonomy support, and low warmth. It often relies on directives, negative criticism, and punishment in order to exert control over children. Authoritarian parenting can impede healthy child development across a variety of domains (e.g., emotional health; Chang, Schwartz, Dodge, & McBride-Chang, 2003) and can negatively impact parent-child and peer relationships (Kuppens, Grietens, Onghena, & Michiels, 2009).

Permissive parenting includes low parental control, high autonomy support, and high warmth. Although permissive parents are extremely warm and supportive, they are often characterized as being overindulgent, allowing children to make decisions before it is developmentally appropriate for them to do so. Despite the low levels of control and high levels of autonomy support offered by these parents, Baumrind (1966, 1971) found that children with permissive parents are less self-reliant and more antisocial.

Uninvolved child rearing is characterized as low control, low autonomy support, and low warmth. In extreme cases, this style could reflect abusive or neglectful parent-child relationships. The development of children with uninvolved parents is typically disrupted in a number of ways, which results in lower levels of self-regulation, difficulties with peers, and poor academic achievement (Ginsburg & Bronstein, 1993).

Finally, authoritative styles emphasize gradual developmentally appropriate control and autonomy support and high warmth. These parents set reasonable limits for their children while maintaining high levels of support and attention, and use positive techniques (e.g., reasoning, negotiation) to create structure around the parent-child relationship. This approach is thought to be the most effective for children's development, and is related to self-control, social-emotional health, and academic achievement (Bernier, Carlson, & Whipple, 2010; Chao, 2001; Kaufman et al., 2000).

The Dynamic Parent-Child Relationship

Historically, children were seen as passive individuals who relied on their parents for environmental inputs that facilitated their development. In other words, the relationship between parents and children and the socialization process was unidirectional. However, many scholars have deemed this perspective too simplistic (e.g., Liable & Thompson, 2006). More recently, there has been a theoretical shift to bidirectional or relational models of parenting which take into account the active role that children play in shaping the parenting process, as well as environmental forces that either enhance or constrain parenting practices. These bidirectional models have led to significant advances in the understanding of family dynamics and child development.

The bioecological model (Bronfenbrenner & Morris, 2006) is grounded in a relational perspective and is a common framework for understanding family group functioning. This theory argues that development occurs within a series of nested environmental systems and places emphasis on the reciprocal nature of parent-child relationships. The bioecological model acknowledges that children's own biologically influenced dispositions have an impact on the interactions they have with the world around them. Environmental systems range from the child's most immediate contexts (e.g., family, peers, school) to the most distal contexts (e.g., cultural values, societal laws). In early childhood, the parent-child dyad is an important context for development; however, according to the bioecological framework, several other layers of the environmental system must be considered. The relationships and interactions that occur in children's proximal contexts (e.g., parent-teacher relationships) have indirect effects on development. Moreover, environmental forces outside the family (e.g., parents' work) have a direct impact on parenting practices.

Interactions that take place within a family (e.g., partner relationship, sibling relationship) can also influence family functioning and child development. According to the family systems theory, individual family members are interrelated and interdependent and cannot be understood in isolation of one another (Broderick, 1993). Every action or behavior of one family member has direct implications for all family members. Suboptimal parental behaviors, like alcoholism, can disrupt the family system and cause chaos and stress for other family members (Finger et al., 2010). More positive parental behaviors, like the provision of emotional support, can facilitate family cohesion. Furthermore, external variables that affect one member of a family also influence other members and their interactions. For example, if a child is diagnosed with a chronic illness, the parent-child relationship will likely change (Coffey, 2006). Within each family system, patterns evolve that govern and regulate each family member's behavior and allow for predictability of the behavior of other family members. These patterns include family rules, roles, and communication styles, and contribute to overall family stability and effective functioning. Family patterns are prone to adaptation over time to adjust to ever-changing developmental abilities and goals. For example, parent communication styles change as children develop more sophisticated verbal abilities (Rowe, 2008), and family rules are negotiated as children become more autonomous (Collins, Madsen, & Susman-Stillman, 2013).

As highlighted by the bioecological and family systems theories, development occurs in the context of a child's larger social and ecological environment. As such, school success is the result of a complex and dynamic set of interactions that take place in classrooms, families, homes, and communities. For this reason, early childhood educators' efforts to provide children with quality educational experiences must include partnerships with families that support parents and other primary caregivers as active contributors to their child's education.

The Role of Parents in Preparing Children for School

Parents play an enormous role in shaping the development of their children's preparedness for formal school entry (Chazan-Cohen et al., 2009). School readiness is a broad construct that consists of many dimensions, including, but not limited to, social-emotional competence, self-regulation, and cognitive skills (e.g., early literacy skills). These skills are foundational for children's positive outcomes in early childhood and beyond (McClelland, Cameron, Wanless, & Murray, 2007). Children's home environments can either attenuate or enhance the development of these important skills. Although several aspects of parenting are important for child development, we focus on three that are particularly salient to school readiness: (1) secure attachment (i.e., parental warmth and responsivity); (2) autonomy support; and (3) cognitive stimulation (i.e., quality of the home learning environment).

The quality of the parent-child attachment relationship lays the foundation for children's social-emotional development. Parents who have secure attachment relationships with their children are positive and affectionate, provide encouragement, convey interest in daily activities, accept children's emotions, and model appropriate social behaviors, all of which support strong social skills, peer group competence, and self-regulatory behaviors (Calkins, 2004; Morris, Silk, Steinberg, Myers, & Robinson, 2007). Importantly, children are active participants in the development of the attachment relationship. Children's behaviors and temperaments, particularly levels of reactivity and responsiveness, help shape the parent-child bond (Maccoby, 1992). In addition to predicting social-emotional skills, secure attachments and parental emotional support during the transition into formal schooling are also strongly related to children's language, emergent literacy, and early math skills (Hirsh-Pasek & Burchinal, 2006; Landry, Smith, Swank, Assell, & Vellet, 2001).

Autonomy support is a second aspect of parenting that promotes strong school readiness. Parents who foster their child's autonomy facilitate independent exploration and assessment, involve children in decision-making and problem solving, and negotiate rules and expectations. A growing body of literature suggests that these autonomy supportive behaviors are related to a smoother transition into formal schooling (e.g., Walker & MacPhee, 2011). For example, research indicates that preschool children whose parents are autonomy supportive demonstrate increased levels of social competence in the form of cooperation (Hindman & Morrison, 2012) and social adjustment (Joussemet, Koestner, Lekes, & Landry, 2005). Furthermore, autonomy support is beneficial for the development of children's self-regulation. In one study of parenting precursors of young children's self-regulation, autonomy support during infancy was the strongest predictor of children's emerging regulatory behaviors (measured at 18 and 26 months of age), above and beyond maternal sensitivity and other important covariates (Bernier et al., 2010). In another study, autonomy supportive language (e.g., parental management language that offers children some degree of choice) was positively associated with preschool children's self-regulation (Bindman, Hindman, Bowles, & Morrison, 2013). Parents who are autonomy supportive promote academic achievement in young children as well (National Institute of Child Health and Human Development Early Child Care Research Network [NICHD ECCRN], 2008).

A final aspect of parenting that is important for school readiness is cognitive stimulation, a broad construct that typically includes resources and learning materials available in the home; the provision of enrichment activities both in and out of the home (e.g., going to the library or zoo); and informal and formal teaching by parents. A common feature of the home learning environment includes available resources (e.g., books) and activities surrounding literacy (e.g., shared parent-child book reading), also called the home literacy environment (HLE). The HLE has been the focus of numerous studies investigating children's language and literacy development, and results indicate that parents' literacy-related behaviors (both formal and informal) and families' literacy resources are directly linked to children's oral language skills (Schmitt, Simpson, & Friend, 2011), print knowledge (Farver, Xu, Lonigan, & Eppe, 2013), and reading (Skwarchuk, Sowinski, & LeFevre, 2014). Recent work has also revealed that the HLE is important for the development of early math skills (Baker, 2014).

As shown above, recent literature recognizes parenting as a multi-dimensional construct, and specific parenting dimensions make domain-specific contributions to the various aspects of school readiness. Hindman and Morrison (2012) estimated a three-dimensional model of parenting involving the home learning environment, autonomy support/expectations, and management/discipline. Their analysis revealed domain-specific relations among parenting dimensions and three aspects of emergent literacy (letter recognition, decoding, and expressive vocabulary), self-regulation, and social competence. Especially, the home learning environment was particularly important for letter recognition, decoding, and social competence; management/discipline was related to self-regulation and social competence, but not literacy; and autonomy support/expectations was only associated with social competence. Findings like these highlight the need for specificity when developing parenting training and engagement programs.

Despite the necessary role that parents play in promoting social-emotional competence, self-regulation, and cognitive skills, several factors can interfere with their efforts to promote these skills. For example, children are born with unique dispositions that lead to varying behavioral tendencies and personality traits. When these individual differences in temperament do not match the temperament of the parents or the family, conflict can arise, making the development of a secure attachment more difficult (Seifer et al., 2014). Furthermore, parents with few resources and high levels of stress can have difficulties engaging in stimulating activities with their children and providing a warm and supportive home environment (Magnusson & Duncan, 2002).

Taken together, the aforementioned research indicates the unequivocal role that parents play in preparing their children for positive experiences in early childhood programs and beyond, but also highlights the barriers and interference factors that some parents must overcome to develop secure attachments and provide quality home environments. Nonetheless, the family remains an important and central context for child development that must be incorporated into early care and education. Early childhood educators who can successfully involve families in the education process will support children's well-being, readiness for school, and long-term academic success.

There are noteworthy strengths and limitations in regard to the current knowledge base around parenting practices. A significant strength is the frequent use of large scale, longitudinal datasets such as the Early Childhood Longitudinal Studies. Scholars also have begun to recognize the need and utility for utilizing diverse samples. Further, mixed methods designs have gained popularity in the study of parenting and have proven particularly useful for the development of culturally sensitive measurement (e.g., McWayne, Melzi, Schick, Kennedy, & Mundt, 2013). There is growing, but limited, knowledge of the role that diverse family structures and experiences play in parenting practices and child development. The definition of the American family is broadening to include redefined single parents (e.g., single parenting by choice), blended families, and same-sex parents, yet empirical work on these family structures is limited. Moreover, family background characteristics, like immigrant status, ethnic minority status, and being an English language learner, have begun to appear as focal variables in some studies; however, a dearth of this type of research remains.

Concept and Dimensions of Family-Centered Practice

Concept of Family-Centered Practice

In the last several decades, the theoretical and empirical literature summarized in the prior section has propelled early care and education programs to recognize the importance of the family system for child development and to involve more family-centered sources of support (e.g., Dunst, Trivette, & Hamby, 2007). The key principles of family-centered practice are integral to the dominant position statements on best practices in early childhood education. Establishing reciprocal relationships with families is one of the five key areas of practice set forth in the National Association for the Education of Young Children's (NAEYC) guidelines for developmentally appropriate practices with young children (Copple & Bredekamp, 2009). The NAEYC position statement indicates that reciprocal relationships entail "mutual respect, cooperation, shared responsibility, and negotiation of conflicts toward achievement of shared goals" (Copple & Bredekamp, 2009, p. 23). Family-centered approaches are fundamental to each of the seven practice areas recommended by the Division for Early Childhood (DEC) of the Council for Exceptional Children (DEC, 2014). For example, early childhood professionals are expected to work with families as team members to identify family preferences for assessment processes and to identify a child's strengths, preferences, and interests to engage the child in active learning.

Family-centered practice in early childhood builds on a tradition of parent involvement in education that promotes parents' school-based participation (parent-teacher conferences, home visits by teacher, classroom visits, and volunteering) as well as program strategies aimed at supporting parents' involvement in children's learning at home (e.g., Hoover-Dempsey et al., 2005). Research indicates that parents' school-based involvement is related to several domains of school readiness, including adaptive behaviors (e.g., coping), social-emotional competence, and academic skills in the early childhood years (Marcon, 1999; Powell, Son, File, & San Juan, 2010). Teacher outreach to families during the transition to kindergarten, including provision of workshops and trainings for parents and invitations to volunteer at school, is also positively related to children's math and literacy development (Hindman, Skibbe, & Morrison, 2013). The benefits of parent involvement extend beyond child outcomes to include parenting beliefs and behaviors as well. When parents are engaged in their children's education, they have greater satisfaction with the early childhood program, stronger beliefs of self-efficacy, self-competence, and sense of control, and more positive perceptions of family and child (Dunst et al., 2007).

The emphasis on partnerships, shared decision-making, and mutual respect represents a major departure from a parent involvement paradigm that assumes the expertise of early childhood educators is the most valuable base of decision-making about children's program experiences. For certain, the idea that effective programs for young children provide focused connections with their parents has long occupied a highly respected position in the field of early childhood education. The traditional paradigm emphasizes a one-way pathway, however. The title of the 1929 yearbook of the National Society for the Study of Education (Whipple, 1929)—*Preschool and Parental Education*—illustrates how the early childhood teacher's work with both children and parents was envisioned as a closely intertwined educational enterprise in an earlier era. The volume title also speaks to the program-to-parent flow of influence that prevailed in images of how programs approach their work with families. The basic assumption was that preschool program experiences must be extended and reinforced in the home if the early childhood program is to exert long-term effects on the child (Powell, 1991).

Many factors prompted the shift to a relationship paradigm that emphasizes family systems and contexts, shared decision-making, and reciprocity. Beginning in the early 1970s, research findings and theoretical treatments broadened the conventional focus on mother-child dyads to include subsystems within families as well as the larger family and community contexts in which children live. Particularly influential was Bronfenbrenner's (1979) ecological perspective on human development, which offered a compelling case for viewing developmental processes as embedded within cultural, community, and family systems, as noted earlier in this chapter. Bronfenbrenner's seminal work also recognized interrelationships among two or more systems in which the developing individual is a participant (called the mesosystem). He theorized that an individual's developmental potential is enhanced when there is goal consensus, a balance of power, supportive linkages, and open, frequent, and personal two-way communication between settings.

Dramatic changes in the demographic characteristics of U.S. families with young children also bolstered interest in the concept of family-centered practices. Beginning in the 1970s, early childhood programs began to serve unprecedented numbers of children from culturally and linguistically diverse families, single-parent families, dual-worker families, and reconstituted or blended families. The wide range of family forms and backgrounds prompted early childhood educators to develop program methods and content that were responsive to and supportive of children and families, and to significantly adapt or abandon long-standing parent involvement practices designed for stay-at-home mothers who were readily available to volunteer in classrooms and lend material support to other program activities (Powell, 1991).

A concomitant interest in empowering families in their child-rearing role also contributed to the growth of interest in family-centered practices in the late 1970s and 1980s. Programs were urged to build on family strengths rather than family deficits, and to take seriously the child development goals and beliefs of parents (Powell, 1991). The family systems and empowerment themes were especially prominent in the scholarly and professional literatures focused on early childhood programs that serve children with special needs (Dunst & Trivette, 1988).

Dimensions of Family-Centered Practice

There is a fledgling line of research in programs of early education and care that seeks to examine specific dimensions of connections between families and early childhood programs. This is a valuable area of investigation because research has tended to combine elements of the relationship into a global or composite measure. This inhibits an understanding of what matters in family-centered practice. Below we describe some research findings and related practices that explicitly or implicitly build on Bronfenbrenner's (1979) theoretical argument that children benefit from home-school relationships characterized by goal consensus, a balance of power, supportive linkages, and open, frequent, and personal two-way communication between settings.

A study of the quality of relationships between mothers and child care providers found that more *communication* between mother and caregiver about the child was associated with more sensitive and supportive caregiver-child interactions in the child care setting. Further, mothers who engaged in more *partnership behavior* with their child's care provider were more supportive and sensitive with children. The measure of partnership behavior, administered to both mothers and caregivers, focused on sharing information about the child, seeking information about the child, and support for one another (Owen, Ware, & Barfoot, 2000).

Recent research points to the perceived *responsiveness* of a preschool teacher to the child and parent as a distinctive dimension of parent-teacher relationships. The investigation of parent-school relationships in public school pre-kindergarten classrooms found that parents' perceptions of teacher responsiveness to child and parent (e.g., takes interest in child, open to new information) was positively related to children's early reading and social skills and negatively related to problem behaviors. Analyses controlled for the quality of teacher interaction with children in the classroom as well as home factors (Powell et al., 2010). Teacher responsiveness to child/parent interests and backgrounds is conceptually related to the growing interest in how schools respectfully accommodate the growing diversity of families.

The growing racial and ethnic diversity of families with young children in the U.S. heightens interest in whether a *match* between home and school is advantageous to children's learning and development. Results of a study of home-school differences in socialization beliefs and practices conducted in public pre-kindergarten programs help to clarify the circumstances in which home-school matches may promote children's outcomes. Findings indicated that a socialization match (similarity) between home and school was associated with positive kindergarten readiness outcomes when both parents and teachers held child-centered beliefs, promoted child autonomy, and demonstrated warmth and support. In contrast, when both teachers and parents were adult-centered, controlling, and unsupportive, children's school readiness indicators were lower (Barbarin, Downer, Odom, & Head, 2010). Thus, it seems that the substance of a match (home and school socialization practices) may be a key factor in the influence of home-school similarity on children's outcomes.

Parent participation in the life of the early childhood program, including their child's classroom, has long been promoted as beneficial to children's outcomes. As indicated earlier, a growing research literature generally supports this view. For example, *parental school involvement* positively predicted children's social skills and mathematics skills and negatively predicted problem behaviors in the Powell et al. (2010) study. Tools have been developed to help teachers and administrators implement family-centered practices. As an illustration, the Harvard Family Research Project (2010) has developed concrete guidelines for teachers, parents, and principals on how to plan and implement parent-teacher conferences. The guidelines include teachers asking questions and actively listening to parents' views of their child's strengths and needs, emphasizing how both family and school can work together to resolve any problems, and jointly developing an action plan for follow-up communication (www.hfrp.org).

The principles of family-centered practice call for thoughtful consideration of how early childhood teachers support a family's *home-based involvement* in their child's learning. Activity suggestions and resources that encourage family members to include their goals and interests are in keeping with the themes of respect and responsiveness. For example, a book club program developed by Neuman (1996) for low-income parents included a choral reading of a children's book and discussion of three questions: What would you want your child to take away from this book? What kinds of questions or comments would you use to stimulate a discussion of the book? How would you help your child revisit this book?

An overriding attribute of family-centered practice is that early childhood programs recognize the value of providing a *range of family engagement opportunities*. Teachers and the programs in which they work may find it beneficial to engage in targeted outreach to learn about the goals and concerns of parents who do not readily access traditional forms of school-based involvement. For example, a collaborative partnership among families, schools, communities, and institutions of higher education used parent focus groups to better understand the interests of Latino parents, many of whom were not responding to school invitations for participation, and then provided opportunities the family requested (e.g., family night sessions in Spanish that provided information requested by parents; Gillanders, Mason, & Ritchie, 2011).

Research on relationships between families and early childhood programs would greatly benefit from more experimental studies as well as improvements in relationship measures. Most of the current knowledge base is correlational in nature, thereby limiting the field's causal understanding of specific strategies for engaging families. Innovative measurement work is needed to precisely capture exchanges between early childhood programs and families. Currently, researchers generally rely on parent and/or teacher self-report measures even though there are persistent concerns about potential response bias, recall accuracy, and respondent interpretations of questionnaire items. In addition, research questions and methods have not kept pace with conceptual changes in connections between families and early childhood programs that emphasize a relationships paradigm. Parental school involvement practices designed to exemplify the family-centered practice principles of shared decision-making, mutual respect, and partnership have received limited systematic research. Little is known about the effects of promising efforts to ensure joint teacher-parent decision-making about a particular child's goals and experiences, for example, or to incorporate family traditions and cultural practices into a classroom. Basic descriptive information on the nature of common elements of program-family relationships, such as the parent-teacher conferences, would go a long way in determining the extent to which family-centered practices are being enacted in early childhood settings. For instance, in a typical parent-teacher conference, what percentage of time do parents and teachers talk; what topics are initiated by parent and by teacher; what amount of turn-taking occurs in the conversation; what is the quality of conversational flow; and, where appropriate, is a follow-up plan developed and actually implemented?

Preparing Teachers to Implement Family-Centered Practice

Our experience is that individuals who enter the field of early childhood education possess a profound interest in the development and learning of young children coupled with a strong desire to positively influence individual trajectories during a sensitive period of development. The idea that effective work with young children entails sustained and meaningful exchanges with their parents and positive regard for their family contexts is often not part of their original interests or image of good teaching. Yet, rigorous professional preparation recognizes that an effective early childhood teacher is a reflective family-centered practitioner. The extant literature includes a number of promising strategies for preparing preservice and inservice teachers to implement family-based practices.

Case studies of teacher preparation programs suggest that the following competencies are important for teachers to develop: welcoming partnerships with families; identifying and using family strengths to support positive child outcomes; positive communication with families; sharing student progress and performance information in an accessible and actionable way; providing families with concrete suggestions to help their children learn inside and outside the classroom; demonstrating respect, particularly culturally and religiously diverse families and families of children with disabilities; and advocating with families for policies and practices to increase children's learning and achievement (Caspe, Lopez, Chu, & Weiss, 2011). These competencies are generally consistent with the NAEYC and DEC standards for family engagement set forth earlier in this chapter.

Teacher educators indicate that efforts to develop these competencies need to recognize the negative attitudes toward parents often held by preservice teachers (Flanigan, 2007). Further, research with preservice teachers suggests that they typically view parent-teacher relationships as a unidirectional, school-to-family flow of communication, and that their own family and student experiences shape their approach to home-school relations (Graue, 2005). Accordingly, a theme in the extant literature is that a first step in preparing teachers to engage in family-centered practices is to broaden and deepen their understandings of a range of family experiences in parenting roles in diverse communities (e.g., Caspe et al., 2011).

Service learning experiences are one promising strategy for exposing preservice teachers to contemporary parenting issues. For example, a course entitled "Working With Socioculturally Diverse Families" offered in the spring semester of preservice teachers' junior year required 30 hours of providing support and service to diverse families and implementing family events at participating schools. Students were paired with diverse families at schools where they participated in internships related to their literacy and social studies method course. Focus group interviews conducted with student participants at the conclusion of the course suggested there were improvements in their understandings of family diversity, the diverse priorities and resources of families, and how family resources and backgrounds influence children's school achievement (Able, Ghulamani, Mallous, & Glazier, 2014). Student teaching experiences are another opportunity to involve preservice teachers with parents in a direct way, including meaningful participation (beyond observation) in parent-teacher conferences (Baum & McMurray-Schwarz, 2004).

Although experts generally see potential value in a stand-alone course on developing relationships with families, it is frequently recommended that family-centered practices should be embedded in all courses in a teacher preparation program (e.g., Caspe et al., 2011). Discussion of shared readings and structured activities related to teacher-family partnerships are among the options for course instructors. For example, Graue (2005) describes a role-play board game used in coursework that involves a teacher and four parents with diverse backgrounds making their way through the school year.

Research is critically needed on best practices in preparing preservice teachers to implement family-centered practices. There is little evidence on whether the promising teacher preparation strategies identified in this chapter are actually beneficial. This leaves the early childhood field with a "cup half empty" situation regarding the implementation of family-centered practices. Fortunately, there is a growing and increasingly sophisticated research literature on family contexts of early development and on the roles of early childhood educators in supporting families that can be marshaled to bolster the impact of early childhood programs.

Conclusion

To effectively engage in family-centered practices, early childhood teachers need to be familiar with two major bodies of knowledge: the contributions of families and parents to children's development in the early years, and the concept and dimensions of family-centered practices in programs of early education and care. Teachers' understandings of parenting practices should include a firm grasp of how contexts such as culture, socioeconomic status, and family structure influence parenting styles and behaviors, particularly parenting practices related to children's readiness for school. Equally important, teachers need a careful understanding of the significant differences across families in the extent to which their child-rearing beliefs and practices reflect cultural and socioeconomic backgrounds. Teachers' familiarity with the concept and dimensions of family-centered practices should include recognition of shared decision-making and reciprocity as central elements of partnerships with parents. Teachers also need specific skills in initiating and sustaining responsive content-focused interactions with parents that promote a range of opportunities for family engagement with children both at school and at home.

Advances in the effectiveness and widespread implementation of family-centered practice in the early childhood field require attention to two priorities. First, rigorous research is needed on effects of innovative approaches to teacher-family interactions and relationships. Practices that facilitate the principles of shared decision-making and mutual respect need a stronger research base than currently exists. Movement in this direction will require improvements in measures of family-school connections. Second, studies are needed on the methods and outcomes of promising strategies for helping teachers acquire family-centered practice knowledge and skills. Currently, the teacher education field has more thoughtful ideas than firm evidence on how to address negative attitudes toward parents, prevailing views of parent-teacher relationships as unidirectional, and work with parents as episodic school-based events rather than ongoing partnerships characterized by a two-way flow of information and influence. The concept of family-centered work requires early childhood educators to move well beyond the field's historic view of parents as tangential to what happens in classrooms. The preparation of early childhood teachers needs to fully embrace the simple yet challenging idea that best practices with young children require meaningful understandings of and connections to their families.

References

Able, H., Ghulamani, H., Mallous, R., & Glazier, J. (2014). Service learning: A promising strategy for connecting future teachers to the lives of diverse children and their families. *Journal of Early Childhood Teacher Education, 35*(1), 6–21.

Baker, C. E. (2014). African American fathers' contributions to children's early academic achievement: Evidence from two-parent families from the Early Childhood Longitudinal Study-Birth Cohort. *Early Education and Development, 25*(1), 19–35.

Barbarin, O. A., Downer, J., Odom, E., & Head, D. (2010). Home-school differences in beliefs, support, and control during public pre-kindergarten and their link to children's kindergarten readiness. *Early Childhood Research Quarterly, 25*(3), 358–372.

Baum, A. C., & McMurray-Schwarz, P. (2004). Preservice teachers' beliefs about family involvement: Implications for teacher education. *Early Childhood Education Journal, 32*(1), 57–61.

Baumrind, D. (1966). Effects of authoritative parental control on child behavior. *Child Development, 37*(4), 887–907.

Baumrind, D. (1971). Current patterns of parental authority. *Developmental Psychology Monograph, 4*(1–2), 1–103.

Bernier, A., Carlson, S. M., & Whipple, N. (2010). From external regulation to self-regulation: Early parenting precursors of young children's executive functioning. *Child Development, 81*(1), 326–339.

Bindman, S. W., Hindman, A. H., Bowles, R. P., & Morrison, F. J. (2013). The contributions of parental management language to executive function in preschool children. *Early Childhood Research Quarterly, 28*(3), 529–539.

Broderick, C. B. (1993). *Family process: Basics of family systems theory.* Thousand Oaks, CA: Sage.

Bronfenbrenner, U. (1979). *The ecology of human development.* Cambridge, MA: Harvard University Press.

Bronfenbrenner, U., & Morris, P. (2006). The bioecological model of human development. In R. M. Lerner (Vol. Ed.), W. Damon & R. M. Lerner (Eds.-in-Chief), *Handbook of child psychology, Vol 1: Theoretical models of human development* (pp. 793-828). Hoboken, NJ: John Wiley & Sons.

Calkins, S. D. (2004). Early attachment processes and the development of emotional self- regulation. In R. F. Baumeister & K. D. Vohs (Eds.), *Handbook of self-regulation: Research, theory, and applications* (pp. 324–339). New York: Guilford Press.

Caspe, M., Lopez, M. E., Chu, A., & Weiss, H. B. (2011). *Teaching the teachers: Preparing educators to engage families for student achievement.* Cambridge, MA: Harvard Family Research Project.

Chang, L., Schwartz, D., Dodge, K. A., & McBride-Chang, C. (2003). Harsh parenting in relation to child emotion regulation and aggression. *Journal of Family Psychology, 17*(4), 598–606.

Chao, R. (2001). Extending research on the consequences of parenting style for Chinese Americans and European Americans. *Child Development, 72*(6), 1832–1843.

Chazan-Cohen, R., Raikes, H., Brooks-Gunn, J., Ayoub, C., Pan, B. A., Kisker, E. E., Roggman, L., . . . Fuligni, A. S. (2009). Low-income children's school readiness: Parent contributions over the first five years. *Early Education and Development, 20*(6), 958–977.

Coffey, J. S. (2006). Parenting a child with a chronic illness: A metasynthesis. *Pediatric Nursing, 32*(1), 51–59.

Collins, W. A., Madsen, S. D., & Susman-Stillman, A. (2013). Parenting during middle childhood. In M. Bornstein (Ed.), *Handbook of parenting: Children and parenting* (Vol. 1) (pp. 73–102). Mahwah, NJ: Lawrence Erlbaum.

Coontz, S. (2006). *Marriage, a history: How love conquered marriage.* New York: Penguin.

Copple, C., & Bredekamp, S. (Eds.). (2009). *Developmentally appropriate practice in early childhood programs serving children from birth through age 8.* Washington, DC: National Association for the Education of Young Children.

Division for Early Childhood (DEC). (2014). DEC recommended practices in early intervention/early childhood special education. Retrieved from http://www.dec-sped.org/recommendedpractices

Dunst, C. J., & Trivette, C. M. (1988). Helping, helpless, and harm. In J. C. Witt, S. N. Elliot, & F. M. Gresham (Eds.), *Handbook of behavior therapy in education* (pp. 343–376). New York: Springer.

Dunst, C. J., Trivette, C. M., & Hamby, D. W. (2007). Meta-analysis of family-centered helpgiving practices and research. *Mental Retardation and Developmental Disabilities Research Reviews, 13*(4), 370–378.

Farver, J.A.M., Xu, Y., Lonigan, C. J., & Eppe, S. (2013). The home literacy environment and Latino Head Start children's emergent literacy skills. *Developmental Psychology, 49*(4), 775–791.

Finger, B., Kachadourian, L. K., Molnar, D. S., Elden, R. D., Edwards, E. O., & Leonard, K. E. (2010). Alcoholism, associated risk factors, and harsh parenting among fathers: Examining the role of marital aggression. *Addictive Behaviors, 35*(6), 541–548.

Flanigan, C. B. (2007). Preparing preservice teachers to partner with parents and communities: An analysis of college of education faculty focus groups. *The School Community Journal, 17*(2), 89–110.

Gillanders, C., Mason, E., & Ritchie, S. (2011). FirstSchool: An approach that prepares pre-k to 3 educators to effectively interpret and respond to school data. *Young Children, 66*(6), 12–19.

Ginsburg, G. S., & Bronstein, P. (1993). Family factors related to children's intrinsic/extrinsic motivational orientation and academic performance. *Child Development, 64*(5), 1462–1474.

Glick, J. E., Hanish, L. D., Yabiku, S. T., & Bradley, R. H. (2012). Migration timing and parenting practices: Contributions to social development in preschoolers with foreign-born and native-born mothers. *Child Development, 83*(5), 1527–1542.

Graue, E. (2005). Theorizing and describing preservice teachers' images of families and schooling. *Teachers College Record, 107*(1), 157–185.

Greenfield, P. M., Trumball, E., Keller, H., Rothstein-Fisch, C., Suzuki, L. K., & Quiroz, B. (2006). Cultural conceptions of learning and development. In P. A. Alexander & P. H. Winne (Eds.), *Handbook of educational psychology* (pp. 675–692). Mahwah, NJ: Lawrence Erlbaum.

Hart, B., & Risley, T. R. (1995). *Meaningful differences in the everyday experience of young American children.* Baltimore, MD: Paul H Brookes.

Harvard Family Research Project. (2010). Parent-teacher conference tip sheets for principals, teachers, and parents. Cambridge, MA: Harvard Family Research Project. Retrieved from www.hfrp.org

Hindman, A. H., & Morrison, F. J. (2012). Differential contributions of three parenting dimensions to preschool literacy and social skills in a middle-income sample. *Merrill-Palmer Quarterly, 58*(2), 191–223.

Hindman, A. H., Skibbe, L. E., & Morrison, F. J. (2013). Teacher outreach to families during the transition to school: An examination of teachers' practices and their unique contributions to children's early academic outcomes. *Early Childhood Education Journal, 41*(5), 391–399.

Hirsh-Pasek, K., & Burchinal, M. (2006). Mother and caregiver sensitivity over time: Predicting language and academic outcomes with variable- and person-centered approaches. *Merrill-Palmer Quarterly, 52*(3), 449–485.

Hoover-Dempsey, K. V., Walker, J. M. T., Sandler, H. M., Whetsel, D., Green, C. L., Wilkins, A. S., & Closson, K. (2005). Why do parents become involved? Research findings and implications. *The Elementary School Journal, 106*(2), 105–130.

Huntsinger, C. S., & Jose, P. E. (2009). Parental involvement in children's schooling: Different meanings in different cultures. *Early Childhood Research Quarterly, 24*(4), 398–410.

Joussemet, M., Koestner, R., Lekes, N., & Landry, R. (2005). A longitudinal study of the relationship of maternal autonomy support to children's adjustment and achievement in school. *Journal of Personality, 73*(5), 1215–1235.

Kaufman, D., Gesten, E., Santa Lucia, R. C., Salcedo, O., Rendina-Gobioff, G., & Gadd, R. (2000). The relationship between parenting style and children's adjustment: The parents' perspective. *Journal of Child and Family Studies, 9*(2), 231–245.

Kuppens, S., Grietens, H., Onghena, P., & Michiels, D. (2009). Associations between parental control and children's overt and relational aggression. *British Journal of Developmental Psychology, 27*(3), 607–623.

Landry, S. H., Smith, K. E., Swank, P. R., Assell, M. A., & Vellet, S. (2001). Does early responsive parenting have a special importance for children's development or is consistency across early childhood necessary? *Developmental Psychology, 37*(3), 387–403.

Lareau, A. (2003). *Unequal childhoods: Class, race, and family life.* Berkeley, CA: University of California Press.

Liable, D., & Thompson, R. (2006). Early socialization: A relationship perspective. In J. Grusec & P. Hastings (Eds.), *Handbook of socialization: Theory and research* (pp. 181–207). New York: Guilford Press.

Maccoby, E. E. (1992). The role of parents in the socialization of children: A historical overview. *Developmental Psychology, 28*(6), 1006–1017.

Magnusson, K. A., & Duncan, G. J. (2002). Parents in poverty. In M. H. Bornstein (Ed.), *Handbook of parenting* (2nd ed.) (pp. 95–121). Mahwah, NJ: Erlbaum.

Marcon, R. A. (1999). Positive relationships between parent school involvement and public school inner-city preschoolers' development and academic performance. *School Psychology Review, 28*(3), 395–412.

McClelland, M. M., Cameron, C. E., Wanless, S. B., & Murray, A. (2007). Executive function, behavioral self-regulation, and social-emotional competence. In O. N. Saracho & B. Spodek (Eds.), *Contemporary perspectives on social learning in early childhood education* (Vol. 7) (pp. 113–137). United States: Information Age Publishing.

McWayne, C. M., Melzi, G., Schick, A. R., Kennedy, J. L., & Mundt, K. (2013). Defining family engagement among Latino Head Start parents: A mixed-methods measurement development study. *Early Childhood Research Quarterly, 28*(3), 593–607.

Morris, A. S., Silk, J. S., Steinberg, L., Myers, S. S., & Robinson, L. R. (2007). The role of the family context in the development of emotion regulation. *Social Development, 16*(2), 361–388.

National Institute of Child Health and Human Development Early Child Care Research Network (NICHD ECCRN). (2008). Mothers' and fathers' support for child autonomy and early school achievement. *Developmental Psychology, 44*(4), 895–907.

Neuman, S. (1996). Children engaging in storybook reading: The influence of access to print resources, opportunity, and parental interaction. *Early Childhood Research Quarterly, 11*(4), 495–513.

Owen, M. T., Ware, A. M., & Barfoot, B. (2000). Caregiver-mother partnership behavior and the quality of caregiver-child and mother-child interactions. *Early Childhood Research Quarterly, 15*(3), 413–428.

Powell, D. R. (1991). Parents and programs: Early childhood as a pioneer in parent involvement and support. In S. L. Kagan (Ed.), *The care and education of American's young children: Obstacles and opportunities. Ninetieth yearbook of the National Society for the Study of Education, Part I* (pp. 91–109). Chicago, IL: University of Chicago Press.

Powell, D. R., Son, S., File, N., & San Juan, R. R. (2010). Parent-school relationships and children's academic and social outcomes in public school pre-kindergarten. *Journal of School Psychology, 48*(4), 269–292.

Rowe, M. L. (2008). Child-directed speech: Relation to socioeconomic status, knowledge of child development and child vocabulary skill. *Journal of Child Language, 35*(1), 185–205.

Schmitt, S. A., Simpson, A. M., & Friend, M. (2011). A longitudinal assessment of the home literacy environment and early language. *Infant and Child Development, 20*(6), 409–431.

Seifer, R., Dickstein, S., Parade, S., Hayden, L. C., Magee, K. D., & Schiller, M. (2014). Mothers' appraisal of goodness of fit and children's social development. *International Journal of Behavioral Development, 38*(1), 86–97.

Skwarchuk, S., Sowinski, C., & LeFevre, J. (2014). Formal and informal home learning activities in relation to children's early numeracy and literacy skills: The development of a home numeracy model. *Journal of Experimental Child Psychology, 121,* 63–84.

Tamis-LeMonda, C. S., Way, N., Hughes, D., Yoshikawa, H., Kalman, R. K., & Niwa, E. Y. (2008). Parents' goals for children: The dynamic coexistence of individualism and collectivism in cultures and individuals. *Social Development, 17*(1), 183–209.

Verma, S., & Sharma, D. (2006). Cultural dynamics of family relations among Indian adolescents in varied contexts. In K. H. Rubin & O. B. Chung (Eds.). *Parenting beliefs, behaviors, and parent-child relations: A cross-cultural perspective* (pp.185–205). New York: Psychology Press.

Vygotsky, L. A. (1962). *Thought and language.* Cambridge, MA: MIT Press.

Walker, A. K., & MacPhee, D. (2011). How home gets to school: Parental control strategies predict children's school readiness. *Early Childhood Research Quarterly, 26*(3), 355–364.

Weisleder, A., & Fernald, A. (2013). Talking to children matters: Early language experience strengthens processing and builds vocabulary. *Psychological Science, 24*(11), 2143–2152.

Whipple, G. M. (Ed.). (1929). *Preschool and parental education. Twenty-eighth yearbook of the National Society for the Study of Education, Part I.* Bloomington, IL: Public School Publishing Co.

10

WHAT TEACHERS NEED TO KNOW

Professional Ethics[1]

Nancy K. Freeman and Stephanie Feeney

The purpose of this chapter is to identify what teachers of young children need to know about professional ethics. We provide an overview of the moral dimensions of teaching; identify the codes of ethics that guide teachers' work, with a particular focus on codes that address early childhood educators; provide an overview of moral development and theories of ethical thinking; consider how to infuse ethics in students' curriculum; and explore how an early childhood teacher educator can go about teaching ethics during every stage of early childhood educators' professional development.

The Moral Dimensions of Teaching

Scholars who investigate the moral dimensions of teaching look at what teachers need to know from two perspectives. The first has to do with teaching students moral behavior. During the first half of the twentieth century the emphasis was on teachers' responsibility to nurture and enhance their students' moral development (Campbell, 2008). One way teachers accomplish this task is by modeling fairness, honesty, caring, and doing what is right every day. Another way teachers support their students' moral development is by implementing an explicit moral development curriculum. These programs, referred to with terms such as "values education," "character education," and "peace education" are designed to shape students' sense of right and wrong and guide them toward becoming productive members of society (Campbell, 2008; Willemse, Lunenberg, & Korthagen, 2008).

The second moral dimension of teaching, the one that is the focus of this chapter, has to do with the particular moral obligations of teaching professionals. Contemporary educational scholars have expressed concerns that the current emphasis on preparing teachers to address rigorous learning standards while readying their students to take high-stakes tests has resulted in teacher education programs that all too often emphasize the technical skills teachers need while either ignoring or taking for granted teachers' ability to navigate the moral dimensions of teaching (Boon, 2011; Campbell, 2008; Hansen, 2001; Shapira-Lishchinsky, 2011; Willemse et al., 2008). Perhaps these moral dimensions were overlooked because many assume that teachers are, after all, good people (Strike, 1990). The fact is, however, that developing teachers need explicit instruction in their moral responsibilities to the students, families, and communities they serve. They need to understand how "matters of what is fair, right, just and virtuous are always present" in classrooms and schools (Fenstermacher, 1990, p. 133), and be prepared to respond to moral issues they encounter in their work thoughtfully and from a clear understanding of their profession's stance about the answer to the question, "What should a good teacher do?"

This strand of inquiry, which has provided the foundation for early childhood educators' interest in professional ethics, attracted the attention of educational philosophers beginning in the 1980s (Campbell, 2008). Discussions of the moral dimensions of teaching begin with the realization that teachers bring their personal morality, that is, their views about their obligations and how they should behave, to their workplace (Kipnis, 1987). Individuals' personal morality is influenced by their family, religious traditions, and the communities to which they belong. Without having established a personal sense of right and wrong, teachers would not be prepared to reflect on the moral dimensions of teaching. This personal moral compass provides an essential foundation for moral professionalism, but it is not enough because our diverse society welcomes those who bring differing perspectives to the workplace. For that reason, teachers need *moral competence,* or knowledge of how members of their profession have collectively and systematically reflected on the field's moral beliefs and practices, and skill applying this collective wisdom to their work (Feeney, 2012).

Educators' Codes of Ethics

Codes of ethics provide teachers with moral guidance. They are important because they extend individuals' personal morality by identifying how they and their colleagues can agree. Codes of ethics articulate practitioners' obligations to society; offer a vision of how teachers should behave; express the field's view of fairness and right and wrong; and address practitioners' professional obligations. They help educators make decisions that are fair to individual children as well as to groups of children, honor their responsibilities to families, guide collegial relationships, and serve the best interest of the community and the larger society. A code of ethics can provide a justification when practitioners are faced with making a difficult decision and create a vehicle for the profession to speak with a collective voice (Feeney et al., 2012; Katz & Ward, 1978; Rich, 1985; Shapira-Lishchinsky, 2011). In fact, codes are so important that when teachers adhere to their code of ethics they are satisfying one of the criteria that distinguishes teaching as a *profession* rather than an *occupation* and help to instill confidence that members of the profession will serve the public good (Feeney, 2012).

Codes for Pre-K-12 Teachers

A number of teachers' organizations have developed codes of ethics to guide their members' work with students from preschool through grade 12. The most widely distributed and broadly applicable code was adopted by the National Education Association in 1975. It has been criticized for being "brief and general and [unable] . . . to serve as a functional standard in cases of any ambiguity" (Strike, 1990, p. 207). The American Montessori Society also has a code, which was first adopted in 1969, expanded in 1975, and updated in 2008 and 2010 (American Montessori Society, 2010).

Codes for Early Childhood Educators

Early childhood organizations throughout many parts of the English-speaking world have taken steps to guide practitioners' ethical decision-making by adopting codes of professional ethics. The National Association for the Education of Young Children (NAEYC) is the United States' largest and most influential professional association devoted to the care and education of young children. Its efforts to map the ethical dimensions of teaching and to support practitioners' efforts to apply its code make it stand out among teachers' professional organizations (Freeman, 2000). Another code of ethics that applies to many early childhood educators is that of the Council for Exceptional Children's Division for Early Childhood (DEC, 1996, 2009). This code was originally approved in 1996 and was reaffirmed in 1999, 2002, and 2009.

In addition to codes developed in the United States, early childhood professional organizations in Australia, New Zealand, Singapore, and several of Canada's provinces have developed codes that reflect their local values and culture (Association for Early Childhood Educators [Singapore], n.d.; Certification Council of Early Childhood Educators of Nova Scotia, n.d.; Early Childhood Australia, 2006; Early Childhood Development Association of Prince Edward Island, n.d.; Early Childhood Educators of British Columbia, 2008; New Zealand Early Childhood Services, n.d.).

The NAEYC Code of Ethical Conduct

The NAEYC Code of Ethical Conduct is the best-known and most widely used code of ethics for early childhood educators in the United States. NAEYC took the first step toward the development of a code of ethics in 1976 when its Governing Board passed a resolution calling for its development. Work on ethics did not begin to move forward, however, until after the 1978 publication of *Ethical Behavior in Early Childhood Education*, a monograph authored by Lilian Katz and Evangeline Ward. They identified two characteristics of the work of early childhood educators that are as important to consider today as they were more than 35 years ago.

The first and most important issue identified by Katz and Ward relates to the power teachers and caregivers have over the vulnerable children with whom they work. Because every aspect of the children's day is controlled by adults, Katz and Ward advised that a code of ethics was needed to remind early childhood educators to protect children from harm and to respect them in the ordinary and not-so-ordinary decisions they make every day. This power disparity between adults and children may be the reason that early childhood educators in many places have committed themselves to ethical behavior as spelled out in a code. The second significant issue they addressed was the multiplicity of clients served by early childhood educators. Katz and Ward recognized that the teachers of young children need guidance about how to balance and prioritize their responsibilities to children, families, their employing agencies, and the community when these interests conflict. What is a teacher to do, for example, when a mother asks her to keep her 4-year-old son from napping even though he needs a nap to be able to function in the afternoon? How should a committed early childhood educator respond when a family needs the services of his program even though they are temporarily unable to pay tuition? What should they do when the administration of their agency asks them to do something they believe is not in the best interests of children? Katz and Ward realized that when teachers' resolutions to these kinds of dilemmas were based on a code of ethics, their decisions would reflect the field's history, values, and collective guidance.

The NAEYC Board did not reach consensus about how to move forward on the development of ethical guidelines until 1984. At that time they established an Ethics Commission and asked Stephanie Feeney to lead efforts to map the ethical dimensions of early childhood education. Working with University of Hawaii ethics specialist and Professor of Philosophy Kenneth Kipnis, Feeney guided NAEYC members in a collaborative process that led to the identification of core values, ideals, and principles that form the moral foundation for the early childhood practitioners' work (Feeney et al., 2012). The first version of the *NAEYC Code of Ethical Conduct* was adopted as a position statement by the NAEYC Governing Board in 1989 (Feeney & Kipnis). The organization made a commitment to review and revise the Code regularly to keep it current and relevant. Members of NAEYC were asked to participate by providing feedback to the Association for the 1992, 1997, and 2005 revisions of the Code and during the development of Supplements to the Code that address the unique ethical responsibilities of adult educators (NAEYC, 2004) and program administrators (NAEYC, 2006, 2011). The NAEYC Governing Board led efforts to update and reaffirm the Code in 2011 (NAEYC, 2011a).

NAEYC has ensured that the Code and supporting resources are readily accessible. The original Code is available in English and Spanish on the NAEYC website and as inexpensive brochures.

The Supplements are also available online. *Ethics and the Early Childhood Educator* (Feeney et al., 2012), a book that examines each section of the Code and models its application, was initially published by NAEYC in 1999 and updated in 2005. A second edition was released in 2012. Its companion book, *Teaching the NAEYC Code of Ethical Conduct: A Sourcebook* (Feeney et al., 2008) was first released in 2000 and updated in 2008. The NAEYC website also provides a "Code of Ethical Conduct Tool Kit" with an introductory PowerPoint, a collection of scenarios, a bibliography of its publications that address professional ethics, and videos of an interview with Stephanie Feeney in which she describes the Code's development and application.

In addition, NAEYC's widely distributed journal, *Young Children*, features a regular column, "Focus on Ethics," which alternates presenting commonly occurring ethical issues with analysis informed by input from practitioners in the field. The organization also grants permission to reprint the Code and its Supplements in textbooks and similar publications at no cost, which increases their distribution and builds awareness among students at every stage of their professional development.

The application and influence of the NAEYC Code has been enhanced by the endorsements of the Association for Childhood Education International (ACEI) and the Southern Early Childhood Association (SECA), and by its adoption by the National Association for Family Child Care (NAFCC). It is notable that early childhood educators in Singapore and British Columbia used the NAEYC Code to inform the codes that they developed for early childhood educators.

The NAEYC Code of Ethics is not enforced because entrance into the field is not regulated (as is entrance to many recognized professions) and membership in NAEYC is open to all. Leaders in the field have taken the stance, nonetheless, that given the vulnerability of young children and the great disparity in power between children and their adult caregivers, even a voluntary code of ethics provides valuable safeguards for children participating in early care and education programs.

Ethical Issues Faced by Early Childhood Educators

Over the years we have learned that early childhood educators face ethical issues on an almost daily basis. Some of the regularly recurring issues include:

- balancing responsibilities to individual children with the needs of their classmates;
- program policies, including assessment practices, that teachers believe are not in children's best interest, including those that may be harmful to children;
- navigating differences between families' wishes and teachers' professional best judgment;
- witnessing colleagues who treat children harshly, are intimidating, sarcastic, or belittling;
- concerns about colleagues' inappropriate behavior including breaches of confidentiality and failure to meet their responsibilities;
- encountering peer pressure from colleagues who do not support practices that are responsive to children's needs; and
- observing violations of licensing or school regulations.

(Feeney & Sysko, 1986)

The NAEYC Code of Ethics has proven to be a valuable resource for individuals facing these kinds of issues. It is noteworthy that researchers have found that early childhood educators are not alone. Elementary and secondary preservice and inservice teachers report that they also encounter issues similar to those faced by the teachers of young children (Campbell, 2008; Colnerud, 1997; Shapira-Lishchinsky, 2011).

The fact that the Code has been endorsed by ACEI, which focuses on children from birth to 13 and "often concerns itself with issues that impact children during their teenage years" (ACEI, n.d.), demonstrates that it has also proven to be applicable to the work of professionals who work with children well beyond the early childhood years. We believe that teacher educators working with preservice teachers preparing to teach in a wide range of settings would benefit from learning to apply the NAEYC Code.

Teaching about Ethics

The first, and most important, reason that every early childhood educator should learn the Code and build it into their professional repertoire is that it is designed to protect children. Principle 1.1, states, "Above all, we shall not harm children. We shall not participate in practices that are emotionally damaging, physically harmful, disrespectful, degrading, dangerous, exploitative, or intimidating to children. *This principle has precedence over all others in this Code*" (emphasis in the original). This is a powerful statement affirming that the first priority of every early childhood educator should be the well-being of children, and that every action and decision should first be considered in light of its potential to benefit or to harm children.

Because teachers who work with young children face ethical issues every day, knowledge of the field's ethical guidelines is now part of the field's core knowledge and required competencies. NAEYC-accredited programs for young children are required to document that staff are aware of and use ethical guidelines and their professional development plans must include regular discussions of ethical issues (NAEYC, 2013).

Accreditation standards of post-secondary early childhood programs require graduates to show increasing competence using the Code. Associate degree programs must demonstrate that their students know about and uphold the NAEYC Code. Graduates of initial certification Early Childhood, Early Childhood Special Education, and Early Intervention programs must demonstrate their knowledge of the NAEYC and/or the DEC Code, and graduates pursuing advanced degrees in early childhood must demonstrate an "*in-depth understanding and thoughtful application of* NAEYC Code of Ethical Conduct" (emphasis in the original) (NAEYC, 2010, p. 56; DEC, 2007a; DEC 2007b). Graduates from ACEI-accredited programs (which includes kindergarten and primary grades) must be able to "reflect on their practice in light of . . . professional ethics, [and] continually evaluate the effects of their professional decisions and actions on students, families and other professionals" (p. 2). These standards reference both the NAEYC and NEA Codes (ACEI, 2007). And finally, the National Board for Professional Teaching Standards (NBPTS) joins these organizations in emphasizing the importance of ethical practice. It describes accomplished teachers of young children as "proactive professionals who conduct themselves in responsible and ethical ways both inside and beyond the classroom" (NBPTS, 2012, p. 101), but does not reference specific ethical guidelines.

Early childhood teacher education faculty members are responsible for ensuring that their students have the knowledge and skills that are prescribed in teacher education standards. This includes the responsibility to teach their students about ethical practice. Accreditation standards for associate degree, initial certification, and advanced degree programs require that instructors in post-secondary programs know about and abide by the NAEYC Code as well as its Supplement for Adult Educators (NAEYC, 2010, 2011b). This requirement acknowledges that future teachers need to understand their moral responsibilities and learn to address the most common ethical situations they face in their work.

There is evidence that time and effort invested in teaching ethics is well-spent. Preservice teachers report that they appreciate the opportunity to study professional ethics and welcome opportunities to practice analyzing ethical dilemmas early in their professional preparation (Boon, 2011). What's more, when ethics is part of students' professional preparation, they report that they are less anxious about assuming full responsibility for their classroom and developing collegial relationships with school staff, believe they have enhanced their classroom management skills, have an increased sense of self-efficacy, and express an increased commitment to the field (Boon, 2011; Daniels, Mandzuk, Perry, & Moore, 2011).

Preparing to Teach Ethics

Faculty preparing to teach professional ethics should be familiar with major theories of moral development and the fundamentals of ethical theory. They must also be familiar with applicable code(s) of ethical conduct. This background knowledge does no good, however, if they do not know how to teach ethics effectively. To do that they must know the content, consider the characteristics of the students with whom they will be working, and tailor their instruction to their audience.

Theories of moral development. An understanding of two prominent theories of moral development, those of Lawrence Kohlberg and Carol Gilligan, can help early childhood teacher educators to understand the moral development and ethical reasoning abilities of their students.

Kohlberg's six-stage theory of moral development (see Table 10.1) was built upon Piagetian stage theory and grew out of 20 years of study during which he followed a cohort of male Harvard students. Kohlberg described the stages of moral development as "systems of thought" that occurred in a hierarchical "invariant sequence" (Kohlberg & Hersh, 1977, p. 54).

Carol Gilligan began studying moral development with Kohlberg, but soon identified gaps in his theory that she believed were created by the fact that his work was based on the study of privileged white men. Gilligan's research on women facing the wrenching decision of whether or not to have an abortion led her to conceptualize a theory of moral development that focuses on relationships and the connections between individuals. Gilligan's feminine perspective of morality sees dilemmas not in terms of right and wrong as did Kohlberg, but rather of conflicting responsibilities. She observed that resolving moral dilemmas requires thinking that is "contextual and narrative rather than formal and abstract" (Gilligan, 1993, p. 19). Like Kohlberg, Gilligan described three stages of moral development, but hers is not a rigid stage theory. She believes individuals' moral growth is a fluid and flexible process. More than thirty years after they were created, Kohlberg's and Gilligan's theories continue to provide a valuable foundation for teacher educators' understanding of their students' approach to moral reasoning and suggest strategies for supporting their developing skills in ethical deliberation. Knowledge of Kohlberg's Stages can help early childhood educators to understand how their students approach moral dilemmas. A student who is bound by rules will have a hard time thinking of alternatives based on a higher level of moral reasoning. A college teacher can help a student reach a higher level, but it takes time and skill, and these efforts are not always successful.

Table 10.1 Kohlberg's Stages of Moral Development

Stage level	*Characteristics*	*Approach to moral decision making*
I & II: Pre-conventional	Thinking is concrete and individual. Goal is to avoid punishment by abiding by the rules.	Resolve ethical issues either in favor of the party with the most power or by looking out for their own best interests.
III & IV: Conventional	Embrace the golden rule and demonstrate loyalty and cooperation with their family or group. Goals are to please others by conforming to their expectations and follow the rules that maintain the social order.	Resolve dilemmas by considering existing social rules and finding resolutions that maintain the social status quo.
V & VI: Post-conventional, autonomous, or principled	Primary goal is the welfare of others. May be guided by universal principles and their individual conscience.	Seek resolutions to moral dilemmas by considering universal principles which lie beyond systems of laws and regulations. Not bound by what has come before. Few adults reach this highest level of moral reasoning.

Table 10.2 Gilligan's States of Moral Development

Stage level	*Characteristics*	*Approach to moral decision making*
I: Pre-conventional	Morality is focused on survival.	Focus is on one's own needs.
II: Conventional	Morality involves responsibility for others, self-sacrifice is seen as desirable.	Prioritizes the responsibility to care for others, sometimes at the expense of one's own self-interest.
III: Post-conventional	Morality involves striving to protect self and others.	Do not hurt self or others. The needs of self and others are equally important. Avoiding conflict and maintaining relationships are priorities.

Gilligan's ideas, found in Table 10.2, are particularly useful for teacher educators because the great majority of those who teach young children are women (Saluja, Early, & Clifford, 2002). Over the years that we have been working on professional ethics in early childhood education (ECE), we have found that many early childhood educators approach ethical dilemmas from the ethic of care. They are often so focused on preserving relationships that they need to be reminded that some situations call for making a difficult decision that will not please everyone.

Ethical theory. As students engage in moral deliberations, their thinking will likely reflect alignment with one of three traditions of moral philosophy. Each of these approaches to moral decision-making offers a different way of thinking about how to resolve the dilemmas of practice (Kidder, 2009; Strike & Soltis, 2009).

The first tradition of moral philosophy is called *utilitarianism* (or *consequentialism*) and derives from the nineteenth-century writings of British philosophers Jeremy Bentham and John Stuart Mill. Philosophers from this school of thought maintain that the ultimate basis for any judgment about the rightness or wrongness of an action should be decided based on its consequences. In other words, the best action is the one that benefits the most people and would result in the most good (Copp, 2006). Utilitarianism has been criticized on the grounds that it is impossible to foresee the consequences of an action and that even if a large number of people benefit from an action, others may be hurt by it, and that it can be very difficult if not impossible to be impartial when one has a personal stake in the outcome of a difficult situation (Frey, 2000).

The principle that can be drawn from this philosophic tradition is, "Do what is best for the greatest number of people" (Kidder, 2009, p. 152). A question that illustrates utilitarian thinking is, "Could I justify this choice to the community at large if I were asked to do so by a television reporter?"

A second tradition is that of the *categorical imperative* (or *universality*) which is based on the writings of Immanuel Kant, an eighteenth-century German philosopher. His approach focuses on individuals' conscience and the *rightness* of an action, not on its consequences. Philosophers from this school believe that people should act so that their actions could become a universal standard that everyone should follow. They believe that acting this way creates the greatest good because it promotes right intentions and actions. Critics suggest that demanding that everyone always follow the same philosophic principles would be impossibly strict and that generally accepted principles can be in conflict with each other, creating the task of prioritizing whose interests and which acts are more "right" than the others (Kamm, 2000).

The philosophic principle that can be derived from this approach is, "Follow your highest sense of principle" (Kidder 2009, p. 152). Questions that early childhood educators can ask themselves based on Kant's approach to moral philosophy are: "Is this the way I think that all professionals in our field should act?" and "Is this action the best one for the profession as a whole?"

The third philosophic approach applies to private realms such as family and friends, as well as to professional practice. Its origins lie in the doctrines of all of the major religions, although it is most often associated with Christianity. This tradition stresses individuals' responsibility to care for others and advises that actions be evaluated based on the extent to which they promote the interests of others and preserve the fabric of relationships (Held, 2006). This approach is consistent with ideas about women's morality, described by Nel Noddings (1992) and Carol Gilligan (1993), referred to as the *ethic of care.* Critics note that the drawback of this approach is that it does not give direct guidance to individuals trying to make difficult ethical choices.

The Golden Rule, "Do unto others as you would have others do unto you," is familiar advice with roots in the philosophic tradition of caring. As you deliberate about this perspective you might ask yourself, "Is this the way I would want others to treat me?" or "Is this solution respectful of people and relationships?"

Considering the implications of these three schools of thought can help early childhood educators to think about the impact of proposed resolutions to dilemmas, but they provide no clear-cut formulas for ethical actions (Feeney et al., 2012).

Teaching Professional Ethics[2]

The sections that follow give a brief introduction to how an early childhood teacher educator might approach the teaching of ethics as part of an early childhood program or course in a college setting, or as part of an inservice training program.

Where Does Ethics Fit in the Curriculum?

As faculty prepare to teach ethics as a part of the curriculum in an accredited degree, they need to consider where ethics will fit into students' program of study. There are two ways in which this can be approached: instruction in ethics can be integrated into several courses and or it can be taught as a stand-alone topic (Boon, 2011). Whether integrated, taught as a stand-alone topic, or a combination of the two, it is important to ensure that instruction in ethics is explicit and that its place is established and formalized. There is a risk that if "everyone" teaches ethics that no one will actually make it a prominent part of their teaching and students will never have the opportunity to develop their knowledge of ethics or the skills they need to apply ethics to their work.

Objectives of Instruction in Ethics

When planning a course, a unit of study within a course, or an inservice session on professional ethics, faculty should remember that early childhood educators need to learn about the NAEYC Code and also need opportunities to learn to analyze, debate, and examine ethical issues (Boon, 2011). Consider these objectives for teaching professional ethics. They demonstrate an appreciation for prior knowledge, include an introduction to professional ethics, and provide opportunities for students to practice applying a code of ethical conduct. Courses devoted to ethics are likely to address all of these objectives, while courses that include ethics as a part of the curriculum and inservice trainings might identify those that are appropriate.

As a result of taking this course (or inservice training) students will:

- be able to identify personal values and morality that they bring to their work with young children;
- be aware of ethical issues early childhood educators may face in professional practice;
- understand the difference between personal values and morality and professional ethics;
- be familiar with the NAEYC Code that will help them address the kinds of ethical issues that occur in work with young children;

- be able to identify ethical issues and to understand the difference between an ethical responsibility and an ethical dilemma;
- develop skill in resolving ethical dilemmas that occur in early childhood settings (that is, they will be able to combine guidance from the Code with good professional judgment to reach an informed resolution to an ethical dilemma); and
- increase their ethical commitment (that is, they will likely apply what they have learned about ethics and ethical analysis in their workplace).

(Brophy-Herb, Kostelnik, & Stein, 2001; Feeney et al., 2012; Keefer & Davis, 2012)

Taking Students' Characteristics into Account

Early childhood educators know how important it is to provide learning experiences that match the needs and interests of their students. This is as true when teaching adults as it is when working with young children. Engaging with professional ethics is beneficial for early childhood educators at every stage in their careers, but activities that are appropriate for teaching professional ethics to preservice and beginning teachers are different from those that one would use with veteran teachers who may have had previous experience learning about ethics. Skillful instructors take their students' characteristics into account and match their teaching to their students' needs and interests.

A person entering the field may first encounter professional ethics in an introductory course or in a preservice training program. Even though novices are likely to be focused on practical teaching skills, learning about the moral and ethical dimensions of teaching early on can help them to focus on the field's shared values and commitments while making it clear that they are not just learning a job, but joining a community. The goal of teaching ethics to this group should be to make the code come alive by demonstrating how it is relevant to teachers' work and to create in novices the disposition to turn to the code to help them honor ethical responsibilities and resolve ethical dilemmas.

Experienced teachers of young children will have had real-life experiences involving ethical issues. They will probably be aware of a code of ethics but will benefit from opportunities to delve more deeply and seek guidance for how to systematically address ethical issues. They will benefit from opportunities to use a code to identify ethical responsibilities, to propose resolutions to real-world dilemmas, and to clearly explain the rationale for the actions they decide to take.

Advanced students are likely to have many years' experience in the field. They may know the code and be eager to share ethical issues they are facing and seek resolutions to these issues. As emerging leaders in the field, they may also be eager for guidance about how they might share their knowledge of the code in their workplace or other settings.

Effective Strategies for Teaching Ethics

Effective teachers begin each session, whether a class meeting or an inservice training, by clearly stating its purpose and the desired learning outcomes. Because discussions of ethical issues may bring to light differing values and beliefs and often involve sharing personal experiences, it is especially important to establish ground rules that will create a nonthreatening environment where participants can trust that their views will be respected and confidences honored. Effective lessons on ethics often begin with a warm-up or ice-breaking activity designed to lay the groundwork for developing trust. Experienced adult educators are likely to have a repertoire of these kinds of exercises, or should see Chapter 1 of *Teaching the NAEYC Code of Ethical Conduct: Activity Sourcebook* (Feeney et al., 2008) for suggestions.

How instruction in ethics is organized will depend on the students: their previous exposure to the study of professional ethics, how much experience they have had with young children, and their level of maturity. Consider these approaches for addressing each of the objectives of ethics instruction identified above.

Exploring personal morality and values. A good place to begin with beginners or students who have not been exposed to instruction in ethics is to have them identify the personal values they bring to their work. We have found it useful to guide students through reflective activities that ask them to identify their personal beliefs and values. They may find that these beliefs are so natural and instinctive that they have difficulty putting them into words or explaining them to classmates whose early experiences, culture, and family backgrounds may be very different from their own. It might then be helpful to ask students to consider the source of some of their personal values, to prioritize their values, or to compare some of their strongly held beliefs with those of their classmates to highlight the fact that the field welcomes individuals with a wide range of beliefs about personal issues that do not relate directly to working with children and families.

Awareness of issues. When introducing ethics to students, the next thing you might do is help them increase their sensitivity to the kinds of ethical issues teachers of young children are likely to encounter. Class discussions might reveal that students have wondered how they should handle the 4-year-old who is so rough that he hurts other children until their parents begin to complain, how they should respond when the father of a 2-year-old demands to know who had bitten his toddler, or how they might approach a teacher who is routinely harsh and disrespectful when disciplining her first graders. Discussions with students about what they should do in these difficult situations should help them to see the value in a code, which can help to guide them toward a response that is right, fair, and just, and that can also back them up when they take a moral position.

Understanding the difference between personal values and morality and professional ethics. Personal values and morals form a necessary foundation for individuals' professional practice, but they need to be complemented with professional values and standards of ethical behavior for members of a profession to be able to speak with one voice about their professional responsibilities.

Guiding students through an exploration of issues like those described above can help them understand why their personal and idiosyncratic values are not sufficient to guide their actions in a professional setting. It will help them understand the contribution the clearly stated standards in the NAEYC Code can make by providing a shared common ground for colleagues who strive to do the right thing for children and families.

Becoming familiar with the NAEYC Code. After having led students in identifying their personal values; exploring the kinds of ethical issues they are likely to face in their work; and illustrating how personal values need to be augmented by the field's code of ethics to ensure that professional decision-making reflects the field's values and ethical guidelines, it is then time to help them become familiar with the NAEYC Code.

One place to begin is by putting the spotlight on the Core Values that are the foundation for the Code. The instructor might ask students to first brainstorm a list of what they believe to be the field's core values, or important principles upon which all early childhood educators can agree, and to then compare their list with the Core Values identified in the NAEYC Code. It is surprising how similar these lists usually are. Other activities that have students reading and thinking about the Code are worthwhile for beginners. For example, they might rephrase its items or re-assemble a Code that has been cut apart (with identifying items removed).

After students have developed some familiarity with the content and organization of the Code, they will benefit from seeing how it can guide their efforts to deal with some of the ethical issues they encounter in their work. It is important to help them understand that the Code is not an instruction manual or a cookbook but is, instead, a tool to guide ethical decision-making. As students grapple with realistic scenarios it may be helpful to remind them that "doing ethics . . . is nothing more than *systematic critical reflection about [their] obligations*" (emphasis in the original; Kipnis, 1987, p. 27), and that a code of ethics provides a framework for this reflection.

We have found that beginners who are not yet facing ethical issues in the classroom particularly enjoy and benefit from games that engage them with the Code. The most effective activity we have found is the "Is it Ethical?" game. It presents short ethical scenarios, describes the way the early childhood educator in the situation chose to respond, and asks "Is it ethical?" Students then refer to specific items in the Code to justify their decision that the suggested response is, or is not, ethical (Feeney et al., 2008).

Learning to identify ethical issues and to respond to them using the Code. After having become acquainted with the Code and practiced identifying ethical and not-ethical responses to scenarios, students may be ready to analyze realistic ethical situations and to develop responses that answer the question, "What should the good early childhood educator do?" In order to be able to engage in this kind of analysis, they need to be able to identify ethical responsibilities that are clearly spelled out in the Code and contrast them with ethical dilemmas— "situation[s] for which there is more than one possible solution, each of which can be justified in moral terms" (Feeney et al., 2012, p. 26).

Instructors may want to begin by having students work with cases found in NAEYC publications such as *Ethics and the Early Childhood Educator* (Feeney et al., 2012), *Teaching the NAEYC Code of Ethical Conduct: Activity Sourcebook* (Feeney et al., 2008), the Ethics Toolkit posted on the NAEYC website, and the "Focus on Ethics" columns in *Young Children.* We suggest beginning with these published sources because developing scenarios that stand up to rigorous analysis is more difficult than it might seem.

It is helpful to provide a framework that guides students in applying professional guidelines to realistic scenarios (Brophy-Herb et al., 2001; Feeney & Freeman, 2014; Warnick & Silverman, 2011). This systematic process is intended to support childhood educators' developing ethical competence:

- Identify the problem and determine if it involves ethics.
- Determine if it is an ethical responsibility or an ethical dilemma.
- Identify the stakeholders affected by the situation and the early childhood professional's responsibilities to each.
- Brainstorm possible resolutions.
- Consider ethical finesse—a way to meet the needs of everyone involved without having to make a difficult decision.
- Look for guidance in the NAEYC Code.
- Identify the most ethical defensible course of action and plan to act.

(Feeney et al., 2012; Warnick & Silverman, 2011)

Another activity that may be valuable for advanced students is to ask them to analyze an ethical dilemma and to develop resolutions that apply each of the three approaches to ethical thinking described previously. That is, would the resolution to the dilemma be based on utilitarianism, universality, or an ethic of care (Strike & Soltis, 2009)?

Advanced students who have had plenty of experience debriefing ethical dilemmas may be ready to develop an ethical dilemma of their own, perhaps a difficult situation they have personally faced. We have used this as a capstone assignment in master's programs. The template below has proved to be useful as students have begun this assignment, but we have found that even mature, experienced, and able students are likely to need a great deal of support to identify a genuine dilemma:

- Your dilemma is to be an engaging story. (Instructors sometimes limit these scenarios to 500 words to encourage students to write precisely and to polish their work carefully.)
- Your scenario must be "a situation for which there is more than one possible solution, each of which can be justified in moral terms" (Feeney et al., 2012, p. 26).
- Your scenario must make you ask the question "What should the good early childhood educator do? Should s/he *do this* or *do that*?"

Increase their ethical commitment. The final goal of instruction in professional ethics is to help increase students' ethical commitment, that is, the disposition to apply what they have learned about ethics and ethical analysis in their workplace. We hear from both beginners and advanced students that studying ethics has had a lasting impact on their practice, but the truth is that this is the most difficult of all the goals to evaluate. We remain hopeful, however, that the influence and reliance on the Code is increasing and that adult educators are seeing evidence that teaching about ethics has had an impact on student's ethical behavior.

Engaging in Ethical Deliberation

Learning about professional ethics involves more than understanding the nature of morality and ethics and learning to use a code. Another essential aspect of ethics instruction is providing students with opportunities to engage in ethical deliberation. There is some evidence to support the idea that professional ethics education can influence the moral reasoning and (to a lesser extent) attitudes of students in professional programs (Warnick & Silverman, 2011). This kind of growth occurs when students have the opportunity to engage in focused discussions about ethical issues.

Ethical deliberation occurs best in small group discussions. Of course it is essential that the groups be structured to ensure that every student's opinions will be heard and respectfully considered.

The opportunity to discuss ethics cases with their peers gives students the opportunity to:

- think clearly, communicate effectively, and listen carefully (Wasserman, 1993);
- be part of a community of learners;
- deal with ambiguity and increase understanding of a range of viewpoints;
- think through a situation and articulate and defend a position;
- articulate principles and arguments, not solutions that go beyond "What should I do?" to "What principles should guide our actions?" (Strike, 1993).

Discussions about ethics, especially with peers whose level of ethical reasoning is just a bit more advanced than their own, can help students to increase their appreciation of the complexity of ethical issues and to reach more mature levels of ethical thinking.

Potential Strands of Inquiry for Future Scholarship

Early childhood educators' work on professional ethics is far from finished. We identify below some opportunities for research and writing that could help us learn more about what early childhood educators understand about ethics, codes of ethics and how they are used, and how they approach moral reasoning. Research on the following topics would fill gaps in the existing literature:

- The kinds of moral reasoning used by early childhood educators and how teacher educators can help their students engage in more advanced levels of moral reasoning.
- What do today's early childhood preservice teachers know about morality and ethics?
- What do today's early childhood preservice teachers know about their field's code of ethics?
- How do teachers of young children perceive and cope with ethical dilemmas they encounter in their work?
- What strategies are teacher educators using to teach ethics? Which strategies are most effective in accomplishing their goals?
- How does the study of ethics translate into workplace attitudes and behavior?

- Are teacher educators aware of the NAEYC Supplement for Adult Educators? How are they using it? What ethical situations have they encountered? How has this Supplement guided their behavior?
- What strategies for teaching and assessing knowledge of ethical standards and ethical practice can early childhood teacher educators learn from other disciplines?

Research on professional ethics may include case studies, surveys, interviews, and other methodologies that are widely used by those who research early childhood teacher education. It is also worth considering "critical incident" qualitative research methods. Critical incidents are events that "mark a significant turning point or change in the life of a person" (Tripp, 1993, as cited in Shapira-Lishchinsky, 2011, p. 649). This strategy has been used to study preservice and inservice teachers' approach to ethical situations in Israel and Sweden (Colnerud, 1997, Shapira-Lishchinsky, 2011, 2013) but has yet to be used to investigate American early childhood teachers' ethical reasoning. Critical incident qualitative research and exploration of the moral reasoning of early childhood educators are two potential strands of inquiry that might yield important insights about professional ethics in early childhood education. We look forward to following the trajectory of this future research.

Notes

1. Sections of this chapter are adapted from Feeney & Freeman, 2009; Feeney, Freeman, & Moravcik, 2008; and Feeney, Freeman, & Pizzolongo, 2012.
2. The discussion in this section refers to the NAEYC Code but can be applied to other codes of professional ethics.

References

American Montessori Society. (2010). *Code of ethics.* New York: Author. Retrieved from http://amshq.org/About-AMS/Who-We-Are/Code-of-Ethics.aspx

Association for Childhood Education International (ACEI). (n.d.). *About us.* Washington, DC: Author. Retrieved from http://acei.org/childhood.html

Association for Childhood Education International. (2007). *2007 ACEI/NCATE elementary education standards and supporting explanation.* Washington, DC: Author. Retrieved from http://acei.org/programs-events/acei-standards-for-elementary-level-teacher-preparation

Association for Early Childhood Educators [Singapore]. (n.d.). *Code of ethics.* Singapore: Author. Retrieved from http://www.aeces.org/files/pdf/coe.pdf

Boon, H. (2011). Raising the bar: Ethics education for quality teachers. *Australian Journal of Teacher Education, 36*(7), 76–93.

Brophy-Herb, E. E., Kostelnik, M. J., & Stein, L. C. (2001). A developmental approach to teaching about ethics using the NAEYC Code of Ethical Conduct. *Young Children, 56*(1), 80–84.

Campbell, E. (2008). The ethics of teaching as a moral profession. *Curriculum Inquiry, 38*(4), 357–385. doi:10.1111/j.1467-873X.2008.00414.x

Certification Council of Early Childhood Educators of Nova Scotia. (n.d.). *Code of ethics.* Halifax, NS: Author.

Colnerud, G. (1997). Ethical conflicts in teaching. *Teaching and Teacher Education, 13*(6), 627–635.

Copp, D. (Ed.). (2006). *The Oxford handbook of ethical theory.* New York: Oxford University Press.

Daniels, L., Mandzuk, D., Perry, R., & Moore, C. (2011). The effect of teacher candidates' perceptions of their initial teacher education program on teaching anxiety, efficacy, and commitment. *Alberta Journal of Educational Research, 57*(1), 88–106.

Division for Early Childhood (DEC). (1996 & 2009). *Code of ethics.* Missoula, MT: Author. Retrieved from http://www.dec-sped.org/About_DEC/Position_Statements_and_Papers

Division for Early Childhood. (2007a). *Early childhood/early intervention initial special education professionals in early childhood special education/early intervention (birth to eight).* Missoula, MT: Author. Retrieved from http://www.dec-sped.org/About_DEC/Personnel_Standards_for_Early_Intervention_and_Early_Childhood_Special_Education

Division for Early Childhood. (2007b). *Early childhood/early intervention advanced special education professionals in early childhood special education/early intervention (birth to eight).* Missoula, MT: Author. Retrieved from http://www.

dec-sped.org/About_DEC/Personnel_Standards_for_Early_Intervention_and_Early_Childhood_Special_Education

Early Childhood Australia. (2006). *Code of ethics.* Deakin, AU: Author. Retrieved from http://www.earlychildhoodaustralia.org.au/code_of_ethics/early_childhood_australias_code_of_ethics.html

Early Childhood Development Association of Prince Edward Island. (n.d.). *Code of ethics.* Retrieved from http://earlychildhooddevelopment.ca/content/ecda-code-ethics

Early Childhood Educators of British Columbia. (2008). *Code of ethics.* Vancouver, BC: Author. Retrieved from www.ecebc.ca/resources/pdf/ecebc_codeofethics_web.pdf

Feeney, S. (2012). *Professionalism in early childhood education: Doing our best for children.* Boston, MA: Pearson.

Feeney, S., & Freeman, N. K. (2009). Professionalism and ethics in early care and education. In S. Feeney, A. Galper, & C. Seefeldt (Eds.), *Continuing issues in early childhood education* (3rd ed.), (pp. 196–211). Upper Saddle River, NJ: Pearson.

Feeney, S., & Freeman, N. K. (2014). Focus on ethics: Standardized testing in kindergarten. *Young Children, 69*(1), 84–88.

Feeney, S., Freeman, N. K., & Moravcik, E. (2008). *Teaching the NAEYC Code of Ethical Conduct: Activity sourcebook.* Washington, DC: National Association for the Education of Young Children.

Feeney, S., Freeman, N. K., & Pizzolongo, P. J. (2012). *Ethics and the early childhood educator: Using the NAEYC Code* (2nd ed.). Washington, DC: National Association for the Education of Young Children.

Feeney, S., & Kipnis, K. (1989). *Code of Ethical Conduct and Statement of Commitment. Young Children, 45*(1), 24–29.

Feeney, S., & Sysko, L. (1986). Professional ethics in early childhood education: Survey results. *Young Children, 42*(1), 15–20.

Fenstermacher, G. D. (1990). Some moral considerations on teaching as a profession. In J. I. Goodlad, R. Soder, K. A. Sirotnik (Eds.), *The moral dimensions of teaching* (pp. 130–151). San Francisco, CA: Jossey-Bass.

Freeman, N. K. (2000). Professional ethics: A cornerstone of teachers' preservice curriculum. *Action in Teacher Education, 22*(3), 12–18.

Frey, R. G. (2000). Act-utilitarianism. In H. LaFollette (Ed.), *The Blackwell guide to ethical theory* (pp. 165–182). Malden: MA: Blackwell Publishers.

Gilligan, C. (1982/1993). *In a different voice: Psychological theory and women's development.* Cambridge, MA: Harvard University Press.

Hansen, D. T. (2001). Teaching as a moral activity. In V. Richardson (Ed.), *Handbook of research on teaching* (4th ed.), (pp. 826–857). Washington, DC: American Educational Research Association.

Held, V. (2006). The ethics of care. In D. Copp (Ed.), *The Oxford handbook of ethical theory* (pp. 537–566). New York: Oxford University Press.

Kamm, F. M. (2000). Nonconsequentialism. In H. LaFollette (Ed.), *The Blackwell guide to ethical theory* (pp. 205–226). Malden, MA: Blackwell Publishers.

Katz, L., & Ward, E. H. (1978). *Ethical behavior in early childhood education.* Washington, DC: National Association for the Education of Young Children.

Keefer, M., & Davis, M. (2012). Curricular design and assessment in professional ethics education: Some practical advice. *Teaching Ethics, 13*(1), 81–90.

Kidder, R. M. (2009). *How good people make tough choices: Resolving the dilemmas of ethical living* (Rev. ed.). New York: Harper.

Kipnis, K. (1987). How to discuss professional ethics. *Young Children, 42*(4), 26–30.

Kohlberg, L., & Hersh, R. H. (1977). Moral development: A review of the theory. *Theory into Practice, 16*(2), 53–49.

National Association for the Education of Young Children (NAEYC). (2004). *Code of ethical conduct and statement of commitment: supplement for early childhood adult educators.* Washington, DC: Author. Retrieved from http://www.naeyc.org/positionstatements/ethical_conduct

National Association for the Education of Young Children (NAEYC). (2006, 2011). *Code of ethical conduct and statement of commitment: Supplement for early childhood program administrators.* Washington, DC: Author. Retrieved from http://www.naeyc.org/positionstatements/ethical_conduct

National Association for the Education of Young Children (NAEYC). (2010). *NAEYC standards for initial & advanced early childhood professional preparation programs.* Washington, DC: Author. Retrieved from http://www.naeyc.org/ncate/files/ncate/NAEYC%20Initial%20and%20Advanced%20Standards%2010_2012.pdf

National Association for the Education of Young Children (NAEYC). (2011a). *Code of ethical conduct and statement of commitment.* Washington, DC: Author. Retrieved from http://www.naeyc.org/files/naeyc/image/public_policy/Ethics%20Position%20Statement2011_09202013update.pdf

National Association for the Education of Young Children (NAEYC). (2011b). *National association for the education of young children associate degree accreditation: Accreditation handbook.* Washington, DC: Author. Retrieved from http://www.naeyc.org/ecada/materials

National Association for the Education of Young Children (NAEYC). (2013). *NAEYC early childhood program standards and accreditation*. Washington, DC: Author. Retrieved from http://www.naeyc.org/academy/primary/viewstandards

National Board for Professional Teaching Standards (NBPTS). (2012). *Early childhood generalist standards* (3rd ed.). Arlington, VA: Author.

National Education Association. (1975). *Code of ethics*. Washington, DC: Author. Retrieved from http://www.nea.org/home/30442.htm

New Zealand Early Childhood Services. (n.d.). *Code of ethical conduct for early childhood services*. Retrieved from http://www.myece.org.nz/code-of-ethical-conduct

Noddings, N. (1992). *The challenge to care in schools: An alternative approach to education*. New York: Teachers College.

Rich, J. M. (1985). The role of professional ethics in teacher education. *Action in Teacher Education*, 7, 21–24.

Saluja, G., Early, D. M., & Clifford, R. M. (2002). Demographic characteristics of early childhood teachers and structural elements of early care and education in the United States. *Early Childhood Research and Practice*, *4*(1), Spring. Retrieved from http://ecrp.uiuc.edu/

Shapira-Lishchinsky, O. (2011). Teachers' critical incidents: Ethical dilemmas in teaching practice. *Teaching & Teacher Education*, *27*(3): 648–656. doi:10.1016/j.tate.2010.11.003

Shapira-Lishchinsky, O. (2013). Team-based simulations: Learning ethical conduct in teacher trainee programs. *Teaching & Teacher Education*, *33*, 1–12. doi:10.1016/j.tate.2010.11.003

Strike, K. (1990). The legal and moral responsibility of teachers. In J. I. Goodlad, R. Soder, & K. A. Sirotnick (Eds.), *The moral dimensions of teaching* (pp. 188–223). San Francisco, CA: Jossey-Bass.

Strike, K. (1993). Teaching ethical reasoning using cases. In K. A. Strike & P. L. Ternasky (Eds.), *Ethics for professionals in education: Perspectives for preparation and practice* (pp. 102–116). New York: Teachers College Press.

Strike, K. A., & Soltis, J. F. (Eds.), (2009). *The ethics of teaching* (5th ed.). New York: Teachers College Press.

Warnick, B. R., & Silverman, S. K. (2011). A framework for professional ethics courses in teacher education. *Journal of Teacher Education*, *62*(3), 273–285.

Wasserman, S. (1993). *Getting down to cases: Learning to teach with case studies*. New York: Teachers College Press.

Willemse, M., Lunenberg, M., & Korthagen, F. (2008). The moral aspects of teacher educators' practices. *Journal of Moral Education*, *37*(4), 445–466. doi:10.1080/03057240802399269

PART III

Models/Approaches to Early Childhood Teacher Education

11
PATHWAYS TO EARLY CHILDHOOD TEACHER PREPARATION

Eun Kyeong Cho

With increasing demand for school readiness and accountability in the early years, the importance of preparing well-trained early childhood (EC) professionals has not only received considerable attention in the literature but also become one of the major foci of EC policy in the past three decades. The field has constantly struggled with a complex set of intertwined issues such as low entry-level requirements for most EC sectors, increasing demand for highly qualified teachers, low compensation, and high turnover. This is compounded by the fact that starkly different qualifications are required of EC teachers (e.g., high school diploma to a master's degree) depending on the employment settings, roles, and age groups they serve. As indicated by the federal government's "silence" on EC workforce standards while defining "highly-qualified" teachers as those with a college degree, public policy on EC teacher preparation "both promotes degree acquisition and depresses workforce qualifications" (Washington, 2008, p. 11). There are also concerns about the "value-added" components of earning higher education degrees due to "the persistently low compensation of people who work with young children, regardless of their credentials or the dynamics of supply and demand" (p. 10) and due to "the historically weak connection, outside of public schools, between credentials and compensation and career or salary growth" (pp. 14–15). In this context, it is not easy for EC teacher candidates to find the time, resources, and support necessary to earn a college degree and teaching certificate. In addition, the route to becoming a teacher is not a clear path but often a circuitous route lacking articulation among systems. Due to these challenges, teacher candidates who try to cross into the more formal system often get stuck in the pathway. Given that different pathways do not always connect, describing pathways in a streamlined fashion for those with less formal education or training is a challenging task.

This chapter reviews different pathways (i.e., Child Development Associate [CDA], two- and four-year programs, and alternative routes) to EC teacher preparation in the U.S. The description starts with entry-level (quick) points of access along the pathway to becoming a teacher and moves to more rigorous and formal (lengthier) points of access, followed by alternative routes to certification. The main features, strengths, and challenges of the pathways are discussed. Available model approaches, promising practices, and future directions for research to improve EC teacher preparation policy and practice are also presented.

Child Development Associate (CDA) Pathway

CDA is a national credential administered by the Council for Early Childhood Recognition that aims to improve the quality of EC practitioners based on demonstrated competence in six CDA competency goals (Table 11.1) and 13 functional areas.

Table 11.1 CDA Competency Goals and Functional Areas

Goal I. To establish and maintain a safe, healthy learning environment
1. Safe
2. Healthy
3. Learning Environment
Goal II. To advance physical and intellectual competence
4. Physical
5. Cognitive
6. Communicative
7. Creative
Goal III. To support social and emotional development and to provide positive guidance
8. Self
9. Social
10. Guidance
Goal IV. To establish positive and productive relationships with families
11. Families
Goal V. To ensure a well-run, purposeful program responsive to participant needs
12. Program Management
Goal VI. To maintain a commitment to professionalism
13. Professionalism

Source: www.cdacouncil.org

CDA requires at least 120 hours of formal training from an agency or organization with at least 10 hours of training in each of the six competency areas, along with at least 480 hours of professional work experience in one of the four credential settings (i.e., preschool, infant/toddler, family child care, and home visitor) that serve young children from birth through age 5. Candidates can apply for one credential setting a time. After getting the required hours of coursework and direct experience with young children, CDA candidates obtain their credential through performance-based assessment that is comprised of an examination of a professional portfolio, a family questionnaire, a verification visit from a CDA professional development specialist and an exam. As it does not require much formal education beyond a high school diploma, typically a person without a postsecondary degree applies for CDA. Since its inception in 1971 (the first CDA credential was awarded in 1975), as of 2014, more than 350,000 CDA credentials have been awarded, with about 18,000 EC practitioners becoming new CDAs annually (Council for Professional Recognition, 2014).

Strengths and Challenges of CDA

CDA is a core competency-based model, a nationally recognized credential, and an entry point credential to advance within an EC teaching career path. Due to its national standards for quality control, flexibility in meeting requirements, and provision of knowledge and competence for EC practitioners who may lack formal education and training, it was originally considered "a realistic alternative training strategy" (Cook, 1973, p. 3) and still is "the most widely recognized credential" and "a key stepping stone on the path of career advancement" in the EC teaching profession (Council for Professional Recognition, 2014).

However, researchers have identified a few challenges in the CDA pathway, such as a limited scope of age range covered, limited target areas of competencies, and a lack of continued mentoring due to high turnover in the field (Cook, 1973; Hinitz, 1996). Also noted are challenges related to quality assurance practices in CDA training (due to a variety of models, options, and instructor qualifications); the need for support by program administration and co-workers; and articulation with two- and four-year degree programs and Child Care Resource & Referral Agencies (New Jersey Professional Development Center [NJPDC] for Early Care and Education, 2004).

Efficacy of CDA

Despite its significant role as the entry-level teacher educational qualification identified in NAEYC accreditation standards, considerably few studies have examined the effectiveness of CDA (Bredekamp, 2000; Heisner & Lederberg, 2011; Tout, Zaslow, & Berry, 2006). A limited number of studies on various groups of EC teachers have included CDA, and these studies show a mixed picture regarding the link between CDA and teaching effectiveness as reflected in classroom quality or students' academic gains. Some studies show a positive link (Torquati, Raikes, & Huddleston-Casas, 2007; Tout et al., 2006), while others show no significant link between the two (Early et al., 2007).

Heisner and Lederberg (2011) urged caution in interpreting research findings on the efficacy of CDA training, as many previous studies did not use control groups. Comparing teachers with and without CDA training, they concluded "the training required for the CDA credential can be an effective means of influencing the beliefs and self-reported practices of teachers with little or no formal education" (p. 229). These findings and previously conducted reviews of literature on CDA demonstrate that, regardless of the level of formal education, when a person does not have specialized training in EC, having a CDA accompanied by EC specific training can be an effective way to prepare entry-level practitioners to be equipped with a necessary competency set of knowledge and skills. In addition, earning a CDA credential has several reported benefits such as salary changes, promotions, earning college credits, and staff retention (Bredekamp, Bailey, & Sadler, 2000; NJPDC for Early Care and Education, 2004).

Higher Education Pathway: Two- and Four-Year Programs

The 2002 reauthorization of Title I, entitled the No Child Left Behind act, required highly qualified teachers in every classroom, which impacted the field of ECE. The NAEYC accreditation of EC programs emphasizes qualifications of teachers as a core requirement. Head Start has been steadily increasing teacher qualification requirements, from requiring a CDA in every classroom, to requiring at least 50% of Head Start teachers in each classroom to have an associate's degree by 2003, to mandating at least half of these teachers have a bachelor's degree by 2012 and that 100% of teachers without a bachelor's degree have at least an associate's degree by 2011 (PL 110–134, Improving Head Start for School Readiness Act of 2007). Since these educational reform initiatives, which focus on improving EC teacher quality, the role of higher education has become more critical than ever.

Main Features of Two- and Four-Year Programs

According to Early and Winton (2001), there are over 1,200 institutions of higher education (IHEs) in the U.S. that offer EC programs designed to prepare teachers for working with children from birth through age 4. About 47% of the 438 EC teacher preparation programs surveyed were four-year institutions and 53% were two-year institutions. Many programs offer more than one degree with 57% offering an associate's degree. In another report, Maxwell, Lim, and Early (2006) indicated that about

40% of degree programs offer a bachelor's degree and 60% an associate's degree. It is also estimated that these programs produce at least 36,000 graduates each year (Hyson, Tomlinson, & Morris, 2009).

There is great variability among IHEs that prepare EC teachers. According to Hyson and her colleagues (2009), there were more similarities than differences between two- and four-year programs in term of "priorities, needs, and challenges." Yet, there were some features that differed between the two, such as the use of standards to guide curriculum, scope of curriculum, faculty capacity, career after graduation, and delivery mode (Early & Winton, 2001; Hyson et al., 2009). Thus, rather than providing a separate picture of each pathway, main characteristics of two- and four-year programs are described and compared below in order to present their relative strengths and features.

Age focus and program priority. Early and Winton (2001) found that about 95% of two-year programs cover infants/toddlers as well as preschoolers and primary ages, and 76% of their graduates work with children birth through age 4. In comparison, only about two-thirds of four-year programs cover infants/toddlers in their course offerings, and the majority (57.2%) of graduates work in a kindergarten or elementary setting. Similarly, Hyson and colleagues (2009) found that faculty at four-year programs were significantly more likely than those at two-year programs to prioritize working with primary-grade children (20.8% vs. 10.3%).

Scope of curriculum. Curriculum for each two- and four-year program is guided by the NAEYC program (Table 11.2) and state standards (Hyson et al., 2009). Based on the standards, each program offers a variety of courses such as child development, EC curriculum, observation and assessment of young children, home-school relations, program administration, and leadership in EC. The minimum number of courses, required coursework, electives, and credit hours vary by college, department, or program. In addition, a minimum number of clock hours for field based training varies by each state. Early and Winton (2001) found that associate's degree programs were more likely to require an entire course or more in infant/toddler care, working in family child care homes, and EC program administration. In comparison, four-year programs were more likely to focus on such areas as cultural and linguistic diversity, children with disabilities, interdisciplinary collaboration, home visiting, and working with families as part of the field experience requirements.

Faculty capacity. Early and Winton (2001) found that only 8.2% of faculty in two-year programs had a doctorate, and that the majority had either a master's degree (66.4%) or a bachelor's degree (24.6%). In four-year programs, about one-third (30.3%) of the faculty had a doctorate and more than half (56.3%) had a master's degree. The faculty members in two-year programs were more likely to have a degree in EC and direct teaching experience with young children than those in four-year programs. Programs reported the need for more faculty with EC expertise such as current knowledge and teaching experience in ECE (Hyson et al., 2009).

Table 11.2 NAEYC Standards for Early Childhood Teacher Preparation

Standard #1. Promoting child development and learning
Standard #2. Building family and community relationships
Standard #3. Observing, documenting, and assessing to support young children and families
Standard #4. Using developmentally effective approaches
Standard #5. Using content knowledge to build meaningful curriculum
Standard #6. Becoming a professional
Standard #7. EC field experiences

Source: NAEYC (2011). 2010 Standards for initial early childhood professional preparation. Washington, DC: Author.

Strengths of Two- and Four-Year Programs

Educational attainment of EC practitioners varies significantly. Herzenberg, Price, and Bradley (2005) reported that the educational attainment of EC educators declined over the past two decades. Though a recent report shows a better picture than previously reported (National Survey of Early Care and Education [NSECE] Project Team, 2013), a significant number of teachers in non-public settings still do not have a four-year college degree (Saluja, Early, & Clifford, 2002; Nelson, Main, & Kushto-Hoban, 2012).

Despite an increasing demand for practitioners who start working in EC with minimal education to receive formal education and training and earn an ECE degree, many inservice practitioners without a college degree are not ready to start a four-year program, due to their work schedules and limited financial means. Rather, they start in two-year programs and earn a four-year degree at a later time. Bragg (2007) emphasizes the critical role of two-year colleges in providing essential job-related education and training, claiming vocational education as "one of the oldest and most firmly entrenched curricular functions associated with the comprehensive mission of the community college, complementing liberal arts and transfer education, developmental and remedial education, and continuing education" (p. 12). As seen from the findings of the study conducted by Early and Winton (2001), the strengths of two-year programs are in the areas of providing practical knowledge and skills in working with children birth to age 4. Particularly, the curricular focus on infants/toddlers, family child care, and program administration demonstrates their significant role in preparing EC teachers to work with this age group in privately funded EC programs and family child care. Thus, with the flexible and affordable access to higher education, training, and completion of credentials, the contribution of two-year colleges in recruiting, preparing, and sending practitioners to the next level of higher education to produce the nation's teaching force has been well documented (American Association of Community Colleges, 2015; NAEYC, 2011).

While the contribution of two-year colleges in producing EC teachers has been enormous, a recent report on EC workforce data collected from an integrated set of four nationally representative surveys shows an increased number of teachers with a four-year degree in the field (NSECE Project Team, 2013). As of 2012, 53% of center-based and 30% of home-based teachers and caregivers reported having college degrees, while almost a third reported a bachelor's or graduate/professional degree (NSECE, 2013, p. 4). This promising picture is in part due to recent policy initiatives aimed at improving the qualifications of the nation's teaching force regardless of the age group they work with. The Committee on Early Childhood Pedagogy of the National Academy of Sciences recommended every EC classroom have a teacher with a bachelor's degree (Bowman, Donovan, & Burns, 2000). Other researchers also recommend that EC teachers earn not only a bachelor's degree but also specialized training, such as ECE and child development (Barnett, 2003; Fuligni, Howes, Lara-Cinisomo, & Karoly, 2009). Four-year programs have more full-time faculty; more faculty with a doctorate; more emphasis on areas such as linguistic and cultural diversity and children with disabilities; and interdisciplinary collaboration than two-year programs (Early & Winton, 2001). As sources of guidance for program design and improvement, four-year programs relied on national and state teacher preparation standards significantly more often than did two-year programs (Hyson et al., 2009). These characteristics allow four-year programs preparing EC teachers to be at the forefront for improving the quality of EC teacher education and the teaching force it produces, along with strengthening relationships with K-12 education. Teacher candidates spend more years of targeted formal education and training to obtain the necessary knowledge and competence in a broad range of areas and ages through a broad and balanced curriculum that focuses on preparing teachers to be critical thinkers, data-driven decision makers, and leaders. Therefore, it is more likely that four-year programs have the potential to contribute to the professionalization of the EC workforce by improving the qualification, knowledge, and competency of EC teachers.

Challenges of Two- and Four-Year Programs

There is a national outcry for true educational reform in teacher preparation programs. Yet educational reform is a challenge because there are "conflicting and competing beliefs on issues as basic as when and where teachers should be educated, who should educate teachers, and what education is most effective in preparing teachers" (Levine, 2006, p. 12). Levine summarized the condition of teacher preparation in higher education with the following terms: "inadequate preparation, a curriculum in disarray, a disconnected faculty, low admission standards, insufficient quality control, disparities in institutional quality" (p. 3).

Similar challenges are true for the IHEs in EC. According to a report (Washington, 2008) on the role and relevance of higher education in the EC field, prepared in partnership with eight organizations (e.g., The Council for Professional Recognition (n.d.), National Head Start Association, Pre-K Now, Wheelock College, and National-Louis University), there are concerns regarding the capacity of IHEs to serve the field, especially in terms of faculty expertise and curriculum to serve the needs of all children. A more pressing issue in EC than in elementary and secondary teacher preparation programs is the accessibility for adult learners. As Washington (2008) noted, "higher education has a long history of being unwelcoming to adult learners, part-time students, new immigrants, and minority groups" (p. 27). Yet, a significant number of the current EC workforce is composed of those who are considered non-traditional students or adult learners. In providing access and support for EC practitioners to earn degrees in higher education, Nelson and her colleagues (2012) categorized challenges in terms of recruitment, preparation, and support: (1) recruitment challenges due to "too varied and too low" entry requirements, issues with articulation and transfer, and insufficient support for matriculation (e.g., financial, social, and academic supports); (2) challenges in preparing candidates for high-quality teaching in all settings due to gaps in curriculum, lack of capacity (e.g., too few financial resources and faculty), and disconnect between coursework and field application; and (3) challenges in supporting a high-quality EC workforce in developing and improving their skills due to a lack of sufficient high-quality placements for diverse field experiences along with a lack of structure for high-quality mentoring and supervision. Early and Winton (2001) identified challenges in terms of curriculum, articulation, and administration: (1) curricular challenges to meet the needs of changing populations; (2) articulation difficulties between two- and four-year colleges; and (3) administrative challenges such as lack of funding, infrastructure, and limited number of full-time faculty. In order to achieve the goal of increasing the credentials of the current workforce, barriers to achieving this goal and the capacity of the IHEs to support this goal need to be considered (Ackerman, 2005; Nelson et al., 2012; Washington, 2008).

Curricular challenges: Breadth and depth. The majority of EC teacher preparation programs require that candidates work with a wide age range (infants through early elementary grades) throughout their coursework and field experience. Having teachers qualified to teach a broad age range has some benefits such as "employment flexibility," yet it may act as a "disservice to the children" if teachers lack depth in their knowledge of development and appropriate curriculum needs of specific age groups, especially when the broad curriculum is to be delivered and mastered during a short period of study (Early & Winton, 2001, p. 298).

Articulation difficulties between two- and four-year programs. Although the main foci of each of the two-year, four-year, and advanced degree programs that prepare EC teachers might be slightly different, there is a strong need to establish continuity and coherence among these programs. Researchers point out a lack of systems, attention, and efforts to establish articulation agreements that allow students to transfer coursework and credits from one type of credentialing system (e.g., vocational high school or CDA) to another (e.g., a two-year or four-year institution) as a major challenge (Early & Winton, 2001; File, 2001; Nelson et al., 2012; Washington, 2008). To realize this goal, efforts are needed not only at the institutional level (to build better collaborative models) but also at a personal level for EC faculty to engage in critical self-examination of their gate-keeping role (File, 2001; Nelson et al., 2012).

Faculty capacity, diversity, and availability. Despite the importance of faculty knowledge and expertise in EC education and the quality of EC degree programs, studies found that only a small fraction of EC faculty have a doctorate in EC education. Many programs depend on part-time faculty, some of whom have inadequate knowledge of current theory and practice in EC (Early & Winton, 2001; Hyson et al., 2009). Also noted are the difficulties of recruiting faculty members who can implement non-traditional course delivery (e.g., evening, weekend, off-site, or online classes) and challenges in recruitment and retention of minority faculty (Early & Winton, 2001; File, 2001).

Meeting adult learning needs. Due to poor working conditions and wages in the field, students enrolled in most community colleges or taking college courses struggle with competing responsibilities between school and work (Early & Winton, 2001). Lack of financial, academic, and social support for matriculation along with a lack of course offerings with non-traditional hours and modes of delivery are reported as challenges in attracting and keeping this group of students (File, 2001; Nelson et al., 2012).

Quality control of programs. A national system of EC teacher preparation accreditation standards and review process is managed by NAEYC. To ensure quality of programs at the bachelor and graduate degree levels, NAEYC works with the Council for the Accreditation of Educator Preparation [CAEP formerly NCATE]. Currently, there are approximately 256 institutions with NAEYC recognized baccalaureate and graduate degree programs in 37 states/territories (NAEYC, n.d.). In 2006, NAEYC launched the EC Associate Degree Accreditation system. Since its inception, a total of 159 programs in 30 states have earned NAEYC EC Associate Degree Accreditation through self-study and external peer review (NAEYC, 2014). The proportion of accredited four-year programs is larger than that of two-year programs and the number of accredited programs is increasing (Hyson, et al., 2009). Yet, limited use of this accreditation system in two-year EC programs and the need to improve the quality of EC teacher preparation programs in general remain problematic (IOM & NRC, 2012).

Efficacy of Two- and Four-Year Programs

There is strong evidence regarding the relationship between the level of teacher qualifications and quality of classroom environments (Barnett, 2003; Bowman et al., 2000; Fuligni et al., 2009; Shonkoff & Phillips, 2000). Yet, researchers have found mixed results regarding the level of education necessary to ensure quality outcomes (e.g., classroom quality and child outcomes).

Several studies have found that teachers with a bachelor's degree were more sensitive in interacting with young children (Howes, Whitebook, & Phillips, 1992) and demonstrated higher quality skills (Burchinal, Cryer, Clifford, & Howes, 2002) than those with an associate's degree or less. Studies on state-funded pre-kindergarten programs have found that programs with more teachers with at least a four-year college degree tend to be of high-quality (Marshall et al., 2002; Roach, Adams, Riley, & Edie, 2002).

A few recent studies have shown contradicting results. Early and her colleagues (2006) compared data from multiple measures of classroom quality and children's academic gains in pre-K for teachers with and without a bachelor's degree. They found no significant difference in classroom quality between teachers with and without a bachelor's degree (e.g., those with an associate's degree) and concluded that having a bachelor's degree alone would not be enough to ensure high-quality teaching in EC classrooms. Similarly, Early and her colleagues (2007) analyzed seven large data sets and found that initiatives focused only on increasing teachers' formal education were not sufficient to improve classroom quality or child outcomes.

Some researchers see instituting a new "bachelor's policy" as a key element to ensure the quality of ECE (e.g., Ackerman, 2005) and recommend not only a bachelor's but also EC-specific training, such as an ECE and child development major, as the proper preparation for EC teachers (Barnett, 2003; Fuligni et al., 2009). Yet, based on the inconsistent findings, the value of having a bachelor's degree has been questioned by some. Overall, researchers agree that teacher qualifications and quality are related and that formal education alone is not sufficient; yet, they have different views on how much education is required to ensure a high-quality teaching and learning environment (Early et al., 2007; Fuligni et al., 2009; Hyson et al., 2009; Washington, 2008).

Alternative Routes

Since the mid-1980s, alternative routes to teacher preparation have been on the rise. Along with a changing trend of measuring quality in teacher preparation from "input-based" (e.g., course credits) to "output-based" (e.g., demonstrated skills) criteria (Hyson et al., 2009), the growth of alternative certificate programs has attracted attention from education researchers (Darling-Hammond, Chung, & Frelow, 2002; Klein-Collins, 2013). At the core of this trend is an emphasis on competencies demonstrated by teacher candidates instead of credit hours or length of preparation. Klein-Collins (2013), who examines competency-based education (CBE) in the higher education system, defines CBE as "one that focuses on what students know and can do rather than how they learned it or how long it took to learn it" and argue that CBE offers "an opportunity to rethink what a college degree means for student learning while addressing concerns regarding higher education's quality and cost" (p. 3).

Main Features of Alternative Routes

There are about 130 alternative routes to enter teaching (National Research Council, 2010). An alternative certification pathway is a non-traditional route to teacher certification that allows candidates to teach "while participating in, or immediately after participation in, the route to certification" (National Association for Alternative Certification, n.d.). Some examples are Teach for America, Peace Corps, and Teacher Opportunity Corps. Programs are offered from a few weeks to several months, covering basic classroom management skills and content knowledge. Each state has a list of approved programs (e.g., colleges, school districts, non-profit education service centers, and private agencies) whose completers may be recommended for a teacher certificate within their respective state. Alternative providers compose one-third of teacher preparation providers (National Association for Alternative Certification, 2014a). About one in five newly certified teachers in 2009 were completers of alternative routes (National Association for Alternative Certification, 2013). EC teacher candidates seeking to teach in public schools or public-funded settings that require a state teacher certificate can start teaching (with paid or non-paid internships) while in this expedited pathway.

While working in public schools requires a teaching certificate (traditional or alternative), there are no nationally set minimum entry requirements (except for a high school diploma) nor any specialized training to begin as an EC teacher serving children birth to age 5 in non-public settings. Entry requirements for non-public EC programs vary by state and funding agency. Alternative routes to EC teacher preparation for those in non-public settings (e.g., child care) that do not require teacher certification or other credentials (e.g., CDA, associate's, or bachelor's degree) depend on coaching, mentoring, and supervision from experienced teachers.

Strengths and Challenges of Alternative Routes

The strengths of these alternative routes include a standards-driven non-traditional teacher preparation path leading to effective staffing, a constant flow of teacher supply in areas of teacher shortage, access to a teaching career for potentially serious teacher candidates without the long years of traditional education and training, and the use of veteran teachers to serve as supervisors and mentors for those who are new to the field (Klein-Collins, 2013; National Association for Alternative Certification, n.d.). In the case of Texas, for example, those who seek to teach in reading, math, science, and special education in early childhood through early elementary grades can apply for an alternative teaching certificate through the Alternative Certificate Program (Texas Education Agency, n.d.).

Despite its contribution to addressing staffing issues, this "open-market approach to entry into teaching" (Darling-Hammond et al., 2002, p. 297) is criticized for its tendency "to treat teaching as a set of empirically proven techniques that can be reduced to their core elements and reproduced" (Friedrich, 2014, p. 3). Friedrich warned that this reductionist approach to teacher preparation is likely to result in teachers who are not trained to be "critical thinkers" (p. 14). There are also increasing concerns regarding the effectiveness, commitment to teaching, and retention rates of teachers certified by alternative routes (Darling-Hammond et al., 2002; Darling-Hammond, Holtzman, Gatlin, & Heilig, 2005; Friedrich, 2014).

Efficacy of Alternative Routes

There are opposing views on the relationship between teacher preparation programs and teacher effectiveness. In response to debates about the necessity and value of teacher preparation programs, researchers compared novice teachers from traditional teacher preparation programs with those from alternative programs in various aspects related to teaching. Darling-Hammond, Holtzman, and colleagues (2005) explored the influence of teacher preparation and certification on teacher effectiveness and retention for both Teach for America (TFA) participants and other teachers. They found that certified teachers were more effective than TFA candidates in producing student achievement gains in reading and math tests over a six-year period. They also found that the majority of TFA recruits left their jobs within three years. Similarly, Darling-Hammond et al. (2002) found that teachers with alternative certification and those with no prior classroom teaching experience rated their initial preparedness significantly lower than those with traditional certification (four-year teacher preparation programs) and were less likely to plan to remain in teaching. However, some researchers (Buchanan, Lang, & Morin, 2013; Carr, 2013) found no statistically significant differences between traditional and non-traditional teachers in terms of their perception of self-efficacy in professionalism, instruction, environment, planning, and classroom management. Also, a retention study (National Association for Alternative Certification, 2014) using 2010–11 and 2011–12 cohorts (n=2,369) found that 78% of non-traditional teachers who were employed three years ago were still teaching in 2014. Researchers agree on the need to conduct more studies on the efficacy of alternative pathways.

Model Approaches and Promising Practices

Instead of highlighting any one approach as a model pathway, some common features of promising practices are shared below. The first set of features is based on community college models and the second is from IHE models. Also shared are national and state initiatives.

Common Features of Promising Community College Models

Bragg (2007) introduced three community-college initiatives that have shown successful records of induction, preparation, and employment of teacher candidates through teacher pipelines starting from high school. One such model is the College and Career Transitions Initiative (CCTI) of Anne Arundel Community College, which is "a consortium model in which the community college partners with K-12 education, university, business, and community organizations to design and deliver an articulated secondary-to-postsecondary curriculum" (Bragg, 2007, p. 15). The main focus is to enhance transfer by articulating two-year programs with four-year programs. High school courses are also "aligned and sequenced" with two-year programs. In this one-stop approach, students receive training (e.g., logical flow of coursework and field experience) that meets professional standards (e.g., NAEYC) and state requirements (e.g., 90 clock-hour certificate to work in a child care center), earn an associate's degree and a letter of recognition in EC, and can easily transfer their degree to a four-year college of education in the state. This program is the result of "enhanced institutional relationships, the creation of new curricular, and improved collaborations" (Bragg, 2007, pp. 15–19). After reviewing three pathway models that demonstrate the active role of community colleges in producing teachers, Bragg (2007) identified the following similarities:

- Decisions to create multiple degree options;
- State support and leadership in the development of degree programs in high-need areas and in the creation of models that other community colleges could follow;
- A high level of understanding of state- and national-level standards governing teacher preparation;
- Articulation with university teacher education programs, often using their own university centers to facilitate the creation of new degree programs; and
- Efforts to create a distinctive model that fit the local region's needs.

Common Features of Exemplary IHE Models

Whitebook and Ryan (2011) posit that the "content and experiences offered" in EC teacher preparation programs and "the capacity of an institution to deliver a curriculum that reflects research wisdom and is relevant to the needs of the field" influence the quality of teacher education (pp. 4–5). The content, experiences, and capacity to deliver relevant curriculum are influenced by many related factors such as faculty, administration, and finances. After researching the nation's schools, colleges, and departments of education using a nine-point template[1] for judging the quality of teacher education programs, Levine (2006) identified the following common features of exemplary teacher education programs.

- Commitment to preparing excellent teachers
- Clear definition of what an excellent teacher needs to know and be able to do
- A coherent, integrated, comprehensive, and up-to-date curriculum
- A field experience component of the curriculum that is sustained, begins early, and provides immediate application of theory to real classroom situations
- A close connection between the teacher education program and the schools in which students teach, including ongoing collaboration between academic and clinical faculties
- High graduation standards
- Faculty committed to their programs and their students
- Collaboration with faculty colleagues within and outside of the education school
- Administrative support from top university administrators
- Public recognition of the high quality of the program and of its graduates (pp. 81–82).

Similarly, Boyd and colleagues (2009) studied the effective features of teacher preparation pathways[2] (including both traditional and alternate routes) and the teachers they produced to work in New York City schools and compared their students' achievement in Math and English Language Arts. Common features that make a difference in teaching and student outcomes include:

- More oversight of student teaching experiences;
- Requiring a capstone project of teacher preparation programs;

- Focusing more on the work of the classroom; and
- Providing opportunities for teachers to review state curriculum and to engage in actual teaching practices.

Darling-Hammond and colleagues (2002) also found similar characteristics from two teacher education programs that allowed graduates to feel particularly well prepared:

- Strong relationships with partner schools; and
- An emphasis on extensive, carefully supervised clinical work (24 or more weeks of student teaching in settings selected to ensure modeling of desired teaching strategies) tightly linked to coursework that places significant attention on the development of content-based pedagogy (p. 293).

In terms of meeting adult learners' needs, Whitebook and Ryan (2011) highlighted a cohort model—"BA completion cohort programs, combined with targeted financial, academic, and technological supports for adults working in ECE settings" (p. 6)—as an approach to support students to enter and complete a four-year program through more peer and administrative support. Beyond specific approaches, Washington (2008) calls for a "systematic thinking" about IHEs in EC, based on "nation-wide and state-wide agreements about the field," and joined by broader leadership from the entire IHEs and community (p. 8).

National and State Initiatives

Washington's (2008) report on the role and relevance of higher education introduces promising practices to reinvent the mechanism of EC teacher preparation. Some national organizations (e.g., NAEYC, National Head Start Association) have created mechanisms to control quality and to provide easy access to training while partnering with IHEs. Some states have reorganized their state agency (e.g., New Mexico) or teacher certification programs (e.g., New Jersey) to create a streamlined system. Shared below are some promising practices of these initiatives introduced in the report (for more, see Washington, 2008, pp. 19–24).

National Head Start Association: The HeadsUp! Network. The National Head Start Association offers one of the nation's largest distance learning programs with a comprehensive set of quality components, such as high-quality content developed by leading experts in the field, low and affordable cost, convenient access to local training sites (e.g., Head Start centers, libraries, and colleges), and partnership with state governments and IHEs (for college credits toward a degree, CDA credential, and in-service training hours; Washington, 2008, pp. 19–20).

New Mexico: A comprehensive statewide model. The state created a framework for "universal articulation" between two- and four-year programs, in which over 20 colleges and universities forged an agreement for a seamless system from an associate's to a bachelor's degree, in combination with "a common catalogue of courses" and "a unified use of the certification and licensure lattice" shared by different systems that allow individuals to move between systems (e.g., Head Start, public school, child care, and early intervention) (Washington, 2008, pp. 21–22).

New Jersey: New teacher certification program and state division on EC. As a result of a series of court rulings, the New Jersey Supreme Court mandated that the state's poorest school district, known as "Abbot," offer high-quality preschool to all 3- and 4-year-olds. The mandate ordered a research-based curriculum, small class size, teacher qualifications (a four-year degree and specialized training in EC), and salary equity (between teachers in public and those in private preschool settings). To meet the mandate, the IHEs in the state created a preschool through third grade certification program; the State Department of Education created a division focusing on EC; the state government provided funding to IHEs to hire EC faculty; and a state-funded scholarship program was initiated to provide tuition support for upgrading teacher qualifications (Washington, 2008, pp. 23–24).

Evident in the promising initiatives are the importance of shared definition and vision (regarding quality EC, EC teachers, and EC teacher preparation programs); collaboration among stakeholders (e.g., policy makers, IHE administrators, professional organizations, and community leaders); and support from state leadership with an understanding of the context of IHEs in EC. Areas for future research remain, including finding ways to improve policy and practice regarding pathways to EC teacher preparation.

Areas for Future Research

Insights gained from reviewing studies on the pathway to EC teacher preparation show areas of challenge in understanding how to better prepare EC teachers using available or innovative systems. Research on the efficacy of different pathways (or their relative strengths or weaknesses) demonstrates inconsistent findings in terms of which career pathway is more effective; how much education and specialized training is necessary; and what entities should provide teacher preparation and for how long. This is in part due to a lack of agreement among stakeholders of clear definitions and concepts under investigation (e.g., EC teachers, quality of teachers/teaching/teacher preparation, and meaningful measures of child and teacher outcomes), and in part due to limitations in research methodologies which allow us to better understand the impact of each pathway on children, teachers, and the profession (IOM & NRC, 2012; NSECE, 2013; Washington, 2008; Whitebook & Ryan, 2011).

Research on Core Concepts Related to EC Teacher Preparation

The literature has documented concerns regarding the lack of clear definitions of the EC teaching force, qualified teachers, and teaching effectiveness. There are different views regarding the main purpose and function of EC teachers depending on their settings and the age groups they serve. In a similar vein, there is a lack of research on what constitutes quality in the EC teaching force, EC teacher preparation programs, and their relationship to (and impact on) student outcomes, services provided in EC programs, teacher supply and demand, and professionalization of the EC field. Research to identify, classify, and define concepts related to EC teacher preparation and core elements of each concept will be needed to build a foundation for further studies on the topic. As Winton (IOM & NRC, 2012) states, "individuals take so many pathways to employment, degrees, and certification that clear, agreed-on definitions are difficult, making it hard to interpret the existing data," and also the field "lacks data collection systems that adequately document the education and training" of ECE practitioners (p. 69).

Under currently available data collection systems for the EC workforce, it is challenging to collect, analyze, and interpret data that will produce meaningful and comparable findings among similar studies on a topic of investigation (IOM & NRC, 2012; NSECE Project Team, 2013). The difficulties in comparing findings across similar studies are, in part, due to differences in data sources (e.g., sample groups, sample sizes, geographical regions) and research methodologies. Research needs to be conducted on ways to collect national data that are representative, comprehensive, "accurate, timely, and meaningful" (IOM & NRC, 2012, p. 89) and that can be aligned with K-12 teacher data.

Future research endeavors need to include how to design and conduct research on the areas mentioned in this chapter using coherent and comprehensive research methods. Also needed are "multiple methods of inquiry . . . synthesizing evidence across multiple studies" (Shonkoff & Phillips, 2000, p. 71). The field especially needs more methodologically sound studies, which often employ characteristics such as a large sample size, random sampling, comparison groups, same measures for same variables (e.g., teacher education measured by degree attainment, number of years of education, and certification in EC), and a longitudinal study design that can be compared with other studies (Burchinal, Hyson, & Zaslow, 2008; Barnett & Ackerman, 2006).

Research on Context, Quality, and Policy: Beyond a Narrow Focus on Formal Education and Training

As Whitebook and Ryan (2011) pointed out, "too much attention has been given to debating the baseline of qualifications required of preschool teachers (e.g., AA vs. BA), failing to take into account the precise nature of the education that teachers have received en route to their degrees" (p. 1). Only a few limited aspects of efficacy of the pathways have been examined. Research on additional outcomes related to these diverse pathways on teaching effectiveness and student achievement, as well as the broader policy context that drives the pathways, needs to be conducted (Fuligni et al., 2009).

IOM and NRC (2012) reported that "the field has too many sets of standards and means of accreditation" and "although each may have value, a lack of integration leads to numerous gaps and duplications" (p. 70). In this context, the role of national and state standards that govern the content and quality of EC teacher preparation needs to be investigated in more depth (e.g., NAEYC accreditation).

Beyond a narrow focus on limited aspects of the pathways to teacher preparation, there is a need to further investigate the relationship between the pathways and outcomes related to teacher effectiveness (e.g., outcomes reflected in self-efficacy on various aspects of teaching, teaching beliefs, observed practices, and child outcomes) and career trajectory (e.g., commitment, promotion, professional development, mobility, and retention rates). The impact of higher education programs (traditional and non-traditional) and their components (e.g., coursework, scope and sequence of curriculum, field experiences, faculty expertise, and infrastructure) on enrolled candidates, graduates, and their students in the classroom, and its relationship to teacher policy, also need to be examined.

Model approaches and promising practices to preparing EC teachers showcased in this chapter demonstrate the significance of collective efforts of stakeholders at every level to improve the system of EC teacher preparation in terms of recruitment, training, and continued support of quality EC teachers. Targeted as well as coordinated research efforts are needed, such as the examinations of the effects and relative strengths of key features (e.g., articulation agreement for a seamless system, statewide coordination of funding, and improved access) of the approaches and their dynamics.

Conclusion

This chapter reviewed different pathways to EC teacher preparation in the U.S., such as CDA, two- and four-year programs, and alternative routes. The main features, strengths, challenges, and efficacy of each pathway were discussed. Identified strengths include CDA's role in preparing entry-level practitioners to be equipped with a necessary competency set of knowledge and skills; IHE's increasingly important role in preparing a more highly qualified teaching force, thus professionalizing the field of EC; and alternative routes' contribution to addressing the staffing issues in critical teacher shortage areas.

While each has strengths, some current challenges and issues in the pathways were identified. The multiple pathways do not always connect for teacher candidates to continue their study from one credentialing system to the next. This is, in part, due to issues with articulation and transfer among programs and across pathways and, in part, due to a lack of coordinated efforts. Further, there are inconsistent findings regarding the efficacy of each pathway to EC teacher preparation, along with the limitations in extant data on the EC workforce and in research (e.g., focus, scope, and methodologies) that meaningfully captures the relationships or impact.

Support for teacher candidates as they enter a teacher preparation pathway, become highly trained, secure employment, remain in the field, and continue to grow professionally requires a carefully planned system (e.g., infrastructure and research). Studies have shown that improving one aspect alone (e.g., bachelor's degree policy) is not enough to produce effective outcomes; rather, collaborative planning and implementation of initiatives will have the potential to actualize our vision for a well-aligned, articulated, coordinated, and effective teacher preparation system. To create or reinvent such a system, joint attention and support from leadership (e.g., state, IHEs, and community) informed by methodologically sound research from the field are required. Model approaches and promising practices highlight some key features (e.g., articulation agreement; aligned and sequenced curriculum with enhanced field components; coordinated funding and support from the respective state; and collaboration among stakeholders) that can be considered in re-envisioning the system of EC teacher preparation. Within the system, well-crafted content and experiences in a logical flow supported by faculty expertise and administration will contribute to preparing and sustaining high-quality EC teachers.

Notes

1. The nine areas include purpose, curricular coherence, curricular balance, faculty composition, admissions, degrees, research, finances, and assessment (for more, see Levine, 2006, pp. 28–29).
2. Pathways included *Teach for America* and the *Teaching Fellows* program; traditional college-recommended; individual evaluation; temporary license; other certificates, including internship certificates, other Transitional B teachers, and those with certification through reciprocity agreements with other states.

References

Ackerman, D. J. (2005). Getting teachers from here to there: Examining issues related to early care and education teacher policy. *Early Childhood Research and Practice,* 7(1), 1–17. Retrieved from http://ecrp.uiuc.edu/v7n1/ackerman.html

American Association of Community Colleges. (2015). 2015 fact sheet. Washington, DC: Author.

Barnett, W.S. (2003). Better teachers, better preschools: Student achievement linked to teacher qualifications. *Preschool Policy Matters, 2.* New Brunswick, NJ: National Institute for Early Education Research.

Barnett, W.S., & Ackerman, D. J. (2006). Costs, benefits, and long-term effects of early care and education programs: Recommendations and cautions for community developers. *Community Development, 37*(2), 86–100.

Bowman, B. T., Donovan, M. S., & Burns, M. S. (Eds.). (2000). *Eager to learn: Educating our preschoolers.* Washington, DC: National Academy Press.

Boyd, D., Grossman, P., Lankford, H., Loeb, S., & Wyckoff, J. (2009). Teacher preparation and student achievement. *Education Evaluation and Policy Analysis, 31*(4), 416–440.

Bragg, D. D. (2007). Teacher pipelines: Career pathways extending from high school to community college to university. *Community College Review, 35*(1), 10–29.

Bredekamp, S. (2000). CDA at 25: Reflections on the past and projections for the future. *Young Children, 55*(5), 15–19.

Bredekamp, S., Bailey, C. T., & Sadler, A. (2000, June-July). *The 1999 national survey of child development associates.* Paper presented at the 5th Head Start National Research Conference, Washington, DC.

Buchanan, T., Lang, N., & Morin, L. L. (2013). *Perception of preparedness of novice teachers from alternative and traditional licensing programs.* Capstone dissertation. Lipscomb University, Nashville, TN. Retrieved from http://www.alt-teachercert.org/Research%20and%20Reports.asp

Burchinal, M., Cryer, D., Clifford, R., & Howes, C. (2002). Caregiver training and classroom quality in child care centers. *Applied Developmental Science, 6*(1), 2–11.

Burchinal, M., Hyson, M., & Zaslow, M. (2008). Competencies and credentials for early childhood educators: What do we know and what do we need to know? *NHSA Dialog Briefs, 11*(1), 1–7. Alexandria, VA: National Head Start Association.

Carr, D. (2013). *The effects of teacher preparation programs on novice teachers regarding classroom management, academic preparation, time management and self-efficacy* Doctoral dissertation. Liberty University, Lynchburg, VA. Retrieved from http://www.alt-teachercert.org/Research%20and%20Reports.asp

Cook, N. (1973). *A review of the Child Development Associate training projects: National and Texas and competency-based training.* Retrieved from http://eric.ed.gov/?id=ED089840

Council for Professional Recognition. (n.d.). *About the CDA credential.* Retrieved from http://www.cdacouncil.org/the-cda-credential/about-the-cda

Council for Professional Recognition. (2014). Head Start nears 50th Anniversary. *CounciLink Newsletter. http://www.cdacouncil.org/councilink-newsletter*

Darling-Hammond, L., Chung, R., & Frelow, F. (2002). Variation in teacher preparation: How well do different pathways prepare teachers to teach? *Journal of Teacher Education, 53*(4), 286–302.

Darling-Hammond, L., Holtzman, D., Gatlin, S. J., & Heilig, J. V. (2005). Does teacher preparation matter? Evidence about teacher certification, Teach for America, and teacher effectiveness. *Education Policy Analysis Archives, 13*(42), 1–51.

Early, D. M., Bryant, D. M., Pianta, R. C., Clifford, R. M., Burchinal, M. R., Ritchie, S., Howes, C., & Barbarin, O. (2006). Are teachers' education, major, and credentials related to classroom quality and children's academic gains in pre-Kindergarten? *Early Childhood Research Quarterly, 21*(2), 174–195.

Early, D. M., Maxwell, K. L., Burchinal, M., Alva, S., Bender, R. H., Bryant, D., Cai, K., Clifford, R. M., Ebanks, C., Griffin, J. A., Henry, G. T., Howes, C., Iriondo-Perez, J., Jeon, H.-J., Mashburn, A. J., Peisner-Feinberg, E., Pianta, R. C., Vandergrift, N., & Zill, N. (2007). Teachers' education, classroom quality, and young children's academic skills: Results from seven studies of preschool programs. *Child Development, 78*(2), 558–580.

Early, D. M., & Winton, P. J. (2001). Preparing the workforce: Early childhood teacher preparation at 2- and 4-year institutions of higher education. *Early Childhood Research Quarterly, 16*(3), 285–306.

File, N. (2001). Practitioner perspective: Response to preparing the workforce. *Early Childhood Research Quarterly, 16*(3), 307–311.

Friedrich, D. (2014). We brought it upon ourselves: University-based teacher education and the emergence of boot-camp style routes to teacher certification. *Education Policy Analysis Archives, 22*(2). Retrieved from http://dx.doi.org/10.14507/epaa.v22n2.2014

Fuligni, A. S., Howes, C., Lara-Cinisomo, S., & Karoly, L. (2009). Diverse pathways in early childhood professional development: An exploration of early educators in public preschools, private preschools, and family child care homes. *Early Education and Development, 20*(3), 507–526.

Heisner, M. J., & Lederberg, A. R. (2011). The impact of Child Development Associate training on the beliefs and practices of preschool teachers. *Early Childhood Research Quarterly, 26*(2), 227–236.

Herzenberg, S., Price, M., & Bradley, D. (2005). *Losing ground in early childhood education: Declining workforce qualifications in an expanding industry, 1979–2004.* Washington, DC: Economic Policy Institute.

Hinitz, B. F. (1996, March). *National policies and training frameworks for early childhood education in the United States: The Child Development Associate and other credentialing frameworks for paraprofessionals.* Paper presented at the Warwick International Early Years Conference, Warwick, UK.

Howes, C., Whitebook, M., & Phillips, D. (1992). Teacher characteristics and effective teaching in child care: Findings from the national child care staffing study. *Child & Youth Care Forum, 21*(6), 399–414.

Hyson, M., Tomlinson, H. B., & Morris, C.A.S. (2009). Quality improvement in early childhood teacher education: Faculty perspectives and recommendations for the future. *Early Childhood Research and Practice, 11*(1). Retrieved from http://ecrp.uiuc.edu/v11n1/hyson.html

IOM (Institute of Medicine) & NRC (National Research Council). (2012). *The early childhood care and education workforce: Challenges and opportunities. A workshop report.* Washington, DC: The National Academies Press.

Klein-Collins, R. (2013). Sharpening our focus on learning: The rise of competency-based approaches to degree completion. *Occasional Paper #20.* Champaign, IL: National Institute for Learning Outcomes Assessment.

Levine, A. (2006). *Educating school teachers.* Washington, DC: The Education Schools Project.

Marshall, N. L., Creps, C. L., Burstein, N. R., Glantz, F. B., Robeson, W. W., Barnett, W. S., Schimmenti, J., & Keefe, N. (2002). *Early care and education in Massachusetts public school preschool classrooms.* Cambridge, MA: Wellesley Center for Women and Abt Associates.

Maxwell, K. L., Lim, C.-I., & Early, D. M. (2006). *Early childhood teacher preparation programs in the United States: National report.* Chapel Hill, NC: University of North Carolina, FPG Child Development Institute.

National Association for Alternative Certification. (n.d.). Definition of alternative certification. Retrieved from http://www.alt-teachercert.org/Definition.asp

National Association for Alternative Certification. (2013). NAAC Newsletter, *22*(4), 5.

National Association for Alternative Certification. (2014a). NAAC Newsletter, *23*(2), 2–3.

National Association for Alternative Certification. (2014b). *Non-traditional teacher and candidate retention: Measures of educator preparation, certification and school staffing effectiveness linked to student achievement.* Retrieved from http://www.alternativecertification.org/NAAC%20retention%20study%20_6.pdf

National Association for the Education of Young Children. (n.d.). NAEYC recognition of baccalaureate and graduate degree programs. Retrieved from http://www.naeyc.org/ncate/

National Association for the Education of Young Children (NAEYC). (2011). *2010 Standards for initial early childhood professional preparation.* Washington, DC: Author.

National Association for the Education of Young Children (NAEYC). (2014). *Programs at three colleges earn NAEYC early childhood associate degree accreditation; Programs at twelve colleges renew accreditation.* Washington, DC: Author.

National Research Council. (2010). *Preparing teachers: Building evidence for sound policy.* Washington, DC: The National Academies Press.

National Survey of Early Care and Education (NSECE) Project Team. (2013). *Number and characteristics of Early Care and Education (ECE) teachers and caregivers: Initial findings from the National Survey of Early Care and Education (NSECE)* (OPRE Report #2013–38). Washington, DC: Office of Planning, Research and Evaluation, Administration for Children and Families, U.S. Department of Health and Human Services.

Nelson, C. C., Main, C., & Kushto-Hoban, J. (2012). *Breaking it down and building it out: Enhancing collective capacity to improve early childhood teacher preparation in Illinois.* Chicago, IL: University of Illinois at Chicago.

New Jersey Professional Development Center (NJPDC) for Early Care and Education. (2004). *The Child Development Associate (CDA) delivering quality education in the State of New Jersey.* Union, NJ: Author.

Public Law 110–134. *Improving Head Start for School Readiness Act of 2007.* Retrieved from http://eclkc.ohs.acf.hhs.gov/hslc/standards/law/hs_act_pl_110–134.pdf

Roach, M., Adams, D., Riley, D., & Edie, D. (2002). *Wisconsin child care research partnership Issue Brief #8: What characteristics relate to child care quality?* Madison, WI: University of Wisconsin-Extension.

Saluja, G., Early, D. M., & Clifford, R. (2002). Demographic characteristics of early childhood teachers and structural elements of early care and education in the United States. *Early Childhood Research & Practice, 4*(1), n1. Retrieved from http://ecrp.uiuc.edu/v4n1/saluja.html

Shonkoff, J., & Phillips, D. (Eds.). (2000). *From neurons to neighborhoods: The science of early childhood development.* Washington, DC: National Academy Press.

Texas Education Agency. (n.d.). *Becoming a certified Texas educator through an Alternative Certification Program (ACP).* Retrieved from http://www.tea.state.tx.us/index2.aspx?id=7073

Torquati, J. C., Raikes, H., & Huddleston-Casas, C. A. (2007). Teacher education, motivation, compensation, workplace support, and links to quality of center-based child care and teachers' intention to stay in the early childhood profession. *Early Childhood Research Quarterly, 22*(2), 261–275.

Tout, K., Zaslow, M., & Berry, D. (2006). Quality and qualifications: Links between professional development and quality in early care and education settings. In M. Zaslow & I. Martinez-Beck (Eds.), *Critical issues in early childhood professional development* (pp. 77–110). Baltimore, MD: Brookes Publishing.

Washington, V. (2008). *Role, relevance, reinvention: Higher education in the field of early care and education.* Boston, MA: Wheelock College.

Whitebook, M., & Ryan, S. (2011). *Degrees in context: Asking the right questions about preparing skilled and effective teachers of young children. Preschool Policy Brief. Issue 22.* New Brunswick, NJ: National Institute for Early Education Research.

12

REIMAGINING TEACHER EDUCATION TO ATTRACT AND RETAIN THE EARLY CHILDHOOD WORKFORCE

Addressing the Needs of the "Nontraditional" Student

Vicki Garavuso

Many early childhood teacher education faculty have come to recognize how particular features of university-level early childhood education programs can, in their efforts to comprehensively address a formidable range of competencies, deter early childhood workers from matriculating into their programs. As a result, these teacher educators have begun to design degree programs that specifically acknowledge and address the needs of early childhood workers seeking college-level credentials, many of whom are "nontraditional" students. Often taking an ecological approach, these teacher educators recognize that changing particular structures and cultural assumptions of their programs is crucial to the project of attracting, supporting, and successfully graduating early childhood educators. This is especially poignant for students who come from backgrounds in which there have been minimal expectations and few precedents for obtaining college degrees. Most prominently, these changes call for the cultivation of diversified teacher education faculty who are well versed in the literature on adult learning, including the concepts of andragogy (Knowles, 1984), critical reflection (Brookfield, 1987), and transformative learning (Mezirow, 1991). Faculty must therefore be able to develop curricula that exploit the benefits of these learners' knowledge, experience, and beliefs that they bring to college classrooms. This chapter will offer examples of university early childhood teacher education programs that are actively contending with traditionally structured programmatic obstacles, are employing narrative pedagogies, which encourage students to consider their "lived situatedness" (McLaren & da Silva, 1993, p. 69), and are developing programs that make use of mentoring and cohort models (see Chu, Martínez-Griego, & Cronin, 2010; Exposito & Bernheimer, 2012; Garavuso, 2010; Haynes Writer & Oesterreich, 2011; Kipnis, Whitebook, Almaraz, Sakai, & Austin, 2012).

The definitions of the early childhood care and education workforce are as varied as the care settings in which we find young children. Here, as is found throughout early childhood education literature, data collection systems, and the workforce itself, terminology tends to obfuscate actual responsibilities. The field interchanges "caregiver", "child care provider", or "child care worker" for those who work in daycare programs, which were historically developed to enable parents to work. The term "teacher" connotes settings in which enrichment or educative experiences are offered, often based on traditional school day hours. For providers who may not fit any of the above categories, such as friends or family members caring for a child, there may be no professional titles (Institute of Medicine and National Research Council, 2012). For the purposes of this chapter and, "(as) derived from focusing on the function of being paid to provide care or instruction for young children, regardless of the setting or program in which it occurs" (Maroto & Brandon, 2012, p. 108), the terms "early childhood care and education (ECCE) worker", caregiver, and teacher will be used interchangeably. This approach also recognizes the current trend of public school systems to "subcontract" teachers and classrooms in community based organizations (CBO) to provide universal pre-K programs, thereby requiring certified teachers and mandated curricula.

Multiple research studies link positive outcomes for young children with higher levels of teacher education (Barnett, 2011; Kelley & Camilli, 2007; Whitebook & Ryan, 2011). The National Research Council's *Eager to Learn* (Bowman, Donovan, & Burns, 2001) recommends all early childhood educators have mastery of information on the pedagogy of teaching preschool-aged children, including knowledge of teaching, learning, and child development. The authors maintain that the early childhood educator must know how to provide rich conceptual experiences that promote growth in specific content areas such as language (vocabulary) and cognition (reasoning), as well as activities that build social-emotional relationships in the classroom. Additionally, her instruction must take into account professional standards, including assessment procedures such as observation/performance records, work sampling, and interview methods. Moreover, she must be cognizant of techniques to teach English language learners, as well as "children from various economic and regional contexts, and children with identified disabilities" (Bowman et al., 2001, p. 312). The teacher of young children must be collaborative, especially acknowledging and valuing roles played by the child's family. She must be able to work with teams of professionals and use regularly shifting standards of accountability. However, many ECCE workers who wish to obtain higher education degrees and qualifications, and who are mindful of these requirements, may discover that pathways for accessing and successfully completing college-level teacher education programs are riddled with numerous situational, dispositional, and institutional obstacles (Cross, 1981). Lastly, many of the caregivers and educators described here are women currently working in early childhood care and education settings, and for whom returning to school as "nontraditional" college students is a way to obtain the credentials necessary to move up the career ladder, better serve their communities, and take part in their profession as lifelong learners.

Why ECCE Workers Tend Not to Seek College Degrees

Although all 50 states require that kindergarten teachers complete sufficient college coursework to earn a bachelor's degree, only 13 states require that center-based ECCE providers have specialized instruction in early childhood education (National Association of Child Care Resource & Referral Agencies [NACCRRA], 2011). This has resulted in insufficient impetus for those already working in early childhood settings to seek degrees in higher education. Consequently, Maroto and Brandon's (2012) study found that 33 percent of child care center and family child care providers' highest level of education is high school. Thirty-nine percent have some college coursework, 12 percent have associate's degrees, between 13 and 21 percent have bachelor's degrees, and 4 percent have graduate or professional degrees.

While there are many confounding statistics (for example: inadequate job definitions, separate funding streams, different types of programs, data which include or exclude preschool and elementary teachers), data collected by Brandon, Stutman, & Maroto (2011) approximate that, including support and administrative staff, there are 2.2 million paid ECCE workers in the U.S. It is additionally estimated that there are 3.2 million unpaid ECCE workers, including, for example, kith and kin caregivers. This produces a total of 5.5 million caregivers (cited in Maroto & Brandon, 2012). Women make up 97% of the ECCE workforce. The median age range for child care workers is 35–39 years, while the median age for preschool teachers is 39 years. Caregivers in private households, including family child care providers are, on average, 43 years of age (Maroto & Brandon, 2012).

Rhodes & Huston (2012) found that average annual salaries for preschool and kindergarten teachers are approximately $31,000, while assistant teachers make an average of $21,000. Other child care workers average $18,000 while family child care providers make an average of $14,000. Blau (cited in Institute of Medicine and National Research Council [IMNRC], 2012) contends that early childhood workers' wages have remained low as compared to wages for jobs requiring a similar level of skills. Although he acknowledges that the number of child care workers has grown by an average of 4.6 percent over the last 10 years, Blau has contended that the labor supply in early childhood remains relatively unsettled, noting that "early childhood teachers who possess the required qualifications may choose to leave a preschool position for higher wages in a K–12 teaching position" (cited in IMNRC, 2012, p. 29).

Thus while many ECCE providers believe that going to school is a worthwhile endeavor (Deutsch & Riffin, 2013), the fact that most states do not require early childhood workers to have college credentials combined with the comparatively low salaries they can expect to earn—not to mention other situational, dispositional, and institutional barriers (Cross, 1981) which will be described further on—actively deter early childhood workers from seeking advanced degrees. This has, in turn, produced a situation in which teachers who work in early childhood settings have little-to-no educational background that has specifically prepared them to work with young children.

Why ECCE Workers *Need* to Seek College Degrees

Despite the above-described disincentives for ECCE workers to seek college degrees, the National Educational Association recommends that all teachers working in publically funded preschool programs hold a bachelor's degree in child development and/or early childhood education; all instructional assistants working in publically funded preschool programs hold an associate's degree in child development or early childhood education; lead teachers in private child care centers hold a minimum of an associate's degree in child development or early childhood education; and that all teaching assistants in private child care centers hold a minimum of a Child Development Associate (CDA) or a state issued certificate that meets or exceeds CDA requirements (National Education Association [NEA], 2010).

In a like-minded move, Head Start has recently made changes to required qualifications, launching initiatives geared toward increasing the early childhood educational backgrounds of its workforce. For example, federal mandates for Head Start teachers require that at least 50 percent of Head Start teachers nationwide have a baccalaureate or advanced degree in early childhood education or a baccalaureate or advanced degree in any subject, and coursework equivalent to a major related to early childhood education, including experience teaching preschool-age children (U.S. Congress, 2007). Assistant teachers in Head Start must have at least a CDA credential and be working toward completion of at least an associate's degree within two years.

In addition to the qualifications recommended by the NEA, researchers have discussed the importance of teachers having diversified linguistic and cultural knowledge to effectively work in early childhood settings. Many have pointed out that when teachers are fluent in a preschooler's home language, offering children opportunities to use both English and their home language, proficiency in that home language improves while progress in English is not hindered (Barnett et al., 2007; Durán et al., 2010; Farver et al., 2009; Gormley, 2007; Kersten et al., 2009, as cited in IMNRC, 2012). Along these lines, Villegas, Strom, and Lucas (2012) have argued that teachers of color are uniquely positioned to teach children of color, since they bring funds of knowledge (Gay, 2002; Nieto, 2000; Villegas & Lucas, 2002, as cited in Villegas et al., 2012) and act as role models (Gordon, 2000; Ochoa, 2007; Su, 1997, as cited in Villegas et al., 2012) for all children.

Yet, since current statistics on the child care workforce in the U.S. indicate that it is made up of predominately White, non-Hispanic women (Maroto & Brandon, 2012), such linguistic and cultural diversity is lacking. African-American, non-Hispanic ECCE personnel comprise 9 to 18 percent across sectors with the fewest working in family child care settings. Additionally, Maroto & Brandon (2012) compare the nearly 18 percent of ECCE workers across sectors who identified as Hispanic (sic) to the higher percentage (22.3 percent) of Hispanic children in care. They point to the growing Hispanic population as an example of the increasing diversity in the U.S. and therefore to the requisite need for an ECCE workforce that shares the categories of cultural and linguistic knowledge of the children in their care.

Indeed caregivers and teachers in early care and education settings who have worked in their own communities with children and families much like themselves are uniquely positioned to work with these children. Nonetheless, those who—despite all the obvious disincentives—make the move to obtain college credentials, still find themselves faced with numerous, formidable obstacles in university settings.

Obstacles for ECCE Workers as "Nontraditional Students"

Since the majority of those who work in early care and education settings have only obtained high school diplomas or associates degrees, and the average age of the early childhood care and education workforce is often older than 35 years old (Maroto & Brandon 2012), many of those who choose to attend university level early childhood education certification programs fall squarely within the definitions of the "nontraditional" college student. As Choy (2002) summarizes, the majority of the nontraditional college student population identify themselves as "workers returning to school", having been out of school for a period of time before entering college, and enter by way of two-year community colleges. They most often hold full-time jobs necessitating part-time college attendance, and come from working class and lower income families. According to the U.S. Department of Education's National Center for Education Statistics (U.S. Department of Education, 2013), between 2000 and 2010 overall college enrollment of older students rose by 42 percent. Many are the first in their family to attend college, and, as Cross (1981) has pointed out, these nontraditional students necessarily confront a number of *situational, dispositional, and institutional* obstacles and barriers as they seek to better their qualifications for working with young children by obtaining a college degree.

Situational Obstacles

Situational barriers faced by adult learners in general include responsibilities beyond their studies such as financial pressures, caring for their own children and often their elders, simultaneously holding down full-time jobs, having poor access to transportation, and having extensive time and energy consuming commitments to the larger community. Additionally, many nontraditional and first generation undergraduate hopefuls have experienced a silencing of their first languages in their previous schooling and a not-so hidden curriculum that gave them a clear message that they were not expected to succeed, let alone to attend college. Many come out of remedial, vocational, and underserved high schools in which they were poorly counseled with regard to higher educational pathways (Carter, Mosi Locks, & Winkle-Wagner, 2013).

Dispositional Obstacles

Closely related to situational barriers, dispositional barriers commonly center on nontraditional students' beliefs and attitudes regarding their relationships to schooling. For example, over 50 percent of today's college student population consists of first generation attendees (Mehta, Newbold, and

O'Rourke, 2011). Often they come to college from underserved school settings that did not prepare them for the rigors of higher education, and they therefore find it difficult to see themselves as successful college students. This image of oneself as "deficient" can be exacerbated by the fact that these students often have fewer sources for information about college life, including academic protocols, access to financial aid, and knowledge of how to develop supportive and mentored relationships with faculty, employers, or peers (Garavuso, 2010). Nonetheless, nontraditional students cited being role models for their children as an incentive for their return to school (Choy, 2002).

Lambert, Sibley, and Lawrence (2010) added elements to this list of dispositional obstacles that are specific to early childhood workers as teacher candidates. They pointed out that many in this group come from backgrounds of "low literacy levels, a history of low wages, their own experiences in poverty, and personal histories with *traditions of compliance* rather than professionalism," (p. 69, italics added). That is to say that for these early childhood workers, school was not necessarily a place for exploration and expression.

Along these lines, Exposito and Bernheimer (2012) described "the challenge of social and cultural incongruence" (p. 179) faced by "nontraditional" students when they

> enter higher education with a cultural capital that differs profoundly from the capital that defines success in these institutions. Since most educational institutions are not concerned with knowing a student's history, culture, or experience, it is assumed that students have the capital needed to succeed . . . the discrepancies between students' home and academic culture . . . are often left unaddressed and lead to a breakdown in motivation and participation.
>
> *(p. 180)*

Exposito and Bernheimer (2012) point out that many nontraditional early childhood undergraduates come from communities that have familial bonds and close social networks, which support students' identity through cultural, linguistic, and racial commonalities. Yet, the absence of these familiar ways of being in the university may ultimately underscore students' perceptions of overt and subtle exclusion in academic settings.

Institutional Obstacles

Institutional barriers include factors such as colleges scheduling daytime classes and college administrative office hours when many nontraditional students are at work. State certification requirements that mandate field assignments, which must also be completed during the school day, add to this list.

Other institutional barriers stem from accredited universities' reliance on standardized tests scores or grade point averages for determining candidates' eligibility for teacher education programs. As Goldhaber and Hansen (as cited in Saracho, 2013) noted, "minority teachers usually perform considerably less well than White teachers on tests that have an unrelated effect on their qualifications to teach" (p. 574). As a result, "documented achievement disparity" (p. 574) may lead candidates from underserved communities and those from nondominant cultures to forgo application.

Another institutional barrier stems from the makeup of the early childhood teacher education faculty itself. Washington (2008) pointed out that most teacher education faculties are much less diverse than their student populations. For example, "although most students in California early childhood teacher preparation programs are people of color, nearly one half of programs have a 100 percent White, non-Hispanic, full-time faculty" (p. 17). Washington cited comparable statistics for faculty in New York State: 82 percent female and 93 percent White. Washington additionally claimed there are insufficient doctoral programs in early childhood curriculum and teaching such that only 36 percent of ECE faculty members hold doctoral degrees.

A fourth institutional barrier arises from the fact that the cost of a recommended or mandated early childhood degree often represents a large percentage of the yearly income of most early childhood workers. Moreover, less than two thirds of caregiver/educators work a full year, often taking second jobs for the remainder of the calendar year. For the adult student of early childhood education, these monetary restrictions make financial aid essential; however, many do not know how to gain access to that aid (Unverfeth, Talbert-Johnson, & Bogard, 2012). Furthermore, many financial aid programs require full-time enrollment, which, as explained previously, is usually not an option for adult early childhood workers. Additionally, many aid packages do not cover living expenses that may be incurred by the adult college student (Dukakis, Bellm, Seer, & Lee, 2007). Finally, many ECCE workers are reluctant to take on the burden of a loan in a profession that is as poorly compensated as early childhood education.

A fifth institutional barrier stems from nontraditional students' customary choice of a community college as an entry point to higher education. Community colleges are generally less expensive, may not have entry requirements more demanding than a high school diploma, and require fewer credits for a degree. But this choice does not necessarily ensure the student a problem-free educational trajectory. The community college may have focused on basic skills and preparing early childhood students for jobs as assistant teachers with associate's degrees. When they advance to four-year programs, students often find that the rigor of their coursework at the community college does not match that of the four-year institution. As most four-year colleges' early childhood programs must prepare students for head teaching positions which require certification and licensure, bachelor's degree-level academics are often more rigorous in these teacher education programs. As a result, students who come from community colleges are often expected to repeat courses to fulfill program requirements, presenting an additional financial burden and time commitment. And, as the number and complexity of professional entry tests have grown, along with higher fees for these, nontraditional and minority teacher candidates face additional obstacles to graduation and certification.

If the Head Start initiatives and NEA's recommendations as stated above are to be heeded, steps must be taken to encourage and support the diverse group of individuals who do not fit the profile of the "traditional" student. Following are examples of university programs developed to benefit and sustain the nontraditional student of ECCE as she surmounts obstacles to higher education and advances to professional qualifications.

Programs for ECCE Workers Seeking Credentials and Degrees

The following programs serve as entry points and pathways for the ECCE workforce to gain certification at various levels, often allowing them to keep their current jobs, move up the career ladder from teacher's aide or assistant teacher to lead teacher, and resourcefully mature as educators.

The Child Development Associate (CDA)

The CDA is currently administered by the Council for Professional Recognition (CPR). The National Association for the Education of Young Children (NAEYC) has also worked with the Council on the design of the CDA with the objective of improving the performance and professional recognition of early childhood educators. Since its inception in 1975 over 300,000 CDA credentials have been awarded, with approximately 18,000 completing the credential annually (Council for Professional Recognition, 2013).

The CDA does not lead to a college degree but rather to a nationally recognized certificate for beginning-level early childhood teachers. Although the CDA's function as a platform for credentialing is important, the courses it requires as part of its "professional education" component are entry level relative to the coursework required for a professional degree in early childhood education. The bar for the professional education component is set relatively low at eight credits, compared to the 60 credit professional education component required for an associate's degree. Most often, these credits are not articulated into university degree granting programs. And, importantly, in order to obtain an associate's degree, one must also complete general education coursework that includes academic skills and content knowledge beyond early childhood pedagogies.

Teacher Education and Compensation Helps (T.E.A.C.H.®)

Another avenue for pursuing professional and educational qualifications for work with young children that has been opened to the early childhood workforce is Teacher Education and Compensation Helps or, T.E.A.C.H.®. As Sue Russell, T.E.A.C.H.'s founder, wrote in this organization's 2011–12 National Report,

> We have focused a good deal of our energy on studying models of student support to track and increase persistence rates toward degree and certificate completion for our workforce, which is dominated by women (many of whom are people of color), who, overall, earn poverty level wages without basic benefits like health insurance, who have little formal education beyond high school and who are often the first person in their families to attend college.
>
> *(Russell, 2012, n. p.)*

With over 17,000 educational scholarships offered in 22 states and the District of Columbia, the T.E.A.C.H. Early Childhood® Project partners with 317 two-year and 200 four-year institutions of higher education. Within these programs, 45 percent of students were people of color, of whom 12 percent were Latina (Russell, 2012). The T.E.A.C.H.® scholarship model provides access to "scholarships . . . for defined periods of time for achieving small steps along (the way) . . . participants' employers pay(ing) for release time and offer(ing) additional support" (Morgan, 2009, p. 101) including incremental pay increases as students reach academic milestones. Students are required to commit to stay in their current early childhood educational setting or in the field for at least six months once they have received the bonus or raise, depending on their specific scholarship. T.E.A.C.H.® also requires that participating institutions of higher education offer all necessary courses, accept and assist part-time students, and facilitate transfer credits. This model of financial, academic, workplace, and social supports offers a template for success in providing access to formal education and realization of professional goals for those in the early care and education workforce.

Beneficial Community College Programs

Exposito and Bernheimer's (2012) examination of programs for early childhood college students is based on the recognition that nontraditional early childhood education teacher candidates' experiences in college are often alienating but may be ameliorated by several factors. These include:

- *Enhancing faculty support for students*: it is incumbent on faculty to venture a bridge between the culture of the institution and the cultures of the learner and that within these parameters, faculty must examine their own beliefs and "assumptions about how they teach and what students need to be successful" (p. 181).
- *Developing inclusive pedagogy:* nontraditional students need to learn not only a body of knowledge, but also the ways of the university.
- *Recognizing the value of connected learning:* "reflection, dialogue, personal narrative, and stories related to or used for enhancing theory and practice . . . engender(ed) new possibilities as diverse perspectives surrounding content in early childhood education are explored and integrated" (p. 183).

Perhaps most interestingly, Exposito and Bernheimer (2012) found that the use of narrative and storytelling practices in their community college early childhood education courses

> provided a personally meaningful learning experience for nontraditional students in early childhood programs . . . extend(ed) opportunities for students to connect their cultural capital to content . . . creat(ed) a culture where nontraditional students feel at ease sharing their stories and [began] to establish bonded networks that support them within university life.
> *(pp. 185–186)*

Another effective approach was established by faculty at Skagit Valley College, a Washington State community college, who realized that although their working early childhood education students took a number of courses over time, few were actually graduating with an associate's degree. By identifying the supports and barriers faced by their students, they developed a program that takes serious account of "the working lives . . .values, cultures, and communities of adult students" (Chu et al., 2010, p. 25), using a model found in care and education settings for young children and their families embracing "consistency, predictability, and commitment" (p. 25). Specifically, the designers of this program responded to the particular characteristics and needs of the bourgeoning Latina adult student population they serve. Bilingual faculty were hired in the interest of building bridges across the cultural and educational experiences of the teacher educators, adult students, program administrators, and children and families they served. Chu and her colleagues insisted that the college advisors, faculty mentors, and practitioners who understood the community as a whole and were committed to serving this cohort of teachers were essential to the program's success.

Cohorts were established. Students explained that being in a cohort of peers with whom they shared the experiences of the demands of a full-time job, family responsibilities, and self-doubt about their academic abilities was a motivating factor in their success. Academic supports included advanced language courses for native speakers, and courses in child development and on children's second language acquisition, in both Spanish and English. Students who had completed these courses later became practicum site model teachers for the next cohort.

Students who were already employed as classroom teachers expressed concerns about returning to college and that college faculty would not recognize or value their previous classroom and community-based experiences. In response, and with the intention of establishing partnerships between the early childhood teacher education program and local Head Start and daycare programs, a program consultant and a child care center director were hired as faculty.

Faculty also endeavored to find the best possible times and locations to offer courses for this student population. Evening, weekend, and intensive summer classes answered working students' scheduling needs. Students moreover reported having benefited tremendously from informed advisors who helped them negotiate the maze of documentation necessary in the financial aid application process. On-going student advisement and programmed quarterly meetings between faculty and students helped address social, emotional, and academic issues that arose, corresponding to situational, dispositional, and institutional barriers. As Chu explains, "College advising was key in discerning if the working teacher-student needed time off for a quarter or simply a pep talk to show what little remained in their degree plan" (Chu et al., 2010, p. 28). Essentially, Skagit Community College developed a program, a faculty, and a community of learners that recognized and supported the values, cultures, and communities of working adult students.

Responsive Four-Year Programs

Jeanette Haynes Writer and Heather Oesterreich (2011) presented highlights of an early childhood and elementary four-year education program at a southwestern university, developed expressly to

> increase the number of highly qualified teachers with a foundational imperative of cultural continuance of the Pueblo people . . . and . . . develop a model professional development program that was sustainable and owned by the local Native community to address the specific cultural and contextual needs of the children.
>
> *(pp. 509–510)*

As teacher educators, they address how colonization "continues to render Native people and their cultural continuance invisible in the policies and practices of teacher education and the conceptualization of 'high-quality' teaching" (Haynes Writer & Oesterreich, 2011, p. 511). The women in this program very much fit the definition of the "new" or nontraditional college student: ages ranged from mid-twenties to late fifties; many were mothers or grandmothers; and all were working full-time as assistants in schools or Head Start centers in rural settings.

Professor Haynes Writer directed the program. Her scholarship was an important aspect of her position as role model (Villegas et al., 2012), and her presence supported negotiations that incorporated Native protocol. Additionally, student leaders who encouraged communication and support networks on and off campus strengthened cohorts.

Although online courses were offered to address the issue of access to the college's many campuses, due to inconsistent Internet access this modality did not serve the entire community. But perhaps more importantly, many students rejected online courses which "frequently ignored relational learning" (Villegas et al., 2012, p. 514), which students valued.

Respecting the sacrifices made, faculty fashioned policies that acknowledged school absences as unavoidable in the face of these women's commitment to remain responsible to both their communities and their own growth. Additionally practical measures were taken and students were provided with laptops, printers, and other essential materials, including books, tuition, and exam fees.

Ultimately, Haynes Writer and Oesterreich (2011) summarized, "much of the success of our program has been centered in the world of relational advocacy to sustain the participants' persistence in becoming licensed teachers in their community" (p. 520). For them, characteristics of a "highly-qualified" teacher rest not in test scores and certification, but rather by relationships that nurture and sustain communities and cultivate ownership of and capable leadership in early childhood settings.

Also using cohort models that took advantage of naturally developing nurturing relationships, six universities in California created bachelor's completion programs with the ultimate intention of expanding access to higher education for the early childhood workforce there. In response to numerous policy changes, including expansion of publicly funded pre-kindergarten programs and new Head Start certification requirements, cohorts were developed consisting of women who shared similar interests and characteristics, including years of experience working in care and education settings, being the first in their families to attend college, and ethnic and linguistic characteristics. Some had made previous attempts at college attendance. Researchers at the Center for the Study of Child-care Employment at the University of California, Berkeley, conducted a longitudinal study of these cohorts and the data reported here come from the Year 4 report of graduated cohorts, two or three years after completion (Kipnis et al., 2012).

As is typical of the early childhood workforce, 96 percent of the participants in the *Learning Together* study were women. In these cohorts, the majority were women of color (74%) and nearly half reported their primary language as other than English. The average age was 45 years. Over three quarters of graduates worked in child care, averaging 16 years in the field, often in linguistically diverse settings serving low-income families.

As early childhood educators attending college, more than half identified financial assistance as the linchpin to their success. At the same time, students cited concrete organizational characteristics such as flexibility of class schedules and convenient class locations as being directly responsive to their needs as full-time working women whose schedules also included family and community commitments.

Additionally, students noted that their cohort experience, which created a sense of community within the college setting, was often transferred to their workplaces, both during their time in school and after graduation. About three quarters of the women reported that they had developed relationships with others in the cohort that created a cadre of professional resources including visiting each other's classrooms, discussing how to implement new teaching methods, and keeping each other informed about policy or other developments in the early childhood field. And, importantly, friendships formed as students shared experiences and found emotional support from members of their cohort.

Almost all of the women in the fourth year of this study perceived obtaining their bachelor's degree as not only having a positive influence on their professional lives, including promotions and pay increases, but on their personal lives as well (Kipnis et al., 2012). Students asserted that their general education courses had helped them succeed in upper level early childhood education courses, and had greatly improved their written and oral presentation skills, enhancing their standing as professionals. They also linked these skills to improved relationships with children and families. Finally, many reported plans to pursue a master's degree, since better career opportunities, feelings of competency, increased self-esteem, and greater financial security all appeared to have contributed to their visions of themselves as lifelong learners.

International Perspectives

Much like the Southwestern cohort, a New Zealand study that examined students' impressions of a teacher education program located in a culturally and ethnically diverse community, identified location as a major source of the program's strength (Stephenson, Anderson, Rio, & Millward, 2009). Students found that pragmatic attributes included access to a broader range of study along with early childhood teacher education, and that familiarity with the community provided an additional sense of unity and strength for them as they prepared to teach in diverse urban schools.

In England, Gardner (2008) has meaningfully addressed the recruitment of minority ethnic students to initial teacher education programs. He interviewed students from diverse ethnic minority backgrounds and found that their choice of university had much to do with perceived characteristics of staff and faculty that paralleled familial relationships. Proximity to home and family was cited as the most influential factor in their choice of school.

Gardner (2008) also examined teacher candidates' experiences in student teaching practicum sites, documenting their concerns regarding what they perceived as direct or indirect racism toward children. He describes candidates' sense of powerlessness in these situations and aligns this with Gordon's suggestion that ". . . students who have been marginalised (sic) . . . are particularly unlikely to be prepared and socialised (sic) for the teaching profession" (as cited in Gardner, 2008, p.7).

Gardner's (2008) recommendations for recruiting and retaining diverse teacher candidates included the development of partnerships with local minority ethnic communities, which emphasize the importance of minority ethnic students and teachers working in all types of schools. He further asserted that colleges must address institutional barriers by implementing measures to reduce the financial hardship experienced by some minority ethnic students, increase the proportion of minority ethnic academic staff, and assure students that their concerns about racism will be addressed. Gardner (2008) was optimistic that if universities pay specific attention to and make clear how they will address racism in their curricula and in school placements, minority ethnic students' altruistic motivations for teaching will "win out".

Reimagining Teacher Education for the "Nontraditional" ECCE Student

The exemplary models of early childhood teacher education programs described here both acknowledge and respond to the particular needs of nontraditional early childhood teacher education students seeking college degrees. The successes of these programs suggest structural and relational considerations as crucial to the mission of effectively attracting, supporting, and graduating early childhood workers from working class, ethnic, and language minority backgrounds for whom there have been few expectations or supports for obtaining a college degree. Several of these are practical in nature and involve ensuring that certain structures are firmly in place in teacher education programs serving nontraditional early childhood education students. These include *scheduling* that responds to early childhood educators' working hours, their need for part-time registration, and acknowledgment that graduation will not necessarily take place within four years; *financial aid* allotments providing not only the costs of tuition, books, and technology but also restoration of lost wages when students must leave their jobs to fulfill licensing requirements as interns or student teachers without pay; clear, *well-publicized and streamlined procedures* for helping students access this financial aid; and *full-time academic advising staff* who know the requirements of the early childhood program, and, along with faculty, mentor students while they advance toward program completion and certification. Additionally, as Haberman (1995) suggests, *admissions procedures* that question the validity of standardized test scores, (which have historically skewed pass rates), must include appropriate criteria and include intake interviews that consider candidates' perspectives on the profession, attitudes toward diverse learners and families, as well as management style and expectations of themselves as lifelong learners.

Perhaps what most warrants crucial attention as we reimagine teacher education programs for the early childhood workforce derives from our understanding, as early childhood educators, of the importance of social and emotional nurturing in educational settings. For the group of adult, nontraditional students considered here, this can take the form of engaging in mutual inquiry and justice-focused activism with other adults.

Such a project points, first and foremost, to the importance of concerted efforts on the part of college faculty members to familiarize themselves with the literature on adult learning, in particular, that which draws attention to the academic and cultural dissonance experienced by many new or nontraditional students. As well, early childhood teacher education faculties must, themselves, become more diversified. Such a faculty is more likely to create an environment of relational advocacy (Haynes Writer & Oesterreich, 2011).

This project moreover involves attention to the benefits of a cohort model, namely that students take advantage of cohort supports while in college and often continue to nurture these relationships to create crucial professional and personal networks when they leave college. The first-year report of the *Learning Together* longitudinal study (Whitebook, Sakai, Kipnis, Almaraz, Suarez, & Bellm, 2008) suggested that the cohort approach, combined with advising and counseling and financial, skill-based, and access-based supports, have enabled working adults—nearly one-half of whom had previously tried unsuccessfully to complete a college degree—to enter upper-division degree programs and succeed.

Reimagining teacher education programs for the early childhood workforce also draws attention to the potential of narrative as a means and place for nontraditional early childhood students to share and validate their experiences and funds of knowledge. Using and trusting in experience as a valid starting place for reflection and theory making, adult students of early childhood education can be encouraged to view themselves as creators of pedagogy and theory. Additionally, nontraditional students should be encouraged to identify, speak, and write about the realities they may face. Such open discussion might help the new student decipher expectations of her college experience and to find her place within the university.

Finally, an important recommendation to be made here centers on possibilities presented when nontraditional early childhood education students carefully examine their own past educational experiences. As described above, students must address the historical, social, and economic structures and mechanisms that have determined the life-circumstances in which they currently find themselves (Wilgus, 2013).

Classroom teachers must also be equipped with sufficient multicultural capital (Gardner, 2008) to challenge the status quo. Armed with such understandings, early childhood teacher educators are positioned to

> engender indignation . . . (and) call attention to . . . experiences . . . in which educational inequities are reproduced in current care/education practices. Such indignation might provoke these teacher candidates to examine the mechanisms underlying this reproduction, positioning them to challenge the assumptions and frameworks from which poor children's academic performance (Bartolomé, 2004) has historically been evaluated and discussed.
>
> *(Garavuso, 2013 p. 58)*

This may also provide opportunities to address theories, regulations, and behaviors that ignore the various forms of cultural capital early childhood workers from different ethnic, socioeconomic, and linguistic backgrounds bring to college coursework and which thus ultimately perpetuate normative cultural knowledge in university classrooms. Engaging in this process might additionally open avenues for teacher candidates from a broad range of backgrounds to become part of a shared discourse on early childhood teacher education, creating a clear and accessible pathway to a reconfigured professional identity for the early childhood workforce.

Acknowledgement

Many thanks to Gay Wilgus, for her generous and consistent guidance and support during the writing of this chapter.

References

Barnett, W.S. (2011). *Preparing highly effective Pre-K teachers.* Paper presented at The Early Childhood Care and Education Workforce: A Workshop, Washington, DC.

Barnett, W. S., Yarosz, D. J., Thomas, J., Jung, K., and Blanco, D. (2007). Two-way and monolingual English immersion in preschool education: An experimental comparison. *Early Childhood Research Quarterly,* 22(3), 277–293.

Bartolomé, L. I. (2004). Critical pedagogy and teacher education: Radicalizing prospective teachers. *Teacher Education Quarterly,* 31(1), 97–122.

Bowman, B., Donovan, M. S., & Burns, S. (Eds.) (2001). *Eager to learn: Educating our preschoolers.* National Research Council, Committee on Early Childhood Pedagogy. Washington, DC: National Academy Press.

Brandon, R. N., Stutman, T. J., & Maroto, M. (2011). The economic value of the U.S. early childhood sector. In E. Weiss & R. N. Brandon (Eds.), *Economic analysis: The early childhood sector* (pp. 19–41). Washington, DC: Partnership for America's Economic Success.

Brookfield, S. (1987). *Developing critical thinkers: Challenging adults to explore alternative ways of thinking and acting.* San Francisco, CA: Jossey-Bass.

Carter, D. F., Mosi Locks, A., Winkle-Wagner, R. (2013). From where I enter: Theoretical and empirical considerations of minority students' transition to college. In M. C. Paulson (Ed.), *Higher education: Handbook of theory and research,* (Vol. 28), (pp. 93–149). Dordrecht, The Netherlands: Springer Science & Business Media.

Choy, S. (2002). *Nontraditional Undergraduates, NCES 2002–012.* Washington, DC: U.S. Department of Education, National Center for Education Statistics.

Chu, M., Martínez-Griego, B., & Cronin, S. (2010). Using a culturally and linguistically responsive approach to help working teachers earn degrees. *Young Children, 65*(4), 24–29.

Council for Professional Recognition. (2013). Child Development Associate Council (CDA) Credential™. Retrieved from www.cdacouncil.org

Cross, K. P. (1981). *Adults as learners: Increasing participation and facilitating learning.* San Francisco, CA: Jossey-Bass.

Deutsch, F. M., & Riffin, C. A. (2013). From teachers to students: What influences early childhood educators to pursue college education. *Journal of Early Childhood Teacher Education, 34*(3), 211–230.

Dukakis, K., Bellm, D., Seer, N., & Lee, Y. (2007). *Chutes or ladders? Creating support services to help early childhood students succeed in higher education.* Berkeley, CA: Center for the Study of Childcare Employment, University of California at Berkeley.

Durán, L. K., Roseth, C. J., and Hoffman, P. (2010). An experimental study comparing English-only and transitional bilingual education on Spanish-speaking preschoolers' early literacy development. *Early Childhood Research Quarterly,* 25(2), 207–217.

Exposito, S., and Bernheimer, S. (2012). Nontraditional students and institutions of higher education: A conceptual framework. *Journal of Early Childhood Teacher Education, 33,* 178–189.

Farver, J.A.M., Lonigan, C. J., and Eppe, S. (2009). Effective early literacy skill development for young Spanish-speaking English language learners: An experimental study of two methods. *Child Development,* 80(3), 703–719.

Garavuso, V. (2010). *Being mentored: Getting what you need.* New York: McGraw Hill.

Garavuso, V. (2013). "I'm not just gonna settle for anything": Inciting teacher efficacy through critical pedagogies. In G. Wilgus (Ed.), *Knowledge, pedagogy, and postmulticulturalism: Shifting the focus of learning on urban teacher education,* (pp. 39–62). New York: Palgrave.

Gardner, P. (2008). *The Recruitment of Minority Ethnic Students to Initial Teacher Education.* Paper presented at the British Educational Research Association Annual Conference, Heriot-Watt University, Edinburgh, 3–6 September, 2008.

Gay, G. (2000). *Culturally responsive teaching: Theory, research, and practice.* New York: Teachers College Press.

Gordon, J. A. (2000). *The color of teaching.* New York: Routledge Falmer.

Gormley, W. T., Jr. (2007). Early childhood care and education: Lessons and puzzles. *Journal of Policy Analysis and Management,* 26(3), 633–671.

Haberman, M. (1995). *Star teachers of children in poverty.* West Lafayette, IN: Kappa Delta Pi.

Haynes Writer, J., & Oesterreich, H. A. (2011). Native women teacher candidates "with strength": Rejecting deficits and restructuring institutions. *Action in Teacher Education 33,* 509–523.

Institute of Medicine and National Research Council (IMNRC). (2012). The early childhood care and education workforce: Challenges and opportunities—A workshop report. Washington, DC: The National Academies Press.

Kelley, P. & Camilli, G. (2007). The impact of teacher education on outcomes in center-based early childhood education programs: A meta-analysis. NIEER Working Paper. New Brunswick, NJ: National Institute for Early Education Research.

Kersten, K., Frey, E., and Hähnert. A. (2009). *ELIAS: Early language and Intercultural Acquisition Studies.* Magdeburg, Germany: EU Education, Audiovisual and Culture Executive Agency.

Kipnis, F., Whitebook, M., Almaraz, M., Sakai, L., & Austin, L.J.E. (2012). *Learning Together: A study of six B.A. completion cohort programs in early care and education. Year 4.* Berkeley, CA: Center for the Study of Childcare Employment, University of California at Berkeley.

Knowles, M. S. (1984). *Andragogy in Action.* San Francisco, CA: Jossey-Bass.

Lambert, R. G., Sibley, A., & Lawrence, R. (2010). Choosing content. In S. B. Neuman & M. L. Kamil (Eds.), *Preparing teachers for the early childhood classroom: Proven methods and key principles,* (pp. 67–85). Baltimore, MD: Brooks Publishing.

Maroto, M., & Brandon, R. N. (2012). Summary of background data on the ECCE workforce. In Institute of Medicine and National Research Council (Ed.), *The early childhood care and education workforce: challenges and opportunities: A workshop report.* Washington DC: The National Academies Press.

McLaren, P., and da Silva, T. T. (1993). "Decentering pedagogy: Critical literacy, resistance and the politics of memory." In P. McLaren & P. Leonard (Eds.) *Paulo Freire: A critical encounter* (pp. 47–89). New York: Routledge.

Mehta, S. S., Newbold, J. J., & O'Rourke, M. A. (2011). Why do first-generation students fail? *College Student Journal 4*(2), 1–20.

Mezirow, J. (1991). *Transformative dimensions of adult learning.* San Francisco, CA: Jossey-Bass.

Morgan, G. (2009, Nov/Dec). Higher education: A closer look—Part 2. *Exchange,* 100–102.

National Association of Child Care Resource & Referral Agencies (NACCRRA). (2011). *We can do better: NACCRRA's ranking of state child care center regulations and oversight: 2011 Update.* Retrieved from http://www.naccrra.org/publications/

National Education Association (NEA). (2010). Raising the standards for early childhood professionals will lead to better outcomes. Policy Brief. Washington, DC: NEW Education Policy and Practice Department. Retrieved from http://www.nea.org/assets/docs/HE/PB29_RaisingtheStandards.pdf

Nieto, S. (2000). *Affirming diversity: The sociopolitical context of multicultural education* (3rd ed.). New York: Longman.

Ochoa, G. L. (2007). Learning from Latino teachers. San Francisco, CA: Jossey-Bass.

Rhodes, H., and Huston, A. (2012). Building the workforce our youngest children deserve. *Society for Research in Child Development: Sharing Child and Youth Development Knowledge. 26*(1).

Russell, S. (2012). *College completion for the early education workforce: A focus on student success.* T.E.A.C.H Early Childhood and Childcare WAGES Annual National Program Report 2011–2012. Retrieved from http://www.childcareservices.org/_downloads/TEACH_AnnualReport_2012

Saracho, O. N. (2013). Early childhood teacher preparation programmes in the USA. *Early Child Development and Care, 183*(5), 571–588.

Stephenson, M., Anderson, H., Rio, N., & Millward, P. (2009). Investigating location effects in a multicultural teacher education programme. *Asia Pacific Education, 29*(1), 87–99.

Su, Z. (1997). Teaching as a profession and as a career: Minority candidates' perspectives. *Teaching and Teacher Education, 13*(3), 325–340.

Unverfeth, A. R., Talbert-Johnson, C., & Bogard, T. (2012). Perceived barriers for first generation students: Reforms to level the terrain. *International Journal of Educational Reform, 21*(4), 238–252.

U.S. Congress 42 USC 9801 et. seq. 2007. Sec. 648A Staff Qualifications and Development. Improving Head Start for School Readiness Act of 2007. Retrieved from http://eclkc.ohs.acf.hhs.gov

U.S. Department of Education, National Center for Education Statistics. (2002). *Nontraditional Undergraduates, NCES 2002–012,* by Susan Choy. Washington, DC.

U.S. Department of Education, National Center for Education Statistics. (2013). *Digest of Education Statistics, 2012* (NCES 2014–015), Chapter 3. Retrieved from http://nces.ed.gov/fastfacts/display.asp?id=98

Villegas, A. M., Strom, K., & Lucas, T. (2012). Closing the racial/ethnic gap between students of color and their teachers: An elusive goal. *Equity & Excellence in Education, 45*(2), 283–301.

Washington, V. (2008). *Role, relevance, reinvention: Higher education in the field of early care and education.* Boston, MA: Wheelock College.

Whitebook, M., & Ryan, S. (2011). *Degrees in context: Asking the right questions about preparing skilled and effective teachers of young children* (Preschool Policy Brief Vol. 22). New Brunswick, NJ: National Institute for Early Education Research.

Whitebook, M., Sakai, L., Kipnis, F., Almaraz, M., Suarez, E., & Bellm, D. (2008). *Learning together: A study of six B.A. completion cohort programs in early care and education. Year I report.* Berkeley, CA: Center for the Study of Childcare Employment. University of California, Berkeley.

13

PRESERVICE EARLY CHILDHOOD TEACHER EDUCATION

Sharon Ryan and Megan Gibson

Preservice teacher education refers to any program where learning about how to teach occurs before entering a classroom with full responsibility for the education of young children (Whitebook, Gomby, Bellm, Sakai, & Kipnis, 2009). However, unlike the K-12 sector where it is expected that nearly all teachers participate in some kind of preservice program of preparation to obtain a 4-year degree and teaching certificate, the value placed on the work of teaching in early education and the qualifications a teacher needs has been delineated by whether the focus of the work is on care or on education (Osgood, 2012). Those early childhood practitioners seeking to work in public schooling contexts are typically expected to obtain a 4-year degree and teaching credential. Alternatively, depending on state and program requirements, early childhood teachers working in before-school settings such as child care may be required to have as little as a high school diploma to be a lead teacher, and therefore are not required to engage in any kind of specialized education before assuming their responsibilities with children. As a consequence of there being no agreed upon baseline qualification for all teachers working with young children from birth through age 8 years, the early childhood workforce is comprised of "highly skilled and tertiary trained specialists" (Productivity Commission, 2011, p. 204), teachers with some education and training as well as those with minimal preparation. Preservice teacher education programs therefore are one of a number of pathways early childhood practitioners can take to work with young children. As preservice teacher education programs in institutions of higher education are at a minimum two years and a maximum of four to five years of length, they also are a more elite and longer pathway to the classroom.

Given the length of time preservice programs take, it might be assumed that early childhood practitioners who take this pathway to the classroom are armed with a depth of professional knowledge and expertise that enables them to teach across settings (e.g. child care, public school, Head Start) and age groups (e.g. infants and toddlers, preschool, grades K-3). Unfortunately, not a lot is known about what takes place in early childhood preservice teacher education programs. The research on early childhood higher education is sparse (Hyson, Horm, & Winton, 2012), as the field has been more concerned with determining level of education (BA or AA) rather than the content and delivery of teacher education programs that contribute to improved practices with young children (Whitebook & Ryan, 2011).

The purpose of this chapter is to examine the research base on preservice early childhood teacher education to ask what is known about particular programs and pedagogies, and the relations between program components and preservice teacher learning and practice. Focusing primarily on empirical studies of preservice teacher education conducted over the past decade, we review the methodological and theoretical lenses used to conceptualize early childhood preservice teacher education with the aim of identifying innovations and promising practices as well as gaps in the knowledge base. At a time when so much policy attention is being given to developing the early childhood workforce, we argue that early childhood teacher educators need to develop a carefully targeted program of research along with an advocacy and policy agenda if the important contributions of preservice teacher education programs are to be acknowledged and capitalized upon.

Research on Preservice Early Childhood Teacher Education

Locating empirical studies of early childhood preservice teacher education is no easy task, in part because the scholarship of the field does not always divide neatly into preservice or inservice programs and approaches. For example, in their early volume on teacher education, Goffin and Day (1994) divide approaches to early childhood teacher education into specific age group foci and what it is that early childhood educators, regardless of whether they are preservice or inservice, need to be prepared to do if teaching infants and toddlers, preschoolers, or kindergarten or above. Given that many teaching positions in early childhood have not required a teaching credential or certificate, it is perhaps not surprising that research specifically on preservice teacher preparation is limited. Yet, the preparation needs of those who have never taught and those who are teaching and trying to improve their qualifications are different.

Moreover, preservice early childhood professional preparation is unique compared to the field of K-12 teacher education. Formal education and certification requirements vary according to the age of children being served, regulatory context, and program type (Whitebook et al., 2011). In contrast to K-12 teacher preparation that typically takes place in schools of education on university campuses, preservice teacher preparation can fall within one of several disciplines (e.g. family studies, education, human development) focused on children (Maxwell, Lim, & Early, 2006; Whitebook et al., 2011).

The literature on preservice programs reflects this diversity and ranges from large-scale survey studies of programs of preparation across a state or country (e.g. Maxwell et al., 2006; Lobman, Ryan, & McLaughlin, 2005; Whitebook, Bellm, Lee, & Sakai, 2005), to program descriptions designed in response to particular challenges or issues in the field (e.g. Jones-Diaz, 2004; Kroll, 2013), to qualitative studies of specific pedagogies such as clinical experience (e.g. Ortlipp & Nuttall, 2011) and student experiences and perceptions of their preparation programs (e.g. Brown, 2009). Uniting all of these studies is an emphasis on the responsiveness of programs and coursework to shifts in the socio-political and knowledge contexts shaping the field.

Survey Studies of Preparation Programs

Across many countries, policymakers keen to harness the economic and academic benefits of quality early childhood programs are creating policies to increase early childhood teacher qualifications, often to include a bachelor's or four-year teaching degree. Examples include the United Kingdom (Osgood, 2012), which aims to be "the best in the world, with a better qualified workforce" (Department for Education and Skills [DfES], 2005); the United States, where a number of states are requiring certified teachers in pre-kindergarten programs; Australia (Department of Education, Employment and Workforce Relations [DEEWR], 2009), which has a new national quality framework requiring 4-year-degree-qualified teachers to be employed in prior-to-school contexts, including child care; and New Zealand's strategic plan for early childhood education outlined by the Ministry of Education, which expects that 70% of staff working in regulated services for children birth through 6 years should be teacher qualified, while the other 30% of staff should be enrolled in a program leading to a teacher qualification (Mitchell & Brooking, 2007).

The increasing policy focus on early childhood education has prompted a number of survey studies that examine the content, pedagogy, and capacity of higher education programs. The general question framing these studies is whether current programs are able to prepare a workforce that can enact the intent of policies and ensure that diverse student populations enter school ready to learn. In the United States, for example, where there is a push for publically funded pre-kindergarten programs, several nationally representative surveys (e.g. Early & Winton, 2001; Maxwell et al., 2006) have been conducted of all 2- and 4-year institutions offering early childhood education programs. In these studies researchers interviewed program representatives about content, clinical experiences, institutional context, and faculty characteristics. A common finding of these studies is that participants are less likely to get training in how to work with students from culturally and linguistically diverse backgrounds or who have special needs. Similarly, in a study solely focused on the diversity coursework early childhood educators receive in programs of preparation, Ray, Bowman, and Robbins (2006) surveyed the websites, syllabi, and program descriptions of 226 bachelor degree-granting programs. They found that "few hours of coursework and little practice is devoted to teaching early childhood teachers how to be effective educators of children of color, second language/dialect speakers, and others" (Ray et al., 2006, p. vii).

A series of state-level studies of preschool teacher preparation programs in New Jersey supports these findings (Lobman et al., 2005; Ryan & Ackerman, 2005). Although a specialized P-3 teaching certificate was created in 2002 when previously there had been none, both teacher educators and preservice teachers reported that preparation in addressing diversity issues in the classroom was less available than other content. When teachers were asked a series of questions about their efficacy to teach particular student populations, less than 50% of teachers reported feeling skilled working with students with special needs and English Language Learners.

In Australia the policy emphasis on early childhood teachers having a bachelor's degree to work in child care services led Garvis, Lemon, Pendergast, and Yim (2013) to examine the emphasis on infant and toddler content in the country's higher education programs. According to the researchers, because preservice teachers have typically been prepared for early elementary classrooms, infant and toddler content and pedagogical content knowledge is often not addressed in preservice teacher education within Australia. A content analysis was conducted on program descriptions, and course outlines downloaded from the websites of 55 programs that provide a 4-year undergraduate university degree in early care and education and are approved by the Australian Children's Education and Care Quality Authority (ACECCQA). After coding for content, or presence of a clinical experience and assessment items focused on infants and toddlers, the authors found that only 15 out of the 55 programs stated an explicit focus on this age group in course content, while 18 institutions offered some kind of a practical experience. Interestingly, the majority of programs that provided a clinical experience, in addition to classes and assignments focused on infants and toddlers, were located primarily in one state, raising concerns about the number of teachers qualified to work with this age group given the Australian Government's focus on upskilling the child care workforce.

Recent studies of the early childhood preparation system in various U.S. states illuminate similar trends. For example, in studies of the programs in New Hampshire (Kipnis, Austin, Sakai, Whitebook, & Ryan, 2013) and New Jersey (Kipnis, Whitebook, Austin, & Sakai, 2013), it was found that infant and toddler coursework was not available in many 4-year institutions of higher education, in part because the emphasis in states like New Jersey has been on building a workforce for the state preschool program serving 3- and 4-year olds. As a consequence preservice teachers were unlikely to have field based experiences working with children under the age of 3.

One reason for the limited availability of coursework for diverse student populations and particular age groups may be because the majority of faculty working in higher education teacher education programs are predominantly White. Moreover, faculty with direct experience with young children are more likely to be found in 2-year institutions and not bachelor-degree granting institutions (Maxwell et al., 2006). Perhaps not surprisingly, the topics of working with dual language learners and children with special needs, as well as working with culturally and linguistically diverse college students, were most frequently cited as professional development needs by faculty in several surveys of the capacity of the higher education systems of particular American states (Austin, Kipnis, Sakai, Whitebook, & Ryan, 2013; Kipnis, Austin, et al., 2013; Kipnis, Whitebook, et al., 2013).

Studies of the capacity of institutions of higher education programs to engage in the kinds of quality improvement needed to meet policy aims suggests that the building of faculty capacity such as professional development and hiring full-time faculty in early education and care is not necessarily a priority (Hyson, Tomlinson, & Morris, 2009), in part because early childhood education is not valued by the school or institution (Kipnis, Whitebook, et al., 2013). This devaluing of early childhood education at a time of high expectations and accountability is concerning given that several studies of state systems of higher education in the U.S. report that many faculty are above 50 years of age and little attention has been given to developing a cadre of diverse and qualified faculty to replace them (Kipnis, Austin, et al., 2013; Kipnis, Whitebook, et al., 2013).

These large-scale survey studies of teacher education programs aim to inform policy and therefore tend to use self-reports of program administrators coupled with examinations of documents such as websites and syllabi. While helpful in highlighting the strengths and gaps in program offerings in a particular location as well as the identification of particular capacity issues that may hinder a state or nation's quality improvement policy agenda, these studies offer little wisdom as to programs in action and students' experiences in these programs.

Descriptions of Programs and Courses

Political and conceptual shifts in the field have prompted some teacher education scholars to describe how they have reformed their programs. For example, Davies & Trinidad (2013) describe how they restructured the curriculum of their teacher education program in Australia so that their students were able to meet new policy expectations that 4-year certified teachers be able to work in child care settings. As part of this revising, they report providing opportunities for preservice students to learn about state and national policies, adding more in-depth content focused on infants and toddlers and requiring students to work in wrap-around services so that they had to engage with a range of families.

Much of the program and course description work focuses on how teacher educators are altering the knowledge base and aims of their preservice programs (e.g. Genishi, Huang, & Glupczynski, 2005; Ryan & Grieshaber, 2005; Sumsion, 2005; Viruru, 2005). Critiques of the child development research base (e.g. Burman, 2008; New, 1994) highlight how most of the studies supporting accepted views of development have been conducted with homogenous populations (White, middle-class). As a consequence, it is argued that teachers cannot be culturally responsive or inclusive of all children's learning by relying primarily on child development theory and research or by implementing developmentally appropriate practices (Ryan & Grieshaber, 2005). Instead, these scholars argue for the inclusion of knowledge that helps preservice teachers to understand their own identities and how these identities and their actions as teachers enact relations of power and privilege. For example Sumsion (2005) describes how she uses postmodern theory as a teacher educator while Viruru (2005) explains how she uses postcolonial theory with her students to help them navigate the politics of teaching young children.

Several teacher educators describe how they have designed programs to ensure that their students are prepared to enact social justice pedagogies. Working in the United States in a small, private liberal arts college, Kroll (2013) explains how the program educates prospective teachers about the cultural nature of development and aims to instill an inquiry stance in students so that they learn to critically reflect on knowledge. Similarly, Jones-Diaz (2004) from the University of Western Sydney describes three subjects/courses in the bachelor's degree program that teach preservice teachers about the social construction of identity markers (e.g. race, class, gender, sexuality, ethnicity, etc.) and their own positioning and views of diversity, as well as offering prospective teachers opportunities to work in diverse early childhood settings where they engage in assignments to redress inequities in the classroom.

Building on these program descriptions, several teacher educators have empirically examined specific coursework that attempts to address equity issues with preservice teachers. For example, Agbenyega and Klibthong (2012) asked 120 preservice students about their learning after participating in a course unit that introduced them to a range of theories and tools about difference and diversity. In the unit, "Spaces of Difference," first-year students were encouraged to critically examine their own identities and experiences in relation to people who differed from themselves. To address their main question of whether students changed from the beginning of the unit, students were asked to respond to prompts in weekly online discussion groups over a 10-week period. Analysis of the qualitative data according to the researchers suggested that these students were beginning to develop new teacher identities that embraced differences although they did not follow-up with the same students toward the end of their program of preparation to see whether these perceived changes were long-lasting. In contrast Genishi et al., (2005), in their action research study of 14 preservice students' assignments completed as part of a language and literacy class, found that their efforts to foreground social justice concepts were not as effective as they would have liked.

These programmatic and course descriptions provide a starting point for other teacher educators considering how best to respond to conceptual and political shifts in the field. However, most of the work in this area is descriptive, offering minimal insight into whether changes made to the curriculum of a program are having their intended impact. Moreover, much of the work in this area does not detail the kinds of pedagogies teacher educators are employing to convey new ideas to preservice teachers.

Research on Pedagogies used in Preservice Programs

Much of the research in preservice early childhood teacher education is comprised of qualitative self-studies conducted by teacher educators of various pedagogies that they have tried out in a particular course to achieve certain goals. How one teaches prospective teachers is not only linked to what one teaches but also assumptions about adult learning and how individuals learn to teach (Grossman, 2005). The kinds of pedagogies studied by early childhood teacher educators seem to be shifting in alignment with changing views of teacher learning. Whereas the 1990's saw a lot of research attention given to pedagogies like case methods, journals, and other tools for individual reflection, the past decade has seen a move toward the use of collaborative pedagogies such as lesson study (e.g. Parks, 2008) and co-student teaching models (e.g. Ammentorp & Madden, 2014; Brown & Danaher, 2008). Influencing most of the recent research on pedagogies in preservice teacher education is the increasing diversity of children and families in early childhood programs and how best to prepare future teachers to be responsive to this diversity at a time of increasing standardization and oversight. The most common pedagogy used and researched to address this need is a range of clinical or field based teaching opportunities.

Field based experiences. Field based experiences, such as student teaching, practica, and the like, might be one of the only signature pedagogies of teacher education, although the number, duration, intensity, and age group focus of field based experiences varies widely between early childhood teacher education programs (Whitebook et al., 2011). A number of teacher educators describe how they take this signature pedagogy and build on its structure and focus to help students learn about particular populations.

For example in Australia, it has been documented (Ailwood & Boyd, 2006; Gibson, 2013; Thorpe, Millear, & Petriwskyj, 2012; Vajda, 2005) that preservice teachers have a negative bias to working in child care with very young children despite national policies requiring 4-year certified teachers in child care settings. Several studies conducted in the United States suggest that practical experiences with infants and toddlers may be a viable way to challenge these negative perceptions. In a qualitative analysis of four preservice early childhood students' weekly dialogue journals that students were required to do as part of a semester-long field experience in infant-toddler classrooms, Recchia and Shin (2010) found that encounters with infants-toddlers created conditions for preservice teachers to "re-think their existing beliefs about infants' capacities and capabilities" (p. 143). Similarly, Beck (2013) documents how three preservice teachers who had no prior experience working with infants and toddlers began to rethink their understanding of the role of the teacher and curriculum in the early childhood classroom because they had to partake in a semester-long practicum with babies. Over the course of the semester, the students began to understand how teaching very young children demands a different kind of mindset and skillset and yet is just as demanding as working with older children.

Another group of studies look specifically at how clinical experiences of differing kinds can contribute to preservice teachers' abilities to work with students with special needs. While many studies focus on the importance of preparing prospective teachers to work in inclusive settings, Recchia and Puig (2011) examined how the use of self-contained early childhood settings as one field experience in a series of five sequenced clinical placements for students enrolled in a dual special education and early childhood education program contributed to their understandings of students with disabilities. After qualitatively analyzing five preservice teachers' journal entries that they recorded weekly over one semester, Recchia & Puig (2011) conclude that student teaching in a self-contained setting as one of several field experiences can encourage future teachers to "think flexibly about teaching children with special needs while enhancing their understanding of the principles behind the continuum of services" (p. 150).

Alternatively, Voss and Bufkin (2011) argue that preservice teachers need to engage in a range of inclusive field experiences linked to coursework if prospective teachers are to be able to work with children with special needs effectively. In this teacher education program, students spend a total of 753 hours of field experience in two different inclusive classrooms. Utilizing a mixed methods evaluation design, Voss and Bufkin (2011) asked, *How do preservice teachers perceive their competence based on inclusive field experiences?* One hundred and twenty-three students over six years of the program were interviewed, observed, and asked to complete an inclusion competency scale. Prior to fieldwork, students reported worrying about working with young children with disabilities but working directly in inclusive settings contributed to their feeling increasingly competent. According to Voss and Bufkin (2011), "field experiences helped clarify inaccurate perceptions and helped preservice teachers develop more appropriate belief systems about working with children with disabilities" (p. 353). Recchia, Beck, Esposito, and Tarrant (2009), in their qualitative study of five preservice special education/early childhood education students who had to participate in five diverse clinical experiences over their 2-year program, concur that extensive practice with children of different ages and abilities leads to future teachers having a deeper understanding of their work.

Taken together these studies on field experience highlight that working directly in a range of diversely populated settings is one way to ensure that students integrate what they are learning in coursework about developmental and cultural differences, equity, and social justice into their beliefs and practices as early childhood teachers. However, Ortlipp and Nuttall (2011), in a series of qualitative studies of culturally and linguistically diverse student teachers and field experiences, illustrate that cooperating or supervising teachers may send contradictory messages about what it means to be culturally responsive. After analyzing the observation reports of supervising teachers of a cohort of international preservice students using poststructural social theory, Nuttall and Ortlipp (2012) found that the reports were silent about the diversity of the student teachers. Similarly, observations in the field sites showed how the supervisory teachers seemed to deny that any cultural differences existed by engaging in compensatory behavior to make up for student teachers' mistakes or by attempting to assume certain behaviors were normal (Ortlipp & Nuttall, 2011). A case study of one of these student teachers (Nuttall & Ortlipp, 2009) illustrates how the ethnicity of the student teacher mediated the supervisory teacher's assessment of her ability to teach. Sue, a student from Singapore whose first language was Mandarin, struggled with particular skills and practices like many preservice teachers. Rather than attributing these deficiencies to Sue being a beginning teacher, her supervisory teacher determined that her inability to master some teaching tasks was a result of Sue's background.

This group of studies illustrates the paradox between the discourse and aims espoused in preservice programs to prepare teachers to enact social justice pedagogies and work with a range of learners in inclusive settings and the fact that preservice teachers are being taught by a teacher educator workforce that may not have the kinds of understandings and skills that programs are trying to develop. As Nuttall and Ortlipp (2012) assert, it seems that teacher educators assume that all prospective teachers are White even though countries like Australia are highly diverse and new teachers entering the field reflect this diversity.

The emphasis on studying practice-based experiences is an important line of inquiry, especially given that there is a growing emphasis on integrating the content of higher education programs with real schooling contexts. For example, a recent report by the National Council for the Accreditation of Teacher Education (2010) has argued that preparing teachers for the 21st century requires programs that are fully grounded in practice in real schooling contexts and integrated with professional and academic content. Many of the studies reviewed here appear to be enacting this kind of implementation although too often the linkages between program philosophy and content and practice remain unexplained.

Along with program descriptions and survey studies of the content and capacity of preservice teacher education programs, studies of pedagogies used by teacher educators provide some sense of the common features pertaining to the preparation of early childhood teachers and what teacher educators themselves are doing to respond to social, political, intellectual, and demographic changes in the field. However, the question remains as to what is the impact of programs of preservice early childhood teacher preparation.

Impacts of Preservice Preparation Programs

It is often argued that the experience of students within early childhood preservice teacher education programs is disconnected from the reality of the teaching work that they ultimately engage in (Hatch, 1999). Sorin (2004) notes "student teachers often report a lack of connection between what is learned in university studies and in the classroom, and often report feeling unprepared for the 'real life' situations that face them in their first days of classroom teaching" (p. 102). Yet limited research exists on the "so what" or impact of preservice teacher education programs as "understanding how higher education contributes to teacher performance is a complex undertaking, requiring researchers to determine differences among teacher education programs along a variety of dimensions, and then to identify which variations are most relevant to student learning and teacher practice with young children" (Whitebook et al., 2011, p. 1). Nonetheless, there are some promising lines of inquiry that can be of some help in this regard.

The first of these lines of inquiry is examinations of *how* preservice teachers develop beliefs about teaching and learning (Brownlee, Petriwskyj, Thorpe, Stacey, & Gibson, 2011; Isikoglu, 2008; Stacey, Brownlee, Thorpe, & Class EAB016, 2005; Walker, Brownlee, Exley, Woods, & Whiteford, 2011). Within this small though growing body of empirical research is a focus on epistemologies or teachers' internal theories/systems of beliefs, and how preservice teachers' understandings of their own knowing and learning interact and are shaped by teacher education courses (Peng & Fitzgerald, 2006), and eventually impact outcomes for children (Stacey et al., 2005). The assumption is that teacher education programs shape preservice teachers' beliefs and values (Darling-Hammond, 2007) so that they align with what is known about best practice. As preservice teachers participate in programs, they develop more sophisticated epistemologies and the level of sophistication is related to their ability to function in the role of teacher in ways that have positive impacts on child outcomes.

A small number of studies conducted in Australia use the Epistemology Belief Questionnaire (EBQ) to measure shifts in the beliefs of prospective early childhood teachers within preservice programs over a period of time. For example, Brownlee et al. (2011) investigated changes in preservice teachers' personal epistemologies as they engaged in an integrated teaching program. An integrated approach to teaching, based on both an implicit and explicit focus on personal epistemology, was developed by a team of teacher educators working across four concurrent units/subjects. Quantitative measures of personal epistemology were collected at the beginning and end of the semester using the Epistemological Beliefs Survey (EBS) to assess changes across the teaching period. Results indicated that preservice teachers' epistemological beliefs about the integration of knowledge became more sophisticated over the course of the teaching period. A key conclusion of the Brownlee et al. (2011) study was that integration of unit/subject content had the potential to promote integrated epistemologies, which, in turn, require different assessment approaches.

In another study, Stacey et al. (2005) examined 65 preservice teachers' responses on the EBQ before and after participating in a 12-week student-teaching placement. Along with this field placement, the preservice teachers participated in a class focused on personal epistemology *and* inquiry methods as "evidence-based knowledge [is] key to developing sophisticated personal epistemologies" (Stacey et al., 2005, p. 6). Pre- and post-tests using Schommer's (1998, cited in Stacey et al., 2005) epistemological questionnaire showed that the students' beliefs had changed in that the group was more likely to integrate knowledge, less likely to believe that knowledge is certain or that learning is based on innate ability, and more likely to criticize the authority of experts. These findings resonate with qualitative studies of student experiences in diverse field based settings where researchers document changes in student beliefs about young children (Beck, 2013), teaching and curriculum in early childhood settings, and professionalism (Recchia et al., 2009).

While changes in teacher beliefs might suggest improved teaching practice, a focus on teacher epistemologies alone without any accompanying observational data and measures of children's learning provides only a limited sense of the impact of a particular course of study or program of preservice preparation. One study that attempted to look at these interrelationships qualitatively was conducted by Brown (2009), who followed nine preservice teachers as they participated in their early childhood preparation program and then when they began teaching in their own classrooms. Situated in Texas, the teacher education program aimed to prepare teachers to teach for understanding by providing them with a range of classes linked with field based work over three semesters. Syllabi from classes were analyzed and preservice teachers were interviewed five times about their experiences as a teacher in training and as a professional as they moved through the program and into the field. It was found that despite reporting learning strategies to teach for understanding, the teachers struggled with how to implement such practices in high stakes, accountability school environments. Thus, even with a carefully sequenced curriculum and integrated field experiences, Brown (2009) argues that unless teacher educators can help prospective teachers adapt constructivist teaching approaches to a range of contexts, teacher education programs will remain disconnected from practice.

In summary, very little is known about the impacts of preservice teacher education programs on prospective teacher learning and their practices once they enter the field as professionals. It would seem that if the curriculum of a program is to be effective there should be some measured changes in teachers' epistemologies or understandings of young children, but as the findings of Brown's (2009) case study suggest, the field needs to be looking at how programs contribute to improved practice and children's learning. Without this kind of research, teacher educators will continue to develop programs that may have little relevance to the complexities of practice.

Toward a Robust Research and Program Improvement Agenda

Krieg (2010) points out that along with increased government attention on early childhood education has come increasing scrutiny of preservice teacher education programs and their ability to prepare a workforce for the demands of an information-rich, technologically mediated, and increasingly diverse society. The studies reviewed in this chapter highlight that there is little coordination or synergy between different programs of research and therefore little information that can be used to both inform policymakers about best practice and ensure that teacher educators maintain creative control over their programs. Those interested in "policy-capturing" work often do not work in the field as teacher educators and their suggestions for action are more about addressing gaps or limitations in program offerings, thus potentially leading to a blaming of those who prepare teachers. While teacher educators are doing most of the up-close program investigations, often these studies are being used to inform program improvement on a small, institution-by-institution basis and not in ways that can help shape the policy agenda. Borrowing from an analogy proposed by Lloyd (2013a & b), early childhood preservice teacher education programs are like the London Underground. Preservice teacher education is a complex array of lines that connect and depart to both comply with governing authorities and attempt creativity in course design. If teacher educators are to drive the policy agenda and not simply react to the demands of lawmakers, then the various lines have to find ways to intersect and work together. In other words, those conducting research on early childhood preservice teacher education and those doing early childhood teacher education must find ways to develop and implement a comprehensive research and advocacy agenda. It is with this aim in mind that we make the following recommendations.

A Research Agenda

This review of the literature on preservice teacher education highlights how the field has accrued empirical wisdom on many different aspects of program design but, at the same time, a lot of what we know about what is taught in early childhood programs, how it is taught, and why it is taught is tacit and context specific. Moreover, the research reviewed in this chapter would suggest that programs may or may not be adding content and pedagogies to their curricula in response to shifts in the social, cultural, and political landscape. Thus, whether prospective teachers are getting up-to-date and relevant preparation is somewhat of a hit or miss affair, in part because there is no agreed upon content, and/or pedagogies for the preparation for early childhood educators that span across geographies, age groups, settings, and credentials (Whitebook et al., 2011). Developing such a coherent vision for preservice teacher preparation is also challenging given that programs of preparation have different institutional histories linked to whether their purpose has been to concentrate on preparing practitioners to predominantly work in child care and/or early school settings (Krieg, 2010). Yet, it seems we are at a significant moment in the field's history, a moment when policymakers in many countries are keen to build systems of quality that cross the boundaries of early care and education, when there have been important conceptual shifts that have expanded understandings of teaching young children beyond child development (e.g. research on early childhood teaching, critical theories, economic analyses), and when the work of teaching young children is occurring in a global and diverse world. Such a confluence of factors would suggest that rather than relying on old ways of doing things, teacher educators have an opportunity for rethinking preservice early childhood program design which in turn requires a particular kind of research agenda.

Teacher preparation that equips teachers for these "new times" calls for the consideration of the "knowledges, skills, values and attributes" that are required of "good teachers" (McArdle, 2010, p. 16) who will make a difference in children's lives. The research reviewed in this chapter would suggest that these knowledge, skills, values, and attributes must span the entire age range focus of early childhood education to include infants and toddlers as well as children in the early years of elementary school. Coursework accompanied by an integrated set of intensive fieldwork experiences also appears to be key to helping prospective teachers understand and experience firsthand the costs and benefits of working in different kinds of classrooms and education and care settings. Yet, aside from research on field experiences, there is little information available about the kinds of pedagogies teacher educators have found effective in helping preservice teachers learn how to work with young children. Moreover, the research on pedagogies does not measure how particular pedagogies shape preservice teacher practice. Self-reports in journals or from interviews with preservice teachers in a class or program are informative. However, quantitative and mixed methods studies are needed of particular pedagogies used across programs and geographies if the field is to have a strong case for the use of particular approaches to the education of new teachers. One sensible place to start this line of inquiry might be to conduct a survey of the various pedagogies used by teacher educators before then digging more deeply into the purposes behind such pedagogies, how they are used by teacher educators, and how effective they are in helping preservice teachers learn particular content, skills, and dispositions. As Grossman (2005) has pointed out, the field of teacher education rarely examines its methods of preparation and yet these are the tools teacher educators use every day to ensure preservice teachers are equipped with both knowledge and know-how to work with young children.

In addition to examining the variety and effectiveness of various pedagogical approaches, what knowledges are valued in the teacher education curriculum also require some consideration. The research on the content of early childhood preparation is largely comprised of counts of the presence or absence of particular courses and practica (e.g. Maxwell et al., 2006). A few studies reviewed here build on these surveys to provide descriptions of particular social justice principles and specific classes that aim to teach students about diversity (e.g. Jones-Diaz, 2004). While the former body of work is helpful in showing trends across institutions and states, and the latter provide some guidance on how to address critiques of the developmental knowledge base and the lack of diversity content highlighted by survey studies, the fact remains that little is known about what is taught in the teacher education curriculum, and whether it is up-to-date and relevant to teaching young children in the 21st century. Therefore, there needs to be a carefully designed set of studies that look at the content of teacher education programs across sites, to identify which knowledge is foregrounded, how much attention is given to particular concepts, and why teacher educators value particular knowledge in their programs for preservice teachers. Such a program of research would also scrutinize dominant discourses framing course programs, help to identify missing perspectives, and thus could open possibilities for rethinking early childhood preservice teacher education. The content of programs also has to be critically examined for relevance to teaching young children. This will require observing preservice teachers in their everyday work and asking them which aspects of their programs they use and what content and experiences may need to be included. Matching theory and practice in this way may help to form a consensus on what should be the knowledge base of preservice teacher education programs.

McArdle (2010) warns that without attention to careful planning and design there is the risk that "undergraduate degree programs can become 'patchwork quilts' with traces of the old and new stitched together, sometimes at the expense of coherence and integrity" (p. 60). To address this concern, a third line of inquiry must look carefully at programs in action and their effects. Like the K-12 teacher education research base (Cochran-Smith & Zeichner, 2005), there are few studies that examine the relationships between the curriculum and pedagogies of preservice teacher education programs, the theories and practices of those who participate in these programs, how graduates of programs perform, and which aspects of these performances contribute to improved child outcomes (Hyson et al., 2012). Teasing out this complex set of interrelationships is no easy task and requires an interdisciplinary approach to both conceptualize and design a set of studies that can capture what takes place in different programs and compare different program designs, as well as follow preservice teachers through their programs and out into the field. Longitudinal studies that follow graduates over time examining their teaching and child outcomes in relation to various teacher education programs are also needed given that many other entities are being allowed to engage in preservice teacher education.

Research on early childhood teaching and teacher education is a small field. The research that has attracted the most attention has been examinations of program quality and type in relation to child outcomes. While this body of work, including economic analyses of quality programs, has raised the importance of a qualified and knowledgeable early childhood workforce, those who prepare preservice teachers are in somewhat of a difficult situation because we have a lot of accrued wisdom but little empirically proven practice. By coming together and developing a research program that utilizes a range of designs to both describe and measure the effects of pedagogies, curriculum content, and programs, it will be possible to speak confidently about what kinds of preparation preservice teachers need to ensure every young child receives a high-quality early educational experience.

Advocating for Early Childhood Teacher Education

A rigorous program of research on early childhood preservice teacher education is of no use if it does not reach policymakers and other teacher educators. Therefore, teacher educators must be strategic in how they package what they do and to whom they communicate about their work. One starting point is to think about working with those in K-12 teacher education. The field of early childhood teacher education is small and those researching and working in teacher education have tended to use early childhood as the "principle" discipline or informant of their work. While this choice has worked to distinguish early childhood teacher preparation as unique and different to K-12 teacher education research, one unintended consequence has been that "the voices of early childhood teacher educators have been missing in the major discourse of teacher education" (Benner & Hatch, 2010, p. 92). Because the K-12 teacher education field is much larger and more influential in policy discussions, those working in early childhood might want to think about how they can connect with K-12 teacher education researchers to advocate for the importance of early childhood preservice teacher education and resources to support its development as a field. One way to begin this partnership work might be for teacher education researchers to become key decision makers in organizations for K-12 education and key informants to editorial decisions on more mainstream teacher education journals.

At the same time, teacher educators and others who research early childhood preservice teacher education need to start developing products that translate research into digestible information for key stakeholders. If key stakeholders are to value the important work of preservice early childhood teacher education, they need white papers and policy briefs that distill the research base into information that can drive reform agendas. The funding for research on teacher education in the U.S. and elsewhere is drying up, and early education and care work is often not viewed as an intellectual endeavor requiring university qualified teaching staff. Therefore, teacher educators and researchers interested in early childhood preservice teacher education must package their work in ways that gets the message out to both the research and policy communities to build support for a qualified workforce and articulate why they need high-quality programs of preparation.

Concluding Thoughts

It seems no matter where one looks, teaching and teacher education are under attack. Neoliberal discourses have helped to create a market of teacher education offerings. Those outside of higher education institutions such as charter schools and various private training institutions are claiming that they prepare teachers more effectively because their programs are grounded in practice. These arguments are not helped by a research base that tends to show that preservice teachers perceive a disconnection between what they learn in their programs of preparation and what they are expected to do in the classroom. In many ways, early childhood preservice teacher education has been on the margins of these debates because of the low status of the field in research and practice communities. Yet with increasing policy expectations and the supports and resources accompanying these expectations, early childhood teacher educators find themselves at a pivotal moment in the field's history. On one hand policy is aiming to make the field more mainstream, and yet those working in teacher education are used to being able to be creative and innovative. Addressing this tension will necessitate leadership that will advocate for a program of research that both captures the essential components of effective preservice early childhood teacher education while also supporting diverse programs that are responsive to contexts and communities. Teacher educators can no longer simply respond to policy shifts in the field but must work together both within early education and beyond to create and implement a strategic program of research and policy-informing strategies that can position early childhood teacher education as central to any education improvement agenda.

References

Agbenyega, J. S., & Klibthong, S. (2012). Transforming selves for inclusive practice: Experiences of early childhood teachers. *Australian Journal of Teacher Education, 37*(5), 65–77.

Ailwood, J., & Boyd, W. (2006). *First year early childhood education students' beliefs about children in long day care.* Paper presented at the Australian Teacher Education Association Conference, Fremantle, Western Australia.

Ammentorp, L., & Madden, L. (2014). Partnered placements: Creating and supporting successful collaboration among preservice teachers. *Journal of Early Childhood Teacher Education, 35*(2), 135–150.

Austin, L. J. E, Kipnis, F., Sakai, L., Whitebook, M., & Ryan, S. (2013). *The state of early childhood higher education in Rhode Island: The Rhode Island early childhood higher education inventory.* Berkeley, CA: Center for the Study of Child Care Employment.

Beck, L. (2013). Fieldwork with infants: What preservice teachers can learn from taking care of babies. *Journal of Early Childhood Teacher Education, 34*, 7–22.

Benner, S. M., & Hatch, J. A. (2010). From the editors: Preparing early childhood educators for 21st century children. *Journal of Early Childhood Teacher Education, 31*(2), 103–105.

Brown, C. P. (2009). Helping preservice teachers learn to teach for understanding in this era of high-stakes early education reform. *Early Childhood Education Journal, 36*, 423–430.

Brown, A., & Danaher, G. (2008). Towards collaborative professional learning in the first year early childhood teacher education practicum: Issues in negotiating the multiple interests of stakeholder feedback. *Asia-Pacific Journal of Teacher Education, 36*(2), 147–161.

Brownlee, J. M., Petriwskyj, A., Thorpe, K., Stacey, P., & Gibson, M. (2011). Changing personal epistemologies in early childhood pre-service teachers using an integrated teaching program. *Higher Education Research & Development, 30*(4), 477–490.

Burman, E. (2008). *Deconstructing developmental psychology* (2nd Ed.). London, UK: Routledge.

Cochran-Smith, M., & Zeichner, K. (2005). *Studying teacher education: The report of the AERA panel on research and teacher education.* Mahwah, NJ: Lawrence Erlbaum.

Darling-Hammond, L. (2007). A good teacher in every classroom: Preparing the highly qualified teachers our children deserve. *Educational Horizons, 85*(2), 111–132.

Davies, S., & Trinidad, S. (2013). Australian early childhood education: From Government policy to university practice. *Journal of Early Childhood Teacher Education, 34*(1), 73–79.

Department for Education and Skills (DfES). (2005). *Children's workforce strategy: Building a world-class workforce for children, young people and families.* London, UK: DfES.

Department of Education, Employment and Workplace Relations (DEEWR). (2009). *National early years workforce strategy.* Canberra, ACT: DEEWR.

Early, D. M., & Winton, P. J. (2001). Preparing the workforce: Early childhood teacher preparation at 2- and 4-year institutions of higher education. *Early Childhood Research Quarterly, 16*, 285–306.

Garvis, S., Lemon, N., Pendergast, D., & Yim, B. (2013). A content analysis of early childhood teachers' theoretical and practical experiences with infants and toddlers in Australian Teacher Education Programs. *Australian Journal of Teacher Education, 38*(9), 25–36.

Genishi, C., Huang, S., & Glupczynski, T. (2005). Becoming early childhood teachers: Linking action research and postmodern theory in a language and literacy course. In S. Ryan & S. Grieshaber (Eds.), *Practical transformations and transformational practices; Globalization, postmodernism, and early childhood education: Advances in early education and day care* (Vol. 14), (pp. 161–192). Stamford, CT: JAI/Elsevier Science.

Gibson, M. (2013). *Producing and maintaining professional identities in early childhood* (Unpublished doctoral dissertation). Queensland University of Technology, Brisbane, QLD.

Goffin, S. G., & Day, D. E. (Eds.). (1994). *New perspectives in early childhood teacher education: Bringing practitioners into the debate.* New York: Teachers College Press.

Grossman, P. (2005). Research on pedagogical approaches in teacher education. In M. Cochran-Smith & K. M. Zeichner (Eds.), *Studying teacher education: The report of the AERA panel on research and teacher education* (pp. 425–476). Washington, DC/Mahwah, NJ: Lawrence Erlbaum Associates.

Hatch, J. A. (1999). What preservice teachers can learn from studies of teachers' work. *Teaching and Teacher Education, 15*, 229–242.

Hyson, M., Horm, D. M., & Winton, P. J. (2012). Higher education for early childhood educators and outcomes for young children. In R. C. Pianta (Ed.), *Handbook of early childhood education* (pp. 553–583). New York: Guilford.

Hyson, M., Tomlinson, H. B., & Morris, C. (2009). Quality improvement in early childhood teacher education: Faculty perspectives and recommendations for the future. *Early Childhood Research & Practice, 11*(1). Retrieved from *http://ecrp.uiuc.edu/v11n1/hyson.html*

Isikoglu, N. (2008). The effects of a teaching methods course on early childhood preservice teachers beliefs. *Journal of Early Childhood Teacher Education, 29*(3), 190–203.

Jones-Diaz, C. (2004). Difference and diversity at the Universty of Western Sydney. *Teaching Education, 15*(1), 97–101.

Kipnis, F., Austin, L., Sakai, L., Whitebook, M., & Ryan, S. (2013). *The state of early childhood higher education in New Hampshire: The New Hampshire early childhood higher education inventory.* Berkeley, CA: Center for the Study of Child Care Employment.

Kipnis, F., Whitebook, M., Austin, L., & Sakai, L. (2013). *The state of early childhood higher education in New Jersey: The New Jersey early childhood higher education inventory.* Berkeley, CA: Center for the Study of Child Care Employment.

Krieg, S. (2010). The professional knowledge that counts in Australian contemporary early childhood teacher education. *Contemporary Issues in Early Childhood, 11*(2), 144–155.

Kroll, L. R. (2013). Early childhood teacher prepaartion: Essential aspects for the achievement of social justice. *Journal of Early Childhood Tecaher Education, 34*(1), 63–72.

Lloyd, M. (2013a). *Finding the balance: Managing synergies and tensions in the whole-of-course design. Audit of agencies impacting on course design.* Brisbane, Qld: QUT.

Lloyd, M. (2013b). *Troubled times in Australian teacher education: 2012–2013. Final Report 2013 of the OLT National Teaching Fellowship. Finding the balance: Managing synergies and tensions in whole-of course design.* Sydney, NSW: Office for Teaching and Learning, Department of Education.

Lobman, C., Ryan, S., & McLaughlin, J. (2005). Reconstructing teacher education to prepare qualified preschool teachers: Lessons from New Jersey. *Early Childhood Research and Practice,* 7(2). Retrieved from http://ecrp.uiuc.edu/v7n2/lobman.html

Maxwell, K. L., Lim, C. I., & Early, D. M. (2006). *Early childhood teacher preparation programs in the United States: National report.* Chapel Hill, NC: The University of North Carolina, FPG Child Development Institute.

McArdle, F. A. (2010). Preparing quality teachers: Making learning visible. *Australian Journal of Teacher Education, 35*(8), 60–78.

Mitchell, L., & Brooking, K. (2007). *First NZCER national survey of early childhood education services, 2003–3004.* Wellington New Zealand Council for Educational Research.

National Council for Accreditation of Teacher Education. (2010). *Transforming teacher education through clinical practice: A national strategy to prepare effective teachers.* Washington, DC: National Council for Accreditation of Teacher Education.

New, R. (1994). Culture, child development, and developmentally appropriate practices: Teachers as collaborative researchers. In B. Mallory & R. New (Eds.), *Diversity and developmentally appropriate practices: Challenges for early childhood education* (pp. 65–83). New York: Teachers College Press.

Nuttall, J., & Ortlipp, M. (2009). Teaching practice assessment in early childhood education: The experience of NESB students and their supervising teachers. Paper presented to the Annual New Zealand Research in Early Childhood Education Conference, Wellington, New Zealand.

Nuttall, J., & Ortlipp, M. (2012). Practicum assessment of culturally and linguistically diverse early childhood preservice teachers. *European Early Childhood Education Research Journal, 20*, 47–60.

Ortlipp, M., & Nuttall, J. (2011). Supervision and assessment of the early childhood practicum: Experiences of preservice teachers who speak English as a second language and their supervising teachers. *Australasian Journal of Early Childhood, 36*(2), 87–94.

Osgood, J. (2012). *Narratives from the nursery: Negotiating professional identities in early childhood.* New York: Routledge.

Parks, A. N. (2008). Messy learning: Preservice teachers' lesson study conversations about mathematics and students. *Teaching and Teacher Education, 24*, 1200–1216.
Peng, H., & Fitzgerald, G. (2006). Relationships between teacher education students' epistemological beliefs and their learning outcomes in a case-based hypermedia environment. *Journal of Technology and Teacher Education, 14*(2), 255–285.
Productivity Commission. (2011). *Early childhood development workforce: Productivity Commission research report.* Canberra, ACT: Commonwealth of Australia.
Ray, A., Bowman, B., & Robbins, J. (2006). *Preparing early childhood teachers to successfully educate all children: The contribution of four-year undergraduate teacher preparation programs.* Foundation for Child Development. Chicago, IL: Erikson Institute.
Recchia, S. L., Beck, L., Esposito, A., & Tarrant, K. (2009). Diverse field experiences as a catalyst for preparing high quality early childhood teachers. *Journal of Early Childhood Teacher Education, 30*(2), 105–122.
Recchia, S. L., & Puig, V. I. (2011). Challenges and inspirations: Student teachers experiences in early childhood special education classrooms. *Teacher Education and Special Education: The Journal of the Teacher Education Division of the Council for Exceptional Children, 34*(2), 133–151.
Recchia, S. L., & Shin, S. (2010). 'Baby teachers': How pre-service early childhood students transform their conceptions of teaching and learning through an infant practicum. *Early Years: An International Research Journal, 30*(2), 135–145.
Ryan, S., & Ackerman, D. J. (2005). Using pressure and support to create a qualified workforce. *Education Policy Analysis Archives, 13*(23). Retrieved from http://epaa.asu.edu/epaa/v13n23/
Ryan, S., & Grieshaber, S. (2005). Shifting from developmental to postmodern practices in early childhood teacher education. *Journal of Teacher Education, 56*(1), 34–45.
Sorin, R. (2004). Webfolio: An online learning community to help link university studies and classroom practice in preservice teacher education. *Australasian Journal of Educational Technology, 20*(1), 101–113.
Stacey, P. S., Brownlee, J., Thorpe, K., & Class EAB016, C. (2005). Measuring and manipulating epistelogical beliefs in early childhood pre-service teachers. *International Journal of Pedagogies and Learning, 1*(1), 6–17.
Sumsion, J. (2005). Putting postmodern theories into practice in early childhood teacher education. In S. Ryan & S. Grieshaber (Eds.), *Practical transformations and transformational practices; Globalization, postmodernism, and early childhood education: Advances in early education and day care* (Vol. 14), (pp. 193–216). Stamford, CT: JAI/Elsevier Science.
Thorpe, K., Millear, P., & Petriwskyj, A. (2012). Can a childcare practicum encourage degree qualified staff to enter the childcare workforce? *Contemporary Issues in Early Childhood, 13*(4), 317–327.
Vajda, M. (2005). *Student teachers' perceptions of a childcare work experience.* Paper presented at the Annual Conference of Australian Research in Early Childhood Education, Melbourne.
Viruru, R. (2005). Postcolonial theory and the practice of education. In S. Ryan & S. Grieshaber (Eds.), *Practical transformations and transformational practices; Globalization, postmodernism, and early childhood education: Advances in early education and day care* (Vol. 14), (pp. 139–160). Stamford, CT: JAI/Elsevier Science.
Voss, J. A., & Bufkin, L. J. (2011). Teaching all children: Preparing early childhood preservice teachers in inclusive settings. *Journal of Early Childhood Teacher Education, 32*(4), 338–354.
Walker, S., Brownlee, J. M., Exley, B., Woods, A., & Whiteford, C. (2011). Personal epistemology in pre-service teachers: Belief changes throughout a teacher education course. In J. Brownlee, G. Schraw, & D. Berthelsen (Eds.), *Personal epistemology and teacher education* (pp. 85–99). Routledge: New York.
Whitebook, M., Austin, L. J. E., Ryan, S., Kipnis, F., Almaraz, M., & Sakai, L. (2011). *By default or by design? Variations in higher education programs for early care and teachers and their implications for research methodology, policy, and practice.* Berkeley, CA: Center for the Study of Child Care Employment, University of California, Berkeley.
Whitebook, M., Bellm, D., Lee, Y., & Sakai, L. (2005). *Time to revamp and expand: Early childhood teacher preparation programs in California's institutions of higher education.* Berkeley, CA: Center for the Study of Child Care Employment.
Whitebook, M., Gomby, D., Bellm, D., Sakai, L., & Kipnis, F. (2009). *Teacher preparation and professional development in grades K-12 and in early care and education: Differences and similarities, and implications for research. Part 1.* Berkeley, CA: Center for the Study of Child Care Employment.
Whitebook, M., & Ryan, S. (2011). *Degrees in context: Asking the right questions about preparing skilled and effective teachers of young children.* New Brunswick, NJ: National Institute for Early Education Research, Rutgers University.

14

FIELD EXPERIENCES IN THE PREPARATION OF EARLY CHILDHOOD TEACHERS

Karen M. La Paro

As the number of early care and education programs for young children increase, attention has been focused on discussions of effective teachers and the pathways to preparing well-equipped, high-quality teachers for young children. Effective early childhood teachers contribute to building a solid foundation for children's development and learning in the early years (Gormley, Gayer, Phillips, & Dawson, 2004; Schulman & Barnett, 2005). Recent research has highlighted the benefits of high-quality early experiences for young children and in contrast the poor, if not dangerous, outcomes for young children exposed to ineffective teachers in low-quality programs (Burchinal, Peisner-Feinberg, Bryant, & Clifford, 2000; LoCasale-Crouch et al., 2007).

Learning to teach is a complex process and continues throughout a teacher's career; teacher preparation can provide the foundation for becoming a teacher (Feiman-Nemser, 2001). Although discussion and debate continues about four-year degrees versus two-year degrees and education requirements for early childhood teachers (Early et al., 2007), merely knowing whether a teacher has a certain degree or not, provides very little information about how effective that teacher may be (Whitebook, Gomby, Bellm, Sakai, & Kipnis, 2009). Rather, efforts are moving forth in early childhood teacher preparation programs to examine the potential effectiveness of teachers. In fact, recent attention has shifted to the specialized training within the applied components (i.e., field based experiences) of teacher preparation programs. Examination of teacher preparation programs seeks to address the question of how to prepare early childhood education teachers so that the students who graduate from these programs are well prepared to be effective teachers in both the specific settings in which they will teach and across the range of settings that provide care and education to young children. These efforts can draw from what has been learned in K-12 preparation, but they must also address the uniqueness of early childhood education which includes children in classrooms and programs spanning a range of ages often from birth to kindergarten and diverse settings, including community child care, Head Start, public pre-K programs, and kindergarten and early elementary classrooms. This chapter provides an overview of field based experiences, the theory and historical perspectives related to teacher preparation, and current research focused on field experiences for preservice teachers. The chapter concludes with challenges, as well as promising practices for field based experiences in early childhood education.

What Are Field Based Experiences?

Field based experiences are the classroom experiences that students in teacher preparation programs complete before graduation. Generally, students observe children and teachers, as well as facilitate or lead classroom activities while under the supervision of a cooperating teacher. The National

Association for the Education of Young Children (NAEYC) Standards of Professional Development highlight the "continuous interplay of theory, research, and practice" offered in field based experiences as a critical component of teacher preparation (2009, p. 6) and the need for supervision and reflection during these experiences to provide and facilitate the development of effective teachers (NAEYC, 2009).

Examination of teacher preparation programs have underscored the variability in field based experiences regarding length, focus, and timing and the need for alignment and linkage of field experiences with students' coursework and assignments in teacher preparation programs (Bornfreund, 2011; Rice & McLaughlin, 2007). Programs which grant a teaching license have a culminating field based experience, generally referred to as student teaching, with requirements aligned with state licensing standards, although the method of supervision, quality of feedback, quality of the site, and time in the classroom may vary (La Paro et al., 2014). The field based experiences prior to student teaching, often termed practica, can range from brief observations in a classroom to semester-long participation in a classroom with responsibilities including lesson/activity planning; implementation and facilitation; behavior guidance/management; meeting with families; and other responsibilities associated with being an early childhood teacher. Whereas states' requirements guide the student teaching experience in some regard, there is much less systematic attention paid to the field based experiences prior to student teaching.

Field based experiences in early childhood teacher education programs are critical elements in the training and development of effective teachers. Ritblatt, Garrity, Longstreth, Hokoda, and Potter (2013) report data indicating the overwhelming majority of students (65%) reported that field experiences had the greatest impact on them during their program, compared to coursework (20%) or even program faculty and staff (15%). Similarly, Ziechner (2010) suggests that students recall their field experiences as the most influential component of their preparation. Outcomes-focused research in P-12 (Pre-K to twelfth grade) demonstrates that achievement, retention, and a sense of being prepared are associated with field based experiences; so that teachers who participated in high-quality field based experiences had classrooms with higher levels of learning, stayed in the field longer, and felt better prepared to be in the classroom (American Association of Colleges for Teacher Education [AACTE], 2010). Given the critical importance of field based experiences, one might assume that field based experiences are well-defined experiences using evidence-based practices for planning and implementation, evaluation with students, and systematic training and support for cooperating mentor teachers. Yet, in reality, little data exist relative to content, learning, or teaching and child outcomes from field based experiences in early childhood programs.

Theory

Relying on Bronfenbrenner's expanded system theory (1979), one can begin to understand the contexts of teacher preparation and the role field based experiences and cooperating teachers have in the development of teachers. Following the major premise of this theory, that optimal learning and development for children occurs through rich learning opportunities and positive growth-promoting interactions with teachers, one can extrapolate to student teachers. In field based experiences, students learn through opportunities presented in the classroom and positive interactions (i.e., proximal processes) with instructors and cooperating teachers. These reciprocal interactions, built from experience and learning, should address the individual learning needs of the preservice teacher, and should occur over an extended period of time to contribute to growth and learning (Bronfenbrenner, 2001). Bronfenbrenner (1979) emphasized the importance of studying development in context and proposed nested and interconnected systems of the ecological environment in which development takes place. Pianta (1999) applied this systems perspective to classrooms, viewing the classroom, the children, and the teachers as dynamic systems simultaneously influenced by many external and internal factors.

Although Pianta's (1999) focus was on understanding teacher behavior, the idea of a system can also be applied to understand the learning and development of preservice teachers, placing the preservice teacher in the center of the system, and taking into account the teacher, the early childhood education program, and the cooperating teacher. The interactions between the preservice teacher and cooperating teacher that occur within this system provide learning opportunities in classrooms, supported with institutional knowledge from coursework, the contextual knowledge of the classroom, and the expertise of the cooperating teacher.

Historical Perspective

The current attention focused on teacher education is not new; in the late 19th century the kindergarten movement prompted a similar examination of teacher education (Blank 2010; Dombkowski, 2001; Weber 1969). As the notion of kindergarten expanded from programs to serve children in poverty to establishing kindergarten classrooms in public schools, kindergarten received mixed reactions, some supportive and some considering kindergarten "a dangerous experimental bomb" (Barbour, 1938, p.26; Weber 1969). Concurrently, trained teachers were needed in these classrooms. State normal schools were established to meet the training needs of teachers, to provide a model school with model classrooms, and to model teaching practices for student teachers (Hunter, 1970).

Just as appropriate learning opportunities for teachers were discussed in these normal schools, the question of what constitutes effective teacher preparation continues today. As early as 1906, Temple advocated for field based experience for kindergarten teachers stating, "I believe the prospective kindergarten teacher needs more time to practice teaching than the would-be grade teacher in which to develop the necessary insight and acquire skill . . . I think it is not uncommon in the normal schools to allow no practice during the first year. I believe that is a fatal mistake" (p. 623). Similarly, Vandewalker (1898) argued that the "quickest way to make a good primary teacher is to bring her into actual contact with kindergarten thought and practice" (p. 432). These early training programs used an apprenticeship model, much like the practicum experiences of today (Shapiro, 1983). The apprenticeship model typically had the preservice teacher observed and supervised by an experienced cooperating classroom teacher; the preservice teacher was expected to observe the practices of the cooperating teacher and model teaching strategies and interactions used by the cooperating teacher, components which are very similar to the current model of field based experiences (i.e., the practicum experience).

Recommendations for Field Based Experiences

The support for classroom-based experiences in teacher preparation is widespread, with several professional organizations identifying this component of teacher education programs as critical to the development of effective teachers (Bornfreund, 2011; NAEYC, 2009; National Council for Accreditation of Teacher Education [NCATE], 2010). The Council for the Accreditation of Teacher Education Programs (CAEP, formerly NCATE) is one agency who grants approval to education programs in institutions of higher education. Two of the areas included in their standards are (1) equipping candidates with content knowledge and appropriate pedagogical tools, and (2) working in partnership with districts to provide strong student-teaching practice and feedback (CAEP, 2013). The NCATE (2010) published report, *Transforming Teacher Education through Clinical Practice*, recommends significant changes in teacher education programs that emphasize field experiences and clinical partnerships between teacher education programs and school districts. The report recommends "turning upside down" the education of teachers in the United States (NCATE, 2010, p. ii). The suggested change attempts to center teacher education in classroom-based experiences with academic content and professional courses as support, rather than continue traditional practice, which emphasizes coursework and uses classroom-based experiences as a supplement to the student's preparation experience.

NAEYC also has published standards for the preparation of teachers in early childhood education. Their standards include an overall vision for the field as well as specific guidelines for programs (NAEYC, 2009). The current NAEYC standards underscore the importance of the "interplay of theory, research, and practice," recognizing that well planned and supervised field experience can contribute to "excellence in teaching" (NAEYC, 2009, p. 6). Articulated in these standards are the challenges in identifying and placing students in high-quality field sites that assist students in the development, application, and refinement of their skills with competent mentorship and supervision, noting that "the strongest indicator of quality is the quality of the students' opportunities to learn and practice, not the quality of the site itself" (p. 6).

In addition to recent support for field based experiences from professional organizations, in her review of what is known about effective teacher education, Darling-Hammond (2006) references three key markers for high-quality teacher education programs related to field based experiences: extended field based experiences, carefully selected and intentionally aligned with coursework, a vision of good teaching across both coursework and field placements, and relationships or partnerships across institutions of higher education and schools to facilitate teaching and teacher education. These recommendations align well with those put forth by professional organizations and reports. A common goal or intent of teacher education and preparation programs seems to be to provide students more time in the classroom with appropriate support and supervision, and connections with programs and schools to develop classroom placements that will foster skills necessary to become an effective teacher, yet the rigorous examination and evidence to support these recommendations is scarce.

Critical Components of High-Quality Field Based Experiences

High-quality field based experiences require careful consideration of important elements and systematic implementation of the process of teacher development and learning. The Center for the Study of Child Care Employment has developed the Early Childhood Higher Education Inventory, which provides information on the current status of teacher preparation programs in institutes of higher education (Austin, Kipnis, Sakai, Whitebook, & Ryan, 2013; Kipnis, Austin, Sakai, Whitebook, & Ryan, 2013; Kipnis, Whitebook, Austin, & Sakai, 2013). The Inventory focuses on several aspects of programs including student field based learning at varying levels of education: bachelor's, master's, and doctoral levels. To date, three states have completed the inventory, New Jersey, Rhode Island, and New Hampshire; the reports demonstrate the variability of field based experiences in teacher preparation programs. From these reports it appears that although many early childhood teacher education programs require student teaching, not all do. Many programs require field based experiences prior to student teaching, but not all do, and some differences exist between ages of children and supervision of student teaching and practicum experiences. As highlighted in other research, few field based experiences are required or offered in settings serving infants and toddlers, and even fewer for student teaching. Similar to other research findings, higher education/teacher preparation programs tend to focus coursework and classroom experiences on children 3 to 8 years of age; often what students and new teachers are learning specific to infants and toddlers is theoretical, academic, and somewhat superficial (Norris, 2010). Currently, less than half (49%) of higher education programs that offer a degree in early care and education for children ages 4 and below require even one course specifically focused on infants and toddlers (Maxwell, Lim, & Early, 2006). Also, criteria for cooperating teachers vary across student teaching and practicum experiences.

High-quality field placements need to articulate critical components such as ages of children and supervision, as well as a process for implementing these experiences for students. AACTE (2010) provides eight key components of field-based experiences:

1. strong school-university partnerships,
2. settings,
3. clinical placements,
4. clinical teachers,
5. coordinating faculty,
6. school-based clinical curriculum,
7. length of program, and
8. performance assessment.

Retallick and Miller (2010) proposed one model for implementing early field based experiences in teacher education. In their model, the foundation of the experience includes the conceptual framework and state, professional, institutional, and national standards. Foundation information and knowledge is critical to developing the field based experience for preservice teachers. Merely observing another teacher without content knowledge and a framework of standards limits the preservice teacher's understanding of teaching and developing of appropriate teaching strategies. Upon this foundation, field experiences need to be organized, requirements established, and documents for communication developed and distributed. These activities are critical to the effectiveness of the experience, and each of these components needs careful consideration: Where are placements and who are the cooperating teachers? Is there a course associated with the field based experiences, or is it a stand-alone experience? Is supervision primary course content? How is the experience organized? Is there guidance for the experience provided via a syllabus? Is there a handbook or guiding document outlining the requirements and expectations for the experience for both the student and the cooperating teaching, and perhaps the university supervisor? What documents are used for observations, notes, and feedback and evaluation? Only after careful consideration is given to the planning and organization of the field based experience can it be implemented with the students and cooperating teachers. The implementation includes two major components: (1) interactions among the student, university supervisors, cooperating teachers, and peers and (2) assessment of the outcomes, learning strategies, and intended outcomes. Although this is just one model for field based experiences, the model includes critical components and elements of effective field based experiences important to explore. Below follows a brief discussion of selected critical components of partnerships between institutions of higher education and schools and programs, supervision in terms of cooperating teachers, and the evaluation of the experience.

Partnerships. Encompassing many of these components, NCATE's 2010 report centered on the idea of coordination between school districts and teacher education programs. Recommendations for teacher education programs and placements included shared decision making and oversight on candidate selection and completion, with a shared responsibility to support the development of "complex teaching skills" (NCATE, 2010, p.ii). This vision outlined by the Blue Ribbon Panel included: (1) more rigorous accountability; (2) strengthening candidate selection and placement; (3) revamping curricula, incentives, and staffing; (4) supporting partnerships; and (5) expanding the knowledge base of what works and supporting continuous improvement (p. iv).

Several K-12 and P-12 programs have established partnerships with schools and programs to create professional development schools. In these models, begun in the 1980s and 1990s, institutions of higher education collaborate and partner with public schools to work toward common goals of high-quality teacher preparation. These partnerships are much more common in K-12 schools, with partnerships between institutions of higher education and P-12 schools emerging. Stroud and Clark (2000) examined the process of developing a partnership between one university and a P-12 school. They highlight the challenges such as teacher turnover, resources, and common definitions of professional growth and development. At the same time the partnership held promise to help professionalize pre-K teachers, allowing them to feel a sense of belonging to the profession and the ongoing collaboration that existed, and providing a foundation for the more formal partnership.

Partnerships can support connections between teaching and field based experiences. Zeichner (2010) presents the idea of mediated instruction, a process in which methods courses are taught in the schools to more directly connect methods being discussed to the practices of teachers within the school. Using this model, students have the opportunity to observe the teachers who are teaching the course and have joint observations of classrooms for discussion of their teaching methods (Feiman-Nemser & Beasley, 2007). These models serve to connect students' learning with the work of experts currently teaching and implementing these practices.

Cooperating teachers. Inherent components of field based experiences are the cooperating, mentoring, or supervising teachers. Following common usage, the term "cooperating teachers" will be used here. Cooperating teachers must be considered a part of the program and work with faculty and institutions to create and support quality experiences and consistent expectations for students (Baum, Powers-Costello, Van Scoy, Miller, & James, 2011; Sayeski & Paulsen, 2012). As mentioned previously, strong relationships that support common knowledge and shared beliefs among school- and university-based faculty engaged in transforming teaching, schooling, and teacher education are critical to student success in field based experiences (Darling-Hammond, 2006). E.M. Weiss and Weiss (2001) and Killian and Wilkins (2009) argue that preparation and the way cooperating teachers mentor is the most important aspect in the development of teachers. Mentoring provides opportunities for students to learn new teaching strategies and approaches, so that they grow in their development as a teacher (Smith, 2007). Fairbanks, Freedman, and Kahn (2000) define mentoring in teacher education as "complex social interactions that mentor teachers and student teachers construct and negotiate for a variety of professional purposes and in response to the contextual factors they encounter" (p. 103). Lai (2005) describes three important components of mentoring in terms of relational, developmental, and contextual dimensions:

- **Relational** can refer to the relationships between cooperating teachers and students.
- **Developmental** refers to how cooperating teachers and students interact personally and professionally within the professional relationship.
- **Contextual features** focus on cultural and situational features of the classroom and education setting.

NCATE has recommended that the skills and attributes required for cooperating teachers be identified and cooperating teachers be carefully selected and prepared in these areas (NCATE, 2010). To support high-quality experiences for students, experts have recommended field based learning that includes "observation, apprenticeship, guided practice, knowledge application, and inquiry" (Feiman-Nemser, 2001, p. 1024). These skills, however, cannot be assumed for all classroom teachers serving as cooperating teachers. The experience, mentoring skills, and training of the teachers must be a consideration in placements (Baum & Korth, 2013). Although the teaching skills and qualifications of the classroom teacher are assumed, the mentoring skills and communication abilities of the cooperating teacher to share information and provide feedback may need to be developed through support and training (Hobson, Ashby, Malderez, & Tomlinson, 2009; Korth & Baum, 2011).

Baum and Korth (2013) recently undertook an examination of the preparation of cooperating teachers, asking the questions of what training is provided, do faculty believe this training is important, and what challenges exist for institutions to provide training and support to cooperating teachers. Of the 62 early childhood teacher preparation programs surveyed, 95% reported believing the training was extremely or very important for cooperating teachers, yet, only 28% required cooperating teachers to participate in training. And, this training varied across respondents, from training to be familiar with the course and requirements to training focused on developing effective mentoring skills. Not surprisingly, resources including money and time were reported most frequently as challenges to providing training.

Evaluating the experience. Attention to evaluation and accountability can assist in assuring high-quality experiences and the connection between students' field experiences and progression to becoming effective teachers. Darling-Hammond (2006) noted that standards to evaluate the field experiences of students should be one of the core components of exemplary programs. Recommendations related to field experiences from NAEYC (2009) suggest the experience should focus on child development, individualizing for children's needs, creating environments that support children's positive growth and development, conducting and using observation and assessment of children for curriculum decisions, building relationships with children, and building family and community partnerships (NAEYC, 2009). Although the degree to which programs address these areas during student teaching is a question in the field of early childhood education, efforts have begun to examine what is occurring in the field experience and what learning opportunities are available to students (La Paro et al., 2014; Maynard, King, La Paro, & Johnson (under review); O'Brian, Stoner, Appel, & House, 2007).

The connection between teacher preparation and child outcomes has moved to the forefront of many discussions. Worrell and colleagues (2014) have recently published recommendations for assessing and evaluating P-12 teacher preparation programs. The recommendations from this report present some significant changes across components of teacher education and have a strong focus on the alignment and collaboration among institutions of higher education, other teacher preparation entities, and districts and programs. This alignment includes efforts to collect necessary data to inform programs, CAEP, and states. The report emphasizes "quality control, program improvement and program fidelity assurance" (Worrell et al., 2014, p. 3). Horm, Hyson, and Winton (2013) also have highlighted the need for evaluation of field based experience so that comparisons can be made across programs and child outcomes can begin to be addressed. The degree to which field based experiences are aligned with state standards and the contribution specifically of field experiences to effective teaching and child outcomes remains an area for study.

Research on Field Based Experiences in Early Childhood Education

Interestingly, even with the attention and importance of field based experiences in teacher preparation, there is an extremely limited research base in early childhood education from which to draw information. Each of these components of partnerships, supervision, and evaluation support high-quality field based experiences for preservice teachers, yet each has its own set of challenges to implementation, given the broad array of settings in which early childhood education is provided and the preparation of teachers to work in these settings. Recent research specific to early childhood education field based experiences is emerging, which provides initial information related to several of these critical components. Surveys of early childhood teacher education programs conducted by Early and Winton (2001) and Maxwell et al. (2006) provided descriptive information of context, content, and needs of teacher preparation programs, and specifically the practicum experiences required and content areas addressed in these field based experiences. Data from respondents from over 400 two- and four-year programs indicated that field based experiences are a component of the majority of bachelor degree and associate degree programs, yet variability exists across program type related to the content included in these practicum experiences.

The Center for the Study of Child Care Employment has conducted studies of higher education programs preparing early education teachers with the intent of influencing and developing policy related to training and preparation. One examination of practicum experiences in higher education is the *Learning Together* longitudinal study of adults currently working in the field and completing their bachelor's degree in early childhood education (Kipnis, Whitebook, Almaraz, Sakai, & Austin, 2012). Overall, participants reported that their education program facilitated their development as effective teachers; in Year 3 participants were asked specifically about their practicum experiences. The vast majority of the students completed practica and about three-quarters of them completed practica in their own classrooms or workplace. Interestingly, about half of the program participants who completed their practicum in their own classroom or workplace reported that they would have preferred to do their practicum in another classroom or in another program. This finding is of note as teacher educators often struggle to find high-quality placement sites and work to coordinate with students' work schedules and transportation issues.

Emerging research has begun to look at field based experiences from the perspective of the student as well as the learning that occurs during these experiences (Maynard, La Paro, & Johnson, 2014; Maynard et al., under review). In the first study, students were interviewed about their experiences during their field-based placements. Five notable themes emerged from these interviews: communication, support, freedom, learning, and "the children." Communication appeared to be at the core of several of the themes. Students in field based experiences expressed the desire to either communicate their questions to their cooperating teachers or receive feedback and information from the cooperating teacher. Communication was connected to the ideas of support and freedom expressed by the students; having their role clearly articulated was important to students, as well as having support communicated to help guide their performance in the classroom. For some students, independence was a form of support to try things out in the classroom, yet for other students a lack of communication or guidelines specified by the cooperating teacher was perceived to be challenging or unsupportive.

Taking a look at learning in the practicum experience and the relevance of coursework, Maynard and colleagues (under review) examined students' reported learning during their practicum. Results from this study found that practicum students reported learning the most about language, literacy, adult-child interactions, and behavior guidance during their practicum experience. The coursework related to diversity, tracking children's growth and development, and reflection were the areas which were most relevant to what they were doing and learning in their practicum classrooms. Overall, students affirmed the relevancy of coursework to their practicum experiences, yet at the same time students' reports indicated the most learning in areas focused on the immediate activities involved in teaching and classroom processes, rather than broader areas such as legislation and policy.

Student Teaching

Given the nature of the profession, new teachers are expected to enter the classroom and effectively interact with and teach young children. This, coupled with the fact that expertise is often reliant on experience, makes the field experiences students have during their education program a critical component of their learning, contributing to their experience and ultimate expertise (Gasbarro, 2008). Several studies and reviews have examined different aspects of student teaching in order to understand student learning and experiences (Anderson & Stillman, 2013; Caires, Almeida, & Vieira, 2012). Similar to the practicum experience, one critical element of the student teaching experience is the feedback students receive about their teaching and classroom performance. MacDougall, Mtika, Reid, and Weir (2013) undertook a study of the feedback used in student teaching in a teacher education program in Scotland in terms of the partnerships among universities and placements for students. These results indicated the challenges of three-way communication, yet the critical need of feedback for students. Students want feedback from their cooperating teachers and from the university supervisor, but synthesizing this feedback to be constructive and understandable to students was a challenge. Additionally, the logistics of meetings of all parties to discuss feedback, highlight key aspects, and make suggestions for students' practice present further challenges.

La Paro et al. (2014) examined the additional information related to the feedback and supervision that students receive during student teaching. Results from a survey of approximately 143 two- and four-year institutions in seven states indicated that programs ranked child development areas, adult-child interactions, and planning as the top three teaching strategy areas for feedback provided to student teachers. Areas of less feedback included inclusion of children with disabilities and implementation of routines and transitions. Regarding supervision provided to student teachers, respondents indicated that on-site visits are the most frequently used source of information for evaluating student teachers, but programs varied in the number of visits completed and length of visits. The study also highlighted the use of formal and informal assessment tools to provide feedback and evaluation of students. Approximately a quarter of programs (n = 32) across two-year institutions (n = 20, 27%) and four-year institutions (n = 12, 20%) used a published tool such as the ECERS-R or CLASS for the evaluation of student teachers. However, many more programs reported using state- or program-developed tools to evaluate student teachers. So it seems that although programs valued the evaluation of students, these evaluations were limited by the available tools and the appropriate use of assessment tools. Student teaching in early childhood education warrants additional exploration in itself, and the coordination and alignment with practicum experiences also needs to be addressed.

Research Needs

Within early childhood education, pre-K is rapidly developing a research base. The burgeoning growth of pre-K and the public money supporting these programs has contributed to the examination of teacher qualifications, and effective practices associated with child outcomes (Early et al., 2007; Pianta et al., 2014). Potential exists to compare and apply what we learn from the research of teacher education and quality in pre-K to the broad age range of early childhood education. Several early childhood studies have looked at teacher beliefs, knowledge, and practice (Hollingsworth & Winter, 2013; Wen, Elicker, & McMullen, 2011), all reasonable areas of study, yet limited in their associations with child outcomes and variables across the age ranges included in early childhood education. The associated variables with child outcomes are vast, complex, and complicated. Careful attention to the goals of this type of research may allow the development of a research agenda that can contribute to the development of high-quality and effective field based placements across age ranges from birth through kindergarten.

One research approach may be longitudinal studies of student outcomes related to field placement experiences. These studies need to take into account both the perspective of the student as well as that of the director or principal in the work setting. Although tracking and following-up with students after graduation is a huge undertaking, information from students about what learning and experiences were most helpful, reviews from administrators and parents about teaching effectiveness, or reviews from outside observers are all important components of this research. Adding to the challenges are the numbers of graduates who actually enter the field of early childhood education and the number who stay past the first year and beyond. Similar to the consideration of appropriate child outcomes, what are ultimately the variables of interest for student outcomes? Do student satisfaction and learning moderate child outcomes? How do specific components of the practicum experiences contribute to student outcomes, and at what point in the students' program do these experiences contribute to student outcomes? Future research will need to explore the complexity of students' experiences during practica to begin to address these questions.

Challenges Related to Field Placements

Early childhood education is a complex and challenging field with the goal of providing high-quality experiences to promote learning and development for young children and to provide a foundation for learning success across a range of ages and types of programs. The preparation and development of effective teachers to provide these experiences has many challenges, especially in the area of field based experiences, which include identifying high-quality placements, the supervision of preservice teachers in field based placements, and resources allocated to field based experiences.

Field placement challenges for early childhood educators are real, with some being unique to early childhood education. The diversity of settings coupled with the range of ages within early childhood education challenge partnerships with multiple programs with varied leadership and administration. The sheer number of placements that are needed for early childhood preservice teachers adds to the challenge. Even a large child care program may only have six to eight classrooms and not all classrooms may have a teacher who meets criteria for cooperating teachers and is eligible to supervise preservice teachers. Although the use of campus child care centers and lab schools provide some advantages (i.e., high-quality experiences, experienced teachers), there are also limitations with these settings for teacher preparation. Graduates whose only experience is in a lab school may not be prepared for the diversity found in other settings relative to administration, families, and resources. And, for early childhood preparation programs that include kindergarten or primary grades, teachers need experience in public schools and curriculum specific to early elementary school. How to provide preservice experiences to prepare preservice teachers to work with children from birth to age 5 or grade 3 is a monumental task. The variation in child development across these age ranges makes working with a toddler very different than working with a second grader, and the settings providing services and education to these children have very different characteristics. The challenge to be addressed is how to prepare and graduate teachers who are effective across the range of settings and across the ages of children included in early childhood programs.

Another challenge is understanding who is supervising, providing feedback, and evaluating preservice teachers in field based placements. Eligibility criteria for cooperating teachers can provide some baseline assurance of quality; however, as surveys have indicated, cooperating teachers tend not to have specialized training in mentoring and may not have the support they need from the institute of higher education to provide optimal supervision and mentoring to preservice teachers completing field based experiences in their classrooms (Clarke, Trigg, & Nielson, 2014). Beyond cooperating teachers, who from the university supervises the students varies across institutions of higher education; whether they are trained in mentoring and supervision, how often they observe students, and what criteria are used for supervision and evaluation are challenges to preparing effective early childhood teachers. The lack of longitudinal research to know what supervision methods and what criteria are essential to the development of effective teachers has resulted in wide variation in practices across institutions of higher education. Standards of practice related to training, supervision, and mentoring are lacking in the field, as are reliable and validated evaluation measures. These are both challenges and areas for discussion and research within the field.

Finally, the resources within institutions of higher education allocated to field based experiences are limited. University supervisors may have increasing numbers of students to supervise as well as limited faculty time allocated to supervision, so programs may be relying even more on cooperating teachers for supervision. Oftentimes supervision is outsourced to adjunct supervisors to minimize travel time and distances and because of the extensive time needed for supervision/observation, feedback, and meetings (Beck & Kosnik, 2002). Adding to these logistical challenges are burgeoning online programs with needs for remote supervision within institutions of higher education. Resources are limited and additional information is needed to help prioritize needs and directions of field-based placements for students. All of these challenges are coupled with very real limitations in the research to date on experiences and outcomes for students' field based placements and the development of effective teachers who graduate, become employed, and remain in the field.

Promising Practices

These challenges related to field based experiences can begin to be addressed in varied ways. The strategy of developing partnerships and designating professional development schools used in K-12 and P-12 may assist in ensuring high-quality placements for students. In early childhood education these often include partnerships with university lab schools; field experiences in lab schools have been shown to contribute to improvement in teacher preparation in early childhood education (McBride et al., 2012; Monroe & Horm, 2012; Swartz & McElwain, 2012). Lab schools associated with institutions of higher education typically provide a high-quality, "ideal teaching environment" for many child development activities, and especially for preservice teaching (McBride et al., 2012). And, the majority of program directors in these programs report that teacher preparation is one of their primary missions (McBride & Baumgartner, 2003). Although limitations exist for student learning in these placements, experiences in developing and maintaining these partnerships may serve to inform foundations in communities and with public schools.

Several recent studies which have examined lab schools and their connections to preservice preparation have found these contexts to have potential for research in teacher education. Monroe and Horm (2012) recently examined the connection of theory and practice in a university lab school using a logic model. Their study specifically focused on the connections between program theory and student activities within the lab school. Findings indicated that there was a disconnect or challenge for students to apply theory from knowledge and coursework to practice. This evaluation prompted revisions to the teacher preparation program and mentoring meetings to focus on connections between theory and practice. Swartz and McElwain (2012) examined emotional socialization of preservice teachers in a lab school setting in response to children's positive and negative emotions. Their findings suggested differences in accepting beliefs about children's emotions among students in advanced practicum and students in earlier practica. More advanced students displayed higher levels of accepting beliefs of children's emotions though no differences emerged between beginning and advanced students on responses to child emotions, demonstrating that this may be an area to address in coursework and field based experiences. These research studies support the importance of partnerships between lab schools and teacher preparation programs to inform, improve, and support teacher development in early childhood education. Both studies support the importance of lab schools in preservice teacher preparation and provide several areas for further examination and study to improve experiences for students. These studies also highlight the importance of supervision and communication between cooperating teachers and students in field based experiences.

Inherent in any placements are the supervision skills of the teachers who mentor students. Coaching and mentoring has received a good deal of attention in the field of early childhood education (Clarke et al., 2014; LoCasale-Crouch, Davis, Wiens, & Pianta, 2012). Typically, coaching offers support in varied forms to assist teachers in applications of information to practice, and is defined by NAEYC as a process to build capacity for specific professional skills through relationship-based processes (NAEYC, 2011). Although much of the work in coaching and mentoring has occurred with inservice teachers, coaching strategies may be useful to the supervision of preservice teachers. It stands to reason that preservice teachers are learning many new skills in coursework and during field based experiences, and additional support such as coaching related to these new skills, may facilitate their implementation and students' development as teachers. Several studies have found that teachers who have received coaching implement and use new strategies more often than teachers who did not have coaching (Dickinson & Caswell, 2007; Justice, Mashburn, Hamre, & Pianta, 2008).

Coaching has several anticipated outcomes relevant for preservice teachers: growth in teacher efficacy, increase in reflective and complex thinking, and increase in teacher satisfaction with career and position. Critical components of coaching include definition, focus, relationships, duration, and delivery (Sandefur, Warren, Gamble, Holcombe, & Hicks, 2010). In addition, different types of coaching have been studied (supervisory coaching and side-by-side coaching), which may fit into the realm of preservice development (Kretlow & Bartholomew, 2010). Just as coaching is often a follow-up to high-quality professional development sessions, coaching for preservice teaching may occur in classroom-based experiences, as mentor teachers coach the students on teaching strategies and practices that they have learned through coursework.

Summary

To address recommendations for high-quality, carefully crafted field based experiences and to meet the goal of teacher education programs to prepare effective teachers, preservice teachers need opportunities to apply knowledge, practice their skills, and receive constructive feedback as they develop as teachers. The complexities of early childhood education and the limited research on field based experiences contribute to challenges in providing optimal field based experiences. In order to address the challenges, developing a practice and research agenda to explore models of quality field based experiences and innovative approaches to developing partnerships with community programs and public schools is needed. Communication between institutions of higher education and placement partners can strengthen collaborative efforts among university instructors and classroom teachers, and strengthen the experience for students. These field based experiences have an essential role in teacher preparation, laying the foundation for the development of effective teachers.

References

American Association of Colleges for Teacher Education (AACTE). (2010). *The clinical preparation of teachers—A policy brief.* Washington, DC: Author. Retrieved from http://www.aacte.org/pdf/Government_Relations/Clinical%20Prep%20Paper_03-11-2010.pdf

Anderson, L. M., & Stillman, J. A. (2013). Student teaching's contribution to pre-service teacher development: A review of research focused on the preparation of teachers for urban and high-needs contexts. *Review of Educational Research, 83*(1), 3–69.

Austin, L. J. E., Kipnis, F., Sakai, L., Whitebook, M., & Ryan, S. (2013). *The State of Early Childhood Higher Education in Rhode Island: The Rhode Island Early Childhood Higher Education Inventory.* Berkeley, CA: Center for the Study of Child Care Employment, University of California at Berkeley.

Barbour, C. W. (1938). Kindergarten education in Wisconsin. In C. D. Aborns, S. A. Marble, & L. Wheelcock (Eds.), *History of the kindergarten movement in the mid-western states and in New York* (pp. 23–30). Washington, DC: Association for Childhood Education.

Baum, A. C., & Korth, B. B. (2013). Preparing classroom teachers to be cooperating teachers: A report of current efforts, beliefs, challenges, and associated recommendations. *Journal of Early Childhood Teacher Education, 34*, 171–190.

Baum, A. C., Powers-Costello, B., Van Scoy, I., Miller, E., & James, U. (2011). We're all in this together: Collaborative professional development with student teaching supervisors. *Action in Teacher Education, 33*(1), 38–46.

Beck, C., & Kosnik, C. (2002). Professors and the practicum involvement of university faculty in preservice practicum supervision. *Journal of Teacher Education, 53*(1), 6–19.

Blank, J. (2010). Early childhood teacher education: Historical themes and contemporary issues. *Journal of Early Childhood Teacher Education, 31*, 391–405.

Bornfreund, L. A. (2011). Getting in sync: Revamping licensing and preparation for teachers in pre-k, kindergarten, and the early grades. Education Policy Program: New America Foundation. Retrieved from http://www.newamerica.net/sites/newamerica.net/files/policydocs/Getting%20in%20Sync-%20Revamping%20Licensing%20and%20Preparation%20for%20Teachers%20in%20Pre-K%20Kindergarten%20and%20the%20Early%20Grades.pdf

Bronfenbrenner, U. (1979). *The ecology of human development: Experiments by nature and design.* Cambridge, MA: Harvard University Press.

Bronfenbrenner, U. (2001). The bioecological theory of human development. In N. J. Smelser & P. B. Baltes (Eds.), *International encyclopedia of the social and behavioral sciences* (Vol. 10), (pp. 6963–6970). New York: Elsevier.

Burchinal, M. R., Peisner-Feinberg, E., Bryant, D. M., & Clifford, R. (2000). Children's social and cognitive development and child-care quality: Testing for differential associations related to poverty, gender, or ethnicity. *Applied Developmental Science, 4*(3), 149–165.

Caires, S., Almeida, L., & Vieira, D. (2012). Becoming a teacher: Student teachers' experiences and perceptions about teaching practice. *European Journal of Teacher Education, 35*(2), 163–178.

Clarke, A., Triggs, V., & Nielsen, W. (2014). Cooperating Teacher Participation in Teacher Education A Review of the Literature. *Review of Educational Research, 84*(2), 163-202.

Council for the Accreditation of Teacher Education Programs (CAEP). (2013). CAEP Accreditation Standards. Retrieved from http://caepnet.org/standards/standards/

Darling-Hammond, L. (2006). Constructing 21st-century teacher education. *Journal of Teacher Education, 57*(3), 300–314.

Dickinson, D. K., & Caswell, L. (2007). Building support for language and early literacy in preschool classrooms through in-service professional development: Effects of the Literacy Environment Enrichment Program (LEEP). *Early Childhood Research Quarterly, 22*(2), 243–260.

Dombkowski, K. (2001). Will the real kindergarten please stand up?: Defining and redefining the twentieth-century US kindergarten. *History of Education, 30*, 527–545.

Early, D. M., Maxwell, K. L., Burchinal, M., Alva, S., Bender, R. H., Bryant, D., . . . & Zill, N. (2007). Teachers' education, classroom quality, and young children's academic skills: Results from seven studies of preschool programs. *Child Development, 78*(2), 558–580.

Early, D. M., & Winton, P. J. (2001). Preparing the workforce: Early childhood teacher preparation at 2- and 4-year institutions of higher education. *Early Childhood Research Quarterly, 16*, 285–306.

Fairbanks, C. M., Freedman, D., & Kahn, C. (2000). The role of effective mentors in learning to teach. *Journal of Teacher Education, 51*(2), 102–112.

Feiman-Nemser, S. (2001). From preparation to practice: Designing a continuum to strengthen and sustain teaching. *Teachers College Record, 103*(6), 1013–1055.

Feiman-Nemser, S., & Beasley, K. (2007). Discovering and sharing knowledge: Inventing a new role for cooperating teachers. *Transforming teacher education: Reflections from the field*, 139–160.

Gasbarro, M. (2008). *Educating the Educators: Effective practices for early childhood teachers' training and professional development.* University of Denver: Marisco Institute for Early Learning and Literacy. Retrieved from https://www.du.edu/marsicoinstitute/media/documents/EducatingtheEducators.pdf

Gormley Jr., W., Gayer, T., Phillips, D., & Dawson, B. (2004). *The effects of Oklahoma's universal pre-k program on school readiness: An executive summary.* Washington, DC: Center for Research on Children in the United States, Georgetown University.

Hobson, A. J., Ashby, P., Malderez, A., & Tomlinson, P. D. (2009). Mentoring beginning teachers: What we know and what we don't. *Teaching and Teacher Education, 25*(1), 207–216.

Hollingsworth, H. L., & Winter, M. K. (2013). Teacher beliefs and practices relating to development in preschool: Importance placed on social–emotional behaviours and skills. *Early Child Development and Care, 183*, 1758–1781.

Horm, D. M., Hyson, M., & Winton, P. J. (2013). Research on early childhood teacher education: Evidence from three domains and recommendations for moving forward. *Journal of Early Childhood Teacher Education, 34*(1), 95–112.

Hunter, M. (1970). Expanding roles of laboratory schools. *Phi Delta Kappan*, 14–19.

Justice, L. M., Mashburn, A. J., Hamre, B. K., & Pianta, R. C. (2008). Quality of language and literacy instruction in preschool classrooms serving at-risk pupils. *Early Childhood Research Quarterly, 23*(1), 51–68.

Killian, J. E., & Wilkins, E. A. (2009). Characteristics of highly effective cooperating teachers: A study of their backgrounds and preparation. *Action in Teacher Education, 30*(4), 67–83.

Kipnis, F., Austin, L. J. E., Sakai, L., Whitebook, M., & Ryan, S. (2013). *The state of early childhood higher education in New Hampshire: The New Hampshire early childhood higher education inventory*. Berkeley, CA: Center for the Study of Child Care Employment, University of California at Berkeley.

Kipnis, F., Whitebook, M., Almaraz, M., Sakai, L., & Austin, L. J. E. (2012). Learning together: A study of six BA completion cohort programs in early care and education—Year 4. *Center for the Study of Child Care Employment, University of California at Berkeley*. Retrieved from http://www.irle.berkeley.edu/cscce/wp-content/uploads/2012/02/LearningTogetherYear4Report.pdf

Kipnis, F., Whitebook, M., Austin, L., & Sakai, L. (2013). *The state of early childhood higher education in New Jersey: The New Jersey early childhood higher education inventory.* Berkeley, CA: Center for the Study of Child Care Employment, University of California at Berkeley.

Korth, B. B., & Baum, A. C. (2011). Teachers supporting future teachers: A critical part of early childhood teacher preparation. *Young Children, 66*(3), 20–26.

Kretlow, A. G., & Bartholomew, C. C. (2010). Using coaching to improve the fidelity of evidence-based practices: A review of studies. *Teacher Education and Special Education, 33*(4), 279–299.

La Paro, K. M., Scott-Little, C., Eijimofor, A., Sumrall, T., Kintner-Duffy, V., Pianta, R. C., . . . & Howes, C. (2014). Student teaching feedback and evaluation: Results from a seven state survey. *Journal of Early Childhood Teacher Education, 35*(4), 318–336.

Lai, E. (2005). *Mentoring for in-service teachers in a distance teacher education programme: views of mentors, mentees and university teachers.* Paper presented at the Australian Association for Research in Education International Education Conference, Parramatta, Australia. Retrieved from http://www.aare.edu.au/data/publications/2005/lai05100.pdf

LoCasale-Crouch, J., Davis, E., Wiens, P., & Pianta, R. (2012). The role of the mentor in supporting new teachers: associations with self-efficacy, reflection, and quality. *Mentoring & Tutoring: Partnership in Learning, 20*(3), 303–323.

LoCasale-Crouch, J., Konold, T., Pianta, R., Howes, C., Burchinal, M., Bryant, D., . . . & Barbarin O. (2007). Observed classroom quality profiles in state-funded pre-kindergarten programs and associations with teacher, program, and classroom characteristics. *Early Childhood Research Quarterly, 22*(1), 3–17.

MacDougall, L., Mtika, P., Reid, I., & Weir, D. (2013). Enhancing feedback in student-teacher field experience in Scotland: the role of school–university partnership. *Professional Development in Education, 39*(3), 420–437.

Maxwell, K. L., Lim, C. I., & Early, D. M. (2006). *Early childhood teacher preparation programs in the United States: National report.* Chapel Hill, NC: The University of North Carolina, FPG Child Development Institute.

Maynard, C., King, E., La Paro, K. M., & Johnson A. V. (under review). Early practicum experiences in early childhood education: Student learning and coursework relevance.

Maynard, C., La Paro, K. M., & Johnson, A. V. (2014). Before student teaching: How undergraduate students in early childhood teacher preparation programs describe their early classroom-based experience. *Journal of Early Childhood Teacher Education, 35*(3), 244–261.

McBride, B., & Baumgartner, J. (2003). The changing profile of teaching, research and outreach activities in lab school programs. *Advances in Early Education and Day Care, 12*, 181–200.

McBride, B. A., Groves, M., Barbour, N., Horm, D., Stremmel, A., Lash, M., & Toussaint, S. (2012). Child development laboratory schools as generators of knowledge in early childhood education: New models and approaches. *Early Education & Development, 23*(2), 153–164.

Monroe, L., & Horm, D. M. (2012). Using a logic model to evaluate undergraduate instruction in a laboratory preschool. *Early Education & Development, 23*(2), 227–241.

National Association for the Education of Young Children (NAEYC). (2009). *NAEYC standards for early childhood professional preparation. Position Statement.* Washington, DC: National Association for the Education of Young Children.

National Association for the Education of Young Children (NAEYC). (2011). *Early childhood education professional development: Training and technical assistance glossary.* Washington, DC: National Association for the Education of Young Children, National Association of Child Care Resource & Referral Agencies.

National Council for Accreditation of Teacher Education (NCATE). (2010). *Transforming teacher education through clinical practice: A national strategy to prepare effective teachers.* Washington, DC: National Council for the Accreditation of Teacher Education.

Norris, D. J. (2010). Raising the educational requirements for teachers in infant toddler classrooms: Implications for institutions of higher education. *Journal of Early Childhood Teacher Education, 31*(2), 146–158.

O'Brian, M., Stoner, J., Appel, K., & House, J. J. (2007). The first field experience: Perspectives of preservice and cooperating teachers. *Teacher Education and Special Education, 30*(4), 264–275.

Pianta, R. C. (1999). *Enhancing relationships between children and teachers.* Washington, DC: American Psychological Association.

Pianta, R. C., Burchinal, M., Jamil, F. M., Sabol, T., Grimm, K., Hamre, B. K., . . . & Howes, C. (2014). A cross-lag analysis of longitudinal associations between preschool teachers' instructional support identification skills and observed behavior. *Early Childhood Research Quarterly, 29*(2), 144–154.

Retallick, M. S., & Miller, G. (2010). A model for implementing early field experiences in teacher education. *Journal of Career and Technical Education, 25*(1), 62–75.

Rice, C., & McLaughlin, J. (2007). Providing tools toward quality: The status of P–3 teacher preparation programs in New Jersey. *Policy Brief.* Newark, NJ: Association for Children of New Jersey.

Ritblatt, S. N., Garrity, S., Longstreth, A., Hokoda, A., & Potter, N. (2013). Early care and education matters: A conceptual model for early childhood teacher preparation integrating the key constructs of knowledge, reflection, and practice. *Journal of Early Childhood Teacher Education, 34*, 46–62.

Sandefur, S. J., Warren, A. R., Gamble, A. B., Holcombe, J. M., & Hicks, H. K. (2010). Coaching: It's not just for little league. In S. B. Neuman & M. L. Kamil (Eds.), *Preparing teachers for the early childhood classroom: Proven models and key principles* (pp. 87–103). Baltimore, MD: Paul H. Brookes Publishing.

Sayeski, K. L., & Paulsen, K. J. (2012). Student teacher evaluations of cooperating teachers as indices of effective mentoring. *Teacher Education Quarterly, 39*(2), 117–130.

Schulman, K., & Barnett, W. S. (2005). *The benefits of prekindergarten for middle-income children.* New Brunswick, NJ: NIEER.

Shapiro, M. S. (1983). *Child's garden: The kindergarten movement from Froebel to Dewey.* University Park, PA: The Pennsylvania State University Press.

Smith, E. R. (2007). Negotiating power and pedagogy in student teaching: expanding and shifting roles in expert–novice discourse. *Mentoring & Tutoring, 15*(1), 87–106.

Stroud, J. C., & Clark, P. (2000). Obstacles and opportunities: Creating early childhood professional development schools. *Journal of Early Childhood Teacher Education, 21*(1), 39–46.

Swartz, R. A., & McElwain, N. L. (2012). Preservice teachers' emotion-related regulation and cognition: Associations with teachers' responses to children's emotions in early childhood classrooms. *Early Education & Development, 23*(2), 202–226.

Temple, A. (1906). The kindergarten training course—in the normal school—in the university or college—the specific kindergarten training school. *Kindergarten Magazine, XVIII*, 622–626.

Vandewalker, N. (1898, November). Froebel vs. Herbart in American education. *Kindergarten Magazine, XI*, 151–157.

Weber, E. (1969). *The kindergarten: Its encounter with educational thought in America.* New York: Teachers College Press.

Weiss, E. M., & Weiss, S. (2001). Doing reflective supervision with student teachers in a professional development school culture. *Reflective Practice, 2*(2), 125–154.

Wen, X., Elicker, J. G., & McMullen, M. B. (2011). Early childhood teachers' curriculum beliefs: Are they consistent with observed classroom practices? *Early Education and Development, 22,* 945–969.

Whitebook, M., Gomby, D., Bellm, D., Sakai, L., & Kipnis, F. (2009). *Preparing teachers of young children: The current state of knowledge, and a blueprint for the future. Executive Summary.* Policy Report. Berkeley, CA: Center for the Study of Child Care Employment, University of California at Berkeley.

Worrell, F., Brabeck, M., Dwyer, C., Geisinger, K., Marx, R., Noell, G., & Pianta, R. (2014). *Assessing and evaluating teacher preparation programs.* Washington, DC: American Psychological Association.

Zeichner, K. (2010). Rethinking the connections between campus courses and field experiences in college-and university-based teacher education. *Journal of Teacher Education, 61*(1–2), 89–99.

15

TEACHER INQUIRY AND PROFESSIONAL DEVELOPMENT

Kathryn Castle

Early Childhood Teacher:

> I can no longer teach without using teacher research, whether it is a formal study . . . or the daily analysis of my classroom practices. Teacher research gives me the attitude of a learner and helps me see how to shape my classroom practice to better guide my students and support their learning. Through collecting and analyzing daily events I have a heightened sense of what is happening in the classroom, freeing me up to better listen to and respond to the needs of my students, allowing me to learn from them.
>
> *(Wood, 2005, p. 10)*

Early Childhood Teacher Educator:

> Teacher research has helped me to continually define what I want to achieve in my practice, what my goals are for my teaching and for my students. It helps me achieve clarity in my work, the feeling that I am on the right track with my students, and that I am learning from them how to be the best teacher for them. For my students, my research of my own practice serves as a model of an inquiring practitioner. Yet to some, it has appeared disconcerting to them that I would not already know the answers to my questions.
>
> *(Castle, 2013, p. 279)*

These two quotes from teachers at different levels exemplify several things about teacher inquiry. First, teachers at all levels engage in teacher inquiry. It is not just for classroom teachers with the possible collaboration of teacher educators. Teacher educators research their own practices and can become advocates for teacher research as valid research (Cochran-Smith & Lytle, 2009; Souto-Manning, 2012). Second, it puts the teacher in the role of a learner focused on learning about and from learners and their needs. Third, it involves a continuous disposition as results from one study are applied and lead to new questions to explore (Ellis & Castle, 2010). As such, it becomes a means of professional development for those doing it. In addition, it can be transformative in the sense that what teachers learn changes their teaching in ways that they can no longer return to what they were doing before (Castle, 2006; Megowan-Romanowicz, 2010; Souto-Manning, 2012).

Teacher inquiry is unique and different from other types of research, including how teachers show that their research is credible. Teacher inquiry takes place at all levels, across cultures (Day, Elliott,

Somekh, & Winter, 2002), and across teaching contexts, and contributes to the knowledge base of teaching and best practices even though it may not be recognized by some as "real" research. Those who do it become more knowledgeable about their own teaching, about teaching in general, and become more capable decision makers. Some have called these teachers more autonomous (Castle, 2006) or agents of change (Goswami & Stillman, 1987; Paris & Lung, 2008), not only in their own communities but also on a broader plane, such as policy change (Meyers & Rust, 2003).

One of the reasons teacher inquiry can be transformative to those doing it and to those around them is due to the nature of such activity. It is insider research as opposed to outsider research done by those outside the classroom (Cochran-Smith & Lytle, 2009). As insider research, the teacher conducting the research is in the position of deciding which questions to ask, how to go about answering the questions, and then interpreting what the answers mean and their application to classroom life. This is very different from merely carrying out the research findings of others. Teachers are more likely to apply results from their own inquiries rather than results from the research of others, even if the results come from respected researchers in their fields. Teachers engaged in teacher inquiry may be looking for answers to solve problems within their own classrooms and contexts and thus more invested in finding solutions that are relevant to their own situations. Flake, Kuhs, Donnelly, and Ebert (1995) point out, "By becoming researchers, teachers can take control of their own classrooms and professional lives in ways that confound the traditional definition of teacher and offer proof that education can reform itself from within" (p. 407). One example of sustained school change through teacher inquiry is a report of teachers in a school engaged in teacher research for at least seven years who cited their ongoing research as one of the things that drove renewal in their school (Giles, Wilson, & Elias, 2010).

The Meaning of Teacher Inquiry

In the daily course of teaching, teachers typically ask questions, observe, take notes, interview students, and collect student artifacts; all of these actions are done in teacher inquiry to inform and produce high-quality teaching (Binder, 2012). Some specific examples of teacher inquiry studies include the study of boys' literacy; classroom community; children's understanding of measurement; and children and mapping. Examples of teacher educators' inquiries include the study of the role of reflection in learning about teaching; college students' approaches to teaching about place value; student teachers' assessments of children; and the use of protocols in college teaching.

The term "teacher inquiry" has multiple meanings and interpretations across professionals. A commonly accepted definition of "teacher inquiry" is the study of teaching for the improvement of teaching and learning (Lankshear & Knobel, 2004). Many labels have been applied to teacher inquiry and can be found in the professional literature, including "teacher research", "teacher as researcher", "practitioner inquiry", "practitioner research", "self-study", and, the most common label, "action research". While it would seem that each of these labels means something different, it is the case that different labels are often used to mean the same thing; for example, practitioner inquiry is used to mean the same as teacher research. However, differences do exist across the labels and the context in which a label is used will help to show what is meant. For example, depending on what is done in a study, the label action research may mean teacher inquiry, or it may refer to research conducted by those outside teaching, such as those in the corporate world, to imply that an action plan will follow research results. Or, the term action research may be used by researchers other than teachers to signify research that has a clear political agenda focused on social justice with implications for policy (Orland-Barak, 2009). It is no wonder that early childhood teacher educators have expressed confusion about the meaning of the term teacher research (Castle, 2013).

Some view teacher inquiry in a more general sense of merely asking questions about one's teaching or how one's teaching impacts learners with little or no attempt at systematic study. A questioning disposition coupled with a reflective attitude results in the construction of professional knowledge and is an example of how teachers grow professionally. Others describe teacher inquiry as systematic studies of teaching and learning including question asking, data collection, data analysis, interpretation of data, and sharing of results (Castle, 2012). In the current educational climate of accountability and evidence-based teaching, teacher inquiry goes beyond questioning to attempt to show connections between teaching and student achievement, usually measured in terms of test scores. The expectation is that teachers will collect documentation (evidence) on what they and their students have done to demonstrate that their teaching has made a difference in the students' learning. It is also expected that teachers' practices reflect the most current research on what works best in promoting student learning. This expectation has been expanded to teacher education as well, where teacher educators are expected to demonstrate that their students' learning and teaching practices have a positive impact on children's learning and achievement.

Teacher inquiry refers to the intentional questioning of teaching and what it means for the learner and improving teaching (Hopkins, 2002; Richardson, 1994; Shagoury & Power, 2012). Some consider teacher inquiry as just another add-on to what teachers do and that it may be considered as an overload. Others, such as Shagoury and Power (2012), argue that it is just what good teachers do to inform their practice. It involves an integration of the two roles of teacher and researcher. Studies have shown that teacher research is having an increasingly positive impact on changing schools, student achievement, and teacher professional development (Flake et al., 1995; King & Newmann, 2000; Loughran, Mitchell, & Mitchell, 2002).

Theoretical Perspectives

The action of doing teacher research tends to be highly interpretive. As in any research endeavor, there are multiple theoretical frameworks that inform teacher inquiry, including constructivism, social constructivism, critical and social theory, and hermeneutic phenomenology, to name some of the most frequently cited. The broader views of the purpose of education, research, and educational goals are reflected in each theoretical perspective. A single theoretical perspective or multiple perspectives may influence inquiry, beginning with the questions asked, data collection, and finally interpretation of what the study means. Theory influences not only the types of questions asked but also the choice of methods used to conduct the study. Some teacher research is done to fulfill a mandate or even a course requirement and as such comes from a behavioristic approach in which the purpose of the study is more about achieving an outcome (i.e. a course grade) rather than a desire to become a better teacher (Brock, Helman, & Patchen, 2005). Teacher inquiry done in the name of social justice goes beyond the goal of a better understanding of teaching to the realm of educational change and reform.

In terms of methodology reflecting various theoretical frameworks, teacher inquiry methodology may be quantitative, qualitative, or employ mixed methods. The teacher research professional literature shows more of a tendency toward a qualitative approach, but with an incorporation of quantitative aspects such as performance measures. In general, the data that teacher researchers collect is varied and contains elements whose characteristics can be interpreted (qualitative) and those that have numerical or measurement aspects (quantitative) or that contain both qualitative and quantitative elements. The field of educational research has long debated quantitative versus qualitative approaches. The area of mixed methods has emerged as one of much promise to educators. Some are now calling for the importance of employing multiple paradigms or methodologies in a single study as a way to more appropriately demonstrate the wholeness or richness of data (Denzin, 2010). Perhaps one of the most recent methodologies that best fits the nature of teacher inquiry is that of crystallization, in which data are analyzed through multiple lenses much as light is filtered through a prism (Ellingson, 2009). Crystallization is particularly appropriate for the analysis of data of an artistic nature and of data based on student artifacts, student productions, or data that is greatly varied.

In their theoretical perspective on education in general and teacher inquiry specifically, Cochran-Smith and Lytle (2009) refer to teacher inquiry as taking an "inquiry stance" in the professional work of teachers. As such, it demonstrates a paradigm shift from the positivistic view of "teacher as consumer and implementer" of the work of experts to a more constructivist view of "teacher as decision maker" and active constructor of knowledge about teaching. The movement has been away from teachers as consumers of research and toward teachers as researchers. Cochran-Smith and Lytle (2009) describe their work as a "call for renegotiation of the boundaries of research and practice and reconfiguration of relationships inside and outside schools and universities, all in the interest of school and social change" (p. vii). Their critical social theory approach to teacher inquiry for social justice calls for research that goes against the grain, challenging the power hierarchy of top-down mandates that can shake up the status quo. It has the potential to uncover injustices in education and because it challenges existing systems, it requires courage and determination on the part of those who do it.

Teacher inquiry also has to do with the study of lived experiences and the deepening of understanding through such study (van Manen, 1990). This lived experience, hermeneutic phenomenological approach to inquiry, is focused on better understanding the teaching-learning experience in order to improve learning experiences for children. Such an approach calls on teachers as researchers to take a stand when necessary based on results of inquiry to advocate for what is good for children regardless of what is politically correct. Such a perspective is distinguished by a strong focus on the child and on what is in the best interest of children; involvement of a broader community including children, families, other educators, and community members; and on inquiry that has the potential to shake up the status quo. Such research is risky because of its potential to uncover education inequities and its potential to endanger the careers of practitioners. As one teacher researcher said, "You have to be a bit gutsy to do it!" Examples of teacher research of this type include a study of changing the way science is done in the classroom (Barman, 2000); the work of Crawford and Cornett (2000) who write about the emancipatory potential of teacher research; and the work of teacher research collaboratives in efforts to promote social justice (Meyers & Rust, 2003).

Teacher Inquiry and Professional Development

Teacher inquiry has been linked to teacher identity formation (Goodnough, 2011; McGregor, Hooker, Wise, & Devlin, 2010; Trent, 2010), student learning (Moore & Gilliard, 2008; Smith & Place, 2011), and teacher professional development (Hiebert, Gallimore, & Stigler, 2002; Roberts, Crawford, & Hickmann, 2010). For example, in a study of first grade teachers in three schools engaged in teacher inquiry groups studying the teaching of reading, teacher knowledge and practices improved and there were gains in student achievement in oral vocabulary as a result of their collaborative research (Gersten, Dimino, Jayanthi, Kim, & Santoro, 2010). McGregor and colleagues (2010) studied a cohort of doctoral students in teacher education allowed to do teacher inquiry and found a significant impact on the formation of their identities as professionals and researchers. Zeichner (2002) summarizes several studies showing the impact of teacher inquiry on the professional development of P-12 teachers, describing how teacher inquiry becomes a transformative professional development activity for teachers and that participation with other teachers in teacher inquiry influences teachers to become more learner-centered. Zeichner (2002) describes how teacher inquiry

> helps teachers to become more confident about their ability to promote student learning, to become more proactive in dealing with difficult situations that arise in their teaching, and to acquire habits and skills of inquiry that they use beyond the research experience to analyze their teaching in an in-depth manner. Teacher research under certain conditions,

> seems to develop or rekindle an excitement and enthusiasm about teaching and to provide a validation of the importance of the work that teachers do that seems to be missing from the lives of many teachers.
>
> *(p. 317)*

The conditions that promote this type of teacher professional development through teacher research include the creation of a culture of inquiry where teachers can work together collaboratively over a lengthy period of time in a safe, supportive group environment that respects teachers' voices and knowledge and operates with routines and protocols (group structures) that move the work forward. Although similar studies of the impact of teacher research by teacher educators have not yet been done, similar conditions for doing such research in higher education would likely be beneficial. One group of teacher educators studying their own research found a contradiction in what their institutions valued in research compared to their identities as teacher educators (Houston, Ross, Robinson, & Malcolm, 2010). Such contradiction can result in teacher educators deciding that teacher research may lead to improvements in their teaching but may not be helpful in demonstrating a research agenda for the promotion and tenure process.

In a study of teachers who do teacher research, Hahs-Vaughn and Yanowitz (2009) found that teachers in private schools in midsize or large cities who participated in professional development programs and who were supported by their schools were more likely to engage in teacher research than teachers in schools with large numbers of students on free or reduced lunch. This study showed that administrators play a key role in supporting teacher research efforts by having expectations for teacher participation in teacher research; allocating funds to support such research; and creating professional development activities focused on teacher research. Administrators in less affluent schools may be more concerned with increasing teacher skill level, teacher retention, and raising test scores than teacher inquiry.

In a study of early childhood teacher educators who do teacher research, it was found that teacher educators primarily do research on their own teaching to improve their teaching, to improve the learning experiences of their students, and for their own professional development (Castle, 2013). In this study, members of the National Association of Early Childhood Teacher Educators (NAECTE) were asked to take an online survey and participate in in-depth interviews. There were 97 respondents to the survey, seven of whom further participated in in-depth interviews. In addition, an analysis of 20 years of content of the *Journal of Early Childhood Teacher Education* (*JECTE*) was carried out to determine the extent to which teacher research studies were published in the journal. Findings indicated that early childhood teacher educators are knowledgeable about teacher research; teach about it primarily at the graduate level; require their students to engage in teacher inquiry in field experiences; share their own teacher research results in publications and presentations; participate in teacher research communities; and view teacher research as a high priority in spite of the difficulties and barriers. Further evidence from this study supports the amount of teacher research done by teacher educators: about one fifth of the content of the *JECTE* from 1990 (when it became a journal) through 2010 reflects teacher educator teacher research. Two issues of the journal, volumes 22(4) and 31(3), are almost entirely composed of teacher research studies. Volume 22(4) is a theme issue, focused on research teacher educators have done on teaching through distance learning. Volume 31(3) is another theme issue on early childhood teacher educator teacher research that exemplifies the kinds of teacher research studies being done by early childhood teacher educators, including research focused on undergraduate and graduate programs and teacher research partnerships.

Teacher Education and Teacher Inquiry

Teacher professional development should be grounded in inquiry, reflection, and experimentation that engage students and teachers as active participants (Darling-Hammond & McLaughlin, 2011). Teacher education programs increasingly offer teacher inquiry experiences to students in course content either as units in courses on research or other topics or as complete courses on teacher research, primarily at the graduate level. Cooney, Buchanan, and Parkinson (2001) provide a rationale for including a teacher-as-researcher strand in courses at both the undergraduate and graduate levels. Programs also engage students to complete in teacher inquiry as course or practicum experience requirements or as culminating projects. Teacher inquiry projects primarily focus on studying the impact of teaching on children's learning and performance. Teacher inquiry projects are commonly required during student teaching.

Teacher educators also do their own teacher research on the effectiveness of these experiences for their students' learning. For example, Keat (2005) studied how two graduate students (early childhood teachers) applied their learning about teacher research in the graduate program to their own classrooms as teacher researchers. In a study of teacher education efforts to promote teacher inquiry in students, Ax, Ponte, and Brouwer (2008) concluded that action research in teacher education should reflect different perspectives based on the students' level of experience such as a professional approach, skill sets, and way of improving practice through the development of practice-based knowledge. In another study, teacher educators did an action research study on teaching their preservice teachers about action research. Their students' conceptions of teaching were expanded as a result of their own engagement in action research (Kitchen & Stevens, 2008).

Arnold (1992) found that teacher education programs that were successful at engaging students in inquiry had these characteristics: teacher educators were involved in reflective/critical thinking about their own teaching; concentrated efforts were made to build communities of educators interested in improving and changing the status quo; teacher educators spent time in schools listening and talking to teachers to understand their *ways of knowing*; student teachers, teachers, and university faculty perceived themselves as researchers; participating in research activities after student teaching seemed to promote greater reflection than during or before student teaching; and the research topic was of mutual interest to all members of the team (p. 14). One example of a program reflecting these characteristics was a case study of two preservice teaching teams engaged in collaborative action research. Changes occurred in increased awareness of the value of shared curriculum decisions, self-regulation through reflection-in-action, and the use of documentation to show connections among teacher thinking, practice, and children's learning (Moran, 2007).

While many report successes of incorporating teacher inquiry into teacher education programs, others describe problems in the process. For example, Bryant and Bates (2010) studied an action research course in a master's program over a four-year period. They found student reactions varied from enthusiasm to resistance. The resistance related to a lack of understanding of the purpose of action research, discomfort with the time involvement and the need to multi-task, and lack of willingness to accept action research as part of learning to teach.

Courses designed for students to learn about and engage in teacher inquiry stress the professional development aspects of teacher inquiry. Smith and Sela (2005) describe how they developed such a course, Teacher as Researcher, taken by students engaged in their final year of the teacher education program (which was also their first year of teaching). The course was meant to emphasize the importance of reflection and the systematic examination of teaching for continuous professional development. Similarly, Smith and Place (2011) describe an inquiry-based literacy methods course and practicum experience. Students who participated in the course increased their understanding of individual children, were actively engaged in reflection on assessment and instruction, and developed pedagogical content knowledge as an element of effective teaching.

In a study of student action research in an early childhood teacher education program, Hatch, Greer, and Bailey (2006) concluded that doing action research increased pedagogical knowledge, developed student ability to use professional literature, and increased appreciation for the process of systematic data collection. Teacher inquiry dissertations are now allowed in some doctoral programs and even advocated for by those who perceive them as more appropriate research venues for professionals beginning careers focused on teacher education and school partnerships (Herr & Anderson, 2014; Olson & Clark, 2009).

Professional Development and Credibility through Teacher Research Partnerships

Teachers who do teacher research may also participate in teacher research collaborative groups or partnerships with other educators at various levels including P-12 schools and teacher education programs in higher education. Henderson, Hunt, and Wester (1999) conducted a survey of member institutions in the American Association of Colleges of Teacher Education (AACTE) and found that most institutions engage students in some form of action research including course offerings, student action research projects, and collaborations with P-12 schools in action research projects. Such participation has probably only increased in the years since the survey was conducted. Survey results showed that collaborations improved relationships between teacher education programs and P-12 schools; improved the teacher education curriculum including methods courses and more integrated approaches in elementary education curriculum; created a team-teaching approach in field experiences; and improved teacher induction practices. One drawback of the study was that P-12 school involvement by teacher education programs in design and planning does not always occur. This was cited as a weakness of such partnerships. Collaborative research between teachers and teacher educators is most successful when both participate equitably in the planning and conducting of the research.

> Collaboration is more than a group of researchers gathering together or working on the same project. It is a process that demands a spirit of true cooperation; a genuine partnership; and an equal sharing of power, leadership, ownership, and responsibility.
>
> *(Potter, 2003, p. 3)*

In addition to AACTE, other professional associations support teacher research collaboratives as an increasingly important part of professional development and a means to building the knowledge base in teaching and content areas. The Research Advisory Committee of the National Council of Teachers of Mathematics (NCTM Research Advisory Committee, 2001) views teacher research as a critical and valuable component adding to the knowledge base of teaching and learning and supports communities of inquiry centered on classroom-based research. "The acceptance of classroom-based research as a form of scholarship requires that we interpret that body of work as a new genre of research with its own criteria of rigor and with unique methodology, form, and style" (NCTM Research Advisory Committee, 2001, p. 445). The American Educational Research Association (AERA) has recognized the importance of teacher research as evidenced by the inclusion of teacher research as a specific research category and by the Special Interest Groups (SIGs) that are affiliated with AERA focused on teacher research. The National Writing Project (NWP) also supports teacher inquiry and has very active Teacher Inquiry Communities. The National Association for the Education of Young Children (NAEYC) recognizes the importance of teacher inquiry in its annual conferences and in the *Young Children* journal, and supports an online journal, *Voices of Practitioners*, that publishes early childhood teacher research. NAECTE, sponsor of the *JECTE* (that has consistently published teacher research studies since 1990) has an active ResearchNet focused on Early Childhood Teacher Educator Teacher Research.

In addition to professional associations, many teacher research collaboratives have been established, such as the Collaborative Action Research Networks (CARN) and the journal *Educational Action Research*. The online teacher research journal, *Networks,* not only publishes teacher research studies but also provides a space for discussions about practitioner inquiry. Teacher research collaborative groups provide a place for teachers to connect with others with similar research interests. Teachers who participate in such groups are more likely to do teacher research and to view it as an important professional activity (Little, Gearhart, Curry, & Kafka, 2003). Additional examples of groups include Teacher Professional Learning Communities, the George Mason University Teacher Research website (with resources on teacher research including guidelines for forming teacher research collaborative groups), the Teacher Fellows Inquiry Learning Community of the University of Florida, the Berkeley Teacher Research Group, the Literacy for Social Justice Teacher Research Group, the University of California, Davis, School of Education, the CRESS Center Teacher Research Group, and the National School Reform Faculty Group, to name a few.

Teacher research collaborative groups generally provide a comfortable place for teachers not only to connect with others with similar research interests but also a place where mentoring occurs. Teachers who initiate teacher research collaborative groups are often strong teacher leaders in their schools who become role models and mentors for less established teachers who have an interest in joining the group. It is a way for relatively new teachers to become mentored by their peers who already have well-formed teaching identities. It provides an opportunity for established teachers to share their knowledge and expertise with less established peers and to learn from them as well. The use of protocols (McDonald, Mohr, Dichter, & McDonald, 2007) for collaborative work helps provide an egalitarian climate of mutuality and reciprocity in the mentoring process. For example, Annie Ortiz, an established teacher leader at an elementary school, became aware that she and teachers at her school had a common interest and concern about boys' literacy because boys in their school were not very active in reading and writing. She initiated the formation of a teacher research group composed of teachers at each grade level plus the art and library media teachers in the school. She wrote a grant that was funded for purchasing books about boys' literacy, plus a stipend for classroom materials for each teacher. Over the course of a year, she used protocols in group meetings and shared leadership roles with group members in data collection and analysis. Results surprised the teachers who learned much about boys' literacy and their own students. They applied their findings and made many significant changes to the school. The newer teachers in the group were mentored and also contributed to the professional development of the established teachers (Ortiz et al., 2014).

Teacher educators who partner with P-12 teachers in teacher research, especially in situations in which both sets of teachers are helping to prepare teacher candidates, serve as mentors for teachers and teacher candidates in learning about teacher research. Such mentoring relationships contribute greatly to the professional development of all involved.

Standards of Quality in Teacher Research

Lincoln and Guba (1985) have developed a standard for qualitative research rigor defined as trustworthiness or the extent to which the study is truthful and accurate; this standard has much potential for addressing quality in teacher inquiry. Trustworthiness is traditionally addressed by the teacher researcher in describing research methods and judged by those outside the process such as review committees or those reading or applying research results. Overall quality in teacher educator teacher research can be judged in terms of its impact and improvement of the teaching/learning process in the teacher education program. Creswell (2012) states that the quality of research can be assessed by the subsequent improvement of practice, impact on policy debates, and the advancement of knowledge.

The audience for teacher research may be the larger educational community, other teacher researchers, or just the teacher researcher herself. Answers to what counts as research and who might be interested tend to vary but do influence the direction of any teacher research study. Two types of research evaluation in teacher education also impact the direction of the research. Evaluation of individual performance linked to promotion and tenure is one type and the other has to do with the extent to which the research informs teaching in higher education and pedagogical practice in schools. Teacher educator teacher research has more potential to impact schooling, including pedagogical practices, than more traditional research. As such, it integrates the two university missions of both research and teaching and possibly service as well. Souto-Manning (2012) proposes "that transforming learning in teacher education classrooms requires us to embrace teacher action research, problematizing and transforming our own pedagogies" (p. 55). This idea of the integration of teaching and research, while foreign to some, has much potential for those in teacher education whose mission is usually three-pronged: teaching, research, and service. And it gets at Boyer's (1990) rethinking of scholarship in higher education and its focus on the teacher scholar. As it is currently, and according to a study by Chetty and Lubben (2010), most teacher educators consider teaching and research as dichotomous. But the concept of teacher research unites the two missions of teaching and research, providing a more unified identity for teacher educators.

The benefits of doing quality teacher research for the improvement of teaching and the teacher education program are the primary reasons that early childhood teacher educators say they do teacher research (Castle, 2013). This primary motivation for doing research could be considered a criterion for quality. As Zeichner (1999) says, "This work can both inform the practices of the teacher educators who conduct it and contribute to the knowledge and understanding of teacher education for the larger community of scholars and educators" (p. 11) and in doing so make a major contribution to the field. Early childhood teacher educators' teacher research results are used by teachers to support and/or improve program practices.

Challenges in Teacher Research

Teacher inquiry is a means for professional development. But it is not without challenges. When teachers at all levels comment on the difficulties involved in doing teacher research, the top challenge reported is lack of time, followed by lack of administrative/institutional support for such research. Teachers may be reluctant to engage in teacher research feeling that they cannot add another task to their already overloaded schedules, especially with current accountability and testing expectations (Bryant & Bates, 2010; Castle, 2012; Mohr, Rogers, Sanford, Nocerino, MacLean, & Clawson, 2004; Pine, 2009; Shagoury & Power, 2012; Smith & Sela, 2005). Time for covering academic content is in such short supply that many elementary schools have sacrificed some curriculum areas and even recess in order to give more time to test preparation.

Many teacher researchers have been able to integrate their inquiries into their teaching and view research as an important and necessary role as a professional because of the positive impact on their teaching and student learning. In addition, it gives them an opportunity to work collaboratively with other teachers on common problems. Teacher educators experience different challenges in doing teacher research related to the established research culture at their institutions that either may not recognize teacher research as real research or may not value it.

Some countries and programs have made concerted efforts to incorporate teacher research into the daily routines of teachers making it a function of teaching and not an add-on. Teacher research is done in many countries and areas around the world such as in Australia, New Zealand, Japan, and Great Britain. The teacher research movement in the United States began in the 1970s under the influence of Stenhouse's (1975) work in Great Britain. In some countries, a culture of teacher inquiry has been well established in schools and in teacher education programs. Early childhood educators have long known of the schools of Reggio Emilia, Italy, and the use of teacher documentation to represent children's and teachers' learning as an important aspect of the Reggio schools. Loris Malaguzzi, founder of the Reggio Emilia system, said that teachers should also be researchers learning and relearning with children, through which teachers attain a higher level of professionalism (Edwards, Gandini, & Forman, 1994). Malaguzzi claimed, "Our teachers do research either on their own or with their colleagues to produce strategies that favor children's work or can be utilized by them" (Edwards et al., 1994, p. 82–83). Teachers are carefully prepared in the process of documentation as a form of action research or *cycle of inquiry,* in which documentation becomes a continuous and repeating spiral process, to make children's learning more visible and to deepen understanding (Gandini, Hill, Cadwell, & Schwall, 2005, p. 53).

It is typical for Reggio teachers to engage in a continuous process of forming questions, observing children, recording and collecting artifacts, organizing documentation, analyzing observations and artifacts, building theories, reframing questions, reflection, and planning. Through careful documentation and verification, children's and teachers' thinking becomes visible. Teachers' professional development is enhanced through revisiting the documentation alone and with other teachers. Reading, interpreting, assessing, and analyzing documentation of project work is a form of teacher inquiry and is included in Reggio teacher professional development. Gandini (2005) says, "This process is sustained through documentation, which renders transparent the work of the school and creates evidence of the children's learning and constructions, because without documentation, nothing remains" (p. 72). Terzi and Cantarelli (2001) describe the role of experimentation of teachers and teacher teams as movement from theory to practice in the analysis of specific innovations.

Finland has also attempted to integrate teacher inquiry into teaching. Finland went from a mediocre educational system in the 1980s to one of the best in the world today due to education reforms that include incorporating research-based approaches and inquiry at all levels, from basic schools to university teacher education programs. Students are required to take an inquiry stance in both studying to become teachers as well as ultimately in their teaching and use of inquiry approaches by students. Students in Finland must complete a university degree and alternative routes to teaching are not accepted (Sahlberg, 2010a). Finland has dedicated itself to a research-based professional culture in which teacher use of research methods is stressed (Niemi, 2009). Teacher educators prepare students in the most current educational research as well as require practicum placements in schools in which students engage in reflecting on educational problems and carrying out systematic research on problems to improve teaching and education. Teachers are encouraged to develop a disposition for doing research in their teaching (Niemi & Jakku-Sihvonen, 2011). Teachers are also encouraged and supported to collaborate in research. Such groups follow a cycle of systematic planning, action, reflection, evaluation, and problem-solving for improving teaching and learning. Teachers are given school time for such activity. As a result, Finland has reported an increase in effective teaching (Darling-Hammond, 2010; Sahlberg, 2010b).

Challenges in Teacher Educator Teacher Research

Common challenges affecting teacher educators who do teacher research are lack of time to do teacher research, problems in the Institutional Review Board (IRB; human subjects) approval process, and a higher education culture that may devalue teacher research in the promotion and tenure process. There is a double standard that exists in teacher education. While teacher research is increasingly being advocated for and encouraged by accrediting agencies such as NAEYC, NCATE (CAEP), the National Board for Professional Teacher Certification process, and professional associations such as the National Writing Project's Teacher Inquiry Communities, it is often not recognized by university academics as legitimate research for promotion and tenure.

Cochran-Smith and Lytle (2009) discuss the role of teacher research in higher education as having the potential to be a form of "constructive disruption" or radical challenge to the university culture, particularly to the relationship of teaching and research. They argue that just as teacher research has changed power relationships in the cultures of schools, it may do the same at the university level by challenging the double standard of what is valued research and the very concept of what counts as research and what is rewarded at the university level. Zeichner (1999) says that those who do not recognize the legitimacy of this research do this not because it is of lower quality but because of the knowledge hierarchies and social prejudices that have "plagued teacher education since its inception in colleges and universities" (p. 4).

Overcoming Common Barriers to Teacher Educator Teacher Research

Cochran-Smith and Lytle (2009) claim that the practitioner research movement is thriving worldwide and pushing back against constraints. They identified some current themes in practitioner research such as taking on issues of equity, engagement, and agency. In terms of reforming research and practice in universities, Cochran-Smith and Lytle (2009) claim there is increasing evidence that involvement with practitioner research can have a transformative effect on aspects of university culture. They have found that programs in language and literacy, teaching and curriculum, higher education, and leadership have begun offering formal preparation in using practitioner methodologies and questions to drive the design of doctoral dissertations.

Houston et al. (2010) researched how a group of teacher educators in a university education department used action research to examine their research situation and perceived that the research their university valued was not necessarily the kind that was built into their identities as teacher educators. This realization became empowering to them. As a way to reconcile the barrier of time to do research conflicting with time to address student needs, they found ways to build their research into their everyday work. In another study, early childhood teacher educators said the benefits to promotion and tenure, while very important, are secondary to the primary reason for the research (Castle, 2013). However, in a study of faculty engagement in research, Moore and Ward (2010) found their university participants viewed their work in part as shaped by institutional expectations for faculty to be actively involved in traditional research. Faculty members in their study felt they had to justify their actions in relation to traditional expectations for research.

Related to the most common barrier (reported as lack of time to do research), early childhood teacher educators are often the only faculty members in their academic programs and are responsible not only for teaching a variety of courses but also supervising students and administering the program (Castle, 2013). Such heavy faculty loads make it difficult to conduct research of any kind. It is important to note that doing teacher research on their own teaching, students' learning, and applying results to improving their programs likely requires less time than other types of research because it integrates the roles of teaching with research.

A similar issue is lack of support for doing research. Even if time is available, there may be no encouragement in terms of recognition for doing this type of research. Also, funding for doing teacher research is not readily available from national funding agencies, with the exception of some funding for teacher research projects in P-12 schools not affiliated with university teaching. Lack of funding may not be a major issue at the university level, however, as most university teacher research is done in university classrooms and does not require a great deal of funds for equipment, travel, or participant incentives. One type of support that would be welcomed by early childhood teacher educators is reduced teaching loads for doing research.

Perhaps the most difficult barrier to overcome that is cited by early childhood teacher educators is the restrictive nature of the promotion and tenure criteria at universities that do not recognize teacher research as legitimate for getting promoted and tenured. It would be helpful if teacher educators who conduct teacher research would become more active in the university promotion and tenure policy process and in service on promotion and tenure committees to change the culture to one that accepts the legitimacy of teacher research. Some entrenched biases against teacher research or any research that is not experimentally designed can be overcome by making visible teacher research as a legitimate type of research that has enhanced the knowledge base and professional development of those who do it (Roberts et al., 2010).

Additionally, some university IRBs do not recognize teacher research and may view it as coercive of students and refuse to approve it (Brown, 2010). Teacher educators who serve on their university IRB can help educate those who hold such beliefs. While it is not possible to change everyone's opinions about the value of teacher research, it is possible to change university policies that don't recognize teacher research or bar it from the IRB process when confronted by AERA recognition and guidelines that prohibit IRBs from discriminating against it.

To confront these barriers takes courage, or what Cochran-Smith and Lytle (2009) call taking an "inquiry stance". As one early childhood teacher educator said, "I taught students to question who makes the standards so I need to do the same".

Early childhood teacher educators said they conduct teacher research despite the barriers for several reasons. Doing such research improves their teaching, course content, and reading materials; improves professional development; helps them continually define goals for their teaching and student learning; helps them learn from their students; changes their view of research as well as teaching and learning; helps them maintain interest in teaching; helps ground them in real issues of contemporary teachers; gives them better insight into the effectiveness of their teaching; helps with course modifications and program changes; helps them co-author manuscripts and professional presentations with peers and students; and helps keep them on the cutting edge in the field (Castle, 2013).

In Conclusion

Teacher research at the P-12 level has demonstrated its power in changing schools and transforming teaching for the improvement of education. While P-12 teacher research exists, it is not widespread in the sense that it has not been incorporated into the daily routines of teaching as has been done in other countries. Educators at all levels including educational policy makers should become more informed about the value of teacher research to schooling. One approach to making this happen is for P-12 schools to partner with teacher education programs so that the strand of teacher research is continuous through education programs at all levels.

Teacher research for teacher educators continues to be a challenge. Following Boyer's (1990) call for reconsidering the notion of scholarship, Moore and Ward (2010) say we need to adopt holistic views of faculty work and each aspect of the faculty role. A more holistic view of scholarship would allow the rethinking of research to include other approaches such as teacher research. This would create a conversation in the academy among researchers coming from various approaches. It would also necessitate informing university administrators and other communities about the value of teacher research. To overcome barriers to teacher research in higher education, it is important for teacher educators to play a more active role in university governance. Marilyn Cochran-Smith (2006) speaks about the power of teacher educator teacher research:

> The growing number of teacher educators engaged in self-study or practitioner inquiry are building into teacher education a process wherein research guides curriculum, evidence is continually fed back into decisions, and effectiveness is measured in large part through evidence of teachers' and pupils' learning. Transforming teacher education in these ways represents a culture shift in the profession.
>
> *(p. 22)*

References

Arnold, G.H. (1992). Strengthening student teachers' reflections through collaborative research. *Journal of Early Childhood Teacher Education, 13*(3), 14–15.

Ax, J., Ponte, P., & Brouwer, N. (2008). Action research in initial teacher education: An explorative study. *Educational Action Research, 16*(1), 55–72.

Barman, C.R. (2000). The value of teachers doing classroom research. *Science and Children, 37*(1), 18–19.

Binder, M. (2012). Teaching as lived research. *Childhood Education, 88*(2), 118–120.

Boyer, E.L. (1990). *Scholarship reconsidered: Priorities of the professorate.* Princeton, NJ: The Carnegie Foundation for the Advancement of Teaching.

Brock, C. H., Helman, L., & Patchen, C. B. (2005). Learning to conduct teacher research: Exploring the development of mediated understandings. *Teachers and Teaching: Theory and Practice, 11*(1), 73–94.

Brown, P. U. (2010). Teacher research and university institutional review boards. *Journal of Early Childhood Teacher Education, 31*(3), 276–283.

Bryant, J., & Bates, A. (2010). The power of student resistance in action research: Teacher educators respond to classroom challenges. *Educational Action Research, 18*(3), 305–318.

Castle, K. (2006). Autonomy through pedagogical research. *Teaching and Teacher Education, 22*, 1094–1103.

Castle, K. (2012). *Early childhood teacher research.* New York: Routledge.

Castle, K. (2013). The state of teacher research in early childhood teacher education. *Journal of Early Childhood Teacher Education, 34*, 268–286.

Chetty, R., & Lubben, F. (2010). The scholarship of research in teacher education in a higher education institution in transition: Issues of identity. *Teaching and Teacher Education: An International Journal of Research and Studies, 26*(4), 813–820.

Cochran-Smith, M. (2006). Ten promising trends (and three big worries). *Educational Leadership, 63*(6), 20–25.

Cochran-Smith, M., & Lytle, S. L. (2009). *Inquiry as stance.* New York: Teachers College Press.

Cooney, M. H., Buchanan, M., & Parkinson, D. (2001). Teachers as researchers: Classroom inquiry initiatives at undergraduate and graduate levels in early childhood education. *Journal of Early Childhood Teacher Education, 22*(3), 151–159.

Crawford, P. A., & Cornett, J. (2000). Looking back to find a vision: Exploring the emancipatory potential of teacher research. *Childhood Education, 77*(1), 37–40.

Creswell, J. W. (2012). *Educational research* (4th ed.). Boston, MA: Pearson.

Darling-Hammond, L. (2010). *The flat world and education.* New York: Teachers College Press.

Darling-Hammond, L., & McLaughlin, M. W. (2011). Policies that support professional development in an era of reform. *Phi Delta Kappan, 92*(6), 81–92.

Day, C., Elliott, J., Somekh, B., & Winter, R. (2002). *Theory and practice in action research.* Oxford, UK: Symposium Books.

Denzin, N. K. (2010). Moments, mixed methods, and paradigm dialogs. *Qualitative Inquiry, 16*(6), 419–427.

Edwards, C., Gandini, L., & Forman, G. (1994). *The hundred languages of children.* Norwood, NJ: Ablex.

Ellingson, L. L. (2009). *Engaging crystallization in qualitative research.* Thousand Oaks, CA: Sage.

Ellis, C., & Castle, K. (2010). Teacher research as continuous process improvement. *Quality Assurance in Education, 18*(4), 271–285.

Flake, C. L., Kuhs, T., Donnelly, A., & Ebert, C. (1995). Reinventing the role of teacher, teacher as researcher. *Phi Delta Kappan, 76*, 405–407.

Gandini, L. (2005). The essential voices of the teachers: Conversations from Reggio Emilia. In L. Gandini, L. Hill, L. Cadwell, & C. Schwall (Eds.), *In the spirit of the studio* (pp. 58–72). New York: Teachers College Press.

Gandini, L., Hill, L., Cadwell, L., & Schwall, C. (2005). *In the spirit of the studio.* New York: Teachers College Press.

Gersten, R., Dimino, J., Jayanthi, M., Kim, J. S., & Santoro, L. E. (2010). Teacher study group: Impact of the professional development model on reading instruction and student outcomes in first grade classrooms. *American Educational Research Journal, 47*(3), 694–739.

Giles, C., Wilson, J., & Elias, M. (2010). Sustaining teachers' growth and renewal through action research, induction programs, and collaboration. *Teacher Education Quarterly, 37*(1), 91–108.

Goodnough, K. (2011). Examining the long-term impact of collaborative action research on teacher identity and practice: The perceptions of K-12 teachers. *Educational Action Research, 19*(1), 73–86.

Goswami, P., & Stillman, P. (1987). *Reclaiming the classroom: Teacher research as an agency for change.* Upper Montclair, NJ: Boynton/Cook.

Hahs-Vaughn, D. L., & Yanowitz, K. L. (2009). Who is conducting teacher research? *The Journal of Educational Research, 102*(6), 415–424.

Hatch, A., Greer, T., & Bailey, K. (2006). Student-produced action research in early childhood teacher education. *Journal of Early Childhood Teacher Education, 27*(2), 205–212.

Henderson, M. V., Hunt, S. N., & Wester, C. (1999). Action research: A survey of AACTE-member institutions. *Education, 119*(4), 663–667.

Herr, K. G., & Anderson, G. L. (2014). *The action research dissertation* (2nd ed.). Thousand Oaks, CA: Sage.

Hiebert, J., Gallimore, R., & Stigler, J. (2002). A knowledge base for the teaching profession: What should it look like and how can we get one? *Educational Researcher, 31*(5), 3–15.

Hopkins, D. (2002). *A teacher's guide to classroom research.* Philadelphia, PA: Open University Press.

Houston, N., Ross, H., Robinson, J., & Malcolm, H. (2010). Inside research, inside ourselves: Teacher educators take stock of their research practice. *Educational Action Research, 18*(4), 555–569.

Keat, J. B. (2005). Theory to practice through teacher inquiry courses in a graduate program: Two teachers' perspectives. *Journal of Early Childhood Teacher Education, 26*(3), 207–223.

King, M. B., & Newmann, F. M. (2000). Will teacher learning advance school goals? *Phi Delta Kappan, 81*, 576–580.

Kitchen, J., & Stevens, D. (2008). Action research in teacher education: Two teacher-educators practice action research as they introduce action research to preservice teachers. *Action Research, 6*(1), 7–28.

Lankshear, C., & Knobel, M. (2004). *A handbook of teacher research*. New York: Open University Press.

Lincoln, Y. S., & Guba, E. G. (1985). *Naturalistic inquiry*. Newbury Park, CA: Sage.

Little, J. W., Gearhart, M. C., Curry, M., & Kafka, J. (2003). Looking at student work for teacher learning, teacher community, and school reform. *Phi Delta Kappan, 85*(3), 184–192.

Loughran, J., Mitchell, I., & Mitchell, J. (2002). *Learning from teacher research*. New York: Teachers College Press.

McDonald, J. P., Mohr, N., Dichter, A., & McDonald, E. C. (2007). *The power of protocols* (2nd ed.). New York: Teachers College Press.

McGregor, D., Hooker, B., Wise, D., & Devlin, L. (2010). Supporting professional learning through teacher educator enquiries: An ethnographic insight into developing understandings and changing identities. *Professional Development in Education, 36*(1), 169–195.

Megowan-Romanowicz, C. (2010). Inside out: Action research from the teacher-researcher perspective. *Journal of Science Teacher Education, 21*(8), 993–1011.

Meyers, E., & Rust, F. (2003). *Taking action with teacher research*. Portsmouth, NH: Heinemann.

Mohr, M. M., Rogers, C., Sanford, B., Nocerino, M. A., MacLean, M. S., & Clawson, S. (2004). *Teacher research for better schools*. New York: Teachers College Press and Berkeley, CA: National Writing Project.

Moore, R. A., & Gilliard, J. L. (2008). Preservice teachers conducting action research in early education centers. *Journal of Early Childhood Teacher Education, 29*(1), 45–58.

Moore, T. L., & Ward, K. A. (2010). Institutionalizing faculty engagement through research, teaching, and service at research universities. *Michigan Journal of Community Service Learning, 17*(1), 44–58.

Moran, M. J. (2007). Collaborative action research and project work: Promising practices for developing collaborative inquiry among early childhood preservice teachers. *Teaching and Teacher Education: An International Journal of Research and Studies, 23*(4), 418–431.

National Council of Teachers of Mathematics (NCTM) Research Advisory Committee. (2001). Supporting communities of inquiry and practice. *Journal for Research in Mathematics Education, 32*(5), 444–447.

Niemi, H. (2009, June). *Why Finland on the top? Reflections on the reasons for the PISA success*. Keynote paper presented at the 3rd Redesigning Pedagogy International Conference, Singapore.

Niemi, H., & Jakku-Sihvonen, R. (2011). Teacher education in Finland. In M. V. Zuljan & J. Vogrinc (Eds.), *European dimensions of teacher education-similarities and differences* (pp. 33–52). Ljubljana, Slovenia: Faculty of Education, University of Ljubljana and Kranj, Slovenia: The National School of Leadership in Education.

Olson, K., & Clark, C. M. (2009). A signature pedagogy in doctoral education: The leader-scholar community. *Educational Researcher, 38*(3), 216–221.

Orland-Barak, L. (2009). Unpacking variety in practitioner inquiry on teaching and teacher education. *Educational Action Research, 17*(1), 111–119.

Ortiz, A., Ferrell, D., Anderson, J., Cain, L., Fluty, N., Sturzenbecker, S., & Matlock, T. (2014). Teacher research on boys' literacy in one elementary school. *Voices of Practitioners, 9*(1). Retrieved from https://www.naeyc.org/files/naeyc/images/voices/9_Ortiz%20v9-1.pdf

Paris, C., & Lung, P. (2008). Agency and child-centered practices in novice teachers: Autonomy, efficacy, intentionality, and reflectivity. *Journal of Early Childhood Teacher Education, 29*, 253–268.

Pine, G. J. (2009). *Teacher action research*. Los Angeles, CA: Sage.

Potter, G. (2003). Teacher research for teacher education: School-university partnerships. *Focus on Teacher Education, 3*(4), 3–7.

Richardson, V. (1994). Conducting research on practice. *Educational Researcher, 23*(5), 5–10.

Roberts, S. K., Crawford, P. A., & Hickmann, R. (2010). Teacher research as a robust and reflective path to professional development. *Journal of Early Childhood Teacher Education, 31*(3), 258–275.

Sahlberg, P. (2010a). *The secret to Finland's success: Educating teachers*. Retrieved from Stanford University Center for Opportunity Policy in Education website: https://edpolicy.stanford.edu/sites/default/files/publications/secret-finland%E2%80%99s-success-educating-teachers.pdf

Sahlberg, P. (2010b). Education change in Finland. In A. Hargreaves, M. Fullan, A. Lieberman, & D. Hopkins (Eds.), *Second international handbook of education changes* (pp. 323–348). Dordrecht, Netherlands: Springer Science and Business Media.

Shagoury, R., & Power, B. (2012). *Living the questions* (2nd ed.). Portland, ME: Stenhouse.

Smith, A. T., & Place, N. A. (2011). Fostering teaching and learning through an inquiry-based literacy methods course. *The New Educator, 7*(4), 305–324.

Smith, K., & Sela, O. (2005). Action research as a bridge between pre-service teacher education and in-service professional development for students and teacher educators. *European Journal of Teacher Education, 28*(3), 293–310.

Souto-Manning, M. (2012). Teacher action research in teacher education. *Childhood Education, 88*(1), 54–56.

Stenhouse, L. (1975). *An introduction to curriculum research and development*. London, UK: Heinemann.

Terzi, N., & Cantarelli, M. (2001). Parma: Supporting the work of teachers through professional development, organization, and administrative support. In L. Gandini & C. P. Edwards (Eds.), *Bambini: The Italian approach to infant/toddler care* (pp. 78–88). New York: Teachers College Press.

Trent, J. (2010). Teacher education as identity construction: Insights from action research. *Journal of Education for Teaching: International Research and Pedagogy, 36*(2), 153–168.

van Manen, M. (1990). *Researching lived experience.* New York: State University of New York Press.

Wood, J. W. (2005). Moses's story: Critical literacy and social justice in an urban kindergarten. *Voices of Practitioners*, 1–12. Retrieved from www.naeyc.org/publications/vop/articles

Zeichner, K. M. (1999). The new scholarship in teacher education. *Educational Researcher, 28*(9), 4–15.

Zeichner, K. M. (2002). Teacher research as professional development for P-12 educators in the USA. *Educational Action Research, 11*(2), 301–326.

PART IV

Pedagogical Approaches that Prepare Teachers to Support Diverse Learners

16

PREPARING TEACHERS TO SUPPORT TRANSITION AND BRIDGE DISCONTINUITY FOR CHILDREN AND FAMILIES

Beth S. Rous and Helena P. Mawdsley

Young children and their families often participate in a number of programs and services throughout their early years. Most commonly these programs include private child care, Head Start, public preschool, early intervention, and early childhood special education. Across these programs, funding streams, overall purpose and philosophy, and approaches to services and supports differ, often significantly, based on the state or locale in which services are provided. What these programs have in common however, is a desire to support the health, welfare, and optimal growth and development of young children. The plethora of programs and services available to young children and families has long been recognized as potentially duplicative and incongruent. A report from the U.S. Government Accountability Office (U.S. GAO, 1994) which conducted a review of federal programs found 22 key programs provided services to children under age 5 in the U.S. Often, these programs targeted the same children, though were varied in the approaches and comprehensiveness of the services they provided.

Recent national efforts have focused on more integration and coordination across programs, most notably public preschool, Head Start, and child care, through the Race to the Top, Early Learning Challenge Funds (U.S. Department of Education & U.S. Department of Health and Human Services [U.S. DOE & U.S. DHHS], 2011). This national initiative focused on the establishment of state systems to support coordination of programs across agencies within a state. This coordination was emphasized through the development and implementation of Tiered Quality Rating and Improvement Systems (TQRIS), common standards and assessment systems, integrated professional development systems to support a high-quality and well-compensated workforce, and school readiness.

Given the historically disparate array of programs for young children, it is not surprising a lack of coordination (e.g., Wischnowski, Fowler, & McCollum, 2000; Rous, Hemmeter, & Schuster, 1999; Rosenkoetter, Hains, & Fowler, 1994) and continuity (e.g., Chun, 2003; Kemp, 2003; LeAger & Shapiro, 1995; Love, Logue, Trudeau, & Thayer, 1992) across and among these programs has long been reported in the literature. This chapter will focus on key terms in the literature related to discontinuity, a summary of the current research, conceptual frameworks that have been used to describe and undergird the research, and key practices that have emerged from the literature.

Key Terms and Definitions

One of the difficulties in understanding the research base related to discontinuity of services and supports in the field of early childhood is the vast number of terms used to describe the phenomenon (Rous & Hallam, 2012). These terms include continuity, alignment, transition, and school readiness. Therefore, it is critical to begin the conversation with descriptors of the various terms and how they have been defined and used within the literature.

Continuity and Alignment

Continuity has been referred to as the "coherence and connectedness among a child's experiences at home and school from preschool through the elementary grades" (Bredekamp, 2010, p. 135). It is generally understood from child development frameworks that continuity between settings facilitates children's ability to navigate new demands and expectations required of them in the new setting (Bronfenbrenner & Morris, 2006; Piaget, 1952; Vygotsky, 1963). An example of how a teacher may attempt to facilitate continuity between settings may be a pre-kindergarten teacher's effort to connect with a kindergarten teacher, either for a particular child or about curriculum. Additionally, this effort may provide an opportunity to share relevant developmental or systemic information. The apparent value of linkages that build continuity between settings underscores the National Education Goals Panel's (1998) emphasis on relationships for successful transitions, identifying them as useful tools to improve connections between home, pre-kindergarten, and elementary school, resulting in enhanced competence for all children.

Discontinuity can be defined as the experience for a child when the sending and receiving environments or their elements are "not compatible" (Love et al., 1992, p. 5). The experience of discontinuity may take many forms. For example, discontinuity may be manifested by a dramatic shift in the curriculum (e.g., moving from play-based to a more academically focused curriculum) or moving into a new educational program, which offers fewer opportunities for family involvement than the previous program (Pianta & Kraft-Sayre, 1999; Rous, Hallam, Harbin, McCormick, & Jung, 2007). Discontinuity between programs, coupled with an absence of systems designed to support and facilitate the transition process, may make the transition for children and families difficult (Love et al., 1992).

The term **alignment** in education connotes the coordination of separate elements or parts (Kagan & Kaurez, 2007) and refers to the degree of a correspondence regarding the content of early learning standards, curriculum, and assessment so that the three components work together toward the common goal of educating students effectively (p. 24). The correspondence of what will be expected, what will be taught, and what will be evaluated has been noted as an essential element of an effective education system. The supposition of aligning standards, curricula, and assessments is that such efforts will enable more effective teaching practices and, in turn, result in positive child outcomes. Together alignment and continuity are the efforts that create a continuous, seamless experience across settings through curriculum and education policy (Lo Casale-Crouch et al., 2008; Rous, Hallam, et al., 2007); in other words, they represent the degree to which program structures complement each other.

The alignment and continuity of the service delivery system in terms of programs, curricula, and expectations can be critical to successful transition and adjustment to new settings and services (Rous, Hallam, et al., 2007). This is supported by studies demonstrating that continuity across programs, curricula, and personnel increases the likelihood for a more successful transition to new programs (Entwisle & Alexander, 1998; Hair, Halle, Terry-Humen, Lavelle, & Calkins, 2006). As we will discuss in more detail, research provides insights into the influence of planning and practices that can support better alignment and maintain continuity in children's development and early academic success (e.g., Hair et al., 2006; Schulting, Malone, & Dodge, 2005).

Transition

For the purposes of this chapter the definition of transition comes from both the general and special education literature where we view transition as the process of a child changing settings both within a day and across time, and includes activities initiated by both the sending and receiving programs to bridge the discontinuity between these experiences for the child and family (Kagan, 1991; Love et al., 1992; Rous, Hallam, et al., 2007). The term transition has conventionally, within the early childhood context, referred to the movement of children as they leave the preschool years and enter kindergarten (Kagan, 2010). Other definitions of transition have included the assimilations and accommodations that families, early childhood programs, and schools make to support children as they navigate the disparate worlds of preschool and primary school (Love et al., 1992). Over two decades ago the term transition expanded in scope and complexity resulting in a two-dimensional concept (Kagan 1991): vertical transition and horizontal transition. Vertical transition refers to the transitions that children make as they advance chronologically through the periods of their lives, for example from infancy to toddlerhood, from toddlerhood to the preschool years, and then from preschool to kindergarten. These types of vertical transitions include the corresponding early education and care settings children move into as a result of the chronological advancement. Horizontal transitions encompass the many settings that children experience simultaneously. Each day, a child routinely moves or makes a transition from one setting or service to another. For example, a child may move from home to child care, and then from child care to a Head Start classroom in a single day (Kagan, 1991).

More recently the focus of transition in the early childhood literature expanded from an individual child orientation to a broader systems-level change. Instead of focusing solely on the early childhood years, the field began expanding vertically, conceding transition for children should include birth through age 8 (Kagan, 2010). Much like the field of early childhood special education, the early childhood literature began to recognize that multiple systems and programs support the full range of child development including health, social services, and community programs during the transition. Thus a horizontal expansion evolved and promoting effective vertical and horizontal transitions became associated with establishing linkages within and among programs and systems. As a result, terms such as *continuity* and *alignment* emerged within the transition literature in order to highlight the importance of these linkages.

School Readiness

Research has indicated children experience the transition to school as a qualitative change in expectations for behavior and performance, with an emphasis on more formal instruction and specific academic goals (Margetts, 2002; Rimm-Kaufmann, Pianta, & Cox, 2000). Attempts to expand early childhood transitions and create readiness implies the mastery of certain basic skills or abilities that, in turn, permit a child to function successfully in a school setting, both academically and socially. Thus, the school readiness construct gained national attention when the first of the National Education Goals, or "Goals, 2000," asserted that "all children in America will start school ready to learn" (National Education Goals Panel, 1998, p. 1). This goal is predicated on the belief that children's abilities and skills at school entry determine their success or failure during the transition to formal schooling (Meisels, 1999). Research and policy have focused largely on the importance of cognitive skills and emergent literacy for later academic achievement (Kauerz, 2002; Snow, Burns, & Griffin, 1998); however, children's school readiness is viewed as multidimensional, encompassing not only cognitive and language skills, but also social-emotional development and health. The National Education Goals Panel (1998) identified five developmental domains associated with early development and learning: physical well-being and motor development, socio-emotional development, approaches to learning, language development, and cognitive and general knowledge (Kagan, Moore, & Bredekamp, 1995).

was child- and school-centered (i.e., discontinuity). Parents reported the transition process experience to be "stressful," a finding consistent with other similar studies (Fowler, Chandler, Johnson, & Stella, 1988; Rosenkoetter et al., 1994). Contemporary research suggests parent concerns about the transition process continue at kindergarten entry (e.g., Janus, Lefort, Cameron, and Kopechanski, 2007; McIntyre, Eckert, Fiese, Reed, & Wildenger, 2010).

More recently, the ECSE literature has highlighted key practices that programs serving children with disabilities might utilize to facilitate better adjustment for the family and child (Mawdsley & Hauser-Cram, 2013), characterizing those practices by level of intensity (i.e., low intensity vs. high intensity; Daley et al., 2011; Rous et al., 2010). Rous and colleagues (2010) suggest that programs, specifically teachers, need to reach parents and children before the first day of school and utilize high-intensity practices (e.g., meeting directly with family members, home visiting) that provide personal contact with families in addition to the low-intensity practices (e.g., open houses, form letters to parents) often put in place. The research indicates that practices related to transitions for children with disabilities, into early education programs and into formal schooling, are key to maintaining continuity (Myers, 2007; Myers & Effgen, 2006; Rous et al., 2010) and facilitating alignment (La Paro, Pianta, & Cox, 2000b).

Conceptual and Theoretical Frameworks

Two specific conceptual frameworks have been developed to support transition research and interpretation of findings. Rimm-Kaufman and Pianta (2000) have built upon the work of ecologically oriented system theories and applied them to the period of kindergarten transition through a proposed Ecological and Dynamic Model of Transition. Within the context of transition, children's adjustment to school is the product of relationships among a wide array of contexts and persons, including the child, the family, schools and teachers, peers, preschools and preschool teachers, and the wider community, as well as the continuity or discontinuity of these relationships over time. The relationships between contexts may support or challenge children's transition to school and also influence later school outcomes (Rimm-Kaufman & Pianta, 2000). They conclude the system of relationships among social contexts (including teachers, parents, and preschool care providers) is a critical predictor of successful transitions. Effective communication and regular contact among the various social contexts engender connectedness and flexibility, thereby promoting an optimal transition.

Rous, Hallam, et al. (2007) employed another transition conceptual framework that took into consideration the specific needs of children with disabilities and their families. This framework addressed and described the unique challenges of planning for and coordinating the transition needs of young children receiving early intervention/early childhood special education services across two distinct levels. The first is based upon bioecological theory (Bronfenbrenner & Morris, 1998) and the second level uses organizational systems theory (Shafritz, Ott, & Jang, 2005), which demonstrates how critical interagency variables (e.g., communication, collaboration) exert influence on the outcomes of the transition. Rous et al. (2007) presented these critical interagency variables as consisting of supportive infrastructure, communication and relationships, and alignment and continuity directed at the multiple agencies involved in the process. This level includes child and family preparation, and child and family adjustment, with the resulting outcome of child success in school. This framework further defined and reiterated the concept of a critical window of time for the child and family to adapt to the new setting and proceed in development.

International Perspectives on Early Childhood Transition

In addition to transition studies conducted in the U.S., studies were reviewed from various countries including Australia, Canada, Finland, Iceland, and Denmark. From this review the most applicable work was found in the Australian literature. Einarsdottir, Perry, and Dockett (2008) stated:

> One of the greatest values in making cross-national comparisons is not what they say about the differences or similarities among the countries and systems but, rather, that they provide an alternative lens through which each of the countries and systems can be observed. An alternative lens can highlight: different interpretations of the same practices; reflection on what is important in transition to school and how this can be incorporated into practice; reflection on practices in each context—often focusing on the practices of others is a less threatening starting point for reflexive practice than examining one's own practice; the importance of context; consideration of 'outsider' and 'insider' perspectives with the expectation that there are multiple perspectives on similar issues and practices.
>
> *(p. 56)*

The concept of preparedness for transition to school has arisen out of underlying theories of social maturation or "academic content knowledge readiness" of children. This concept remains prevalent in some areas of Australia, and in a number of countries where school-like reception programs are implemented to respond to the concern about equality of opportunity for immigrants, children with special needs, and the socially disadvantaged (Petriwskyj, Thorpe, & Tayler, 2005; Villeneuve et al., 2013). Similar to the transition literature in the United States, the international literature emphasized continuity for children as they entered new programs, particularly primary school (Carida, 2011; Dockett & Perry, 2013). For example, maintaining continuity between preschool and primary school for (1) the child as co-constructor of knowledge, identity and culture; (2) the teacher and her role; and (3) pedagogical practice have been identified as necessary mutual goals among these institutions (Dahlberg & Lenz Taguchi, 1994). Broström (2002) also emphasized continuity in children's lives as they move from preschool to primary school, focusing particularly on teachers' practice of inviting children to visit new settings. As such, the aim of many "transition programs" as they are called in international communities, was described as "easing" or "smoothing" the transition process (Carida, 2011; Dockett & Perry, 2013), suggesting the start to school was inherently challenging, particularly for children with special needs (Kemp, 2003) or at a socio-economic risk (Dockett & Perry, 2007). Additionally, literature from Australia describes programs to support families and adjustment to school in the form of supporting parents as they manage the transition. For example, three programs, Transition to Primary School Parent Programs (Giallo, Treyvard, Matthews, & Kienhuis, 2010), the Pathways to Prevention programs (Freiberg et al., 2005), and Triple P—Positive Parenting Programs (Sanders et al., 2008) operate on the principle that enhancing parents' skills to manage interactions with their children, as well as with school professionals, builds their capacity to support the children and promote a positive start to school (Dockett & Perry, 2013).

On the other hand, unlike transition studies conducted in the U.S., international studies, such as the Starting School Research Project (Dockett & Perry, 2005a), include the children's perspectives of the transition process. In this project the role of children as "social and cultural actors" was stipulated. Children's perspectives were gathered during group discussions and via photography (Dockett & Perry, 2005b). Kindergarten children were asked, "*What did you need to know about when you started school?* and *"There are some children who are going to start school soon. What is important for them to know about this school?*" (p. 8). Children identified important places within the school and discussed why those places were important to them. For example, playground equipment was photographed and the children explained the playground was an important place for new students to know about because "it is where you play and make friends" (p. 11). Using grounded theory, the researchers identified eight categories (i.e., knowledge, adjustment, skills, disposition, rules, physical, family issues, and educational environments) as key themes to consider when developing practices and strategies for young children moving into a kindergarten. Further, recognition of children's perspectives has led to changes in transition practices (Perry & Dockett, 2011). As a result of the Starting School Research Project, collaboration and cooperation among the study schools and prior-to-school settings (e.g., preschool) improved, opportunities for educators across settings to interact and plan transitions increased, and the confidence of preschool teachers to engage with primary schools increased. These investigations recognize young children are capable and competent narrators of their experiences and much can be gained from the perspectives of those most directly involved in the transition to school (Jackson & Cartmel, 2010; MacDonald, 2009).

Embedding Continuity and Transition into Teacher Education Programs

From a teacher education perspective, continuity and transition can be embedded within the preservice curriculum as most strategies used to support these constructs are consistent with high-quality teaching and instructional practice. In fact, the implementation of developmentally appropriate practices across early care and education settings has been linked to better academic and social outcomes (e.g., Mantzicopoulos, 2005; Marcon, 2002; Huffman & Speer, 2000). Using the explicit definitions of alignment, continuity, and transition, early childhood teacher educators can match core competencies within the preservice curriculum to these constructs to help future educators understand and apply them within their practice settings.

In line with the National Association for the Education of Young Children (NAEYC, 2009a) developmentally appropriate practices, early childhood teacher educators can engage students in assignments/activities to facilitate their understanding of specific practices that support alignment, continuity, and transition. For example, having students engage in role-playing a home visit assuming the role of parent, teacher, and observer can help them to gain insight into ways they might engage families during a home visit. Reflective discussion of how best to support coherence and connectedness among the child's experiences at home, school, and other settings across time can help students see what worked, what didn't, and how they might change their approach. As a subsequent activity, using readings, literature search, and/or teacher interviews (as appropriate), students can identify the types of information that would be helpful to know about a student entering a new program to support continuity. In class, they can work in small groups to compare information and work as a team to develop a process that can be used to gather and share the information across settings to support a child's transition.

Home visits are often used by teachers to connect with families and support the child's development across environments (continuity). By timing a home visit before a child enters a new program, the teacher can help prepare the child and family for that important first day at school (transition). Likewise, timing a home visit in the first few weeks of the child's enrollment can help the teacher work with the family to address any concerns related to the child's adjustment to the new program (continuity). To further solidify preservice students' learning about the home visiting process, early childhood teacher educators can design opportunities for participation in actual home visits within a field based practicum experience or a course on working with families. This approach is in keeping with research that suggests work-embedded practice is more effective in promoting implementation of evidence-based practices than classroom based lectures alone (Joyce & Showers, 2002).

The most valuable concept for new teachers related to continuity and transition is to identify and minimize the number of disruptions in a child's schedule or setting. Incorporating this awareness into teacher preparation and providing students opportunities to observe and reflect on children's transitions into new classrooms can help students to better understand the significance of this experience for young children and families. For instance, many early care and education programs move children from setting to setting based on age. In this way, young children often transition from the infant room to the toddler room, from the 1-year-old room to the 2-year-old room. These decisions are often based on staff-child ratios or other licensing/programmatic requirements. However, this results in children experiencing multiple disruptions over time, meaning they must continually adjust to new settings, instructional approaches, and personnel. In contrast, strategies such as looping (multi-age or

NAEYC Core Standards for Initial and Advanced Early Childhood Preparation Programs

Standard 2: Building Family and Community Relationships

Key elements 2c: Involving families and communities in their children's development and learning.

Within this standard, the supporting explanation states: "Well-prepared early childhood candidates are able to identify such resources and know how to connect families with appropriate services, including help with planning transitions from one educational or service system to another" and "Candidates understand how to go beyond parent conferences to engage families in curriculum planning, assessing children's learning, and planning for children's transitions to new programs" (p. 12).

Standard 4: Using Developmentally Effective Approaches to Connect with Children and Families

Key elements 4c: Using a broad repertoire of developmentally appropriate teaching/learning approaches.

Within this standard, the supporting explanation states: "In making the transition from family to a group context, very young children need continuity between the practices of family members and those used by professionals in the early childhood setting. Their feelings of safety and confidence depend on that continuity" (p.15).

CEC/DEC Initial Standards for Beginning Early Childhood Special Education/Early Intervention

CEC/DEC Standard 4: Instructional Strategies – Possess and use a repertoire of evidence-based instructional strategies that promote the success of children.

ICC4K1 – Evidence-based practices validated for specific characteristics of learners and settings.

ICC4S1 – Use strategies to facilitate integration into various settings.

ICC4S6 – Use strategies that promote successful transitions for individuals with exceptional learning needs.

ECSE4S4 – Link development, learning experiences, and instruction to promote educational transitions.

CEC/DEC Standard 5: Learning Environments and Social Interactions

ICC5S3 – Identify supports needed for integration into various program placements.

CEC/DEC Standard 10: Collaboration

ICC10S2 – Collaborate with caregivers, professionals, and agencies to support children's development and learning.

ECSE10S8 – Assist the family in planning for transition.

ECSE10S9 – Implement processes and strategies that support transitions among settings for infants and young children.

(ICC = initial common core; EC = early childhood; K = knowledge; S = Skills)

Figure 16.1 Transition and Continuity Relevant National Personnel Preparation Standards

multi-year classrooms) can minimize these disruptions, allow for more continuity, and provide more stability for children.

To support the process of embedding the concepts of transition and continuity into teacher education programs, Figure 16.1 presents core teacher standards identified through NAEYC (2009b) and the Council for Exceptional Children (CEC) (2012). Courses within which these skills and competencies can be embedded include those that address:

- Child Growth and Development
- Teaching Young Children with Special Needs
- Family/Parent Involvement in Education

As faculty consider addressing the topic of continuity and transition across their courses, specific transition practices and strategies identified through the literature, as well as those identified by major professional organizations (i.e., NAEYC and DEC), can be helpful and relevant for early childhood teacher preparation. Practices are defined as "key elements of transition planning that are broad and global in nature . . . and are regularly and consistently implemented across staff and programs" (Rous, 2009, p. 3). For each practice, specific strategies reflect the practice in action. Strategies are defined as "specific program or classroom activities used to implement a practice" (Rous, 2009, p. 3). Table 16.1 provides a list of practices and corresponding strategies that have been identified in the literature as facilitating continuity and/or alignment during the transition process (Mawdsley, Snyder, & Rous, 2014). In addition, the Division for Early Childhood (2014)

Table 16.1 Transition Practices, Strategies, and Supporting Research

Practice	*Sample Strategies*	*Supporting Research*
Transition information and timelines identified and communicated refers to the extent to which general information about when certain events are expected to happen regarding the transition (e.g., the specific date of the first day of kindergarten for the approaching school year) is disseminated to families of children either leaving or entering a new setting.	• Letters sent to every child's home. • Flyer about important program dates or deadline posted in or around community. • Program offers a pre-transition open house or orientation.	Daley et al., 2011; Early et al., 2001; Gill et al., 2006; La Paro et al., 2000a; Lo Casale-Crouch et al., 2008; Pianta et al., 1999; Rous, 2009; Rous et al., 2010; Schulting et al., 2005.
Referral process and/or enrollment process & timelines are identified and communicated across programs and to families refers to the extent to which important information about referral and/or enrollment policies is communicated between the sending and receiving programs and is understood by each entity. The practice also refers to the extent to which important information is communicated and understood by families. The practice and strategies may be used more frequently for children with special needs but can be generalized to the transition of children without disabilities as well.	• Provided professional development or training to early childhood professionals re: transition policies. • Develop understanding across programs about expectations for referral/enrollment timelines and process. • Program conducts community referrals and provides specific information re: referral and enrollment to families.	Early et al., 2001; Forest, Horner, Lewis-Palmer, & Todd, 2004; Gill et al., 2006; La Paro et al., 2000b; Myers & Effgen, 2006; Noonan & Ratokalau, 1991; Rous, 2009; Rous et al., 2010.
Communication and coordination is established both within and across programs regarding transition refers to the actions that the receiving and sending programs take to discuss or coordinate the transition for all children or for a specific child and family.	• Receiving and sending professionals contact with each other either before transition, after transition, or at both time points. • Program visit – Sending professional to new program/setting. • Program visit – Receiving professional to sending program/setting. • Receiving program receives child's previous records/information.	Daley et al., 2011; Early et al., 2001; Forest et al., 2004; La Paro et al., 2000a; La Paro et al., 2000b; Noonan & Ratokalau, 1991; LoCasale-Crouch et al., 2008; Pianta et al., 1999; Pianta, Kraft-Sayre, Rimm-Kaufman, Gercke, & Higgins, 2001; Rous, 2009; Rous et al., 2010; Schulting et al., 2005.

Communication and coordination established with family of child refers to the actions early childhood professionals and programs take to establish communication with the family and child in order to facilitate the transition.	• Home Visits – Professional to child's home. • Encourage the family and child to visit new program/setting or professional accompanies family during visit to new program. • Receiving program-initiated contact with family	Daley et al., 2011; Early et al., 2001; Forest et al., 2004; Gill et al., 2006; La Paro et al., 2000a; La Paro et al., 2000b; Noonan & Ratokalau, 1991; Lo Casale-Crouch et al., 2008; Pianta et al., 1999; Myers & Effgen, 2006; Rous, 2009; Rous et al., 2010; Schulting et al., 2005.
Conduct assessment and/or coordinate curriculum information refers to the extent to which the professionals within the program conduct an assessment for a specific child(ren) and/or align curriculum between programs.	• Conduct assessment for incoming child(ren) and use assessment result to inform curriculum • Align curriculum between sending and receiving programs	Forest et al., 2004; La Paro et al., 2000b; Lo Casale-Crouch et al., 2008; Murphy, McCormick, & Rous, 2013; Myers & Effgen, 2006; Pianta et al., 1999; Quintero & McIntyre, 2011; Rous, 2009; Rous et al., 2010.
Professionals and/or interdisciplinary team are engaged in transition planning and placement refers to the extent to which the key professionals who have been and/or will be working with a specific child are supporting the child and family and contributing to the transition process. The strategies associated with this practice are typically used for children receiving special education services.	• Interdisciplinary team provides consultation re: evaluation, placement, curriculum, or care for child and family. • Professionals attend the IFSP/IEP meeting and support families to attend IFSP/IEP meeting.	Daley et al., 2011; Forest et al., 2004; Noonan & Ratokalau, 1991; Myers, 2007; Myers & Effgen, 2006; Rous, 2009; Quintero & McIntyre, 2011.

identified two recommended practices to support the transition process for children who have disabilities and/or special needs.

- DEC Recommended Practice TR1: Practitioners in sending and receiving programs exchange information before, during, and after transition about practices most likely to support the child's successful adjustment and positive outcomes.
- DEC Recommended Practice TR2: Practitioners use a variety of planned and timely strategies with the child and family before, during, and after the transition to support successful adjustment and positive outcomes for both the child and family.

We view all of these transition practices as teachable and appropriate to include in pre-service curriculum.

Summary

Early childhood teachers in today's classrooms face a myriad of opportunities and challenges. The implementation of new integrated systems (e.g., professional development, Quality Rating and Improvement Systems), along with continued movement toward serving children from diverse backgrounds and contexts in integrated settings requires teachers to have a new set of skills and competencies. Understanding how to support continuity, alignment, and transition services exemplifies the skill set needed. As seen in the research literature, teachers in programs must both understand and respond to the settings from which children come, as well as prepare children for the settings to which they will transition. Due to the complex nature of early childhood services and supports, these settings are often administered under the purview of different agencies. In addition, the need to address continuity and transition across both the vertical and horizontal axes requires thought and collaboration between different providers and with families. The practices and strategies provided in this chapter exemplify the skills and knowledge that can support teachers in navigating these complex processes.

Acknowledgements

This chapter was supported, in part, by an Institute of Education Sciences research fellowship training grant (R324B1200002) awarded to the University of Florida.

References

Bredekamp, S. (2010). Aligning curriculum and teaching: A child focused approach. In S. L. Kagan and K. Tarrant (Eds.), *Transitions for Young Children* (pp. 135–159). Baltimore, MD: Brookes Publishing.

Bronfenbrenner, U., & Morris, P. A. (1998). The ecology of developmental processes. In D. William and R. Lerner (Eds.), *Handbook of child psychology: Vol 1: Theoretical models of human development* (5th ed.), (pp. 993–1028). Hoboken, NJ: John Wiley & Sons.

Bronfenbrenner, U., & Morris, P. A. (2006). The bioecological model of human development. In W. D. & R. M. Lerner (Eds.), *Handbook of child psychology: Vol. I. Theoretical models of human development.* (6th ed.), (pp. 793–828). Hoboken, NJ: Wiley.

Broström, S. (2002). Communication and continuity in the transition from kindergarten to school. In H. Fabian and A. W. Dunlap (Eds.). *Transitions in the early years. Debating continuity and progression for children in early education*, (pp. 52–63). London, UK: Routledge.

Bruder, M. B. (1994). Working with members of other disciplines: Collaboration for success. In M. Wolery & J. S. Wilbers (Eds.), *Including children with special needs in early childhood programs* (pp. 45–70). Washington, DC: National Association for the Education of Young Children.

Bruder, M. B., & Bologna, T. (1993). Collaboration and service coordination for effective early intervention. In W. Brown, S. K. Thurman, & L. F. Pearl (Eds.), *Family-centered early intervention with infants and toddlers: Interdisciplinary cross-disciplinary approaches* (pp. 103–127). Baltimore, MD: Brookes Publishing.

Carida, H. C. (2011). Planning and implementing an educational program for the smooth transition from kindergarten to primary school: The Greek project in all-day kindergartens. *The Curriculum Journal, 22*(1), 77–92.

Chun, W. (2003). A study of children's difficulties in transition to school in Hong Kong. *Early Child Development and Care, 173*, 83–96.

Council of Exceptional Children (CEC). (2012). *Personnel standards for early intervention and early childhood special education: DEC initial standards.* Retrieved from http://community.cec.sped.org/dec-beta0/contactus1/personnelstandardsforearlyinterventionandearlychildhoodspecialeducation

Dahlberg, G., & Lenz Taguchi, H. (1994). *Forskola och skolaom tvd skilda traditioner och om visionen om en motesplats* [Preschool and school: Two different traditions and a vision of a meeting place]. Stockholm, Sweden: HLS Forlag.

Daley, T. C., Munk, T., & Carlson, E. (2011). A national study of kindergarten transition practices for children with disabilities. *Early Childhood Research Quarterly, 26*, 409–419.

Division for Early Childhood. (2014). *DEC recommended practices in early intervention/early childhood special education.* Retrieved from http://www.dec-sped.org/recommendedpractices

Dockett, S., & Perry, B. (2003). The transition to school: What's important? *Educational Leadership, 60*(7), 30–33.

Dockett, S., & Perry, B. (2005a). Researching with children: insights from the Starting School Research Project. *Early Child Development and Care, 175*(6), 507–521.

Dockett, S., & Perry, B. (2005b). 'You Need to Know How to Play Safe': children's experiences of starting school. *Contemporary Issues in Early Childhood, 6*(1), 4–18.

Dockett, S., & Perry, B. (2007). *Transitions to school: Perceptions, expectations, experiences.* Sydney, Australia: UNSW Press.

Dockett, S., & Perry, B. (2009). Readiness for school: A relational construct. *Australasian Journal of Early Childhood, 34*(1), 20–26.

Dockett, S., & Perry, B. (2013). Trends and tensions: Australian and international research about starting school. *International Journal of Early Years Education, 21*(2–3), 163–177.

Dunst, C. J., Trivette, C. M., & Cornwell, J. (1989). Family needs, social support, and self-efficacy during a child's transition to school. *Early Education and Development, 1*(1), 7–18.

Early, D. M., Pianta, R. C., Taylor, L. C., & Cox, M. J. (2001). Transition practices: Findings from a national survey of Kindergarten teachers. *Early Childhood Education Journal, 28*(3), 199–206.

Einarsdottir, J., Perry, B., & Dockett, S. (2008). Transition to school practices: Comparisons from Iceland and Australia. *Early Years, 28*(1), 47–60.

Entwisle, D. R., & Alexander, K. L. (1998). Facilitating the transition to first grade: The nature of transition and research on factors affecting it. *Elementary School Journal, 98*(4), 351–364.

Forest, E. J., Horner, R. H., Lewis-Palmer, T., & Todd, A. W. (2004). Transitions for young children with autism from preschool to Kindergarten. *Journal of Positive Behavior Interventions, 6*(2), 103–112.

Fowler, S. A., Chandler, L. K., Johnson, T. E., & Stella, M. E. (1988). Individualized family involvement in school transitions: Gathering information and choosing the next program. *Journal of the Division for Early Childhood, 12*, 208–216.

Freiberg, K., Homel, R., Batchelor, S., Carr, A., Lamb, C., Hay, I., . . ., Teague R. (2005). Pathways to participation: A community-based developmental prevention project in Australia. *Children and Society, 19*, 144–157.

Giallo, R., Treyvard, K., Matthews, J., & Kienhuis, M. (2010). Making the transition to primary school: An evaluation of a transition program for parents. *Australian Journal of Educational & Developmental Psychology, 10*, 1–17.

Gill, S., Winters, D., & Friedman, D. S. (2006). Educators' views of pre-Kindergarten and Kindergarten readiness and transition practices. *Contemporary Issues in Early Childhood, 7*(3), 213–227.

Greenberg, M. T., Lengua, L. J., Coie, J. D., & Pinderhughes, E. E. (1999). Predicting developmental outcomes at school entry using a multiple-risk model: Four American communities. *Developmental Psychology, 35*, 403–417.

Hair, E., Halle, T., Terry-Humen, E., Lavelle, B., & Calkins, J. (2006). Children's school readiness in the ECLS-K: Predictions to academic, health, and social outcomes in first grade. *Early Childhood Research Quarterly, 21*(4), 431–454.

Hanline, M. F., & Halvorsen, A. (1989). Parent perceptions of the integration transition process: Overcoming artificial barriers. *Exceptional Children, 55*, 487–492.

Hanson, M. J., Beckman, P. J., Horn, E., Marquart, J., Sandall, S. R., Greig, D., & Brennan, E. (2000). Entering preschool: Family and professional experiences in this transition process. *Journal of Early Intervention, 23*, 279–293.

Huffman, L. R., & Speer, P. W. (2000). Academic performance among at-risk children: The role of developmentally appropriate practices. *Early Childhood Research Quarterly, 15*, 167–184.

Jackson, A., & Cartmel, J. (2010). Listening to children's experience of starting school in an area of socioeconomic disadvantage. *International Journal of Transitions in Childhood, 4*, 13–25.

Janus, M., Lefort, J., Cameron, R., & Kopechanski, L. (2007). Starting kindergarten: Transition issues for children with special needs. *Canadian Journal of Education, 30*(3), 628–648.

Johnson, T. E., Chandler, L. K., Kerns, G. M., & Fowler, S. A. (1986). What are parents saying about family involvement in school transitions? A retrospective transition interview. *Journal of the Division for Early Childhood, 11*(1), 10–17.

Joyce, B. R., & Showers, B. (2002). *Student achievement through staff development* (3rd ed.). Alexandria, VA: Association for Supervision and Curriculum Development (ASCD).

Kagan, S. L. (1991). Moving from here to there: Rethinking continuity and transitions in early care and education. In B. Spodek & O. Saracho (Eds.), *Yearbook in early childhood education* (pp. 132–151). New York: Teachers College Press.

Kagan, S. L. (2010). Seeing transition through a new prism: Pedagogical, programmatic, and policy alignment. In S. L. Kagan & K. Tarrant (Eds.), *Transitions for young children* (pp. 3–18). Baltimore, MD: Brookes Publishing.

Kagan, S. L., & Kaurez, K. (2007). Reaching for the whole: Integration and alignment in early education policy. In R. C. Pianta, M. J. Cox, & K. L. Snow (Eds.), *School readiness and the transition to kindergarten in the era of accountability* (pp. 11–30). Baltimore, MD: Brookes Publishing.

Kagan, S. L., Moore, E., & Bredekamp, S. (1995). *Reconsidering children's early development and learning: Toward common views and vocabulary*. Washington, DC: National Education Goals Panel Goal One Technical Planning Group.

Kauerz, K. (2002). *Literacy*. No Child Left Behind Policy Brief. Denver, CO: Education Commission of the States (ECS) Retrieved from http://www.ecs.org/clearinghouse/35/66/3566.pdf

Kemp, C. (2003). Investigating the transition of young children with intellectual disabilities into mainstream classes: An Australian perspective. *International Journal of Disability Development and Education, 50*, 403–431.

Kemp, C., & Carter, M. (2000). Demonstration of classroom survival skills in kindergarten: A five-year transition study of children with intellectual disabilities. *Educational Psychology, 20*, 393–411.

La Paro, K., Pianta, R., & Cox, M. (2000a). Kindergarten teachers' reported use of Kindergarten to first grade transition practices. *Elementary School Journal, 101*(1), 63–78.

La Paro, K., Pianta, R. C., & Cox, M. (2000b). Teachers' reported transition practices for children transitioning into kindergarten and first grade. *Exceptional Children, 67*, 7–20.

LeAger, C., & Shapiro, E. (1995). Template matching as a strategy for assessment of and intervention for preschool students with disabilities. *Topics in Early Childhood Special Education, 2*, 187–218.

Lin, H., Lawrence, F. R., & Gorrell, J. (2003). Kindergarten teachers' views of children's readiness for school. *Early Childhood Research Quarterly, 18*, 225–237.

Lo Casale-Crouch, J., Mashburn, A. J., Downer, J. T., & Pianta, R. C. (2008). Pre-kindergarten teachers' use of transition practices and children's adjustment to kindergarten. *Early Childhood Research Quarterly, 23*(1), 124–139.

Love, J. M., Logue, M. E., Trudeau, J. Y., & Thayer, K. (1992). *Transitions to kindergarten in American schools: Final report of the national transition study.* Hampton, NH: ERIC Clearinghouse for Elementary and Early Childhood Education (ERIC Document Reproduction Service No. ED344693).

Lovett, D. L., & Haring, K. A. (2003). Family perceptions of transitions in early intervention. *Education and Training in Developmental Disabilities, 38*(4), 370–377.

MacDonald, A. (2009). Drawing stories: The power of children's drawings to communicate the lived experience of starting school. *Australasian Journal of Early Childhood, 34*(3), 40–49.

Mantzicopoulos, P. (2005). Conflictual relationships between kindergarten children and their teachers: Associations with child and classroom context variables. *Journal of Social Psychology, 43*, 425–442.

Marcon, R. A. (2002). Moving up the grades: Relationship between preschool model and later school success. *Early Childhood Research & Practice, 4*, 26.

Margetts, K. (2002). Transition to school—Complexity and diversity. *European Early Childhood Education Research Journal, 10*(2), 103–114. doi:10.1080/13502930285208981.

Mawdsley, H. P., & Hauser-Cram, P. (2013). Mothers of young children with disabilities: perceived benefits and worries about preschool. *Early Child Development & Care, 183*(9), 1258–1275. doi:10.1080/03004430.2012.719896.

Mawdsley, H. P., Snyder, P., & Rous, B. (2014, February). *Characterizing transition practice intensity in early childhood.* Poster presented at the biennial Conference for Research Innovations in Early Interventions, San Diego, CA.

McIntyre, L. L., Eckert, T. L., Fiese, B. H., Reed, F.D.D., & Wildenger, L. K. (2010). Family concerns surrounding kindergarten transition: A comparison of students in special and general education. *Early Childhood Education Journal, 38*(4), 259–263.

Meisels, S. J. (1999). Assessing readiness. In R. C. Pianta & M. J. Cox (Eds.), *The transition to kindergarten* (pp. 39–66). Baltimore, MD: Brookes Publishing.

Murphy, M., McCormick, K. M., & Rous, B. (2013). Rural influence on the use of transition practices by preschool teachers. *Rural Special Education Quarterly, 32*(1), 29–37.

Myers, C. (2007). The role of independent therapy providers in the transition to preschool. *Journal of Early Intervention, 29*(2), 175–183.

Myers, C. T., & Effgen, S. K. (2006). Physical therapists' participation in early childhood transitions. *Pediatric Physical Therapy: The Official Publication of the Section on Pediatrics of the American Physical Therapy Association, 18*(3), 182–189.

National Association for the Education of Young Children. (2009a). *Developmentally appropriate practice in early childhood programs serving children from birth to eight.* Washington, DC: Author. Retrieved from http://www.naeyc.org/files/naeyc/file/positions/PSDAP.pdf

National Association for the Education of Young Children. (2009b). *NAEYC standards for early childhood professional preparation.* Washington, DC: Author. Retrieved from http://www.naeyc.org/files/naeyc/files/2009%20Professional%20Prep%20stdsRevised%204_12.pdf

National Education Goals Panel. (1998). *Ready schools.* Washington, DC: U.S. Government Printing Office.

Noonan, M. J., & Ratokalau, N. B. (1991). Project PPT: The Preschool Preparation and Transition project. Journal of Early Intervention, 15, 390–398.

Perry, B., & Dockett, S. (2011). 'How 'bout we have a celebration!' Advice from children on starting school. *European Early Childhood Education Research Journal, 19*(3), 373–386.

Petriwskyj, A., Thorpe, K., & Tayler, C. (2005). Trends in construction of transition to school in three western regions, 1990–2004. *International Journal of Early Years Education, 13*(1), 55–69.

Piaget, J. P. (1952). *The origins of intelligence in children.* New York: International Universities Press.

Pianta, R. C., Cox, M. J., Taylor, L., & Early, D. (1999). Kindergarten teachers' practices related to the transition to school: Results of a national survey. *Elementary School Journal, 100*(1), 71–86.

Pianta, R. C., & Kraft-Sayre, M. (1999). Parents' observations about their children's transitions to kindergarten. *Young Children, 54*, 47–52.

Pianta, R. C., Kraft-Sayre, M., Rimm-Kaufman, S., Gercke, N., & Higgins, T. (2001). Collaboration in building partnerships between families and schools: The National Center for Early Development and Learning's kindergarten transition intervention. *Early Childhood Research Quarterly, 16*, 117–132.

Pianta, R. C., & Rimm-Kaufman, S. (2006). The social ecology of the transition to school: Classrooms, families, and children. In K. McCartney & D. Phillips (Eds.), *Blackwell handbook of early childhood development* (pp. 490–507). Malden, MA: Blackwell Publishing.

Quintero, N., & McIntyre, L. L. (2011). Kindergarten transition preparation: A comparison of teacher and parent practices for children with autism and other developmental disabilities. *Early Childhood Education Journal, 38*(6), 411–420.

Rice, M. L., & O'Brien, M. (1990). Transitions: Times of change and accommodation. *Topics in Early Childhood Special Education, 9*(4), 1–14.

Rimm-Kaufman, S. E., & Pianta, R. C. (2000). An ecological perspective on the transition to kindergarten: A theoretical framework to guide empirical research. *Journal of Applied Developmental Psychology, 21*, 491–511.

Rimm-Kaufman, S. E., Pianta, R. C., & Cox, M. J. (2000). Teachers' judgments of problems in the transition to kindergarten. *Early Childhood Research Quarterly, 15*(2), 147–166.

Rosenkoetter, S. E., Hains, A. H., & Fowler, S. E. (1994). *Bridging early services for children with special needs and their families: A practical guide for transition planning.* Baltimore, MD: Paul H. Brookes Publishing.

Rosenkoetter, S., Schroeder, C., Rous, B., Hains, A., Shaw, J., & McCormick, K. (2009). *A review of research in early childhood transition: Child and family studies.* Technical Report #5. Lexington: University of Kentucky, Human Development Institute, National Early Childhood Transition Center. Retrieved from http://www.ihdi.uky.edu/nectc/

Rous, B. (2009). *Recommended and Evidence Based Practice to Support Transition to Inclusive Settings.* Presentation to the National Early Childhood Inclusion Institute Chapel Hill, NC. May 2009. Lexington: University of Kentucky, Human Development Institute, National Early Childhood Transition Center. Retrieved from http://www.ihdi.uky.edu/nectc/

Rous, B., & Hallam, R. (2006). *Tools for transition in early childhood: A step by step guide for agencies, teachers, and families.* Baltimore, MD: Brookes Publishing.

Rous, B., & Hallam, R. (2012). Transition services for children with disabilities: Research, policy and practice. 25th Anniversary Volume. *Topics in Early Childhood Special Education, 31*(4), 232–240.

Rous, B., Hallam, R., McCormick, K., & Cox, M. (2010). Practices that support the transition to public preschool programs: Results from a national survey. *Early Childhood Research Quarterly, 25*(1), 17–32.

Rous, B., Hallam, R., Harbin, G., McCormick, K., & Jung, L. (2007). The transition process for young children with disabilities: A conceptual framework. *Infants and Young Children, 20*(2), 135–148.

Rous, B., Hemmeter, M. L., & Schuster, J. (1999). Evaluating the impact of the STEPS model on development of community-wide transition systems. *Journal of Early Intervention, 22*, 38–50.

Rous, B., Myers, C., & Stricklin, S. (2007). Strategies for supporting transitions of young children with special needs and their families. *Journal of Early Intervention, 30*(1), 1–18.

Rous, B., Schuster, J., & Hemmeter, M. L. (1994). Sequenced transition to education in the public schools: A systems approach to transition planning. *Topics in Early Childhood Special Education, 14*(3), 374–393.

Rule, S., Fiechtel, B., & Innocenti, M. (1990). Preparation for transition to mainstreamed post-preschool environments: Development of a survival skills curriculum. *Topics in Early Childhood Special Education, 9*(4), 78–90.

Sanders, M. R., Ralph, A., Sofronoff, K., Gardiner, P., Thompson, R., Dwyer, S., & Bidwell, K. (2008). Every family: A population approach to reducing behavioral and emotional problems in children making the transition to school. *The Journal of Primary Prevention, 29*(3), 197–222. doi:10.1007/s10935–008–0139–7.

Schulting, A. B., Malone, P. S., & Dodge, K. A. (2005). The effects of school based kindergarten transition practices on child academic outcomes. *Developmental Psychology, 41*(6), 860–871.

Shafritz, J. M., Ott, J. S., & Jang, Y. S. (2005). *Classics of organization theory* (6th ed.). New York: Harcourt College Publishers.

Snow, C. E., Burns, M. S., & Griffin, P. (Eds.). (1998). *Preventing reading difficulties in young children.* Washington, DC: National Academies Press.

U.S. Department of Education (U.S. DOE) & U.S. Department of Health and Human Services (U.S. DHHS). (2011). *Race to the top—early learning challenge executive summary.* Accessed January 10, 2014. Retrieved from http://www.acf.hhs.gov/sites/default/files/ecd/rtt_elc_executive_summary_final.pdf

U.S. Government Accountability Office (U.S. GAO). (1994). *Early childhood programs: Multiple programs and overlapping target groups.* (GAO Publication No. HEHS-95-4FS). Retrieved from U.S. Government Printing Office, http://www.gao.gov/assets/90/89793.pdf

Villeneuve, M., Chatenoud, C., Hutchinson, N., Minnes, P., Perry, A., Dionne, C., . . . Weiss, J. (2013). The experience of parents as their children with developmental disabilities transition from early intervention to kindergarten. *Canadian Journal of Education, 36*(1), 4–43.

Vygotsky, L. S. (1963). Learning and mental development at school age. In B. Simon and J. Simon (Eds.). *Educational psychology in the USSR* (pp. 21–34). Redwood City, CA: Stanford University Press.

Wesley, P. W., & Buysse, V. (2003). Making meaning of school readiness in schools and communities. *Early Childhood Research Quarterly, 18,* 351–375.

Wischnowski, M. W., Fowler, S. A., & McCollum, J. A. (2000). Supports and barriers to writing an interagency agreement on the preschool transition. *Journal of Early Intervention, 23,* 294–307.

Wolery, M. (1989). Transitions in early childhood special education: Issues and procedures. *Focus on Exceptional Children, 22*(2), 1–16.

17

ADDRESSING THE NEEDS OF YOUNG CHILDREN WITH DIVERSE ABILITIES AND DEVELOPMENTAL DIFFERENCES

Leslie J. Couse

One proven avenue to improving educational access and outcomes for all young children is to prepare teachers to address the educational needs of children with diverse abilities. While research shows that teachers who possess the requisite knowledge and skills are effective in supporting the educational needs of young children with disabilities, teacher education is challenged with adequately preparing teachers to effectively do so (American Association of Colleges for Teacher Education [AACTE], 2002; Couse & Recchia, 2011; Maxwell, Lim, & Early, 2006). The education of children with disabilities in the least restrictive environment has been law in the U.S. for 40 years, yet a divide remains between early education and special education in the preparation of teachers.

Teacher preparation has historically been constructed to prepare teachers separately for general education (typically developing students) and for special education (students with disabilities). This bifurcated nature of preparation has left teachers with the notion of "my children" and "your children," with many educators believing that only special education teachers who are specially prepared are suited to teach children whose development or ability is outside of typical norms. Yet, our societal expectations have evolved to give early educators and early childhood special educators shared responsibility in working with young children and their families (IDEA, 2004). Given the diagnosis of delay or disability often emerges during early school experiences, quality early learning opportunities are foundational to a child's later success. When discontinuity among teachers and recommended practice exists, quality and outcomes are compromised.

This chapter seeks to bridge the divide by examining teacher preparation holistically, looking at both early childhood education and early childhood special education to understand teacher preparation for young children with diverse abilities and developmental differences. It examines the constraints of our history and the elements of high-quality teacher education, along with the challenges, promising practices, and future directions for teacher preparation for all young children. This synthesis of research brings together what we know to be effective practices for preparing teachers for inclusive early childhood teaching.

Development and Ability Vary for All Children

The United Nations estimates that globally 10% of the population has a disability (2006). Over 15% of U.S. children up to the age of 17 experience a developmental disability or special health care need (National Survey of Children with Special Health Care Needs, 2011) and recent estimates of autism spectrum disorder (ASD), suggest a prevalence of 1 in every 68 children (Centers for Disease Control, 2014). Each year thousands of children across the United States are diagnosed with a disability or delay. The U.S. Department of Education Office of Special Education Programs (OSEP) reports that in 2011, the number of children, birth to 2 years in early intervention was 336,519 (3% of children). Correspondingly, 745,349 children (6% of children) ages 3 to 5 years, received special education services (Data Accountability Center, 2012). As children age, the prevalence of disability or developmental delay increases, with 11% of students receiving special education services by 8 years of age (Data Accountability Center, 2012). The majority of children with a delay or disability are educated in typical classroom environments (OSEP, 2012).

Early educators meet young children at the beginning of their school experiences, building a foundation for their educational future. Therefore, there are many reasons why early childhood teachers need to be prepared to teach a developmentally diverse group of children. First, the range of development and abilities in early educational settings vary widely. Early childhood, the period from birth to 8 years, is characterized as a time of rapid growth and learning in all areas of development along a continuum where children naturally develop skills and abilities at varied rates and ages (Copple & Bredekamp, 2009). Second, adding to this natural diversity, young children's development and ability may be affected by heredity, health, or environmental factors. For some children, early intervention may ameliorate delays, bringing development within the typical range, while other children may need ongoing intervention and support throughout their lifetimes (DEC, 2014). Third, in early education settings, it is common for children to be in multiage groups, where the toddler classroom is comprised of 18- to 36-month-olds, preschool of 3- to 5-year-olds, and primary classrooms of 6- to 8-year-olds, thus creating a naturally occurring broad range of abilities. And finally, U.S. law (IDEA, 2004) decrees that children with disabilities have the same access to educational opportunities as their typical peers, which poses a legal and ethical responsibility for teachers to be ready to teach children with diverse abilities and developmental differences. With increasing diversity among children, and growing attention and resources focused on the importance of early education, how then can we better prepare teachers to support the diverse needs of children in their care?

Constrained by Our History

Historically, the United States has had a two-tiered system of care and education for children birth to 8 years old. Within this system there exist two dimensions: general early childhood education (ECE) and early childhood special education (ECSE). The slow progress to integrate the preparation of early childhood teachers and improve educational practice for *all* young children can be better understood through our historical context in the United States where the care and education of infants and preschool children has been largely viewed as the responsibility of families, with the government only stepping in to provide financial support in times of national security or as social welfare. The roots of child care began with *Day Nurseries* (child care centers) for the children of poor working immigrant mothers and charity-funded *American Infant Schools* designed for preschoolers deemed developmentally at-risk (Nourot, 2004). These efforts gave birth to the social stigma of child care as assistance to less competent parents. This opened the door to a two-tiered system of child care and early education, with a divide in the professional standards of teacher education: child care and early intervention under the jurisdiction of health and human services, and pre-K-12 in the purview of the department of education (Cho & Couse, 2008).

The care and education of children with disabilities has historically fallen to families, resulting in their exclusion from general education settings. Parent advocacy led to the availability of specialized schools in segregated settings and eventually legislation in 1975, *Education for All Handicapped Children Act* (PL 94–142), which provided education for children 5–21 years old. Currently known as the

Individuals with Disabilities Education Act (IDEA, PL 105–17), this law entitles children with disabilities (birth–21 years) to a free and appropriate public education in the least restrictive environment (Turnbull, Turnbull, Erwin, Soodak, & Shogren, 2011).

Inclusive education provides access and instructional supports that enable children with disabilities to be educated and have meaningful relationships with their age-typical peers. While the practice of inclusion takes many forms and a universal definition does not exist (Odom et al., 2004), the joint position statement of the National Association for the Education of Young Children (NAEYC) and the Division for Early Childhood (DEC) of the Council for Exceptional Children agree that:

> Early childhood inclusion embodies the values, policies, and practices that support the right of every infant and young child and his or her family, regardless of ability, to participate in a broad range of activities and contexts as full members of families, communities, and society.
>
> *(DEC/NAEYC, 2009, p. 2)*

The National Professional Development Center on Inclusion (NPDCI, 2011) has identified four movements in the education of young children that bring to light the need for teachers to develop competency with inclusion: qualifications of early education teachers; legal and ethical responsibility; growing diversity of young children in the U.S.; and the cross-sector integration of early education systems toward more inclusive and collaborative approaches to educating young children. While young children with disabilities are regularly included in typical early educational settings, the professional identities and teacher preparation of early childhood and early childhood special educators remain largely separate (Cho & Couse, 2008). The expansion of the education law to include infants and toddlers with the passage of PL99–457 in 1986 (Turnbull et al., 2011) gave rise to practical challenges to include children with disabilities in community-based settings with typically developing peers. Early research in this area examined whether common ground existed between the distinct ideologies across fields (McLean & Odom, 1993; Wolery & Bredekamp, 1994).

Separate Professional Identities

The preparation of teachers to work with young children draws its philosophical underpinnings from two disciplines within education, ECE and ECSE. As a discipline, ECE grew from the fields of education and psychology, specifically child development, operating within a developmental and constructivist framework. The educational approach is that of developmentally appropriate practices (DAP) with a child-centered, intentional curriculum (Copple & Bredekamp, 2009). Settings for early education have typically been in center- and home-based child care, preschools, and public school K-3rd grade. While considerations of development inform instruction, the instructional focus for ECE teachers has primarily been on group lesson planning, classroom organization, and teaching children in group settings (Copple & Bredekamp, 2009; NAEYC 2009).

ECSE, with origins in the second half of the 20th century, grew from the fields of early education, special education, and psychology, strongly informed by behaviorism and learning theory. Shaped by the integrated nature of health care and disability in early life along with the funding of services, ECSE practice has been highly influenced by the medical model (Wolery & Bredekamp, 1994). The developmental needs of the individual drive instruction in ECSE with the focus on assessing the needs of the learner, individualized planning and instruction, behavior modification, and providing accommodations to make the learning environment accessible (DEC, 2014). Traditional settings for ECSE have been clinics and public schools, however with movement toward inclusion, as a result of legislation (IDEA, 2004), the focus became natural settings, which has brought ECSE into home and community schools. Including children with disabilities in typical early education settings brings ECSE and ECE teachers together to work with the same children, often with conflicting ideas, based on their professional preparation, about how to best support children's learning.

Each of these early education professions has separate professional organizations that guide teacher practice and licensure. NAEYC's mission is to promote excellence and improve professional practice in ECE for all young children. The more specialized DEC is for individuals who work with or on behalf of children (birth to 8 years) with special needs and their families. A growing movement to link the professions through their shared practice with young children and families is evidenced through the development of joint position statements defining best practice. While movement in the 1980s and 1990s toward uniting the ECE and ECSE teacher preparation has slowed (Piper, 2007), recent work toward the alignment of personnel preparation standards has revealed areas of significant overlap between the two sets of teacher standards (Chandler et al., 2012).

Professional Standards for Early Childhood Educators

Guidelines set by both NAEYC (2009) and DEC (2008) emphasize that early childhood professionals need appropriate coursework and field placements at the undergraduate and graduate level to meet the diverse needs of all young children. For this chapter, the focus is on the professional teacher standards that guide accredited 2- and 4-year teacher preparation programs in higher education. Regarding what tomorrow's early childhood teachers should know and be able to do, the NAEYC standards are framed around the following areas: (1) promoting child development and learning; (2) building family and community relationships; (3) observing, documenting, and assessing; (4) using developmentally effective approaches to connect with children and families; (5) using content knowledge to build meaningful curriculum; and (6) becoming a professional. Similarly, DEC has ten areas of competence, with more in-depth knowledge and skill in understanding atypical development, particularly in the area of language development, targeted intervention, assessment of learning, and collaboration with professionals. An alignment of the NAEYC and DEC teacher preparation standards are presented in Table 17.1. These national standards, along with varied state-to-state teacher licensure standards, guide faculty in each institution in determining the nature and scope of curriculum and practical training for preservice teachers.

Table 17.1 Comparison of Teacher Preparation Standards of the National Association for the Education of Young Children (NAEYC) and the Division for Early Childhood (DEC)

NAEYC Teacher Standards	*DEC Teacher Standards*
1. Importance of Knowing Child Development	1. Foundations 2. Development and Characteristics of Learners 6. Language
2. Building Family and Community Relationships	10. Collaboration (families, professionals, and community)
3. Observing, Documenting, and Assessing to Support Young Children and Families	8. Assessment
4. Teaching Methods and Strategies	3. Individual Learning Differences 4. Instructional Strategies
5. Curriculum	5. Learning Environments and Social Interactions 7. Instructional Planning
6. Becoming a Professional	9. Professional and Ethical Practice

Teacher Education Practices that Support Developmental Diversity

Teacher preparation typically includes the development of knowledge, skills, and dispositions for working with a given age group or in a subject area. Specific to educating children with disabilities, additional constructs deemed essential for teacher education include collaborative interdisciplinary clinical practices and family partnerships (AACTE, 2002; DEC, 2014). A review of the research literature for effective methods to ready teachers for work with young children with delayed development and disability falls into three areas: (1) knowledge of disability through coursework and clinical field experiences; (2) building relationships with families; and (3) interdisciplinary collaboration with professionals. Within these three areas, a summary and critique of current research follows.

Knowledge of Disability through Coursework and Clinical Field Experience

Teacher candidates need field experiences that include children with diverse abilities. A candidate's beliefs about inclusion and self-efficacy as a teacher in an inclusive classroom are positively influenced by experience and exposure to individuals with disabilities. When students have the opportunity in a practice setting like student teaching or an internship to develop skills in lesson planning and teaching that include differentiation of instruction, positive support strategies, and collaborative work with parents, they exit confident in their ability to teach in inclusive settings (AACTE, 2002). Yet, a national survey of early childhood teacher preparation programs uncovered that only about half the 4-year degree programs that prepare ECE teachers include a required course on children with disabilities, only 42% require coursework on families, and a mere 11% require coursework on collaboration. When the teacher education program's mission was to prepare teachers for ECSE, the results were slightly better, with 63% requiring a course on children with disabilities (Chang, Early, & Winton, 2005). Further, recent studies (Early & Winton, 2001; Maxwell et al., 2006) indicate the majority of ECE programs in the U.S. do not require a full course specific to working with infants and toddlers, students with special needs, nor children and families from diverse ethnic, linguistic, and cultural backgrounds. This raises concerns about the quality and consistency of the nation's early childhood teacher education programs (Tarrant, Greenberg, Kagan, & Kauerz, 2008), and their ability to prepare teachers for children with diverse abilities.

Curriculum increases teacher knowledge of developmental diversity. Foundational to teacher preparation is a strong knowledge of child development both typical and atypical, along with strong ECE and ECSE content knowledge. Coursework with content focused on children with disabilities (McMurray-Schwartz & Baum, 2000, Voss & Bufkin, 2011) is crucial for developing teacher competence. While the vast majority of states require at least one course in teaching children identified for special education services, there are still states where general teacher certification does not require any course content in this area (Geiger, Crutchfield, & Mainzer, 2003). Teacher preparation programs need to offer coursework with a focus on understanding disability, the law, differentiation of instruction to meet a variety of developmental levels, and positive support strategies. This lack of content in understanding developmental difference and specialized educational need leaves teachers less prepared and students at educational risk.

Beyond a basic understanding of disability, teachers need tools and strategies to fully include children in early educational settings. Marchant (1995) found teachers were supportive of having children with disabilities in their classrooms, but that they needed knowledge and skills in how to individualize instruction to assure children were learning (Odom, Buysee, & Soukakou, 2011). Understanding and applying principles such as universal design for learning (UDL), how to differentiate instruction based on children's development, as well as how to embed instruction into daily routines (McGuire-Schwartz & Arndt, 2007) are recommended practices (DEC, 2014) for teachers to support the learning of all students, but particularly for those with diverse ability and developmental differences.

Teacher beliefs about inclusion. Teacher beliefs have widely been found to influence practice. Teachers make hundreds of decisions daily that influence the lives of children and how learning is constructed. These decisions affect the degree to which children with disabilities are included with peers and what access they have to the general curriculum. Research on teacher beliefs about inclusion focuses primarily on two aspects: the *notion* of whether inclusion is a worthwhile practice and the *efficacy* of whether the teacher can effectively carry out the practice of inclusion to meet a child's educational needs.

Teacher beliefs are influenced by positive personal experiences with children with disabilities. Niemeyer and Proctor (2002) found that preservice teachers perceived that the combination of coursework and placement in an inclusive classroom for student teachers positively influenced their beliefs about inclusion and their abilities to successfully implement it in the future. Shippen and colleagues examined the dispositions toward inclusion of over 300 preservice teachers from both general and special education, across three universities (Shippen, Crites, Houchins, Ramsey, & Simon, 2005). Students who completed an introductory course on exceptionality significantly decreased their anxiety and hostility toward including children with disabilities.

Jeon and Peterson (2003) in their survey of preservice ECE and Elementary teachers (N=297) found that having a personal relationship with a person with a disability and the number of specialized teaching courses taken were predictive of a positive attitude toward inclusion. Similarly, Campbell, Gilmore, and Cuskelly (2003) conducted surveys of 274 preservice teachers enrolled in a semester unit on children with Down Syndrome (DS). Post-surveys found that students had less anxiety along with a more positive and accurate perception of individuals with DS. There was a significant drop in their fear and anxiety related to interacting with children with DS. The course combined formal instruction with a field experience. Upon completion of the course, students reported less anxiety and hostility toward children with disabilities in general and toward their inclusion in general education. Preservice teachers reported influential experiences, which contributed to their beliefs in efficacy, were formal learning opportunities (content and theoretical knowledge, field experience, student teaching) and personal experience outside of their teacher preparation (e.g., family, work, volunteering).

However, even when preservice teachers have coursework focused on understanding disability, misconceptions about children with developmental differences persist. Barned, Knapp, and Neuharth-Pritchett (2011) surveyed and interviewed 15 preservice teachers about Autism Spectrum Disorders (ASD), an increasingly prevalent diagnosis. They found that while preservice teachers were generally supportive of inclusive education, they had multiple misconceptions about ASD and strong concerns about behavior disruption that may result from the inclusion of students with more severe disabilities.

For countries beginning reform toward inclusive education, similar issues arise. A qualitative study of 20 undergraduate ECE preservice teachers in Jordan examined attitudes, preparation, and teacher concerns about inclusion. Preservice teachers were supportive of inclusion from a social justice frame; their concerns were with the preparation and lack of specialized training received, and desired hands-on opportunities to gain experience (Fayez, Dababneh, & Jumiaan, 2011). The influence of teacher beliefs upon inclusive practice has been explored in many countries. A meta-analysis of 26 international empirical studies, reflective of 13 countries, conducted between 1998 and 2008, examined primary teachers' perspectives on inclusion (deBoer, Pijl, & Minnaert, 2011). The majority of teachers held a neutral or negative attitude (viewpoint or disposition) toward the inclusion of students with disabilities in general primary education. Factors related to teacher attitudes were their specialized training, prior experience with inclusion, and the type of disability present. In six of the studies, teachers did not feel competent or confident in their ability to teach children with disabilities. Teachers with fewer years teaching were more positive toward inclusion than highly experienced teachers, which may speak to the currency of their preparation and contemporary notions of inclusion. However, those teachers who had experience and specialized training with inclusive education held more positive attitudes overall than those without experience or specialized training in inclusion.

Teacher beliefs about inclusion influence teacher practice. Combining knowledge with experience allows preservice teachers to integrate practical and theoretical knowledge, thereby supporting both aspects of teacher beliefs, the notion of inclusion and teacher efficacy toward its practice. Increasing preservice teachers' knowledge, comfort, and familiarity regarding children with diverse abilities increases the likelihood of children's successful inclusion in early education settings.

Clinical field experience. The American Association of Colleges for Teacher Education (AACTE, 2010) recommends extended clinical opportunities for students to practice and develop skills as teachers in supervised and supportive settings as a key to improving teacher education. Similarly, the standards for early childhood teacher preparation set out by NAEYC (2009) and DEC (2008) also recommend field experiences to give teacher candidates knowledge of disability and the law, as well as opportunities to develop skills and competency in teaching young children with developmental differences. Working with children who experience delays or diverse abilities through field experiences, provides teacher candidates with situated learning opportunities to apply newly acquired knowledge and skills in teaching young children and develop competence under the guidance and supervision of an experienced teacher. The competence of beginning teachers is affected by the intensity of their preparation and the alignment of practical experiences to teaching standards during their preservice teacher preparation (Macy, Squires, & Barton, 2009). Further, children in classrooms also benefit from the additional instructional opportunities that student teacher interns provide (Maheady, Jabot, Ray, & Michielli-Pendl, 2007). However, despite the strong guidance and benefits associated with clinical learning experiences in the field, at least one-third of teacher preparation programs neither include nor require field experiences in educational settings serving young children with delayed development and disabilities. Even in ECSE programs, 20% of teachers graduate without clinical field experience with children with disabilities (Chang et al., 2005). This lack of supervised opportunity to gain practical knowledge puts children in the classrooms of beginning teachers at a disadvantage.

While most early childhood classrooms are inclusive, some children are still educated for part or all of their school day in segregated settings. Recchia and Puig (2011) found that using segregated classrooms as one of several supported placements allowed student teachers the opportunity to think flexibly about their teaching, gain a multidisciplinary perspective as part of a collaborative team of professionals, and draw on previous experiences in both general and special education to consider a continuum of services for children with disabilities. Reflective journals allowed them to make connections between their coursework and fieldwork and supported developing a sense of self as a teacher.

Building Relationships with Families

In order to prepare preservice teachers to work with families, teacher education needs to include opportunities for students and families to engage in meaningful interactions (Hansuvadha, 2009). Teacher preparation that includes self-advocates and family members of individuals with disabilities as experts have been found to be very successful in not only building understanding but also in modeling collaboration with families for teachers to use in their practice (Jorgensen, Bates, Frechette, Curtin, & Sonnenmeier, 2011; Maude et al., 2011; Silverman, Hong, & Trepanier-Street, 2010). Several models exist for incorporating parents and self-advocates into teacher preparation through involvement on advisory boards (Couse & Miller Sallet, 2011; Mandell & Murray, 2005; Smith, 2010; Stayton, Whittaker, Jones, & Kersting, 2001), guest lecturing, co-teaching, and field supervision (Jorgensen et al., 2011; Prosser, 2009; Mandell & Murray, 2005; Murray & Curran, 2008; Stayton et al., 2001; Trepanier-Street, 2010). Other curricular approaches involve the use of video clips (Kim & Vail, 2011), performance role-playing (Maude et al., 2011), and eco-maps (Baumgartner & Buchanan, 2010) to engage teachers in thinking beyond the child in the classroom to holistically consider the home and school contexts. Preservice teachers who are actively engaged with families have opportunities to challenge their assumptions about children and families and gain skills in supporting productive relationships to promote learning.

Developing reciprocal relationships with families is a competency that is vitally important in supporting children with diverse abilities and developmental delays. The foundation of these relationships is built on trust and understanding (Blue-Banning, Summers, Frankland, Nelson, & Beegle, 2004). Zygmunt-Fillwalk (2011) studied the effect that taking a course on families, as part of teacher preparation, had on the practice of teachers post-graduation. While those who took the course did not demonstrate a significant difference in the types of activities offered to parents from those who did not take the course, they differed in their approach to and in the value they placed upon family involvement. Those who took the course viewed family involvement as supporting the child's education, while those who did not have the course placed less emphasis on parent involvement in their teaching and were more likely to characterize parent relationships as antagonistic.

While family involvement is espoused as important for early learning, Murray and Curran (2008) note there is a limited amount of parent involvement in preservice programs. A national study found that only 42% of ECE and 67% of ECSE teacher preparation programs require a course focused on families (Chang et al., 2005). Yet when preservice programs offer students time to interact with parents through a variety of opportunities in a variety of settings, students are better able to generalize skills needed to form successful parent-professional partnerships (Murray & Mandell, 2004; Sheldon &Van Voorhis, 2004).

Much of the research on preparing teachers to work with families is highly qualitative, based on specific experiences with a particular group of students or at one university. The research also tends to come from early childhood special education, which has a legal mandate (IDEA, 2004) for working with families and where critical teacher shortages have resulted in federal grant opportunities to support targeted research priorities (Horm, Hyson, & Winton, 2013). Early childhood teacher education would benefit from larger studies with generalizable results and ones that are longitudinal, which follow preservice teachers into their practice with children and families.

Collaboration with Interdisciplinary Professionals

The education of young children is a collaborative venture that involves multiple adults. In addition to the family, early childhood classrooms often have at least a teacher and assistant working together. When a child has specialized learning needs additional specialists (speech, occupational or physical therapist, child specific aide, etc.) provide related services. Coordinating the services across disciplines and synthesizing the efforts of all invested adults necessitates teachers have skills in interdisciplinary teaming.

Collaborative teaching. Co-teaching, an important component of inclusion and a moderator of child outcomes, is an instructional strategy for students with disabilities in general education settings (Buysee & Hollingsworth, 2009). In the co-teaching model, all students receive collaborative instruction by general education and special education teachers in one or more content areas (Panscofar & Petroff, 2013) or learning centers. Students with disabilities remain in general education classroom settings rather than being pulled out for instruction in separate classrooms. Therefore, a teacher needs to be ready to share teaching responsibilities with another teacher in an effort to promote learning for all children. Co-teachers share responsibility for designing the learning environments, curriculum development, intervention strategies, and lesson planning to intentionally include children with a range of abilities in learning.

While collaboration with other professionals is a recommended practice (DEC, 2014; NAEYC, 2009) in quality inclusive early education, teachers are not consistently receiving preparation in this area. A large national survey found that nearly 90% of ECE and 73% of ECSE graduates were not specifically receiving coursework focused on collaboration (Chang et al., 2005). More recently, a national survey of preservice K-12 special education teacher preparation programs found that 70% required a course on collaboration for special education majors as compared to only 16% for general education majors (McKenzie, 2009), representing a significant difference in the perceived importance of collaboration competencies between special education and general education. While special education emphasizes building skills in collaboration, there is little emphasis (coursework and field experience) in most general education teacher preparation curricula. Joint experiences for general and special education preservice teachers to collaborate rarely exist within teacher preparation. New teachers are challenged by a lack of experience and must develop collaboration skills as new professionals, which likely hinders efforts to improve collaboration among practicing teachers. ECE and ECSE teacher education programs will produce more effective collaborators when a collaborative culture, which includes co-teaching as part of preparation, is embraced (Chiasson, Yearwood, & Olsen, 2006).

Interdisciplinary collaboration. Working with professionals outside of education is an important aspect in supporting children with diverse abilities. Evidence of successfully pairing social work (SW) and early childhood graduate students in their professional preparation is found repeatedly in the literature. Banach and Couse (2012) intentionally paired social work and ECSE graduate students as co-facilitators of post-diagnosis parent support groups as part of their professional preparation. The discipline-specific knowledge of social workers focuses on group work theory, community systems, resources, and advocacy, while early childhood special educators possess specialized knowledge in child development, learning supports, and educational systems. The interdisciplinary co-facilitation of parent support groups provided preservice students with an authentic experience to collaborate with parents and another group of professionals. Further, parents in the support group benefited as well; their empowerment regarding education and community services and knowledge of how to access the system increased significantly over the course of the support group (Banach, Iudice, Conway, & Couse, 2010). In another study, experienced ECSE graduate students who understood the culture and power structure of schools were paired with social work graduate students with knowledge of forces affecting student achievement and community resources to collaboratively develop social skills and transition groups in inclusive elementary schools (Tourse, Mooney, Kline, & Davoren, 2005). Through co-facilitating an activity, student interns gained a greater understanding of the problems that children may encounter, options for solving them, and professional communication necessary for collaborative work.

Anderson (2013) also paired ECE and SW graduate students in collaborative activities as part of their professional preparation. Two classes (N=29) joined together for a two-hour interprofessional training. The students, in interdisciplinary groups, developed a referral protocol for addressing challenging behavior and bullying. This helped with understanding discipline-specific roles and reasons to access another discipline as a resource in their work. While all three of these studies demonstrated success in pairing ECE and social work as part of their professional preparation, all were characterized as pilot studies with few students involved. Banach and Couse (2012) and Tourse et al. (2005) engaged students in authentic activities of curriculum development, role negotiation, and collaborative work with another discipline. The efficacy of these collaborative interdisciplinary activities in teacher preparation is limited by a small sample size and the use of participant report, rather than a statistical measure of teacher collaboration skills.

Other areas of interdisciplinary collaboration in preparation are found between early education and health care professionals (e.g., physicians, and physical, occupational, and speech language therapists). Given delayed development or disability is often first discovered through the health care system, linking professional preparation across these disciplines is consistent with the integrated nature of early intervention services. Silverman et al. (2010) present a university partnership with a local health care center to incorporate a transdisciplinary model of inclusive practice into early childhood teacher preparation. Components include a transdisciplinary faculty, clinical observations, mentoring, implementation of inclusive playgroups, creative arts and activities with specialists, and family-centered inclusive events. Analysis of student reflection papers discovered preservice teachers had a more positive attitude toward family-centered partnerships after participating in family events, a shared philosophy with professional partners that aided in understanding, and acceptance of inclusive practice and interdisciplinary teaming.

Challenges to Improving Practice

There are several challenges to improving the preparation of early childhood teachers for inclusive education. First, the separate professional identities for ECE and ECSE limit the effectiveness of practice in providing high-quality inclusive education for all children. The separate identities perpetuate the vestiges of the roots of each profession and the boundaries of responsibility forged from the practice of segregated special education. Second, ECE teacher preparation programs do not adequately prepare teachers to work with children with special needs (Chang et al., 2005; Early & Winton, 2001). Many teachers lack the knowledge and skills necessary to effectively work with children with diverse development and abilities. While family involvement has been found to improve educational outcomes (Sheldon & Van Voorhis, 2004), is legally required (NCLB, 2001; IDEA, 2004), and is a recommended practice (DEC, 2014; NAEYC 2009), the emphasis in teacher preparation is inconsistent. Until teacher preparation programs consistently require content and clinical field experiences with children of diverse abilities, interactions with families, and interdisciplinary collaboration, teachers will continue to lack the tools and confidence they need to effectively engage in inclusive teaching (Macy et al., 2009). Third, to improve inclusive practice, beginning teachers need support in deepening their knowledge and skills as they become experienced teachers.

Various levels of collaboration exist in teacher preparation between general and special education. The future trend is toward new models of collaborative teacher education with a systematic unified approach to prepare teachers for inclusive classrooms (Blanton & Pugach, 2007; Piper, 2007). Collaboratively co-taught courses (Chiasson et al., 2006) that model the practice of co-teaching can provide a link between general and special education in teacher preparation. "Interdisciplinary teaming has been described as the pivotal component of blended interdisciplinary teacher preparation for early childhood" (Miller & Stayton, 2006, p. 56). The challenges to interdisciplinary teaming and program development may result from structures and policies in higher education (Mellin & Winton, 2003; Miller, 2003; Miller & Stayton, 1998; Miller & Stayton, 1999), such as the traditional departmental structures separating faculty by discipline, which promote a climate of isolation rather than collaboration; faculty reward structures that promote competition; and a lack of faculty and administrator knowledge about interdisciplinary teacher preparation practices that limits efforts for innovative learning opportunities for students (e.g., faculty co-teaching courses).

The first five years of teaching are viewed as critical for the development of new teachers. New teachers face the transition from being students learning to teach with support from cooperating teachers, university faculty, and their peers (Lava, Recchia, & Giovacco-Johnson, 2004), to becoming effective independent teachers. The loss of support for novice teachers post-graduation can be daunting. Current estimates of teacher attrition in the first three years range from 40–50% (Ingersoll, Merrill, & Stuckey, 2014; Carroll & Foster, 2010). Moreover, teacher turnover contributes to discontinuity, poor quality, and increased cost.

Promising Practices

The movement to develop joint practice documents and begin to align teacher preparation standards between NAEYC and DEC holds much promise for improving the inclusion of children with diverse abilities in early childhood settings. Many teacher preparation programs have moved to blended preparation, where early childhood teachers are prepared in both ECE and special education resulting in dual certification and teacher competence (Pugach & Blanton, 2009; Miller & Stayton, 2006; Piper 2007). Likewise other programs have increased the pathways by allowing students to add a secondary area and extend their certification. Field experiences that include children with disabilities increase teacher readiness and efficacy for inclusive classrooms. Further, teacher preparation that includes opportunities to collaborate with families and other professionals will benefit teachers and children alike.

Linking the professional development of teachers as a continuum from preservice through inservice is an evolving trend, where teacher education is viewed as lifelong and not finished at graduation. The use of early career mentors and supported practice are examples of ways that new teacher growth is enabled. Couse and Miller Sallet (2011) facilitated the expansion of an existing early education professional development network to include preservice teachers, who were linked with a practicing professional in the field of inclusive education for mentoring. This gave preservice teachers early access to experts in the network and opportunities for application and feedback on practice (Buysee, Winton, & Rous, 2009), along with early career linkages to the professional community.

Formalized mentoring relationships are one of the ways new teachers are supported and inducted into the profession. Schools may include mentoring as part of their professional development support for beginning teachers. Post-graduation, university-school district partnerships are an effective way to navigate the educational needs of novice teachers (Boyer, 2005). Further, adult learning strategies, such as coaching and mentorship, have been found to be highly effective for improving practice and are elements of effective evidence based-practice for adult learners (Trivette, Dunst, Hamby, & O'Herin, 2009). Through ongoing professional development that seeks to deepen knowledge and skills, early childhood teachers can develop competency with inclusion (Buysee et al., 2009; NPDCI, 2011) and more collaborative approaches to educating young children.

Future Directions

Early childhood teacher education and practice needs to forge a professional identity for early educators that embraces teaching all children. It is time to move beyond thinking of children with disabilities as needing special education support to thinking about how teachers are prepared to support children of diverse abilities in early childhood settings. This notion will be furthered through increased articulation between DEC & NAEYC. Wrestling with questions such as, "*Would we be better served by a single joint professional organization and standards?*" will take considerable discussion, aligning of goals, and political will. In the meantime, continued alignment of position statements and professional standards, which bring both organizations to the table to begin to align practice expectations in an effort to serve children, their families, and teachers well, is paramount.

Exploring the development of a joint set of personnel preparation standards, endorsed by both DEC and NAEYC, could guide the preparation of early childhood teachers to support children of diverse ability. Joint standards could improve the preparation of all early education teachers, and also promote the development of blended ECE programs where teachers are dually certified (Chandler et al., 2012; Piper, 2007). Curricula that includes specialized training and authentic experiences in inclusive settings will prepare teachers to work with the diverse development of young children. All early educators, regardless of the teacher education program they graduate from, should have course content and field experiences with children of diverse abilities. Key to this type of preparation are opportunities for preservice teachers to build relationships with families and develop collaboration skills with other adults, including professionals from other disciplines. Many faculty in early childhood preparation programs endorse change that will benefit their students, yet this type of collaborative reform effort will require support, along with significant professional and institutional will to implement (Miller & Stayton, 2006; Winton & Catlett, 2009). The resultant blended continuous path of preparation and development for teachers (Buysee et al., 2009) will result in teachers feeling competent in their ability to promote learning, thereby improving the access and educational outcomes of all young children.

And finally, there is a critical need to identify what teacher education practices are most effective to prepare teachers to address a diverse range of abilities in early education. There is a critical need for developing a robust research base on early childhood teacher education, comprised of rigorous studies that examine the efficacy of teacher preparation practices that support inclusion (Horm et al., 2013). The existing teacher education research suffers from being comprised largely of single program evaluation studies that rely heavily on small convenience samples, which is likely due to a lack of research funding and the heavy workload demands of preservice teacher educators (Hyson, Tomlinson, & Morris, 2009). Seizing on the growing public support for early education, particularly in the U.S., could produce funding opportunities for systematic research resulting in larger generalizable results, to truly move the field forward toward identifying a more robust evidence-base in early childhood teacher education.

Conclusion

Children in early childhood settings are becoming increasingly diverse. Teacher preparation needs to move beyond its historical roots in ECE and ECSE so teachers leave their programs with the knowledge and skills needed to successfully teach all young children, including those with diverse abilities and developmental differences. By better preparing teachers to understand and support diversity, including disability, and to have the skills to collaborate with families and other professionals (Odom et al., 2011), we will improve the quality of early education for all children.

References

American Association of Colleges for Teacher Education (AACTE). (2002). *Preparing teachers to work with students with disabilities: Possibilities and challenges for special and general teacher education*. Washington, DC: Author.

American Association of Colleges for Teacher Education (AACTE). (2010). *The clinical preparation of teachers—A policy brief.* Washington, DC: Author. Retrieved from http://www.aacte.org/pdf/Government_Relations/Clinical%20Prep%20Paper_03-11-2010.pdf

Anderson, E. M. (2013). Preparing the next generation of early childhood teachers: The emerging role of interprofesssional education and collaboration in teacher education. *Journal of Early Childhood Teacher Education, 34*(1), 23–35.

Banach, M., & Couse, L. J. (2012). Interdisciplinary co-facilitation of groups for parents of children with Autism: An opportunity for professional preparation. *Social Work with Groups, 35*(4), 313–329.

Banach, M., Iudice, J., Conway, L., & Couse, L. J. (2010). Family support and empowerment: Post Autism diagnosis support group for parents. *Social Work with Groups, 33*(1), 69–83.

Barned, N., Knapp, N. F., Neuharth-Pritchett, S. (2011). Knowledge and attitudes of early childhood preservice teacher regarding the inclusion of children with Autism spectrum disorder. *Journal of Early Childhood Teacher Education, 32*(4), 302–321.

Baumgartner, J. J., & Buchanan, T. K. (2010). "I have HUGE stereotypes:" Using eco-maps to understand children and families. *Journal of Early Childhood Teacher Education, 31*(2), 173–184. DOI: 10.1080/10901021003781270.

Blanton, L. P., & Pugach, M. C. (2007, June). *Collaborative programs in general and special teacher education: An action guide for higher education and state policy makers*. Washington, DC: Council of Chief State School Officers. Retrieved from http://www.ccsso.org/projects/center_for_improving_teacher_quality/Resources_Links/

Blue-Banning, M., Summers, J., Frankland, H., Nelson, L., & Beegle, G. (2004). Dimensions of family and professional partnerships: Constructive guidelines for collaboration. *Exceptional Children, 70*(2), 167–184.

Boyer, L. (2005). Supporting the induction of special educators: Program descriptions of university-school district partnerships. *Teaching Exceptional Children, 37*(3), 44–51.

Buysee, V., & Hollingsworth, H. (2009). Program quality and early childhood inclusion: Recommendations for professional development. *Topics in Early Childhood Special Education, 29*(2), 119–128.

Buysee, V., Winton, P., & Rous, B. (2009). Reaching consensus on a definition of professional development for the early childhood field. *Topics in Early Childhood Special Education, 28*(4), 235–243.

Campbell, J., Gilmore, L., & Cuskelly, M. (2003). Changing student teachers' attitudes toward disability and inclusion. *Journal of Intellectual and Developmental Disability, 28*(4), 369–378.

Carroll, T., & Foster, E. (January 2010). "Who Will Teach?: Experience Matters" (Washington, DC: National Commission on Teaching and America's Future). Retrieved from http://nctaf.org/wp-content/uploads/2012/01/NCTAF-Who-Will-Teach-Experience-Matters-2010-Report.pdf

Centers for Disease Control. (2014, March 28). Prevalence of autism spectrum disorder among children aged 8 years—autism and developmental disabilities monitoring network, 11 Sites, United States 2010. *Autism and Developmental Disabilities Monitoring Network Surveillance Summaries. 63(SS02)*; 1–21. Retrieved from http://www.cdc.gov/mmwr/preview/mmwrhtml/ss6302a1.htm?s_cid=ss6302a1_w

Chandler, L., Cochran, D., Christensen, K., Dinnebeil, L., Gallagher, P., Lifter, K., . . . Spino, M. (2012). The alignment of CEC/DEC and NAEYC personnel preparation standards. *Topics in Early Childhood Special Education, 32*(1), 52–63.

Chang, F., Early, D. M., & Winton, P. J. (2005). Early childhood teacher preparation in special education at 2- and 4-year institutions of higher education. *Journal of Early Intervention, 27*(2), 110–124.

Chiasson, K., Yearwood, J., & Olsen, G. (2006). The best of both worlds: Combining ECE and ECSE philosophies and best practices through a co-teaching model. *Journal of Early Childhood Teacher Education, 27*(3), 303–312. DOI: 10.1080/10901020600843707.

Cho, E. K., & Couse, L. J. (2008). Early childhood teacher policy in the United States: Continuing issues, overcoming barriers, and envisioning the future. *International Journal of Child Care and Education Policy, 2*(2), 15–30.

Copple, C., & Bredekamp, S. (Eds.). (2009). *Developmentally appropriate practice in early childhood programs serving children from birth through age 8* (3rd ed.). Washington, DC: National Association for Education of Young Children.

Couse, L. J., & Miller Sallet, P. (2011). *Transforming Professional Development: Community of Practice Uses the Evidence-Base, I-Tunes and Mentoring.* Paper presented at the Annual Conference of the Teacher Education Division of the Council for Exceptional Children, November 12, 2011.

Couse, L. J., & Recchia, S. L. (2011). Editorial: Inclusive early childhood teacher education. *Journal of Early Childhood Teacher Education, 32*(4), 299–301.

Data Accountability Center. (2012). *Individuals with disabilities education act (IDEA) data: Part B child count.* Retrieved from https://www.ideadata.org/PartBChildCount.asp/

deBoer, A., Pijl, S. J., & Minnaert, A. (2011). Regular primary school teachers' attitudes towards inclusive education: A review of the literature. *International Journal of Inclusive Education, 15*(3), 331–353, DOI: 10.1080/13603110903030089.

DEC/NAEYC. (2009). *Early childhood inclusion: A joint position statement of the Division for Early Childhood (DEC) and the National Association for the Education of Young Children (NAEYC).* Chapel Hill, NC: The University of North Carolina, FPG Child Development Institute.

Division for Early Childhood (DEC). (2008). *Early childhood special education/early intervention (birth to age 8) professional standards with CEC common core.* Arlington, VA: Council for Exceptional Children.

Division for Early Childhood (DEC). (2014). DEC recommended practices in early intervention/early childhood special education. Retrieved from http://www.dec-sped.org/recommendedpractices

Early, D., & Winton, P. J. (2001). Preparing the workforce: Early childhood teacher preparation at 2- and 4-year institutions of higher education. *Early Childhood Research Quarterly, 16*, 285–306.

Education for All Handicapped Children Act. (1975). Pub. L. No. 94–142, 20 U.S.C. § 1401–1420.

Fayez, M., Dababneh, K., & Jumiaan, I. (2011). Preparing teachers for inclusion: Jordanian preservice early childhood teachers' perspectives. *Journal of Early Childhood Teacher Education, 32*(4), 322–337. DOI: 10.1080/10901027.2011.622239.

Geiger, W. L., Crutchfield, M. D., & Mainzer, R. (2003). *The status of licensure of special education teachers in the 21st century* (COPSSE Document No. RS-7E). Gainesville, FL: University of Florida, Center on Personnel Studies in Special Education.

Hansuvadha, N. (2009). Compromising in collaborating with families: Perspectives of beginning special education teachers. *Journal of Early Childhood Teacher Education, 30*(4), 346–362. DOI: 10.1080/10901020903320270.

Horm, D. M., Hyson, M., & Winton, P. J. (2013). Research on early childhood teacher education: Evidence from three domains and recommendations for moving forward. *Journal of Early Childhood Teacher Education, 34*(1), 95–112. DOI: 10.1080/10901027.2013.758541.

Hyson, M., Tomlinson, H. B., & Morris, C. A. (2009). Quality improvement in early childhood teacher education: Faculty perspectives and recommendations for the future. *Early Childhood Research and Practice 11*(1). Retrieved from http://ecrp.uiuc.edu/v11n1/hyson.html

Individuals with Disabilities Education Act (IDEA). (2004). Pub. L. No. 108–446, U.S.C. 20, 1400 et seq.

Ingersoll, R., Merrill, L., & Stuckey, D. (2014). Seven trends: The transformation of the teaching force. CPRE Research Report # RR-80. Philadelphia: Consortium for Policy Research in Education. DOI: 10.12698/cpre.2014.rr80.

Jeon, H. J., & Peterson, C. A. (2003). Preservice teachers' attitudes toward inclusion: Early childhood education and elementary education programs. *Journal of Early Childhood Teacher Education, 24*(3), 171–179. DOI: 10.1080/1090102030240306.

Jorgensen, C. M., Bates, K., Frechette, A., Curtin, J., & Sonnenmeier, R., (2011). "Nothing about us without us": Including people with disabilities as teaching partners in university courses. *International Journal of Whole Schooling,* 7(2). Retrieved from http://www.wholeschooling.net/Journal_of_Whole_Schooling/IJWSIndex.html

Kim, E. J., & Vail, C. (2011). Improving preservice teacher perspectives on family involvement in teaching children with special needs: Guest speakers versus video. *Teacher Education and Special Education, 34*(4), 320–338.

Lava, V. F., Recchia, S. L., & Giovacco-Johnson, T. (2004). Early childhood special educators reflect on their preparation and practice. *Teacher Education and Special Education, 27*(2), 190–201.

Macy, M., Squires, J. K., & Barton, E. E. (2009). Providing optimal opportunities: Structuring practicum experiences in early intervention and early childhood special education preservice programs. *Topics in Early Childhood Special Education, 28,* 209. DOI: 10.1177/0271121408327227.

Maheady, L., Jabot, M., Ray, J., & Michielli-Pendl, J. (2007). Early field-based experience and its impact on preservice candidates teaching practice and their pupil's outcomes. *Teacher Education and Special Education, 30*(1), 24–33.

Mandell, C., & Murray, M. (2005). Innovative family-centered practices in personnel preparation. *Teacher Education and Special Education, 28*(1), 74–77.

Marchant, C. (1995). Teachers' views of integrated preschools. *Journal of Early Intervention, 19,* 61–73.

Maude, S. P., Brotherson M. J., Summers J. A., Erwin E. J., Palmer, S., Peck, N. F., . . . Weigel, C. J. (2011). Performance: A strategy for professional development in early childhood teacher preparation. *Journal of Early Childhood Teacher Education, 32*(4), 355–366. DOI: 10.1080/10901027.2011.622244.

Maxwell, K. L., Lim, C. I., & Early, D. M. (2006). *Early childhood teacher preparation programs in the United States: National report.* Chapel Hill, NC: The University of North Carolina, FPG Child Development Institute.

McGuire-Schwartz, M. E., & Arndt, J. S. (2007). Transforming universal design for learning in early childhood teacher education from college classroom to early childhood classroom. *Journal of Early Childhood Teacher Education, 28*(2), 127–139. DOI: 10.1080/10901020701366707.

McKenzie, R. (2009). A national survey of pre-service preparation for collaboration. *Teacher Education and Special Education, 32*(4), 379–393.

McLean, M., & Odom, S. (1993). Practices for young children with and without disabilities: A comparison of DEC and NAEYC identified practices. *Topics in Early Childhood Special Education, 32*(1), 38–51.

McMurray-Schwartz, P., & Baum, A. (2000). Infusing special education content into teacher education courses. *Journal of Early Childhood Teacher Education, 21*(2), 249–253. DOI: 10.1080/0163638000210217.

Mellin, A. E., & Winton, P. J. (2003). Interdisciplinary collaboration among early intervention faculty members. *Journal of Early Intervention, 25*(3), 173–188.

Miller, P. S. (2003). Understanding and meeting the challenges to implementation of recommended practices in personnel preparation. In V. D. Stayton, P. S. Miller, & L. Dinnebeil (Eds.), *Personnel preparation in early childhood special education: Implementing the DEC recommended practices* (pp. 183–196). Longmont, CO: Sopris West.

Miller, P. S., & Stayton, V. D. (1998). Blended interdisciplinary teacher preparation in early childhood education and intervention: A national study. *Topics in Early Childhood Special Education, 18*(1), 11–21.

Miller, P. S., & Stayton, V. D. (1999). Higher education culture—A fit or misfit with reform in teacher education? *Journal of Teacher Education, 50*(4), 290–302.

Miller, P. S., & Stayton, V. D. (2006). Interdisciplinary teaming in teacher preparation. *Teacher Education and Special Education, 29*(1), 56–68. DOI: 10.1177/088840640602900107.

Murray, M. M., & Curran, E. M. (2008). Learning together with parents of children with disability: Bringing parent-professional partnership education to a new level. *Teacher Education and Special Education, 31*(1), 59–63. DOI: 10.1177/088840640803100106.

Murray, M. M., & Mandell, C. J. (2004). Evaluation of a family-centered early childhood special education preservice model by program graduates. *Topics in Early Childhood Special Education, 24,* 238–249.

NAEYC (National Association for the Education of Young Children). (2009, July). *NAEYC Standards for preparation of early childhood teachers: Position Statement.* Washington, DC: National Association for the Education of Young Children. Retrieved from http://www.naeyc.org/files/naeyc/files/2009%20Professional%20Prep%20stdsRevised%204_12.pdf

National Professional Development Center on Inclusion (NPDCI). (2011, August). *Competencies for early childhood educators in the context of inclusion: Issues and guidance for states.* Chapel Hill, NC: The University of North Carolina, FPG Child Development Institute, Author.

National Survey of Children with Special Health Care Needs. (2011). Data resource center on child and adolescent health: Child and adolescent health measurement initiative. Retrieved from http://www.childhealthdata.org/learn/NS-CSHCN

Niemeyer, J., & Proctor, R. (2002). The influence of experience on student teacher's beliefs about inclusion. *Journal of Early Childhood Teacher Education, 23*(1), 49–57.

No Child Left Behind (NCLB). Act of 2001, Pub L. No. 107–110, § 115, Stat. 1425 (2002).

Nourot, P. M. (2004). Historical perspectives on early childhood education. In J. L. Roopnarine & J. E. Johnson (Eds.), *Approaches to early childhood education* (4th ed.). Upper Saddle River, NJ: Merrill.

Odom, S. L., Buysee, V., & Soukakou, E. (2011). Inclusion for young children with disabilities: A quarter century of research perspectives. *Journal of Early Intervention, 33*(4), 344, 356. DOI: 10.1177/1053815111430094.

Odom, S. L., Vitztum, J., Wolery, R., Lieber, J., Sandall, S., Hanson, M., . . . Horn, E. (2004). Preschool inclusion in the United States: A review of research from an ecological systems perspective. *Journal of Research in Special Educational Needs, 4*(1), 17–49.

Panscofar, N., & Petroff, J. (2013). Professional development experiences in co-teaching: Associations with teacher confidence, interest, and attitudes. *Teacher Education and Special Education, 36*(2), 83–96.

Piper, A. (2007). What we know about integrating early childhood education and early childhood special education teacher preparation programs: A review, a reminder, and a request. *Journal of Early Childhood Teacher Education, 28*(2), 163–180. DOI: 10.1080/10901020701366749.

Prosser, T. M. (2009). Personnel preparation for preservice early intervention providers: Supporting families' participation in university classrooms. *Journal of Early Childhood Teacher Education, 30*(1), 69–78.

Pugach, M. C., & Blanton, L. P. (2009). A framework for conducting research on collaborative teacher education. *Teaching and Teacher Education, 25*, 575–582.

Recchia, S. L., & Puig, V. I. (2011). Challenges and inspirations: Student teachers' experiences in early childhood special education classrooms. *Teacher Education and Special Education, 32*(2), 131–151. DOI: 10.1177/0888406410387444.

Sheldon, S. B., & Van Voorhis, F. L. (2004). Partnership programs in U.S. schools: Their development and relationship to family involvement outcomes. *School Effectiveness and School Improvement, 15*(2), 125–148.

Shippen, M. E., Crites, S. A., Houchins, D. E., Ramsey, M. L., & Simon, M. (2005). Preservice teachers' perceptions of including students with disabilities. *Teacher Education & Special Education, 28*(2), 92–99.

Silverman, K., Hong, S., & Trepanier-Street, M. (2010). Collaboration of teacher education and child disability health care: Transdisciplinary approach to inclusive practice for early childhood pre-service teachers. *Early Childhood Education Journal, 31*, 461–468.

Smith, J. (2010). An interdisciplinary approach to preparing early intervention professionals: A university and community collaborative initiative. *Special Education and Teacher Education, 33*(2), 131–142.

Stayton, V., Whittaker, S., Jones, E., & Kersting, F. (2001). Interdisciplinary model for the preparation for related services and early intervention personnel. *Teacher Education and Special Education, 24*(4), 395–401.

Tarrant, K., Greenberg, E., Kagan, S. L., & Kauerz, K. (2008). The early childhood workforce. In S. Feeney, A. Galper, & C. Seefeldt (Eds.), *Continuing issues in early childhood education* (pp. 134–157). Upper Saddle River, NJ: Pearson Education.

Tourse, R., Mooney, J., Kline, P., & Davoren, J. (2005). A collaborative model of clinical preparation: A move toward interprofessional field experience. *Journal of Social Work Education, 41*(3), 457–477.

Trepanier-Street, M. (2010). Education and medical professionals collaborating to prepare early childhood teachers for inclusive settings. *Journal of Early Childhood Teacher Education, 31*(1), 63–70. DOI: 10.1080/10901020903529739.

Trivette, C. J., Dunst, C. J., Hamby, D. W., & O'Herin, C. E. (2009). Characteristics and consequences of adult learning methods and strategies. *Research Brief,* 3(1). Tots & Tech Research Institute. Retrieved from http://tnt.asu.edu

Turnbull, A. P., Turnbull, H. R., Erwin, E. J., Soodak, L. C., & Shogren, K. A. (2011). *Families, professionals, and exceptionality: Positive outcomes through partnerships and trust* (6th ed.). Boston, MA: Pearson.

United Nations Convention on the Rights of Persons With Disabilities. (2006, December). Retrieved from http://www.un.org/disabilities/convention/conventionfull.shtml

United States Department of Education Office of Special Education Programs. Data Analysis System (DANS). (2012). Table C1–9: Number and percent of infants and toddlers receiving early intervention services under IDEA, Part C, by age and state: Fall 2011 (data file). Retrieved from https://www.ideadata.org/TABLES35TH/C1–9.pdf

Voss, J. A., & Bufkin, L. J. (2011). Teaching all children: Preparing early childhood preservice teachers in inclusive settings. *Journal of Early Childhood Teacher Education, 32*(4), 338–354.

Winton, P., & Catlett, C. (2009). Statewide efforts to enhance early childhood personnel preparation programs to support inclusion: Overview and lessons learned. *Infants & Young Children, 22*(1), 63–70.

Wolery, M., & Bredekamp, S. (1994). Developmentally appropriate practices and young children with disabilities: Contextual issues in the discussion. *Journal of Early Intervention, 18*(4), 331–341.

Zygmunt-Fillwalk, E. (2011). Building family partnerships: The journey from preservice preparation to classroom practice. *Journal of Early Childhood Teacher Education, 32*(1), 84–96. DOI: 10.1080/10901027.2010.547653.

18

"MY MOMMY DOESN'T SPEAK ENGLISH"

Supporting Children as Emergent Bilinguals

Celia Genishi and Tara Lencl

Language is a remarkable human invention. Almost all human beings, without formal instruction, are able to speak or otherwise convey meaning through the language used in their communities. As adults we seem to take this ability to learn and use language for granted; it is ever present and thus like the air we breathe. When we stop to reflect, we may realize how remarkable language is, how complicated yet practical it is; and if we go a step further, we may wonder whether knowing two languages is twice as remarkable. Of course knowing two languages—bilingualism—is not that simple. The purpose of this chapter is to discuss what it might mean to learn and know two or more languages, within the framework of early childhood teaching and teacher education. The kindergartner's statement in the chapter title, "My mommy doesn't speak English," was overheard in her classroom and was her comment on why she is in a bilingual program. We take her declaration to be an invitation to address the following organizing questions:

- What are theoretical and historical contexts for childhood bilingualism?
- How do young children become bilingual?
- What kinds of programs and what kinds of teachers support the process of becoming bilingual?
- How effective is bilingual education for young children?
- Which researchers identify practices in early childhood teacher education programs that support young emergent bilinguals?

We answer these questions partly by countering persistent myths about bilingualism, young bilingual learners, and bilingual education and by including research and examples of practice that shed light on the questions.

We begin by clarifying terms since there are so many that refer to children learning one or more languages that are not used in their homes. *Bilingualism* refers to knowing two languages, although in practice there is a continuum of knowing: some bilinguals understand or comprehend two languages; others understand and speak them with differing degrees of fluency; some read and/or write them and become *biliterate*. Moreover, there are different kinds of bilingualism in terms of acquisition. Some bilinguals acquire or learn their languages *simultaneously* from birth, usually at home, whereas others learn them *sequentially*, having learned their home language first and then learning the language of the broader community in school—for example, English in the United States (Tabors, 1997).

Other terms seem self-explanatory, such as *English learner* or *second-language learner.* Some terms convey a negative meaning, for example, *limited English-proficient.* A more positive term, *emergent bilingual* (Garcia, Kleifgen, & Falchi, 2008), emphasizes the process through which children become bilingual or, in some cases, multilingual. Each of these terms has drawbacks: children may be learning a language other than English or a third rather than a second language. Children may be learning a second language proficiently and so do not demonstrate limitations; or they may be emergent *multi*linguals. Further, when young children use their two or more languages in a balanced or equally proficient way, some might argue that they are no longer *emergent*, but rather they have become bilingual or multilingual. Because in this chapter we address the process of *becoming* bilingual primarily in educational settings, we have chosen the term *emergent bilingual* as the one that captures in a positive way what many children are experiencing. Choosing a positive term helps to position bilingualism as an asset and resource, rather than as a deficit or problem to be fixed. This view of bilingualism captures the stance we take throughout this chapter, and we address opposing views by further explaining our stance and presenting theories, research, and practices that support it. In the next section we offer theoretical frameworks that have influenced our understanding of bilingualism and bilingual persons.

Theoretical Frameworks: Understanding Bilingualism

The ways that educators understand a phenomenon as complicated as bilingualism vary depending on their theoretical framework. Two persistent frameworks that have underlain research and practice related to children, including young emergent bilinguals, are *behaviorism* and *interactionism*. Proponents of these frameworks differ in their definitions of language and in their conceptions of how children learn language.

Since the early 20th century psychologists like Edward L. Thorndike (1938) theorized that behavior is learned and that things external to the learner determine how well something is learned. As B. F. Skinner, one of the pioneers of *behaviorism* of the mid-20th century, described it, a stimulus outside the learner, sometimes specified and administered by an experimenter, is presented to the learner; the learner responds; and that response is reinforced. According to Skinner (1957), language is learned like everything else. In short, words are verbal behavior, like stimuli that are responded to, and the learner's response is then reinforced. One of the complexities of behaviorist theory is the variety of reinforcements, beyond simply positive or negative reinforcers. Some current approaches to managing children's behavior in classrooms are based on behaviorist theory (Greer & Ross, 2007), as are highly structured language lessons for children (Engelmann, Haddox, & Bruner, 1983) and teachers (Moats, 2000), demonstrating the power that this theory has retained over time.

A contrasting theory, which we refer to as *interactionism,* defines language and language learning more broadly (Genishi & Dyson, 1984). In this view language is *not* like every other kind of behavior, but is a genetic given—some would say a gift—that must be developed through interactions that vary socially and culturally, depending on each learner's community. Psycholinguists—psychologists who study children's language development—laid the foundation for understanding the strengths that very young children bring to the task of learning one or more languages (Brown, 1973; Brown, Cazden, & Bellugi, 1969; Bruner, 1983; Hakuta, 1986). Beginning in the 1970s there was a movement away from the internal or psychological toward the external or social or, more accurately, toward acknowledging that the social and cultural always influence the psychological. Those who eventually identified themselves as *sociolinguists* came from various traditions, including anthropology, developmental psychology, education, and linguistics (Cazden, John, & Hymes, 1972; Heath, 1983; Labov, 1970; Schieffelin, 1990).

It would be simplistic to reduce theory and research influencing our understanding of bilingualism solely to the work of pioneers in the fields of verbal behavior and psycholinguistic, sociolinguistic, or interactionist research. There is a large body of work stemming from these traditions that has advanced our understanding of how children learn language(s), some of which is reviewed below. Further, there is extensive research in the area of second-language acquisition, which often focuses on learners beyond the early childhood years (Mitchell, Myles, & Marsden, 2013), although McLaughlin's work (1984, 1985) is an exception. To take a step away from theory and toward contexts of language use, we turn now to a historical and sociocultural framework that addresses one of the myths about bilingualism.

Historical and Sociocultural Context

Here we counter *the myth that bilingualism is atypical, exotic, or historically rare.* Although there are areas of the United States and other countries that seem "monolingual" in the public imagination, there have been bilingual populations and populations speaking languages other than English since before the United States was founded. Indigenous or Native American groups of course preceded English speakers by centuries, and many of these indigenous languages have unfortunately been lost. Elsewhere, for example, in Africa and Europe, speaking more than one language or dialect has been typical because of many countries' close proximity to others where different languages or dialects are spoken.

Since the 19th century the attitudes toward bilingual students and their education in the United States have shifted many times. Legislation providing the first federal funding for bilingual education was enacted in 1968 and was called the Bilingual Education Act (BEA). It was significant historically and educationally because it cast bilingual education as compensatory for students of "limited English proficiency" from families of low income. A long-term consequence of this characterization was a deficit view of bilingual students and bilingualism (Garcia, 2005).

There have been educational efforts to change the discourse from a negative one to one that constructs bilingualism as an asset or resource. An early advocate of a German-English dual-language program in the 19th century, Klemm (cited in Ferguson & Heath, 1981), was a precursor of educators who developed programs that aimed to maintain home languages and educate young children bilingually (Escobedo, 1983; Garcia & Garcia, 2012; John & Horner, 1971). These educators have threaded the history of early childhood education with a positive, asset-based perspective on bilingual children that belies the myth that bilingualism is atypical, exotic, or rare. In the next sections we counter other myths about children who are becoming bilingual and about the kinds of programs that educate them.

Young Children Becoming Bilingual: Myths and Counter-Myths

The next myth we address is that becoming bilingual is confusing or harmful to children. During the first half of the 20th century, it was widely believed that bilingualism and second language learning confused young children and hindered their cognitive and linguistic development and school success. While we have noted that attitudes toward bilingualism have fluctuated over the years, the myth that bilingualism is confusing or harmful to children still persists, even in light of considerable research pointing to the benefits of childhood bilingualism (Bialystok, 2009).

One of the earliest studies of childhood bilingualism was published between 1939 and 1949 by linguist Werner Leopold, in which he meticulously recorded the bilingual development of his daughter Hildegard in German and English from the time she was 8 months until she was 8 years of age (Hakuta, 1986). Other researchers have also used case studies across time and contexts to illustrate the language learning of emergent bilinguals. For example, Hakuta (1986) documented the English-learning of Uguisu, a 5-year-old Japanese girl who moved from Japan to the U.S. with her parents, and Long (1997) described the emergent bilingualism of her 7-year-old English-speaking daughter Kelli when the family moved to Iceland. The children in each of these studies became successful communicators in more than one language and showed bilingualism to be an advantage.

Moreover, rather than being confusing and harmful, recent research in childhood bilingualism has shown several cognitive benefits, including increased metalinguistic awareness and executive control (Adesope, Lavin, Thompson, & Ungerleider, 2010). Metalinguistic awareness refers to the ability to think about language and how it works. Researchers investigating the impact of bilingualism in this area have noted that bilingual children typically show a higher level of metalinguistic awareness than their monolingual peers (Adesope et al., 2010). Executive control refers to brain functions including working memory, mental flexibility, inhibitory control, and self-regulation. Each of these capacities is considered foundational to school success, forming the cognitive processes that underlie many skills necessary in school. For example, executive control influences a student's ability to plan, organize, focus their thinking, filter out distractions, make decisions, switch gears appropriately, and regulate their own behavior. Researchers in this area have found that bilingual children typically outperform their monolingual counterparts on tests that measure executive control, especially when children know both languages in a relatively balanced way (Adesope et al., 2010; Bialystok, 2009; Espinosa, 2013).

Overall, bilingualism can be seen as a positive experience for young children, offering benefits in both linguistic and cognitive development. However, while research on the benefits of bilingualism helps us to challenge the myth that bilingualism is confusing and harmful to children, there is often little direct connection between this research and what actually happens to and with young children in early childhood classrooms. In order to bring us closer to the actual experiences of emergent bilinguals in their early childhood settings, and to further consider how this research can impact practice, we turn our attention now to the remaining myths related to the education of emergent bilinguals.

The Ineffectiveness of Bilingual Education: Unpacking the Myth

A long-standing myth related to bilingual education is that it has been ineffective. Like the myths related to children's language learning, this one needs to be carefully unpacked. First, what is meant by *bilingual education* and, second, what is meant by *ineffective*?

Conceptualizing and Defining Bilingual Education

The term *bilingual education* resembles *bilingualism*. It may bring to mind curiosity about what it is, positive or negative feelings about its value, and questions as to how best to understand it. In addition, it prompts us to think about a continuum, rather like the continuum of bilingualism. In this case the continuum has multiple dimensions to be discussed next: a *conceptual* one that is based on the definitions and values of involved persons; a *practical* one that incorporates different models of bilingual education; and an *evaluative* one that raises the policy-related question of how effective bilingual programs are.

The processes of conceptualizing and defining bilingual education are underlain by individuals' values. Because we authors place a high value on learning and knowing two (or more) languages, we see bilingual education as positive and define it as a form of education that promotes the learning and maintenance of two (or more) languages. In an ideal world bilingual learners eventually understand, speak, read, and write two languages, while also appreciating the culture in which the languages are embedded. In reality we know that there is great variation in the forms of bilingual education and therefore in learner outcomes, or to what extent learners become bilingual.

In the U.S. context most programs focus on two languages, English and a language that may be the home or heritage language of children's communities. The emphasis placed on maintaining the home language in bilingual programs varies along a continuum. Educational programs whose aim is to maintain the home language while English is learned are at one end aiming for *maintenance*, whereas those that seek to provide a bridge or transition into English are in the middle. This *transitional* model anticipates a phasing out of the use of home languages in classrooms, at least for instructional purposes. At the other end of the continuum are programs that are enacted *mostly in English*, with little support for learners in the home language. These are nominally bilingual or are officially categorized as "general education" or "general ed" classrooms. They may reflect a lack of funding for bilingual programs or a community's or family members' desire to encourage the use of English in school settings since it is the dominant language of society in the United States. There are many points along this continuum that reflect the complexity of programs and family attitudes toward being bilingual. In the next section we offer examples of programs that illustrate different points along the continuum.

Practicing Bilingual Education

Searching for programs for young bilingual children reveals a contradiction: there is a plethora of examples, available through school districts or local and state departments of education, at the same time that there are few published curricula that specify child learners in the birth through grade 2 range. The curricula or classroom materials that are available are generally focused on content areas, primarily literacy, for kindergarten through grade 2. This dearth of published materials, however, is misleading since visits to classrooms in the pre-kindergarten (pre-K) to grade 2 range in school districts with culturally and linguistically diverse learners reveal a continuum of practices corresponding to the continuum of bilingual education described in the previous section. Some of these classrooms are categorized as "bilingual" or "dual-language," whereas others are called "general education" or "inclusive" settings. We present some vignettes from our own studies to illustrate our points.

Practicing bilingual education in general education "mostly English" classrooms: When the teacher is bilingual. In areas where teachers happen to speak the language of the children who are emergent bilinguals, some teachers modify their curriculum to make it accessible to children who enter the classroom with no knowledge of the dominant language. In a public pre-K in New York City the bilingual teacher Ms. Yung allows children to speak Cantonese, the home language of many of her children, including Andy and James, and she occasionally speaks Cantonese to clarify content to children whose English is just emerging. In this example, however, she helps Andy communicate a complaint in English in the midst of story-sharing time:

Andy: Ms. Yung! Ms. Yung! (Andy says something in Cantonese, about James bothering him.)
Ms. Yung: Well, tell him. Tell James, "I don't like to be bothered when I'm listening to a story." Tell him, tell him, Andy.
Andy: Don't bother me (turning to James).
Ms. Yung: James, he doesn't like to be bothered. So, what do you need to say to him?
James: Sorry.

(Genishi, Yung-Chan, & Stires, 2000, field notes, 5/98)

Ms. Yung extends a mini-lesson in using one's words in English to include a reminder to be polite, even if in a perfunctory way. This brief exchange with Andy and James is a "teachable moment" that we describe as bilingual even though the classroom is not designated as such. Because the teaching or maintenance of Cantonese is not an overall goal, Ms. Yung illustrates what is possible at the *mostly English* end of the continuum of bilingual education. Many other classrooms at that end of the continuum would differ significantly from Ms. Yung's because the teacher would use *only* English, making the model monolingual or in some cases "sink or swim."

Practicing bilingual education in transitional classrooms. Transitional bilingual classrooms are noted for their variety. Some have a majority of children who are emergent bilinguals, whereas others have a minority. Thus teachers in such classrooms make decisions about how to support the emergent bilinguals, in which language, and for how long.

A pre-K classroom in the New York City public schools is an example of a setting where almost all children start the year with Spanish as their home language and English as their school language or language of wider communication. The teacher Ms. Garza speaks both Spanish and English and toward the end of the pre-kindergarten year is heard alternating between Spanish and English during read-alouds (authors' oberservation, 2014). The children chat with each other at choice time in English and Spanish, and Ms. Garza and the class sing "The Hokey Pokey" and "The Wheels on the Bus" in English with jazzy embellishments and movements and great energy as they transition from one activity to another or before they leave school for the day. *Transition* in Ms. Garza's pre-K curriculum means using both the home language and English throughout the year, as the children become bilingual to differing degrees. In her school a greater number of parents want their children to maintain the home language in the classroom than not. In other schools more parents might prefer a rapid transition into English so administrators and teachers may accommodate this parental preference.

Practicing bilingual education in dual-language programs. Classrooms within the same program categories can of course vary. A public school kindergarten teacher in a dual language setting in Flushing, New York explains that many Korean-speaking parents in the community want their children to have teachers who are prepared to support the learning of Korean. However, by the end of the school year, children and their teacher clearly speak more English than Korean. Further, for the first grade some parents prefer not to place their children in a bilingual classroom.

We present a contrasting example of a dual-language program that would place itself on the "maintenance" end of the practice continuum; that is, the staff at the school aim for children to maintain their home language while English-speaking children are taught a second language. In places like New York City there are multiple home languages, although at the time this chapter was written Spanish and Mandarin/Chinese were most frequently offered in dual-language programs. Their structure usually follows a 50–50 plan, in which teachers and children experience two full days in Spanish, for example, two full days in English, and one day divided between Spanish and English. In some schools the eventual goal is a 90–10 format, so that English is used 90% and Spanish 10% of the instructional time. Teachers vary in terms of using only Spanish or only English on assigned days, depending on the linguistic abilities of their students.

Here is an example from Ms. A's second-grade science lesson in a dual language program on a Spanish day. (Translations are included in parentheses for readers; they were not provided by the teacher):

Ms. A: *Quiero que describan las rocas, como se sienten, como pesan. . . si son brillantes, lisas, ásperas. Les voy a dar frases que pueden usar* (I want you to describe the rocks, how they feel, how much they weigh, if they're shiny, smooth, rough. I'm going to give you sentences that you can use):
[The teacher's sentence starters:]

Mi roca es (My rock is)
Algo que yo noto en mi roca es (Something that I notice about my rock is)
Yo pienso que mi roca (I think that my rock)
El color de mi roca es (The color of my rock is)
La textura de mi roca es (The texture of my rock is)
Mi roca se siente (My rock feels)
Mi roca tiene (My rock has)

Ms. A: *Tienen que escribir una página y luego vienen a la alfombra para compartir.* (You have to write a page and then come to the rug to share.) (Gives them 20 minutes)

Children go back to tables where they were writing in the morning. Teacher sets up rocks and hands out magnifying glasses.

> A, As, and J are in a group, playing with the magnifying glasses, looking through them putting them up to their eyes. When the teacher puts the rocks on their table they collectively [say] "oooooooo" and then notice that there are little numbers on the rock samples.
>
> A says, "*Parece un meteoro*" ("it looks like a meteor") and demonstrates by having the rock fly towards the table and pretends to crash into table.
>
> J and As are speaking in English, A switches between English and Spanish although mostly Spanish.
>
> (Falchi, Axelrod, & Genishi, 2014, field notes, 1/10)

Ms. A teaches in Spanish on the "Spanish days" and in English on the "English days" and as long as children are talking softly does not interrupt their talk. Thus although the lesson is presented in Spanish, children may choose between their languages within small groups.

Evaluating Bilingual Education

The myth that bilingual education is ineffective is complicated by our two previous topics, the meaning of bilingual education and the practices that define it. As importantly, it is tightly linked to the ongoing emphasis in U.S. education on core standards and the tests that assess student performance on them. In general, large-scale evaluations of bilingual programs focus on the question of whether bilingual education is effective or ineffective. Because individual studies vary in their definitions of bilingual classrooms and their measures and because researchers often have strong opinions about bilingual education, findings have been contested and energetically debated. For example, a well-known meta-analysis of evaluations of bilingual education by Baker and de Kanter asserting ineffectiveness was assertively countered by Willig on methodological grounds (Baker, 1987; Baker & de Kanter, 1983; Willig, 1987). Surprisingly, however, there are relatively few individual evaluative studies that include data on student outcomes, such as comparisons of standardized test scores (August & Hakuta, 1997). August and Hakuta (1997) analyzed findings from 33 studies, only one of which included pre-K classrooms, focused on schools and programs for English language learners and do not offer conclusive answers to the question of whether bilingual education is effective. Rather, they identified the following attributes from the studies' findings that are associated with effective schools and classrooms:

> A supportive school-wide climate, school leadership, a customized learning environment, articulation and coordination within and between schools, some use of native language and culture in the instruction of language minority students, a balanced curriculum that incorporates both basic and higher-order skills, explicit skills instruction, opportunities for student-directed activities, use of instructional strategies that enhance understanding, opportunities for practice, systematic student assessment, staff development, and home and parent involvement.
>
> *(August & Hakuta, 1997, p. 171)*

One of the few experimental studies of pre-K classrooms comparing bilingual and monolingual classrooms is that of Barnett, Yarosz, Thomas, Jung, and Blanco (2007). The researchers randomly assigned children to English Immersion (English only) or Two-way Immersion or Dual Language Spanish-English classrooms, identified as of high quality. The main findings were that there were no significant differences between the achievement in English in language, literacy, and mathematics in comparisons between the two kinds of classrooms. There were, however, significant gains in Spanish vocabulary and rhyming skills for the children in the Dual Language classrooms. Thus bilingual education offered advantages in the children's home language while not adversely affecting learning in English. The researchers point out that this is a single study that demonstrates particular strengths of bilingual education and that it needs to be replicated in many other sites. Of interest is consistency across the study's pre-K programs, which all used the same curriculum, i.e., High/Scope (Hohmann, Banet, & Weikart, 1979) and which employed "licensed" or certified teachers in the state of New Jersey, where a court decision mandated increased funding for under-resourced school districts across the state (Abbott v. Burke, 2000). These features of defined curriculum and licensed teachers were interpreted as indicators of "high quality" and may be hard to replicate in some locales, given the variability of the early childhood teaching workforce (Kagan, Kauerz, & Tarrant, 2008).

Still, identifying positive features of schools and districts as August and Hakuta (1997) and Barnett et al. (2007) have done is echoed in recent research in Union City, New Jersey. Kirp (2013) describes the transformation over more than 20 years of an urban school district from failure to widely publicized success. Since the late 1960s the district has had a student population that is largely Latino, from every part of Latin America. What is impressive about Union City's success story is that it is one of evolution, not revolution, in which "there are no quick fixes, no miracle cures" (Kirp, 2013, p. 5). Rather, many elements came together to lead up to a graduation rate of 89.4% in 2011, 15% higher than the national average. Based on his own observations and analyses, Kirp asserts that the practices and policies that contribute to this statistic include the following:

- High-quality full-day preschool for all children starts at age 3.
- Word-soaked classrooms give youngsters a rich feel for language.
- Immigrant kids become fluent first in their native language and then in English.
- Teachers and students get hands-on help to improve their performance.
- The schools reach out to parents, enlisting them as partners in the education of their children.

(Kirp, 2013, p. 9)

The research findings point to practices and policies that incorporate some form of bilingual education for emergent bilinguals, within an educational context that supports and embraces learners, families, and teachers throughout the pre-K to 12 range.

Teachers Supporting Emergent Bilingualism: An Inclusive Approach

The final myth to address is that only teachers prepared to teach English as a second language (TESOL/ESL) are able to work successfully with bilingual children. Emergent bilinguals make up the fastest growing population of students in U.S. schools, and this number is highest during the early years (Garcia, Jensen, & Scribner, 2009; National Center for Education Statistics, 2014). In light of this growing population an increasing number of monolingual early childhood teachers without specific training in teaching emergent bilingual students will be in classrooms with children who speak a language other than English at home. However, this situation does not have to be a hindrance to working successfully with emergent bilingual children for these teachers. Early childhood teachers who do not have specific training in teaching English as a foreign language (such as TESOL and ESL) can learn a variety of strategies and approaches to support emergent bilingual children in inclusive settings. Indeed, given this demographic imperative, Nieto and Bode (2007) note:

> It is clear that the responsibility for educating these children can no longer fall only on those teachers who have been trained specifically to provide bilingual education and ESL services. This responsibility needs to be shared by all teachers and all schools.
>
> *(pp. 238–239)*

Through thoughtful teaching that is responsive to children's linguistic and cultural backgrounds and includes intentional strategies that both value the home language and support learning English, all teachers can work successfully with young emergent bilinguals (Reyes & Vallone, 2008).

A number of strategies to support language learning can be drawn on by teachers who may be monolingual English speakers, may be bilingual but not speak the home languages of the children in their classrooms, and/or may have little to no training in teaching English as a second language. A few key strategies that help to foster environments that are supportive of emergent bilinguals' language development include valuing the home language, creating an inclusive environment, providing scaffolds, building on the children's interests, and encouraging peer interaction (WestEd, 2006).

Even in classrooms where the teachers do not speak the home languages of emergent bilingual children, these languages can be valued and supported. Supporting the home language has many benefits, including supporting cognitive development, encouraging self-esteem, strengthening family ties, and enhancing social interactions (Nemeth, 2012). By valuing the home language teachers convey to children and families that their language is respected and important in the classroom. This can be done in a number of ways, such as including books, music, and environmental print in the classroom in each of the languages represented. One of the strongest ways is to learn a few words in each of the languages represented in the classroom. Not only does this place value on the language and show children and families that they are welcome, but it shows that the teacher is a language learner too (Stires & Genishi, 2008; WestEd, 2006).

Tara, the second author, is a teacher in a toddler classroom in New York City. The three teachers in the classroom are all monolingual English speakers, while each year several languages are represented by the children. Tara tries to learn a few key words and phrases in each of these languages. One evening she was leaving at the same time as her student Elina, a Russian speaker, and Elina's father. The following brief conversation took place:

Tara: *Poka Elina! Spokojnoj nochi.* (Bye Elina! Good night.)
Elina: *Poka!*
Father: *(smiling)* I think you speak more Russian than her now!
Tara: *(laughing)* No! I can only say like six things.
Father: Yes, but it shows that you really care.

Similarly, Rosie, a first grade teacher in New York City, encouraged her Cantonese- and Spanish-speaking students to teach her words in their home languages. In this way she showed them that she valued their language and provided a space for them to draw on their home languages as strengths in the classroom (Stires & Genishi, 2008).

Valuing the home language is also one way to enact the next strategy, creating an inclusive environment. Young emergent bilinguals develop their use of English along their own unique timelines (Genishi & Dyson, 2009). Teachers can create an inclusive environment that welcomes children as competent and sees their linguistic diversity as a strength, while at the same time supporting their language development in multiple ways. Teachers can provide time and space for children to observe and listen to language as well as ample opportunities to interact with teachers and peers across contexts and in various group sizes (WestEd, 2006). Such a setting provides the space for young children to draw on multiple ways of communicating as they to listen to, experiment with, and practice language along their own individual paths.

Within this context, teachers who are not specifically trained in teaching English as a second language can support emergent bilinguals through scaffolding and responding to children's interests. Scaffolds provide multisensory ways to support understanding, such as the use of the home language, building on familiar activities and concepts, using pictures and other props, and drawing on music, movement, and body language. By focusing on the interests of the children, teachers have the opportunity to build on their knowledge by responding to their language and actions through modeling and extending language (Nemeth, 2012; WestEd, 2006). For example, returning to Tara's classroom, we meet Martina, a 2-year-old, Spanish-speaking child who is learning English in the classroom. Martina is playing at the water table with a small group of children. Some of the children are standing on towels, but there is no towel at Martina's spot. When she realizes the floor is getting wet the following conversation ensues:

Martina: *Necesito . . . necesito . . .* this one. (I need . . . I need . . . this one. *Pointing at the towel her friend was standing on.*)
Tara: Oh! You need a towel!
Martina: *Necesito* towel. (I need towel)
Tara: Here's a towel. (*Handing a towel to Martina*)
Martina: Towel. (*Spreading the towel on the floor and standing on it*)

(Lencl, observation, 1/12)

Here Martina draws on her knowledge of both Spanish and English as well as the use of gesture to express her need. By responding to Martina's interest and using the scaffold of the actual item combined with language, the teacher is able to model English and teach new vocabulary within the natural context of Martina's play at the water table.

Finally, teachers can support the language development of emergent bilingual children by creating settings that offer many opportunities for peer interactions (Nemeth, 2012; August & Pease-Alvarez, 1996; WestEd, 2006). Through these interactions emergent bilinguals have access to their peers as language models and have the opportunity to experiment with and practice English in a nonthreatening context. For example, we meet Jin, another child in Tara's classroom. Jin started school in September speaking his home language of Korean, but by March has learned quite a bit of English. Jin is building in the block area when Jeremy joins him:

Jeremy: What is that, Jin? What is that?
Jin: This house.
Jeremy: House?
Jin: This my house. This my house book corner. Book corner big. So big. That bed. My Jin's bed. That's my daddy's bed. This my mommy's bed. Jin mommy bed. (*Jin explains to Jeremy as he points to different parts of his structure*)
Jeremy: Hey! How 'bout this one? (*Taking a block from the shelf*)
Jin: What?
Jeremy: A bed!
Jin: OK! Here, here! This my *Harabuji* (grandpa) bed.

(Lencl, observation, 3/13)

Through this interaction with Jeremy during block play Jin has the opportunity to explore his use of English in many ways, answering and asking questions, describing what he is doing, experimenting with the use of grammar, welcoming his friend in, and giving directions. In this way peer interactions can offer emergent bilinguals multiple ways to build their linguistic repertoires.

The Importance of Play

An important arena for the implementation of these strategies in early childhood classrooms is play. Genishi and Dyson (2009) describe the mutually supportive relationship between language and play, each one moving forward the development of the other. Here, drawing on the words of Vivian Paley, play is described as the ideal "habitat" (p. 59) for language learning, providing children a context rich with opportunities for using communication and language in multiple ways. Paley (2004) refers to play as the work of children and eloquently describes the importance of fantasy (or sociodramatic) play in fostering all areas of development, including language. Researchers specifically examining the play of young emergent bilingual children note this importance as well.

Long, Volk, and Gregory (2007) describe three studies examining the play of emergent bilingual children. Across each study the authors note that play provided a space for children to jointly create new ways of teaching and learning about language, literacy, and cultural practices. While all forms of play fostered second language learning, sociodramatic play provided the most dynamic and varied opportunities for learning and using language. Axelrod (2014) supports this point as well with her research in a bilingual Head Start classroom, illustrating the ways the children's sociodramatic play provides a rich context in which they negotiate and blend multiple languages and cultural practices as they put their developing language to work. Her work further extends the research in this area by illuminating the important role of the classroom teachers in supporting this play.

Unfortunately, despite its importance, play has lost much of its footing in early elementary classrooms due to an increased focus on academics and standardization. Today even preschool teachers feel the pressure of this academic push down as it encroaches on spaces once occupied by children's play (Genishi & Dyson, 2014). In this context early childhood teachers and teacher educators may have to increasingly take on the role of advocates for children's right to play. As Paley (2004) notes, "we perform a grave error when we remove fantasy play as the foundation of early childhood education" (p. 102). However, in their review of research examining teachers' views of play and their competence to include it in the early childhood curriculum, Ryan and Northey-Berg (2014) found that teachers often lack the knowledge necessary to "assert their authority about the use and relevance of play in the early childhood curriculum" (p. 207). These researchers argue that advocacy for and inclusion of play in early childhood classrooms will continue to diminish unless specific attention to play is increased in teacher preparation.

By engaging in intentional teaching practices aimed at supporting children from diverse linguistic backgrounds, all teachers can learn to work successfully with young emergent bilingual children. We now turn to general ways in which students in teacher education programs might learn to support children learning more than one language.

Implications for Early Childhood Teacher Education: How Do We Learn to Support Emergent Bilinguals?

With the growing number of emergent bilingual children in early childhood education settings, it is imperative that early childhood teacher education programs prepare preservice teachers to work successfully with the linguistically diverse students in their classrooms. Research on early childhood teacher education is limited (Ryan & Northey-Berg, 2014); however, researchers in this area have begun to examine a variety of promising practices in early childhood teacher education to better support teachers in working with emergent bilingual children and families. One important commonality across these studies is the acknowledgement of bilingualism as a strength rather than a deficit. Additionally, these studies illustrate in multiple ways the importance of providing opportunities for connecting theory to practice by combining information learned in courses with hands-on opportunities for implementation. Szente (2008) describes a service-learning project in conjunction with university coursework in which preservice teachers volunteered as academic (literacy) tutors for culturally and linguistically diverse students in kindergarten through third-grade classrooms. She found that the 105 preservice teachers in her study broadened their pedagogical understandings through applying what they learned in their courses in their field placements. Through this process the preservice teachers gained a better understanding of both their students and themselves (Szente, 2008).

Hooks (2008) notes that while the population of emergent bilingual children in early childhood classrooms is rapidly increasing, the vast majority of preservice teachers in early childhood teacher education programs in the U.S. do not have bilingual backgrounds. In her study Hooks responded to anxiety her preservice students expressed about working with linguistically diverse children and especially with their families. To support her students Hooks (2008) partnered her early childhood university course with a community-based adult English language class. During this partnership the preservice teachers engaged in mock parent-teacher conferences with the adult language students, as well as casual conversations to get to know each other. Preservice students engaged in reflections before and after the mock conferences. Prior to the conferences the main themes in these reflections were anxiety about the conference and concern over being able to communicate effectively. After the conferences, the reflections included increased confidence, a broader awareness and appreciation for diversity, greater knowledge of what is involved in communication, and a commitment to working with parents (Hooks, 2008).

The research of Hardin et al. (2010) focuses on a professional development program for inservice pre-K teachers. The program was developed to support teachers in classrooms with a high percentage of emergent bilingual children (27% or above) and consisted of three interactive training sessions. These covered: (1) strategies for identifying cultural practices, (2) classroom strategies that support second language acquisition, and (3) effective methods for strengthening teacher, family, and community organization relationships. Participants included 48 teachers in 24 pre-K classrooms across 17 schools. Hardin and her colleagues found that the project teachers strengthened their practices with emergent bilingual children and their families in multiple ways. The teachers also found the support of knowledgeable mentors during coaching sessions to be very beneficial for connecting theory to practice (Hardin et al., 2010).

Rather than focusing on specific interventions for preservice (or inservice) teachers, McCrary, Sennette, and Brown (2011) documented a program-wide, grant-funded effort to include attention to emergent bilinguals across the curriculum, in order to better prepare preservice teachers to meet the needs of emergent bilinguals during their program and in their future classrooms. The activities of the faculty study team included attending lectures by visiting scholars with expertise in working with emergent bilinguals, participating in book study groups, attending conferences, making classroom visits, and engaging in course development and revision. In this way McCrary and colleagues (2011) combined gaining new knowledge with hands-on application (through restructuring the content of their teacher education program). Preservice teachers and faculty both expressed positive responses to the changes made in the program, noting increased knowledge and repertoires of strategies for working with emergent bilingual students (McCrary et al., 2011).

Taken together these studies highlight the importance of taking a strength-based stance toward bilingualism in teacher education, combining theory with opportunities for hands-on practice, preferably in conjunction with a knowledgeable mentor or field supervisor, and making an effort to infuse content related to emergent bilinguals throughout general early childhood teacher preparation programs in order to better prepare all teachers for the linguistic diversity they are likely to meet in their future classrooms. Additionally, the paucity of this research points to the need for further studies examining teacher preparation strategies for working with emergent bilingual children and families to strengthen these practices in early childhood teacher education programs.

Teacher Diversity and Recommendations for the Future

The process of learning to support emergent bilinguals varies across a broad continuum. We acknowledge each reader's individual uniqueness; we all come to the learning/teaching task with prior experiences, knowledge, and dispositions. Some of us are born into bilingual families. We may advocate for, resist, or feel neutral about practices that help children become bilingual. Others of us may never have lived in bilingual or multilingual homes or communities but may similarly favor, resist, or feel neutral about the idea of supporting emergent bilingual children.

Regardless of our individual dispositions toward bilingualism and multilingualism, early childhood teacher education programs are positioned to make decisions about the place of bilingual language development and education. This means that all of us, regardless of our dispositions, have a responsibility to reflect on these decisions and their importance to the future of early childhood teacher education.

The recommendations that follow grow out of the stances we have articulated earlier and the research we reported on bilingualism, bilingual education, and early childhood teacher education. That is, we have viewed bilingualism or multilingualism as a resource and not a deficit, and we have presented studies showing that educational sites or programs with particular features may be effective in supporting emergent bilinguals. Thus we propose teacher education that incorporates multiple ways to:

- Learn about language development in young learners, including bilingual and multilingual children, through courses that focus on language and communication that include but are *not* dominated by early literacy objectives, such as letter-sound correspondence.
- Plan curricula that embed many opportunities for emergent bilingual children to interact with peers and adults and practice the languages they are learning.
- Enact plans based on knowledge of language development and a range of practices, including child-chosen play, that support young learners whose unique developmental timelines are respected and whose curiosities and interests are nurtured.
- Assess through observation and documentation how children respond to and learn from enacted practices so that plans for next steps build on these teacher- and classroom-based assessments.
- Infuse curricula related to teaching linguistically diverse children throughout early childhood teacher education programs, rather than isolating this information in an individual course.
- Teach the skills and knowledge necessary for teachers to advocate for, implement, and engage in language learning through play once they enter the work force.
- Offer hands-on experiences working with emergent bilinguals in the field, in combination with a knowledgeable mentor or supervisor.
- Seek out field placements in schools that share at least some of the characteristics of the positive environments for emergent bilinguals described in the research, and with classroom teachers who are skilled at teaching linguistically diverse children.

These are challenging recommendations for teacher educators who may find that their institutions lack a course on language development or that classrooms in their locales lack opportunities for children's play or critical numbers of emergent bilinguals. Demographic changes in the United States, however, suggest that reforms in early childhood education and teacher education would be timely and clearly needed. In addition, early childhood classrooms across the globe will need teachers who are able to work with children whose home languages are different from the dominant school language. Like the child in our chapter title who states that her mommy doesn't speak English, increasing numbers of children will want to learn a language of wider communication; and they will be best positioned to do this when their teachers are prepared to work with them.

References

Abbott v. Burke. (2000). 163 New Jersey 95, 48.2d82.

Adesope, O. O., Lavin, T., Thompson, T., & Ungerleider, C. (2010). A systematic review and meta-analysis of the cognitive correlates of bilingualism. *Review of Research in Education, 80*(2), 207–245.

August, D., & Hakuta, K. (Eds.). (1997). *Improving schooling for language-minority children: A research agenda.* Washington, DC: National Academy Press.

August, D., & Pease-Alvarez, L. (1996). *Attributes of effective programs and classrooms serving English language learners.* Santa Cruz, CA: National Center for Research on Cultural Diversity and Second Language Learning.

Axelrod, Y. (2014). "Todos vamos a jugar, even the teachers"—Everyone playing together. *Young Children, 69*(2), 24–31.

Baker, K. (1987). Comment on Willig's "A meta-analysis of selected studies in the effectiveness of bilingual education. *Review of Educational Research, 57*(3), 351–362.

Baker, K., & de Kanter, A. (1983). Effectiveness of bilingual education. In K. Baker & A. de Kanter (Eds.), *Bilingual education: A reappraisal of federal policy* (pp. 33–86). Lexington, MA: Lexington Books.

Barnett, W. S., Yarosz, D. J., Thomas, J., Jung, K., & Blanco, D. (2007). Two-way and monolingual English immersion in preschool education: An experimental comparison. *Early Childhood Research Quarterly, 22*, 277–293.

Bialystok, E. (2009). Bilingualism: The good, the bad, and the indifferent. *Bilingualism: Language and Cognition, 12*(1), 3–11.

Brown, R. (1973). *A first language: The early stages.* Cambridge, MA: Harvard University Press.

Brown, R., Cazden, C. B., & Bellugi, U. (1969). The child's grammar from I to III. In J. P. Hill (Ed.), *Minnesota symposium on child psychology* (vol. 2). Minneapolis, MN: University of Minnesota Press.

Bruner, J. (1983). *Child's talk: Learning to use language.* New York: W. W. Norton & Company.

Cazden, C. B., John, V. P., & Hymes, D. (Eds.). (1972). *Functions of language in the classroom.* New York: Teachers College Press.

Engelmann, S., Haddox, P., & Bruner, E. (1983). *Teach your child to read in 100 easy lessons.* New York: Simon & Schuster.

Escobedo, T. H. (Ed.). (1983). *Early childhood bilingual education: A Hispanic perspective.* New York: Teachers College Press.

Espinosa, L. M. (2013). *Pre-K-3rd: Challenging common myths about English language learners* (Policy to action brief 10). New York: Foundation for Child Development.

Falchi, L., Axelrod, Y., & Genishi, C. (2014). "*Miguel es un artista*"—and Luisa is an excellent student: Seeking time and space for children's multimodal practices. *Journal of Early Childhood Literacy, 14*(3), 345–366.

Ferguson, C. A., & Heath, S. B. (Eds.). (1981). *Language in the U.S.A.* New York: Cambridge University Press.

Garcia, E. E. (2005). *Teaching and learning in two languages: Bilingualism and schooling in the United States.* New York: Teachers College Press.

Garcia, E. E., & Garcia, E. H. (2012). *Understanding the language development and early education of Hispanic children.* New York: Teachers College Press.

Garcia. E. E., Jensen, B. T., & Scribner, K. P. (2009). The demographic imperative. *Educational Leadership, 66*(7), 9–13.

Garcia, O., Kleifgen, J., & Falchi, L. (2008). *From English language learners to emergent bilinguals.* Equity Matters: Research Review No. 1. Retrieved from http://www.tc.columbia.edu/i/a/document/6468_Ofelia_ELL__Final.pdf

Genishi, C., & Dyson, A. H. (1984). *Language assessment in the early years.* Norwood, NJ: Ablex.

Genishi, C., & Dyson, A. H. (2009). *Children, language, and literacy: Diverse learners in diverse times.* New York: Teachers College Press & Washington, DC: National Association for the Education of Young Children.

Genishi, C., & Dyson, A. H. (2014). Play as the precursor for literacy development. In L. Booker, M. Blaise, & S. Edwards (Eds.), *The SAGE handbook of play and learning in early childhood* (pp. 228–239). Los Angeles, CA: SAGE Publications.

Genishi, C., Yung-Chan, D., & Stires, S. (2000). Talking their way into print: English language learners in a prekindergarten classroom. In D. S. Strickland & L. M. Morrow (Eds.), *Beginning reading and writing* (pp. 66–80). New York: Teachers College Press.

Greer, R. D., & Ross, D. E. (2007). *Verbal behavior analysis: Inducing and expanding new verbal capabilities in children with language delays.* Boston, MA: Allyn & Bacon.

Hakuta, K. (1986). *Mirror of language: The debate on bilingualism.* New York: Basic Books.

Hardin, B. J., Lower, J. K., Smallwood, G. R., Chakravarthi, S., Li, L., & Jordan, C. (2010). Teachers, families, and communities supporting English language learners in inclusive pre-kindergartens: An evaluation of a professional development model. *Journal of Early Childhood Teacher Education, 31*(1), 20–36.

Heath, S. B. (1983). *Ways with words: Language, life, and work in communities and classrooms.* New York: Cambridge University Press.

Hohmann, M., Banet, B., & Weikart, D. (1979). *Young children in action.* Ypsilanti, MI: High/Scope Press.

Hooks, L. M. (2008). Help! They don't speak English: Partnering preservice teachers with adult English language learners. *Journal of Early Childhood Teacher Education, 29*(2), 97–107.

John, V. P., & Horner, V. M. (1971). *Early childhood bilingual education.* New York: Modern Language Association.
Kagan, S. L., Kauerz, K., & Tarrant, K. (2008). *The early care and education teaching workforce at the fulcum: An agenda for reform.* New York: Teachers College Press.
Kirp, D. L. (2013). *Improbable scholars: The rebirth of a great American school system and a strategy for America's schools.* New York: Oxford University Press.
Labov, W. (1970). The logic of nonstandard English. In F. Williams (Ed.), *Language and poverty* (pp. 153–189). Chicago, IL: Markham.
Long, S. (1997). Friends as teachers: the impact of peer interaction on the acquisition of a new language. In E. Gregory (Ed.), *One child, many worlds: early learning in multicultural communities* (pp. 123–136). New York: Teachers College Press.
Long, S., Volk, D., & Gregory, E. (2007). Intentionality and expertise: Learning from observations of children at play in multilingual, multicultural contexts. *Anthropology and Education Quarterly, 38*(3), 239–259.
McCrary, D. E., Sennette, J., & Brown, D. L. (2011). Preparing early childhood teachers for English language learners. *Journal of Early Childhood Teacher Education, 32*(2), 107–117.
McLaughlin, B. (1984). *Second-language acquisition in childhood: Preschool children* (vol. 1). Hillsdale, NJ: Erlbaum.
McLaughlin, B. (1985). *Second-language acquisition in childhood: School-age children* (vol. 2). Hillsdale, NJ: Erlbaum.
Mitchell, R., Myles, F., & Marsden, E. (2013). *Second language learning theories* (3rd ed.) New York: Routledge.
Moats, L. C. (2000). *Speech to print: Language essentials for teachers.* Baltimore, MD: Paul H. Brookes.
National Center for Education Statistics. (2014). *English Language Learners update.* Retrieved from http://nces.ed.gov/programs/coe/indicator_cgf.asp
Nemeth, K. N. (2012). *Basics of supporting dual language learners: An introduction for educators of children from birth through age 8.* Washington, DC: National Association for the Education of Young Children.
Nieto, S., & Bode, P. (2007). *Affirming diversity: The sociopolitical context of multicultural education.* Upper Saddle River, NJ: Allyn & Bacon.
Paley, V. G. (2004). *A child's work: The importance of fantasy play.* Chicago, IL: University of Chicago Press.
Reyes, S. A., & Vallone, T. L. (2008). *Constructivist strategies for teaching English language learners.* Thousand Oaks, CA: Corwin Press.
Ryan, S., & Northey-Berg, K. (2014). Professional preparation for a pedagogy of play. In L. Booker, M. Blaise, & S. Edwards (Eds.), *The SAGE handbook of play and learning in early childhood* (pp. 204–215). Los Angeles, CA: SAGE Publications.
Schieffelin, B. B. (1990). *The give and take of everyday life: Language socialization of Kaluli children.* New York: Cambridge University Press.
Skinner, B. F. (1957). *Verbal behavior.* New York: Appleton Century-Crofts.
Stires, S., & Genishi, C. (2008). Learning English in school: Rethinking curriculum, relationships, and time. In C. Genishi & A.L. Goodwin (Eds.), *Diversities in early childhood education: Rethinking and doing* (pp. 49–66). New York: Routledge.
Szente, J. (2008). Preparing preservice teachers to work with culturally and linguistically diverse children: A service learning experience. *Journal of Early Childhood Teacher Education, 29*(2), 140–145.
Tabors, P. O. (1997). *One child, two languages: A guide for preschool educators of children learning English as a second language.* Baltimore, MD: Brookes.
Thorndike, E. L. (1938). Studies in the psychology of language. *Archives of Psychology*, 231. New York: University Microfilms International.
WestEd. (2006). *A world full of language: Supporting preschool English learners.* Sacramento, CA: The California Department of Education.
Willig, A. (1987). Examining bilingual education research through meta-analysis and narrative review: A response to Baker. *Review of Educational Research, 57*(3), 363–376.

19

MULTICULTURALLY SUSTAINING PEDAGOGY IN EARLY CHILDHOOD TEACHER EDUCATION

Mariana Souto-Manning and Ranita Cheruvu

"What is multicultural education?" If you pose this question to a group of early childhood educators, you are likely to hear many different responses. Because there are many ways to define and practice multicultural education, it is rare that any two early childhood educators will share the same understanding of multicultural education. Multiple researchers (Banks & McGee Banks, 1995; Derman-Sparks & Ramsey, 2011; Gay, 2004; Sleeter, 1996; Souto-Manning, 2013) have found evidence of superficial implementation of multicultural curriculum and teaching in preschool-12th grade settings, often resulting from the action of well-intentioned educators who consider multicultural education to be merely adding so-called "multicultural materials" or "multicultural celebrations" to their classrooms. A specific example of this would be purchasing "multicultural dolls" (often identified as such in popular educational catalogues) and adding them to the dramatic play area in an infant, toddler, or preschool classroom (Souto-Manning, 2013). In pre-kindergarten and primary grades, some early educators believe that learning about important historical figures and holidays from cultures around the world (read: foreign and exotic) is multicultural education. For example, learning an abbreviated and incomplete story of Rev. Dr. Martin Luther King, Jr., during February, Black History Month, or learning about Kwanza and Hannukah during the dominant Christmas season, are considered to be forms of multicultural education by many. However, the action of adding new materials labeled "multicultural" does not solely or necessarily comprise a change in teaching and learning or in the interactions and beliefs present in a classroom; nor does a "holidays and heroes" approach to learning about non-dominant cultures (De Gaetano, Williams, & Volk, 1998; Ramsey & Williams, 2003).

This lack of or limited understanding regarding multicultural education reflects the myriad of ways the field of early childhood education has understood and responded to the diversities of young children. Historically, in the U.S., diversities have been thought of as inherently inferior, as comprising deficits, or as being an add-on to the so-called "normal" curriculum (Carter & Goodwin, 1994; Goodwin, Cheruvu, & Genishi, 2008). Although there is an emerging understanding that the growing diversity of young children in early childhood care and educational settings necessitates a shift in teaching practices, there is a lack of a clear vision as to what this practice should be or should look like (Souto-Manning, 2013). Early childhood educators often feel unprepared to teach diverse young children and may be reluctant to engage in multicultural teaching (Ray & Bowman, 2003; Valli & Rannert-Ariev, 2000).

In 1988, Moultry found that almost 40% of preservice teachers did not see the point in multicultural teaching as they did not believe in institutionalized racism and were not aware of how teachers' beliefs, values, and stereotypes influence the educational experiences of children from non-dominant backgrounds. Such attitudes remain today (Souto-Manning & Price-Dennis, 2012). Similarly, early childhood teacher educators lack a shared conception of multicultural education (Laman, Miller, & Lopez-Robertson, 2012). Given the fact that children of color, children from low- or no-income families, and children who are linguistically "minoritized" (McCarty, 2004) continue to face inequitable and unjust early educational and care experiences, it is imperative that early childhood educators—those who teach young children and those who prepare teachers—work toward a shared vision of multicultural education. In this chapter we take on the project of moving toward a common understanding of multicultural education and, in turn, (re)conceptualize how early childhood teacher education might go about preparing teachers to engage in multicultural teaching practices.

What Is Multicultural Education? Reviewing the Literature

"Multicultural education can be traced historically to the civil rights movement" (Sleeter & McLaren, 2009, p. 17). During this time, African Americans began the fight for equity and equality in schooling policies and practices, as well as other political, economic, and cultural rights (Banks, 2004). However, the seeds of multicultural education were planted much earlier. The works of W.E.B. Dubois, Carter G. Woodson, and the Intergroup and Intercultural movements have all been identified as historical antecedents to multicultural education (Banks, 2004). The "myriad of responses" (Banks, 2009, p. 1) to ethnic studies reform movements in schools led to the initial development of multicultural education. Over the next four decades, multicultural education scholars in the United States developed and deepened their conceptualizations of multicultural education. These conceptualizations (to be discussed below) have informed multicultural education efforts internationally in various nation states.

There are many definitions of multicultural education. Banks and McGee Banks (2004) defined multicultural education as "a field of study designed to increase educational equity for all students" (p. xii). In refining his definition of multicultural education, Banks (2004) developed five dimensions of multicultural education: (1) *content integration* (bringing together multiple cultural perspectives, knowledges, and experiences as central and imperative to teaching and learning); (2) *knowledge construction process* (locating the social, cultural, and historical construction of knowledge—coming to trouble culture-free notions of knowledge, teaching, and learning); (3) *prejudice reduction* (developing positive cross-cultural and intergroup attitudes and actions in the classroom while troubling privileges and seeking to move away from inferiority and deficit perspectives); (4) *equity pedagogy* (implementing teaching strategies that honor multiple groups—in terms of race, language, culture, etc.—regardless of their representation in the classroom community and that honor children as unique human beings who are members of communities and families); and (5) *empowering school culture and social structure* (changing the status of diverse groups in schools, fostering more equitable experiences). Gay (1994) defined multicultural education as:

> Policies, programs, and practices employed in schools to celebrate cultural diversity. It builds on the assumption that teaching and learning are invariably cultural processes . . . As used in this definition, celebration means to know, believe, accept, value, use, and promote cultural diversity as a normal feature of humankind, a characteristic trait of U.S. society, and an essential component of quality education for all students. Effective implementation of multicultural education requires a combination of the personal attitudes and values of educators, curriculum content, instructional methods and materials, classroom climates, and the participation of individuals at all levels of the educational enterprise.
>
> *(p. 17)*

Nieto (2002) defined multicultural education critically, within a complex sociopolitical context, acknowledging and reaffirming the need for multicultural education which

> challenges and rejects racism and other forms of discrimination in schools and society and accepts and affirms the pluralism (ethnic, racial, linguistic, religious, economic, and gender, among others) that students, their communities, and teachers reflect. Multicultural education permeates schools' curriculum and instructional strategies, as well as interactions among teachers, students, and families, and the very way that schools conceptualize the nature of teaching and learning. Because it uses critical pedagogy as its underlying philosophy and focuses on knowledge, reflection, and action (praxis) as the basis for social change, multicultural education promotes democratic principles of social justice . . . is antiracist . . . [and] important for all students.
>
> *(pp. 29–30)*

From a critical perspective, multicultural education focuses on challenging the idea of diverse individuals possessing deficits (lacking something or needing to be fixed) or being considered inferior. Thus, "multicultural teaching is good teaching for *all* children" (Souto-Manning, 2013, p. 15).

Multicultural education is about fostering and forming an equitable and socially just society (Ramsey & Williams, 2003). Multicultural education "uses the transformation of self and school as . . . metaphor[s] and point[s] of departure for the transformation of society. Ultimately, social justice and equity in schools can, and should, mean social justice and equity in society" (Gorksi, 2010, p. 1). This is important because:

> A large white and female teaching force may bring negative, unacceptable attitudes toward the growing numbers of students of color in their classrooms; these attitudes coupled with the attendant lower expectations, are major contributing factors to the widespread academic failure among minority students.
>
> *(Garmon, 1996, p. 5)*

Situating multicultural education within the context of early childhood education, Souto-Manning (2013) proposed that multicultural education is an

> approach to education [that] holistically critiques and responds to discriminatory policies and practices in education. It involves contextualizing, historicizing, and problematizing inequities in classrooms and beyond (Souto-Manning, 2010b). Thus, instead of finding fault with traditionally disenfranchised families, it is important to work towards eradicating teaching practices that disenfranchise—teaching practices that are not inclusive of multiple perspectives and points of view (Derman-Sparks & Ramsey, 2006).
>
> *(p. 5)*

Multicultural education invites early childhood educators to honestly consider the following questions:

- Do I tend to find fault with students of color or other students and families from non-dominant, minoritized, and traditionally disenfranchised groups (e.g., gay and lesbian families, low/no-income families, families of color)?
- Do I examine ways in which (pre)school policies and my teaching practices influence educational outcome disparities and further disadvantage students and families from non-dominant, minoritized, and traditionally disenfranchised groups?

- Do I tend to blame individual students and their families for educational failure, or do I tend to examine how larger societal factors (e.g., health care, wages, housing) influence educational outcome disparities (e.g., high school graduation)? And, when students do not do well, do I believe that they are responsible for their failure, or do I understand how they have been failed by the educational and social systems?

These questions serve as starting points for teachers to begin the journey of transforming themselves, their practices, and, ultimately, schools and society.

(Re)Conceptualizing Multicultural Education as Transformative Education

Multicultural education is grounded in ideals of social justice, educational equity, and educational experiences that allow each child to reach his/her full potential as a learner and as a socially aware and active human being (Banks, 1994; Nieto, 1999). Multicultural education acknowledges that teachers, classroom communities, and schools as a whole are essential to laying the foundation for the transformation of society and the elimination of social injustices. The aim of multicultural education is to initiate positive social change and transform society and schools through education. Multicultural education, when conceived as education for transformation, involves the interrelated transformation of self, teaching, and society (Gorski, 2010; Souto-Manning, 2013). Below, we explore specific facets of this interrelated transformation at the heart of multicultural education.

The Transformation of Self

To teach multiculturally, one starts by acknowledging his/her identities, beliefs, experiences, privileges, oppressions, and values as culturally shaped. Researchers have documented how teachers may not view themselves as cultural beings (Derman-Sparks & Ramsey, 2006; Goodwin & Genor, 2008)—especially those who grew up in cultures that are not deemed to be "different" (i.e. White, speaker of Mainstream American English, economically comfortable). This is also true of teacher educators who often position diversities as add-ons to their traditional curricula and teaching. All individuals are cultural beings, so it is essential to identify the cultural threads that make up their identities. Unless educators understand how their cultures shaped and continue to shape who they are, they will not be able to teach multiculturally. This is due to the fact that individuals (especially those from privileged backgrounds, who historically have been in positions of power) will continue to revere their own culture(s) as the norm, and teach (mono)culturally (Goodwin, Cheruvu, & Genishi, 2008; Souto-Manning, 2010a).

In addition to viewing their own selves as cultural beings and their identities, values, experiences, and practices as culturally-shaped, educators have a dual responsibility to engage in a critical and continual process of examining how their socializations and biases inform their teaching and thus the educational experiences of their students (Freire, 1998; Goodwin & Genor, 2008). Educators have the responsibility to examine and problematize how they perceive the people, events, and practices that influence their lives so that they can have a sense of how their own perceptions and values are developed in relation to their life experiences. In doing so, they can come to understand how their place in and perception of the world are culturally-situated constructs. From this perspective, they are more prone to successfully negotiate and navigate relationships with the young children they teach. Educators have a responsibility to young children (and teacher educators to the teachers of young children), to work toward eliminating our prejudices, examining who is (and who is not) being reached by our teaching, and rediscovering who we are. After all, whether in early childhood education or in early childhood teacher education settings, their identities will affect their students' learning experiences. Critical multicultural educators engage in a constant process of self-examination and transformation—asking if they are advantaging some students over others, and how their own upbringing and experiences influence their teaching and the learning climate in their classrooms.

The transformation of self is an imperative first step toward embarking on the multicultural education journey. After all, multicultural education is about equity. In the early childhood teacher education classroom, equity has to do with whose voices are valued—that is, heard and read. Multicultural education is about helping "all students acquire the knowledge, attitudes, and skills needed to participate in cross-cultural interactions and in personal, social, and civic action that will help make our nation more democratic and just" (Banks, 2007, p. xii). It is about developing these knowledges, attitudes, and skills as a teacher educator as well. "To teach multiculturally means to teach inclusively, to create spaces of possibility, to bring differences front and center in the life of the classroom" (Souto-Manning, 2013, p. 17). This involves positioning power differentials and conflicts (Souto-Manning, 2014) at the center of teaching. After all, it is not possible to address race, language, income, sexuality, and gender or to question structures of power and privilege unless we consider power relationships. "The connection between practical strategies and issues of power lies with teachers, which is why the continual critical examination and reflection of self is so important" (Souto-Manning, 2013, p. 17).

The Transformation of Teaching

Multicultural education calls for a critical examination of all aspects of schooling (Grant & Sleeter, 1990). Here, we consider two aspects of transforming teaching to be key: fostering student-centered ways of teaching and designing a multicultural curriculum.

Student-centered ways of teaching. One of the key premises of multicultural education is that the experiences of students (and their families and communities) are brought to the center of the curriculum, making learning active, interactive, relevant, and engaging (Nieto, 2010; Souto-Manning, 2010b; Souto-Manning, 2013). Thus, traditional teaching approaches—teachers as the sole experts in the classroom, transmission of knowledge from teacher to student—are deconstructed to examine how they contribute to and support educational injustice and inequity (Freire, 1970; Nieto, 1999). Known inequitable practices like tracking—determining who is ready for kindergarten (even if informally), early intervention requirements, standardized test scores, and school rankings—are problematized and critically examined. To practice student-centered ways of teaching, all aspects of teaching and learning in schools are re-examined, and redirected to the students themselves. Emphasis is placed on critical thinking, learning skills, and deep social awareness as well as the contextualization and problematization of facts and figures—recognizing that knowledge is culturally shaped (Grant & Sleeter, 1990). Multicultural teaching provides all students with the opportunity to reach their full potential as learners, as it is universally designed and inclusive.

Multicultural curriculum. "A multicultural curriculum rests on two ideals: (a) equal opportunity and (b) cultural pluralism" (Grant, 2008, p. 895). A multicultural curriculum necessitates all subjects to be considered from multiple perspectives, to improve accuracy and completeness (De Gaetano et al., 1998; Ladson-Billings, 1994). An "inclusive curriculum" means both paying close attention to multiple ways of representing and providing multiple ways of acting and expressing in the classroom. It also means including the voices of the students in the classroom, their families, and communities (Souto-Manning, 2013), focusing on the what, how, and why of learning within the context of families, communities, and societies. Thus, educational materials should be inclusive of diverse voices and perspectives (Bishop, 2007; Derman-Sparks & Ramsey, 2011). As part of a multicultural curriculum, teachers *and* students are encouraged to think critically about materials and media and consider questions such as: Whose voices are they hearing or not hearing? Why did that company produce that film? Who wrote this book? What is the bias this author brought to her or his writing? The idea of published media sanctioning "real" and "worthy" knowledge is thus deconstructed.

The Transformation of Society

Ultimately, the goal of multicultural education is to contribute to the positive transformation of society and to the negotiation of social justice and equity. This stands to reason, as the transformation of schools necessarily transforms a society that puts so much stock in educational attainment, academic degrees, and test scores. In fact, it is this competitive stance that is so prevalent in the United States (and increasingly the world, with the so-called "help" of the U.S.) that multicultural teaching aims to challenge, unsettle, problematize, expose, and critique (Souto-Manning, 2013).

By imposing standards that do not take into account the contextual while ignoring practices such as critical thinking and problem solving, schools employ so-called traditional (read: normative) curriculum in spite of the fact that they serve more and more diverse students. Employing traditional curricula and ways of teaching, schools continually provide privilege to the privileged and on-going struggle to the struggling with very little hope of transformation. Thus, those who have historically succeeded in our schools (mostly White children living in economically-comfortable households) continue to succeed, and those who have been failed by schools continue to be pushed out—children of color and/or low-income families (Derman-Sparks & Ramsey, 2011; Goodwin & Genor, 2008). "Informal" tracking, standardized testing, discrepancies in the quality of schools within and across regions, and other inequitable practices remain. These have historically shaped schooling—even before school integration—and continue to do so today.

We propose that to promote change and create equitable learning communities, early childhood educators must engage in multicultural teaching and learning principles both inside and out of the classroom (Nieto, 2003; Souto-Manning, 2013). We cannot equate the perception that the vast majority of schools are "well-intentioned" with the assumption that schools are immune to the inequity of society. They are not.

Thus, teacher educators are charged with the responsibility of preparing teachers who are equipped with the knowledge, skills, and dispositions to engage in transformative multicultural teaching practices. In order to reconceptualize early childhood teacher education, it is imperative to interrogate where the field has been with respect to attending to the diversities of our young children and how we have prepared teachers to work with children from diverse racial, cultural, and linguistic backgrounds.

Considering the History of Early Childhood Education in the United States

The history of early childhood education in the United States is built upon two foundational assumptions:

> (1) early learning experiences, and the environments in which they occur, strongly influence children's capacities to become productive learners and citizens in schools and society—and some environments are considered to be better than others (e.g., wealthier families and English-speaking families are seen as superior); and
>
> (2) children's homes and families are the primary physical and interactional settings for care and education, yet not all families are considered to be well-suited to raise America's future citizens.
>
> (Goodwin et al., 2008)

These assumptions have shaped the trajectory of early childhood education and the ways in which the field has attended to the care and education of young children. As with any assumption, these are cultural and normative, built-on values associated with White Anglo-Saxon Protestant values (Bloch, 1987; Goodwin et al., 2008), the values of power or, as Delpit (1996) posits, the values of those who have power.

According to researchers (Bloch, 1987; Goodwin et al., 2008), the early childhood years are critical years. The care and educational experiences of the early years are believed to lay the foundation for the future of a child and therefore, of his/her family, community, and ultimately, the welfare of the nation. Thus, early education and care outside of the home are justified under the pretense of building national security and prosperity—considering some families to be better than others. This reasoning can be traced back to Plato who advocated for education for the early years (Conklin & Lee, 2010, p. 240) and raised the notion that not all families were well suited to raise future citizens (Canella, 1997), an ethnocentric, exclusionist, and deficit-ridden perspective (Goodwin et al., 2008). This rationale still exists today, as evidenced by the underlying argument of President Obama's Early Learning Initiative (White House, Office of the Press Secretary, 2013).

Inherent in these assumptions is that families that have low/no-income and minoritized racial, cultural, and linguistic backgrounds are not able to provide the early experiences that are required for successful participation in society as adults. These assumptions reflect the three dominant paradigms of diversity (Carter & Goodwin, 1994) that have justified and shaped the types of early care and education afforded to children and families from diverse backgrounds—racial inferiority, cultural deficiency, and cultural difference. Furthermore, they have ultimately led to a two-tiered system of early childhood care and education that is divided along the intersecting lines of race, culture, linguistic background, and socioeconomic status (Wright, 2011).

The racial inferiority paradigm suggests that children and families who are not White are racially and culturally inferior. Given this belief, although Native Americans had their own system of early education, English colonists established schools for them that focused on erasure of their language and culture. In the 1600s and 1700s, missionaries attempted to convert them to Christianity. The Puritans created "praying towns" for Native Americans and printed the Bible and related texts in their native languages (Wright, 2011). Lascarides and Hinitz (2000) wrote that in 1819 Congress passed an act that provided a "civilization fund" to teach Native Americans agriculture, trade work, and basic reading, writing, and arithmetic. In the 19th century, tribal school systems and governments were shut down and reservation schools were opened. These schools were focused on assimilating children into society by erasing children's names, languages and cultures and forcing them to speak only in English.

The racial inferiority paradigm is also evident in the 18th and early 19th century Sunday Schools, infant schools, and nursery schools that focused on the moral development and "spiritual salvation" of non-White children (Bloch, 1987) who, by virtue of their racial background and culture, were assumed to have an inferior upbringing and value system. Similarly, the day nurseries, modeled after the French crèches and founded on a missionary stance, provided care and education for impoverished and migrant workers. Serving primarily African Americans, these day nurseries focused on child care, hygiene, and nutrition (Nourot, 2004). With the first great immigration wave toward the end of the 19th century, European immigrants, who at the time were not considered to be the dominant majority and thus were seen as racially and culturally inferior, were provided with schools that focused on their moral and character development.

During the 1960s, the War on Poverty established a paradigmatic shift in understandings of racial and cultural diversity. Sociologists furthered the idea that the home environments and cultures of Native Americans, African Americans, and immigrants could negatively impact a child and thus, it was the responsibility of schools to provide early care and education that would counter the deprivation of children's home culture (Carter & Goodwin, 1994). While White children from middle- and upper-income families had access to kindergartens and schools that valued play and learning, children of color, immigrant children, and poor children only had access to nursery schools and free kindergartens that valued assimilation and provided children with the proper care that was believed to be absent at home. During the 1960s researchers also purported that proper and early intervention was crucial to children from "disadvantaged" backgrounds so that they would not begin elementary school with the deficits afforded by their home environments and backgrounds (Goodwin, Cheruvu, & Genishi, 2008).

Consequently, Head Start was born out of the Economic Opportunity Act of 1964. The program was established to provide equal opportunity in schooling and in later life. Inherent in the sweeping reforms aimed to assist the poor in the 1960s was the belief that the poor and people of color are racially and culturally inferior and deficient, therefore they were at a disadvantage; it was the duty of the welfare state to provide opportunities that could counter and "fix" the disadvantages associated with their home cultures and languages (Goodwin et al., 2008).

The cultural difference paradigm emerged in the mid-20th century from the work of social researchers who argued that the values, beliefs, and norms of people of color were culturally specific and therefore not "deviant" or "deficient" but rather different from White, middle-class norms. During this time, interest in multicultural education and culturally responsive teaching was garnered in the field of education, although it is important to note that the roots of both were established much earlier. Scholars purported that schools had marginalized children of minoritized racial, cultural, and linguistic backgrounds by focusing on their presumed deficiencies rather than their differences. There was also a movement to acknowledge and represent the cultures of children of color in schools, as it served to improve their educational experiences and outcomes. As suggested by Goodwin and colleagues (2008), with this paradigmatic shift, there have been changes made to curricula and the services provided to children that reflect cultural sensitivity and multi- vs. monoculturalism.

Despite these paradigmatic shifts, within the cultural difference paradigm the assumptions of the inferiority and deficiency paradigms still linger (Carter & Goodwin, 1994). Thus, while "each paradigm might be associated more with one era over another" (Goodwin et al., 2008, p. 5), all three simultaneously exist, shaping early childhood educational policies, institutional structures, and practices, thereby both advancing and hindering equitable experiences and opportunities for young children.

In early childhood education one of the most pertinent ways that all three paradigms of diversity simultaneously exist is in the field's adoption and application of child developmental theories. The adoption of and alignment with child development theories can be traced to the professionalization of early childhood teachers. As teacher education shifted from "teacher institutions to normal schools to universities and their laboratory schools, teachers and teacher educators incorporated the latest scientific discourses from the psychological, educational, health, and social sciences in their work and both groups gained status as scientific professionals" (Bloch & Popkewitz, 2005, p. 22). As such, dominant perspectives in early childhood education are deeply rooted in child development theories.

The dominant developmental perspectives adopted by the field reflect the three grand theories of Piaget, psychoanalysis, and learning theory, which describe development as universal across time and space (Lee, 2010). Although developmental science has moved to consider the systems and contexts in which children learn over time, the field of early childhood education holds steadfast to universalistic child developmental theories (Lee, 2010). These developmental theories are grounded in modernist thought that favors dichotomous and linear ways of observing and understanding children. The developmental knowledge base rests on research that has been conducted on White, middle-class children, and thus does not account for the ways that growth is mediated across multiple cultures or social classes (Lubeck, 1994). Rather, these developmental theories dictate a universal Eurocentric, middle-class norm for development that judges any different developmental trajectory as deviant. Thus, children whose development is nurtured within the contexts of non-Eurocentric cultures and lower socioeconomic contexts are deemed to be developmentally abnormal.

Even more troublesome is that universalistic, Eurocentric models of child development have provided the foundation for the field's discourse on developmentally appropriate practice (DAP; Copple & Bredekamp, 2009; Mallory & New, 1994). Early childhood curricula and teaching practices are deemed to be of quality provided they meet the standards of DAP (Charlesworth, 1998). Scholars in the field of early childhood education have critiqued the discourse on developmentally appropriate practice due to its over-reliance on child development theories that marginalizes, and at times pathologizes, the developmental trajectory of children of color and children from lower income families. Many have argued that by using monocultural and hierarchical developmentally appropriate practice guidelines, teachers have regulated children's learning to fit what is considered to be normal (Williams, 1994) and thus, have overlooked children's agency in their own learning (Silin, 1995).

On Early Childhood Teacher Education

The preparation of early childhood professionals has primarily involved "learning about child developmental theories and research and the curricula and teaching practices that are informed by this knowledge" (Bredekamp cited in Ryan & Grieshaber, 2005, p. 34). Early childhood teacher educators who recognize the problems with child development theories and developmentally appropriate practice (DAP), and who have sought to prepare teachers from a postmodern perspective, have incorporated a broader view of the ways children learn and of teacher-generated knowledges and theories. Such teacher educators have facilitated an understanding of early childhood education as it has been shaped through social, historical, philosophical, and political contexts. While incorporating different knowledges has been an important step in preparing teachers to teach children from diverse backgrounds and in multiple contexts, this additive approach has still centered on normative child development theory (Isenberg, 2000). Thus, despite the efforts to expand the Eurocentric, monocultural knowledge base of early childhood education to include multiple knowledges, values, and ways of teaching and learning, nothing has really changed. A closer look at how teacher education has attended to issues of diversity sheds light on the resistance toward multiplicity. Issues of diversity and multicultural education have been part of the teacher education landscape since the 1970s. "Diversity" and "multicultural education" became part of the rhetoric of teacher education over forty years ago, as evidenced by the American Association of Colleges for Teacher Education (AACTE) 1973 Commission on Multicultural Education and their statement on multicultural education, *No One Model American*. In this statement cultural pluralism was said to be a valuable resource that should be preserved and extended in schools as well as in the preparation of teachers. Following AACTE's statement on diversity, the National Council for the Accreditation of Teacher Education (NCATE) introduced a multicultural education standard in 1979 (Nieto, 2000). Later, in the 1980s, the multicultural education standard was replaced with the diversity standard and multicultural education was implicitly alluded to in other standards (Nieto, 2000). NCATE's diversity standard puts emphasis on preparing teachers to teach "all children." The National Association for the Education of Young Children (NAEYC) does not have a licensure standard that states that teachers need preparation to work with diverse children (Ryan & Lobman, 2008). Instead, NAEYC merely suggests in its guidelines for initial licensure that teachers should be able to support and empower children from diverse backgrounds by creating connections between their home cultures and languages.

Multicultural teacher educators have critiqued these standards and reports as being vague (Vavrus, 2002; 2010), thereby allowing the field of teacher education "to deal with the demographic statistics of diversity without grappling with the sociopolitical dimensions" (Grant & Gibson, 2011, p. 44). This vagueness has resulted in peripheral and superficial commitments to and implementation of multicultural education initiatives in teacher education in which programs have loosely addressed or mentioned diversity. Thus, although the rhetoric of multicultural education and diversity has been present in teacher education for over four decades, most scholars conclude that nothing has really changed with respect to how teachers are prepared to engage in equitable and successful teaching practices with diverse learners (Gorski, 2009; Ladson-Billings, 2005; Sleeter & McLaren, 1995).

In early childhood teacher education, most programs do not have courses that address issues of diversity or multicultural education (Early & Winton, 2001; Ryan & Lobman, 2008). In fact, Lim, Maxwell, Able-Boone, and Zimmer (2009) pointed out that the presence of such courses in the field of early childhood education is more dependent on contextual factors, most notably the presence of teacher educators of color. To date, those programs, which attend to multicultural education, have done so as isolated topics in courses, stand-alone workshops, or specific courses devoted to "diversity" or "multicultural education," rather than with an integrated approach in which multicultural education permeates coursework, field experiences, and other programmatic structures and processes (Cochran-Smith, 2003; Nieto, 2000; Sleeter, 2001).

Amidst the broad array of definitions and commitments to multiculturalism and diversity, there still remains an undercurrent of racial inferiority and cultural deficit paradigms in teacher education practice and theory (Gorski, 2009; Ladson-Billings, 2005; Sleeter & McLaren, 1995). Preservice teachers still hear about the dangers and challenges of teaching students in urban areas, and are advised about the signs (read: symptoms) of those who are "at-risk": children of single parents and eligible for free and/or reduced lunch. This single story is dangerous (Adichie, 2009) and obscures the promise, resilience, creativity, and strengths that students' racial, cultural, and linguistic backgrounds, experiences, and histories afford them (Goodwin et al., 2008; Ladson-Billings, 2005). Although having the "veneer of diversity," teacher education programs have had "limited success in promulgating diversity as a value-added factor" (Ladson-Billings, 2005, p. 231). Rather, diversity is often positioned as a "challenge" or "problem" that needs to be addressed (Goodwin et al., 2008).

Necessary Conceptual Shifts

Given the history of the field with respect to diversity and, the influence of child development theories on teacher education, we argue that the preparation of early childhood educators to engage in transformative multicultural education necessitates conceptual shifts.

Reconceptualizing Diversities

We argue that there is a need for a paradigmatic shift in how we conceptualize diversity. Although the cultural difference paradigm moves beyond racial and cultural ideologies of inferiority and deficiency, it positions the racial, cultural, and linguistic backgrounds of minoritized populations as "Other." That is, it still privileges White, middle class, monolingual ways of being and ways of thinking as the norm. Rather, we argue that the norm should not privilege any single worldview but rather multiple worldviews. As such, we conceptualize diversity as part of the natural order and embrace diversity as the norm (Genishi & Dyson, 2009).

The vision of multicultural education as transformative, as described earlier in the chapter, is grounded in this conception of diversity. Thus, we argue that multicultural education is not merely something that early childhood educators need to practice in response to an increasingly diverse population of children. Rather, teaching multiculturally is a stance that educators must bring to their classrooms in order to *respond to* and *sustain* the inherent diversities that exist in society. Engaging in multicultural teaching practices from this conception of diversity means that teachers not only engage in culturally responsive teaching (Gay, 2000) practices that build upon children's funds of knowledge, but also engage in culturally sustaining practices that "perpetuate and foster . . . cultural pluralism as part of the democratic project of schooling" (Paris, 2012, p. 93).

In the remainder of the chapter we discuss the necessary conceptual shifts in early childhood teacher education that are needed to prepare early childhood teachers to engage in transformative multicultural education. We conclude with an invitation to *re-vision* early childhood teacher education by describing a few promising practices in contemporary early childhood teacher education.

Reframing Child Development Theories

The critiques of child development theories and their framing of developmentally appropriate practice, as described earlier, point toward the need for developmentally appropriate practices that are multiculturally sustaining. The critique is "not whether child development is important but the ways it is embedded into a system of reason that shapes and fashions how educators 'see,' think, talk, and act toward teaching children, and schooling" (Bloch & Popkewitz, 2000, p. 7). Similarly, with respect to DAP, as Mallory and New (1994) suggested, there is a need to ask who determines what is developmentally appropriate and on what and whose knowledge, values, and goals it is based.

Ryan and Grieshaber (2005) posited that teacher educators should bring a postmodern orientation to child development and developmental perspectives in early childhood education. Such an orientation requires teacher educators to engage students in thinking about the power and subjectivity of child development theories. In doing so, students are able to develop "a set of analytic tools (something like a theoretical toolbox) that they can use to view practices from different perspectives, providing alternative ways of seeing, understanding, and acting on the same situation" (Ryan & Grieshaber, 2005, p. 43). In turn, early childhood teacher educators can move toward acknowledging that there are multiple developmentally appropriate *practices,* which are culturally responsive and situated, thus privileging cultural pluralism rather than a normative perspective with respect to developmental theories.

Students and Teachers as Cultural Beings

The first step toward change is the critical (meta)awareness of and reflection on one's cultural identity—as teachers and as children who are distinct members of classroom communities (Freire, 1970; Souto-Manning, 2010b; Souto-Manning, 2011a). While histories shape individuals through questioning and problematizing, and by enacting change, individuals can (re)shape their own histories as they consider their past, live the present, and author their futures. While reconceptualizing our stances toward diversities is complex, time consuming, and a long-term project involving critical and often political perspectives about self (Oakes & Lipton, 1999; Goodwin & Genor, 2008), in order to practice multicultural education, early childhood teacher educators need to engage in reflection on their stances as an ongoing part of their personal and professional lives.

Examining privileges and identities. Derman-Sparks and Edwards (2010) proposed that anti-bias education goals must foster, for all children, self-awareness, confidence, family pride, and positive social identities; comfort and joy with human diversity; accurate language for human differences; deep, caring human connections; recognition of fairness; language to describe unfairness; understanding that unfairness hurts; and the empowerment and skills to act against prejudice and/or discrimination—collectively or individually. These goals apply to teachers and teacher educators as well (Souto-Manning, 2013). After all, a prerequisite to seeing all students (children and/or teachers of children) as worthy human beings is to acknowledge that everyone is a cultural being who sees the world contextually and culturally, and to move toward troubling one's own culturally-situated beliefs and assumptions. The identities early childhood teacher educators occupy—in terms of race, gender, class, sexuality, or ability—position them in certain ways, thus affording them certain privileges or conferring deficit-ridden stereotypes. In such a process, it is important to consider questions such as:

- What cultural threads make up the fabric of who I am? What aspects of my identity afford me privileges?
- What is the racial and linguistic background of those who surround me in school/at work? Why?
- What assumptions do outsiders associate with me? What do these assumptions tell me about the privileges and oppressions I experience?
- Do I see and actively question inequities that exist in the (pre)schools where I work? If not, why?

These are simple, yet important questions to consider (Souto-Manning, 2013).

Saluja, Early, and Clifford (2002) documented that most (78%) early childhood educators are White females. For the great majority of early childhood educators, the first step is to recognize that White persons are cultural beings too. Even though larger institutional discourses perpetuate the idea of White being merely normal (Souto-Manning, 2013), this is a very problematic construct. Unless the idea of *White = Normal* is challenged, we will continue imposing Whiteness as the standard against which all others are scaled and rated. It is imperative to recognize "the ideological mechanisms that shape and maintain our racist order" (Bartolomé & Macedo, 1997, p. 223). To do so, it is essential to become critically (meta)aware of and to problematize (Freire, 1970) society's "deeply rooted assumptions that schools are inherently fair, that children's capacities to learn are predetermined and unalterable, and that meritocratic competition is the route to equal educational opportunity" (Goodwin & Genor, 2008, p. 201). We must acknowledge and trouble pervasive inequities as

> too many children of color, poor children, or children who are new immigrants continue to experience troubled and limiting school lives. As a society, we have come to accept too easily as "business as usual" what should stand out as stark aberrations and deep contradictions: race and socioeconomic status as "predictors" of poor school performance; gifted classrooms that exclude most children of color; "minorities" and the poor always doing less well on standardized tests than those in the white middle class; children of color disproportionately labeled as behavior problems and assigned to special education; and schools serving culturally and linguistically diverse children invariably being resource poor.
>
> *(Goodwin & Genor, 2008, pp. 214–215)*

There is a need to interrupt this racist way of seeing the world, this ideology of inequity. To engage in multicultural pedagogy, early childhood educators must constantly practice self-reflection and analysis so that they can come to more clearly identify existing inequities and injustices in (pre)schools and classrooms today. While this is not easy work, it is necessary, as the vast majority of today's teachers are White females who come from economically-comfortable households, and have monolingual backgrounds (Cochran-Smith, 2004) while by the next U.S. Census children of color will comprise the majority of students in American early educational settings (Frey, 2011).

Promising Practices

It is imperative to recognize that in order to engage in multicultural pedagogy one's cultural location has to become a site of "interruption," with lenses utilized to critically examine how one's lived cultural experiences mediate his/her ways of knowing the world, the ways that schools structure inequality, and the ways in which one can make a firm and deliberate commitment to multicultural education, social justice, and social change. To this end, Goodwin and Genor (2008) highlighted the importance of such critical reflection as they discussed the possibilities of autobiographical analysis. The authors invited preservice teachers to write their autobiographies in which they explored their racial, cultural, and social locations and how these shaped their ideas about education and schooling. They engaged in this autobiographical analysis in their preservice programs, documenting how their understanding of themselves changed over time, as well as their ideas about teaching children from diverse backgrounds. In doing so, preservice teachers disrupted their ideologies and comfort zones.

Extending the "interruption" of one's racial and cultural location, Souto-Manning (2011b) discussed her use of Boalian theatre games as a tool for interrogating privilege and positionality with preservice teachers. By playing these games in class followed by problem-posing dialogue, her preservice teachers were able to "unveil, unsettle, and start to question White privilege" (Souto-Manning, 2011b,

p. 999) and the myth of meritocracy. Boalian theater games served as an entry point to discussions that are often avoided in teacher education programs. Souto-Manning (2011b) described how playing the games and debriefing via anonymous written reflections followed by problem-posing dialogue helped preservice teachers recognize and understand the ways their positionalities in society privileged them.

As preservice teachers engage in critical reflections of their worldviews and racial, cultural, and social locations, they must also learn about the myriad of ways that children develop across space, time, and multiple cultures. Ryan and Grieshaber (2005) described how they have sought to overturn the traditional developmental discourse in which early childhood education is deeply rooted. Calling for postmodern teacher education practices that consider the political and sociocultural nature of child development knowledge, the authors utilized three strategies in their coursework to disrupt universalistic, Eurocentric perspectives about child development and DAP. Ryan and Grieshaber (2005) suggested that by (1) situating knowledge as historically and culturally bound; (2) providing spaces for multiplicity of interpretations of observations about children, teachers, and classroom practices; and (3) engaging with images that deconstruct dominant societal views of early childhood education settings, children, teachers, and preservice teachers can develop the analytical tools needed to critically consume and produce knowledge related to children's learning and development.

Just as Ryan and Greishaber (2005) argued for critically examining and repositioning the knowledges that inform the field of early childhood education, Souto-Manning and Price-Dennis (2012) described the benefit of using popular culture media texts with preservice teachers as a tool in preparing them to engage in multicultural practices. The authors described how they utilized a popular culture media text—a song from a children's animated movie that used elements of African American Language (AAL)—with preservice teachers to uncover the marginalization of AAL in schools and society. Additionally, the media text served as a vehicle to deconstruct teacher-student binaries that preservice teachers held onto from their own schooling experiences. As such, preservice teachers were able to read and reposition the text in their field experiences. The authors utilized critical pedagogies in bringing critical media literacy to the teacher education course. Souto-Manning and Price-Dennis (2012) suggested that "engaging preservice teachers in critical media literacy through critical pedagogy allows them to (a) experience how texts can be sites of exclusion, (b) collectively raise questions about how this further marginalizes groups in our society, and (c) begin designing ways to contest these manifestations" (p. 307).

These promising practices bring to life the necessary conceptual shifts required for engaging in multiculturally responsive early childhood teacher education. Early childhood teacher educators must carefully and critically consider ways to revision their programs and practices to:

- reconceptualize diversities, placing them front and center and coming to regard cultural pluralism as central to early childhood teaching and teacher education;
- reframe child development knowledge, recognizing how development is "biologically cultural" (Rogoff, 2003, p. 34); and
- reposition students and teachers as cultural beings.

If early childhood teacher educators are truly committed to fostering multicultural practices, they must embrace multiculturally sustaining early childhood pedagogies.

References

Adichie, C. N. (2009). *The danger of a single story.* TED Talk. Retrieved from http://www.ted.com/talks/chimamanda_adichie_the_danger_of_a _single_story.html

American Association of Colleges for Teacher Education. (1973). *No one model American.* Washington, DC: Author.

Banks, J. (1994). Transforming the mainstream curriculum. *Educational Leadership*, 51(8), 4–8.

Banks, J. (2004). Multicultural education: Historical development, dimensions, and practice. In J. A. Banks & C. A. Banks (Eds.), *Handbook of research on multicultural education* (2nd ed.) (pp. 3–29). San Francisco, CA: Jossey Bass.

Banks, J. (2007). Series foreword. In C. D. Lee. *Culture, literacy, and learning: Taking bloom in the midst of the whirlwind* (pp. xi-xv). New York: Teachers College Press.

Banks, J. (Ed.). (2009). *The Routledge international companion to multicultural education*. New York: Routledge.

Banks, J., & McGee Banks, C. (Eds.). (1995). *Handbook of research on multicultural education* (2nd ed.). San Francisco, CA: Jossey Bass.

Banks, J., & McGee Banks, C. (Eds.). (2004). *Multicultural education: Issues and perspectives* (5th ed.). Hoboken, NJ: John Wiley.

Bartolomé, L., & Macedo, D. (1997). Dancing with bigotry: The poisoning of racial and ethnic identities. *Harvard Educational Review, 67*(2), 222–244.

Bishop, R. S. (2007). *Free within ourselves: The development of African American children's literature*. Portsmouth, NH: Heinemann.

Bloch, M. (1987). Becoming scientific and professional: An historical perspective on the aims and effects of early education. In T. Popkewitz (Ed.), *The formation of school subjects: The struggle for creating an American institution* (pp. 25–62). New York: Falmer Press.

Bloch, M., & Popkewitz, T. (2000). Constructing the parent, teacher, and child: Discourses of development. In L. D. Soto (Ed.), *The politics of early childhood education* (pp. 7–32). New York: Peter Lang.

Canella, G. (1997). *Deconstructing early childhood education: Social justice and revolution*. New York: Peter Lang.

Carter, R., & Goodwin, A. L. (1994). Racial identity and education. *Review of Research in Education, 20*, 291–336.

Charlesworth, R. (1998). Developmentally appropriate practice is for everyone. *Childhood Education, 74*, 274–282.

Cochran-Smith, M. (2003). Learning and unlearning: The education of teacher educators. *Teaching and Teacher Education, 19*(1), 5–28.

Cochran-Smith, M. (2004). *Walking the road: Race, diversity, and social justice in teacher education*. New York: Teachers College Press.

Conklin, H. G., & Lee, K. (2010). Walking the borderlands. In K. Lee & M. D. Vagle (Eds.), *Developmentalism in early childhood and middle grades education: Critical conversations of readiness and responsiveness* (pp. 233–254). New York: Palgrave Macmillan.

Copple, C., & Bredekamp, S. (Eds.). (2009). *Developmentally appropriate practice in early childhood programs serving children from birth through age 8* (3rd ed.). Washington, DC: NAEYC.

De Gaetano, Y., Williams, L. R., & Volk, D. (1998). *Kaleidoscope: A multicultural approach for the primary classroom*. Upper Saddle River, NJ: Merrill Prentice Hall.

Delpit, L. (1996). *Other people's children: Cultural conflict in the classroom*. New York: New Press.

Derman-Sparks, L., & Edwards, J. (2010). *Anti-bias education for young children and ourselves*. Washington, DC: National Association for the Education of Young Children.

Derman-Sparks, L., & Ramsey, P. (2006). *What if all the kids are white? Anti-bias multicultural education with young children and families*. New York: Teachers College Press.

Derman-Sparks, L., & Ramsey, P. (2011). *What if all the kids are white? Anti-bias multicultural education with young children and families* (2nd ed.). New York: Teachers College Press.

Early, D. M., & Winton, P. J. (2001). Preparing the workforce: Early childhood teacher preparation at 2- and 4-year institutions of higher education. *Early Childhood Research Quarterly, 16*, 285–306.

Freire, P. (1970). *Pedagogy of the oppressed*. New York: Continuum.

Freire, P. (1998). *Teachers as cultural workers: Letters to those who dare teach*. Boulder, CO: Westview Press.

Frey, W. H. (2011). *The new metro minority map: Regional shifts in Hispanics, Asians, and Blacks from census 2010*. Washington, DC: Brookings Institution.

Garmon, M. A. (1996, April). *Missed messages: How prospective teachers racial attitudes mediate what they learn about diversity*. Paper presented at the annual meeting of the American Educational Research Association, New York.

Gay, G. (1994). *At the essence of learning: Multicultural education*. West Lafayette, IN: Kappa Delta Pi.

Gay, G. (2000). *Culturally responsive teaching: Theory, research, and practice*. New York: Teachers College Press.

Gay, G. (2004). The importance of multicultural education. In D. Flinders & S. Thornton (Eds.), The curriculum studies reader (2nd ed.) (pp. 315–321). New York: RoutledgeFalmer.

Genishi, C., & Dyson, A. H. (2009). *Children, language, and literacy: Diverse learners in diverse times*. New York: Teachers College Press and Washington, DC: NAEYC.

Goodwin, A. L., Cheruvu, R., & Genishi, C. (2008). Responding to multiple diversities in early childhood education. In C. Genishi & A. L. Goodwin (Eds.), *Diversities in early childhood education: Rethinking and doing* (pp. 3–10). New York: Routledge.

Goodwin, A. L., & Genor, M. (2008). Disrupting the taken-for-granted: Autobiographical analysis in preservice teacher education. In C. Genishi & A. L. Goodwin (Eds.), *Diversities in early childhood education: Rethinking and doing* (pp. 201–218). New York: Teachers College Press.

Gorski, P. (2009). What we're teaching teachers: An analysis of multicultural teacher education coursework syllabi. Journal of Teaching and Teacher Education, 25(2), 309–318.

Gorski, P. (2010). *The challenge of defining multicultural education.* Retrieved from http://www.edchange.org/multicultural/

Grant, C. (2008). An essay on searching for curriculum and pedagogy for African American students: Highlighted remarks regarding the role of gender. *American Behavioral Scientist, 51*, 885–906.

Grant, C., & Gibson, M. (2011). Diversity and teacher education: A historical perspective on research and policy. In A. F. Ball & C. A. Tyson (Eds.), *Studying diversity in teacher education* (pp. 19–61). New York: Rowman & Littlefield.

Grant, C., & Sleeter, C. (1990). *After the school bell rings* (2nd ed.). Philadelphia, PA: Falmer.

Isenberg, J. P. (2000). The state of the art in early childhood professional preparation. In National Institute on Early Childhood Development and Education, U.S. Department of Education (Eds.), *New teachers for a new century: The future of early childhood teacher preparation* (pp. 15–52). Washington, DC: The National Institute on Early Childhood Development and Education, U.S. Department of Education.

Ladson-Billings, G. (1994). *The dreamkeepers: Successful teachers of African American children.* San Francisco, CA: Jossey-Bass.

Ladson-Billings, G. (2005). Is the team all right? Diversity and teacher education. *Journal of Teacher Education, 56*(3), 229–234.

Laman, T. T., Miller, E. T., & López-Robertson, J. (2012). Noticing and naming as social practice: Examining the relevance of a contextualized field-based literacy course. *Journal of Early Childhood Teacher Education, 33*(1), 3–18.

Lascarides, V. C., & Hinitz, B. F. (2000). *History of early childhood education.* New York: Falmer Press.

Lee, K. (2010). Who is normal? Who is abnormal? Rethinking child development from a cultural psychological perspective. In K. Lee & M. D. Vagle (Eds.), *Developmentalism in early childhood and middle grades education: Critical conversations on readiness and responsiveness.* New York: Palgrave Macmillan.

Lim, C-I., Maxwell, K. L., Able-Boone, H., & Zimmer, C. R. (2009). Cultural and linguistic diversity in early childhood teacher preparation: The impact of contextual characteristics on coursework and practica. *Early Childhood Research Quarterly, 24*, 64–76.

Lubeck, S. (1994). The politics of developmentally appropriate practice: Exploring issues of culture, class and curriculum. In B. L. Mallory & R. S. New (Eds.), *Diversity and developmentally appropriate practices: Challenges for early childhood curriculum* (pp. 17–43). New York: Teachers College Press.

Mallory, B. L., & New, R. S. (Eds.). (1994). *Diversity and developmentally appropriate practices: Challenges for early childhood education.* New York: Teachers College Press.

McCarty, T. (2004). Brown plus 50 and beyond: Anthropology and the ongoing challenge of the "great divide." *Anthropology and Education Quarterly, 35*(1), 1–9.

Moultry, M. (1988). Senior education students' attitudes about multicultural education. In C. Heid (Ed.), *Multicultural education: Knowledge and perceptions.* Bloomington, IN: Indiana University Press.

Nieto, S. (1999). *The light in their eyes: Creating multicultural learning communities.* New York: Teachers College Press.

Nieto, S. (2000). Placing equity front and center: Some thoughts on transforming teacher education for a new century. *Journal of Teacher Education, 51*(3), 180–187.

Nieto, S. (2002). *Language, culture, and teaching: Critical perspectives for a new century.* Mahwah, NJ: Lawrence Erlbaum Associates.

Nieto, S. (2003). *What keeps teachers going?* New York: Teachers College Press.

Nieto, S. (2010). *Language, culture, and teaching: Critical perspectives* (2nd ed.). New York: Routledge.

Nourot, P. (2004). Historical perspectives on early childhood education. In J. Roopnarine & J. E. Johnson (Eds.), *Approaches to early childhood education* (4th ed.). Columbus, OH: Prentice Hall.

Oakes, J., & Lipton, M. (1999). *Teaching to change the world.* Boston, MA: McGraw-Hill.

Paris, D. (2012). Culturally sustaining pedagogy: A much needed change in stance, terminology and practice. *Educational Researcher, 41*(3), 93–97.

Ramsey, P. G., & Williams, L. (Eds). (2003). *Multicultural education: A sourcebook.* New York: Routledge.

Ray, A., & Bowman, B. (2003). *Learning multi-cultural competence: Developing early childhood practitioners' effectiveness in working with children from culturally diverse communities.* Chicago, IL: Center for Race, Class, and Culture in Early Childhood, Erikson Institute.

Rogoff, B. (2003). *The cultural nature of human development.* Oxford, UK: Oxford University Press.

Ryan, S., & Grieshaber, S. (2005). Shifting from developmental to postmodern practices in early childhood education. *Journal of Teacher Education, 5*(1), 34–45.

Ryan, S., & Lobman, C. (2008). Catching up with globalization: One state's experience of reforming teacher education in the 21st century. In C. Genishi & A. L. Goodwin (Eds.), *Diversities in early childhood education: Rethinking and doing* (pp. 167–182). New York: Routledge.

Saluja, G., Early, D. M., & Clifford, R. M. (2002). Demographic characteristics of early childhood teachers and structural elements of early care and education in the United States. *Early Childhood Research and Practice, 4*(1). Retrieved from http://ecrp.uiuc.edu/v4n1/saluja.html

Silin, J. (1995). *Sex, death and the education of our children: Our passion for ignorance in the age of AIDS.* New York: Teachers College Press.

Sleeter, C. E. (1996). *Multicultural education as social activism.* Albany, NY: State University of New York Press.

Sleeter, C. E. (2001). Preparing teachers for culturally diverse schools: Research and the overwhelming presence of whiteness. *Journal of Teacher Education, 52*(2), 94–106.

Sleeter, C. E., & McLaren, P. (Eds.) (1995). *Multicultural education and critical pedagogy: The politics of difference.* Albany, NY: State University of New York Press.

Souto-Manning, M. (2010a). Challenging ethnocentric literacy practices: (Re)Positioning home literacies in a Head Start classroom. *Research in the Teaching of English, 45*(2), 150–178.

Souto-Manning, M. (2010b). *Freire, teaching, and learning: Culture circles across contexts.* New York: Peter Lang.

Souto-Manning, M. (2011a). A different kind of teaching: Culture circles as professional development. In V. Kinloch (Ed.), *Urban literacies: Critical perspectives on language, learning, and community* (pp. 95–110). New York: Teachers College Press.

Souto-Manning, M. (2011b). Playing with power and privilege: Theatre games in teacher education. *Teaching and Teacher Education, 27*(6), 997–1007.

Souto-Manning, M. (2013). *Multicultural teaching in the early childhood classroom: Approaches, strategies, and tools (preschool-2nd grade).* New York: Teachers College Press and Washington, DC: Association for Childhood Education International (ACEI).

Souto-Manning, M. (in press). Making a stink about the "ideal" classroom: Theorizing and storying conflict in early childhood education. *Urban Education.*

Souto-Manning, M., & Price-Dennis, D. (2012). Critically redefining and repositioning media texts in early childhood teacher education: What if? And why? *Journal of Early Childhood Teacher Education, 33*(4), 304–321.

Valli, L., & Rennert-Ariev, P. L. (2000). Identifying consensus in teacher education reform documents: A proposed framework and action implications. *Journal of Teacher Education, 51*(1), 5–17.

Vavrus, M. (2002). *Transforming the multicultural education of teachers: Theory, research, and practice.* New York: Teachers College Press.

Vavrus, M. (2010). Critical multiculturalism and higher education: Resistance and possibilities in teacher education. In S. May & C. E. Sleeter (Eds.), *Critical multiculturalism: Theory and praxis* (pp. 19–32). New York: Routledge.

Williams, L. R. (1994). Developmentally appropriate practice and cultural values: A case in point. In B. L. Mallory & R. S. New (Eds.), *Diversity and developmentally appropriate practices: Challenges for early childhood education* (pp. 155–165). New York: Teachers College Press.

White House, Office of the Press Secretary. (2013). Fact sheet: President Obama's plan for early education for all Americans [Press release]. Retrieved from https://www.whitehouse.gov/the-press-office/2013/02/13/fact-sheet-president-obama-s-plan-early-education-all-americans

Wright, T. (2011). Countering the politics of class, race, gender, and geography in early childhood education. *Educational Policy, 25*(1), 240–261.

20

A SOCIAL JUSTICE APPROACH TO DIVERSE FAMILIES

Beatrice S. Fennimore

All children who are born into the world have unique families that will play a central role in their survival and continued well-being. Early childhood educators, who are charged with the care and optimal development of children, are responsible for developing a positive and productive relationship with the families of all the children in their care. In the post–World War II social context in the United States, it was most likely assumed that these families would be composed of a married mother and father with children (Coontz, 1992). However, that uniform assumption has since been permanently altered by a host of dynamic social, cultural, and political changes over time (Berman & Enjoli, 2010). Early childhood educators today must thus be well-prepared to work successfully and respectfully with many different family structures. This chapter is written to support the work of early childhood teacher educators as they strive to prepare future teachers for strong and meaningful relationships with families. The social justice approach, the foundation of this chapter, is one that embraces differences, inquires into strengths, critiques bias and unfairness, and opens spaces of opportunity and respect for families.

The Social Justice Approach to Families

All early childhood educators have the ethical responsibility to treat children and families with equal regard and respect (National Association for the Education of Young Children [NAEYC], 2011). This expectation is a challenging one in a nation mirroring inequalities including huge gaps in the income and resources available to families. Poverty, often reflecting complex interrelated issues such as racism, gender discrimination, and inequitable educational and employment opportunities, has an incalculable and harmful impact on the well-being of children and families (Jiang, Ekono, & Skinner, 2012). Currently poverty is on the rise. At the beginning of the 21st century more than 12 million children in the United States lived in poverty—this number increased to 15.7 million in 2012. Children from single-mother households and children of color face the highest poverty rates (Bratter & Damaske, 2013). These and other serious family dilemmas underscore the critical contribution that must be made by well-prepared early educators who know how to transcend traditional deficit-based models of children and families to support them with dynamic interest and expertise.

What Is a Family?

For the purpose of this chapter, a "family" is defined as the adult or adults with whom the child is living or spending the most time while enrolled in the school or program. The term "parents" will be used flexibly to indicate the adult or adults who have major responsibility for the child and who are the primary source of communication between home and school. These definitions have been created by the author to avoid unwieldy terminology as well as the risk of leaving some variability of family life out of consideration. They are also used to emphasize that early childhood educators are always responsible for communicating with those who are currently acting in the role of parent, even if they are well outside of the realm of what might traditionally be considered to be parents.

A family, according to the U.S. Census Bureau, is a group of two people or more (one of whom is the householder) related by birth, marriage, or adoption and residing together (U.S. Census Bureau, 2012). This definition is permeable and includes many different family groupings in the United States. For example, one in ten children in the United States, 7.7 million overall, are living with grandparents and many other children are in relative-based caring arrangements (Pew Research Center, 2013). Many children live with heterosexual and homosexual cohabitating parents who are unmarried; while the overall marriage rate is dropping (Lewis, 2013) the current legislative trends in same-sex marriage will undoubtedly result in more children living with married same-sex parents. Other children experience temporary family arrangements, such as foster care, for reasons including imprisonment of parents; currently 2.7 million children under the age of 18 have a parent in prison or jail (Owens, 2013). There are so many other variations in family structure in the United States that right now it appears that if you consider yourself to be a family, you are a family (Berman & Enjoli, 2010). Early childhood educators who seek to engage all families must embrace these dramatic and enduring changes in human relationships with knowledge and enthusiasm. Classroom curriculum as well as communications with families will need to be flexible enough to include many different home-based relationships. While some educators may question or disagree with these shifts in family structure, all the families in communication with early childhood educators deserve support and respect of the professionals they entrust with the care of their children.

What is a "diverse" family? The term "diverse families" in this chapter is all-inclusive—every family is considered to be part of the world of diversity in which we all live. Specifically, neither White families, economically thriving families, nor married heterosexual families will be viewed as the *norm*, with other families considered *diverse*. The changing demographics and legislative trends in our nation are an imperative for inclusivity. Honoring some families as *normal* while setting others aside as *different* undermines our sense of community, our full ethical alignment with all families, and our imperative to treat every family as equally valued and worthy of our consideration and respect. In this chapter, *diversity itself* is considered to be the *norm* of family life in the United States; such an approach requires positive and creative attitudes on the part of all early childhood educators.

That being said, the suggested movement toward inclusiveness in our consideration of diversity should not be confused with a new form of "colorblindness." Differences between families should be recognized and articulated; the dangers of racism, discrimination, and bias must be acknowledged. Further, it should be expected that different groups of people will want to carve out their own identities and will expect recognition of their unique cultural, political, and economic realities (Fennimore, 2014). The task of the early childhood educator is to balance the acknowledgement of difference with determination to avoid the valuing of some forms of family over others. All families should be viewed as interesting, important, and worthy of dedicated professional attention.

What Is a Social Justice Approach?

A social justice approach to families recognizes the myriad ways in which the strengths and challenges of families has been shaped by complex cultural and social experiences over time—experiences that have forged privilege for some and discriminatory marginalization for others. It embraces the ecological approach to human development (Bronfenbrenner, 1981) that considers all the interrelated and interactive systems of social, economic, and political relationships affecting the lives of children and their families. Further the social justice approach has a focus on the unique role of educators to view families through a lens of fairness and compassion, seeking always to recognize their challenges and invoke their strengths and abilities in all interactions.

Social justice for families is underscored by three values: (1) resources should be distributed so everyone can live a decent life, (2) human beings should all have equal human rights and should be recognized in all their diversity, and (3) all people should be represented and should be able to advocate on their own behalf. Further, a social justice approach seeks to address the root and avoidable causes of inequities experienced by those who are systematically excluded from opportunity (Klugman, 2010).

The theory of John Rawls (1971, 2001) lends itself well to a social justice approach to families. He conceptualized social justice as evident when responsible citizens are working in social institutions with a spirit of fairness and cooperation—seeing equal treatment of every individual. If any citizens in a society are unable to get access to resources considered essential to well-being, Rawls believed that everyone in that society must necessarily be concerned and take action. This theory underscores the essential importance of advocacy for social justice for families on the part of early childhood educators. Through advocacy they can demonstrate the values and virtues that lead them to seek fundamental fairness (Novak, 2000). In order to have integrity, early childhood educators must accept responsibility for standing up to the contradictions between stated commitments to equality on the part of their society and the documented existence of divisiveness and injustice (Thrupp & Tomlinson, 2005). Further, they should question the claims of those who say they are treating all people equally and fairly when they are in fact clearly acting otherwise (Bender-Slack & Raupach, 2008).

Unique Social Justice Role of Early Childhood Educators

An important aspect of the social justice approach to families is determined avoidance of efforts to judge and blame them for perceived shortcomings. Instead, there should be a clear professional articulation of what early childhood programs and teachers are committed to doing for every child regardless of circumstances. Expressions such as "the parents are the most important teachers" or "the parents are the first teachers" can serve to blur the differences between the responsibilities of the primary family relationship and the professional responsibilities of teachers. In truth, it is not families but *teachers* who are the first *teachers.* The professional role of early childhood educators (often confused with motherhood in the past [Braun & Edwards, 1972]) should be kept separate and clearly defined. Parents have a constant and intimate relationship with their children, with whom they share a collective life. They are responsible for all aspects of their children's care at home and balance that responsibility with the need to maintain the employment that ensures family survival. Early childhood educators, on the other hand, have bordered professional relationships with children based on the expectation that they have achieved a specified level of expertise. They are expected to enact an established knowledge base gained through academic study, they are fiscally compensated for time spent with children, they are academically prepared to promote child development in cultural and group contexts, and they are responsible for following a specific code of ethical conduct (NAEYC, 2011).

Children do of course learn a great deal from their families, but the complex roles and responsibilities of families *differ* from those of teachers. It is always important to consider the ecological-developmental-theoretical perspective that families are trying to meet their responsibilities in social, political, and economic contexts (such as the local availability of affordable child care, the policies of their workplace, the quality of local public education, and federal funding for family supports) that add to or detract from their ability to support their children as well as they might (Bronfenbrenner, 2004).

The social justice approach to families by early educators is characterized by inquiry rather than assumption—inquiry that seeks the full picture of family strengths and values the voices of parents and family members. This should be *caring* inquiry that strengthens parents and professionals alike through preservative love and nurtured growth (Swick, Da Ros, & Kovach, 2001). Caring inquiry is also reflected in the words that early childhood educators use in the everyday—words that avoid denigration and deficit and seek understanding and recognition of competence and possibility (Fennimore, 2000).

The social justice approach inevitably leads to the need for advocacy on the part of early childhood educators. This is a natural and important extension of being aware of injustices that stand in the way of optimal child and family development. Advocacy for social justice on the part of educators is directly aligned with the deeply held values espoused by the United States of America. The social justice approach is centered in the very values of liberty and equality protected by the Constitution of the United States: it provides protection and hope to every family encountered in our professional lives. A social justice approach is further aligned with the internationally adopted United Nations Convention on the Rights of the Child (UNCRC) of 1989. Although the United States is one of two nations that have failed to ratify this convention, it is important to know that the UNCRC has provided greater support for the rights of children throughout the world (Fennimore, 2014). Ultimately, "social justice is based on the belief that all people in the world are equally valuable, have human rights worth recognizing and respecting and deserve to be in a just and democratic society of equal opportunity" (Griffin & Steen, 2011, p. 76).

Social Justice and Teacher Praxis

There is no shortage of availability of comprehensive and informative literature about parent and family involvement in schools. Much of this literature has emphasized cultural sensitivity and equal respect for parents for many years! In spite of this, the problem of privileging some parents (often the more affluent parents) and dispriviliging others (often parents who are poor, parents of color, or parents who are immigrants) has persisted. Traditional deficit-based beliefs about some families can still be deeply and historically embedded in the language and practice of a school or program.

Another complicating factor is the possibility that many educators have read books or encountered professional development experiences that support and enhance the deficit approach to families. One example might be the popular professional development of Dr. Ruby Payne (1998), whose approaches to the poor focus on their perceived deficits and inadequacies rather than on the complex issues of historic discrimination and exclusion from opportunity that create economic and educational inequalities (Boomer, Dworin, May, & Semingson, 2008). Another example might be the book *Class and Schools: Using Social, Economic, and Educational Reform to Close the Black-White Achievement Gap* by Richard Rothstein (2004), which suggests that the powerful influence of class-based differences in social characteristics (specifically including the characteristics of "lower class families" versus "professional" families) are unlikely to be overcome by schools—no matter how well their teachers are trained or their instructional programs designed.

The social justice approach requires educators to read and listen critically; they have the power to resist rather than embrace deficit models—including when they are promoted in some professional contexts. The commitments of early childhood educators to enact a social justice approach to families will inevitably come down to the idea of "praxis"—real talk and real action (Fennimore, 2014). This talk and action must resist deficit thinking and focus on the hard work of liberating parents from models of thought that blame them for their own challenges and those of their children.

There are many opportunities during teacher preparation for students to confront the complex layers of cultural assumptions that underlie deficit thinking. A critical first step is the opportunity to reflect on the ways in which their current thinking about differences has been shaped. Such reflection should include thoughts on personal identity, recognition of the cultural threads that led to this identity, and aspects of identity that afforded privilege and/or prejudice and discrimination. This can be achieved through readings, course projects, autobiographies, and other relevant cultural activities (Souto-Manning, 2013). A study by Hyland and Noffke (2005) indicated the effectiveness of social and community-based inquiry projects that help students to analyze bias that emerges in real experiences with children and families different from themselves. With the support and guidance of committed teacher educators, they can explore perspectives that are more empathetic and accepting of a variety of human characteristics and experiences.

Traditional Approaches to Families in Early Childhood Education

Programs and interventions for young children past and present have focused on traditional forms of parent education and parent involvement. These approaches have frequently sought to assist parents in caring for their children through hygiene, improved nutrition, social skills, and readiness for early schooling. The field of early childhood education and related parent involvement came of age in the 1960s and 1970s when the federally funded Head Start Program focused the public eye on the promise of early childhood education to offset the negative effects of poverty. Head Start parents were included in numerous opportunities, including enhanced education and leadership within the Head Start programs (Braun & Edwards, 1972).

More recently there has been a strong national focus on the importance of parent participation in the schooling of their children. The involvement of parents is assumed to result in higher academic achievement, improved attendance, better grades, positive attitudes of parents and children toward schooling, and improved parent satisfaction with teachers (Graue, 2005). Parent involvement has also been a major component in the ongoing school reform movement; Goals 2000 focused on the need for every school to promote partnerships with parents. The emphasis on parent involvement was based on what is called the *family support hypothesis;* parents who are active participants in the schooling of their children learn skills and attitudes that will assist them in increasing their child's success in school (Meidel & Reynolds, 1999). The emphasis on parent involvement has intensified with the passage of *No Child Left Behind,* with a focus on home-based activities that would increase child readiness and future success in school (Souto-Manning & Swick, 2006).

Children as Workforce Capital

The argument for funding for early childhood programs is often based in the concept of human capital—preparing children for a strong and competent national workforce. Children are viewed as investments that will pay off in the future; lifted from poverty, they will be more likely to adopt the values and work ethic of the middle class. Such views lend themselves to standardization of selected forms of knowledge with the underlying values of competition in school and in the future workforce (Zipin, Sellar, & Hattam, 2012).

This approach frequently leads to implementation of questionable and constraining early academics (Genishi & Dyson, 2009) in the programs specifically designed to educate young children who are poor. Already unable to get access to the enrichments made available for the more affluent children likely to be deemed to be "ready" for school, children who are poor can become frustrated and bored with developmentally mismatched rigidity of academic routines. Subsequent disinterest or resistance through what is viewed as misbehavior can serve to deepen the already existing inequalities of opportunity for privileged and dispriviliged children (Wright, 2011). This unfortunate situation can also increase bias toward children and tension in the relationship of families with educators.

Conflict Inherent in Normative Approaches to Families

In spite of the good intentions of many educators, there has been a deep and harmful chasm between the desire to help and include parents and enactment of deficit-based assumptions about them. This long-standing situation has been exacerbated by current pressures of curriculum standardization and testing. Early assessments at school entry can be used to label very young children "unready" before they have had any opportunity to benefit from early education. This can lead to a host of denigrating assumptions and negative expectations. Their families, on whom the entire responsibility for the perceived lack of readiness in the child is often placed, are also placed at risk for being judged to be inadequate and undesirable (Fennimore, 2014). The result of this tension and negativity is a "deficit glaze" of pathology placed on children and families that results in harmful institutional dispositions and practices (Dudley-Marling, 2007). The enduring mismatch between a widely-held focus on the importance of family involvement and practices that devalue and marginalize families can be rectified to a great degree by a commitment to social justice and a critical approach that questions and resists traditional and deficit-based views of family.

Early childhood teacher educators are in a position to help students understand that there is little or no agreed-on definition of readiness, and that researchers have found that many readiness tests are relatively poor predictors of future school performance (Weigel & Martin, 2006). When students in education learn to focus on funds of knowledge—the skills and abilities that children *do* bring to school—they are better able to demonstrate the compassion and deep regard for the individual encouraged by the Gesell Institute early in the emergence of the concept of readiness (Gesell & Ilg, 1943). Because children of poverty are more likely to be profiled as "unready," teacher educators can widen the perspectives of their students through community visits and interviews with parents and representatives of community agencies who present compassionate and committed views of the strengths and abilities of children who are poor (Fennimore, 2014; Souto-Manning, 2013).

Embracing a Critical Perspective

A critical perspective to family engagement moves beyond harmful deficit-based assumptions to questions about the reasons why inequalities exist in the first place. The critical approach "seeks to tease out sources of inequity and power imbalance in order to effect more equitable distribution of resources and success" (Wright, 2011, p. 241). Simply put, this means that teachers would look beyond long-standing bias to see that present and historic inequalities have persisted in privileging and harming the same groups of people for a long time. What is going on beneath the surface that might perpetuate these inequalities? Who is benefitting from them? Who is losing out? The critical approach should strengthen the determination of teachers to find as many ways as possible to help the disprivileged children and their families to have more of a fair share of resources—including positive expectations, cultural understanding, ethical descriptions of their potential to further develop in the school setting, and curriculum materials that are engaging and culturally relevant (Souto Manning & Swick, 2006). Several case studies have documented the importance of critical approaches to deficit thinking about children during field experiences in teacher education. Student teachers who have been steadily engaged in collaborative dialogue with their university supervisors about the importance of fair treatment and equal educational opportunity have demonstrated enhanced intentions to embody social justice teaching in present and future practice (Abt-Perkins, & Hauschildt, 2000; Lee, 2011).

Promising Practices in the Social Justice Approach

We live in a nation in which many families are struggling personally and financially to cope with complex social demands. Clearly early childhood education with a strong focus on parent *engagement* can offer compassion and meaningful support to these families. Family engagement "occurs when there is an on-going, reciprocal, strengths-based partnership between families and their children in early childhood education programs" (Halgunseth, Peterson, Stark, & Moodie, 2009, p. 1). Further, it is in evidence when educators purposefully counter potential bias with intentional words and actions that honor family strengths and abilities. There are six factors that add to a comprehensive definition of family engagement: (1) families are participatory partners and advocates, (2) families are part of consistent two-way communication between home and school, (3) families and educators collaborate and exchange knowledge, (4) families and educators create and sustain learning activities at home and in the community to enhance early learning, (5) families create a home environment that values learning and supports programs while programs collaborate with goals at home and at school, and (6) family engagement is supported through training and supports that enhance the ability of dedicated teachers and administrators to sustain it (Halgunseth et al., 2009).

The social justice approach to family engagement helps educators to be *imaginative* and to recognize that there is a great deal that *they do not know* about the possibilities that may arise for families in the future (Graue, 2005). *Acting* as though families are valued and competent is the essential first step to a strong relationship. Early childhood educators are in a position to utilize and adapt ideas from a number of promising programmatic approaches to families.

The Strengths Approach

The strengths approach to families is a solution-based and ecologically-based approach that avoids focus on deficits and recognizes the importance of the multiple contexts that influence people's lives. The approach seeks to build family resilience through recognition of strengths, abilities, and interests. The six key stages in the strengths approach are (1) listen to people's stories, (2) develop a picture of the future, (3) highlight strengths and exceptions to the problems in the family, (4) identify additional resources that will be of assistance, (5) mobilize strengths and resources, and (6) continually review and evaluate progress and change (Fenton, McFarland, & Piazza, 2014). This approach can be applied broadly to any communication with or about families; it leads to the development of positive language about what can be done that enhances a positive climate and sense of ever-present possibility (Fennimore, 2000).

Focusing on Family Resilience

The approach of Focusing on Family Adjustment and Adaptation Response (FAAR model) also places a strong emphasis on resilience and competencies within the family. While the term "resilience" is often used to identify individuals who somehow managed to rise above circumstances related to family dysfunction, this model uses it more to focus on strengths than on deficits. A particular focus in the family resilience approach is acknowledgement of the adaptive processes that aid families in competent functioning when exposed to risk. This approach seeks to help families develop a balance between the demands they face and the capabilities that they have. Further, families that have experienced extreme stress or loss are helped to move forward through construction of a new view of the world that allows them to make greater sense of what has happened and what they need to do as a result (Patterson, 2002).

Funds of Knowledge and Funds of Identity

The Funds of Knowledge (FOK) approach develops a view of the knowledge and skills that are essential for the well-being of an entire household. Young children, for example, who seem "unready" for school may have very well-developed family-based skills. The Funds of Identity (FOI) approach takes a closer look at how people actively use their Funds of Knowledge to describe themselves. Their actual identities as described would be composed of cultural factors such as socio-demographic conditions, social institutions, artifacts, significant others, activities, and practices. Vygotsky's perspective theory provides the structure for the theory of Funds of Identity; it focuses on historically accumulated, culturally developed, and socially distributed resources that strengthen the functional well-being of a household (Moises & Moll, 2014).

The Funds of Knowledge and Funds of Identity approaches "take fuller account of the diverse and complex spaces of social-historical life in high-poverty regions in new times" (Zipin et al., 2012, p. 179). For educators, this can lead to acknowledgement and utilization of assets from the real-world lives of families. Further, they can lead to "thoughtful social imagining" (p. 191) of highly intelligent ways in which educators and teachers might work together to build conditions for desirable futures (Zipin et al., 2012). A good example of this concept can be found in a qualitative study of the effectiveness of the funds of knowledge approach (Moll, Amanti, Neff, & Gonzalez, 1992). In this study, teachers as coresearchers had the opportunity to engage in the household knowledge of their students. Through a series of home visits, the teacher-investigators became able to redefine the households of students as rich in knowledge. Thus, they were able to begin to develop new approaches to the development of culturally relevant classroom pedagogy inclusive of the lives and strengths of the students.

All three of the above approaches are characterized by positive thinking, inquiry into family strengths, and inclusion of the family in efforts to construct the future.

New Visions for Early Childhood Teacher Educators

Teacher educators play a central role in the development of a social justice approach to families in their students. Their own modeling of attitude and action in the field is essential, as is their active listening to the perceptions and beliefs of their students. It is always important to promote inquiry, and to ask students to reflect on multiple interpretations of family beliefs and behaviors. Promoting the understanding of skilled dialogue, along with opportunities to practice it, supports the ability of students in teacher education to communicate with respect, reciprocity, and responsiveness (Barrera & Corso, 2003). Any emergent deficit-based assumptions of students (sometimes modeled by other educators during field experiences) should be explored and gently but pointedly interrupted with discussion of new interpretations and multiple solutions to tensions between home and school. In their article *Skilled Dialogue: Weaving Webs of Connectedness across Diverse Voices and Identities* (2007), Barrera and Kramer provide the example of a meeting between a parent who believes the teacher is too permissive while the teacher believes the parent does not allow enough space for exploration and free play. The teacher becomes aware of her assumption that her way of doing things is the best and allows the apparently contradictory views of the parent to stand side by side with her own until a sense of respectful partnership is established. The teacher takes time to listen in full relationship with the parent's ideas and seeks what she might value in what the parent has to say. Finally, the teacher takes the steps necessary to harmonize both views into a way in which she and the parent can work together. This would be a good example for students to study and put into practice through role modeling.

Unique Qualities of Students in Teacher Education

It is important to remember that students in education live in a figured world. Their world is formed in the context of their lived experience; figured worlds are a socially and culturally constructed realm of interpretation. Students come to early childhood teacher education with a history of inclusions and exclusions that will affect their interpretations of daily events. Further, undergraduate students in teacher education are in the process of constructing adult identities as they move away from their own parents. This identity task must be completed in conjunction with the development of a new identity as a professional educator (Graue, 2005).

Students already engaged in the construction of the above new identities can become confused by the mixed-messages of parent engagement in schools. Once they enter field placements, students often become aware of the ideological mismatches between parents and teachers within schools.

While a stated interest in parent involvement often exists, parents and teachers may often find themselves in opposition to one another (Graue, 2005). Particularly when faced with families in the direst conditions, sometimes called excluded families (because of their isolation in communities [Mitchell & Campbell, 2011]), students may start to lose their earlier enthusiasm about constructing positive relationships with families.

The social justice approach to families is frequently more embedded in teacher dispositions than it is in curriculum or strategies. Early childhood teacher educators are challenged to strengthen positive values in prospective teachers as they begin to relate to special needs and cultural considerations of all kinds in the early childhood classroom. Through the lens of these values future teachers must inquire into the forms of societal and cultural power that can skew their perceptions of parents and families. In this process, teaching must be seen as a moral and value-laden responsibility that requires careful individual consideration on a daily basis. Teachers must accept responsibility for constant improvement of their practice; this improvement is often made through an insistent intention to value the personal and cultural attributes of every parent and child to whom they have a professional responsibility (Williams, 2005). An effective way to imbed the development of such intentions into teacher preparation is to create meaningful opportunities for students to critically analyze examples of well-accepted books or articles on education that reflect deficit-based assumptions of children (e.g. poor children come to school with fewer vocabulary words). They might be encouraged to wonder about the life experiences that led the researchers to their positions in prestigious universities. How did they obtain the power to "tell the story" about the shortcomings of those who are less privileged in society? How might the parents of these children argue with the assumptions of the researchers if they had the opportunity? What might we discover if we had the chance to engage many poor children in personal conversations? By learning to use multiple perspectives to question what they read, future teachers can develop skills necessary for critical inquiry and respectful acknowledgement of differences (that are not necessarily deficits) in their future practice (Derman-Sparks & Ramsey, 2011; Fennimore, 2014; Souto-Manning, 2013).

Promoting Postmodern Critique

To achieve these goals future teachers will benefit from a postmodern framework allowing them to move from constrained normative expectations into open-minded interest in the actual conditions, needs, and strengths of every family (Ryan & Grieshaber, 2004). In the postmodern context, future teachers can recognize that learning and development are always both cultural and constructivist. This means that they must be active and inquiring learners; passive biased assumptions must be viewed as unethical and harmful to children and families. Importantly, future teachers must concentrate on the value of enhancing the life of the child in the here and now rather than focusing on the child as a future wage earner. When children are considered important only for their future economic value, they are in danger of being tokenized or exploited. The fullness of their everyday life, enhanced by the connected caring of their homes and early childhood teachers, should be sought and valued as a good unto itself (Kroll, 2013). All of these efforts, made in a postmodern context, should also recognize that the education of young children is a community privilege as well as a serious responsibility.

Future teachers should be encouraged to rise above ethnocentric suggestions that their role is to teach all students the tools of the White middle class (Payne, 1998). This is not to suggest that there are not strategies and tools that have enhanced those in the White middle class that could be of equal value to all children. Harm is done, however, when children are expected to abandon their funds of knowledge and identity in a blind trade for blanket teacher-based assumptions of "White middle-class values." We must always start with the strengths, capacities, and cultural understandings of our students. It is important to note that teacher educators are in a prime position to model such respect and regard for the diversity of ideas and values of the preservice teachers in their university classrooms.

Through creation of discourse that encourages divergent and critical thought, teacher educators can model ways of honoring and including multiple perspectives.

Supporting Social Justice Commitments in Future Teachers

Future early childhood teachers need constant opportunities to blend their understanding of developmental processes with deepening acceptance of differences and the ways in which those differences affect the relationship of families with schools. Their vision and imagination of possibilities for all families can be enhanced with the use of *story* in teacher education. It is through the development of stories, about themselves and others, that students can think vigorously and creatively about experience and possibility. How has their experience shaped them? How might different experiences have shaped them differently? Through awareness of their own emergent developmental story—personal and professional—future teachers can become more fully interested and engaged in the life stories of others (Graue, 2005). Kyles (2008) found through a mixed-methods study that multiple opportunities to write and reflect on cultural autobiographies supported preservice teachers' empathetic understanding of others. Le Fevre (2011) also found qualitative evidence that preservice students experience transformative growth when they share and witness autobiographical narrative.

As our students in early childhood education grow and change, it is important to continue to offer them opportunities to use their tools of identity in new and creative ways. They need more than one required course or set of methodological "strategies" if they are going to construct a new figured world of teaching. In fact, they need to move continually toward the understanding that "home-school relations are the ultimate crucible of culture" (Graue, 2005, p. 183). Their entire university preparation should be permeated with a vision of social justice embedded in constant consideration of the possibilities of good, true, and productive relationships with parents and families. Hopefully their journey to professionalism will be guided by university-based instructors whose own explicit commitments to a social justice approach to families is articulated and modeled with depth and consistency. Early childhood teacher educators, along with their students, have the power to make schools places where parents and families are welcomed and supported, places in which their love and concern for their children can be honored and respectfully enhanced.

References

Abt-Perkins, D., & Hauschildt, P. (2000). Becoming multicultural supervisors: Lessons from a collaborative field study. *Journal of Curriculum and Supervision, 16*(1), 28–47.

Barrera, I., & Corso, R. (2003). *Skilled dialogue: Strategies for responding to cultural diversity in early childhood*. Baltimore, MD: Paul H. Brookes.

Barrera, I., & Kramer, L. (2007). Skilled dialogue: Weaving webs of connectedness across diverse voices and identities. *Childhood Education, 83*(5), 304–308.

Bender-Slack, D., & Raupach, M. P. (2008). Negotiating standards and social justice in social studies: Educators' perspectives. *Social Studies, 99*(6), 255–259.

Berman, J., & Enjoli, F. (2010). *What makes a family? Children, say many Americans*. Retrieved from abcnews.go.com/WN/defines-family-children-americans-survey/story? id=11644693

Boomer, R., Dworin, J. E., May, L., & Semingson, P. (2008). Miseducating teachers about the poor: A critical analysis of Ruby Payne's claims about poverty. *Teachers College Record, 110*(12), 2497–2531.

Bratter, J. L. & Damaske, S. (2013). Poverty at a racial crossroads: Poverty among multiracial children of single mothers. *Journal of Marriage and the Family, 75*, 486–502.

Braun, S. J. & Edwards, E. P. (1972). *History and theory of early childhood education*. Belmont, CA: Wadsworth.

Bronfenbrenner, U. (1981). *The ecology of human development: Experiments by nature and design*. Cambridge, MA: Harvard University Press.

Bronfenbrenner, U. (Ed.). (2004). *Making human beings human: Bioecological perspectives on human development*. Thousand Oaks, CA: Sage Publications.

Coontz, S. (1992). *The way we never were: American families and the nostalgia trap*. New York: Basic Books.

Derman-Sparks, L., & Ramsey, P.G. (2011). *What if all the kids are white: Anti-bias multicultural education with young children and families* (2nd ed.). New York: Teachers College Press.

Dudley-Marling, C. (2007). Return of the deficit. *Journal of Educational Controversy, 2*(1).

Fennimore, B.S. (2000). *Talk matters: Refocusing the language of public schooling.* New York: Teachers College Press.

Fennimore, B.S. (2014). *Standing up for something every day: Ethics and justice in early childhood classrooms.* New York: Teachers College Press.

Fenton, A., MacFarland, M., & Piazza, L. (2014). Supporting early childhood preservice teachers in their work with children and families with complex needs: A strength approach. *Journal of Early Childhood Teacher Education, 35*(1), 22–38.

Genishi, C., & Dyson, A.H. (2009). *Children, language, and literacy: Diverse learners in diverse times.* New York: Teachers College Press.

Gesell, A., & Ilg, F.L. (1943). *Infant and child in the culture of today.* New York: Harpers.

Graue, E. (2005). Theorizing and describing preservice teachers' images of families and schooling. *Teachers College Record, 107*(1), 157–185.

Griffin, D., & Steen, S. (2011). A social justice approach to school counseling. *Journal for Social Action in Counseling and Psychology, 3*(1), 74–85.

Halgunseth, C., Peterson, A., Stark, D.R., & Moodie, S. (2009). Family engagement, diverse families, and early childhood education programs: An integrated review of the literature. Retrieved from www.naeyc.org/files/naeyc/file/eeprofessional/EDF/LiteratureReview.pdf

Hyland, N.E., & Noffke, S.E. (2005). Understanding diversity through social and community inquiry: An action research study. *Journal of Teacher Education, 56*(4), 367–380.

Jiang, Y., Ekono, M., & Skinner, C. (2012). Basic facts about low-income children: Children under 18 years. *National Center for Children in Poverty.* Retrieved from http://www.nccp.org/

Klugman, B. (2010). Evaluating social justice advocacy: A values-based approach. *Center for Evaluation Innovation.* Retrieved from http://www.evaluationinnovation.org

Kroll, L.R. (2013). Early childhood teacher preparation: Essential aspects for the achievement of social justice. *Journal of Early Childhood Teacher Education, 34*(1), 63–72.

Kyles, C.R. (2008). Uncovering preservice teachers' beliefs about diversity through reflective writing. *Urban Education, 43*(5), 500–518.

Lee, Y.A. (2011). What does teaching social justice mean to teacher candidates? *The Professional Educator, 35*(2), 1–20.

Le Fevre, D.M. (2011). Creating and facilitating a teacher education curriculum using preservice teachers' autobiographical stories. *Teaching and Teacher Education, 27*(4), 779–787.

Lewis, J. M. (2013). Married couples are not the only kind of two-parent family. *Random Samplings: The Official Blog of the U.S. Census Bureau.* Retrieved from http://blogs.census.gov/2013/11/25/married-couples-are-not-the-only-type-of-two-parent-family/

Meidel, W.T., & Reynolds, A. J. (1999). Parent involvement for disadvantaged children: Does it matter? *Journal of School Psychology, 37*(4), 379–402.

Mitchell, G., & Campbell, L. (2011). The social economy of excluded families. *Child and Family Social Work, 6*, 422–433.

Moises, E., & Moll, L. C. (2014). Funds of identity: A new concept based on the funds of knowledge approach. *Culture and Psychology, 20*(1), 31–48.

Moll, L. C., Amanti, C., Neff, D., & Gonzalez, N. (1992). Funds of knowledge for teaching: Using a qualitative approach to connect homes and classrooms. *Theory into Practice, XXXI*(2), pp. 132–141.

National Association for the Education of Young Children. (2011). *NAEYC code of ethical conduct and statement of commitment.* Retrieved from https://www.naeyc.org/files/naeyc/image/public_policy/Ethics%20Position%20Statement2011_09202013update.pdf

Novak, M. (2000). Defining social justice. *First Things, 108*, 11–13.

Owens, M.L. (2013). *2.7 million children under the age of 18 have a parent in prison or jail—we need criminal justice reform now.* Retrieved from http://www.alternet.org

Patterson, J.M. (2002). Integrating family resilience and family stress theory. *Journal of Marriage and Family, 64*, 349–360.

Payne, R.K. (1998). *A framework for understanding poverty: Modules 1–7 workbook.* Highlands, TX: Aha!

Pew Research Center. (2013). *At grandmother's house we stay: One-in-ten children are living with a grandparent.* Washington, DC: author.

Rawls, J. (1971). *A theory of justice.* Cambridge, MA: Harvard University Press.

Rawls, J. (2001). *Justice as fairness: A restatement.* Cambridge, MA: Belknap Press of Harvard University Press.

Rothstein, R. (2004). *Class and schools: Using social, economic, and educational reform to close the black-white achievement gap.* New York: Economic Policy Institute and Teachers College.

Ryan, S., & Grieshaber, S. (2004). It's more than child development: Critical theories, research, and teaching young children. *Young Children, 59*, 44–92.

Souto-Manning, M. (2013). *Multicultural teaching in the early childhood classroom: Approaches, strategies, and tools Preschool-2nd Grade.* New York: Teachers College Press.

Souto-Manning, M., & Swick, K. J. (2006). Teachers' beliefs about parent and family involvement: Rethinking our family involvement paradigm. *Early Childhood Education Journal, 34*(2), 187–193.

Swick, K. J., Da Ros, D. A., & Kovach, B. A. (2001). Empowering parents and families through a caring inquiry approach. *Early Childhood Education Journal, 29*(1), 65–71.

Thrupp, M., & Tomlinson, S. (2005). Introduction: Education policy, social justice, and "complex hope." *British Education Research Journal 31*(5), 545–566.

UN General Assembly, *Convention on the Rights of the Child*, 20 November 1989, United Nations, Treaty Series, vol. 1577, p. 3. Retrieved from http://www.refworld.org/docid/3ae6b38f0.html

U.S. Census Bureau. (2012). Families and living arrangements: 2012. Retrieved from census.gov/hhes/families/data/cps2012.html

Weigel, D. J., & Martin, S. S. (2006). Early childhood research and practice. *Early Childhood Research Quarterly, 15*(1), 295–317.

Williams, L. R. (2005). Greetings from the editor. *Journal of Early Childhood Teacher Education, 26*(1), 1.

Wright, T. S. (2011). Countering the politics of class, race, gender, and geography in early childhood education. *Educational Policy, 25*(1), 240–261.

Zipin, L., Sellar, S., & Hattam, R. (2012). Countering and exceeding "capital": A "funds of knowledge" approach to re-imagining community. *Discourse Studies in the Cultural Politics of Education, 33*(2), 179–192.

PART V

Contemporary Influences in Early Childhood Teacher Education

21

EMERGING ROLE OF TECHNOLOGY TO SUPPORT EARLY CHILDHOOD PEDAGOGY

Claire E. Hamilton and Ellen Edge

Technology, specialized tools or techniques, has always been a part of the early childhood classroom. Technological tools can be high-tech, simple-tech, or no-tech. High-tech tools, the focus of this chapter, are those related to digital technology—newer tools like smartphones, tablet computers, and interactive white boards as well as older forms like television and video, desktop computers, and digital cameras. When we first began working with young children, a core piece of technology, and an indicator of classroom quality, was the woodworking bench (Harms & Clifford, 1980). As novice teachers, we approached this piece of technology with some trepidation: What classroom learning goals were supported by a woodworking bench? What safety issues did we need to consider when we weighed what tools or materials we should include with the woodworking bench—realistic but child-size metal hammers and real saws or plastic replicas? What social interactions, between children, and between teachers and children, were appropriate for the woodworking bench? And, perhaps equally important, what training did we have in using these materials—had we ever used a vise grip, a cross cut, or a rip saw? The questions we ask as we introduce new forms of technology into the classroom are the same; what changes are the tools themselves.

The technology in today's early childhood classrooms includes digital cameras, smartphones, tablets, document and liquid-crystal display (LCD) projectors as well as crayons, building blocks, puzzles, and perhaps, occasionally, a woodworking bench. Digital technology is viewed as both disruptive and transformative—changing how adults and children manage their lives and interact with the world and perhaps how we view education and learning. There are promises that technology is "moving U.S. education to the level required for our global age" (Barron et al., 2011) and concerns that media consumption may lead to a generation of young children with "play deficit disorder," deprived of the physical and social interactions they need for optimal development (Levin, 2013). As early childhood professionals grapple with issues around digital technology and media, the questions remain the same as those surrounding the woodworking bench: What technological tools (e.g. computers, LCD projectors, interactive white boards, digital cameras, or smartphones) should we include in early childhood classrooms? Are these technological tools and the media content available on them beneficial or potentially harmful for young children? How do we integrate this technology into our classrooms in meaningful ways that support the learning and developmental goals we have for young children? And perhaps, most importantly for early childhood teacher educators, how do we support teachers' use of technology in their classrooms?

Children as Digital Natives

Today's children are digital natives surrounded by technology before birth. This does not mean that children experience technology in the same ways. Consider for a moment two contexts that illustrate how children may differ in their experiences with technology. In the first, technology exposure begins with parents posting their ultrasound images on Facebook and texting their birth photos to friends and relatives from the delivery room, and then continues as the child begins to make use of technology independently. We see toddlers who delight in the "selfies" taken with their parents' smartphones while waiting in the doctor's office, preschoolers who Skype with grandparents, kindergarteners who program Lego robots that deliver pencils to their classmates, and second graders creating and sharing stop-action digital movies on a classroom website. These experiences with technology are interactive, creative, and collaborative. A second, and equally plausible picture of technology, similarly begins before birth though in this case the fetus is presented with "auditory exercises" via speakers strapped to its' mother's belly. Infants are propped in front of the television to watch educational baby videos for an hour or two, and independent use includes toddlers whose bedtime story routines rely on an e-reader, preschoolers who fall asleep each night with the television on in their bedrooms, and 8-year-olds who have discovered that the internet connects not only to child-friendly sites like Club Penguin but also to the unrestricted, adult content available through YouTube. These experiences are far too typical for many children and are unlikely to support, and in fact may be harmful to, their development. As we consider how to integrate technology into our early childhood classrooms we first need to examine how children use technology and media outside of the classroom.

Research on Young Children's Use of Media and Technology

The first systematic study on children's media use was conducted about a decade ago (Rideout, Vandewater, & Wartella, 2003). Children then and now are clearly exposed to and consuming media, beginning early in infancy and increasing throughout early childhood. Most children become daily consumers of screen media as preschoolers, typically with about two hours of exposure per day, half of which is television viewing. Infants are less likely to engage with screen media but those that do spend about an hour a day with screen time (Common Sense Media, 2013). The overall amount of screen time exposure has actually changed very little in the last decade, and there is some indication that screen exposure may in fact be decreasing (Common Sense Media, 2013; Rideout et al., 2003). How children are engaged with screen media, however, has changed. While live-time television was once the dominant form of screen exposure, and still accounts for about half of children's screen time exposure, television and video are now more likely to be accessed through DVR and DVD players, gaming systems, and mobile devices. Beginning in 2013 there has been a dramatic increase in family access, across socioeconomic and ethnic groups, to mobile devices (e.g. smartphones, tablets, iPods). Most families now own a smartphone and over 40% of families have tablets (Common Sense Media, 2013). Visit a dentist's waiting room, a grocery store, or an airport and it is clear that many parents feel comfortable sharing mobile technology devices with young children and even infants. Almost all children over the age of two years have used some form of mobile device and children who have regular access spend up to an hour a day on mobile devices and typically they use these devices independently. Are children engaging with these new technological tools in more innovative ways? Typically no, children are using mobile devices most often for watching videos and playing games (Common Sense Media, 2013).

Concerns about Children's Use of Technology

While young children are clearly using technology and have been for decades, there have been long-standing concerns about the impact that screen media may have on their development. The evidence on the value of technology is controversial (Levin, 2013; National Association for the Education of Young Children [NAEYC] & the Fred Rogers Center, 2012). Screen media is a broad concept that refers to any children's use of any technology platform with a screen. In practice much of the research on screen media has more directly focused on television viewing, but screen media includes video games, DVD players, televisions, and computers as well as mobile devices. The American Academy of Pediatrics (AAP) has long had concerns about the impact of children's exposure to media evident in the release of their first policy statement on Media Education in 1999 (AAP, 1999), followed with more age-specific policy recommendations for children younger than two years (AAP, 2011) and revised policy recommendations for children and adolescents most recently in 2013. Current AAP policy for children under two years discourages parents from allowing infants access to any screen media, which parents seem largely to ignore, and suggests that older children be restricted to less than two hours of screen time per day, a recommendation generally followed (Vandewater et al., 2006). These AAP policy guidelines stem from numerous studies on the impact of media exposure or screen time that have been conducted over a number of years focusing on television, as well as computers, gaming systems, or mobile devices. Given that even with the increased access to potentially more interactive digital technology tools children continue to spend substantial amounts of time viewing video, either through traditional television viewing or through mobile devices, this research remains relevant. For preschoolers and older children the evidence is mixed. Some research has found that children with more screen time exposure and higher rates of media consumption are at-risk for higher rates of obesity, increased sleep disturbances, increased aggressive behavior and attentional issues, both concurrently and in later childhood, and poorer academic achievement (for reviews of the literature and policy statements see AAP, 2013; Center on Media and Child Health, 2005; Kirkorian, Wartella, & Anderson, 2008; NAEYC, 2012). At the same time, studies have also found positive impacts of media exposure, particularly of educational television, though also including the use of computers and the internet. Again for children older than two years, media exposure is associated with improved social skills, language competence, and school readiness (Kirkorian & Anderson, 2008; AAP, 2011). There is less research on children's use of emerging technology, but there is some evidence that children can and do learn valuable skills related to early literacy when using research-designed apps (Chiong & Shuler, 2010). However most commercially available apps are less likely to provide high-quality educational learning opportunities (Guernsey, Levine, Chiong, & Severns, 2012).

For infants and toddlers the risks of screen time exposure seems to outweigh any potential benefits that may occur. Infants and toddlers seem to have difficulty making sense of video content. This "video deficit" means that generally infants learn best from their direct experiences and interactions with the social and physical world. Under very controlled, researcher-designed situations in which the video content is specific and shown repeatedly, infants do seem able to process some information from video presentations (DeLoache & Chiong, 2009). However infants also seem highly susceptible to adverse effects of media exposure, particularly background television. For infants and toddlers, just being present while the television is on may reduce their play behavior, and even when parents are asked to interact with their children, having the television on depresses the interactive behaviors of the adults (Barr, 2008). Interaction seems to be key. In co-viewing situations with older toddlers in which parents are given direct instructions on how to interact, children may show some evidence of learning new vocabulary (Guernsey, 2013). Newer technologies, such as touch screens and e-books, are certainly tools that have the potential for more interactivity, however the limited research on parent-child use of such technology suggests that parents themselves use these tools in less interactive ways with their young children (Common Sense Media, 2013; Guernsey, 2013).

In a recent set of guidelines distributed by *Zero to Three*, Lerner and Barr (2014) offer research-based suggestions for using screen technology with children under three. They found no research support for enhanced development through infants' independent use of these technologies, and reiterate the overarching importance of interactive experience for this age group. Mindful of the ways that screen use has become an integral part of adults' and children's everyday lives, however, they offer the following guidelines for using these technologies with children under two years old:

- Participate and make screen use interactive, talking about what children are seeing, and encouraging them to use their minds and bodies as much as possible to maximize learning.
- Help children bridge the gap between content they are exposed to on screens—new words and concepts—and their real-life experiences.
- Be sure that the content reflects the child's everyday experiences. Ideally, the program or game should engage children interactively (Lerner & Barr, 2014, p.8).

We share the concerns expressed in the NAEYC (2012) Position Statement on Technology and recommend that early childhood educators should generally limit the use of technology with infants and toddlers.

Dan Anderson and his colleagues have argued that the mixed evidence on the impact of technology and media on young children's development can best be conceptualized within the metaphor of a "well-balanced media diet" (Anderson & Hanson, 2009). This metaphor suggests that there is no singular effect of the amount of media exposure or screen time, rather that the effect of technology use reflects the content of the media (e.g. educational programming, adult entertainment, advertising), the potential interactivity of the technology tool (e.g. touch screens, games, video), as well as the total amount of screen exposure and the context in which technology use occurs. This metaphor is helpful in guiding the use of technology in early childhood classrooms. Nutritional dietary recommendations for infants and toddlers are more restrictive than those for preschoolers, older children, or adults. So too there may be a need to have more restrictive recommendations for technology use by the very youngest. Infancy is a period of intense neurological growth and during this time synaptic development occurs in response to external stimuli (Christakis & Zimmerman, 2009). The introduction of technology use during this period may pose more risks for development given the "salient features of the medium itself . . . that could overstimulate the brain" (pp. 1178) and the simple fact that time spent with technology and media may displace the developmentally critical learning opportunities infants need for direct interaction with the social and physical world (Christakis & Zimmerman, 2009). How we feed children not only reflects dietary recommendations but also their individual needs, preferences, and cultural backgrounds. The media diets we provide should also reflect the needs of diverse learners.

Useful Applications of Technology in the Early Childhood Classroom Universal Design for Learning

The focus of Universal Design for Learning (UDL) is on how we increase all children's access and participation in the general curriculum through the provision of multiple means of representation, action and expression, and engagement (Hitchcock, Meyer, Rose, & Jackson, 2002; Rose & Gravel, 2010). Typically early childhood classrooms have addressed UDL through the use of low-tech tools or no-tech approaches. In a preschool classroom the teacher might introduce a project on farm animals by providing a variety of materials in different center-based activities—small farm animal manipulatives in the block area, animal masks in the dress-up corner, traditional print picture books, or even a field trip to a local farm. A second grade teacher could introduce the concept of two-digit subtraction by drawing problems on a chalk or dry erase board, providing students with unifix cubes or other math manipulatives, assigning individual worksheets, or embedding counting activities in authentic classroom routines (i.e. taking class attendance during morning meeting). In these ways teachers are using UDL, however the curriculum may still not be fully accessible for all learners and the use of digital technology can afford additional routes of access to the curriculum. In the preschool classroom the teacher could support the needs of English language learners by providing multilingual alternatives to print books—e-book apps, audio books, or even audio recordings created by parents on their smartphones. Digital cameras (or tablets) could be used as part of the farm field trip to capture children's experience in still or video images, so children could revisit the field trip back in their classroom. The second grade teacher might increase student engagement through the use of an interactive white board and virtual math manipulatives or by modeling the use of traditional math manipulatives using a document camera (i.e. Elmo) during group presentations and by providing access to computer-based math 'games' and activities. For the primary grade classrooms, in which students are expected to access academic material through text and demonstrate their understanding through writing, text-to-speech and voice recognition software affords access to students who might struggle in reading or writing. Digital technology can also offer multiple forms of documenting and assessing children's progress—digitized audio recordings of early reading fluency, video clips of students' use of manipulatives to solve math problems, and even the computer-based activities that include student progress monitoring. Within a UDL framework digital media and technology offer powerful opportunities for early childhood educators to help their students to access the general curriculum. Many of the technology tools used within UDL are also tools that play a role in assistive technology.

Assistive Technology

Assistive technology (AT) refers to tools that are "individually matched to and uniquely required for a child to participate in the curriculum or classroom and to make educational progress" (Parette & Blum, 2013, p. 9). Even with the application of UDL, some children will need additional assistance to participate in classroom activities. As with UDL, assistive technology tools can be low-tech (pencil grips or positioning aids), simple-tech switches, or high-tech, including augmentative communication devices and specialized computer software. There is overlap in some of the technology tools used within UDL and provided to students through assistive technology, however even with the use of UDL, specific assistive technologies are essential for some children to access classroom activities.

For example, the use of text-to-speech software may provide alternative means of representation for all students (UDL) but may be the only way for visually impaired students to access and engage in print material available in their classrooms. The use of AT devices is associated with increasing young children's access to a wide range of classroom (and home) activities by supporting mobility, communication, specific literacy skills, increased peer interactions and play, and technology use (Parette, Blum, & Boeckmann, 2009). While AT must be considered as part of children's Individual Education Plans or Individual Family Service Plans under IDEA 2004, and the use of assistive technology seems to be effective for young children with disabilities, research suggests that these devices are not regularly used by educators (Dunst, Trivette, & Hamby, 2012; Naraian & Surabian, 2014).

How Are Early Childhood Teachers Using Technology in Their Classrooms?

Many individual teachers use technology creatively in their classrooms; over the last few years, many articles written by early childhood practitioners have appeared in *Young Children*, the leading publication for early childhood educators. These articles reflect the use of various forms of technology as tools to enhance classroom curriculum. Technology is used to document children's experiences with the use of digital cameras, to access the internet to provide children with virtual field trips, to provide multilingual versions of print and audio materials, to support early mathematics learning through the use of virtual manipulatives, and to communicate with families. These articles demonstrate the creative ways with which technology can support and enhance children's development in early childhood classrooms. Some early childhood teachers can and do use technology in ways that can contribute to children's learning, communication with families, documentation of children's progress, and their own professional development.

The research literature also documents many ways that technology has been incorporated into early childhood classrooms and the positive impacts of this technology integration. Bers, Flannery, Kazakoff, and Sullivan (2014) found that children whose kindergarten teachers were supported by research assistants in the implementation of lessons on robotics and basic programming demonstrated increased competence in basic programming skills, including program debugging, non-sequential programming, and sequencing. While the focus was on basic computer programming skills, these skills are reflected in more general problem solving and cause-and-effect skills typically targeted in an early childhood curriculum. Kazakoff, Sullivan, and Bers (2013) demonstrated the generalizability of computer programming skills to picture story telling. Research on children's use of LOGO, a child-friendly computer programing language, introduced through the use of an interactive white board, also demonstrates that children in the early primary grades are able to learn and use computer programming languages and that use of LOGO or similar programming languages may support children's collaboration, social, language, mathematics, and general problem-solving skills (Fessakis, Gouli, & Mavroudi, 2013). Best practices, whether developed by individual teachers as published in *Young Children*, or as applied in classrooms as part of research-based designs, provide many models for positive uses of technology in early childhood settings. Questions remain regarding how most teachers are typically using technology in their classrooms and how early childhood teacher preparation programs are supporting teachers in developing their skills in integrating technology into the early childhood curriculum.

Technology Access and Use in Early Childhood Programs

Early childhood education settings include home-based family child care programs, group care settings for infants, toddlers, and preschoolers, school-based and child care–based prekindergarten programs, and public and private kindergarten through second grade classrooms. Much of the research on classroom-based technology use has been conducted in K-12 settings and is not easily generalized to the diverse contexts found in early childhood education. Non–school-based early childhood settings are more variable in overall quality—teacher education levels, group or class size, and physical resources—as well as in program and curricular goals. Early childhood educators may also be more diverse in their belief systems about the value of technology for children because of ongoing controversies within the field (Blackwell, Lauricella, Wartella, Robb, & Schomburg, 2013). The accessibility of technology and the internet in K-12 schools has steadily been increasing since the early 2000s and with increased accessibility, the actual use of technology has also increased (PBS & Grunwald Associates, 2010). Virtually all K-12 teachers regularly use digital media in their classrooms and elementary teachers are overall the most frequent users (Gray, Thomas, & Lewis, 2010; PBS & Grunwald Associates, 2010, 2011). Teachers utilize a wide variety of digital content and resources for their students, for their own professional growth, and for administrative purposes including assessment and communication (Gray et al., 2010). Elementary teachers as a group appear to be the most frequent technology users within K–12 teachers (PBS & Grunwald Associates, 2010) and early childhood educators in public school settings report access to and use of a variety of technological tools including computers, interactive white boards, and mobile devices (McMannis, Nemeth & Simon, 2013; Wartella, Blackwell, Lauricella, & Robb, 2013). However prekindergarten teachers, even those in public school settings, are far less likely than K–12 teachers to use digital media (PBS & Grunwald Associates, 2010). Access to technology is more limited in non–school-based early childhood settings. Virtually all early educators in these settings have access to digital cameras, computers, and TVs/DVDs, however few have access to mobile devices or interactive whiteboards (Wartella et al., 2013).

On a basic level, early childhood teachers lack accessibility to technology tools. Most report that digital cameras, computers, and TV/DVDs are available, however, less than one-third report that they have tablet computers, interactive white boards, or mobile technology available for classroom use, and the availability of technology tools is related to program type (Wartella et al., 2013). School-based programs are far more likely to have access to a broad range of technology tools. Usage is clearly related to accessibility, and the lack of accessibility remains a barrier for technology use in early childhood classrooms (Wartella et al., 2013). As we think of how technology can be integrated into the early childhood curriculum, access is not the only barrier. Teachers who have access to technology do use technology in their classrooms, and most report feeling very confident in their abilities to use various tools (Wartella et al., 2013). This is not surprising given that most adults use technology, including computers, mobile technologies, and video, in their own lives. For more "classroom-based" technology tools such as interactive white boards or LCD projectors, the teachers that do have access to these tools generally report feeling fairly confident in using these devices with children (McMannis et al., 2013).

Challenges to Using Technology in the Early Childhood Classroom

While teachers may be confident in how to use many of the technology tools available in their classrooms, the question remains as to how they integrate technology into the curriculum in ways that support and enhance children's development. Despite the availability of various forms of technology in most early childhood classrooms, teachers' actual use of these tools illustrates some of the challenges beyond accessibility that they may face in effectively integrating technology into their curricula.

Computers, whether desktops, laptops, or tablet computers, are increasingly part of adults' and children's lives outside of the classroom, and surveys indicate that early childhood teachers are very confident computer users (McMannis et al., 2013). We could expect that most have used computers as students themselves as part of their teacher preparation programs and many primary grade teachers use computers regularly as part of their professional responsibilities. Confidence in computer use does not, however, translate into effective classroom practices. We draw on two examples. In the first we draw on an observation we made in a second grade classroom and in the second on a series of research studies conducted by Plowman and Stephen (2005, 2007) in preschool classrooms.

Typically primary school teachers have greater access to technology than their early childhood colleagues in non-public early care settings (McMannis et al., 2013). Access however can take many forms. In observing in a second grade classroom located in an inner city school serving predominantly low-income English Language Learners, one of us observed the following:

> The teacher led her class of 18 students into the computer lab for their twice-weekly 40-minute block of computer time. The computer lab included 24 computers distributed on round tables; each contained six computers separated by desktop dividers. The teacher settled her students into their individual seats and asked them to log into their school accounts to use the reading software. Immediately problems arose. Some children seemed to have forgotten their login codes or login procedures, others who successfully logged in struggled to find the reading software, for some the computers didn't seem to boot up at all, only a small number of the children seemed successful in accessing the appropriate software. The teacher, who was alone, began to troubleshoot—distributing index cards with names and login codes to various students, rebooting computers, and helping individual students find the appropriate software. As a few children continued to work independently on the software programs the teacher moved among individual students trying to help them get started. Eventually, it seemed that some computers were not even working and she ended up distributing paper and pencils to those unfortunate children with no computer access and establishing a turn-taking system with the functioning computers.

The end result was that the 40 minutes of computer time became for many students 20 minutes or less of independent work time with a computer. Also, as we watched, we saw that some children were actually using the reading software, while the more computer savvy seemed to have found alternative software more to their liking. To be sure, by a broad definition the students and their teacher had access to technology and perhaps the reading software itself provided affordances for literacy learning, however, the teacher clearly faced many challenges in structuring this activity for her students. The school's policies and structures established when and how these young students interacted with computers, and the school resources limited access to functioning computers and technical support. From this observation it was not clear what if any instructional options this teacher had.

Research on computer use in preschools may present a different set of challenges. Plowman and Stephen (2005, 2007) used case-study methodology to examine how teachers integrated computer use in early childhood centers that espoused child-centered learning and free play opportunities. Teachers in these programs typically provided children with independent opportunities for "playing with the computer" during the day, much as they provided child-choice activities with blocks, puzzles, and art materials. The computer center was typically tucked into a less busy corner of the room presumably to support children's independent exploration but making adult supervision and monitoring difficult, given teachers' supervision responsibilities for other classroom activities. Beyond perhaps an initial introduction in how to use the computer or access the media content, typically teachers rarely interacted with children as they used the computer. Most often teachers' involvement in children's computer use was in the form of distal monitoring. Teachers may or may not have provided a child with some assistance in getting started; they monitored turn-taking; and while most children who experienced problems simply left the computer area after a minute or two, teachers did respond to children's requests for help. As Plowman and Stephen (2005, 2007) suggested, the use of guided interaction and scaffolded adult support for learning with the technology was rarely seen. As the teachers in these child-centered programs integrated technology in their classrooms they tried to actively avoid direct instruction and provided opportunities for child-directed exploration. Their beliefs and attitudes about the developmentally appropriate use of technology, however, in many ways seemed to actually restrict children's learning experiences with technology.

Based on this research Plowman and Stephen (2007) concluded that desktop computers are not suitable technology tools for preschool classrooms and suggest that more interactive tools might have an advantage. While it may be that some technology tools by the nature of their user interface and interactivity may be less suitable for children of different ages, the more fundamental difficulty may reflect teachers' lack of confidence not in the technology tools themselves but in integrating technology tools into instruction. Even when teachers have access to more interactive technology tools, such as interactive whiteboards and tablet computers, there seems to be a disconnect between their beliefs on developmentally appropriate usage and their classroom practices (Simon, Nemeth, & McMannis, 2013). So while teachers seem to have concerns about the amount of classroom time children are exposed to technology, their actual classroom practices may exceed what they themselves consider to be developmentally appropriate. Thus, teachers may be using technology in teacher-directed, often large group settings, rather than in child-initiated experiences (Simon et al., 2013). The beliefs and attitudes teachers hold about technology use in the classroom, above and beyond the access to and confidence in using technology, play a powerful role in classroom practices (Blackwell et al., 2013).

The use of television and video are perhaps the most controversial technology. In some measure this seems consistent with the guidance provided by the NAEYC (2012) Position Statement, which characterizes television and video as non-interactive media, and also with concerns about television viewing that have been part of early childhood for decades (Levin, 2013). Early childhood teachers, with the exception of those in home-based settings (Wartella et al., 2013), avoid the use of video in the classroom. In contrast, video is one of the most commonly used forms of media in K-12 classrooms and K-12 teachers feel very positive about the use of video as a way to stimulate class discussions and illustrate complex concepts (PBS & Grunwald Associates, 2011). Perhaps our image of video in early childhood needs to shift from that of children glued to a television screen for an hour of commercial TV to the K-12 model of video, which involves students engaged in a lively discussion and classroom activity sparked by the presentation of a very short video segment (rather than an entire program). In the case of video, our challenge may be to help early childhood educators begin to think about the potential affordances of easily accessible technology and media in ways that extend and enhance children's learning.

The research on classroom video and computer use suggests that teachers feel fairly confident in their use of commonly accessible technology tools and may feel fairly confident in their own use of a broad range of technology tools. Their confidence and abilities in integrating these tools and the media content into their classrooms remains challenging. The issue of media content, beyond the technology tools themselves, is an ongoing concern. Research on children's television viewing has demonstrated that educational programming can promote the learning of specific academic skills, facts, and general concepts and is associated with long-term academic success (Kirkorian & Anderson, 2008). These positive effects are mediated by the age of the viewers, and the amount and context of viewing. Educational programs designed for preschoolers do not have the same educational benefits when viewed by older children or toddlers (Kirkorian & Anderson, 2008). Unfortunately while guidelines and policies exist for distinguishing between educational and "entertainment" television programming (Kirkorian & Anderson, 2008), decisions about the educational value of media available on emerging technology platforms is less clear.

The NAEYC (2012) Position Statement encourages teachers to exclude non-interactive media and in choosing interactive technology to "take the time to evaluate and select technology and media . . . to identify opportunities and problems . . . to make appropriate adaptations and to become familiar with new technologies as they are introduced" (p. 6). This is a daunting task complicated by the rapid market expansion of newer media forms in large part through commercial venues. For example, a recent review of the top preschool literacy apps and e-books identified as educational in the iTunes store indicated that the apps targeted only very basic literacy skills, that there was a lack of clarity in terms of how the features included with the e-books would in fact support the development of pre- or early literacy skills, and in most instances there was no evidence presented on how the educational value of this media was determined (Guernsey et al., 2012). The end result is that, as McMannis and Gunnewig (2012) stated, there is a critical need to provide support for early childhood practitioners in developing their knowledge and skills to evaluate new technologies.

Role of Early Childhood Teacher Preparation

Our role as early childhood teacher educators and teachers of teachers is to help our own students become digitally literate so that they in turn can integrate technology and digital literacy into their classrooms. We would expect our preservice teachers to develop competencies in the basic operations related to technology, the ethical issues surrounding technology usage, how technology can be used to create new knowledge and ideas and to communicate and collaborate with others, how to access and evaluate information, and how to use technology in solving problems and thinking critically (International Society for Technology in Education [ISTE] Standards for Students, 2007; and Standards for Teachers, 2008). We can support our students as technology learners as individual instructors within our classes and through our early childhood teacher preparation programs.

The students now entering our teacher preparation programs have grown up with digital technology (Bers & Kazakoff, 2013). Though there continue to be differences by ethnicity, gender, and social class in the ownership and patterns of use for different technology tools, most young adults will have had a computer, some form of video game system, a mobile phone, and access to the internet in their home (Rideout, Lauricella, & Wartella, 2011). While they may have used technology previously as students, by far their primary form of technology use is likely to have been entertainment—watching videos, accessing social networking sites, listening to music, and texting (Rideout et al., 2011). While our students are likely to have had a great deal of experience in consuming media and in using technology to communicate with their peers, they are perhaps less likely to have developed the student competencies identified by ISTE (2007). They do, however, have rich experiences in the use of technology. We can ask ourselves as instructors how we build on our students' digital experiences in our own courses. Do we fight the battle of silencing cell phones in our classes or construct ways to integrate students' use of cell phones as part of class activities? Most higher education institutions have adopted some form of a learning management system (e.g. Blackboard, Moodle, Sakai) and most faculty use these systems as part of face-to-face classes (Jaschik & Lederman, 2013). Learning management systems typically offer features for collaborative learning, peer communication, the integration of multimodal resources, and the provision of adaptive learning experiences, however typically faculty do not make use of these features and utilize learning management software for basic functions such as to post course syllabi, communicate with students, and manage grades (Jaschik & Lederman, 2013). Do we incorporate multimedia presentations into our course assignments or rely on traditional essays and paper and pencil exams? The infusion of technology into instructional practices has long been identified as a key element in preparing new teachers to use and integrate technology into their own teaching practices (Cradler, Freeman, Cradler, & McNabb, 2002; Tondeur et al., 2012), and while the NAEYC (2012) Position Statement on Technology is clear that "teacher educators need to provide technology-mediated and online learning experiences that are effective, engaging and empowering," it is less certain that early childhood teacher educators have been able to meet this challenge individually or programmatically.

Most teacher education programs rely on an introductory educational technology course as the primary means of supporting student technology learning, with technology less typically integrated throughout methods courses and field experiences (Polly, Mims, Shephard, & Inan, 2010; Tondeur et al., 2012). Furthermore student use of technology in their teacher preparation programs typically does not reflect the use of technology by practicing teachers (Ottenbreit-Leftwich et al., 2012). Practicing pre-K-12 teachers who express a high comfort level in using technology in their classrooms report that they typically and regularly use technology for administrative purposes, including personal productivity and analysis of student achievement data, professional development, and communication, and within the classroom to present information, teach specific concepts, support diverse learning styles, and support higher order thinking. In contrast, teacher educators tended to report the inclusion of less classroom-based technology activities, such as information presentation and personal productivity, as regular elements within their teacher preparation programs (Ottenbreit-Leftwich et al., 2012). This disconnect between the technology activities included in teacher preparation programs and the actual use of technology by practicing teachers is problematic given the difficulties our students may have in translating their technology knowledge as students into their professional lives as teachers (Laffey, 2004). In addition, the rapid change in technology itself—in the technology tools available and the uses of these tools—suggests that our early childhood teacher preparation programs face the challenge of preparing our preservice teachers to use technology that is only now being imagined (for example trends in wearable technology and the "internet of things" as reported in the 2014 New Media Consortium Horizon K-12 Report (Johnson, Becker, Estrada, & Freeman, 2014).

Promising Practices in Early Childhood Teacher Education

Koehler & Mishra (2008) characterize the complex problem of teaching with technology as a "wicked problem" which involves "incomplete, contradictory, and changing requirements". Their concept of technological pedagogical content knowledge (TPACK) provides a framework for how we think about how and why we integrate technology in the early childhood curriculum. The application of TPACK relies on the intersection of three sources of knowledge. In the case of early childhood curriculum this would be the pedagogy and knowledge of how children think, learn, and develop; the content or subject-based knowledge of early childhood; and technological knowledge including the affordances and constraints of different technology tools and media. TPACK has been used as a framework for describing pre- and inservice teachers' understanding and skills in integrating technology and to analyze how faculty and preservice teacher preparation programs support technology integration (Polly et al., 2010; Schmidt et al., 2009; Tondeur et al., 2012).

Early childhood educators demonstrating TPACK in planning a classroom literacy activity that, for example, introduces unfamiliar vocabulary words, might use their content knowledge of early literacy and choose to embed the introduction of new vocabulary words as part of a book sharing activity, thus supporting other literacy goals as well. Their understanding of early literacy content would guide their choice of text (fiction or expository), text complexity, and quality of illustration. Pedagogical knowledge would be reflected in their understanding of developmentally appropriate practice and the needs of their learners: whether to structure the activity as a teacher-directed whole class circle time, small group activity, or child-choice independent activity; whether there were English language learners in their classroom; and the learning support needed by individual learners. Technological knowledge would be reflected in their choice of which technology tools would be most appropriate—traditional print picture book, Big Book, digital book, or e-book app—and perhaps whether to use a presentation tool, either an LCD projector or an interactive whiteboard. Within each area of knowledge teachers skilled in TPACK would be able to weigh the affordances and constraints of the various choices within the unique context of their classrooms based on their depth of knowledge within each area. A preparation program that supports learning in this way would emphasize learning activities that build knowledge and skills in all three areas, not only in the course content but also in applying this knowledge in students' clinical field experiences.

Field experiences as collaborative partnerships. Clinical field experiences have the potential to provide students with the hands-on technology experiences that they need to apply the knowledge base acquired as students in their courses to authentic classroom practice. Field experiences in which preservice teachers are able to work with early childhood educators who successfully integrate technology in their classrooms are critical (Laffey, 2004). The current state of technology use and accessibility of technology in early childhood classrooms, as reviewed earlier, may pose challenges in finding appropriate placements that support these experiences for our students. Collaborative partnerships between teacher preparation programs and community-based early education settings may facilitate these opportunities (Polly et al., 2010). Such partnerships are often a goal of many teacher preparation programs and are consistent with national accreditation expectations and standards (e.g. NCATE). However, the issue of technology access within early childhood settings may still be a barrier even within partnership models.

We may also want to consider how we could capitalize on our students themselves to bridge these access issues. In a student-led conference, two student teachers in our middle school teacher preparation program presented a workshop on technology. Both student teachers were enthusiastic personal users of technology, both were motivated to use technology with their students, and both were placed in schools located in low-income communities, one rural and one urban. The technology available to their middle school students, as is typical of many early childhood settings, was limited. The solution for these student teachers was to bring their technology tools—their own smartphones and tablets—into the classroom and to then model and share these tools with their students. Though there are differences between middle school and early childhood classrooms, these ideas can be applied within our early childhood teacher preparation programs. For example, in our methods courses students could be asked to address technology integration based on the personal technology they could bring into their field settings (rather than the technology that may or may not be available in these settings). Student teachers could be asked how they could use the applications typically found on cell phones (i.e. photos, videos, audio recordings) to document children's progress, how they could integrate open source applications into their lesson plans (for example, the Educreation app is a free interactive whiteboard and screencasting tool that teachers and students can use to create simple instructional videos or animations), or how they could utilize freely available assistive technology to support the needs of diverse learners (for example, the VL2 Storybook apps are freely available through Gaullaudet University and include text narrations in both English and American Sign Language).

Conclusion

As teacher educators we are being asked to prepare our students to become practitioners who are knowledgeable in how to evaluate media content that has not yet been developed, to become skilled in using technology that is now only imagined, and to be able to integrate this media and technology in developmentally appropriate ways in early childhood settings. In the opening of this chapter we identified the questions that we faced as beginning teachers as we considered how to integrate a far more simple form of technology, the woodworking bench, into the early childhood classroom. These questions are relevant as we consider the integration of more complex and emerging technology tools and media. Our students need to understand and be able to evaluate the learning goals supported by the use of digital technology tools and media. Our teacher education programs should include opportunities for students to explore and apply frameworks such as TPACK and Universal Design for Learning principles across their content and methods courses. Our students need to be aware of the research on the potential affordances and benefits of digital technology as well as the potential harmful impacts of media exposure. And perhaps most importantly we cannot prepare our students to become digitally literate until we, as their teachers, are digitally literate ourselves (Donohue & Schomburg, 2015).

References

American Academy of Pediatrics, Committee on Public Education. (1999). Media education. *Pediatrics, 104*(2 pt 1), 341–343.

American Academy of Pediatrics, Council on Communications and Media. (2011). Media use by children younger than 2 years. *Pediatrics, 128*(5), 1–6.

American Academy of Pediatrics, Council on Communication and Media. (2013). Children, adolescents, and the media. *Pediatrics, 132*(5), 958–961.

Anderson, D. R., & Hanson, K. G. (2009). Children, media, and methodology. *American Behavioral Scientist, 52*(8), 1204–1219.

Barr, R. (2008). Attention and learning from media during infancy and early childhood. In S. L. Calvert & B. J. Wilson (Eds.), *Handbook of child development and the media*, pp. 143–165. Malden, MA: Blackwell.

Barron, B., Cayton-Hodges, G., Bofferding, L., Copple, C., Darling-Hammond, L., & Levine, M. (2011). *Take a giant step: A blueprint for teaching young children in a digital age.* New York: The Joan Ganz Cooney Center at Sesame Workshop. Retrieved from http://www.joanganzcooneycenter.org/publication/take-a-giant-step-a-blueprint-for-teaching-young-children-in-a-digital-age/

Bers, M. U., Flannery, L. P., Kazakoff, E. R., & Sullivan, A. (2014). Computational thinking and tinkering: Exploration of an early childhood robotics curriculum. *Computers & Education, 72*, 145–157.

Bers, M. U., & Kazakoff, E. R. (2013). Techno-Tykes: Digital technologies in early childhood. In O. N. Saracho with B. Spodek (Eds.), *Handbook of research on the education of young children*, pp. 197–205. New York: Routledge.

Blackwell, C. K., Lauricella, A. R., Wartella, E., Robb, M., & Shomburg, R. (2013). Adoption and use of technology in early education: The interplay of extrinsic barriers and teacher attitudes. *Computers and Education, 69,* 310–319.

Center on Media and Child Health, Children's Hospital Boston. (2005). *The effects of electronic media on children ages zero to six: A history of research.* Kaiser Family Foundation. Retrieved from www.kff.org/entmedia/loader.cfm?url=/commonspot/security/getfile.cfm&PageID=50552

Chiong, C., & Shuler, C. (2010). *Learning: Is there an app for that? Investigations of young children's usage and learning with mobile devices and apps.* New York: The Joan Ganz Cooney Center at Sesame Workshop.

Christakis, D. A., & Zimmerman, F. J. (2009). Young children and media: Limitations of current knowledge and future directions for research. *American Behavioral Scientist, 52*(8), 1177–1185.

Common Sense Media. (2013). *Zero to eight: Children's media use in America 2013.* Retrieved from https://www.commonsensemedia.org/research/zero-to-eight-childrens-media-use-in-america-2013

Cradler, J., Freeman, M., Cradler, R., & McNabb, M. (2002). Research implications for preparing teachers to use technology. *Learning and Leading with Technology, 30*(1), 50–55.

DeLoache, J. S., & Chiong, C. (2009). Babies and babies' media. *American Behavioral Scientist, 52*(6), 1115–1135.

Donohue, C., & Schomburg, R. (2015). Teaching with technology: Preparing early childhood educators for the digital age. In C. Donohue (Ed.), *Technology and digital media in the early years*, pp. 36–53. New York: Routledge.

Dunst, C. J., Trivette, C. J., & Hamby, D. W. (2012). Assistive technology and the communication and literacy development of young children with disabilities. *CELL Review, 5*(7), 1–7.

Fessakis, G., Gouli, E., & Mavroudi, E. (2013). Problem solving by 5–6 years old kindergarten children in a computer programming environment: A case study. *Computers & Education, 63*, 87–97.

Gray, L., Thomas, N., and Lewis, L. (2010). *Teachers' use of educational technology in U.S. public schools: 2009 (NCES 2010–040).* Washington, DC: National Center for Education Statistics, Institute of Education Sciences, U.S. Department of Education.

Guernsey, L. (2013). Toddlers, electronic media, and language development. *Zero to Three, 33*(4), 11–17.

Guernsey, L., Levine, M., Chiong, C., & Severns, M. (2012). *Pioneering literacy in the digital Wild West: Empowering parents and educators.* New York: The Joan Ganz Cooney Center at Sesame Workshop.

Harms, T., & Clifford, R. M. (1980). *Early childhood environment rating scale.* New York: Teachers College Press.

Hitchcock, C., Meyer, A., Rose, D., & Jackson, R. (2002). Providing new access to the general curriculum. *Teaching Exceptional Children, 35*(2), 8–17.

International Society for Technology in Education (ISTE). (2007). *ISTE Standards for students.* Retrieved from http://www.iste.org/STANDARDS

International Society for Technology in Education (ISTE). (2008). *ISTE Standards for teachers.* Retrieved from http://www.iste.org/STANDARDS

Jaschik, S., & Lederman, D. (Eds.). (2013). *The 2013 Inside Higher Ed survey of faculty attitudes on technology.* Conducted by Gallup. Retrieved from http://www.insidehighered.com/news/survey/survey-faculty-attitudes-technology#sthash.FctGVJka.dpbs

Johnson, L., Becker, A., Estrada, V., & Freeman, A. (2014). *NMC Horizon Report: 2014 K—12 Edition.* The New Media Consortium: Austin, Texas. Retrieved from http://www.nmc.org/publication/nmc-horizon-report-2014-k-12-edition/

Kazakoff, E., Sullivan, A., & Bers, M. U. (2013). The effect of a classroom-based intensive robotics and programming workshop on sequencing ability in early childhood. *Early Childhood Education Journal, 41*(4), 245–255.

Kirkorian, H. L., & Anderson, D. R. (2008). Learning from educational media. In S. L. Clear & B. J. Wilson (Eds.), *The Blackwell handbook of children, media, and development*, pp. 319–360. Boston, MA: Blackwell.

Kirkorian, H. L., Wartella, E. A., & Anderson, D. R. (2008). Media and young children's learning. *Future of Children, 18*(1), 39–61.

Koehler, M. J., & Mishra, P. (2008). Introducing technological pedagogical knowledge. In AACTE (Ed.), *The handbook of technological pedagogical content knowledge for educators.* New York: Routledge for the American Association of Colleges of Teacher Education.

Laffey, J. (2004). Appropriation, mastery and resistance to technology in early childhood preservice teacher education. *Journal of Research on Technology in Education, 36*(4), 361–382.

Lerner, C., & Barr, R. (2014). Screen sense: Setting the record straight: Research-based guidelines for screen use for children under 3 years old. Washington, DC: Zero to Three.

Levin, D. E. (2013). *Beyond remote-controlled childhood: Teaching young children in the media age.* Washington, DC: National Association for the Education of Young Children.

McMannis, L. D., & Gunnewig, S. B. (2012). Finding the education in educational technology with early learners. *Young Children, 67*(3), 14–24.

McMannis, L. D., Nemeth, K., & Simon, F. (2013, April). What's really happening with technology in early childhood education? Voices from the field: 2012 National Early Childhood Technology Today Survey. Paper presented at the annual meeting of the Early Education and Technology for Children, Salt Lake City, UT. Retrieved from http://www.slideshare.net/FSSimon/eetc-2013-ecetechsurveymcmanisnemethsimonpdf

Naraian, S., & Surabian, M. (2014). New literacy studies: An alternative frame for preparing teachers to use assistive technology. *Teacher Education and Special Education, 37*(4), 330–346.

National Association for the Education of Young Children & The Fred Rogers Center. (2012). *Technology and interactive media as tools in early childhood programs serving children from birth through age 8.* Washington, DC: Authors.

teaching has been elusive (Darling-Hammond, 2000; Wright, Horn, & Sanders, 1997). Researchers argue that this lack of conceptual clarity poses the main obstacle to achieving a widely accepted approach to teacher assessment (Cruickshank & Haefele, 1990). Yet clarification in this area is critical for two reasons, "First, what is measured is a reflection of what is valued, and as a corollary, what is measured is valued" (Goe, Bell, & Little, 2008, p. 4).

Keeping in mind the lack of agreement on a definition of teacher effectiveness, we feel that a conceptual framework is needed around which to organize our discussion of promising teacher assessment practices. Therefore, we begin with a broad description of three unique but related approaches to teacher evaluation: the measurement of inputs, processes, and outputs (Goe et al., 2008). Teachers bring inputs, their personal qualities and characteristics, into the classroom. Inputs include a teacher's knowledge, skills, beliefs, and qualifications. Processes are made up of the interactions that take place between teachers and students in the classroom. These include instructional decisions, relationship characteristics, and organizational structures in their classrooms. Finally, outputs are the results of these processes including student achievement and indicators of positive child development. In summary, inputs are what teachers *bring*, processes are what they *do*, and outputs are the *results* of their efforts.

The current legislative climate suggests the ultimate measure of teacher effectiveness is student achievement (Goe, 2007). However, understanding the intermediary steps, or more proximal outcomes, in the causal chain of effects between teacher characteristics and student achievement gains provides researchers and policy makers with leverage on the development of teacher effectiveness (Sheridan, Edwards, Marvin, & Knoche, 2009). The Measures of Effective Teaching (MET) Project, one of the most extensive research studies on teacher assessment in K-12 settings, supports the measurement of inputs, processes, and outputs in early childhood teacher assessment. The project created and evaluated measures of teacher effectiveness, as well as provided feedback and supports for teachers who were found less effective.

Data from over 3000 teachers revealed that the use of multiple measures to determine teacher effectiveness (classroom observations, surveys, and student achievement data) produced more consistent and stable estimates of teacher effectiveness from one year to the next (Bill & Melinda Gates Foundation, 2013). The results suggest caution when emphasizing a single measure. For example, an emphasis on academic achievement tests might push teachers to focus primarily on academic goals to the detriment of other important developmental child outcomes, such as learning positive social interactions. Exclusive measurement, a single outcome measure, creates an incentive structure that is not aligned with the multifaceted goals of early childhood education. Teacher evaluation systems in more than 40 states use multiple measures of student achievement and observations to determine effectiveness and improve teacher quality (Kane et al., 2014).

Promising Teacher Assessment Practices

The following sections describe assessment tools used in varying combinations to evaluate early childhood teacher effectiveness around the country. These widely used or empirically supported tools represent assessment strategies in the areas of teacher inputs, processes, and outputs. Some have been developed specifically for use in early childhood classrooms, while others are being adapted to meet the needs of early childhood settings. While these tools are promising, none of them are considered comprehensive. The most complete picture of the strengths and challenges of teachers is generated through a combination of assessments.

Assessing Teacher Inputs

Teacher inputs are the characteristics of teachers. Although teacher inputs can be conceptualized to include aspects of a teacher's education and credentials, this information tends to be more informative of teacher quality at the school level, rather than as an indicator of individual teacher effectiveness.

For example, a school might use the percentage of teachers at the school with advanced degrees as a point of differentiation from other schools. Similarly, for early childhood education settings, parents might consider the percentage of teachers with state certification or a Child Development Associate (CDA) credential when selecting a child care center. Empirical evidence for the efficacy of teacher qualification in measuring teacher efficacy is mixed (Early et al., 2006, 2007).

Yet a recent investigation of the relationship between preschool teachers' knowledge of effective teaching practices (input) and their ability to enact effective teacher practices (process) suggests that a transactional relationship exists between these two aspects of teacher effectiveness (Pianta et al., 2014). This means that as teachers try to practice more effective teaching behaviors, they understand them better and can more accurately identify them in others. As teachers develop a deeper understanding of effective teaching behaviors, their teaching becomes more effective. These findings further highlight the challenge of assessing effective teaching: teachers do not become skilled in their classroom practices simply through a linear increase in pedagogical or content knowledge. That knowledge must be synthesized into their classroom behaviors through extensive practice, classroom observation, reflection, and feedback (Hamre, Downer, Jamil, & Pianta, 2012). In order to capture a teacher's level of expertise, and his or her growing effectiveness over time, assessment systems must include measures of teacher knowledge, but consistently incorporate that information with assessments of how that knowledge is applied in the classroom across time to truly characterize the teacher's professional skills.

Teacher Knowledge Measures

Assessing teacher knowledge is necessary at different junctures in the teacher preparation and professional development process. Two promising areas of research are the assessment of teacher content knowledge and pedagogical content knowledge for early math and reading.

Nearly a decade of research in teacher knowledge for mathematics instruction by Heather Hill and colleagues (see Hill, Ball, & Schilling, 2008) furthered the conceptualization and measurement of pedagogical content knowledge in math. Their recent efforts focus on the explication of teachers' knowledge of content and students (KCS). They posit that KCS is "content knowledge intertwined with knowledge of how students think about, know, or learn this particular content" (Hill et al., 2008, p. 375). They propose that KCS is important for teacher effectiveness because it is the knowledge base that good teachers use to simultaneously address the subject matter and how students typically master it, including predicting common mistakes and misconceptions that may arise. Teachers use KCS to design instructional activities that meet the needs of their students based on what the students already know and what they need to learn. Hill and colleagues assessed aspects of KCS with over 5,000 teachers over three years, but in spite of rigorous measurement work were unable to produce an assessment with strong psychometric properties. The authors reported that the work helped them refine their conceptualization of KCS. They reflected that formulating more open-ended assessment items, as opposed to multiple choice, might produce a clearer picture of KCS.

More recently, McCray and Chen (2012) focused specifically on pedagogical content knowledge in preschool math through the use of open-ended interview questions. Their Preschool Mathematics Pedagogical Content Knowledge Interview (PM-PCK Interview; McCray & Chen, 2012) focused on three areas: (1) teachers' subject matter understanding for preschool math, (2) their teaching techniques for teaching these concepts, and (3) their awareness of how students develop in their mastery of these concepts. During the interview, teachers were presented with two different scenarios in a preschool classroom. The interviewer asked the teachers questions about incorporating mathematical concepts in naturalistic play settings through the use of specific materials at hand and the comments made by children in the scenarios. Teachers who identified more mathematical instruction opportunities in the course of these play scenarios and made comments that helped extend these opportunities scored higher on the interview. In a study of 113 children in 22 Head Start classrooms, McCray to better understand teacher impacts on student achievement or for high stakes evaluations of teachers, which impact their employment and compensation. In order to support effective education, it is important that observation protocols are used in ways that align with the purpose for which they were developed, and meet acceptable standards of validity and reliability for the context in which they are employed (Goe et al., 2008).

It is very important that classroom observers are consistently monitored and trained because of the high inference nature of classroom observations, and the often high-stakes applications of observation data. Initial training or certification ensures that all raters apply the observation protocol in the same way, so that scores are comparable across classrooms and raters. Regular calibration is also required to ensure that raters continue to apply the protocol in the same way over time. This is especially important when observation protocols are used to measure changes in teacher effectiveness across time, because changes in scores need to reflect actual changes in classroom process quality, not a drift in the implementation of the observation protocol (Meyer, Cash, & Mashburn, 2011). For example, if classroom observers apply an observation protocol to a classroom very stringently at the beginning of the year, and then become lenient as the year progresses, it may appear that teachers are becoming more effective. But in reality, the apparent growth in teacher effectiveness is a function of rater calibration error. Although challenging, research suggests it is possible to successfully calibrate a large number of raters over time (Cash, Hamre, Pianta, & Myers, 2012). Indications that classroom observations can be associated with children's learning outcomes (Curby et al., 2009; Kimball, White, Milanowski, & Borman, 2004) suggest that this may be a useful teacher assessment tool if used with careful attention to issues of reliability and validity. As such, we will discuss two of the most widely used and studied observation protocols, Charlotte Danielson's (1996) Framework for Teaching and the Classroom Assessment Scoring System (Pianta et al., 2008).

Classroom Assessment Scoring System

The Classroom Assessment Scoring System (CLASS) is a theoretically and empirically driven observation measure of proximal processes, or the moment-to-moment interactions, that take place between teachers and students and among students in the classroom. This observation instrument was initially developed as a measure of teacher-student interactions in preschool classrooms at the University of Virginia, although versions of the CLASS have subsequently been developed and studied for observing classrooms from infancy through high school. The CLASS organizes classroom interactions into three broad domains: emotional support, classroom organization, and instructional support. The emotional support domain focuses on the types of interactions that teachers use to establish caring relationships in classrooms, including responding to students' individual needs and promoting independence. Classroom organization captures interactions that organize students' attention, time, and behavior. The instructional support domain relates to interactions that teachers use to provide feedback that encourages student persistence and promotes higher-order thinking. Each of the CLASS domains is divided into dimensions that capture more specific areas. These dimensions are outlined with indicators and behavioral markers that help observers identify specific behaviors that define effective teaching interactions in each of these areas. Observers rate teachers on each dimension using a 7-point scale, with 1 to 2 representing low-quality interactions, 3 to 5 representing mid-range interaction quality, and 6 to 7 representing high-quality interactions. The CLASS framework covers a broad range of interactions that are associated with children's positive socio-emotional, self-regulatory, and cognitive development (Downer, Sabol, & Hamre, 2010), while providing enough specificity in each dimension to identify what effective interactions look like depending on the development stage and age of the students. Furthermore, the protocol can be used to observe classroom interaction quality across content areas.

One of the strengths of the CLASS is the great deal of reliability and validity work that has accompanied its development and implementation over the years. CLASS observers must undergo two days of standardized training and pass a certification test that requires them to score five 20-minute classroom videos with 80 percent accuracy within one point when compared to master codes, established through a rigorous consensus process with multiple expert raters. The developers of the protocol recommend that a minimum of four 20-minute observations, scored using classroom video or through live observation, be aggregated to obtain CLASS scores to ensure that observers obtain stable and representative estimates of teacher interaction quality, (see Mashburn, Downer, Rivers, Brackett, & Martinez, 2014). Research on validity of the CLASS revealed associations between the interactions measured in the CLASS and a variety of measures of child development, behavior, and learning in over 4,000 classrooms in urban, rural, and suburban schools across the country (Hamre & Pianta, 2005; Burchinal et al., 2008; Rimm-Kaufman, La Paro, Downer, & Pianta, 2005). This is part of the reason that the CLASS is used as a primary teacher evaluation tool in over 50,000 Head Start classrooms across the United States.

Framework for Teaching

Another classroom observation protocol generating consistent associations between classroom processes and student achievement (Gallagher, 2004; Kimball et al., 2004; Milanowski, 2004) is Danielson's (1996) Framework for Teaching. The Framework for Teaching is one of the most commonly used observation tools in public school districts in the United States (Brandt, Mathers, Oliva, Brown-Sims, & Hess, 2007). Much like the CLASS, the Framework for Teaching has a hierarchical structure, with four broad domains: planning and preparation, classroom environment, instruction, and professional responsibilities. These domains are divided into 22 components, each with two to five descriptive elements. Teachers receive a score on each of the components that rates them as *Distinguished*, *Proficient*, *Basic*, or *Unsatisfactory*. The planning and preparation domain captures the ways teachers use their understanding of content, pedagogy, and the students to design instruction and assessment. The classroom environment domain focuses on the ways in which teachers arrange the classroom and interact with students to maximize positive relationships and behavior. The instruction domain reflects the ways in which teachers engage students and promote their learning. Finally, the professional responsibilities domain includes the activities outside of instructional time, like positive engagement with parents and the school community and continued professional growth. Unlike the CLASS, which focuses specifically on teacher-child interactions that take place in the moment of teaching, the first and fourth domains of the Framework for Teaching requires the evaluation of artifacts as evidence of teacher planning and professional activities (Danielson, 1996).

The Framework for Teaching has been used for many purposes, both summative and formative, but the developer suggests that its greatest value is in its use as a feedback tool to help teachers continue improving their teaching skills (Danielson, 2007). Similar to the CLASS, it provides evaluative information on teacher effectiveness as well as a basis for mentoring programs, instructional coaching, and other professional development activities (Gallagher, 2004; Kimball et al., 2004; Milanowski, 2004). Unlike the CLASS, for which different versions highlight developmentally aligned interactions within the same broad domains for different grade levels, the Framework for Teaching can be used in classrooms of any age level or content area. The rationale presented by the developer for using the same tool across contexts is that the underlying elements of good teaching transcend age and content area, although there has been little investigation into whether the instrument functions differently at different age levels.

Content-Specific Classroom Observation

Although the instruments discussed above are both widely used and provide useful information about classroom processes, there is growing interest in content area-specific instruments that focus on teachers' use of subject-specific knowledge for teaching. There are a variety of content-specific classroom observations in use, but the majority were developed as part of specific research projects. Examples of protocols with promising early childhood applications include the TEX-IN3 (Hoffman, Sailors, Duffy, & Beretvas, 2004) and the Mathematics Quality of Instruction (MQI; Hill et al., 2008; Hill, Kapitula, & Umland, 2011). The TEX-IN3 focuses on the instructional interactions that involve literacy in the classroom. Observations consider the quality of texts used, the ways teachers engage students around text, and the understandings they develop about the uses of text. The MQI focuses on similar aspects involving mathematics. This tool considers the richness, clarity, and connectedness of mathematics in the classroom, as well as student engagement in mathematical reasoning and meaning-making. This growing body of observational assessments is based on the recognition that the classroom processes for effective content-area instruction are distinct from more foundational pedagogical interactions focused on classroom climate, organization, and instructional engagement. Although these instruments have not been widely used beyond the developers, they show a promising new direction in the assessment of classroom processes that warrant further investigation. Collectively, the research suggests classroom observation measures have the ability to capture the complexity of interactions in classrooms. Although, a significant threat to the reliability of the scores is ever-present with the use of this teacher assessment method. Consistent efforts must be made to ensure that raters are well-trained and stay calibrated over time, in order for observations to serve as a credible assessment of teacher effectiveness.

Assessing Educational Outputs

The assessment of educational outputs remains the least developed or standardized approach to teacher assessment in early childhood contexts. Educational outputs are the results of effective teaching, including academic achievement as well as indicators of positive child development. While statistical techniques for measuring and isolating the impact that teachers have on student learning has been an area of growth for the field of education in upper elementary and secondary contexts (see Raudenbush, 2004), the translations of these techniques to non-tested early childhood classrooms has proven to be a challenge (Connors-Tadros & Horowitz, 2014). Furthermore, the common use of educational artifacts to provide rich information about the ways in which teachers are impacting student learning lacks sufficient reliability and validity to be used in high-stakes teacher evaluation contexts.

Student Achievement Data

Examining changes in student achievement data is one of the most widely used methods of determining teacher effectiveness. Achievement data are often used in value-added models—a set of complex statistical techniques using students' prior achievement on standardized tests to arrive at a predicted score for subsequent years, and determining teacher effectiveness as a function of whether students meet, exceed, or fail to reach expected scores (Goldhaber & Anthony, 2003). A teacher is deemed effective when the majority of the students in the classroom exceed their expected scores; if students fall below expectations teachers are considered less effective. Two important factors can potentially affect the utility of the value-added model's ability to provide useful information about teacher effectiveness. First, these complex statistical models are susceptible to specification errors without a consensus from the field on the best modeling strategies (Bracey, 2004; Rockoff, 2004). In addition, the accuracy of value-added is highly dependent on the reliability and validity of the student achievement data. Because standardized achievement data are rarely collected in early childhood classrooms, using value-added models to assess teacher effectiveness in these settings is difficult (Connors-Tadros & Horowitz, 2014). This issue is particularly challenging for early childhood teachers who are required to take part in state evaluation systems for a variety of reasons (i.e. they teach for school districts, are state licensed, or are paid through public school funds).

Early childhood teachers often conduct formative, observation-based, authentic assessments of children to help guide instructional decisions, but using these methods for teacher evaluation can be problematic due to a lack of standardization (Goe & Holdheide, 2011). Moreover, there is a conflict of interest when teachers are asked to use such subjective means to document student growth that is connected to their own evaluation. Although some schools counteract this issue by having objective observers assess children's learning in classrooms, this can be a costly and time-consuming solution. A lack of empirical evidence on how to measure teacher effectiveness from educational outputs in early childhood has led states and school districts to a variety of approaches. More than 20 states have been experimenting with the use of student learning objectives (SLO), specific learning goals with aligned assessments that are used to determine teacher effectiveness as a function of student learning (Connors-Tadros & Horowitz, 2014). An SLO is set for the whole class or for a subset of students and includes three main components: (1) a clear student objective or goal; (2) a target for growth based on students' beginning achievement level; and (3) a specific assessment tool used to determine the extent to which the learning goal is met (Bornfreund, 2013).

Austin Independent School District (AISD) in Texas, and the Denver Public School District in Colorado are two examples of well-researched implementations of SLOs. Both of these districts started using SLOs as part of teacher incentive pay programs that reach across age levels; however, neither has reported effectiveness results separately for their early childhood teachers. Early evidence of the association between teacher SLO achievement and student performance on standardized tests suggests it may be a promising alternative for measuring teachers' contribution to student learning in non-tested classrooms, such as early childhood settings. In Austin, teachers were asked to develop two SLOs with the help of the district, one of which had to be attainable for 75 percent of the students in their class. They were also asked to determine a measurement strategy for these objectives (e.g. existing assessments or assessments they developed and were approved by the district). Administrators were required to assess the quality of the SLOs based on a standard rubric provided by the district. Findings from tested grades in Austin classrooms suggest that teachers whose students met SLOs were also able to show growth on state administered achievement tests (Schmitt and Ibanez, 2011). Similarly, in Denver, teachers who attained SLO targets also performed well on established measures of effectiveness, such as value-added scores (Goldhaber & Walch, 2012).

More evidence is needed in early childhood classrooms to understand the extent to which SLOs are viable as an assessment of teacher effectiveness. The flexibility of SLOs is attractive; SLOs can be based on a set of standards, such as the Common Core, or on local school growth priorities. They can also be used in the context of value-added models, or as separate measures of student learning that are customized to content. Student learning objectives can be assessed using externally developed or teacher developed assessments, provided these assessments are rigorous and allow for comparison across classrooms. However, SLOs also come with their own distinct challenges (Bornfreund, 2013). First, it is difficult to create SLOs that provide appropriate levels of challenge, are achievable, and utilized in high-stakes evaluation. Second, they require reliable measures of children's learning. And finally, teachers often require support and supervision to ensure successful implementation of SLOs to meet the first two challenges. As such, the flexibility and autonomy provided by SLOs in teacher evaluation create the greatest threats to reliability and validity of the approach (Harris, 2012).

Teacher Portfolios

Another method commonly used to assess teacher effectiveness through the examination of education outputs is the teacher portfolio, a curated sampling of evidence of teachers' exemplary practice and student progress. Portfolios can exhibit teacher effectiveness through the use of lesson plans, assignments, student work samples, assessments, classroom videos, and teacher reflective writing that describes why selected artifacts are included (Painter, 2001). Portfolios are most often used in teacher preparation programs to document candidate progress for licensure, but are also utilized by several states as part of broader teacher evaluation systems. For example, portfolio-based performance assessment has served as a large component of teacher evaluation in Vermont for several decades (Koretz, Stecher, Klein, & McCaffrey, 1994). Although this approach is unusual at the state level, the system has stakeholder support because it creates a comprehensive representation of the complex impacts that teachers have on students beyond test scores. On the other hand, the same complexity has posed a challenge to establishing inter-rater reliability in evaluating the portfolios (Koretz et al., 1994). These measurement challenges and the lack of empirical support for the use of portfolios in teacher assessment suggest that portfolios be used in conjunction with multiple teacher evaluation measures, and not as a summative assessment (Johnson, McDaniel, & Willeke, 2000).

The Connecticut Beginning Educator Support and Training (BEST) Program is another example of a successful portfolio assessment system. Teachers in this two-year induction program worked with a mentor and received several types of professional development as they made the transition into the first year of teaching. During the second year of teaching, they submitted a portfolio of their teaching practice for assessment and completion of certification requirements (Connecticut State Department of Education, 2007). Portfolio evaluation was based on Connecticut's Common Core of Teaching standards, focusing both on foundational pedagogy and grade-level and content-specific knowledge and skills. Furthermore, portfolio assessors were experienced teachers from the same content area as the teacher being assessed. These assessors had at least 50 hours of training and passed reliability tests on portfolio assessment protocols. Although heralded as an exemplary portfolio assessment and model of state level standardization and guidance, the task of assembling the portfolio was stressful for novice teachers (Ellis, 2013). In 2010, the state of Connecticut replaced the BEST program with the Teacher Education and Mentoring (TEAM) induction program, which changed foci from teacher assessment to teacher skill development and support. The new induction program helps new teachers set student learning goals and demonstrate progress by incorporating classroom observations and reflective writing in modules (Ellis, 2013).

The transition occurring in Connecticut highlights several specific issues concerning the use of portfolios in teacher assessment and teacher assessment in general. The comprehensive nature of portfolios can be a double-edged sword—even though they allow teachers to show evidence of effectiveness in domains not easily captured in classroom observations or even student achievement tests, the detailed documentation required can be time consuming and distracting from the actual work of teaching. This problem persists even if reliable scoring of portfolios is maintained over time. Clarifying the purpose of the portfolio assessment is also among the most salient challenges. Teacher development and evaluation need to drive the design and implementation of portfolio assessment. Unfortunately, as evidenced in this overview of several current teacher assessment practices, function does not always drive form.

Challenges and Next Steps in Teacher Assessment

Our review of several different teacher assessment approaches, currently in use or gaining traction in the field, raises some important questions and concerns. These challenges fall mainly into two areas: conceptualization and measurement. In order for teacher educators and educational professionals to obtain greater clarity on how to move early childhood teacher assessment toward a more coherent, research-based science, these challenges need careful consideration. Although more research is needed on the conceptualization and measurement of teacher effectiveness, the aim of this section is to highlight the questions that will guide the discussion of next steps.

The first challenge current teacher assessment practices face is a lack of a clear purpose of assessment in schools, districts, or the state level. All too often, teacher assessments are selected without asking the most foundational question: Why are these teachers being assessed? Are we assessing teachers to support workforce decisions about hiring and compensation? Is the purpose of the assessments to show accountability to a baseline standard? Or are we assessing teachers systematically to help gather information that will serve as the basis of ongoing professional development? Is the purpose of teacher assessment to sort more effective teachers from less effective teachers, or to help the current teacher workforce attain a higher level of effectiveness? The usefulness of teacher assessments is highly dependent on their alignment with their broader purpose. For example, value-added measures may provide information about which teachers make greater contributions toward student learning, but they do not provide information on how to help teachers improve their effectiveness. On the other hand, teacher knowledge assessments or classroom observations might help identify target areas for teacher professional development. Each approach is expected to increase student learning, but they assume different underlying mechanisms for attaining this ultimate goal (Firestone, 2014).

The question of purpose also has strong implications for assessment validity. Because teacher assessments are validated for particular purposes or contexts, a clear purpose is essential for the appropriate selection of measures (Kane, 2006). For example, a teacher math knowledge assessment might be validated for use in initial screening to decide which type of professional development a teacher will receive, but not be valid to decide if the teacher has enough content area knowledge to receive teacher certification. The high stakes nature of the second scenario would warrant a much stronger evidence base than the first, showing associations between the types of math knowledge that the assessment measures and student achievement. Therefore, determining the validity of the assessment would require clearly understanding the purpose for which it was intended.

In addition to validity, reliability issues are also of great concern in teacher assessment. Although many of the assessments discussed in this chapter come with recommendations from the developers on how to maintain reliability, once a teacher assessment is in the field the data it generates are only as reliable as the diligence with which they are gathered. For example, if classroom observers are initially trained and certified to use an observation tool, but they fail to maintain inter-rater reliability with other observers over time, teacher assessment data cannot be compared across classrooms or from one point in the year to the next. But going back to our previous point about assessment purpose, it is also important to remember that the answers do not all lie in the psychometric properties of an assessment but also in capturing that which is meaningful—a measure can reliably and consistently capture the number of math manipulatives that are present in a preschool classroom, but if this construct is unrelated to how much math children actually learn, then the value of this measure in assessing teacher effectiveness is questionable (Goe et al., 2008).

If the goal of teacher assessment is to improve teacher practice in areas that are critical for children's learning and development, then we need to make sure that teachers are being assessed in those areas. Sensible measures must fit into a widely accepted framework of early childhood teacher effectiveness. The NAEYC Standards for Early Childhood Teacher Preparation (National Association for the Education of Young Children, 2009) are one example of a framework that articulates different dimensions believed to represent the qualities of an effective teacher in the field of early childhood education. According to this framework, being an effective early childhood teacher extends far beyond understanding curriculum and instructional practices (see NAEYC, 2009). Effective teachers build relationships with parents and communities, understand healthy environments for child development, and follow the ethical principles of the profession.

Reflection on these standards reinforces two important points: (1) the needs of early childhood teacher assessment are unique and (2) there are a dearth of valid and reliable measures that could be useful for meeting these unique needs. This means that the field of early childhood education cannot depend solely on the research of teacher assessment that is conducted in K-12 settings, although these studies can inform early childhood teacher evaluation (Bill & Melinda Gates Foundation, 2013). There is a need to develop measures that align with the NAEYC (2009) framework and go beyond teachers' contributions to student achievement gains. These frameworks might include measures to document the quality of a teacher's family-sensitive caregiving practices (Bromer et al., 2011) or health promotion practices (Hegland et al., 2011). The growing diversity in early childhood classrooms today requires assessment research on culturally responsive practices (Shivers, Sanders, & Westbrook, 2011). These especially influential aspects of teaching young children have yet to be captured in more widely used classroom observation tools such as the CLASS or Danielson's Framework for Teaching. Although developing, validating, and reliably using this wide array of measures may be expensive and complicated, it is also essential to understanding early childhood teacher effectiveness in all of its complexity.

Conclusion

Taken as a whole, this chapter highlights a growing need for valid and reliable assessments of early childhood teachers in order to document and improve teacher effectiveness. Although there have been strides in the development and validation of observational measures of teacher quality, more work is needed to develop measures of teacher inputs and outputs. Some informative research has been done regarding outputs in K-12 teacher evaluation contexts, but the need remains for equally valid and reliable assessments for early childhood teachers. Furthermore, there is an urgent need for early childhood teacher assessments to capture the unique aspects of effective early childhood teaching. The field is at risk for becoming overly dependent on single observational tools to assess teacher effectiveness. Given that the sheer complexity of defining the components of effective teaching is one of the impediments to proper assessment, taking this oversimplified approach would surely be a mistake. Early childhood teacher assessments serve teachers, administrators, parents, students, and researchers. The development of an evaluation system, which successfully assesses early childhood teachers will require the use of a range of tools that are conceptually aligned with a definition of teacher effectiveness that captures the voices of all of these stakeholders.

References

Bill and Melinda Gates Foundation. (2013). *Ensuring fair and reliable measures of effective teaching: Culminating findings from the MET Project's three-year study.* Seattle, WA: Author.

Bornfreund, L. (2013). *Ocean of unknowns: Risks and opportunities in using student achievement data to evaluate preK-third grade teachers.* Washington, DC: New America Foundation.

Bracey, G.W. (2004). RESEARCH: Serious questions about the Tennessee value-added assessment system. *Phi Delta Kappan, 85*(9), 716.

Brandt, C., Mathers, C., Oliva, M., Brown-Sims, M., & Hess, J. (2007). *Examining district guidance to schools on teacher evaluation policies in the Midwest region (Issues & Answers, REL 2007-No. 030).* Washington, DC: U.S. Department of Education, Institute of Education Sciences.

Bromer, J., Paulsell, D., Porter, T., Henly, J.R., Ramsburg, D., Weber, R.B., & Families, and Quality Workgroup Members. (2011). Family-sensitive caregiving: A key component of quality in early care and education arrangements. In M. Zaslow, I. Martinez-Beck, K. Tout, & T. Halle (Eds.), *Quality measurement in early childhood settings* (pp. 161–190). Baltimore, MD: Brookes.

Burchinal, M., Howes, C., Pianta, R., Bryant, D., Early, D., Clifford, R., & Barbarin, O. (2008). Predicting child outcomes at the end of kindergarten from the quality of pre-kindergarten teacher–child interactions and instruction. *Applied Development Science, 12*(3), 140–153.

Campbell, R. J., Kyriakides, L., Muijs, R. D., & Robinson, W. (2003). Differential teacher effectiveness: Towards a model for research and teacher appraisal. *Oxford Review of Education, 29*(3), 347–362.

Carlisle, J. F., Kelcey, B., Rowan, B., & Phelps, G. (2011). Teachers' knowledge about early reading: Effects on students' gains in reading achievement. *Journal of Research on Educational Effectiveness, 4*(4), 289–321.

Cash, A.H., Hamre, B.K., Pianta, R. C., & Myers, S.S. (2012). Rater calibration when observational assessment occurs at large scale: Degree of calibration and characteristics of raters associated with calibration. *Early Childhood Research Quarterly, 27*(3), 529–542.

Connecticut State Department of Education. (2007). *A guide to the BEST program for beginning teachers: 2007–2008.* Hartford, CT: Author.

Connors-Tadros, L., & Horowitz, M. (2014). *How Are Early Childhood Teachers Faring in State Teacher Evaluation Systems?* (CEELO Policy Report). New Brunswick, NJ: Center on Enhancing Early Learning Outcomes.

Cruickshank, D., & Haefele, D. (1990). Research-based indicators: Is the glass half-full or half-empty? *Journal of Personnel Evaluation in Education, 3*, 33–40

Cunningham, A. E., Zibulsky, J., & Callahan, M. D. (2009). Starting small: Building preschool teacher knowledge that supports early literacy development. *Reading and Writing, 22*(4), 487–510.

Curby, T. W., LoCasale-Crouch, J., Konold, T. R., Pianta, R. C., Howes, C., Burchinal, M., . . . Barbarin, O. (2009). The relations of observed pre-K classroom quality profiles to children's achievement and social competence. *Early Education and Development, 20*(2), 346–372.

Danielson, C. (1996). *A framework for teaching.* Alexandria, VA: Association for Supervision and Curriculum Development.

Danielson, C. (2007). *Enhancing professional practice: A framework for teaching.* Alexandria, VA: Association for Supervision and Curriculum Development.

Darling-Hammond, L. (2000). How teacher education matters. *Journal of Teacher Education, 51*(3), 166–173.

Downer, J., Sabol, T. J., & Hamre, B. (2010). Teacher–child interactions in the classroom: Toward a theory of within-and cross-domain links to children's developmental outcomes. *Early Education and Development, 21*(5), 699–723.

Early, D. M., Bryant, D. M., Pianta, R. C., Clifford, R. M., Burchinal, M. R., Ritchie, S., . . . Barbarin, O. (2006). Are teachers' education, major, and credentials related to classroom quality and children's academic gains in pre-kindergarten? *Early Childhood Research Quarterly, 21*(2), 174–195.

Early, D. M., Maxwell, K. L., Burchinal, M., Alva, S., Bender, R. H., Bryant, D., . . . Zill, N. (2007). Teachers' education, classroom quality, and young children's academic skills: Results from seven studies of preschool programs. *Child Development, 78*(2), 558–580.

Ellis, C. D. (2013). *Making sense, making do: Local district implementation of a new state induction policy* (Unpublished doctoral dissertation). University of Connecticut, Storrs, CT.

Feldon, D. F. (2007). Cognitive load and classroom teaching: The double-edged sword of automaticity. *Educational Psychologist, 42*(3), 123–137.

Firestone, W. A. (2014). Teacher evaluation policy and conflicting theories of motivation. *Educational Researcher, 43*(2), 100–107.

Gallagher, H. A. (2004). Vaughn elementary's innovative teacher evaluation system: Are teacher evaluation scores related to growth in student achievement? *Peabody Journal of Education, 79*(4), 79–107.

Goe, L. (2007). *The link between teacher quality and student outcomes: A research synthesis.* Washington, DC: National Comprehensive Center for Teacher Quality.

Goe L., Bell C., & Little O. (2008). *Approaches to evaluating teacher effectiveness: A research synthesis.* Washington, DC: National Comprehensive Center for Teacher Quality.

Goe, L., & Holdheide, L. (2011). *Measuring teachers' contributions to students' learning growth for nontested grades and subjects.* Washington, DC: National Comprehensive Center for Teacher Quality.

Goldhaber, D. D., & Anthony, E. (2003). *Teacher quality and student achievement.* ERIC Clearinghouse on Urban Education, Teachers College, Columbia University.

Goldhaber, D., & Walch, J. (2012). Strategic pay reform: A student outcomes-based evaluation of Denver's Pro-Comp teacher pay initiative. *Economics of Education Review, 31*(6), 1067–1083.

Hamre, B., Downer, J., Jamil, F., & Pianta, R. (2012). Enhancing teachers intentional use of effective interactions with children. In R. C. Pianta, W. S. Barnett, L. M. Justice, & S. M. Sheridan (Eds.), *Handbook of early childhood education* (pp. 507–532). New York: Guilford Press.

Hamre, B. K., & Pianta, R. C. (2005). Can instructional and emotional support in the first-grade classroom make a difference for children at risk of school failure? *Child Development, 76*(5), 949–967.

Hamre, B. K., Pianta, R. C., Burchinal, M., Field, S., LoCasale-Crouch, J., Downer, J. T., . . . Scott-Little, C. (2012). A course on effective teacher-child interactions effects on teacher beliefs, knowledge, and observed practice. *American Educational Research Journal, 49*(1), 88–123.

Harris, D. (2012). *How do value-added indicators compare to other measures of teacher effectiveness?* (Carnegie Knowledge Network What We Know Series: Value-Added Methods and Applications, Knowledge Brief 5). Stanford, CA: Carnegie Foundation for the Advancement of Teaching.

Hegland, S. M., Aronson, S. S., Isbell, P., Neelon, S. B., Rous, B. S., & Krajicek, M. J. (2011). Measuring health-related aspects of quality in early childhood settings. In M. Zaslow, I. Martinez-Beck, K. Tout, & T. Halle (Eds.), *Quality measurement in early childhood settings*, (pp. 135–160). Baltimore, MD: Brookes.

Hill, H. C., Ball, D. L., & Schilling, S. G. (2008). Unpacking pedagogical content knowledge: Conceptualizing and measuring teachers' topic-specific knowledge of students. *Journal for Research in Mathematics Education, 39*(4), 372–400.

Hill, H. C., Kapitula, L., & Umland, K. (2011). A validity argument approach to evaluating teacher value-added scores. *American Educational Research Journal, 48*(3), 794–831.

Hoffman, J. V., Sailors, M., Duffy, G. R., & Beretvas, S. N. (2004). The effective elementary classroom literacy environment: Examining the validity of the TEX-IN3 observation system. *Journal of Literacy Research, 36*(3), 303–334.

Horm, D. M., Hyson, M., & Winton, P. J. (2013). Research on early childhood teacher education: Evidence from three domains and recommendations for moving forward. *Journal of Early Childhood Teacher Education, 34*(1), 95–112.

Jamil, F., Sabol, T., Hamre, B., & Pianta, R. (in press). Assessing teachers' skills in detecting and identifying effective interactions in the classroom: Theory and measurement. *Elementary School Journal.*

Johnson, R. L., McDaniel, F., & Willeke, M. J. (2000). Using portfolios in program evaluation: An investigation of interrater reliability. *American Journal of Evaluation, 21*(1), 65–80.

Kane, M. (2006). Content-related validity evidence in test development. In S. M. Downing & T. M. Haladyna (Eds.), *Handbook of test development* (pp.131–154). Philadelphia, PA: Erlbaum.

Kane, T., Kerr, K., & Pianta, R. (2014). *Designing teacher evaluation systems: New guidance from the measures of effective teaching project.* San Francisco: John Wiley & Sons.

Kimball, S. M., White, B., Milanowski, A. T., & Borman, G. (2004). Examining the relationship between teacher evaluation and student assessment results in Washoe County. *Peabody Journal of Education, 79*(4), 54–78.

Knudsen, E. I., Heckman, J. J., Cameron, J. L., & Shonkoff, J. (2006). Economic, neurobiological, and behavioral perspectives on building America's future workforce. *Proceedings of the National Academy of Sciences of the United States of America, 103*(27), 10155–10162.

Koran, M. L., Snow, R. E., & McDonald, F. J. (1971). Teacher aptitude and observational learning of a teaching skill. *Journal of Educational Psychology, 62*(3), 219.

Koretz, D., Stecher, B., Klein, S., & McCaffrey, D. (1994). The Vemont Portfolio Assessment Program: Findings and Implications. *Educational Measurement: Issues and Practice, 13*(3), 5–16.

Mashburn, A. J., Downer, J. T., Rivers, S. E., Brackett, M. A., & Martinez, A. (2014). Improving the power of an efficacy study of a social and emotional learning program: Application of generalizability theory to the measurement of classroom-level outcomes. *Prevention Science, 15*(2), 146–155.

McCray, J. S., & Chen, J. Q. (2012). Pedagogical content knowledge for preschool mathematics: Construct validity of a new teacher interview. *Journal of Research in Childhood Education, 26*(3), 291–307.

Meyer, J. P., Cash, A. H., & Mashburn, A. (2011). Occasions and the reliability of classroom observations: Alternative conceptualizations and methods of analysis. *Educational Assessment, 16*(4), 227–243.

Milanowski, A. (2004). The relationship between teacher performance evaluation scores and student achievement: Evidence from Cincinnati. *Peabody Journal of Education, 79*(4), 33–53.

Moats, L. C. (1994). The missing foundation in teacher education: Knowledge of the structure of spoken and written language. *Annals of Dyslexia, 44*(1), 81–102.

Moreno, R., & Valdez, A. (2007). Immediate and delayed effects of using a classroom case exemplar in teacher education: The role of presentation format. *Journal of Educational Psychology, 99*(1), 194.

Muijs, D. (2006). Measuring teacher effectiveness: Some methodological reflections. *Educational Research and Evaluation, 12*(1), 53–74.

National Association for the Education of Young Children (NAEYC). (2009). *NAEYC standards for early childhood professional preparation: A position statement of the National Association for the Education of Young Children.* Washington, DC: Author.

National Scientific Council on the Developing Child. (2007). *The timing and quality of early care experiences combine to shape brain architecture.* Washington, DC: Author.

Painter, B. (2001). Using teaching portfolios. *Educational Leadership, 58*(5), 31–34.

Peisner-Feinberg, E. S., Burchinal, M. R., Clifford, R. M., Culkin, M. L., Howes, C., Kagan, S. L., & Yazejian, N. (2001). The relation of preschool child-care quality to children's cognitive and social developmental trajectories through second grade. *Child Development, 72*(5), 1534–1553.

Pianta, R. C., Burchinal, M., Jamil, F. M., Sabol, T., Grimm, K., Hamre, B. K., . . . Howes, C. (2014). A cross-lag analysis of longitudinal associations between preschool teachers' instructional support identification skills and observed behavior. *Early Childhood Research Quarterly, 29*(2), 144–154.

Pianta, R. C., La Paro, K. M., & Hamre, B. K. (2008). *Classroom Assessment Scoring System.* Baltimore: Paul H. Brookes.

Raudenbush, S. W. (2004). What are value-added models estimating and what does this imply for statistical practice? *Journal of Educational and Behavioral Statistics, 29*(1), 121–129.

Reutzel, D. R., Dole, J. A., Read, S., Fawson, P., Herman, K., Jones, C. D., . . . & Fargo, J. (2011). Conceptually and methodologically vexing issues in teacher knowledge assessment. *Reading & Writing Quarterly, 27*(3), 183–211.

Rimm-Kaufman, S. E., La Paro, K. M., Downer, J. T., & Pianta, R. C. (2005). The contribution of classroom setting and quality of instruction to children's behavior in kindergarten classrooms. *The Elementary School Journal, 105*(4), 377–394.

Rockoff, J. E. (2004). The impact of individual teachers on student achievement: Evidence from panel data. *American Economic Review, 94*(2), 247–252.

Schmitt, L., & Ibanez, N. (2011). *AISD REACH Program Update: 2009–2010 Texas Assessment of Knowledge and Skills (TAKS) Results and Student Learning Objectives (SLOs).* Austin, TX: Austin Independent School District Department of Program Evaluation.

Sheridan, S. M., Edwards, C. P., Marvin, C. A., & Knoche, L. L. (2009). Professional development in early childhood programs: Process issues and research needs. *Early Education and Development, 20*(3), 377–401.

Shivers, E. M., Sanders, K., & Westbrook, T. R. (2011). Measuring culturally responsive early care and education. In M. Zaslow, I. Martinez-Beck, K. Tout, & T. Halle (Eds.), *Quality measurement in early childhood settings* (pp. 191–225). Baltimore, MD: Brookes.

Shonkoff, J. P., & Phillips, D. A. (Eds.). (2000). *From neurons to neighborhoods: The science of early childhood development.* Washington, DC: National Academy of Press.

Shulman, L. S. (1987). Knowledge and teaching: Foundations of the new reform. *Harvard Educational Review, 57*(1), 1–23.

Wright, S. P., Horn, S. P., & Sanders, W. L. (1997). Teacher and classroom context effects on student achievement: Implications for teacher evaluation. *Journal of Personnel Evaluation in Education, 1*(1), 57–67.

Zaslow, M., Tout, K., Halle, T., & Forry, N. (2009). *Multiple purposes for measuring quality in early childhood settings: Implications for selecting and communicating information on quality.* Washington, DC: Office of Planning, Research and Evaluation, Administration for Children and Families, U.S. Department of Health and Human Services.

23

GLOBALIZATION

International Perspectives on Early Childhood Teacher Education

James L. Hoot, Fortidas Rwehumbiza Bakuza, Masoud Gholamali Lavasani, Sungok R. Park, Maryam S. Sharifian, and Tunde Szecsi

We live in an increasingly interdependent society. This is readily seen in the accumulating evidence of the impact of environmental warming on rapidly changing weather extremes throughout the world. Likewise, growing global interdependence is seen in diverse nations sharing their resources to locate missing passenger planes and school girls abducted from their classrooms, or international collaboration in fighting terrorism. If the world's increasing interdependence is to result in the creation of a better world, the need for more competent and caring global citizens has never been greater. Since education plays a pivotal role in creating such a citizenry, the world's teachers have a critical role to play—especially teachers of very young children. Relatively little is known, however, about global challenges facing the preparation of such teachers in the 21st century. This chapter attempts to begin such a dialogue by sharing current issues and concerns facing early childhood teacher educators in diverse areas of the world (Africa, Middle East, Central Europe, and Asia). Unlike much of the literature on global teacher education written primarily by monolingual Americans sharing their impressions of short visits abroad, problems and issues concerning early childhood teacher education (ECTE) from the four regions of the world sampled for this snapshot were shared by *native* EC teacher educators. Collaborators on this project were asked to share information obtained from the most credible and most recent literature (e.g. Ministry of Education, professional journals, and conferences in their national languages). It is hoped that the conversations shared herein will spark further international sharing that will result in better teachers for our worlds' children.

ECTE in Africa—The Case of Tanzania

The government of Tanzania is party to many international agreements designed to improve access, equity, and quality of education for its children (United Republic of Tanzania [URT], 2008, 2009a). Since 1995, Tanzania initiated a series of policies to increase the likelihood that it will achieve its stated commitments (URT, 2002). In 1997, for example, the government launched its Education Sector Development Programme (ESDP; URT, 2000). The implementation of ESDP brought about major educational reforms that have greatly improved enrollment in both primary and secondary schools. Concomitant with this rapid increase in enrollment, however, remains the urgent demand for increasing both the numbers and competence of those who will be teaching the emerging masses of very young children—caregivers, pre-primary teachers, and primary grade teachers. ECTE for these teachers is described below.

Child Care Teachers ("Caregivers")

The Ministry of Health and Social Welfare (MHSW) is responsible for children from birth to age 4. From ages birth to 3 children are expected to be at home where home-based care is provided. The MHSW has programs across the country for training home-based care service providers who interact with parents on appropriate early care and early stimulation.

Those who work with children ages 3–4 in child care centers fall under the administration of the Ministry of Health and Social Welfare. Currently around 38% of children this age access child care services. At present the Ministry oversees nearly 2,000 child care centers (mostly private) that enroll about 300,000 children. This suggests that the number of child care centers is still very small (less than half) compared to the demand (Social Welfare Department, 2014).[1] Educators teaching in these programs are referred to as "caregivers" and are trained by institutions that are owned and operated by the Ministry of Health and Social Welfare as well as private institutions. The minimum education requirement to be a caregiver is a certificate of secondary education (i.e. U.S. equivalent of Grade 10).

Pre-primary Teachers (Teachers of 5- and 6-Year-Old Children)

Children ages 5–6 are required to attend pre-primary schools. These may be public or private but they are registered and regulated by the Ministry of Education and Vocation Training (MoEVT). Teachers working with pre-primary children are expected to have a minimum of four years of secondary education and a two-year certificate from a recognized teacher training college. In 2012, 8,354 out of 9,352 (89.3%) ECE teachers met these requirements. This percentage, however, indicates only the number of documented teachers as reported in government documents. Major differences remain in these numbers between urban and rural schools and from region to region. Likewise, teacher qualifications also differ. In a recent study, pre-primary teachers indicated that their training ranged from a few seminars and workshops to a year of formal coursework (Bakuza, 2014). Further, teachers in this study received ECE training solely as part of inservice training. These teachers also indicated that they needed more focused training opportunities for this age level.

Primary Teachers (Teachers of 7- and 8-Year-Old Children)

Seven- and 8-year-old children are required to enroll in Tanzania's 16,001 public primary schools (URT, 2012). Yet, there are currently no specialized courses to specifically teach children at this level. Further, recent findings indicate that current teachers in public schools at this level tend to be women who are in their mid-career or close to retirement without any specialized training (Bakuza, 2014). Despite great demand for well-trained teachers at this level, training of preservice and inservice teachers to teach the increasing numbers of primary grade children has received little governmental attention. For example, between 1996 and 2004 there was no official documentation regarding ECE-specific teacher training. Since then, sporadic ECE workshops lasting between a few weeks to a year have begun to emerge. Yet, even today there is no data regarding how many teachers have taken part in these emerging short courses, or, perhaps more importantly, no evaluation of the quality of such courses.

Recent Government Strategies to Address ECTE

To address the urgent need for ECTE, a number of government strategies are beginning to emerge. These include creating specialized diploma programs in ECE and implementation of the Teacher Development and Management Strategy of 2008–2013.

Creating an Early Childhood Specialist Diploma

In 2009 the Tanzania Institute of Education (TIE) developed the "Curriculum for Diploma in Teacher Education Programme in Tanzania". In this curriculum TIE describes a specific diploma program—Teacher Education Diploma in Early Childhood Education (URT, 2009b). In order to enroll in this course a candidate must have completed six years of secondary education (i.e. U.S. equivalent of Grade 12). The duration of the two courses is two years. In Tanzania, formal ECE refers to two years of pre-primary education for 5- and 6-year-old children and Grades 1 and 2 for children ages 7 and 8. The curriculum for the two-year diploma program in ECE includes three major areas of study: (1) Professional Studies (Curriculum Implementation, Education Foundations, and Educational Research and Measurement); (2) Academic Content Knowledge and Pedagogical Knowledge; and (3) Education Media and Information Communication and Technology.

As mentioned above, in 2012, 89.3% of teachers met minimum standards to teach in pre-primary classes. However, this basic training was not designed to prepare teachers who specifically specialize in ECE. In an attempt to prepare specialized ECE teachers, the government very recently started to enroll preservice teachers in an entire ECE curricular program. While the government appears to be initiating formal ECE academic preparation, the sheer number of children in classrooms provides serious challenges to those wishing to provide a quality education to very young children. The current national teacher/student ratio computed by dividing the total number of children documented as enrolled in preschool education by the number of qualified teachers is 1:124. This ratio in no way meets the BEST (URT, 2013) standard of one teacher for a class of 25 children in each pre-primary class. These data become even more concerning when one considers that very recent reports (e.g. URT, 2012) suggest that these teacher/student ratios of 1:124 include *secondary school* graduates with no prior training in teaching preschool children. These data suggest that teachers with an ECE-specific Diploma in Teacher Education in Tanzania remain in critically short supply.

Teacher Development and Management Strategy

To address the growing demand for well-qualified ECE teachers in public schools in Tanzania, the government recently developed the Teacher Development and Management Strategy 2008–2013 (TDMS). The main goal of this policy document is "to have and sustain adequate numbers of competent teachers and tutors to effectively support pre-primary, primary, secondary, adult and non-formal education, as well as Teachers' Colleges" (URT, 2008, p. 10). The implementation of TDMS is also attempting to improve the quality of teaching that is related to teacher professionalism, management, and motivation. Expected outcomes of TDMS include increasing the number of qualified candidates joining the teaching profession and improved teacher retention. Achievement of these goals is seen as being especially critical in rural areas and in areas of high poverty.

Expansion of ECE Preparation Programs in Higher Education

The government recently began implementation of programs to increase the quality of preparation of teachers by selecting a few teacher training colleges that will have ECE cohorts of preservice ECE teachers. The first cohort of teachers was enrolled in 2013. However, this ECE cohort met a number of challenges such as a shortage of competent instructors and learning materials, as well as crowded classes due to a rapid increase in enrollment (Lukanga, 2013).

A number of public institutions are also expanding their program offerings. The University of Dodoma, University of Dar es Salaam, and the Institute of Education Development for East Africa of Aga Khan University are some of the public universities that have now begun offering bachelor's degrees specifically in Early Childhood Education. The later program now also offers a one-year master's program for ECE teachers. The Open University of Tanzania is also developing ECE teacher training courses at certificate, diploma, and degree levels. It is expected that these training opportunities will greatly increase the number of better-trained ECE teachers. However, providing *enough* quality teachers to meet the expected demand remains problematic.

To help achieve its goal, the government has increasingly turned to opportunities provided by the private sector, which has long been viewed as the leader in ECE teacher preparation (URT, 2008). One of the best-known private teacher training programs in this area is the Montessori Teacher Training College in Dar es Salaam. This college is sponsored by the Roman Catholic Church and trains teachers at the certificate level. Another well-established private teacher training college is Tanzania Early Childhood Education Teacher Training College. This privately owned teacher training college exclusively prepares ECE teachers at both the certificate and diploma levels. There are also increasing numbers of small private colleges that are providing short courses for ECE teachers.

The Need for ECE Leadership Training

While the Education and Training Policy 1995 (URT, 1995) requires all primary schools to establish pre-primary classes, head teachers of these primary schools generally have no formal EC leadership training. Muijs, Aubrey, Harris, and Briggs (2004) suggest that lack of EC leadership preparation is a serious threat to improved practice. This researcher further reports that "It seems almost inconceivable that the leadership practices of those working within EC are not being taken seriously" (p. 167). Yet, these leaders recently expressed a greatly increased desire to receive such training (Bakuza, 2014).

Final Thoughts—Tanzania

While education policies and programs are becoming better documented, major implementation concerns remain. In a recent study of differences between stated and implemented policies in ECE leadership, ECE teachers indicated that they had very limited information about policies developed at the national level (Bakuza, 2014). Teachers also commonly lament frequent changes in the ECE curriculum—without preparation to implement these changes in severely overcrowded classrooms (Bakuza, 2014). The voices of teachers and their head teachers suggest a picture of ECTE that needs immediate attention in providing greatly expanded support structures (Muijs et al., 2004).

While major challenges remain for EC teacher preparation, the future appears promising. Experiences from other contexts suggest that the successful implementation of Education Policy in ECE is determined by many factors that include respect for pedagogical approaches which influence training and employment of well-trained teachers for ECE (Taguchi & Munkammar, 2003; Taguma, Litjens, & Makowiecki, 2013). The goal now should be to advocate for government and other employers to improve the working conditions of teachers in order to attract more teachers to join and remain in an EC teaching career. In closing, deliberate efforts from the government and other key stakeholders are greatly needed to invest in ECE teaching and ECE leadership training in Tanzania.

Early Childhood Teacher Education in Central Europe—the Case of Hungary

Recent political, economic, and social changes in Hungary have shaped the Hungarian National Core Curriculum for Preschool Education (Magyar, 2012). This curriculum defines preschool education as being "inclusive, and therefore promotes all children's personal development in a quality and loving environment ensuring access to equal opportunities without prejudice" (para. 3). This document also outlines core values to be developed such as respect for families' diverse socio-cultural contexts, strong support for physical and mental health, and inclusive education for children with special needs. To address these expectations, the more than 170-year-old ECTE in Hungary has embraced new

Educating Children with Special Needs

Historically, both Hungarian children with special needs and teachers of these children were schooled separately from general education students. In 1998, the Decree for Equal Opportunities (Magyar, 1998) required the integration of students with special needs and mainstream students starting at the preschool level. This mandate created a need for a transformation in ECTE. Because of the ongoing philosophical dispute regarding integration versus segregation in professional circles, changes in ECTE have been slow and poorly implemented (Rózsáné, 2013). Currently, most programs require students to take one or two courses in differentiated pedagogy. However courses in inclusive pedagogy are offered only as electives. This limited exposure to coursework and student teaching experience in inclusive classrooms is likely to result in preschool teachers with superficial knowledge in special education content and a lack of competence in working in inclusive classrooms (Baloghné, 2013). In a pilot integration program in Szeged, preschool teachers expressed openness to inclusion. However, they felt unprepared for educating children with special needs. Ultimately, they urged in-depth preparation and ongoing multidisciplinary collaboration for effective implementation of inclusion (Benkő & Lippai, 2004). It is clear that competence in serving children with special needs will only be achieved with a more systematic approach in both initial preparation and inservice professional development.

Final Thoughts—Hungary

Hungarian society clearly recognizes the crucial role early education plays in nurturing 21st century global citizens. In light of this, the government recently extended mandatory public preschool education starting at age 3 to ensure all children become healthy, happy, and successful adults (Magyar, 2011). Accordingly, early childhood teacher educators in Hungary are striving to revitalize their curricula to meet these expectations. Embracing century-long traditions of quality preschool teacher preparation in Hungary, professionals in ECTE are currently paving the road toward competence-based preparation and giving equal attention to content knowledge and professional skills and attitudes. In the more global context of the European Union, it is imperative that preschool teachers become competent professionals prepared to educate children regardless of their disadvantaged backgrounds, minority culture and language, and special needs. Although this transition in ECTE is built on research-based recommendations, political, social, and economic barriers must be overcome before meaningful changes will emerge.

ECTE in the Middle East—the Case of the Islamic Republic of Iran

Expansion and development of preschools in Iran has been uneven in recent years—especially since the Islamic Revolution in 1979. Moreover, clear policies for the preparation of those teaching very young children are largely unavailable. Rather, the major focus of current educational policy is upon preparing teachers for primary school and higher education. Because of this, there is limited concern for preparing kindergarten and preschool teachers. Perhaps the major reason for this is that tradition holds that training children under age 7 has been considered the family responsibility, particularly mothers. In addition, scarcity of funding for teacher training due to global sanctions following the revolution has been an additional detriment to growing concerns for better preparing teachers of very young children. In this context, a number of challenges currently face those concerned with preparing teachers of very young children in Iran. These include upgrading the importance of EC teacher education in Iran, improving the quality of ECTE curriculum, diminished long-term job aspirations of preservice teachers, gender issues, and preparing future teachers for diversity.

Upgrading the Importance of EC Teacher Education

Currently, early childhood teacher training in Iran is presented in two forms—preservice and inservice training. Preservice degree programs (associate's degrees through master's degrees) are available at universities. Short-term inservice training is provided to prepare both people with high school diplomas interested in ECE and to apprise inservice teachers of developing knowledge in the field. There are some advantages in preservice versus inservice training. For example, preservice certificates allow candidates to become directors of child care centers which provide much higher salaries.

In addition to training provided by public colleges of education and private sector institutions, EC teacher training in Iran is always accompanied by Jahad Daneshgahi. This organization is the public non-profit institution founded in 1991, which provides short-term training for upgrading kindergarten and preschool teacher skills. Courses at Jahad Daneshgahi include the study of child growth and development, psychology, educational play, child health and nutrition, children with special needs, storytelling, and dramatic arts. Further, faculties include members of the university with professional expertise in psychology and child health or PhD/master's degree students in these content areas (Ebrahimi Ghavam & Karimi, 2011). Priority for enrolling in Jahad Daneshgahi programs is given to kindergarten teachers who have a high school diploma without higher academic education in early childhood. The length of the training periods in these centers is about three to four weeks annually for degreed teachers. For those with only high school diplomas the training is generally six months to a year. This additional training allows high school diploma teachers permission to teach but does not allow them to open child care centers or serve as child care directors.

In 2004, the Welfare University launched the first bachelor's degree program in early childhood education. Soon after other public and private universities also provided associate's, bachelor's, and master's degrees in ECE. Students in these programs must successfully complete courses such as sports movement and special rhythms for children, psychology of reading, physical health, mother and child nutrition, individual differences of children, psychology of play, methods of teaching, experimental science, creative storytelling and playing, children's literature, and children's counseling. Since this is a new degree program specifically designed for teachers of very young children, it is criticized by many practicing teachers as being too heavy on theory with limited theoretical application for actual classrooms.

Improving Quality in ECTE

Recent research in Iran has indicated a number of challenges in the EC teacher training curriculum. Mullayenejad (2012), for example, describes problems regarding the curriculum of teacher training institutions over the past two years. Mullayenejad suggests that current programs are not preparing ECE preservice professionals for working in real classrooms. Likewise, results in Liaghatdar's (2001) research regarding the quality of internship courses in teacher training centers suggest internship experiences are viewed very negatively by student teachers. The main reason provided is that interns do not receive relevant support from university instructors. For example, Liaghatdar found that associate degree students had no accompanying seminar course to address practical concerns of students while engaged in field work. This lack of ongoing practical support during student teaching results in a lack of confidence in interns regarding their ability to teach.

In addition to issues associated with student teaching, the pedagogical tradition at teacher preparation institutions often diminishes the value of practical experiences with children under the supervision of a master teacher with expertise in child development. Farahani, Nasr, and Sharif (2012), for example, recently stated that teacher-training institutions do not value *practical* education of teachers of very young children. These researchers reviewed current studies suggesting practical training is minimized in teacher education programs in favor of emphasis upon memorization of academic facts.

Moreover, where internship courses are available, they are not viewed as serious academic experiences. Thus, it appears competencies needed for professionals to translate research and theory into practice with very young children are not being addressed in teacher training in Iran.

Diminished Long-Term Job Aspirations of Preservice Teachers

The majority of graduates of teacher training facilities in Iran do not see working in child care centers as ultimate career goals, since teachers are generally employed with only short-term contracts. Lack of long-term employment security often results in a lack of enthusiasm for teaching as a career. This is especially true for men considering EC teaching as a career since men are traditionally the major financial supporters of the family.

Another issue contributing to a lack of preservice teacher enthusiasm for the teaching profession is poor working conditions. The national teacher-child ratios, for example, should be one teacher for every 10 infants, 15 toddlers, or 15 preschool children. While these ratios are on the books, these standards are achieved in very few preschools (Pooshneh, Khosravi, & Purali, 2013). To keep costs down, most ECE center directors do not limit the number of children enrolled in classrooms. Moreover, the pay for preschool teachers is very low compared to the pay of primary grade teachers. For example, a preschool teacher typically makes around 1,500 U.S. dollars (45,000,000 Reial Iranian currency) per year. Primary teachers, on the other hand, might receive a salary around $3,000 (90,000,000 Reial) (Nabati, 2014). Perhaps this situation results from the general societal view that nurturing children in homes is sufficient. Thus, most people (including many professors) are unaware of the cost-effectiveness and long-term benefits of quality education in the earliest of years (Abbasi, 2003; Zaare & Ghoshuni, 2008). Thus, because of relatively low pay and lack of prestige of preschool teachers, many preservice teachers have long-term goals of becoming center directors rather than classroom teachers. Teacher trainers are now becoming increasingly concerned with how to begin to change this public perception, which is a serious threat to the selection and retention of promising ECTE candidates.

Another factor contributing to a lack of enthusiasm for EC as a career is the lack of practical knowledge of professors. Karshaki, Jafari Sani, and Arfa Balouchi, (2013), for example, studied student teachers evaluations of professors in ECE. Results suggest students felt professors lacked both ECE content knowledge and experience in teaching in the early grades.

Gender Issues in Early Childhood Teacher Education

Gender issues are yet another challenge faced by teacher educators after the revolution. Prior to the revolution, more female teachers taught in preschool and primary schools. After the revolution, however, boys and girls were separated by gender beginning with primary grades. (The exception to this is the rural areas where the number of teachers and students of both sexes are so low that such separation is not economically feasible.) Research is beginning to emerge regarding potential issues resulting from gender segregation in the primary grades. Farahani and colleagues (2012), for example, studied the relative impact of female teachers in teaching students in the first to third grade. Researchers compared women teaching girls and men teaching boys in Grades 1 to 3. Data suggests that emotional needs of children might be better met by allowing women to teach both genders in the primary grades.

Diversity Challenges in ECTE

Iran is a culturally diverse society. Yet, it is becoming increasingly evident from emerging research that the preparation of teachers for very young children pays very little attention to diversity issues. Azizi, Bolandhematan, and Soltani (2010), for example, studied teacher education in Sanandaj Kurdish regions of Iran and reported that student teachers in Kurdish centers were very unsatisfied with the preparation they had received to work with culturally diverse children. Student teachers were especially concerned that preschool directors and teachers were not sensitive to the cultural traditions of the Kurdish populous. Student teachers in this region specifically mentioned that the content of textbooks demonstrated little sensitivity to diversity.

Another major related teacher education issue is the lack of preparation of preservice teachers for addressing language diversity. While Farsi is the national language of Iran, numerous other languages are spoken in homes (e.g. Turkish, Kurdish, Gilaki). This is especially the case in rural areas where 29% of the population of the country live (Barnameh, 2012). Thus, Farsi is not the home language of many teacher candidates. Likewise, teachers who do speak the native Farsi are often presented with difficulties in working with parents of very young children who may speak little, or no, Farsi. Teacher preparation programs provide little training to prepare student teachers for these challenges.

Adding to the challenges of preparing teachers for rural areas is that recruiting quality teacher candidates is even more difficult. During the past decade, the rural population has decreased. Even if teachers from these remote areas do graduate from teacher preparation programs, as with younger people in most nations, they prefer greater opportunities in major cities. Even recent government incentives to recruit and retain teachers for rural areas have not mitigated this problem (Fallahi, 2010).

Final Thoughts—Iran

Early childhood education in Iran is beset with numerous challenges. Foremost among these are concerns for better educating the general populous regarding the importance of education in the earliest years, paying much more attention to teaching *practices* rather than primarily theory in teacher preparation, finding ways to make the general perception of teaching as a career more attractive to current and future teachers, more research regarding implications of gender separation in teaching, and issues of diversity. If more competent and caring global citizens are to emerge, research, resources, and global collaboration are urgently needed to address the above challenges.

Early Childhood Teacher Education in Asia—the Case of South Korea

Over the past half century Korea has moved from a nation devastated by war to a major global economic powerhouse. Much of this nation's success is attributed to its system of education. Maintaining its standing in the world, however, presents serious challenges to those responsible for educating future citizens for the 21st century. This is especially true regarding the preparation of those who will teach children in the earliest years. Two major challenges currently confronting early childhood teacher education in Korea are (1) how to prepare future teachers for greatly increasing diversity and (2) preparing ECE teachers for increasing numbers of children.

Preparing Teachers of Young Children for Diversity

Korea has been a traditionally homogeneous nation steadfast in its preference for *pure Korean blood, one language,* and *one history*. This nationalistic bias is easily seen in textbooks used by children in every public school until 2007 when the Korea Education Development Institute (KEDI) revised textbooks for its national curriculum. The impetus for such revision was two major socio-economic changes since the late 1990s. The first such change was the realization that continued economic prosperity was not possible in a nation with a declining birthrate. Since workers are desperately needed for industrial production, Korea is forced to invite greatly increasing numbers of foreign immigrants (especially from Southeast Asia) to work what are referred to as "3D jobs" (i.e. dirty, demeaning, and dangerous jobs). According to a recent report, for example, 1,604,703 foreigners were given legal permission of stay in South Korea in 2013 (Korean Statistical Information Service [KOSIS], 2013a). Secondly, the process of building stronger ties in the global marketplace has resulted in greatly increased numbers of international marriages, which were previously viewed negatively by Korean citizens. In 2013, there were 25,963 international marriages (KOSIS, 2013b). This suggests that international marriages now make up about 7% of annual marriages.

This rapid change in diversification presents a major challenge to those preparing teachers of young children. By analyzing multicultural educational policy documents, Lee (2013) found that national educational institutions (e.g. Ministry of Education Science and Technology, Ministry of Health and Welfare) and government-financed educational policy and program research institutes (e.g. KEDI, Korean Institute of Child Care and Education) are currently taking a leading role in addressing this challenge.

Besides government financed institutes, a number of universities are beginning to work toward much better preparation for increased diversity education. Busan National University of Education (BNUE), for example, is seen as a model for providing diversity training for teachers of very young children. The university opened its *Center for Multicultural Education* in 2009 and since then has received about $500,000 annually from the university to expand its diversity program offerings. Specifically, this center was among the first in the nation to offer courses devoted entirely to diversity issues. Such courses include Multiculture and Korean Language Education, Multiculture and Korean Society, and Korean Language Education in Multicultural Society. The center also organized club activities called WF (We are Friends) and Mentoring that encourages university students to be actively involved in multicultural education. Currently 230 university students in this program volunteer as one-to-one mentors to children from multicultural backgrounds. As mentors, students visit children twice a week to help with homework, teach Korean language, and share cultural experiences.

Despite efforts of BNUE to promote increased preparation for diversity, however, little is known about how other major universities in South Korea are preparing teacher candidates to work with diverse young children in classrooms. In order to determine the diversity preparation of top-ranking teacher education programs in Korea, Park (2013) interviewed ECE teacher education candidates and found that Korean preservice teachers expressed much interest in better preparation for classroom diversity. Teachers also felt such interest could be better addressed via semester-long courses in diversity as opposed to occasional lectures to better prepare them for multicultural classrooms. Yet, a recent review of top-ranked Korean teacher education universities revealed that diversity-related courses in early childhood teacher education remain scarce, at best (Park, 2012). Thus, if Korea is to maintain and expand its place as an economic force in the world, greatly improved education for diversity is urgently needed.

Preparing Early Childhood Teachers for Increasing Numbers of Children in Programs

In addition to greatly increasing numbers of international children, Korea is also being confronted by another unique problem—rising enrollment in a nation with a declining birth rate. South Korea is currently confronting a low "birthrate crisis" (Korea Herald, 2014). According to the Korean Statistical Information Service, there were 490,543 births in 2003. Ten years later, there were only 436,600 births (National Index, 2014). The main cause attributed to this lowered birthrate is parental fear of not being able to afford future higher education expenses for children (Ministry of Education Science and Technology [MEST] & Ministry of Health and Welfare [MHW], 2013).

While the birthrate is dropping, the number of children in programs is on the rise (Korean Institute of Child Care and Education [KICCE], 2013a). KICCE suggested that in 2010, about 90% of all 5-year-old children in South Korea were registered in kindergarten or daycare centers. Those not in programs, however, stayed at home mainly because parents could not afford tuition fees, or chose to home school. In addition, two different early childhood systems often confuse parents since curricula for 3- to 5-year-olds overlap. Early childhood programs in South Korea are offered and supervised by two separate government Ministries. The Ministry of Education Science and Technology (MEST) is responsible for kindergarten programs for children ages 3–5. The Ministry of Health and Welfare (MHW) is responsible for childcare centers for children from birth to age 5. Distinct differences exist in the curricula of these two programs. Kindergarten programs usually place an emphasis primarily on academics while daycare centers are more focused on daily care of children (i.e. children's health and safety).

In order to provide equity education and care for all children from the beginning, the government recently placed early childhood education at the forefront of its education policy agenda. As a result, a greatly revised national common curriculum (i.e. *Nuri Curriculum*) has been established for children ages 3–5. The major goal of this curriculum is to assure that all children have quality education and care with equal opportunity. As a result, since 2013, *all* children ages 3–5 are now provided free public preschool programs with the *Nuri Curriculum*.

The *Nuri Curriculum* differs from previous curricula in terms of both content and administration. The previous Kindergarten Curriculum and Standard Childcare Curriculum have been modified and combined into the Nuri Curriculum. The focus now encompasses both education and care. Specifically, former Kindergarten Curriculum consisted of five domains (i.e. health, social, expression, language arts, and explorations) and Standard Childcare Curriculum consisted of six domains (i.e. fundamental living habits, physical activities, social interactions, communication, arts experiences, and nature exploration). The current Nuri Curriculum consists of five domains with the balance of education and care: physical activity and health, communication, social interactions, arts experiences, and nature explorations. Nuri curriculum is unique in that it aims to provide equal opportunity for education to *all* children—especially those from immigrant families. It also emphasizes character and diversity education. In its teachers' manual, for example, it states that teachers must "assist children to understand that there are diverse people from around the world and to respect their beliefs and different life styles." According to urgent discourse on issues of diversity as described above, the Nuri Curriculum Handbook highlights a new direction for teacher education as "preparing teachers as global citizens" who "reinforce multicultural education" (KICCE, 2012).

Implementing this universal common curriculum presents many challenges for those preparing teachers of very young children. Implementing Nuri Curriculum requires two major ministries (MEST and MHW) to work collaboratively in administering both kindergartens and child care centers. Because two separate administrative bodies regulate not only the curriculum but also preparation of those teaching children ages 3 to 5 respectively, teacher preparation institutions are presented with unique challenges.

Because two government bodies regulate these programs, Korea currently has two separate initial certifications for those teaching children ages 3–5. Through MHW, certification (for daycare teachers) can be earned by taking 17 courses, which include 160 hours teaching practice at MHW-accredited institutions. Teacher education programs for child care teachers are currently offered in two- and three-year colleges and through online institutions. In 2011, there were 166,937 certified child care teachers. Two years later this number increased to 204,946 (Korea Statistics, 2014). The majority of these teachers were certified through online courses. Kindergarten teachers, on the other hand, are initially certified only after completing 50 courses at accredited Early Childhood Teacher Education programs at a four-year university. As of today, 181 institutions offer specific Early Childhood Education programs in Korea (MEST, 2013). These programs argue that standard child care teacher certification needs to be upgraded to meet higher qualifications.

While separate certifications remain, the government is strongly encouraging unification of early childhood teacher certification to meet the demands of high-quality programs for all children. Yet, quality is difficult to achieve when preservice teachers have differing certifications for teaching children of the same age. Moreover, while it is anticipated that teacher certification in Korea will soon

KICCE: Korean Institute of Child Care and Education. (2013b). *Nuri Curriculum Handbook* (Publication No. 11–1341000–002339–01). Seoul, Korea: MEST & MHW, Government Printing Office.

Koloszár, I. (2010). Az angol nyelv az óvódában [English language in preschool]. *Létünk, 4*, 75–84.

Korea Herald. (2014, March 9). Birthrate crisis. *The Korea Herald*. Retrieved from http://www.koreaherald.com/view.php?ud=20140309000070

Korea Statistics. (2014). Certified Childcare Teachers. Retrieved from http://kostat.go.kr/wnsearch/search.jsp

KOSIS: Korean Statistical Information Service. (2013a). 2013 Status of Foreigners Report (111_DT_1B040A15_20140924083405). Retrieved from http://kosis.kr/statHtml/statHtml.do?orgId=111&tblId=DT_1B040A15&conn_path=I2

KOSIS: Korean Statistical Information Service. (2013b). International Marriages (101_DT_1B83A24_20140924084623). Retrieved from http://kosis.kr/statHtml/statHtml.do?orgId=101&tblId=DT_1B83A24&conn_path=I2

Kwon, K., & Choi, S. J. (2007). Comparison and analysis for integration of early childhood education law and childcare law. *Journal of Early Childhood Education, 27*(6), 67–100.

Lee, Y. (2013). Analysis of Korean early childhood multicultural education policies based on critical perspective. *International Journal of Early Childhood Education, 19*(1), 109–127.

Liaghatdar, M. J. (2001). گزارش تحقیقی از وضعیت آموزش معلمان در ایران [Research report regarding teacher training in Iran]. فصلنامه پژوهش در مسائل آموزش و پرورش. *[Journal of Research in Education]*, *13*(14), 105–113.

Lukanga, A. L. (2013). *Teacher education in Tanzania: The experience of pre-service and in-service teacher preparation for quality education.* Retrieved from http://www.tenmet.org/Droop/Docs/QEC 2013/Lukanga.pdf

Magyar Akkreditációs Bizottság. (2012). *Akkreditációs jelentés MAB 2012/10/IX/1–35. sz. Határozata [Report of accreditation. MAB Regulation of 2012/10/IX/1–35]*. Retrieved from http://www.mab.hu/web/tir/jelentesek/p13_121207_jelentesH.pdf

Magyar, K. (1998). *Fogyatékos személyek jogairól és esélyegyenlőségük biztosításáról. 1998. évi XXVI. Törvény [Governmental decree of equal opportunities for people with special needs, 1998 XXVI]*. Retrieved from http://net.jogtar.hu/jr/gen/hjegy_doc.cgi?docid=99800026.TV&celpara=13#xcelparam

Magyar, K. (2011). *A nemzeti köznevelésről CXC. Törvény [Governmental decree of public education 2011 CXC]*. Retrieved from http://net.jogtar.hu/jr/gen/hjegy_doc.cgi?docid=A1100190.TV

Magyar, K. (2012). *Óvódai nevelés országos alapprogramja. Kormányrendelet 363/2012. XII. 17 [National core curriculum for preschool education. Decree of Government 363/2012. XII. 17]*. Retrieved from http://net.jogtar.hu/jr/gen/hjegy_doc.cgi?docid=A1200363.KOR&celpara=#xcelparam

MEST: Ministry of Education Science and Technology. (2013). Early childhood education program institutions. Retrieved from http://www.mest.go.kr/web/107261/ko/board/list.do?bbsId=342

MEST & MHW. (2013). *Handbook for Nuri Curriculum, Ages 3–5* (Publication No. 11–1341000–002339–01). Seoul, Korea: Ministry of Education, Science and Technology & Ministry of Health and Welfare.

Muijs, D., Aubrey, C., Harris, A., & Briggs, M. (2004). How do they manage?: A review of the research on leadership in early childhood. *Journal of Early Childhood Research, 2*, 157.

Mullayenejad, A. (2012) .صلاحیت های حرفه ای مطلوب دانشجو معلمان دوره آموزش ابتدایی [Professional qualifications desirable for student teachers in elementary schools]. فصلنامه نوآوری های آموزشی *[Journal of Educational Innovations]*, *11*(44), 33–62.

Nabati, R. (2014, May 11). Income subsidies allocated to the livelihood of teachers. Moallempress. Retrieved from http://moallempress.ir/fa/news-details/1879/

National Index. (2014). National Birthrate (National Approval Statistics No. 10103: Birthrate). Retrieved from http://www.index.go.kr/potal/main/EachDtlPageDetail.do?idx_cd=1428

Oh, C. S. (2011). The exploration of teacher professionalism in early childhood and care according to policy change. *Early Childhood Education Research Review, 15*(5), 249–277.

Oktatási Minisztérium. (2006). *Alap- és mesterképzési szakok képzési és kimeneti követelményeiről. 15/2006. (IV. 3.) rendelet* [*Outcome requirements for bachelor and master programs. Decree of Ministry of Education 15/2006. IV. 3*]. Retrieved from http://net.jogtar.hu/jr/gen/hjegy_doc.cgi?docid=A0600015.OM

Orosz, J. (2007) Tréningtechnikák a pedagógusképzésben [Training techniques in teacher education]. In I. Bollokne (Ed.) *Gyermeknevelés-Pedagógusképzés [Childhood education-Teacher education]* (pp. 149–154). Budapest: Trezor Kiadó.

Park, S. O. (2012). Korea in rapid transition toward a multicultural society: Challenges in preparing teachers of young children. *International Journal of Early Childhood Education and Care, 1*(1), 61–75.

Park, S. O. (2013). Mixed method study on multicultural teaching competence of Korean early childhood educators: Directions for teacher education. *Journal of Teaching and Education, 2*(4), 19–33.

Pooshneh, K., Khosravi, A., Purali, P. (2013). ارزشیابی میزان کیفیت برنامه‌های مراکز پیش دبستانی شهر تهران [Evaluation the quality of preschool programs in Tehran]. اندیشه‌های نوین تربیتی. *New Thought Education*, *8*(1), 58–29.

Rózsáné Czigány, E. (2013). A gyógypedagógia szemlélet integrálása a budai tanítóképzésbe [The integration of special education into the teacher preparation in College at Buda]. *Gyermeknevelés, 1*(1), 23–31.

Social Welfare Department (2014, January 13). Differences between stated and implemented policies in Early Childhood Education Leadership; A case study of Tanzania [Personal interview].

Szécsi, T. (2007). A tanítóképzésben résztvevők véleménye az eltérő kultúrák kezeléséről az általános iskolában [Diversity as perceived by administrator, teacher educator, mentor teacher and teacher candidates in Hungary]. *Pedagógusképzés, 34*(5), 29–47.

Taguchi, H. L., and Munkammar, I. (2003). Consolidating governmental early childhood education and care services under the Ministry of Education and Science: A Swedish case study. UNESCO; Early Childhood & Family Policy Series N°6.

Taguma, M., Litjens, I., and Makowiecki, K. (2013). Quality matters in early childhood education and care: Sweden 2013. *OECD Better Policies Better Lives.*

Trentinné Benkő, É. (2013a). Kétnyelvi pedagógusképzésben résztvevő hallgatók nézeteinek megjelenése kreativ vizuális alkotásaikban [Views of teacher candidates in bilingual teacher preparation through their creative visual representation]. *Gyermeknevelés, 1*(1), 73–105.

Trentinné Benkő, É. (2013b). A kétnyelvi képzésre jelentkező óvódapedagógus hallgatók nézetei és motivációi az ELTE TOK-on [The views and motivation of early childhood teacher candidates at ELTE College of Education]. In V. Árva & É. Márkus (Eds.), *Education and/und Forschung II. ELTE TÓK Tudományos Közlemények XXXV* (pp. 251–276). Budapest: Eötvös Kiadó.

United Republic of Tanzania. (1995). *The Education and Training Policy 1995.* Dar es Salaam.

United Republic of Tanzania. (2000). *The Education Sector Development Programme Document.* Dar es Salaam.

United Republic of Tanzania. (2002). *Primary Education Development Programme.* Dar es Salaam.

United Republic of Tanzania. (2008). The Teacher Development and Management Strategy (2008–2013).

United Republic of Tanzania (URT). (2009a). Basic Standards for Pre-Primary and Primary Education in Tanzania.

United Republic of Tanzania (URT). (2009b). Curriculum for Diploma in Teacher Education Programmes in Tanzania. Developed by Tanzania Institute of Education (TIE), Dar es Salaam, Tanzania.

United Republic of Tanzania (URT). (2012). Takwimu za Kielimu kwa baadhi ya miaka ya Uhuru wa Tanzania.

United Republic of Tanzania (URT). (2013). Basic Education Statistics in Tanzania (BEST).

Zaare, H., & Ghoshuni, A. (2008). آموزش پیش از دبستان: وضعیت موجود، کاستی ها، پیشنهادها و تدوین سیاست ها [Early childhood education: Current situation, shortcomings, recommendations and existing policies]. فرهنگ و علم *[Journal of Culture and Science], 1*(1), 241–248.

24

ALTERNATIVE PERSPECTIVES ON EARLY CHILDHOOD TEACHER EDUCATION

Shifting Pedagogies

J. Amos Hatch

In my office I have a sign I picked up in a little shop on a side street in Avignon, France. The sign reads: *PLACE DES BRICOLEURS*. For me, the sign symbolizes the kind of paradoxical thinking, writing, and teaching that have characterized the most recent period of my academic career. In ordinary translation, a *bricoleur* is a handyman (a *bricoleuse* a handywoman). A *bricoleur* or *bricoleuse* is one who solves problems using whatever materials and tools are readily available (i.e., he or she practices *bricolage*). *Bricolage* can be practiced in the arts, in philosophy, in architecture, in research, and in education (see e.g., Derrida, 1978; Hatton, 1989; Kincheloe, 2005a).

Here's the paradox. Teachers and teacher educators have been maligned for not basing their practice on a codified, "scientifically-based" body of knowledge (Hatch, 2006). Their approach to solving classroom problems by using any means available has been characterized as tantamount to "tinkering," the most unflattering characterization of *bricolage*. On the other hand, as I have worked with advanced doctoral candidates and preservice early childhood teachers, I have encouraged them to search about for whatever research and pedagogical tools they can find to accomplish the ends of their work.

I feel like a *bricoleur* as a teacher and scholar, so my surroundings at the university seem like a kind of place where *bricolage* is practiced. My way around complaints of merely tinkering is to provide my students and readers with a variety of powerful tools and materials from which to choose when they confront issues that make their work difficult. This chapter takes that stance. Early childhood teacher educators have the daunting task of preparing teachers to work in settings so complex and dynamic that the application of formulaic "Truths" based on traditional early childhood orthodoxy will no longer suffice. My goal is to lay out several alternative perspectives on early childhood pedagogy, describe their basic elements, identify ways these pedagogical approaches can enrich the learning and life chances of young children, and provide examples of how early childhood teacher educators can model these approaches in their teaching. The examples of early childhood teacher education practice are drawn from the literature, from my own experiences as a teacher educator, and from my imaginings of what might be possible.

The range of perspectives that I explore below may seem too broad to many experienced early childhood teacher educators. I divide the body of my exposition into sections on: direct instruction; scaffolding; teaching for thinking; multiple literacies pedagogy; culturally responsive teaching; critical pedagogy (including critical literacy approaches); and postmodern pedagogies (as influenced by queer theory, deconstruction, postcolonial theory, poststructuralism, and feminist poststructuralism). I acknowledge from the outset that there is occasional overlap among these approaches, but describing them individually is necessary for clarity and efficiency. I further realize that by including approaches as dramatically different as direct instruction and feminist poststructuralism, I may surprise colleagues on the ideological left, right, and middle of our field. More glaring for some will be the lack of attention paid to what I count as traditional "developmentally appropriate practices" codified in materials from the National Association for the Education of Young Children (NAEYC; e.g., Copple & Bredekamp, 2009) that continue to dominate the discourse of early childhood and early childhood teacher education.

But, the point of the chapter is to challenge traditional thinking by offering alternative perspectives on early childhood teaching and early childhood teacher education. It is clear that we are living in a world that is strikingly different from what existed when traditional approaches to early childhood education were developed. The experience of being a child in the early 21st century is already different from what it was like a generation ago, and it is vastly different from when the developmental principles that guide mainstream early childhood practice were promulgated (Hatch, 2005). Further, the knowledge base related to how children learn and develop has exploded, and many contributions from disciplines such as brain research, cognitive psychology, sociology, and educational psychology, as well as findings from early childhood researchers, tell us that many of the tenets of traditional early childhood practice are flawed at best (e.g., Ginsburg et al., 2006). In addition, the expectations for children's learning in preschool and beyond have escalated dramatically, and for better or worse, society through its approach to schooling is saying that "developmental" approaches to providing early education are insufficient (Stone, 1996).

Ignoring the reality of these changes seems foolish. Waving the flag of developmentally appropriate practice seems like an act of denial. As teacher educators, we have the opportunity to directly impact what will be happening in the classrooms our students will teach. It is our responsibility to prepare them to work with children who are experiencing postmodern childhoods, who deserve to be taught using the best knowledge available about teaching and learning, and who need to be prepared to be successful in contemporary school settings. The alternatives outlined in this chapter are designed to provide a framework for shifting our thinking about the pedagogical approaches we utilize in our university teaching so that we can respond effectively to these and other challenges our students will face.

I hope that my colleagues from across the political spectrum will consider the potential richness that the application of these alternative pedagogies can bring to their own understandings and to the preparation of future early childhood teachers. If *bricolage* is an appropriate metaphor, then what follows are resources for raising early childhood teacher education practice from making do with what we have always had available to creating something new and important to meet the needs of future educators who will be teaching in a rapidly changing postmodern world.

Direct Instruction

The terms "direct instruction" and "direct teaching" are most often used to describe general classroom practices that are characterized as teacher directed or teacher centered. These generic approaches were labeled as "developmentally inappropriate practice" (DIP) in the original version of the *Developmentally Appropriate Practices Handbook* published by NAEYC in the 1980s (Bredekamp, 1987). Since that time, mainstream early childhood scholars have perpetually favored constructivist "developmentally appropriate" strategies over behaviorist "direct instruction" approaches (e.g., Hart, Burts, & Charlesworth, 1997). Authors of widely adopted early childhood textbooks continue to emphasize developmental approaches, often excluding direct teaching entirely or casting it as inappropriate for young children (e.g., Essa, 2011). It appears that direct instruction continues to be perceived as DIP by the mainstream early childhood community because it is based on principles of learning derived from behaviorist theory and is seen to ignore the constructivist assumptions that are the bedrock of developmentally appropriate practices.

Here, I describe a specific set of instructional steps that make up the direct instruction model and explain why early childhood teachers should be competent in using this model to teach basic skills and concepts that young children need. I am not interested in promoting the notion that teacher directed activity should make up all or most of the school day; I am suggesting that the specific teaching steps in direct instruction (and knowing when and when not to use them) should be part of every early childhood teacher's repertoire.

The direct instruction model is based on findings from "process-product" research that has been ongoing since the 1970s (e.g., Rosenshine & Stevens, 1986). In this research, trained observers chart teaching behaviors (process) of thousands of instructors, then these data are correlated with test scores (product) of those teachers to determine which teaching behaviors were positively related to improved test performance. While there are slight differences among models, I have adapted Slavin's (1997) version, which is based on his synthesis across the process-product literature, supplementing it with explanations found in my kindergarten text (Hatch, 2005) and Moore and Hansen's (2012) instructional strategies book. A direct instruction sequence includes the following steps:

1. *Set the stage for learning.* Teachers orient students to the lesson by stating the learning objectives, reviewing prerequisite knowledge, making connections to students' experience, and/or providing an attention getter.
2. *Present new material.* Teachers tell students what it is they want them to learn, giving varied and concrete examples, demonstrating skills and defining concepts, and modeling what students are supposed to be able to do at the end of the lesson.
3. *Monitor and adjust.* Teachers ask questions and give practice problems, assessing students' level of understanding, correcting misconceptions, and reteaching on the spot when necessary.
4. *Provide independent practice.* Teachers give students the opportunity to practice newly acquired skills or concepts, assigning independent activities to be completed in the classroom or at home to help children consolidate their learning.

Direct instruction has shown to be an effective and efficient way to teach important skills and concepts to young children (Meyer, 1984; Rosenshine, 2008). My view is that it would be "inappropriate" to make direct instruction the major or only strategy utilized in early childhood classrooms, but that can be said of any of the pedagogical approaches to follow. The importance of young children's mastery of basic skills and concepts (especially in math and early literacy) is hard to overestimate, given the curricular expectations that characterize contemporary early schooling. While some students will learn basic skills and concepts using strictly constructivist approaches, many will take a long time to discover the learning they need, and others will not "get it" at all. Future teachers need to understand that a combination of direct instruction and more integrated approaches are needed to meet the needs of every child (e.g., Clements, Sarama, & DiBiase, 2004; Xue & Meisels, 2004).

In my preservice teacher coursework, I require students to write lesson plans that follow the four-step model described above. They have to identify appropriate content, write objectives, and detail how they will teach using the direct instruction model. They then "micro-teach" their lessons in small groups, making videotapes while they are teaching four or five of their peers. Following micro-teaching procedures described in the teacher education literature (e.g., Darling-Hammond, Hammerness, Grossman, Rust, & Shulman, 2007; Grossman, 2005), students also review the tapes along with their peers and the instructor, who offer critiques of how closely the lessons matched the intent and letter of the model. Although not required, many of my university students use these lessons in real classrooms in their field experiences and internship placements. The message is consistent: direct teaching is great for teaching basic skills and concepts, but it is not a good choice for teaching the myriad other content elements, cognitive processes, and dispositions children need to acquire in early childhood classrooms.

Scaffolding

I have made the case in other writing that for too long early childhood education as a field has overemphasized children's development at the expense of their learning (Hatch, 2010, 2012). I contrast the perspectives of Piaget and Vygotsky on the relative positionings of learning and development, arguing that Vygotsky's (1978) notion that *learning leads development* has been basically ignored in favor of Piaget's (1964) dictum that *learning is subordinated to development.* The point here is to help preservice teachers see that learning has a vital place in early childhood classrooms and to provide future teachers with knowledge and instructional tools to bring Vygotsky's conceptualization of how learning happens to life through their teaching. I use the construct of "scaffolding" to show how Vygotsky's ways of thinking can be enacted to enhance the capabilities of early childhood educators to impact the learning of their students.

Scaffolding is the "process of providing temporary guidance and support to children moving from one level of competence to another" (MacNaughton & Williams, 2004, p. 331). Effective scaffolding takes place within the child's zone of proximal development; that is, the child completes tasks with the support of an adult or more competent peer that he or she could not complete alone. Scaffolding takes form in verbal and non-verbal instructional techniques that extend children's understandings and skills, including questioning, demonstrating, prompting, confirming, pointing out, modeling, simplifying, directing, restating, redefining, and repeating (Bedrova & Leong, 2007; MacNaughton & Williams, 2004). In their book about how to apply Vygotskian principles in early childhood classrooms, Berk and Winsler (1995) describe the elements that make up a framework for the scaffolding process:

1. *Joint problem solving.* Children are engaged with the teacher in a collaborative effort to solve a meaningful problem.
2. *Intersubjectivity.* Through social negotiation, the teacher and child come to a mutual understanding and shared definition of the task at hand.
3. *Warmth and responsiveness.* When children feel safe and supported, they are much more likely to be fully engaged in challenging tasks that (by definition) they could not complete alone.
4. *Keeping the child in the ZPD.* Since each child's zone of proximal development is always changing, it is important for teachers to monitor children's progress, adjusting the tasks assigned and the level of scaffolding provided.
5. *Promoting self-regulation.* As children's competence increases, teachers need to reduce the amount of scaffolding provided and turn over to children increasing responsibility for regulating the learning task at hand.

As early childhood teacher educators, we never fail to mention Vygotsky when we talk about the theoretical bases of our work, but I am afraid that many of our students are sent into classrooms without a full understanding of or appreciation for the implications of some of Vygotsky's key contributions. I am concerned that these future teachers will not be exposed to or ignore all the evidence that suggests that young children are capable of learning much more than we have thought in the past (Hatch, 2010). Vygotsky and his interpreters argue that all classroom instruction ought to take place within a child's zone of proximal development. Instead of teaching preservice teachers all of the limitations a child's stage of development places on his or her learning potential, we should be showing future teachers the capacity of scaffolding to accelerate important dimensions of children's development. If learning leads development, then our students need the knowledge and skills to make learning the central feature in their future classrooms.

In my preservice teaching, I highlight the potential of scaffolding to be an invaluable instructional tool in contemporary early childhood teaching (Berk & Winsler, 1995). I assign readings and provide classroom instruction directly related to effective scaffolding. I also model scaffolding strategies and lead in-class activities, during which university students role-play how they would scaffold the learning of specific content from early childhood curriculum. Role-playing pedagogies have a long history in teacher education (Grossman, 2005), and playing the role of student and teacher gives future early childhood teachers opportunities to experience the scaffolding process from both perspectives. These activities require students to design a task that would get at some specific curricular content, plan a hierarchy of scaffolding strategies that might be needed for a child to accomplish the task, and then scaffold that task with another student who plays the role of a young child who cannot accomplish that task without the teacher's support. We then debrief together about what makes a good task for teaching certain content and how well the teachers in the role-playing met the five guidelines for effective scaffolding described above.

Teaching for Thinking

Teaching young children to think is another construct that rubs many early childhood educators the wrong way. Traditionalists who rely on Piagetian-based understandings of cognitive development believe that children are incapable of abstract reasoning until they are about twelve years of age and that cognitive development needs to be in place before meaningful learning can be accomplished. The assumption is that no amount of instruction will be effective if the mental processing involved is beyond the child's level of cognitive development. In the words of one of Piaget's most prominent interpreters: "Learning is inconceivable without a theoretically prior interior structure" (Furth, 1970, p. 160).

As we have learned from research done within disciplines as varied as cognitive psychology, brain physiology, social psychology, and cultural anthropology, children as young as three and four are capable of mental processing that was considered impossible based on Piagetian notions of cognitive development (see Hatch, 2010, 2012). For example, cognitive scientists (e.g., Bransford, Brown, & Cocking, 2000; Meadows, 2006) who study how children learn have discovered that young children can think about their own thinking, metacognitively monitor their own learning, and intentionally adjust their own mental processes to adapt to different learning situations. Understanding that children are fully capable of "learning to think" creates possibilities and responsibilities for early childhood teacher educators that were unimaginable within Piagetian worldviews. Again, the application of Vygotskian principles offers one way to build teaching for thinking into our teacher preparation programs.

The literature on teaching thinking processes is vast and complex, but little has been done that specifically focuses on preschool-aged children. As part of an ongoing project, I have synthesized a taxonomy of thinking skills and developed some sample activities designed to guide early childhood educators interested in teaching young children to think. A working version of that taxonomy is included in Table 24.1.

The activities I have developed to address the skills on the taxonomy apply Vygotsky's notions that all learning is social, thinking is interiorized speech, and children develop tools of the mind by thinking out loud with others (Bedrova & Leong, 2007; Berk & Winsler, 1995; Vygotsky, 1978). For example, one activity that teachers can use to teach comparing (an information processing skill on the taxonomy) is to think aloud with a child about what is the same and different about two familiar objects (e.g., forks and spoons). The adult explicitly states what he or she is thinking as the pair notes similarities and differences. As with scaffolding above, the teacher gradually gives more responsibility to the children who verbalize their own thinking as additional familiar objects are compared.

Such activities are examples of ways to address the larger point: Young children can learn to think in much more complex ways than we have traditionally understood; and early childhood teacher educators should guide the preservice teachers with whom they work toward understanding young children's cognitive capacities and finding ways to scaffold children's development as thinkers. With

Table 24.1 Taxonomy of Thinking Skills for Young Children

I. Information Processing Skills
- A. Comparing
- B. Sorting
- C. Classifying
- D. Ordering/Sequencing
- E. Analyzing Relationships
- F. Generalizing
- G. Forming Concepts
- H. Inferring
- I. Concluding
- J. Predicting
- K. Considering Other Points of View

II. Reasoning Skills
- A. Inductive Reasoning
- B. Deductive Reasoning
- C. Metaphoric Reasoning
- D. Mathematical Reasoning

III. Creative Thinking Skills
- A. Brainstorming
- B. Divergent Thinking
- C. Flexible Thinking

refe[illegible] teaching thinking skills in early childhood classrooms, Costello (2012) argues that teachers s[illegible]

- [illegible]d with opportunities to think critically;
- [illegible]cit training in how to enhance their own critical thinking skills (as part of initial teacher education courses);
- [illegible] training in how to promote and extend children's thinking skills; and
- [illegible]llingness to think critically. (p. xii).

In or[illegible] to think, [illegible]ir own thinking capacities and explore the processes of teaching children, but [illegible]ity students thinking tasks that parallel those I developed for young children, [illegible] content. Modifying "Jigsaw" cooperative learning strategies (Aronson & Patnoe, [illegible] they think [illegible]rt groups," in which a set of participants is given the same task and group that [illegible] a solution. Individuals then pair up with a student from another [illegible] different task; then, one at a time, the students in each pair teach each other [illegible]ir respective tasks, applying the Vygotskian principles described above. Given [illegible]ing that thinking is such a prominent feature of the Common Core State St[illegible] [illegible]st prepare our students to address (Bellanca, Fogarty, & Pete, 2013), activit[illegible]ng are all the more important for early childhood teacher educators to a[illegible]

Multiple Literacies Pedagogy

The young children our university students will spend their careers teaching are growing up in a different world than we experienced in childhood. New technologies are being developed faster than ever, and children's out-of-school experiences with literacy have been altered in significant and dramatic ways. Critics point out that the text-based literacy practices that characterize early education settings ignore the multimodal texts that children are exposed to before entering classrooms. The multimodal texts that young children now experience very early in their lives incorporate sound, music, written and spoken words, still and moving pictures, and animation, and are closely associated with television, computers, cell phones, video games, tablets, and the Internet (Kress, 2010; Yelland, Lee, O'Rourke, & Harrison, 2008). The traditional printed text emphasized in school is disconnected from how children experience literacy at home and fails to give them the skills they will need in the new media age (Marsh, 2005). Thus, early childhood teacher educators and preservice teachers need to broaden their thinking about literacy instruction to include a multiple literacies pedagogical approach.

Taking a multiple literacies approach when teaching young children means going beyond an emphasis on the basic numeracy and literacy skills that make up what's usually taught (and tested) in contemporary early childhood classrooms. In the words of Cope and Luke (2000),

> A pedagogy of multiliteracies, focuses on modes of representation much broader than language alone. . . . Multiliteracies also create a different kind of pedagogy: one in which language and other modes of meaning are dynamic representational resources, constantly being remade by their users.
>
> (p. 3)

A multiple literacies pedagogy for young children should include opportunities for learning, multimodal texts and use multiple forms of representation through the application of approp technologies. Yelland and colleagues (2008) collected examples of such pedagogical practices in education classrooms, including the following activities and their associated technologies: (a) acc information using the Internet; (b) creating representations using computerized painting and programs; (c) using digital cameras to document activities; (d) making videos with music, images using cameras and specialized editing software; (e) creating portfolios utilizing a electronic communication tools; (f) incorporating digital representations as part of child dramatic play; and (g) finding ways to link multiple literacy activities with traditional writing instruction.

Most of the university students we teach came of age in the technological era. As we teachers, we should build on our students' familiarity and comfort with the emergi that have a direct impact on the literacy experiences of the young children they wi teachers, we can add knowledge and experiences that will improve future teache utilizing multiple literacy pedagogies in their classrooms. For example, adapting fra been used to encourage early childhood teachers' adoption of multiliteracy prac 2008), we can create assignments that require preservice teachers to assess the l operating in classrooms they visit and/or complete analyses of how well the of individual children are being met. Additionally, we can demonstrate som multiple literacies pedagogy in our own teaching and challenge students t teaching as they plan and implement literacy lessons with young children. A have worked with primary teachers to form "multiliteracies book clubs" of practice approach to exploring multiple literacies pedagogies. These jointly experience, explore, and discuss multimodal communication ar with traditional literacy practices (Gardiner, Cumming-Potvin, & Hesterman, 2013). Facilitating such experiences with preservice teachers is another way teacher educators can emphasize the importance of going beyond standardized literacy practices in early childhood teaching.

Culturally Responsive Teaching

No one doubts the need for future early childhood teachers to be able to effectively teach children from cultural backgrounds different from their own. The majority of students entering the education system in the United States are children of color, many of whom do not speak English as their home language. At the same time, over 75 percent of teachers are White, monolingual speakers of mainstream American English (Souto-Manning, 2013). It is vital that we as teacher educators do a better job of preparing our students for the complexities and opportunities these demographic changes signal for the present and future.

Gay (2010) describes culturally responsive teaching (CRT) as a framework for addressing the learning needs of all children. CRT is a pedagogical approach that uses the cultural knowledge, prior experiences, frames of reference, and performance styles of students from diverse backgrounds to make learning more relevant and effective for them. Gay (2010) describes culturally responsive teaching as having the following characteristics:

- acknowledging the cultural heritages of different ethnic groups, both as legacies that affect students' dispositions, attitudes, and approaches to learning and as worthy content to be taught in the formal curriculum;
- building bridges of meaningfulness between home and school experiences as well as between academic abstractions and lived sociocultural realities;
- using a wide variety of instructional strategies that are connected to different learning styles;
- teaching students to know and praise their own and each others' cultural heritages; and
- incorporating multicultural information, resources, and materials in all the subjects and skills routinely taught in schools. (p. 31–32).

The principles of CRT can be applied in classrooms for students of all age levels and represent a useful guide for creating learning opportunities for future early childhood teachers. In addition, early childhood scholars provide specific guidance for working with young children from diverse backgrounds (e.g., Doucet & Adair, 2013; Genishi & Goodwin, 2008; Souto-Manning, 2013); and "anti-bias" strategies (e.g., Derman-Sparks & ABC Task Force, 1989; Derman-Sparks & Edwards, 2010) continue to be invaluable resources for early childhood teachers and teacher educators.

An essential element of CRT or other approaches to providing culturally relevant pedagogy is teacher awareness of and respect for the cultural backgrounds and experiences of their students. In the urban-multicultural teacher education program in which I work, we have students complete "cultural autobiographies" as a way to help them acknowledge their own cultural identities so that they can understand and appreciate others' ways of knowing and being. We invite individuals from a variety of cultural backgrounds within the community to share their stories, then have our students record, transcribe, and fill-in their own stories, which we revisit periodically throughout their time in our program. We also require that students complete "community mapping" activities, in which they work in teams to produce multimedia presentations that portray the strengths they found in the urban school communities in which they complete their internships. We also have preservice teachers conduct a videotaped family interview in the home of one of their students in order to help them see the importance of learning about individual children and their families. They analyze and edit the tapes, then present their findings to their peers. We also spend a great deal of time reading about and discussing anti-bias, anti-racist, and culturally relevant teaching.

Table 24.2 Generalizations from Postmodern Theories

- Truth claims (grand narratives) are historically, socially, and politically situated constructions—not universal constants.
- Knowledge is always partial, local, and subjective.
- Knowledge and power are inextricably connected.
- Queer theory questions the assumption that there is any "normal" expression of anything.
- Deconstruction involves reading experience as if it were text, examining it for what is said and not said.
- Postcolonial thought values indigenous worldviews and challenges an uncritical acceptance of the notion of progress.
- Poststructuralists debunk the modern belief that science is capable of objectively determining universal laws.
- Feminist poststructuralists reveal for inspection the heteronormative discourses that dominate considerations of gender and take seriously the active role individuals play in their own gender development.

Early childhood educators from around the globe have developed ways to apply pedagogical approaches based on queer theory, deconstruction, postcolonial theory, and poststructuralism/feminist poststructuralism in their classrooms. Blaise and Taylor (2012) describe an activity designed to develop awareness of heteronormative assumptions by having children sort clothes and accessories from the dress-up area into girl, boy, and girl/boy piles, then asking thought-provoking questions such as, "How did you decide to make these piles of dress-ups?" and "Why might some children not like to use those (girl, boy, girl/boy) dress-ups?" (p. 96). To help young children begin to see how language can be taken apart in order to understand what is fair and unfair, MacNaughton and Williams (2004) illuminate activities that encourage children to critically explore word pairs such as rich and poor, asking questions such as, "When and why might it be good to be poor?" or "What things do poor people do better than rich people?" (p. 242). Ritchie (2013) details activities undertaken in Maori kindergarten classrooms that make possible the deliberate "unlearning" of colonialist assumptions and practices by infusing indigenous ways of being, knowing, and doing. And Robinson and Jones Diaz (2006) contend that early childhood teachers need to observe children's classroom positionings through poststructural lenses and learn to link their interpretations to programming and planning—for example, "bilingual children's rejection of their home language; or the young boy who bullies other children as a performance of his masculinity" (p. 42).

Early childhood teacher educators have the opportunity to expand their students' perspectives on teaching young children by exposing future teachers to postmodern pedagogies and by modeling ways these can be applied in classroom settings. Some examples of activities utilized by university-based postmodern pedagogues include having pre- or inservice teachers locate television or print advertisements that could be used to help young children deconstruct the idea that only mothers should care for babies or having them find historical and contemporary posters of underrepresented or oppressed peoples and say how those images perpetuate or challenge stereotypes (MacNaughton & Williams, 2004). Others have emphasized the importance of improving future teachers' awareness of "the various forms of cultural capital children 'bring' with them to school in terms of linguistic and cultural knowledge" (O'Connor, 2011, p. 124). And, Yelland and Kilderry (2005) offer the following questions that can be posed to preservice early childhood educators to stimulate discussions and initiate change:

- How can we act as *critical advocates* for early childhood education?
- Is the *overemphasis on developmental theory* in early childhood education a problem? In what ways is it or is it not?
- What is the value of disrupting the way we view *play materials* that are commonly found in early childhood settings?

- Is there a time and place for *risky teaching*?
- How can we enact socially-just teaching? (p. 246, emphases in original)

In their article encouraging early childhood teacher educators to move from developmental to postmodern practices, Ryan and Grieshaber (2005) argue that a postmodern teacher education seeks to provide students with a set of analytical tools (something like a theoretical toolbox) that they can use to view practices from different perspectives, providing alternative ways of seeing, understanding, and acting on the same situation (p. 43).

Ryan and Grieshaber (2005) have developed a three-pronged approach to introducing their students to postmodern pedagogies: situating knowledge, multiple readings, and engaging with images. *Situating knowledge* means "examining the historical, social, political, economic, and cultural contexts that give rise to various understandings and practices associated with educating young children" (p. 36). These teacher educators give the example of having preservice teachers explore the biographical, historical, and political contexts in which Piaget's developmental theories were created. *Multiple readings* are designed to help students make sense of the ways that discourses shape education and social life by "reading aspects of early childhood theory and practice from various perspectives to ask who benefits from particular knowledges and what other practices might be possible" (p. 37). Ryan and Grieshaber (2005) provide students with data excerpts from classroom interactions and have students explore competing systems of meaning operating in the classroom vignettes. *Engaging with images* is a strategy Ryan and Grieshaber (2005) use to help students explore their professional identities through the use of visual representations. One of their activities is to ask preservice teachers to draw their own images as early childhood educators, then examine these images as texts "that reflect particular values about the identities of early childhood teachers" (p. 40).

Conclusions

Ryan and Grieshaber's (2005) portrayal of postmodern pedagogical approaches as "something like a theoretical toolbox" (p. 43) takes me back to my premise that early childhood teaching and teacher education represent a kind of *bricolage,* in that both classroom teachers and university instructors are engaged in solving problems using whatever materials and tools are readily available. I have argued elsewhere that, "modern ideas such as the possibility of uncovering universal truths through the application of scientific principles are being replaced with the postmodern understanding that multiple truths exist and that these are always local, partial, and in flux" (Hatch, 2005, p. 14). Helping our students understand that there is no single "correct" solution to any issue they may face in the classroom is vital to their success. Providing future early childhood teachers with the disposition to apply a wide assortment of materials and tools, including pedagogical approaches like those outlined in this chapter, seems essential to preparing them to teach in an increasingly complex and rapidly changing world. Expanding our own theoretical toolboxes and demonstrating how to use the knowledge and skills necessary to participate in postmodern schooling should be a high priority for all contemporary early childhood teacher educators. I hope the examples here will expand my colleagues' understanding of what's possible in their work and encourage them to challenge the boundaries of what's appropriate as they prepare early childhood education teachers for the future.

Beyond our immediate impact in university classrooms, early childhood teacher educators should be engaged in shaping policy in early childhood education and in our specialized segment of that field. Early childhood education needs strong voices to articulate the necessity for adopting a wider view of what constitutes appropriate pedagogical practices. The field of early childhood teacher education needs powerful examples of how alternative pedagogies like those described in this chapter can be enacted in university and early childhood classrooms. Both disciplines need leadership in shifting our perspectives on what constitutes best practices in early childhood classrooms. If we do not speak out in professional settings, publish evidence for the efficacy of alternative teaching approaches, and advocate for policies that encourage a broader approach to early childhood pedagogy, the myopia that has characterized the mainstream of our field may lead us into irrelevance.

References

Aronson, E., & Patnoe, S. (2011). *Cooperation in the classroom: The jigsaw method* (3rd ed.). London, UK: Pinter & Martin.

Bedrova, E., & Leong, D. J. (2007). *Tools of the mind: The Vygotskian approach to early childhood education* (2nd ed.). Upper Saddle River, NJ: Pearson.

Bellanca, J. A., Fogarty, R. J., & Pete, B. M. (2013). *How to teach thinking skills within the common core.* Bloomington, IN: Solution Tree Press.

Berk, L. E., & Winsler, A. (1995). *Scaffolding children's learning: Vygotsky and early childhood education.* Washington, DC: National Association for the Education of Young Children.

Blaise, M., & Taylor, A. (2012). Using queer theory to rethink gender equity in early childhood education. *Young Children, 67*(1), 88–98.

Bransford, J. D., Brown, A. L., & Cocking, R. R. (Eds.). (2000). *How people learn: Brain, mind, experience, and school.* Washington, DC: National Academy Press.

Bredekamp, S. (Ed.). (1987). *Developmentally appropriate practice in early childhood programs serving children from birth through age 8.* Washington, DC: NAEYC.

Cannella, G. S. (1997). *Deconstructing early childhood education.* New York: Peter Lang.

Clements, D. H., Sarama, J., & DiBiase, A. M. (Eds.). (2004). *Engaging young children in mathematics: Standards for early childhood education.* Mahwah, NJ: Erlbaum.

Comber, B. (2003). Critical literacy in the early years: What does it look like? In N. Hall, J. Larson, & J. Marsh (Eds.), *Handbook of early literacy* (pp. 355–368). London: Sage.

Cope, B., & Luke, C. (2000). Multiliteracies: The beginning of an idea. In B. Cope & M. Kalntzis (Eds.), *Multiliteracies: Literacy learning and the design of social futures* (pp. 3–8). South Yarra, AU: Macmillan.

Copple, C., & Bredekamp, S. (Eds.). (2009). *Developmentally appropriate practice in early childhood programs* (3rd ed.). Washington, DC: National Association for the Education of Young Children.

Costello, P. J.M. (2012). *Thinking skills and early childhood education.* New York: Routledge.

Darling-Hammond, L., Hammerness, K., Grossman, P., Rust, F., & Shulman, L. (2007). The design of teacher education programs. In L. Darling-Hammond & J. Bransford (Eds.), *Preparing teachers for a changing world: What teachers should learn and be able to do* (pp. 390–441). San Francisco, CA: Jossey-Bass.

Davies, B. (1993). *Shards of glass: Children reading and writing beyond gendered identities.* Sydney, AU: Allen and Unwin.

Derman-Sparks, L., & ABC Task Force. (1989). *Anti-bias curriculum: Tools for empowering young children.* Washington, DC: National Association for the Education of Young Children.

Derman-Sparks, L., & Edwards, J. O. (2010). *Anti-bias education for young children and ourselves.* Washington, DC: National Association for the Education of Young Children.

Derrida, J. (1978). *Writing and difference.* Chicago, IL: University of Chicago Press.

Doucet, F., & Adair, J. K. (2013). Addressing race and inequality in the classroom. *Young Children, 68*(5), 88–97.

Essa, E. L. (2011). *Introduction to early childhood education* (6th ed.). Belmont, CA: Wadsworth.

Freire, P. (1970). *Pedagogy of the oppressed.* New York: Continuum.

Furth, H. G. (1970). *Piaget for teachers.* Englewood Cliffs, NJ: Prentice-Hall.

Gay, G. (2010). *Culturally responsive teaching: Theory, research, and practice* (2nd ed.). New York: Teachers College Press.

Gardiner, V., Cumming-Potvin, W., & Hesterman, S. (2013). Professional learning in a scaffolded 'multiliteracies book club': Transforming primary teacher participation. *Issues in Educational Research, 23*(3), 357–374.

Genishi, C., & Goodwin, A. L. (Eds.). (2008). *Diversities in early childhood education: Rethinking and doing.* New York: Routledge.

Ginsburg, H. P., Kaplan, R. G., Cannon, J., Cordero, M. I., Eisenband, J. G., Galanter, M., & Morgenlander, M. (2006). Helping early childhood educators to teach mathematics. In M. Zaslow & I. Martinez-Beck (Eds.), *Critical issues in early childhood professional development* (pp. 171–202). Baltimore, MD: Paul H. Brookes.

Grossman, P. (2005). Research on pedagogical approaches in teacher education. In M. Cochran-Smith & K. M. Zeichner (Eds.), *Studying teacher education: The report of the AERA panel on research and teacher development* (pp. 425–476). Washington, DC: American Educational Research Association.

Hart, C. H., Burts, D. C., & Charlesworth, R. (Eds). (1997). *Integrated curriculum and developmentally appropriate practice: Birth to age eight.* Albany, NY: State University of New York Press.

Hatch, J. A. (2005). *Teaching in the new kindergarten.* Clifton Park, NY: Thompson Delmar.

Hatch, J. A. (2006). Qualitative studies in the era of scientifically-based research. *Qualitative Studies in Education, 19*(4), 403–407.

Hatch, J. A. (2010). Rethinking the relationship between learning and development: Teaching for learning in early childhood classrooms. *The Educational Forum, 74,* 258–268.

Hatch, J. A. (2012). Developmental theory and its relationship to curriculum and instruction in early childhood education. In N. File, J. J. Mueller, and D. B. Wisneski (Eds.), *Curriculum in early childhood education: Re-examined, rediscovered, renewed* (pp. 42–53). New York: Routledge.

Hatch, J. A., & Groenke, S. L. (2009). Issues in critical teacher education: Insights from the field. In S. L. Groenke & J. A. Hatch (Eds.), *Critical pedagogy and teacher education in the neoliberal era: Small openings* (pp. 63–82). New York: Springer.

Hatch, J. A., & Meller, W. B. (2009). Becoming critical in an urban elementary teacher education program. In S. L. Groenke & J. A. Hatch (Eds.), *Critical pedagogy and teacher education in the neoliberal era: Small openings* (pp. 219–232). New York: Springer.

Hatton, E. (1989). Levi-Strauss's "bricolage" and theorizing teachers' work. *Anthropology and Education Quarterly, 20*(2), 74–96.

Kincheloe, J. L. (2005a). On to the next level: Continuing the conceptualization of the bricolage. *Qualitative Inquiry, 11*(3), 323–350.

Kincheloe, J. L. (2005b). *Critical pedagogy.* New York: Peter Lang.

Kress, G. (2010). *Multimodality: A social semiotic approach to contemporary communication.* New York: Routledge.

Kuby, C. R. (2013). *Critical literacy in the early childhood classroom: Unpacking histories, unlearning privilege.* New York: Teachers College Press.

Larson, J., & Marsh, J. (2005). *Making literacy real: Theories and practices for learning and teaching.* Thousand Oaks, CA: Sage.

MacNaughton, G., & Williams, G. (2004). *Teaching young children: Choices in theory and practice.* London, UK: Open University Press.

Marsh, J. (2005). Digikids: Young children, popular culture and media. In N. Yelland (Ed.), *Critical issues in early childhood education* (pp. 181–196). New York: Open University Press.

McLaughlin, M., & DeVoogd, G. (2004). *Critical literacy: Enhancing students' comprehension of text.* New York: Scholastic.

Meadows, S. (2006). *The child as thinker: The development and acquisition of cognition in childhood.* New York: Routledge.

Meller, W. B., Richardson, D., & Hatch, J. A. (2009). Using read-alouds with critical literacy literature in K-3 classrooms. *Young Children, 64*(2), 76–78.

Meyer, L. A. (1984). Long term academic effects of the direct instruction Project Follow Through. *The Elementary School Journal, 84*(4), 380–394.

Moore, K. D., & Hansen, J. (2012). *Effective strategies for teaching in k-8 classrooms.* Thousand Oaks, CA: Sage.

O'Connor, J. (2011). Applying Bourdieu's concepts of social and cultural capital and habitus to early years research. In T. Waller, J. Whitmarsh, & K. Clarke (Eds.), *Making sense of theory and practice in early childhood* (pp. 115–127). New York: Open University Press.

Piaget, J. (1964). Development and learning. In R. E. Ripple & V. N. Rockcastle (Eds.), *Piaget rediscovered: A report of the conference on cognitive studies and curriculum development* (pp. 7–20). Ithaca, NY: Cornell University School of Education.

Quintero, E. P. (2004). *Problem-posing with multicultural children's literature: Developing critical early childhood curricula.* New York: Peter Lang.

Ritchie, J. (2013). Indigenous onto-epistemologies and pedagogies of care and affect in Aotearoa. *Global Studies of Childhood, 3*(4), 395–406.

Robinson, K. H., & Jones Diaz, C. (2006). *Diversity and difference in early childhood education: Issues for theory and practice.* New York: Open University Press.

Rosenshine, B. (2008). *Five meanings of direct instruction.* Lincoln, IL: Center for Innovation and Improvement.

Rosenshine, B. V., & Stevens, R. J. (1986). Teaching functions. In M. C. Wittrock (Ed.), *Third handbook of research on teaching* (pp. 376–391). New York: Macmillan.

Ryan, S., & Grieshaber, S. (2005). Shifting from developmental to postmodern practices in early childhood teacher education. *Journal of Teacher Education, 56*(1), 34–45.

Slavin, R. E. (1997). *Educational psychology: Theory and practice.* Boston, MA: Allyn and Bacon.

Souto-Manning, M. (2010). *Freire, teaching and learning: Culture circles across contexts.* New York: Peter Lang.

Souto-Manning, M. (2013). Teaching young children from immigrant and diverse families. *Young Children, 68*(4), 72–80.

Stone, J. E. (1996). Developmentalism: An obscure but pervasive restriction on educational improvement. *Education Policy Analysis Archives, 4*(8), 1–32.

Swadener, B. B., & Mutua, K. (2007). Decolonizing research in cross-cultural contexts. In J. A. Hatch (Ed.), *Early childhood qualitative research* (pp. 185–205). New York: Routledge.

Tobin, J. (1995). Post-structuralist research in early childhood education. In J. A. Hatch (Ed.), *Qualitative research in early childhood settings* (pp. 223–243). Westport, CT: Praeger.

Vasquez, V. (2004). *Negotiating critical literacies with young children*. Mahwah, NJ: Lawrence Earlbaum Associates.

Vygotsky, L. S. (1978). *Mind in society: The development of higher psychological processes.* Cambridge, MA: Harvard University Press.

Xue, Y., & Meisels, S. J. (2004). Early literacy instruction and learning in kindergarten: Evidence from the Early Childhood Longitudinal Study—Kindergarten Class of 1998–1999. *American Educational Research Journal, 41*(1), 191–129.

Yelland, N., & Kilderry, A. (2005). Postmodernism, passion, and potential for future childhoods. In N. Yelland (Ed.), *Critical issues in early childhood education* (pp. 243–248). New York: Open University Press.

Yelland, N., Lee, L., O'Rourke, M., & Harrison, C. (2008). *Rethinking learning in early childhood education.* New York: Open University Press.

25

FUTURE DIRECTIONS FOR EARLY CHILDHOOD TEACHER EDUCATION

Leslie J. Couse and Susan L. Recchia

The *Handbook of Early Childhood Teacher Education* (ECTE) was undertaken with the intent to bring together, analyze, and articulate the current research and knowledge on preparing teachers to work with children from birth through age 8. Taking broad strokes to reflect the breadth of the field, our diverse group of authors illuminates the multiple dimensions of influence in ECTE. Through their expertise and passionate interest in particular perspectives within the field, chapter authors look deeply at what we know thus far, what we need to explore further, and some promising ways to move forward.

This final chapter serves as a synthesis of what we have learned from the chapter authors about the diversities, complexities, strengths, and challenges of ECTE, as well as a vehicle for highlighting the enduring questions for research and practice that have emerged for the field. In this chapter, we articulate what is needed to solidify and enrich ECTE to harness our strengths and further legitimize the field as a distinct area within teacher education, and to push the field forward to deepen and apply our knowledge and understanding.

Contributions and Tenets of the Field: What Matters Most in Early Childhood Teacher Education?

The complexities inherent in early childhood education (ECE) make it difficult, at best, to clearly describe the field as a single entity, or to generate simple or straight-forward recommended practices and policy. As a consequence, the field of early childhood teacher education is also fraught with complexity and challenged by expectations to generate streamlined models of early childhood teacher preparation. In the current landscape, we are struggling as a field to hold on to core beliefs that have long guided work with the youngest children and undergird what we have come to know over time about how children learn and what components are most essential to building a foundation for lifelong learning and well-being. At the same time, we are aware of and want to capitalize on new opportunities and resources that will require connecting more firmly to K-12 schooling.

In a recent article, Halpern (2013) described the ways that early childhood has historically been different from "schooling," articulating the values reflected in our perspectives on children and learning. These include a high regard for children as active agents in their own learning; an appreciation of the social and emotional conditions that promote children's learning; flexibility regarding assessment and evaluation; a sense of responsibility to families as integrally important to their children's learning;

a valuing of the contributions of individual and cultural diversity; attention to social-emotional and physical needs as a part of curriculum; and an emphasis on play, creative problem-solving, integrated knowledge, and cooperative learning. These strengths of the field resonate throughout the pages of this handbook, as our chapter authors draw on what we have learned from research and practice about educating young children, and preparing teachers for this work.

Beyond historical foundations and current innovations in the field of ECE, early childhood teachers and teacher educators have created through their work an enduring sense of what Halpern (2013) refers to as our "identity as a public good." He posits that the field is "struggling to hold on to a generous, inclusive view of children (and of learning), and likewise to its historic emphasis on community and the valuing of diversity" (p. 2). He makes a case for preserving early childhood as a separate and distinct entity in the educational trajectory by stating: "We need a distinct ECE because we cannot afford the loss of another institution that expresses and nurtures such non-market values as sense of community, empathy, and the importance of diversity to a healthy society" (Halpern, 2013, p. 11). Like Halpern, we see the work of ECTE as a way of contributing to a better future.

Current Challenges to the Field of ECE

With growing numbers of children entering infant/toddler and pre-K programs both in the U.S. and abroad, and changes in policy to support and expand early care and education programs, preparing teachers for the field has taken on a new significance. The demand for ECE is growing faster than we are able to prepare qualified early childhood teachers in ECTE. Preparing teachers for the diverse professional early childhood settings that are represented in ECE and through the multiple pathways for teacher preparation in the field of ECTE make this challenge quite daunting, as described by Pianta:

> Unlike the K-12 system, in which the supply chain for teachers is regulated by a single state entity, training of the early childhood and child-care work force is widely distributed and loosely regulated. . . . there is no easily identifiable and easily regulated pipeline for training the early education workforce, a clear challenge for policymakers.
>
> *(Pianta, 2007, p. 7)*

Further, increasing diversity in U.S. children across the birth through 8 years age range, as well as a growing move toward inclusive early childhood classrooms globally, adds to the complexity of preparing a quality workforce ready to teach all children. Too few children, particularly those in the direst socio-economic circumstances, are receiving high-quality ECE (Cochran-Smith, 2004; Halpern, 2013; Pianta, 2007). Despite what we have learned from interdisciplinary research about early learning, much of this knowledge has been slow to translate to practice.

> Though we now have substantial knowledge about children's developmental tasks and support needs during this age period, there is less and less place for this knowledge in school policy and practice. The discrepancy between what we know and what we practice is especially notable in learning settings serving economically disenfranchised children and children of color.
>
> *(Halpern, 2013, p. 2)*

Rethinking Program and Teacher Evaluation

Increased government spending on early childhood education programs comes with new accountability standards and a move toward homogenizing curriculum for ease in measuring outcomes. This policy change "creates a tension between the reality of an increasingly diverse, and in some instances vulnerable, population of young children and both greater and more standardized expectations at each age" (Halpern, 2013, p. 3). A focus on school readiness in ECE takes over the curriculum, increasing direct instruction and overriding young children's natural ways of learning through play and exploration. The need for increased quality and equity across ECE delivery systems should neither disenfranchise diverse children and families, nor should it reduce opportunities to create curricula that reflect the needs and interests of local communities. As Halpern states:

> Ultimately the risk in binding ECE and schooling more closely together is not just about the power of schools and their agendas. It derives from a set of related cultural problems. The first can best be described as losing the present to the future—the very problem with school readiness as the central goal of ECE. We still seem not to have taken to heart Dewey's insight over a century ago that to meet children's needs, schooling has to be understood not as preparation for life but as life itself, broadly envisioned.
>
> *(p. 11)*

Measures of program and teacher quality and effectiveness have focused narrowly on teacher qualifications and program components, with much less attention paid to how teachers teach and children learn. Pianta (2007) describes these measures as proxies for teacher-child interactions, both instructional and social, which tell us little about what we know from research is most important to children's learning—effective, high-quality teaching (Darling-Hammond, 2007).

Implications for ECTE

These overarching issues challenging the field of ECE practice are reflected in parallel ways in ECTE. Current knowledge about the importance of early learning as foundational to children's future well-being (Shonkoff & Phillips, 2000) compels us as a field and a society to pay attention to our work with young children. Growing numbers of infants, toddlers, and preschoolers in early care and education programs, more rigorous requirements for preparing the workforce for quality teaching, and changes in the population of children in ECE and in expectations for their learning necessitate changes in teachers' roles and the nature of teachers' work. Preparing early childhood teachers to address this broad range of learners, negotiating often mandated curricular content, while also attending to the social and emotional dimensions so important to early learning, including family, community, cultural, and linguistic contexts, is a highly complex task.

Our strengths as an area of teacher education are our emphasis on the development and learning of the whole child, reciprocity with families in that venture, and embracing diversity as a natural part of the education process. Community-based education is a hallmark of early education. As a distinct area of teacher education, with increasing standardization (certification, public funding, public programs, etc.), how do we keep our unique features without losing our identity? How do we continue to value and enact practices that support vulnerable learners, in line with research that informs the long-term social, intellectual, and economic gains of high-quality early learning experiences (Heckman, 2011)?

What Do We Still Need to Learn and What Do We Do Next?

These questions help to guide a much needed research agenda for ECTE. As the emphasis on early learning brings opportunities to grow the field, we need a clearer understanding of the impact of early childhood teacher education on teaching and learning. Overwhelming agreement regarding the limitations in our current research base, and the need for more systematic studies to inform the field, is echoed throughout this handbook. Given the diversity and complexity of ECE, we need more information on what kinds of content and process are most effective within which contexts, as well as a clearer sense of how to integrate the coursework and experiences that best prepare ECE teachers for the complexities of the field. Although studies in the broader field of teacher education can inform our research (Grossman & McDonald, 2008), issues particular to younger children require a distinct focus that recognizes developmental and learning differences unique to infants, toddlers, preschoolers, and children in the primary grades. Attention to such issues as the nature of children's learning, the role of the teacher, the impact of high-stakes testing, and the involvement of family and community must be considered, while attending to the "non-school factors that powerfully shape children's availability to learn" (Halpern, 2013, p. 9).

Better Ways of Creating Continuity between ECTE and K-12 Teacher Education Research

Historically we have worked hard to successfully set the field of ECE apart, highlighting our differences and calling attention to the unique capacities and characteristics of young children as learners which must be addressed in ECTE (NAEYC, 2009). But to what degree have we, as a field, avoided bigger questions in teacher education by focusing on the early years as separate from K-12 schooling (New, 2013)? Have we compromised opportunities to create stronger systems of continuity between early childhood and elementary and secondary teacher education systems and have we inadvertently missed out on resources that could strengthen our ability to increase professionalism in ECE/ECTE? Examining innovative models of teacher education that utilize a common framework built on what all teachers need, yet allow for specialization (e.g., birth to age 8) and a concentration (e.g., preschool and early elementary), hold promise for linking ECTE to the work of our colleagues in K-12, as well as embedding teacher preparation and development within communities (Kennedy & Heineke, 2014). How can we move forward to create more fully integrated teacher education policy, funding streams, teacher certification standards, and teacher assessments that reflect children's learning needs across early care and education systems and provide clearer linkages with the K-12 continuum, to better support children and families, and strengthen our profession?

Grossman and McDonald (2008) put forth a strong argument for looking back at the ways that teacher research has evolved as a means of helping the field move forward. They suggest that more current research on teaching has focused for too long on the cognitive aspects of teaching, with less regard for teaching practices and relationships between teachers and their students. Teacher education "in turn, must attend to preparing novices for the relational as well as the intellectual demands of teaching" (Grossman & McDonald, 2008, p. 185). They encourage researchers across teacher education programs to find a common research agenda to lend power to our knowledge base.

> Just as in research on teaching, researchers in the area of teacher education need a common research agenda, a shared language, and more precise methodological and theoretical tools for addressing critical questions about how best to prepare teachers. Such research could focus both on burning policy issues regarding preparing teachers and on research that improves the actual practice of teacher education.
>
> *(p. 198)*

These authors urge teacher education researchers to move beyond the small case studies of individual programs commonly found in teacher education research to engage in more large-scale studies that focus on teaching practices across teacher education programs, which aligns with the recommendations of chapter authors in this handbook. Using similar measurement strategies, researchers need to track more carefully the impact of programs on outcomes for both children and teachers to further inform teacher education in general and ECTE specifically.

Creating a Robust Teacher Education Research Agenda

There is a strong need for robust research that considers ECTE in all its complexities, including the proximal and distal factors that influence the field—workplace, resources, faculty, ECE settings, policies, and regulations (Horm, Hyson, & Winton, 2013). This research agenda requires consideration of ways to capitalize on similar needs and components (e.g., resources, service delivery, individual teacher needs) between preservice and inservice teacher development. As articulated throughout the handbook, the multifaceted nature of ECE/ECTE adds layers of challenge to our task of expanding and empowering its research base. In large part, the current research in ECTE has looked narrowly at particular programs and preparation practices. Although there is much to be learned from this body of research, until concerted efforts are made by ECTE researchers to rise to the call for more large-scale, cross-program, systematic studies focused on process as well as outcomes, we will be unable to move our knowledge base forward to make evidence-informed decisions for the field. Pianta (2007) reminds us of the importance of keeping the particular needs of ECE at the center of our work, while also thinking more directly about making stronger connections with K-12 education.

> Thoughtful and effective policies for developing a professional workforce will have to include a mix of incentives for pre-K teachers that may be different from those designed for teachers in K-12; provide training that is focused on classroom practices and the specific challenges of teaching young children; and improve the alignment of early childhood education with K-12.
>
> *(Pianta, 2007, p. 8)*

As we develop a broad scale research base, there is also a need to attend to the process of teaching—the nuances of what teachers do. We need to know more about the elements of teaching practice, including how decision-making is informed and strengthened as a teacher grows in her practice. As teacher educators, we need to know more about what best supports the development of sound decision-making in teachers. We believe engaging in research that fundamentally respects the work of teachers, recognizes the complexity of teaching, and reflects the voices of teachers (Castle, 2013) is integral to expanding our knowledge. We can further understand the complexity of teaching and learning by partnering with teachers to promote inquiry as a means to deepening, more fully understanding, and improving their own practice.

Balancing our approach to research will allow opportunities for practice knowledge to inform policy decisions. While a common perception is that theory informs practice, theory does not always lead practice (Williams, 1996). Rather, there is a natural reciprocity between theory and practice, as practice helps us see and understand what theory does not explain. With increasing diversity and globalization in our societies around the world, we need better ways to interpret the subtleties of difference—what is the impact of the "human factor" in teaching, and how does this change under different conditions? Interestingly, the more diverse the group under study, the less likely large-scale research will be able to fully explain the variability in outcomes. It is in the critical decision making of teachers in practice, where the power of teaching and learning lies. How do we access this power within teacher-child interactions in moving ECTE forward, more clearly articulating the insider perspective (Cochran-Smith & Lytle, 1993) both as a form of professional development and a tool to enhance practice? How do we engage in this work, fully acknowledging the role of teacher knowledge as not only a legitimate component of our research in ECTE, but an essential one?

Articulating Systems of Teacher Development

The complexity of early childhood has been articulated repeatedly throughout this handbook. Early childhood encompasses children from birth to age 8, yet our systems of teacher development, accreditation, and licensure are fragmented. Moving forward, there is need to assure continuity among those systems, to develop a framework where teachers are viewed as developing professionals and lifelong learners, with a recognition that teaching practice grows and becomes stronger over time with access to further knowledge and resources.

Community-based agreement. As we articulate systems of teacher preparation and professional development, we must carefully consider who is working with children to prepare them for school; how are we growing and developing the workforce and the profession? As communities search for ways to improve student achievement and success, efforts are afoot to create a seamless system of education, which considers preschool through college (P-20). Particular to early childhood, known as PK-3 (Graves, 2006), are efforts to improve pre-K to 3rd grade alignment in both systems that educate children and in the preparation of their teachers. The highly fragmented approach to preparing teachers for early childhood differs not only across systems (education and child care), but across states within the U.S. (Bornfreund, 2011). Articulating a clear system of early childhood teacher development would bring continuity to the field across municipalities to bring together more power, ideas, resources, and people.

Preservice education. The multiple pathways for preparing teachers to work with children from birth through age 8 focus on distinct but sometimes inconsistent teacher knowledge, skills, and requirements (Washington, 2008). Preservice expectations, program courses and experiences, earned certifications, and access to job opportunities vary both within and between these different preparation pathways. This creates discontinuities for teachers' professional advancement. Relationships between 2-year and 4-year ECTE programs are often non-existent or tenuous at best. Lower admission standards and the practice orientation that are typical of 2-year programs may be at odds with the more theoretical orientation and higher admission requirements of 4-year programs. These issues have implications for increasing the diversity of the ECE workforce, as many 2-year programs serve more diverse teacher candidates. If we want to increase the diversity of our teaching workforce, we must attend to access. Stronger articulation between 2- and 4-year EC teacher preparation programs will improve the probability that teachers continue their formal education.

Ongoing professional development in the lives of teachers. ECTE researchers increasingly understand teacher preparation and development as a process that extends beyond initial preparation programs and into teaching practice. As teachers gain knowledge and skills through more years of teaching, teacher education can support their engagement in reflective practice as a means to guide their decisions and interactions with others. By applying a critical lens to their early childhood settings, teachers can become more effective agents of change (Guaravuso, 2007). A need exists to develop a system of ongoing support for teachers, beyond initial preparation, that sustains them in making meaning of their practice. In preservice education we see this taking place in the triad of collaboration (Watkins, 2005) between a student teacher, field supervisor, and cooperating teacher through reflection, coaching, and planning. The provision of this type of supported teacher education, through ongoing reflective practice and mentoring to refine and further develop their skills, is sorely lacking for novice teachers. Developing mechanisms that support induction, at least through the first three years, the most critical time for determining whether a new teacher stays or goes, would improve quality (Carroll & Foster, 2010). Ongoing changes in the landscape of policy and practice have implications for teachers' skills and knowledge. More knowledge is needed about systems of professional development that are effective throughout teachers' lives, and responsive to innovation.

Re-envisioning Curriculum in ECTE

Teacher education scholars across the continuum posit the need for changes in how teachers are prepared to teach, not only to better meet the changing needs of an increasingly diverse population, but also to address inequities and increase social justice. "Bridging the chasm between the school and life experiences of those with and without social, cultural, racial, and economic advantages requires fundamental changes in the way teachers are educated" (Cochran-Smith, 2004, p. 7). Although in theory the field of ECE has long supported notions of inclusivity and diversity in its approaches to teaching and learning, there are still many inequities in children's and families' experiences in early childhood education settings. Increases in the numbers of infants, toddlers, and preschoolers receiving early care and education and in the diversity of these populations, as well as changes in family structure, require a transformative shift in how we prepare early childhood teachers to meet the needs of the children and families they will serve in the field. Changes in policy to support greater inclusion of children with disabilities in general education and community settings also requires integrated teacher preparation so that teachers are prepared for all the children they will teach. With increasing numbers of immigrant, multilingual, and multicultural families accessing ECE services for their young children, teachers need preparation programs that provide the skills they will require to be culturally and linguistically responsive educators.

While the teacher is recognized as a crucial component in the success of a child's educational experience, formal education alone is not a direct determinant of teacher quality. Teacher education in general has moved beyond the construct of "inputs" (e.g., SAT, GPA, coursework,) as the best determinants of quality, to recognize that competency is based on the integration and implementation of research based practices, and must be measured in the moments which comprise decision making and teacher-child relationships (Early et al., 2006; Pianta et al., 2014). Further, identifying the critical features of teacher education, their timing, and duration is important for advancing our knowledge. For example, field experiences have been identified generally as a key feature in quality ECTE and specifically in preparing teachers to support the diverse learning needs of children in their classrooms. However, at what points, at what intensity, and for how long in teacher preparation are these features most effective? How are the relational ratios of these features maximized (Ronfeldt, Schwartz, and Jacob, 2014)? A recent study suggests teacher education may have preliminary answers to some of these questions. Ronfeldt and colleagues (2014) found that teacher preparation and teacher retention can be improved through increased practice teaching and increased teaching methods courses. Rather than faster and easier pathways to teaching, which are often promoted as solutions for teacher education, it is a path of greater immersion and rigor in preparation that holds more promise. How does this translate for ECE, which is struggling with the notion of increased expectations to professionalize the field? Until we are able to answer questions about the key features of ECTE, and enact them in teacher preparation, the quality and effectiveness of teachers of young children will remain widely varied.

Global connections. Throughout this handbook, authors have highlighted the challenges of ECTE practice and policy. Examining ECTE in a global context, it is striking that regardless of whether countries have strong economies and are recognized as world powers, or are emerging nations experiencing cultural change, the overarching challenges in ECTE are remarkably similar. Issues of access, teacher preparation, teaching quality, and ongoing professional development are found across the world. Similarly, teacher educators in many societies are experiencing challenges in preparing teachers with the tools to support increasing classroom diversity. This offers evidence of an increased commitment to social justice and the global nature of our world. Across societies, we appear to be at different points on the same path poised to learn from each other, presenting opportunities for ECTE curriculum development and research.

Quality, Accountability, and Sustainability

Measuring quality teaching. We all want effective teachers, but measuring high-quality teaching remains elusive. Tools that accurately assess the learning and effectiveness of teachers at various points throughout their careers need to be developed, as a means of understanding how teaching changes over time and with experience. Measures of competency for teacher candidates, novice teachers, and mature teachers who continue to strengthen their practice need to be grounded in research that addresses the complexity of teaching (Horm et al., 2013; Hamre, Dower, Jamil, & Pianta, 2012). As we develop new systems for assessing teacher quality it is important that we keep in mind those elements we deem most essential to quality teaching and learning in ECE. Current measures of quality tend to focus more on program components or structural features, rather than on the nature of interactions between teachers and students, where teaching and learning takes place (Darling-Hammond, 2007; Pianta, 2007).

Faculty development. What should teacher educators know and be able to do? Most teacher educators indicate they were prepared to be educational researchers rather than to be educational researchers knowledgeable in the preparation of teachers. Their doctoral preparation lacked focus on how to teach adults and specifically how to educate teachers (Goodwin et al., 2014). Particularly interesting is the lack of study about the field of teacher education in doctoral preparation. For teacher education in general and ECTE in particular, the development of robust foundational research on the knowledge base of ECTE faculty and faculty development is overdue.

This handbook has focused on preparing early childhood (EC) teachers to work with young children. But how do we best prepare faculty and professional development specialists for the work of educating EC teachers? Given the changing nature of education and its continually evolving research base, how do ECTE faculty stay current? If our goal is high-quality EC teachers, then we need to attend to how we prepare faculty for ECTE (Hyson, Tomlinson, Morris, 2009; Horm et al., 2013). ECE faculty are already over-extended, with high demands (student ratios, labor-intensive field practice) and few resources, and their contributions to education are undervalued (Hyson et al., 2009). If we are to sustain and nourish our field, we must build leadership capacity in ECTE.

Final Thoughts

As we bring the Handbook of ECTE to a close, it is our hope that the rich array of ECTE practices, policies, and ideas for the future of the field presented here will serve as both a resource and guide for looking back and moving forward. These chapters reflect our rich history, and bring to light the enduring values and strengths of the field. They also challenge us to question what we think we know, how we study what we do, and the ways we prepare early childhood teachers, not only for today, but for the dynamic changes presented by the world of the future. There is much work to be done to transform early childhood teacher preparation. We hope that this volume serves as a springboard to move the field forward for the 21st century and beyond.

References

Bornfreund, L. (2011). *Getting in sync: Revamping licensing and preparation for teachers in pre-K, kindergarten, and the early grades.* Washington, DC: New America Foundation.

Carroll, T., & Foster, E. (January 2010). "Who Will Teach?: Experience Matters" (Washington, DC: National Commission on Teaching and America's Future). Retrieved from http://nctaf.org/wp-content/uploads/2012/01/NCTAF-Who-Will-Teach-Experience-Matters-2010-Report.pdf

Castle, K. (2013). The state of teacher research in early childhood teacher education. *Journal of Early Childhood Teacher Education, 34*, 268–286.

Cochran-Smith, M. (2004). *Walking the road: Race, diversity, and social justice in teacher education.* New York: Teachers College Press.

Cochran-Smith, M., & Lytle, S. L. (1993). *Inside/Outside: Teacher research and knowledge.* New York: Teachers College Press.

Darling-Hammond, L. (2007). A good teacher in every classroom: Preparing the highly qualified teachers our children deserve. *Educational Horizons, 85*(2), 111–132.

Early, D. M., Bryant, D. M., Pianta, R. C., Clifford, R. M., Burchinal, M. R., Ritchie, S., . . . Barbarin, O. (2006). Are teachers' education, major, and credentials related to classroom quality and children's academic gains in pre-kindergarten? *Early Childhood Research Quarterly, 21*(2), 174–195.

Goodwin, A. L., Smith, L., Souto-Manning, M., Cheruvu, R., Tan, M. Y., Reed, R., & Taveras, L. (2014). What should teacher educators know and be able to do? Perspectives from practicing teacher educators. *Journal of Teacher Education, 65*(4), 284–302. DOI: 10.1177/0022487114535266.

Graves, B. (2006). PK-3: *What is it and how do we know it works?* (Policy Brief: Advancing PK-3 No.4). New York: Foundation for Child Development. Retrieved from http://fcd-us.org/sites/default/files/PK-3WhatIsItand-HowDoWeKnow.pdf

Grossman, P., & McDonald, M. (2008). Back to the future: Directions for research in teaching and teacher education. *American Educational Research Journal, 45(1)*, 184–205.

Guaravuso, V. (2007). A non-traditional teacher's experience after Student Teaching: Implications for Early Childhood Teacher Education. *Journal of Early Childhood Teacher Education 28*, 393–410. DOI: 10.1080/10901020701686682.

Halpern, R. (2013) Tying early childhood education more closely to schooling: Promise, perils and practical problems. *Teachers College Record, 115*(1), 1–28.

Hamre, B., Downer, J., Jamil, F., & Pianta, R. (2012). Enhancing teachers' intentional use of effective interactions with children. In R. C. Pianta, W. S. Barnett, L. M. Justice, & S. M. Sheridan (Eds.), *Handbook of early childhood education* (pp. 507–532). New York: Guilford Press.

Heckman, J. J. (2011). The economics of inequality: The value of early childhood education. *American Educator, 35*(1), 31–47.

Horm, D. M., Hyson, M., & Winton, P. J. (2013). Research on early childhood teacher education: Evidence from three domains and recommendations for moving forward. *Journal of Early Childhood Teacher Education, 34*(1), 95–112. DOI: 10.1080/10901027.2013.758541.

Hyson, M., Tomlinson, H. B., & Morris, C. A. (2009). Quality improvement in early childhood teacher education: Faculty perspectives and recommendations for the future. *Early Childhood Research and Practice, 11*(1). Retrieved from http://ecrp.uiuc.edu/v11n1/hyson.html

Kennedy, A. S., & Heineke, A. (2014). Re-envisioning the role of universities in early childhood teacher education: Community partnerships for 21st-century learning. *Journal of Early Childhood Teacher Education, 35*(3), 226–243. DOI: 10.1080/10901027.2014.936072.

National Association for the Education of Young Children (NAEYC). (2009). *NAEYC standards for early childhood professional preparation. Position Statement.* Washington, DC: National Association for the Education of Young Children.

New, R. (2013). Commentary: Looking back and moving forward. *Journal of Early Childhood Teacher Education, 34*(1), 113–118.

Pianta, R. C. (2007). Preschool is school, sometimes. Hoover Institute, Education Next No 1. *Making Early Childhood Education Matter.* 1/9/2007. Retrieved from http://www.hoover.org/publications/ednext/4612287.html

Pianta, R. C., Burchinal, M., Jamil, F. M., Sabol, T., Grimm, K., Hamre, B. K., . . . Howes, C. (2014). A cross-lag analysis of longitudinal associations between preschool teachers' instructional support identification skills and observed behavior. *Early Childhood Research Quarterly, 29*(2), 144–154.

Ronfeldt, M., Schwartz, N., & Jacob, B. (2014). Does preservice preparation matter? Examining an old question in new ways. *Teachers College Record, 116* (100305), 1–46.

Shonkoff, J. P., & Phillips, D. A. (Eds.). (2000). *From neurons to neighborhoods: The science of early childhood development.* Washington, DC: National Academy of Press.

Washington, V. (2008). *Role, relevance, reinvention: Higher education in the field of early care and education.* Boston, MA: Wheelock College.

Watkins, C. (2005). *Classrooms as learning communities: What's in it for schools?* New York: Routledge.

Williams, L. R. (1996). Does practice lead theory? Teachers' constructs about teaching: Bottom-up perspectives. In J. A. Chafelt & S. Reifel (Eds.) *Advances in early education and care, v8,* (pp. 153–184). Greenwich, CT: JAI.

CONTRIBUTORS

Charlotte Jean Anderson, Ph.D., has worked with preschool and primary school-aged children since 1987. After owning and directing her own child care center for five years, she earned her doctorate and taught Early Childhood Education coursework at Texas State University, San Marcos. In 2008, Charlotte began her speaking and teaching practice, *Teaching Those Who Raise Our Children*, through which she leads teacher and parenting seminars. She has presented papers at the National Association for the Education of Young Children (NAEYC) Annual Conferences and the 2008 conference of the International Froebel Society. She coordinates a part of the NAEYC History Seminar, and co-edits the "Our Proud Heritage" column in *Young Children*.

Fortidas Rwehumbiza Bakuza, Ph.D., is a lecturer in Early Childhood Education at Aga Khan University Institute for Education Development in East Africa. Dr. Bakuza has more than 20 years of experience as a teacher, administrator, teacher educator, and researcher. Prior to receiving his Ph.D. from the State University of New York at Buffalo, he served as the National Coordinator of the Tanzania Early Childhood Development Network. He has also served in a variety of capacities in numerous national and international organizations supporting the rights and needs of the world's children. His primary research interest is in the area of early childhood education leadership and policy.

W. Steven Barnett, Ph.D., is a Board of Governors Professor and Director of the National Institute for Early Education Research (NIEER) at Rutgers University. Dr. Barnett is a Fellow of the American Educational Research Association and a member of the National Academy of Education. He advises national governments, international agencies, and foundations of early care and education policy, research, and evaluation. Dr. Barnett is co-editor of the *International Journal of Child Care and Education Policy* and a member of the Editorial Board of *Early Childhood Research Quarterly*. Dr. Barnett's research includes studies of the effectiveness and economics of early care and education including the well-known benefit-cost analyses of the Perry Preschool and Abecedarian programs. He has also studied the impacts of program duration and intensity, dual language models, curriculum, alternative staffing structures, professional development, and parental engagement.

Kathryn Castle, Ed.D., Professor Emeritus and Chuck and Kim Watson Endowed Chair in Education, has authored seven books including two children's books, numerous book chapters and monographs, over 30 peer-reviewed journal articles, and numerous other publications. In addition to two national research awards, she is the recipient of the NAECTE Outstanding Early Childhood Teacher

Educator Award, the OSU Regents Distinguished Teaching Award, and the OSU Regents Distinguished Research Award. She has been an early childhood teacher, the director of test evaluations for a national learning foundation, professor, and graduate coordinator. She is a teacher researcher, a member of the NAEYC teacher research Advisory Group for the online journal *Voices of Practitioners*, and has taught graduate courses on teacher research and authored the book *Teacher Research in Early Childhood Education* (Routledge, 2012).

Ranita Cheruvu, Ed.D., is an Assistant Professor of Early Childhood Education at William Paterson University. Her scholarship and teaching are grounded in a critical perspective with respect to issues of diversity and equity in early childhood education. Her research focuses on culturally responsive and sustaining pedagogies and the preparation of preservice teachers of color, and more generally in the areas of early childhood teacher education, multicultural teacher education, and teacher education action research.

Eun Kyeong Cho, Ed.D., is an Associate Professor at the University of New Hampshire. Dr. Cho earned an Ed.D. from Teachers College, Columbia University, concentrating in early childhood education with a focus on early childhood teacher policy. She has published articles, book chapters, and professional development training manuals on topics such as early childhood teacher policy, professional development, technology integration in teacher preparation, and supporting families from diverse backgrounds. She currently serves as a consulting editor for the research journal, *Early Childhood Research Quarterly*, and the professional journal, *Young Children*, published by the National Association for the Education of Young Children (NAEYC), and is a member of the Governing Board of the National Association for Early Childhood Teacher Educators (NAECTE).

Nitasha M. Clark, M.Ed., is a Research Assistant with FirstSchool. Prior to joining FirstSchool, she spent over 18 years in various educational positions supporting adult and child learners as a coordinated early intervention specialist, university lecturer, research project coordinator, elementary and middle school special education teacher, and preschool teacher. A native of North Carolina, Ms. Clark received her B.A. from the University of North Carolina at Wilmington and M.Ed. from the University of Southern Mississippi.

Leslie J. Couse, Ph.D., is Associate Professor of Education at the University of New Hampshire and Adjunct Assistant Professor of Pediatrics at the Geisel School of Medicine at Dartmouth. Her expertise lies in preparing teachers for inclusive early childhood settings through interdisciplinary collaboration with parents, teachers, and service providers. Through community partnerships, she researches inclusive teacher education, leadership development for the field of disability, and the use of technology in early education. She is Chair of the Education Department and Project Director for the U.S. Department of Education Office of Special Education-funded *Early Childhood Special Education Assistive Technology Project*. Dr. Couse is co-editor of *The Handbook of Early Childhood Teacher Education* (Routledge, 2016), served as guest editor for a special issue and is a member of the editorial board for the *Journal of Early Childhood Teacher Education*, and past Governing Board member of the National Association for Early Childhood Teacher Educators (NAECTE).

Gisele M. Crawford, M.A.A., is a Research Specialist at the Frank Porter Graham Child Development Institute at the University of North Carolina at Chapel Hill. Early in her career, Ms. Crawford served as an assistant teacher in a classroom for 4-year-olds and a lead teacher for two-and-a-half to 3-year-olds, as well as a teacher of English for children and adults in Taiwan. Since then she has worked on numerous studies of young children and their environments and experiences, including large-scale studies of public prekindergarten in the United States. She is currently on the staff of FirstSchool, a prekindergarten through third grade initiative to improve the school experiences and outcomes of

African American, Latino, and low-income children. She has published articles and book chapters relating to serving diverse populations of children in early education settings, and is a contributing author to *FirstSchool: Transforming PreK-3rd Grade for African-American, Latino, and Low-Income Children.*

Ellen Edge, M.Ed., is the Director of the Child Development Center, an NAEYC accredited demonstration affiliated with the Keene State College Teacher Preparation Program. She has been involved with the field of early education since the early 1990s working in many diverse settings as a teacher and administrator. Ms. Edge has been active in the area of public policy within New Hampshire and Massachusetts and is a member on the Communication and Public Awareness subcommittee for the New Hampshire Early Childhood Advisory Council. She has participated on Head Start Review Teams in various capacities and is currently a reviewer for Head Start's Monitoring System. Ms. Edge is a doctoral student in the Children, Families, and Schools concentration at the University of Massachusetts. Her research interests include infant mental health, social/emotional development, and teacher-child relationships.

Stephanie Feeney, Ph.D., is Professor Emerita of Education at the University of Hawaii. Since the 1980s she has been involved in work on professional ethics for the National Association for the Education of Young Children (NAEYC). She is co-author of the NAEYC Code of Ethical Conduct, supplements to the Code for Adult Educators and Program Administrators and the books *Ethics and the Early Childhood Educator* and *Teaching the NAEYC Code of Ethical Conduct.* She is co-editor of the "Focus on Ethics" column in *Young Children.* Her other publications include *Who Am I in the Lives of Children?* (10th edition), *Continuing Issues in Early Childhood Education* (3rd edition), and *Professionalism in Early Childhood Education: Doing Our Best for Young Children.* Dr. Feeney has served on the Governing Boards of NAEYC and the National Association for Early Childhood Teacher Educators (NAECTE). She has lectured and taught throughout the United States, the Pacific, and Asia.

Beatrice S. Fennimore, Ed.D., is a Professor in the Department of Professional Studies at Indiana University of Pennsylvania. Her teaching, scholarship, and activism have focused on child advocacy, social policy, public school equity, social justice, and multicultural/anti-bias education. Dr. Fennimore was recently a visiting professor at Teachers College, Columbia University, where she also served as an adjunct professor for many years. Her publications include *Talk Matters: Refocusing the Language of Public Schooling* (Teachers College Press), *Promoting Social Justice for Young Children* (co-edited with A. Lin Goodwin, Springer), *Brown and the Failure of Civic Responsibility* (Teachers College Record), *Equity is Not an Option in Public Education* (Educational Leadership), *Know Where You Stand and Stand There,* and *Responding to Prejudiced Comments: A Four-Step Method That Works* (Childhood Education). Dr. Fennimore recently published her book *Standing Up for Something Every Day: Ethics and Justice in Early Childhood Classrooms* (2014, Teachers College Press).

Nancy K. Freeman, Ph.D., is Professor Emerita of Instruction and Teacher Education in the College of Education at the University of South Carolina. She has written and presented extensively on professional ethics since the 1990s. Dr. Freeman is co-author of two books on ethics, *Ethics and the Early Childhood Educator* and *Teaching the NAEYC Code of Ethical Conduct,* and is co-editor of the "Focus on Ethics" column in *Young Children.* She was a leader in the development of supplements for program administrators and adult educators and was involved in the Code's revisions. Other publications include *Planning and Administrating Early Childhood Programs* (11th edition). Dr. Freeman served as President of the National Association of Early Childhood Teacher Educators (NAECTE). For many years she chaired the Governor's Advisory Committee on Child Care Regulation and held many leadership positions in South Carolina. In 2012, she was recognized as the NAECTE Outstanding Early Childhood Teacher Educator.

Doris Pronin Fromberg, Ed.D., is Professor Emerita, Hofstra University, where she has served as chairperson of the Department of Curriculum and Teaching, as well as director of Early Childhood Teacher Education. She serves on the NYS Governor's Early Childhood Advisory Council, editorial boards of professional journals, and continues to advocate for high-quality early childhood teacher and administrator education. She served as president of several national professional associations and received national and state awards. Among her publications are articles, chapters, and books, including *The All-Day Kindergarten and Pre-K Curriculum: A Dynamic-Themes Approach* (Routledge, 2012); *Play from Birth to Twelve 3rd Edition* co-edited with D. Bergen (Routledge, 2015); *Play and Meaning in Early Childhood Education* (Allyn & Bacon); *The Full-Day Kindergarten* (Teachers College Press); *The Encyclopedia of Early Childhood Education* with L.R. Williams (Routledge); and *The Successful Classroom* with M. Driscoll (Teachers College Press), with some publications in translations.

Vicki Garavuso, Ed.D., is an Associate Professor of Early Childhood Education at The City College of New York's Center for Worker Education. Her research focuses on working class undergraduate students' experiences in early care and education settings and mentoring. Her book, *Being Mentored: Getting What You Need* (2010) was written as a support for the "non-traditional" undergraduate students in early childhood education. Dr. Garavuso is a member of the editorial board of the *Journal of Early Childhood Teacher Education.*

Celia Genishi, Ph.D., is Professor Emerita of Education at Teachers College, Columbia University. She is a former secondary Spanish and preschool teacher and has taught courses related to early childhood and qualitative research methods in the Department of Curriculum and Teaching at Teachers College. Her books include *Ways of Assessing Children and Curriculum*; *Diversities in Early Childhood Education* (with A. Lin Goodwin); and *Children, Language, and Literacy: Diverse Learners in Diverse Times* (with Anne Haas Dyson). The author of many articles for researchers and practitioners, her research interests include childhood bilingualism; children's language use, play, and early literacy in classrooms; and collaborative research and assessment with teachers. She is a recipient of an Advocate for Justice Award from the American Association of Colleges for Teacher Education and the Distinguished Career Contribution Award from the American Educational Research Association Special Interest Group on Critical Perspectives on Early Childhood Education.

Megan Gibson, Ph.D., is a Lecturer in the School of Early Childhood, QUT. Dr. Gibson uses a range of qualitative methodologies to examine early childhood workforce issues, preservice teacher education, professionalism, leadership, and sustainability. Dr. Gibson's award-winning doctoral research examined the discursive production of early childhood teachers' professional identities, with particular implications for preservice teacher education course design. She is part of a federally funded Early Years Collaborative Research Network involving over 80 researchers from three universities in Australia. Current research with this network includes a large-scale research project that examines the complexity of work in early childhood settings. Dr. Gibson's research builds on extensive experience working in diverse early childhood contexts, most notably 10 years as director of an internationally recognized child care center in Australia.

Stacie G. Goffin, Ed.D., is Principal of the Goffin Strategy Group. Established in 2004, the Goffin Strategy Group dedicates itself to building early childhood education's ability to provide effective programs and services for young children through leadership, capacity, and systems development. Dr. Goffin works with local and state non-profits, governments, national organizations, and philanthropy. A widely published author, Dr. Goffin's conceptual leadership focuses on advancing early childhood education as a professional field of practice. Prior to forming the Goffin Strategy Group, Dr. Goffin led the five-year effort to redesign the National Association for the Education of Young Children's

[NAEYC] early childhood program accreditation system. She is a former senior program officer at the Ewing Marion Kauffman Foundation, higher education faculty member, and preschool educator. More information can be found at http://www.goffinstrategygroup.com.

Claire E. Hamilton, Ph.D., is the Chair of the Department of Teacher Education and Curriculum Studies at the University of Massachusetts in Amherst. She has been involved in the field of early childhood education as a child care teacher, coordinator of the Children, Families and Schools division, and faculty coordinator of the early childhood education specialization. She teaches graduate and undergraduate courses in child development, early childhood, and elementary education through traditional face-to-face and fully online formats. Her research interests include early literacy, early childhood curriculum, the social context of schooling, and technology-based learning and teaching. Dr. Hamilton utilizes innovative technology in her teaching and in one of her recent studies, published in *Educational Research and Technology Development,* explored the affordances of multi-user virtual environments in supporting college students' collaborative learning strategies and child development knowledge.

J. Amos Hatch, Ph.D., is Professor of Theory and Practice in Teacher Education at the University of Tennessee. He has published widely in the areas of early childhood education, qualitative research, and teacher education. He served as co-executive editor of *Qualitative Studies in Education* from 1991 to 1996 and the *Journal of Early Childhood Teacher Education* from 2008 to 2012. He has written or edited a number of books, including *Doing Qualitative Research in Education Settings* (SUNY Press, 2002), *Teaching in the New Kindergarten* (Thompson, 2005), *Early Childhood Qualitative Research* (Routledge, 2007), and (with Susan Groenke) *Critical Pedagogy and Teacher Education in the Neoliberal Era* (Springer, 2009). His latest book is *Reclaiming the Teaching Profession: Transforming the Dialogue on Public Education* (Rowman & Littlefield, 2015).

Blythe Farb Hinitz, Ed.D., is Professor of Elementary and Early Childhood Education at The College of New Jersey, where she serves as President of the Honor Society of Phi Kappa Phi. She was named a Distinguished Professor by the New Jersey Secretary of Higher Education in 2012, and honored as a Hero by the NAEYC History Seminar in 2011. A past Treasurer of NAECTE and winner of the 2007 Outstanding Teacher Educator Award, she currently serves on the Boards of the World Organization for Early Childhood Education—U.S. National Committee (OMEP-USA) and Professional Impact New Jersey. Research interests include history of early childhood education and teacher education, anti-bullying, and the social studies. Publications include *The Hidden History of Early Childhood Education* (2013), *History of Early Childhood Education* (2011), the Spanish edition of *The Anti-Bullying and Teasing Book for Preschool,* and "History of Early Childhood Education in Multicultural Perspective" in *Approaches to Early Childhood Education* (6th edition).

Adam Holland, Ph.D., is currently an Investigator on the FirstSchool PreK-3 Initiative at the Frank Porter Graham Child Development Institute located at the University of North Carolina at Chapel Hill. He has taught first grade, pre-kindergarten, and 3-year-olds with special needs but spent most of his teaching career in kindergarten. Dr. Holland's chief interest is in children's motivation and engagement. He has presented on these topics across the U.S. and internationally to a variety of audiences ranging from teachers and administrators to other researchers and professors.

James L. Hoot, Ph.D., is Professor at the Department of Learning and Instruction at The State University of New York at Buffalo. His primary research interest is issues concerning early childhood education globally. Dr. Hoot has served as Guest Editor of 12 annual theme issues of professional journals and is a member of the editorial boards for nine journals. Dr. Hoot is a member of the Executive Board of the World Organization for Early Childhood Education (OMEP USA) and has served two terms as President of the Association for Childhood Education International (ACEI).

Marilou Hyson, Ph.D., is a consultant in early child development and education and adjunct professor at the University of Pennsylvania's Graduate School of Education and the University of Massachusetts-Boston. Formerly Associate Executive Director with the National Association for the Education of Young Children, Dr. Hyson is the author of publications on early childhood services, teacher education, and professional development, as well as the recent books *The Early Years Matter* and *Enthusiastic and Engaged Learners: Approaches to Learning in the Early Childhood Classroom.* Internationally, she has consulted for the World Bank and Save the Children, with emphasis on professional development. Formerly, Dr. Hyson was Professor and Chair of the University of Delaware's Department of Individual and Family Studies, served as editor-in-chief of *Early Childhood Research Quarterly,* and was an SRCD Fellow in the U.S. Department of Education. She holds a Ph.D. in Child Development and Early Childhood Education from Bryn Mawr College.

Faiza M. Jamil, Ph.D., is an Assistant Professor of Child Development at the Eugene T. Moore School of Education at Clemson University in South Carolina. Her research follows two complementary strands: (1) understanding the underlying psychological processes—cognitive, social, and emotional—that influence teachers' classroom behaviors and career decisions, and (2) understanding the ways in which teacher-child interactions influence children's learning and development. She serves on the research council of the Institute of Child Success, a research and policy organization that fosters public and private partnerships to support the positive development of young children in South Carolina. Dr. Jamil also teaches child development courses in the Elementary and Early Childhood teacher preparation programs at Clemson University, to which she brings her own experiences as a teacher in early childhood and upper elementary classrooms in three countries.

Karen M. La Paro, Ph.D., completed her Ph.D. in Early Childhood Special Education at the University of New Orleans and is currently an Associate Professor in the Department of Human Development and Family Studies at the University of North Carolina at Greensboro. She teaches undergraduate and graduate courses focused on early childhood education and coordinates practicum courses and placements. As part of the National Center for Research on Early Childhood Education, Dr. La Paro worked on a survey focused on the supervision of student teaching in early childhood education programs across seven states. She was a Co-Principal Investigator for a DHHS Innovation grant focused on personnel preparation in the context of cultural and linguistic diversity. She has co-authored an observational measure of classroom quality related to teacher-child interactions, the Classroom Assessment Scoring System; and conducts observation, reliability, and professional development trainings related to the CLASS across the country.

Masoud Gholamali Lavasani, Ph.D., is Associate Professor of Psychology at the University of Tehran. His major research interests include motivation, cooperative learning, and the development of social skills in children. Dr. Lavasani has published more than 100 scientific articles and he participates in numerous national and international professional organizations. He has more than 14 years of experience teaching research methods in psychology, developmental psychology, and motivation in education courses.

Tara Lencl, Ed.M., is a doctoral student and instructor in the Program in Early Childhood Education, the Department of Curriculum and Teaching at Teachers College, Columbia University. She is also a toddler teacher at a preschool in New York City, where she has worked with young children and their families for 13 years. Her interests focus on equity and diversity in early childhood education and teacher preparation, as well as on multicultural education, culturally responsive teaching, and language development and bilingualism in young children. She has presented her work at numerous national and international conferences.

Betty Liebovich, Ed.D., lectures and tutors at Goldsmiths University of London in Early Years Education on the B.A. (Hons.) Education, Culture, and Society course, Primary PGCE course, M.A. Education program, Ph.D. program, and is Deputy Head of the B.A. (Hons.) Education, Culture, and Society degree. Her current research interests include the history of the open-air nursery, the Rachel McMillan Nursery and the Rachel McMillan Training College in Deptford, London, and the history of early childhood teacher education in England and the U.S. Current and pending publications have centered on the history of early years education, the educational philosophy of Margaret McMillan, the experiences of graduates of the Rachel McMillan Training College to establish a history of pedagogy for early years teacher education in England, and the influence that Margaret McMillan's philosophy has had on contemporary early years teacher education and practice in England and the U.S.

Helena P. Mawdsley, Ph.D., is currently an Institute of Education Sciences (IES) Postdoctoral Fellow in Early Intervention and Early Learning in Special Education at the University of Florida. Her research interests include contextual-, educational-, and policy-level influences on young children with disabilities and their families. Specifically, Dr. Mawdsley has focused on two areas: early childhood transition practices and psychological processes of the caregivers of young children with disabilities. Dr. Mawdsley has conducted program evaluations for state-sponsored early childhood initiatives and is currently the on-site coordinator for an IES-funded study.

Marica Cox Mitchell, M.S., is Deputy Executive Director for Early Learning Systems at the National Association for the Education of Young Children (NAEYC). She previously led the Early Childhood Professional Development Unit at the District of Columbia Office of the State Superintendent of Education. In that capacity, she developed and monitored a wide range of professional development resources designed to increase the quality of early learning programs and advance cohorts of early childhood professionals. Ms. Mitchell also facilitated the pilot and implementation of the Full Service Community School Model while serving as a specialist with the District of Columbia Public Schools. During a previous five-year tenure at NAEYC, she supported the launch of the NAEYC Early Childhood Associate Degree Accreditation system. Ms. Mitchell began her early childhood professional journey working in local early childhood programs as a teacher assistant, teacher, and curriculum specialist.

Rebecca S. New, Ed.D., has been a teacher since 1968, just prior to the court-mandated integration of Florida's public schools. After teaching for several years in primary-grade classrooms, she returned to graduate school where she earned a master's degree in Early Childhood Education. She returned to teaching at the University of Florida's P. K. Yonge Laboratory School where she taught and learned from a multi-age classroom of children ages 4–7. Doctoral studies at Harvard University's Graduate School of Education established her life-long curiosity about the cultural nature of child development. She has spent several decades studying early care and education in Italy, including the municipal early childhood services in Reggio Emilia. This work informed her early critique of NAEYC's *Guidelines for Developmentally Appropriate Practices* and continues to inform her work in early childhood teacher education. She is currently directing a longitudinal ethnographic study of Chinese and Mexican immigrant parenting of young children.

Sam Oertwig, Ed.D., is the Director of School Implementation for FirstSchool, a PreK-3 school improvement initiative focused on improving the school experience of African American, Latino, and low-income children. Previously, Dr. Oertwig served 25 years in public education as an elementary teacher, principal, director of elementary programs, and director of professional development. For the past 12 years, her work has focused on achieving educational equity for minority students by assisting teachers and schools to become more culturally proficient in practice and policy; and, she has been recognized at the local, state, and national level as a leader in this area. Dr. Oertwig has also facilitated the development of professional learning communities and cultures of collaborative inquiry that use data and research to improve practice. She has published articles and chapters related to her work and is a contributing author to *FirstSchool: Transforming PreK-3rd Grade for African-American, Latino, and Low-Income Children*.

Sungok R. Park, Ph.D., has had a lifelong interest in learning from people from diverse cultures. Her international experiences include working with young children and families in the Philippines, India, Korea, and in a highly diverse preschool in Western New York. Dr. Park's research foci include multicultural teacher education, global advocacy for children's rights, equity, and diversity. Currently, she is engaged in the study of educational implications of migration for very young children and their families. She is currently a professor in the College of Education at Northern Arizona University.

Robert C. Pianta, Ph.D., is the Dean of the Curry School of Education, Novartis Professor of Education, Professor of Psychology, and founding director of the Center for Advanced Study of Teaching and Learning at the University of Virginia. Dr. Pianta's research and policy interests focus on the measurement and production of effective teaching in classrooms from preschool to high school. He has authored more than 300 scholarly papers and several influential books related to teaching and the intersection of education and human development. Dr. Pianta's assessments of teacher-student interaction are widely used in research and in a number of at-scale applications in the U.S. and internationally. His recent work on improvement of teacher-student interactions has implications for teacher preparation and workforce development. Dr. Pianta consults regularly with foundations as well as state and federal agencies.

Douglas R. Powell, Ph.D., is a Distinguished Professor in the Department of Human Development and Family Studies at Purdue University. His research focuses on programs designed to strengthen family and early childhood program contributions to children's development. This includes a series of experimental studies of effects of a technologically-based program aimed at improving Head Start children's literacy and language skills via professional development with teachers, supported by grants from the Institute of Education Sciences. He also has developed and investigated community-based parenting support programs. Currently, Dr. Powell is leading a large curriculum development project for the U.S. Department of Defense Child Development Program. He is former Editor of the *Early Childhood Research Quarterly* and current editorial board member of five scholarly journals.

Susan L. Recchia, Ph.D., is Professor and Co-Coordinator of the Integrated Early Childhood Program at Teachers College, Columbia University. Drawing on her own diverse experiences in the fields of infancy, early childhood, and special education, Professor Recchia explores issues of diversity and development in her research and teaching. She serves as Faculty Director of the Rita Gold Early Childhood Center, an inclusive, culturally responsive center for early care and education, professional preparation, research, and outreach. Her research focuses on social and emotional experiences in early learning; adult-child relationships across contexts; issues in inclusive early care and education, and early childhood teacher development. She serves on the executive board of the New York Zero to Three Network and the editorial board of the *Journal of Early Childhood Teacher Education*. Professor Recchia's recent publications include *Inclusion in the Early Childhood Classroom: What Makes a Difference?* (Teachers College Press, 2013) with Yoon-Joo Lee.

Shannon Riley-Ayers, Ph.D., is an Associate Research Professor at The National Institute for Early Education Research at Rutgers University. Dr. Riley-Ayers conducts research and provides technical assistance on issues related to literacy, performance-based assessment, and professional development—often working with teachers and early childhood leaders. She is co-author of the policy brief *Early Literacy: Policy and Practice in the Early Years* (NIEER) and the book *Literacy Leadership in Early Childhood: The Essential Guide* (2007, Teachers College Press). She is first author of the Early Learning Scale (Lakeshore Learning Materials), a comprehensive performance-based assessment system for preschool and kindergarten children. Before joining NIEER, Dr. Riley-Ayers was co-director of the Office of Early Literacy at the New Jersey Department of Education and was instrumental in developing and implementing the New Jersey Early Literacy Initiative. She is a certified teacher and reading specialist, with several years of experience in public school classrooms.

Sharon Ritchie, Ed.D., participation in the field of education includes experiences as a teacher, program director, teacher educator, and researcher; teaching all ages from 3-year-olds to graduate students in special, general, and gifted education in multiple roles with K-12 schools and early childhood programs. On the UCLA faculty, she prepared elementary educators for 11 years and worked extensively with Head Start as project director for several national studies examining children in early learning settings. Currently, she is a Senior Scientist and Director of FirstSchool at the FPG Child Development Institute at UNC-Chapel Hill, leading the effort to rethink schools to improve the school experiences of African American, Latino, and low income children. The work reconceptualizes early education to increase professionalism, use data as a tool for inquiry, and enrich curriculum to portray and value diversity, caring instructional practices, competence and excellence, and positive changes in relating with families.

Beth S. Rous, Ed.D., is Professor in Educational Leadership Studies and Director of the Kentucky Partnership for Early Childhood Services at the University of Kentucky. Her primary research interests focus on the intersection of child care, early intervention, early childhood special education, Head Start, and public pre-kindergarten programs and services across three major areas: transitions, standards and accountability, and quality of the workforce and service systems. Dr. Rous has served as PI/Co-PI on over 30 projects and centers funded through the U.S. Department of Education, U.S. Department of Health and Human Services, private foundations, and state agencies.

Frances O'Connell Rust, Ed.D., is a Senior Fellow and Director of Teacher Education at the University of Pennsylvania Graduate School of Education. She is Professor Emeritus at New York University's Steinhardt School of Education where she was a professor of education between 1991 and 2007 and directed the undergraduate programs in Early Childhood and Elementary Education. She is a winner of the AERA Outstanding Dissertation Award (1985), the ATE Award for Distinguished Research in Teacher Education (2001), and the NAECTE Outstanding Teacher Educator Award (2008). She is a member of the AERA—Division K Summit on Teacher Education and the International Forum for Teacher Educator Development (InFo-TED). She has published widely on topics related to teacher preparation and teacher quality. She serves on the editorial boards of the journals, *Teachers and Teaching—Theory and Practice, Voices of Practitioners* (an online journal for early childhood teacher research), and the *Teacher Education Quarterly*.

Sharon Ryan, Ed.D., is Professor of Early Childhood Education and Chair of the Department of Learning & Teaching at the Graduate School of Education, Rutgers University. She is also a Research Fellow at the National Institute of Early Education Research. Before undertaking graduate studies in the United States Dr. Ryan worked in the early childhood field in Australia as a preschool teacher, program leader, curriculum advisor, and special educator. Dr. Ryan uses a range of qualitative and mixed methods designs to research early childhood teacher education and professional development, curriculum, policy implementation, and the potential of critical theories for rethinking early childhood practices. She has published a number of articles, book chapters, and reports in these areas.

Sara A. Schmitt, Ph.D., is an Assistant Professor in the Department of Human Development and Family Studies at Purdue University. She is also a member of Purdue's Center on Poverty and Health Inequities. She completed her doctoral work in Human Development and Family Sciences at Oregon State University and has interdisciplinary training in human development, public health, and developmental psychology. Dr. Schmitt's research is broadly focused on optimizing young children's development in multiple contexts. Specifically, she studies contextual factors that support or inhibit the development of important school readiness skills, including self-regulation, executive function, social competence, and pre-academic achievement. Dr. Schmitt has received research support from Purdue as well as the Indiana Clinical and Translational Sciences Institute. She is also Co-Principal Investigator on a longitudinal study evaluating a pilot prekindergarten program for the state of Indiana.

Maryam S. Sharifian, M.A., is from the Islamic Republic of Iran. Currently she is completing Ph.D. studies in Early Childhood Education at the State University of New York at Buffalo. She received her Bachelor's Degree in Guidance and Counseling from Allame Tabatabiee University and her Master's Degree in School Counseling from the University of Tehran. Her major research interests include international early childhood education, issues of equity, diversity, access, and socio-emotional development. She is actively involved in professional international organizations supporting the rights and needs of children. Most recently, she was elected to the Executive Board of the Association for Childhood Education International. Her dissertation research focuses on the education of children and teacher educators in war zones, using Syria as an example.

Patricia A. Snyder, Ph.D., is a Professor and the David Lawrence Jr. Endowed Chair in Early Childhood Studies and founding director of the Anita Zucker Center for Excellence in Early Childhood Studies at the University of Florida. Among her research interests are professional development approaches that enhance teachers' and caregivers' confidence and competence to implement evidence-based interactional and teaching practices with infants, toddlers, and preschoolers. Her other research interests include interactional and instructional quality, social-emotional foundations of early learning, and early childhood assessment. She is a past editor of the *Journal of Early Intervention* and a member of the Division for Early Childhood Recommended Practices Commission.

Mariana Souto-Manning, Ph.D., is Associate Professor of Education, Coordinator of the Early Childhood Education Program, and Director of the QUIERE (Quality Universally Inclusive Early Responsive Education) Project at Teachers College, Columbia University. Formerly a preschool and primary grades teacher, she is now a teacher educator whose teaching and research focus on early bilingual development, literacy teaching, and critical multicultural education. Her most recent book is entitled *Multicultural Teaching in the Early Childhood Classroom: Approaches, Strategies, and Tools (Preschool-2nd Grade) (Teachers College Press, 2013)*. Her research has been published in journals such as *Teachers College Record* and the *Journal of Teacher Education*. She has received research awards from major professional organizations, including the American Educational Research Association (AERA), the National Conference on Research in Language and Literacy (NCRLL), the American Educational Studies Association (AESA), and the National Association of Early Childhood Teacher Educators (NAECTE).

Tunde Szecsi, Ph.D., is an Associate Professor at Florida Gulf Coast University, where she is Co-Coordinator of the Elementary Teacher Education Programs. She earned her Master's degrees in Hungarian, Russian, and English language and literature in Hungary. For 17 years she taught at the high school and college level in Hungary. In 2003, she obtained her Ph.D. in Early Childhood Education at the State University of New York at Buffalo and has since taught courses in elementary and early childhood education and teaching English as a second language. She served as co-editor of the 2007 and 2012 "International Theme Issues" and the "Teaching Strategies" column of *Childhood Education*. Over the past decade, she has made numerous presentations throughout the world, and has contributed over 30 articles and five book chapters in child development, multicultural education, culturally responsive teacher preparation, and humane education.

Pamela J. Winton, Ph.D., is a Senior Scientist and the Director of Outreach at the Frank Porter Graham (FPG) Child Development Institute at the University of North Carolina at Chapel Hill. Dr. Winton has been involved in research, outreach, professional development, and scholarly publishing related to early childhood for the last three decades. She has taught courses on families, teaming, and professional development for many years. Dr. Winton has served as principal investigator (PI) or co-principal investigator (Co-PI) on multiple national centers and on numerous U.S. national, state, and local advisory boards, review panels, and editorial boards of journals. Dr. Winton has published numerous books, articles, chapters, and curricula on topics related to professional development, systems change, collaboration among professionals and families, and inclusion.

INDEX

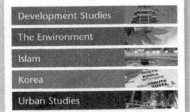